A PROFESSIONA
SUBCONSCIOUS STORY DEVELOPMENT
AND SYSTEMATIC OUTLINING

THE SUBCONSCIOUS NOVELIST

A. M. BLANCO

BEST SELLING AUTHOR OF *VULTURE*

A PROFESSIONAL NOVELIST'S GUIDE TO SUBCONSCIOUS STORY DEVELOPMENT AND SYSTEMATIC OUTLINING

THE SUBCONSCIOUS NOVELIST

A. M. BLANCO

BEST SELLING AUTHOR OF *VULTURE*

9TH HOUSE BOOKS, LLC.

Hialeah, Florida 33013

The Subconscious Novelist: A Professional Novelist's Guide to Subconscious Story Development and Systematic Outlining / A. M. Blanco

Published by 9th House Books, LLC

Book & Cover Design by A. M. Blanco

For more information contact 9th House Books at: www.9thhousebooks.com

To reach the author directly contact A. M. Blanco at: amblancowriter@gmail.com

ISBN: 979-8-9920687-1-9

First 9th House Books LLC Edition March 2025

Table of Contents

For all the master storytellers—living and dead—who through their narratives have inspired and taught us the secret of drawing from the infinite well of the subconscious mind and who have illuminated our collective imagination with the most profound truths—your stories live in us all, teaching even when we don't realize we're learning

A PROFESSIONAL NOVELIST'S GUIDE TO SUBCONSCIOUS STORY DEVELOPMENT AND SYSTEMATIC OUTLINING

THE SUBCONSCIOUS NOVELIST

A. M. BLANCO

BEST SELLING AUTHOR OF *VULTURE*

Welcome to The Subconscious Novelist

As writers, we all know that feeling—the sense that there's a story within us waiting to be told, characters eager to come alive on the page, and worlds yearning to be explored. Yet, the journey from initial concept to completed novel can often feel overwhelming, especially when we're trying to figure out our own unique creative process. I've been there, and it's what led me to develop this systematic approach to novel writing that I'm about to share with you.

This guidebook emerged from a deeply personal realization: despite being a natural plotter and having written multiple novels and screenplays, I noticed that my approach to each project was inconsistently different. Some outlines took a week, others three weeks, and some stretched into months. While the stories themselves turned out well, I couldn't shake the feeling that I was reinventing the wheel each time, relying on some combination of natural storytelling ability, reader's intuition, and plain luck. I knew there had to be a better way—a repeatable process that would allow writers to consistently access their creative depths while maintaining structural integrity.

What you hold in your hands is the result of years of research, experimentation, and refinement. I've created a comprehensive yet flexible 12-day framework that bridges the gap between your conscious crafting mind and your subconscious storytelling wisdom. This system isn't about forcing creativity into a box; rather, it's about creating the optimal conditions for your subconscious mind to reveal the story it wants to tell, while providing the structural support needed to shape that story into a compelling novel.

The beauty of this approach lies in its integration of both creative freedom and systematic development. Each day of the program is carefully designed to engage different states of consciousness—from the deep theta state where breakthrough ideas originate, to the focused beta state where we organize and structure our narrative. By working with rather than against these natural mental states, we create a harmonious writing process that honors both the mysterious nature of creativity and the practical demands of novel construction.

One of the most powerful aspects of this system is its emphasis on building a deep, trusting relationship with your creative subconscious. Through specific exercises and techniques, you'll learn to access that infinite well of creativity where your most authentic stories reside. The process shown in this book isn't just about outlining a novel; it's about developing a sustainable partnership with your deeper storytelling mind that will serve you throughout your writing career.

The 12-day timeline is a suggested framework, one that I've found allows for optimal creative development while maintaining momentum. However, the system is flexible enough to accommodate your personal pace and needs. Whether you dedicate two hours or four hours daily to the process, whether you extend certain phases or compress others, the fundamental structure remains sound. The goal is to provide you with a reliable roadmap while allowing space for your unique creative journey.

What makes this approach particularly effective is its integration of both conscious craft and subconscious creativity. You'll find that as you work through each day's tasks, you're not just organizing plot points and character arcs—you're actually deepening your understanding of the story on multiple levels. The systematic nature of the framework frees your creative mind from structural concerns, allowing it to focus purely on the storytelling elements that will make your novel unique and compelling.

Through this guidebook and its accompanying workbook, you'll discover how to:

- Access and trust your deeper storytelling wisdom
- Develop a consistent, repeatable creative process
- Create detailed, workable outlines in a structured timeframe
- Balance creative freedom with narrative organization
- Build a sustainable writing practice that honors both structure and inspiration

Remember, this system wasn't developed in a vacuum—it's been tested and refined through practical application. The framework you're about to learn has helped writers move from vague story ideas to detailed, actionable outlines in less than two weeks. It's designed to eliminate the uncertainty and overwhelm that often accompanies novel development, replacing it with a clear, step-by-step path to a complete and compelling story.

So, whether you're a natural plotter looking to refine your process, a pantser curious about the benefits of structure, or somewhere in between, I invite you to approach this system with an open mind and willing spirit. Whether you're consciously aware of it or not, your subconscious mind already knows the story you need to tell—this guidebook simply provides the tools and framework to bring that story into clear, coherent focus. Let's begin the journey of bringing your novel to life, one consciously crafted, subconsciously inspired step at a time.

Throughout this book, you may notice certain elements and concepts repeated in different contexts. This repetition is intentional—it's designed to help these crucial ideas sink deeply into your subconscious mind, where they can take root and flourish. Just as a master craftsman internalizes their tools through repeated use, you'll internalize these storytelling principles through multiple exposures and applications.

The structure of this guidebook reflects my own journey as a writer, influenced by masters like Michael Crichton, Anne Rice, James Ellroy, William Peter Blatty, Dan Brown, James Rollins, David Baldacci, Robert Ludlum, and Eric Van Lustbader. From Crichton, I learned the power of cinematic storytelling. From Rice, I discovered how cadence and structure can carry an entire novel. From Ellroy, Blatty, and Baldacci, I gained insights into crisp, sharp tone and impactful sentence structure. Through the works of Brown, Rollins, Ludlum, and Lustbader, I mastered the art of maintaining suspense—that crucial ability to keep readers on the edge of their seats, turning pages deep into the night.

As I absorbed these influences, I began to recognize a crucial pattern: the best storytellers weren't just writing by the seat of their pants (even if some of them wrote their first draft that way)—they were orchestrating their narratives with precision and purpose. What's fascinating is that this recognition wasn't a conscious, analytical process—it was my subconscious mind making connections and revealing insights about story structure and development. When I consciously began to work with my subconscious mind rather than trying to force the creative process, my stories not only improved dramatically, but the entire writing process became more fluid, natural, and organically coherent.

This understanding deepened significantly through my professional work as a Certified Hypnotist, Astrologer, and Metaphysician. Helping countless clients resolve deep-seated subconscious issues gave me unique insights into how the subconscious mind works and how to access its infinite creative potential. This expertise proved invaluable in developing my approach to writing and story development. While I still maintain my practice in these fields, my passion for helping writers access their creative depths has led me to focus primarily on writing coaching, where I can help others tap into the same powerful subconscious storytelling abilities that transformed my own writing.

This realization led me to develop a robust outlining process that allows writers to plan their novels thoroughly before writing the first draft. By understanding the what, how, and why of your story before you begin, you can create an remarkably clean first draft that requires minimal revision. What's particularly powerful about this approach is that the detailed outlining process essentially becomes your true first draft—a complete exploration and development of your story. This means that in ***The Subconscious Novelist*** system, what we traditionally call the "first draft" is technically more like your second draft, since you've already worked through the story's major elements in your outline. By the time you reach the editing and revision phase—if revisions are even necessary—you're effectively working on what would traditionally be considered a third draft. This system synthesizes all these influences and insights into a practical, repeatable approach that you can adapt to your own unique voice and style.

One of the most powerful aspects of this system is its integration of hypnotic principles into the creative process. You'll learn specific techniques for accessing different states of consciousness—from the active beta state where we edit and organize, to the deeper theta state where breakthrough ideas often originate. These aren't just theoretical concepts; they're practical tools that you'll use throughout your novel-writing journey to access and maintain creative flow.

The system also includes what I call the ***Sleep Story Seeding Method***—a technique that helps you partner with your subconscious mind during sleep to develop your stories. This method, combined with other specialized approaches like ***The Subconscious Story Writing Process***, creates a comprehensive framework for accessing and utilizing your full creative potential. Even if you don't remember your dreams, this practice strengthens the connection between your conscious and subconscious storytelling minds, leading to richer, more authentic writing.

Let me be clear: this isn't just another book about writing—it's a complete system for developing your story from the inside out. Whether you're working on your first novel or your fifteenth, whether you write thrillers, literary fiction, or fantasy, these techniques will help you access deeper levels of creativity while maintaining professional-level structure and organization. The goal is to make the novel-writing process not just manageable, but genuinely enjoyable and consistently repeatable.

So, take a deep breath, and prepare to embark on a transformative writing journey. Your subconscious mind is an infinite source of creativity, and this system will help you tap into that source with confidence and clarity. Trust the process, trust your deeper mind, and let's begin creating something extraordinary together.

As you embark on this journey with The Subconscious Novelist process, consider enhancing your experience with the companion workbook: "***The Subconscious Novelist's Workbook: A 12-Day Guide to Subconscious Story Development and Systematic Outlining***." While this guidebook provides everything you need to understand the process, the workbook serves as a powerful, hands-on tool for deepening your practice. Its carefully designed exercises create a direct channel to your creative subconscious, engaging your mind kinesthetically while maintaining the structural support your conscious mind craves. The workbook's daily tasks follow the same proven framework—and remember, there's no rush. Whether each day's work takes you hours or days to complete, the structure will keep you on track. Trust the process, honor your unique pace, and prepare to discover the extraordinary stories waiting within you.

Welcome to ***The Subconscious Novelist!***

CHAPTER 1

Understanding the Writer's Subconscious Mind: Your Infinite Creative Source

As writers, we often sense there's something deeper at work when we create—a wellspring of creativity that seems to flow from beyond our conscious awareness. This is your writer's subconscious mind, and understanding its nature and laws is crucial to becoming what I call a "Subconscious Novelist."

The Two Minds of a Writer

Every novelist possesses two distinct creative forces: the conscious and subconscious minds. Understanding how these two aspects of your creative self interact and complement each other is crucial to mastering the art of storytelling.

Your conscious mind serves as your skilled editor and external architect. Like a master craftsman, it excels at:

- Shaping raw narrative material into structured form
- Analyzing plot mechanics and story logic
- Organizing scenes and chapters into coherent sequences
- Refining language for precision and impact
- Managing the technical aspects of storytelling Yet for all its strengths, the conscious mind has its limitations. It operates linearly, focusing on one element at a time, and often lets critical judgment stifle creative potential before it can fully emerge.

Your subconscious mind, however, is your master storyteller and internal architect. It works on a deeper level, where:

- Infinite creative potential flows without bounds
- Multiple story threads weave together effortlessly
- Characters reveal their true essence and motivations
- Seemingly disconnected elements form brilliant connections

- Universal human truths emerge naturally in your narrative
- The wellspring of creativity never runs dry

Think of your conscious mind as the skilled sculptor who shapes the clay, while your subconscious mind is the rich earth from which that clay is drawn. Both are essential, but the subconscious holds the raw material of all possibility.

The Laws of the Writer's Subconscious Mind

1. **The Law of Creative Acceptance**
   Your subconscious mind accepts and acts upon whatever your conscious mind deeply believes about your writing abilities. If you believe you're creatively blocked, it will manifest that reality. If you believe you're an endless source of stories, it will prove you right. *I dive deeper into this topic in the section titled ***The Infinite Well -Faith in Your Subconscious Creative source.***
2. **The Law of Story Gestation**
   Your subconscious mind never stops working on your story, even when you're not actively writing. It continues developing characters, plotting scenes, and solving narrative problems during sleep, walks, or while you're engaged in other activities.
3. **The Law of Creative Resonance**
   Your subconscious mind transforms everything you experience into potential story material. This includes not just reading and life experiences, but also focused research, chance encounters, overheard conversations,

dreams, and even seemingly unrelated fields of study. The more diverse and rich your inputs, the more unique and compelling your creative output becomes. Research plays a particularly powerful role here—when you deeply immerse yourself in a subject, your subconscious mind weaves that knowledge into your outline and narrative drafts in ways your conscious mind could never predict. This is why some of the most surprising and delightful story elements often emerge after intense research and varied experiences.

4. **The Law of Non-Judgment**
   Unlike your conscious mind, your subconscious doesn't judge ideas as "good" or "bad." It offers up all possibilities, leaving your conscious mind to select what serves the story best. This is why the free association writing we do the first day and brain-dumping techniques can be so productive.
5. **The Law of Story Truth**

   Your subconscious mind always knows the deeper truth of your story—the real conflicts, the authentic character motivations, the genuine thematic resonance. When you're stuck, it's often because your conscious mind is fighting against this deeper truth.

Working With Your Writer's Subconscious

Think of your conscious and subconscious minds as creative collaborators, but understand this crucial truth: the conscious mind cannot work independently of the subconscious. Your subconscious mind is the master storyteller with infinite creative resources, while your conscious mind is the skilled craftsperson who shapes those raw materials into a polished narrative. Yet even this crafting process relies on subconscious wisdom—every creative decision, every edit, every refinement draws upon the deeper well of your storytelling mind.

To access your subconscious storytelling power:

1. **Build Trust** *More on this in the section titled: ***The Infinite Well -Faith***

in Your Subconscious Creative source.

- Accept all ideas without immediate judgment
- Write down everything, even fragments that seem nonsensical
- Look for patterns and connections in what emerges
- Trust that your subconscious knows where the story needs to go

2. **Create Optimal Conditions**

- Write at the same time daily to train your subconscious
- Establish a dedicated writing space
- Use rituals to signal "story time" to your deeper mind
- Practice entering the creative state through meditation or self-hypnosis

3. **Maintain the Connection**

- Keep a dream journal by your bed
- Carry a notebook for random insights
- Record story ideas immediately when they arise
- Pay attention to sudden intuitions about your story

4. **Feed Your Creative Well**

- Read widely in and outside your genre
- Experience art in all forms
- Observe people and nature
- Live fully—everything becomes story material

The Power of Integration

The goal of the Subconscious Novelist process is to gradually integrate your conscious and subconscious writing minds until they work in seamless harmony. This doesn't happen overnight—although it could happen that way to some of you—it's a journey of developing trust, establishing communication, and learning to recognize and honor the gifts your subconscious mind offers.

As you practice this integration, you'll find that:

- Writer's block becomes rare or nonexistent
- Stories develop more organically and powerfully
- Characters take on genuine depth and authenticity
- Plots emerge with natural complexity and resonance
- Your unique voice becomes stronger and clearer
- Writing becomes more joyful and less stressful

Remember: Your subconscious mind is always ready to help you tell powerful stories. Your job is to create the conditions that allow this deeper creativity to flow freely, while maintaining the conscious craft needed to shape it into compelling fiction.

Through consistent practice and trust in this process, you'll develop what feels like a direct line to your creative source—a state where stories seem to write themselves through you rather than being forced onto the page by conscious effort alone.

This is the true power of becoming a Subconscious Novelist: learning to dance between the infinite creative potential of your deeper mind and the skilled craftsmanship of your conscious awareness, creating stories that resonate deeply with readers because they emerge from the depths of authentic creative truth.

The Infinite Well - Faith in Your Subconscious Creative Source

The Divine Connection to Story

Every story that has ever been told and every story yet to be told exists within the infinite mind of the Universe. As novelists, we stand at the threshold of this boundless realm, not as creators in the strictest sense, but as channels through which these stories flow into conscious reality. The greatest secret of prolific writers is not that they possess superior intellect or talent, but that they have—consciously or unconsciously—developed an unshakeable faith in the inexhaustible creative source that exists within their own subconscious mind.

The universe is an infinite and eternal spiritual system which is responsive to our belief. This principle applies powerfully to the novelist's craft. Your subconscious mind does not distinguish between what you vividly imagine and what you experience in the physical world. It accepts the thoughts, beliefs, and feelings you impress upon it and works ceaselessly to bring these impressions into tangible form—in our case, as compelling narratives that move our readers.

When you sit before the blank page with anxiety, believing the story must come from your conscious intellect alone, you effectively close the channel to this infinite source. However, when you approach your writing with absolute faith that the perfect story already exists within you, waiting to be revealed, you open yourself to receive the infinite intelligence within your subconscious depths.

The Law of Subconscious Faith

"According to your faith is it done unto you." (Matthew 9:29) This timeless principle forms the cornerstone of understanding the subconscious mind and applies with remarkable precision to the novelist's journey. Your subconscious creative faculty can only give you what you truly believe is possible. If you harbor doubts about your ability to access profound story ideas, if you believe in writer's block, if you accept the notion of creative limitation—then these become your experience.

Conversely, when you cultivate an unwavering faith in your connection to the infinite creative source, the floodgates begin to open. This is not wishful thinking or metaphorical encouragement—it is the practical application of a psychological and spiritual law that has been demonstrated by the most prolific and inspired writers throughout history.

Consider the novelist who rises early each morning, sits at their desk, and begins to write without anxiety or doubt. They have trained their subconscious to believe in the abundance of creative inspiration. They expect the words to flow, the characters to speak, the plots to unfold. And so they do. This is not merely habit or discipline—though these play their part—it is the manifestation of subconscious faith in action.

The Conscious Mind as Gatekeeper: The Paradox of Control

Your conscious mind serves as both gatekeeper and gardener to your subconscious creative soil. The thoughts you habitually entertain regarding your creative abilities, the emotions you associate with the writing process, and the beliefs you hold about the source of your stories—all these are seeds planted in the fertile ground of your subconscious.

The subconscious mind is subject to the conscious mind in the local, day-to-day operations of creativity. Yet this represents only half of the truth. In the deeper, non-local spiritual reality, the subconscious mind remains the true sovereign of your creative kingdom. This creates a fascinating paradox for the novelist to navigate: while your conscious mind appears to direct the creative process, it is actually your subconscious that holds the ultimate creative authority.

Think of it this way: Your conscious mind is like a ship's captain who can steer the vessel and give orders to the crew, but it is the vast ocean beneath—your subconscious—that possesses the true power, depth, and mystery that makes the journey possible at all. The captain may determine the immediate course, but the ocean determines what is ultimately possible or impossible for the ship.

As novelists, we must become vigilant guardians of our conscious thoughts about our writing, precisely because they act as instructions to the more powerful subconscious. Every time you declare, "I don't know what happens next in my story," or "I've run out of ideas," or "I'll never create something as good as my last work," you are programming your subconscious to manifest exactly these limitations. The gatekeeper is restricting access to the kingdom's treasures.

Instead, affirm with conviction: "The perfect unfolding of this story is already complete in my subconscious mind." "I am connected to an infinite source of creative ideas." "My best work flows through me with ease and joy." These declarations, especially when accompanied by genuine feeling, redirect your subconscious toward the abundance that has always been available to you. In making these affirmations, you are not so much commanding your subconscious as acknowledging its true nature and removing the barriers your conscious mind has erected.

This understanding transforms your relationship with the creative process. Rather than struggling to generate ideas through conscious effort alone, you learn to humble your conscious mind before the vast creative intelligence of your subconscious. The conscious mind becomes not a taskmaster but a devoted servant to the subconscious—asking the right questions, creating the proper conditions, and then stepping aside to allow the true creative boss to work its magic.

The Divine Creative Principle at Work

At the core of human creativity lies what we metaphysicians might call Divine Intelligence or the Creative Principle that operates through all things, including the human mind. For the novelist, understanding this principle transforms the writing process from one of forced mental effort to one of inspired reception.

There is a power for good in the universe greater than you are, and you can use it. The subconscious novelist knows that they do not write alone. They are participating in a cosmic creative process that transcends individual identity while expressing uniquely through their particular consciousness.

This creative paradox can be understood elegantly: The subconscious mind is the storehouse of memory and the workshop of infinite intelligence. As you write, you are both accessing the universal storehouse of all possible stories and engaging the unique workshop of your individual subconscious, which filters and shapes these universal elements through your personal experience and viewpoint.

This understanding liberates you from the burden of believing you must generate every aspect of your novel from scratch. Instead, you become a skilled listener, attuned to the whispers of your subconscious as it draws from the infinite well of universal creativity and presents you with exactly what your story needs.

Cultivating Faith Through Practice

Faith in your subconscious creative source is not something you can fake or force. Like any profound relationship, it must be cultivated through consistent practice and demonstrated experience. The novelist who claims to believe in unlimited creative inspiration but never sits down to write is like the person who claims to believe in abundance but never plants a garden.

Faith is a thought in your mind which causes the power of your subconscious to be distributed into all phases of your life according to your thinking. For the novelist, this means establishing practices that align your conscious activities with your faith in the subconscious creative process.

Consider establishing these faith-building practices:

1. **Morning Receptivity:** Before rising, spend several minutes in a relaxed state (you can use the techniques I teach in this book) affirming your connection to the infinite creative source and mentally asking your subconscious to reveal the perfect next steps in your current project.
2. **Pre-Writing Meditation:** Before beginning each writing session, enter a state of calm receptivity. Acknowledge that you do not write alone but in partnership with your subconscious mind and the universal creative intelligence.
3. **Questions Before Sleep:** As you drift toward sleep each night, pose specific questions about your novel to your subconscious. "What is the perfect resolution to this conflict?" "How can I deepen this character's motivation?" Your subconscious will work on these questions as you sleep. You can also use **The Sleep Story Seeding Method I teach in this book.**
4. **Record Inspirational Moments:** Keep a dedicated journal of moments when inspiration flowed effortlessly. Review these regularly to strengthen

your faith in the process.

5. **Gratitude Practice:** Express genuine gratitude for each insight, plot solution, or character revelation that emerges from your subconscious. Gratitude reinforces the connection and invites further abundance.

Overcoming Doubt and Fear

Every novelist, regardless of experience or success, encounters moments of doubt and fear. These emotional states are the primary saboteurs of subconscious faith and creative flow. Fear is the absence of faith in your good. For the novelist, fear manifests as anxiety about the blank page, worry over reader reception, comparison with other writers, or doubt in the value of your unique voice.

When these fears arise—and they will—recognize them not as truth but as invitations to reaffirm your faith in the subconscious creative process. The thing to do is to replace fear with faith, for fear is a negative faith; it is faith in evil instead of good.

A powerful practice for transmuting fear into faith is to meet each moment of creative anxiety with a concrete question directed to your subconscious: "If I were absolutely certain that the perfect words would flow through me, what would I write next?" This question bypasses the conscious mind's doubts and directly engages your subconscious creative faculty.

Remember that doubt itself is merely a thought pattern that has been accepted by your subconscious. It can be replaced through consistent mental discipline and the evidence that comes from acting despite the doubt. Each time you sit down to write when you don't feel inspired and find that the words begin to flow, you build experiential evidence for your subconscious faith.

The Abundance Mindset for Novelists

Central to understanding the creative mind is the principle of abundance. The universe is not characterized by scarcity but by endless creativity and renewal. The possibility of a new idea coming forth from the infinite mind is endless. For the novelist, this means releasing the fear that you will "use up" your best ideas or exhaust your creative well.

The subconscious novelist cultivates an abundance mindset that trusts in the limitless nature of creative inspiration. When you complete one novel, you do not approach the next with trepidation, wondering if you have anything left to say. Instead, you approach it with excited anticipation, knowing that your connection to the infinite creative source remains undiminished—indeed, it has likely been strengthened by your previous act of creative faith.

This abundance mindset extends beyond ideas to encompass all aspects of the novelist's journey. There is abundant time to write, abundant paths to share your work, abundant readers waiting to be moved by your stories, and abundant rewards—both tangible and intangible—for your creative expression.

The Universal Storehouse of Story

Every story element imaginable exists within what we might call the Universal Mind. Character archetypes, plot structures, thematic explorations, settings, conflicts, resolutions—all are present in infinite variation within this universal storehouse, accessible through your subconscious mind.

When you request a specific creative element from your subconscious—a compelling antagonist, a surprising plot twist, a resonant thematic revelation—you are not asking it to manufacture something new but to select and present what already exists in potential form. Your subconscious, that faithful servant, searches the universal storehouse and brings forth exactly what is needed for your unique creative expression.

This understanding transforms how you approach creative "blocks." When you feel stuck, you are not experiencing a lack of available material but a temporary constriction in your receptive capacity. The solution is not to force creativity but to restore your faith in the abundance and accessibility of the universal storehouse.

There are specific techniques for this restoration: What you mentally picture, you materialize. What you feel, you attract. What you mentally accept, you experience. Visualize your novel completed in perfect form. Feel the satisfaction and joy of its creation. Accept mentally that the entire story already exists within your subconscious mind, needing only your participation to bring it into form.

From Seeking to Finding

Many novelists approach the creative process as a seeker, constantly looking for inspiration, hunting for ideas, searching for the perfect narrative path. The subconscious novelist, however, understands that they are not a seeker but a finder. All that you need for your novel already exists within the infinite creative source to which your subconscious mind is connected.

This shift in perspective is profound: We should not be seeking inspiration, but we should be finding it. Similarly, we should not be seeking stories but finding the stories that already exist within us, waiting to be revealed through our conscious awareness.

This shift transforms the writing process from one of anxious pursuit to one of joyful discovery. You are not trying to create something that doesn't exist; you are uncovering what has always existed in potential form within the universal creative mind and your own subconscious connection to it.

The practical application of this principle is profound. Rather than asking, “What should I write next?” ask instead, “What is already waiting to be written through me?” Rather than wondering, “How will I create a compelling character?” ask, “Which character is already formed within my subconscious, waiting to be revealed?” This subtle shift in questioning redirects your subconscious from the mode of creation to the mode of revelation—and revelation is infinitely more accessible and effortless.

The Subconscious and Writing Flow

The state of "flow" that many writers describe—when time seems to disappear, when words emerge without conscious effort, when characters seem to act of their own accord—is not mysterious when understood through the lens of subconscious faith. This flow state represents the perfect alignment of conscious intention and subconscious expression.

The conscious mind is the reasoning mind, and it's the realm of effect. The subconscious mind is the realm of cause. When you experience writing flow, you are witnessing the causal power of your subconscious mind as it expresses through your conscious activity. The stories, characters, and themes that emerge in these moments have their origin not in your conscious reasoning but in the deeper creative intelligence of your subconscious.

To experience this flow more consistently, practice surrendering conscious control of your writing process. Set clear intentions for your outlining or writing session, and follow the daily structure I provide in this book, then release the need to direct every aspect of the creative unfolding. Trust that your subconscious—infused with the universal creative principle—knows the perfect path for your story, even when that path differs from your conscious expectations.

Beyond Technique to Trust

The craft of writing involves numerous techniques and skills that must be consciously learned and applied. Structure, characterization, dialogue, description, pacing—these elements of craft cannot be neglected. However, the subconscious novelist understands that technique alone cannot produce truly resonant fiction. Technique must be balanced with trust in the subconscious creative process.

Principle is not bound by precedent. Your subconscious creative faculty is not limited by conventional approaches to novel writing. It may guide you to break traditional rules, experiment with unexpected forms, or blend genres in innovative ways. When you trust this guidance—when you have faith that your subconscious is drawing from a deeper wisdom than conscious technique alone can access—you open yourself to creating work of genuine originality and power.

This does not mean abandoning craft but transcending it. Master the technical elements of fiction writing, then surrender them to your subconscious mind, which will apply them in perfect measure for the unique story you are bringing forth.

The Faith-Filled Novelist

The novelist who establishes unshakeable faith in the subconscious creative source experiences a transformation that extends beyond their writing to encompass their entire relationship with creativity and life itself. They recognize that life is a mirror and will reflect back to the thinker what he thinks into it.

When you think thoughts of creative abundance, when you feel emotions of gratitude for your connection to the infinite well of inspiration, when you act from the certainty that your subconscious mind is constantly working to bring forth your perfect creative expression—these thoughts, feelings, and actions are reflected back to you as a writing life characterized by flow, joy, and prolific output.

The subconscious novelist writes not from desperation or force but from a place of centered faith in the creative principle that flows through all things, including their own mind and imagination. The feeling of wealth produces wealth; the feeling of health produces health. How do you feel?

How do you feel about your creative capacity? How do you feel about the stories waiting to emerge through you? How do you feel as you approach the blank page? These feelings, more than any technique or strategy, determine what your subconscious mind will deliver to your conscious awareness as you write.

Cultivate the feeling of creative abundance. Nurture your faith in the infinite well of inspiration within you. Trust that your subconscious mind, in partnership with the universal creative principle, holds every story you will ever need to tell. Then write from this place of faith-filled certainty, and watch as the perfect words flow through you onto the page, revealing stories more powerful and profound than your conscious mind alone could ever conceive.

The subconscious novelist knows this truth: There is no limit to Mind, no boundary to the possibilities of understanding. Your creative potential as a novelist is equally boundless when you establish unwavering faith in the subconscious source of all storytelling.

Seven Mindset Rules for the Subconscious Mind

1. Commitment to Process

Embrace the power of structural commitment. The 12-day outline process isn't just about organization—it's a covenant with your creative self. By honoring each day's designated task, you're training your subconscious to recognize that you're serious about this work. This reliability creates a safe space for your deeper mind to release its treasures, knowing they'll be captured and developed rather than abandoned.

2. Type Hard, Type True

Establish non-negotiable daily writing goals and honor them as sacred appointments with your creativity. "Type hard" means bringing intensity and presence to each session—it's about engagement, not just word count. When you show up consistently, your subconscious learns to prepare for these sessions, arriving ready with material it's been secretly developing between writing sessions.

3. Velocity Before Verdict

Let words flow without immediate judgment. Your first draft—whether of an outline component or narrative chapter—should prioritize momentum over perfection. The subconscious works best when it isn't interrupted by the critical mind. Remember: your creative unconscious works at lightning speed when unhindered by doubt. You can refine later, but first, capture the raw material your deeper mind is offering.

4. Cultivate Deep Listening

Before and during each writing session, practice conscious receptivity to what lies beneath surface thoughts. Your subconscious communicates through impressions, images, emotional resonance, and unexpected connections. Train yourself to recognize and honor these signals, especially when they contradict your logical planning. The most powerful story elements often arrive as whispers, not shouts.

5. Trust the Fertile Void

Embrace periods of apparent emptiness or confusion as essential parts of the creative process. When you feel stuck during your 12-day journey, resist the urge to force progress. Instead, step away briefly, engage in a mindless activity, and allow your subconscious to continue working in the background. What seems like a void is actually a fertile space where connections are forming beneath awareness.

6. Honor Emotional Truth

The subconscious speaks the language of emotion before logic. When developing characters, plot points, and thematic elements, prioritize what feels emotionally authentic over what seems clever or original. Ask yourself regularly: "Does this resonate on a gut level?" "Does this resonate on a gut level with this character?" Your subconscious knows the emotional landscape of your characters and your story before your conscious mind can map it.

7. Practice Radical Surrender

At every stage of the 12-day process, be willing to abandon preconceptions when your subconscious offers something better. The most powerful outlines emerge when you hold your conscious plans loosely, allowing deeper currents to reshape them. This surrender isn't about abandoning structure—it's about recognizing that the most compelling structure emerges from your subconscious mind, not from your conscious mind. Plus, you already have a pre-determined chapter by chapter structure I am providing you with to ease your conscious mind's worry with structure.

CHAPTER 2

AN OVERVIEW OF THE SUBCONSCIOUS STORY OUTLINING SYSTEM

This comprehensive overview provides essential context before you begin working on your outline, and before diving into The Subconscious Novelist Workbook. Take time to familiarize yourself with these elements—understanding them deeply will enhance your creative process and story development. Consider this chapter your roadmap to the territories we'll explore together, a conceptual framework that will support your journey from initial inspiration to finished outline.

Introduction to the System

The Subconscious Story Writing System is designed to help you tap into both conscious and subconscious elements of storytelling. By understanding and implementing these foundational elements, you'll create richer, more engaging narratives that resonate with readers on multiple levels.

The core philosophy of this system acknowledges a fundamental truth about creativity: our most powerful stories emerge from the dialogue between our conscious craft knowledge and the deeper wisdom of our subconscious minds. Most writing methods emphasize one at the expense of the other—either rigid structural formulas that can feel mechanical or purely intuitive approaches that often lack cohesion. This system creates a bridge between these worlds, honoring both the architect and the dreamer within you.

In the pages that follow, we'll explore the essential building blocks of compelling fiction—from character development to plot structure, from thematic resonance to genre conventions. But we'll approach these elements differently than traditional craft books. Rather than imposing external frameworks onto your creative vision, we'll use these elements as doorways into your subconscious storytelling mind, accessing the narrative wisdom you already possess at deeper levels.

Think of this system not as a set of rules to follow but as a conversation between your analytical and intuitive selves. The conscious mind excels at organization, logic, and structure; the subconscious excels at connection, symbolism, and emotional truth. When these aspects work in harmony, the resulting stories possess both coherence and depth, both professional craft and authentic voice. Let's begin exploring the elements that will facilitate this creative partnership.

Core Story Elements

Title Development

The journey of your novel begins with its name. While this might seem simple, your title serves multiple purposes beyond mere identification. A powerful title creates the first impression for readers, establishing tone and creating immediate expectations. It hints at the story's themes and content without revealing too much, offering an intriguing preview that invites readers to discover more. A well-crafted title also sets genre expectations, signaling to readers what kind of experience they can anticipate. Finally, it influences marketing potential, affecting everything from cover design to search engine optimization.

Start with a working title that captures your story's essence. This can evolve as your narrative develops, but having a strong working title helps anchor your creative process. Consider both literal and metaphorical meanings, and how they might resonate with your intended audience.

When developing your title, explore multiple layers of meaning. A truly effective title works on several levels simultaneously. Consider "The Old Man and the Sea" by Ernest Hemingway—this seemingly straightforward title identifies the protagonist and setting while simultaneously establishing the thematic conflict between human determination and natural forces. It creates visual imagery while hinting at deeper existential questions.

Allow yourself to generate numerous possibilities before settling on your final choice. Sometimes the perfect title emerges early in the process; more often, it reveals itself gradually as you develop your story's themes and characters. Be open to unexpected inspirations—sometimes a line of dialogue or a seemingly minor image captures your story's essence perfectly.

Remember that your title creates a promise to readers—about genre, tone, content, and reading experience. The most effective titles fulfill these promises while offering surprising depths as readers engage with your work. Whether you choose something evocative and poetic ("The Road") or directly descriptive ("Murder on the Orient Express"), ensure your title establishes the appropriate expectations for the journey you're inviting readers to undertake.

Genre Foundation

Understanding Genre's Role

Genre is far more than a marketing category—it's the architectural framework that shapes your entire narrative. Each genre represents a set of established patterns, expectations, and narrative conventions that guide nearly every aspect of your storytelling process. These conventions have evolved over centuries because they satisfy fundamental human desires for specific types of stories.

Genre conventions guide story structure, establishing the expected rhythm and progression of your narrative. Mysteries typically move from crime to investigation to revelation; romances progress from meeting to conflict to resolution. Understanding these patterns helps you create satisfying structures that feel both familiar and fresh to readers who love these genres.

Genre also influences crucial pacing decisions—action-oriented genres like thrillers demand faster pacing with frequent tension points, while literary fiction might allow more space for contemplation and character development. Being fluent in your genre's typical rhythm helps you make informed decisions about where to accelerate and where to linger.

Character development similarly follows genre patterns. Romance protagonists must undergo emotional growth that enables lasting connection; mystery detectives require observational skills and determination. These character expectations create a foundation upon which you can build unique, memorable personalities that still fulfill readers' genre-specific desires.

Perhaps most importantly, genre defines reader expectations—the implicit contract between writer and audience about what kind of experience your story will deliver. Horror promises fear; comedy promises laughter; romance promises emotional satisfaction. Understanding these expectations allows you to fulfill them while finding fresh approaches that prevent your work from feeling derivative.

Genre knowledge also informs your marketing strategies, helping you identify your target audience, comparable titles, and appropriate promotional approaches. Finally, it creates opportunities for innovation—you can only effectively subvert conventions once you thoroughly understand them.

Early genre exploration helps you establish clear story parameters, identifying which elements are essential and which are optional for your particular narrative. It helps you understand which story elements deserve emphasis based on reader expectations. And it provides a roadmap for planning your marketing approach, from cover design to promotional language.

Perhaps most excitingly, understanding genre deeply allows you to find unique angles within established conventions. The most memorable stories in any genre tend to fulfill core expectations while introducing innovative elements that surprise and delight readers. This balance between familiarity and novelty creates the sweet spot where commercial success and artistic satisfaction often meet.

Genre Requirements and Cross-Pollination

Modern storytelling often thrives on genre hybridization. Understanding core genre requirements allows you to blend elements effectively, creating fresh narratives that still satisfy reader expectations. Consider these detailed genre requirements not as rigid rules but as essential ingredients that can be combined in creative ways.

Thriller/Suspense centers around high-stakes scenarios with clear consequences that matter deeply to characters and readers. These narratives maintain sustained tension through strategic pacing and calculated information reveals, creating an emotional rollercoaster for readers. Time pressure elements—deadlines, countdowns, or rapidly deteriorating situations—create urgency that propels the narrative forward.

A compelling thriller requires a complex antagonist with a credible threat level—whether a brilliant serial killer, an intimidating organization, or a natural disaster. The antagonistic force must pose a genuine challenge that readers believe could potentially defeat the protagonist. The narrative employs strategic information revelation, controlling exactly what readers know and when they discover it to maximize suspense.

Physical or psychological danger permeates these narratives, with characters facing threats to their safety, sanity, or moral integrity. Escalating complications prevent easy resolution, forcing protagonists to adapt repeatedly as situations worsen. This genre demands particularly tight plot structure with precisely engineered cause-and-effect relationships and multiple tension points that prevent reader disengagement.

Mystery revolves around a central crime or puzzle requiring resolution, creating the foundational question that drives the narrative forward. The genre demands strategic placement of clues and evidence that allows readers the satisfaction of potentially solving the mystery themselves while maintaining sufficient challenge. Calculated red herrings and misdirections create false paths that test both protagonist and reader without feeling manipulative.

The genre promises a satisfying resolution that holds up to scrutiny—the solution must feel both surprising and inevitable when revealed. This requires meticulous planning to ensure all clues lead logically to the conclusion without telegraphing it too early. A compelling detective figure or investigator serves as the reader's surrogate, possessing the determination, intelligence, or specialized knowledge necessary to unravel the truth.

The narrative follows logical investigation progression, showing the methodical process of gathering and interpreting evidence. Multiple suspect possibilities maintain tension through competing explanations for the central crime or puzzle. Information gathering scenes—interviews, research, evidence examination—form the structural backbone of these narratives. The overall structure follows progressive revelation, with understanding deepening in satisfying increments throughout the story.

Horror creates escalating tension and atmospheric dread, building unease through setting, tone, and strategic uncertainty. The genre requires a compelling threat or monster—whether physically tangible like a creature or killer, or psychological like madness or existential dread. This threat creates immediate or looming danger that characters cannot easily escape or defeat.

Dark atmosphere and tone permeate these narratives, established through setting, imagery, and language choices that evoke unease. The genre may include supernatural elements, though psychological horror can be equally effective without them. Psychological manipulation of both characters and readers creates disorientation and vulnerability. Fear-inducing scenarios exploit common phobias and primal anxieties—isolation, unknown threats, loss of control, or violation of natural order.

Visceral descriptions engage readers' senses to create immersive fear experiences, making the threat feel immediate and personal. The most effective horror activates primal fear triggers—darkness, confined spaces, contamination, predatory threats—that resonate with readers across cultural boundaries because they connect to evolutionary survival mechanisms.

Science Fiction builds upon scientific or technological foundations, extrapolating from current knowledge to create plausible future developments. These narratives typically feature speculative future or alternate reality settings that provide fresh contexts for exploring human nature and societal questions. The genre excels at exploration of technology's societal impact, examining how scientific developments might transform human experience.

Consistent internal logic creates believable speculative worlds with clear rules and limitations. World-building elements establish how technology, politics, economics, and culture operate in these alternate realities. Scientific plausibility, even when highly speculative, maintains reader engagement by grounding fantastic elements in recognizable principles. The narrative explores technological consequences—both intended and unintended—as innovations reshape societies and individuals.

The genre examines social implications of scientific developments, using speculative scenarios to comment on contemporary issues like inequality, surveillance, or human connection. These narratives offer future extrapolation that extends current trends to their logical conclusions, whether utopian, dystopian, or more nuanced outcomes.

Historical Fiction demands historically accurate details and settings that immerse readers in past eras without anachronism. These narratives often integrate real events and figures alongside fictional characters, requiring meticulous research to represent historical personalities authentically. Period-appropriate dialogue and behavior prevent modern sensibilities from creating jarring disconnections from the historical context.

Cultural accuracy in representing social structures, beliefs, and practices grounds these narratives in genuine historical understanding. Historical research integration weaves factual elements seamlessly into the fictional narrative without creating information dumps. Period-specific details about clothing, technology, medicine, and daily life create immersive historical environments.

The genre requires authentic characterization that reflects period-appropriate values and worldviews while remaining accessible to modern readers. Era-appropriate conflicts emerge organically from historical contexts—whether wars, social movements, or technological changes. Historical context provides both backdrop and active influence on character decisions and plot developments.

Literary Fiction typically features character-driven narrative focus, emphasizing psychological depth and inner experience over plot-driven action. The genre engages in complex thematic exploration, addressing significant human questions without simplistic answers. There's a particular emphasis on craft and style, with language itself becoming an essential element of the reading experience rather than merely a vehicle for plot.

These narratives often embrace open-ended resolution potential, avoiding neat conclusions in favor of thought-provoking ambiguity. Deep psychological insight reveals the complexities of human motivation and behavior. Symbolic elements create layers of meaning beyond literal interpretation. Multilayered meaning invites multiple valid interpretations of the same text.

Artistic expression takes precedence over commercial conventions, allowing for experimental approaches to structure, perspective, or language. Thematic depth explores complex ideas about human experience, ethics, society, or existence itself, challenging readers to engage intellectually and emotionally with difficult questions.

Romance centers on a central love story driving plot development—the relationship must be the primary narrative focus rather than a subplot. These narratives trace an emotional development arc as characters grow through their romantic experience. The genre promises a satisfying relationship resolution that fulfills the emotional needs established throughout the story.

Relationship conflicts and obstacles prevent easy union, creating the narrative tension that drives the story forward. Character chemistry must be palpable enough to justify the central relationship's importance. Emotional depth prevents the romance from feeling superficial or merely physical. The narrative typically traces relationship stages from initial meeting through challenges to ultimate commitment.

Personal growth occurs through the romantic relationship, with characters becoming more complete or authentic through their connection. The genre traditionally promises happy ending expectations—either "happily ever after" or "happy for now"—though some subgenres may offer more complex resolutions while still providing emotional satisfaction.

Fantasy requires detailed worldbuilding systems with consistent rules governing magic, politics, geography, and culture. These narratives establish coherent magic system rules that create both possibilities and limitations for characters. Hero's journey elements often provide structural backbone as protagonists leave familiar environments to face extraordinary challenges.

Good versus evil dynamics frequently drive conflict, though contemporary fantasy often explores moral complexity within this framework. Mythological elements—whether directly borrowed from existing traditions or freshly invented—create resonant symbolic dimensions. Magical consistency prevents convenient solutions that undermine narrative tension.

Quest structure often drives plot development as characters pursue specific objectives through dangerous territories. World rules establish the physics, biology, and metaphysics of the created realm. Fantastic elements—creatures, powers, or realms—provide the genre's distinctive wonder and spectacle while exploring themes through metaphorical means.

Young Adult fiction features teen protagonist perspective, addressing challenges specific to adolescent experience. Coming-of-age themes explore the transition from childhood dependency to adult identity formation. The content remains age-appropriate while honestly addressing challenging aspects of teen experience.

Identity exploration focus examines questions of self-definition central to adolescent development. Relatable challenges reflect genuine teen concerns—social acceptance, family conflict, future uncertainty, or romantic awakening. Peer relationships play crucial roles as characters navigate friendship dynamics, group pressure, and social hierarchies.

Self-discovery drives character development as protagonists learn their capabilities, values, and authentic desires. First experiences—whether romantic, ethical, or achievement-oriented—create significant growth moments. Growing independence from parental authority or societal expectations creates both opportunity and conflict as characters establish their unique identities.

Understanding these genre requirements allows you to either work purely within established conventions or strategically blend elements to create hybrid narratives. For instance, a science fiction mystery would maintain the puzzle-solving structure and clue placement of mystery while incorporating the technological speculation and societal examination of science fiction. A historical romance would feature the central relationship focus and emotional development of romance within the carefully researched period setting of historical fiction.

The most innovative contemporary fiction often emerges from thoughtful genre cross-pollination—using the strengths of multiple traditions to create fresh narrative experiences. By understanding the essential elements that make each genre work, you can combine them intentionally rather than haphazardly, creating hybrids that satisfy multiple reader expectations simultaneously.

Character Architecture

The Hero (Protagonist)

Your protagonist serves as the story's heart, driving both narrative and character development. Their journey should resonate on multiple levels, creating a character readers will follow willingly through hundreds of pages. This multidimensional development begins with core elements that establish both surface details and deeper significance.

Core Elements

Begin with your protagonist's name, considering potential symbolic resonance. Names carry weight in fiction, often subtly reinforcing character traits or thematic elements. Consider how names like Ebenezer Scrooge (suggesting miserliness) or Holly Golightly (suggesting carefree movement through life) encapsulate character essence. Your character's name might reflect family background, cultural heritage, parental aspirations, or personal reinvention.

Age selection carries significant implications for your character's life stage, perspective, capabilities, and challenges. A teenage protagonist brings different concerns than a middle-aged or elderly one. Consider both the literal age and its significance within your character's cultural context—what expectations, freedoms, or limitations does this age carry?

Occupation choice reveals values, skills, interests, and socioeconomic position. Even a character's unemployment or resistance to conventional work reveals important character information. Consider not just what your protagonist does professionally but why they've chosen this path and how they feel about it—is it a calling, a compromise, or merely survival?

Personal history provides essential context for current behavior and attitudes. Significant past experiences—triumphs, traumas, turning points—shape how your character perceives and responds to present challenges. This history need not be fully revealed immediately but should inform every aspect of characterization.

Current life situation establishes the status quo that will be disrupted by your story's inciting incident. Where does your protagonist live? What is their financial situation? What daily routines structure their life? What recent changes have created new pressures or possibilities?

Social connections define your character through relationships—family dynamics, friendships, romantic entanglements, professional networks, community ties. These connections reveal how your protagonist functions interpersonally and provide essential secondary characters who can support, challenge, or complicate the central journey.

Skills and abilities determine what your protagonist can realistically accomplish within your narrative. These include not just professional expertise but personal aptitudes, whether intellectual, physical, emotional, or interpersonal. These capabilities should balance with meaningful limitations to create a character who is competent enough to be credible but challenged enough to create tension.

Personal challenges—internal obstacles like fears, flaws, wounds, or external problems like financial pressures, relationship conflicts, or professional setbacks—create the resistance against which your character will develop. These challenges should connect meaningfully to your story's central conflict rather than existing as isolated character traits.

Growth potential establishes the distance your character can credibly travel during your narrative arc. What learning, healing, or transformation is possible for this specific character? What internal or external factors might facilitate or resist this development? This potential evolution creates the character arc that will parallel your external plot.

Symbolic Layering

Consider how every aspect of your protagonist can enhance your story's themes. For example, the name analysis of Tom Vogel, the hero from my police thriller/horror novel "Vulture" demonstrates multiple layers of meaning that enrich the narrative on several levels:

1. Surface Level His professional identity as Miami Homicide Detective establishes his role in investigating a cannibalistic serial killer who mimics vulture behavior. This creates immediate genre positioning and clear story function. The name itself sounds appropriate for a detective character—strong but not flashy, memorable without being eccentric. The first-person present tense structure allows for the dynamics of the story's plot structure to occur organically through his immediate perceptions and responses.

2. Symbolic Connections The initials T.V. connect to Turkey Vulture, the type of vultures common to Miami, Florida, where the novel takes place. This creates a subtle link between hunter and hunted, suggesting deeper connections that emerge throughout the narrative. The surname "Vogel," meaning "Bird Catcher" in German, reinforces his story function of trying to capture a killer who mimics vulture behavior. This linguistic connection adds a layer of meaning that attentive readers might appreciate without being heavy-handed. The Biblical reference through the name "Thomas" connects to significant thematic elements about doubt and evidence that run throughout the story.

3. Thematic Layers The connection to the doubting Thomas theme reinforces the character's skeptical nature and need for tangible evidence—attributes essential for both his detective work and his personal spiritual journey. Links to Gnostic traditions add philosophical depth to what might otherwise be a straightforward thriller. His symbolic role in the story's redemption arc gains additional resonance through these biblical connections, adding mythic dimension to the contemporary crime narrative.

4. Psychological Depth The name reflects the character's journey from doubt to belief, from isolation to connection. It creates connections to his internal conflicts about trust, faith, and certainty. It mirrors external challenges as he pursues a killer who represents something beyond ordinary human understanding.

These layers create depth that rewards attentive readers who recognize connections between character names and story themes. They strengthen thematic resonance by reinforcing central ideas through multiple narrative elements. They add interpretive possibilities beyond surface plot, inviting readers to engage with deeper patterns and meanings. They create discussion points for readers sharing their experience of the book. Perhaps most importantly, they enhance literary value while maintaining genre accessibility.

The layered connections help you build story more organically because everything becomes subconsciously connected to something else in the narrative. These connections often emerge intuitively during the writing process, revealing how your subconscious mind creates meaningful patterns that your conscious crafting can then refine and strengthen.

The Villain (Antagonist)

Your antagonist should serve as a powerful counterforce to your protagonist, embodying opposing values while maintaining credible motivation. The most compelling villains are not merely obstacles but complex characters with understandable (if misguided) purposes, creating conflict that tests your protagonist on multiple levels.

Essential Elements

1. Personal Background Your antagonist's age carries significance beyond chronology—it positions them generationally in relation to your protagonist and influences their formative experiences. Historical context shapes their worldview through the cultural, political, and social environment of their development. Formative experiences—particularly traumatic or transformative ones—explain how they developed their current beliefs and methods. Cultural influences establish values, traditions, and perspectives that inform their choices. Social position—whether privileged or marginalized—affects their access to resources and shapes their perspective on power dynamics.

2. Professional Elements Their occupation choice reveals values, skills, and social position—whether they pursue legitimate work, criminal enterprises, or exist outside conventional systems. Status implications of their professional role affect their self-perception and treatment by others. Power dynamics established through their work position create specific relationship patterns with others, including your protagonist. Resource access through professional roles or connections determines what tools, information, or allies they can deploy against your protagonist. Skill development through professional experience provides abilities that make them formidable opponents in your story's central conflict.

3. Core Characteristics Fundamental beliefs form the foundation of their worldview—the principles they consider unquestionable truths about reality, humanity, or morality. Their value system establishes priorities and judgments about what matters most, creating natural conflict with characters holding different values. Their moral framework—whether conventionally ethical, deliberately immoral, or operating on alternative ethical principles—determines what actions they consider justified in pursuing their goals. Psychological makeup encompasses personality patterns, defense mechanisms, and cognitive tendencies that influence decision-making and behavior. Behavioral patterns reveal character through habitual actions, reactions, and interpersonal approaches.

4. Story Function Opposition methods establish how the antagonist creates concrete obstacles for your protagonist—whether through direct confrontation, manipulation, sabotage, or competing for the same objectives. Conflict generation should occur on multiple levels—physical, psychological, moral, or philosophical—creating multidimensional challenges. Theme reflection occurs as the antagonist embodies opposing values or represents thematic questions from a different perspective than your protagonist. Plot advancement happens as antagonistic action forces protagonist response, creating the cause-effect chain that drives narrative forward. Character development in your protagonist occurs through the specific challenges your antagonist creates, testing particular weaknesses or requiring specific growth.

The most compelling antagonists often function as dark reflections of your protagonists—similar in core drives or abilities but making crucially different choices. This mirroring creates thematic resonance while establishing conflicts that test your protagonist's most vulnerable areas. Rather than creating a simplistic villain, develop an antagonist whose perspective makes internal sense, even if their methods or conclusions are ultimately destructive.

Narrative Dynamics

Goal Development

Your hero's objective must be tangible and challenging enough to force meaningful change. Compelling goals create the spine of your narrative, establishing what's at stake and why readers should care about the outcome.

1. Goal Origins Pre-story connections establish how your protagonist's objectives relate to their life before the narrative begins—whether fulfilling long-held dreams, addressing persistent problems, or responding to recent developments. The inciting incident relationship clarifies how your story's catalyzing event either creates new goals or transforms existing ones. Personal motivation links connect objectives to internal needs, values, or wounds that make these goals matter deeply rather than remaining merely external achievements. External pressures—from family expectations to societal demands to financial necessities—can compel pursuit of goals that might not otherwise be priorities. Internal drives—ambition, curiosity, restlessness, fear—similarly push characters toward specific objectives that reflect psychological needs.

2. Goal Evolution Initial objectives establish starting motivations that engage your protagonist in the story's central conflict. Changing priorities occur as new information, obstacles, or internal development shift what your character values most. Growth-related shifts happen as the protagonist's evolving self-awareness and capabilities create new possibilities or recognition of more meaningful objectives. Obstacle impacts force adaptation as initial approaches fail, requiring new strategies or even reconsidered goals. Final aims may differ significantly from initial objectives as your character's journey transforms their understanding of what truly matters.

3. Achievement Requirements Necessary steps create the structural progression of your narrative as your protagonist moves toward their objective. Required resources—whether material objects, information, allies, or internal qualities—establish what your protagonist must acquire to succeed. Skill development creates meaningful character growth as your protagonist builds new capabilities specifically required by their goal pursuit. Personal growth parallels external achievement as internal limitations must be overcome to reach objectives. External support from secondary characters provides both assistance and relationship development opportunities.

4. Implementation Strategy Action planning reveals character through the specific approaches chosen to pursue objectives. Resource gathering demonstrates resourcefulness, connections, or limitations as your protagonist assembles necessary tools. Skill acquisition shows commitment and adaptability as your protagonist develops new capabilities required for success. Alliance building reveals interpersonal dynamics and the protagonist's ability to inspire, negotiate, or manipulate others. Obstacle assessment demonstrates analytical thinking and adaptation as your protagonist recognizes and responds to barriers.

Goals function most effectively when they're specific enough to create clear success/failure conditions, significant enough to justify the narrative's length and complexity, and personal enough to engage your protagonist's deepest values and vulnerabilities. The most compelling objectives often require both external achievement and internal growth, creating parallel character and plot arcs that reinforce each other.

Motivation Architecture

Hero's Motivation

Create compelling reasons for your protagonist's actions through multi-layered motivation that makes their choices both believable and revealing of character.

1. Internal Drivers Personal desires establish what your protagonist actively wants—whether tangible achievements, emotional states, or specific experiences. Emotional needs create deeper motivational currents, often operating below conscious awareness—the need for connection, recognition, security, or purpose that drives surface behaviors. Psychological pressures arising from insecurities, traumas, or identity issues create powerful motivational forces, sometimes manifesting as compensatory behaviors or avoidance patterns. Value systems establish priorities and principles that guide choices, creating potential internal conflicts when different values compete. Belief structures about how the world works, what's possible, or what's deserved shape both goals and methods for achieving them.

2. External Catalysts Environmental factors—physical settings, available resources, geographical limitations—shape what actions are possible or likely. Social pressures from family expectations, cultural norms, or peer influences create external motivation through the desire for acceptance or fear of rejection. Situational demands created by crises, opportunities, or responsibilities force choices that might not otherwise be made. Relationship influences—desires to protect, please, prove oneself to, or rebel against others—create powerful motivational forces. Cultural expectations establish socially approved goals and methods that characters may either pursue or deliberately reject.

3. Development Impact Character growth occurs as motivations evolve through experience, creating measurable character development. Decision making reveals character through the specific motivations prioritized when values conflict. Behavioral changes reflect motivational shifts as internal transformations manifest in observable actions. Relationship effects emerge as motivational patterns create recurring dynamics with others. Plot advancement occurs as motivations drive specific actions that generate consequences, creating the cause-effect chain of narrative.

The most compelling character motivations operate on multiple levels simultaneously—the conscious objective alongside deeper psychological needs, the stated rationale alongside unexpressed emotional drives. This multi-layered approach creates characters who feel authentically complex rather than simplistically driven by single motives.

Villain's Motivation

Develop complex, believable motivations that make your antagonist compelling rather than cartoonishly evil. The most effective antagonists have understandable—even occasionally sympathetic—motivations implemented through problematic methods or taken to destructive extremes.

1. Psychological Foundation Personal trauma often creates the formative experiences that shape antagonistic worldviews—loss, betrayal, abuse, or injustice that distorts perspective. Value distortion develops as initially positive values like justice, loyalty, or excellence become warped through extreme application or divorced from balancing principles. Belief systems establish the antagonist's understanding of how the world works or should work, often containing elements of truth taken to harmful conclusions. Moral framework creates the internal justification system that allows antagonists to view their actions as necessary or even righteous. Emotional damage—unhealed wounds, unintegrated grief, or overwhelming fear—drives destructive behavior through psychological mechanisms like projection, displacement, or compensation.

2. Goal Structure Primary objectives establish what the antagonist actively pursues—the central aim that brings them into conflict with your protagonist. Secondary aims create additional motivational dimensions that make the character more complex and potentially unpredictable. Implementation methods reveal character through the specific approaches chosen to achieve goals—whether violent, manipulative, systematic, or opportunistic. Resource utilization demonstrates intelligence and capability through how effectively the antagonist deploys available tools, connections, or knowledge. Strategy development shows foresight and adaptability through planned approaches to obstacles—including your protagonist's opposition.

3. Opposition Elements Conflict areas identify where antagonist and protagonist inevitably clash based on incompatible goals or methods. Value clashes create deeper thematic conflicts as characters embody opposing principles or priorities. Goal interference occurs when characters pursue mutually exclusive objectives or compete for the same resources or positions. Personal antipathy may develop through history, temperamental incompatibility, or representing everything each character rejects. Ideological differences about fundamental questions—how society should function, what constitutes justice, or who deserves power—create conflicts that transcend personal animosity.

Villains who believe themselves to be heroes in their own stories create particularly compelling antagonists. Their conviction in the righteousness or necessity of their actions makes them more determined, more consistent, and ultimately more dangerous than those motivated simply by greed or cruelty. This moral conviction also creates opportunities for more complex thematic exploration than simplistic good-versus-evil dynamics allow.

Conflict Development

Conflict drives your narrative through multiple layers of opposition, creating the resistance against which your story develops. Well-crafted conflict operates simultaneously across different dimensions, testing characters physically, emotionally, intellectually, and morally.

1. Direct Opposition Character confrontations create immediate dramatic scenes where opposing agendas clash through dialogue, physical action, or psychological manipulation. Goal conflicts establish the fundamental story tension as characters pursue incompatible objectives or compete for the same resources or positions. Value clashes create deeper thematic conflicts as characters embody opposing principles, priorities, or worldviews. Resource competition forces difficult choices about allocation of limited means—whether material resources, time, attention, or opportunity. Power struggles over control, influence, or autonomy create dynamic relationship conflicts with shifting advantages.

2. Internal Struggles Personal doubts create inner conflict between different aspects of the protagonist's own nature—confidence versus insecurity, hope versus pessimism, ambition versus contentment. Moral dilemmas force choices between competing values with no perfect solution, revealing character through which principles are ultimately prioritized. Value conflicts emerge when different cherished principles require contradictory actions. Fear responses create resistance to necessary actions despite conscious desire to proceed. Growth resistance occurs as characters cling to familiar limitations rather than risking the discomfort of change, even when that change is ultimately desirable.

3. External Obstacles Environmental challenges from weather, terrain, or physical environment create practical problems requiring resourceful solutions. Social barriers including prejudice, bureaucracy, or social conventions limit available options based on identity or status. Resource limitations force creativity and prioritization as characters work with insufficient tools, information, allies, or capabilities. Time constraints create urgency and force difficult choices about allocation of limited attention. Physical impediments including distance, barriers, or bodily limitations require specific strategies to overcome.

4. Progressive Complications Escalating difficulties prevent resolution through initial approaches, forcing adaptive responses that reveal character under increasing pressure. Increasing stakes raise the consequences of both success and failure as the narrative progresses, intensifying emotional investment. Compounding problems create multiple simultaneous challenges that test prioritization and resource allocation. Growing pressure intensifies emotional states and relationship dynamics as stress reveals core character traits. Mounting tension builds toward climactic confrontations where multiple conflict dimensions converge.

The most compelling narratives develop conflict across all these dimensions, creating multifaceted challenges that test characters completely rather than in isolated aspects. This layered approach ensures that resolution requires both external action and internal growth, creating satisfying narratives that feel both exciting and meaningful.

Character Depth

Hero's Profile Development

External World Building

Establish your protagonist's concrete reality through specific details that create both believability and thematic resonance. This external characterization provides the tangible foundation upon which deeper psychological development can build.

1. Current Situation Living conditions—physical environment, neighborhood, home design, possessions—reveal socioeconomic status, priorities, and daily realities. Professional status establishes not just occupation but position within that field—level of achievement, reputation, satisfaction, and trajectory. Social connections map relationships that shape the character's life—family structures, friendships, romantic entanglements, community ties, professional networks. Financial state creates both practical limitations and psychological pressures through abundance, scarcity, or uncertainty. Daily routines reveal character through habitual behaviors, time allocation, and the balance between obligation and choice in how life is structured.

2. Active Pursuits Professional goals reveal ambition, values, and self-concept through what achievements the character considers worthy of effort. Personal objectives beyond career—whether relationship goals, creative pursuits, or lifestyle aspirations—similarly reveal core values and identity concepts. Relationship aims show interpersonal needs and attachment patterns through what the character seeks from connections with others. Skill development demonstrates growth orientation and specific interests through what capabilities the character actively cultivates. Life changes actively pursued—relocations, career shifts, relationship transitions—reveal dissatisfaction with current situations and visions of preferred futures.

3. Environmental Factors Cultural context establishes norms, expectations, and available life patterns that either support or conflict with the character's personal inclinations. Social pressures from family expectations, peer influence, or community standards create external forces that shape choices. Economic conditions—both personal financial circumstances and broader economic environment—create both constraints and opportunities that influence decisions. Political climate affects everything from career options to personal safety depending on the character's identity and the story's setting. Technological level establishes available tools, communication methods, and information access that shape how characters solve problems and connect with others.

Internal World Construction

Develop your protagonist's inner landscape with the same attention to detail given to external circumstances. This psychological dimension creates the depth that allows readers to understand motivations and identify with experiences different from their own.

1. Personality Elements Core traits establish consistent patterns of behavior, thought, and emotional response that define character—whether introversion/extroversion, optimism/pessimism, caution/risk-taking, or other fundamental temperamental qualities. Value system reveals what the character considers most important—whether security, achievement, creativity, justice, connection, or autonomy—creating the priorities that guide choices. Belief structure establishes how the character understands how the world works, what's possible, and what's deserved. Emotional patterns reveal typical responses to challenges—whether anger, withdrawal, humor, problem-solving, or seeking connection. Behavioral tendencies establish predictable responses to typical situations, creating both consistency and opportunities for meaningful deviation that signals character development.

2. Capability Assessment Natural talents identify innate abilities that come easily to your character—whether analytical thinking, physical coordination, emotional intelligence, creative expression, or interpersonal influence. These inherent strengths provide foundation for character competence while suggesting areas where development has likely occurred naturally. Learned skills represent capabilities developed through deliberate practice, formal education, or life experience—the expertise your character has intentionally acquired. Knowledge base encompasses both formal education and practical understanding acquired through life experience, establishing what information your character can reasonably access without research. Experience level in relevant domains creates credibility for character competence while establishing realistic limitations based on exposure. Growth potential identifies capabilities that could be developed during your narrative, creating opportunities for meaningful character evolution in response to story challenges.

3. Challenge Areas Personal limitations establish realistic constraints on character capability—whether physical disabilities, knowledge gaps, temperamental challenges, or skill deficiencies. These limitations create both vulnerability and opportunity for growth when confronted with obstacles requiring these underdeveloped capacities. Skill gaps identify specific capabilities your character lacks that will be required to overcome story challenges, creating natural points of tension and development. Knowledge deficits similarly create vulnerabilities when characters must operate in unfamiliar domains without necessary information or context. Emotional blocks—fear, trauma responses, defense mechanisms—prevent effective action despite adequate skill, creating psychological rather than practical obstacles. Behavioral patterns that once served protective functions but now limit growth—avoidance tendencies, control needs, people-pleasing—create habitual responses that must be overcome for character development.

These challenge areas create the friction necessary for compelling character development. A protagonist without meaningful limitations lacks the vulnerability that creates both tension and relatability. By establishing specific areas where your character struggles, you create natural opportunities for growth directly connected to the obstacles your plot presents.

Psychological Architecture

Wound Development

The psychological wounds your characters carry create the emotional foundation for your story's internal journey. These unresolved hurts shape perception, behavior, and development potential, establishing both limitations to overcome and vulnerabilities that antagonists can exploit.

1. Trauma Identification Key events establish the specific experiences that created psychological wounding—whether childhood neglect, betrayal, loss, failure, or abuse. While some traumas may be dramatically significant, others might be relatively commonplace experiences that carried particular impact for this specific character based on timing, vulnerability, or meaning assigned. Impact assessment examines how these experiences affected the character's self-concept, worldview, and behavioral patterns. Ongoing effects reveal how past wounds continue to influence present functioning through triggers, fears, or compensatory behaviors. Coping mechanisms identify the specific strategies developed to manage painful emotions—whether healthy adaptations like creative expression or problematic patterns like substance abuse, emotional avoidance, or relationship sabotage. Growth barriers emerge from these coping mechanisms as protective strategies that once provided safety now prevent healthy risk-taking or vulnerability.

2. Fear Integration Core fears establish the fundamental anxieties that drive avoidance behaviors—whether fear of abandonment, failure, exposure, insignificance, or loss of control. These deep concerns often operate below conscious awareness while powerfully influencing decisions. Manifestation patterns show how these abstract fears appear in concrete situations—specific triggers, avoidance behaviors, or compensatory actions. Behavioral impacts demonstrate how fear shapes choices, relationships, and life paths through excessive caution, perfectionism, people-pleasing, isolation, or overachievement. Growth limitations emerge as fear prevents experiences necessary for development—whether intimacy, creative risk, leadership opportunities, or authentic self-expression. Resolution potential identifies pathways toward healing through specific experiences, relationships, or insights that could transform the character's relationship with fear.

3. Vulnerability Mapping Emotional triggers identify specific situations, words, or behaviors that activate old wounds, creating disproportionate reactions based on past rather than present reality. Understanding these triggers allows you to deliberately activate them through plot and character interaction, creating emotionally resonant conflict. Weakness areas establish domains where the character lacks confidence or competence due to past experiences, creating natural growth opportunities within your narrative. Defense mechanisms reveal how the character protects against psychological pain—whether through intellectualization, humor, denial, projection, or other protective strategies. Growth opportunities emerge precisely at these vulnerable points, as healing occurs through facing rather than avoiding psychological pain. Healing potential identifies specific experiences, relationships, or insights that could transform wounds into wisdom over the course of your narrative.

Well-developed psychological wounding creates characters with believable limitations and authentic growth trajectories. Their flaws and struggles emerge naturally from their histories rather than appearing as arbitrary traits, creating coherent psychological portraits that feel like real people rather than collections of characteristics. This psychological depth also creates natural connections between external plot events and internal character development, as story challenges specifically activate and address established wounds.

Plot Structure Integration

External Plot (A Story)

The external plot creates the visible architecture of your story—the tangible events, conflicts, and developments that readers can directly observe. This "A

Story" provides the primary narrative throughline that organizes your novel's progression.

1. Physical Events Action sequences create dynamic scenes where conflict manifests through tangible movement and confrontation. These high-energy moments punctuate your narrative, creating variation in pacing and demonstrating character capability under pressure. Environmental changes—whether gradual transformations or sudden disruptions—create evolving settings that influence character options and relationships. Character interactions form the backbone of scene structure as personalities clash, connect, and negotiate through dialogue and behavior. Plot developments advance the central narrative through discoveries, decisions, and consequences that change character circumstances. Concrete outcomes create measurable progress or setbacks in pursuit of established goals, maintaining reader engagement through tangible stakes.

2. Tangible Challenges Physical obstacles create literal barriers that characters must overcome through strength, skill, or strategy. These concrete challenges demonstrate character capability while creating visceral tension easily understood by readers. Resource limitations—whether shortage of money, time, information, or materials—force creative problem-solving and difficult prioritization. Time constraints create urgency that pressures decision-making and limits available options. External opposition from antagonistic forces—whether individuals, organizations, or natural forces—creates conflict that drives narrative forward. Environmental barriers from geographical features, weather conditions, or built structures create physical challenges requiring specific approaches to overcome.

3. Observable Actions Character behaviors demonstrate personality, values, and emotions through concrete actions rather than stated traits. These observable choices reveal who characters truly are rather than who they claim to be, creating authenticity through specificity. Event sequences create the cause-effect chain that drives narrative forward as actions generate consequences that necessitate further actions. Visible changes in circumstances, relationships, or environments create measurable progression that maintains reader engagement. Physical conflicts provide dynamic scenes that test character capabilities while creating visceral reading experiences. Measurable outcomes create clear markers of progress or setback in relation to established goals, maintaining narrative tension through tangible stakes.

The external plot provides the primary structure readers consciously track—the "what happens" that creates the story's forward momentum. This visible architecture supports the more subtle internal developments, giving concrete expression to psychological and thematic content through specific actions and events.

Internal Plot (B Story)

The internal plot creates the psychological and philosophical architecture of your story—the invisible but essential developments occurring within characters as they experience external events. This "B Story" provides the emotional and thematic depth that makes your narrative meaningful rather than merely entertaining.

1. Thematic Development Core message establishes the central insight or truth your story explores—not as explicit statement but through the pattern of events and consequences. While external plot shows what happens, thematic development reveals what it means within your story's moral universe. Moral exploration examines ethical questions through character choices and their outcomes, allowing readers to consider complex questions through concrete scenarios rather than abstract discussion. Value examination similarly tests the relative worth of competing priorities—security versus risk, connection versus independence, tradition versus innovation—through specific character decisions. Truth revelation occurs as characters discover previously unacknowledged realities about themselves, others, or the world through narrative experiences. Understanding growth tracks how character perspective evolves through story events, creating the wisdom gained through narrative journey.

2. Emotional Journey Feeling progression traces the emotional arc characters experience—from initial states through complications that trigger new feelings to ultimate emotional resolution. This affective journey creates the reader's emotional experience alongside intellectual engagement with plot developments. Relationship development tracks changing connections between characters as trust builds, betrayals occur, alliances form, or romances develop. These interpersonal dynamics create emotional resonance while revealing character through interaction rather than isolation. Personal growth traces character development through changing responses to similar situations, demonstrating evolution through behavior rather than stated transformation. Understanding expansion occurs as characters gain new perspective on themselves, others, and their situations through narrative experiences. Wisdom acquisition—the integration of experience into meaningful insight—creates the lasting change that makes character journeys significant beyond immediate plot resolution.

3. Psychological Growth Belief changes track how character worldview evolves through story experiences—how assumptions are challenged, certainties questioned, or new possibilities recognized. These cognitive shifts create meaningful character development as perceptions align more closely with reality or expand to include previously rejected perspectives. Value adjustments similarly trace how character priorities evolve through narrative challenges that test what truly matters when choices must be made. Understanding development occurs as characters gain insight into their own motivations, others' perspectives, or the complex dynamics of their situations. Perspective shifts create meaningful growth as characters see themselves, others, and their circumstances from new angles that reveal previously unrecognized truth. Wisdom acquisition integrates these cognitive and emotional developments into lasting character change that persists beyond immediate story resolution.

4. Spiritual Development Faith exploration examines characters' relationship with belief systems, meaning structures, or larger questions of purpose and existence. Whether through religious traditions, philosophical frameworks, or personal meaning-making, this dimension addresses how characters understand their place in the universe. Truth seeking traces character journeys toward greater authenticity as they discard false self-images or social masks to embrace more genuine identity. Meaning discovery follows characters' search for purpose and significance beyond material achievement or social recognition. Purpose understanding develops as characters recognize their unique contributions and callings within larger contexts. Value integration occurs as abstract principles become embodied in concrete choices, transforming intellectual understanding into lived reality.

The internal plot creates the psychological and philosophical resonance that makes stories meaningful beyond momentary entertainment. While readers consciously track external developments, they unconsciously absorb these deeper patterns that create emotional impact and lasting impression. The most powerful narratives create perfect alignment between external events and internal developments, using physical action to express psychological truth.

Implementation Guide

Practical Application

Translate theoretical understanding into concrete creative practice through systematic implementation of these story elements. This practical approach ensures that your novel emerges with both organic authenticity and professional structure.

1. Story Development Outline creation provides the architectural blueprint for your narrative, establishing key structural elements while leaving room for discovery during drafting. Whether you prefer detailed planning or minimal scaffolding, some level of structural awareness prevents major revisions later. Scene planning builds this structure at more granular level, establishing purpose, conflict, and progression for individual narrative units. Character development transforms conceptual understanding into specific individuals with consistent traits, compelling motivations, and clear growth trajectories. Plot structuring arranges events in sequences that create optimal pacing, tension, and revelation. Theme integration weaves conceptual concerns throughout narrative elements, creating coherent philosophical exploration without heavy-handed messaging.

2. Writing Process Draft development transforms outline and planning into actual narrative, focusing on forward progress rather than perfection. Initial drafting emphasizes discovery and generation rather than refinement, allowing unexpected elements to emerge from your subconscious creativity. Revision strategy approaches rewrites systematically, addressing different elements—structure, character, prose, theme—in separate passes rather than attempting simultaneous correction. Detail enhancement adds sensory specificity, emotional nuance, and environmental texture during revision, creating immersive reading experience. Consistency checking ensures character traits, plot logistics, and thematic elements remain coherent throughout the manuscript despite extended creation time. Quality improvement focuses on prose-level refinement after larger structural elements are solidified, polishing language to professional standards.

3. Review Methods Structure assessment examines overall narrative architecture—act divisions, key turning points, pacing patterns, subplot integration—ensuring coherent progression and appropriate tension development. Character evaluation focuses on consistency, distinctiveness, and developmental arcs across your cast, ensuring compelling and believable personalities. Plot analysis examines cause-effect relationships, tension patterns, and resolution satisfaction, identifying logical gaps or missed opportunities. Theme verification ensures philosophical elements develop coherently without becoming heavy-handed or contradictory. Quality control addresses prose-level concerns from sentence rhythm to dialogue authenticity to descriptive effectiveness.

Remember

This system serves as your foundation for creating deep, engaging narratives that resonate with readers on multiple levels. Take time to understand and implement each element, allowing your creative process to flow naturally while maintaining structural integrity.

The approach outlined in this chapter represents not a rigid formula but a flexible framework designed to support your unique creative vision. These elements provide architectural support that actually enhances creative freedom by establishing clear parameters within which your imagination can flourish. Like the sonnet form for poets or tonal structure for composers, narrative conventions provide productive constraints that channel creativity rather than limiting it.

As you work with these elements, maintain balance between conscious craft and subconscious inspiration. Use these concepts as entry points into your creative mind rather than mechanical checkboxes. The most compelling fiction emerges when structural understanding supports rather than suppresses authentic artistic expression—when craft and inspiration become partners rather than competitors in the creative process.

In the chapters that follow, we'll explore specific techniques for accessing your subconscious storytelling wisdom while maintaining professional-level structure. This integration of depth and architecture creates narratives that satisfy both commercial and artistic standards—stories that entertain while revealing authentic truth about human experience. The journey toward this integration begins with the foundational understanding presented here and continues through the practical exercises and techniques in subsequent chapters.

CHAPTER 3

An Overview of the Elements of Fiction

Lets take a look at the elements of fiction. These elements will help you write your novel.

The essential elements of fiction writing are:

1. Plot - The sequence of events that make up the story
2. Character - The people who drive the narrative
3. Setting - The time and place where the story occurs
4. Theme - The central idea or meaning behind the story
5. Point of View - The perspective from which the story is told
6. Conflict - The central problem or struggle
7. Dialogue - The conversations between characters
8. Tone - The story's emotional feel or attitude
9. Style - The writer's distinct way of using language
10. Pacing - The story's rhythm and forward momentum

Plot: Plot is story and story is plot. Think of plot as the structured sequence of events that form a story's narrative arc, typically following a pattern that fits into the 3 act structure, it has areas of exposition, rising action, climax, falling action, and resolution. It encompasses both the physical events and emotional developments that transform characters while maintaining causality - each event should logically lead to the next while building tension and stakes throughout the story. Remember, as you begin to brainstorm any story you are going to write, that character and plot are intrinsically connected. Story informs character and character informs plot. There is no one without the other (for the novel's sake).

Character: Character(s) are the living elements of fiction that drive the story through their thoughts, actions, emotions, decisions, and growth. They must be believable individuals with distinct personalities, histories, motivations, dilemmas, flaws, and thematic arcs that engage readers emotionally and carry the narrative's thematic weight through their experiences and transformations. Remember, as you begin to brainstorm any story you are going to write, that character and plot are intrinsically connected. Story informs character and character informs plot. There is no one without the other (for the novel's sake).

Setting: Setting encompasses both the physical location and time period of a story, as well as the social, cultural, and environmental contexts that shape the narrative world. It influences character behavior, scenes, plot possibilities, and thematic resonance while providing atmosphere and grounding the story in a specific reality that readers can visualize and understand. When you brainstorming your novel's setting think about how it can connect to the theme of your story, how it can play a role in the behavior of your characters. Setting is sometimes belittled or overlooked by inexperienced novelists but it is one of the most powerful tools at your disposal to create an amazing novel.

Theme: Theme is the most important element in fiction writing, it is the central message or underlying meaning that a story explores through its plot, characters, and conflicts. It represents the universal or spiritual truth or even an insight about human nature that emerges organically through the narrative's events rather than being explicitly stated, giving the story deeper significance beyond its surface entertainment value. Theme is unequivocally linked to your hero's flaw, his history and in specific the event that created a psychological wound or trauma, or belief system that needs healing. This wound and the need to resolve or heal it allows the internal story to carry the external story. In my opinion, theme is everything. Theme is the glue that keeps your story's plot together. I personally love to explore theme in the very early stages of brainstorming and when I am exploring the world of the story. This ensures I can build upon the theme's discovery and let it guide me to powerful scenes. The more you think about theme the more possibilities open up from the well of your subconscious about scenes and events that can occur in your story and this will help the story have a greater impact on your reader. I have included a section devoted to the subconscious power of theme, make sure you read that and really understand the importance of theme. It will impact your relationship with your subconscious mind and its ability to reveal stories and it will change your writing approach for the best.

Point of View (Overview): Point of view is the perspective through which a story is told, determining who narrates events and how much information readers receive. This choice affects narrative distance, reliability, and emotional connection while shaping how readers experience and interpret the story's events. I go deeper into POV in the last chapter.

First Person Present Tense: In this immediate and intimate perspective, the narrator tells their story as it happens using "I" and present tense verbs, creating a sense of urgency and allowing readers to discover events alongside the narrator with no knowledge of future outcomes.

First Person Past Tense: The narrator recounts their story after it has occurred using "I" and past tense verbs, allowing for reflection on past events while maintaining personal connection and potentially offering hints about future developments through narrative distance. I used this POV in my novel ***Vulture.*** It's a great POV to use when you want an intimate and psychologically tense feel for your novel. It's great for unreliable narrators and for confusing your readers (something typically done in psychological thrillers).

Third Person Present Tense: The story follows a character (not "I") as events unfold in real-time, creating immediacy while maintaining some narrative distance and allowing for more objective observation of the protagonist's experiences. Screenwriters use this POV almost exclusively, even when they become novelists. I personally like this for thrillers and suspense novels a lot. Although it is not as common as Third Person Past Tense.

Third Person Past Tense: Events are narrated about a character (not "I") after they've occurred, providing traditional storytelling distance while allowing for broader perspective on events than first-person narration. This is the most common POV in use by most fiction writers. It's unequivocally the most flexible.

Third Person Omniscient: The narrator knows and can reveal all characters' thoughts, feelings, and motivations across time and space, offering complete insight into the story world while potentially sacrificing intimate character connection.

Third Person Limited (Past): The narrator follows one character's perspective in past tense, revealing only what that character knows, thinks, and feels, combining the focus of first-person with the narrative distance of third-person.

Third Person Limited (Present): Similar to past tense but events unfold in real-time, creating immediacy while maintaining focus on a single character's perspective and limiting information to what they can know or observe in the moment.

Conflict: Conflict is the central tension that drives story action through opposition between characters' goals, internal struggles, or external challenges. It creates the narrative's dramatic foundation by presenting obstacles that must be overcome, forcing character growth and maintaining reader engagement through escalating stakes.

Dialogue: Dialogue consists of character conversations that advance plot, reveal personality, provide information, and create tension while mimicking natural speech patterns. It serves multiple narrative functions including character development, conflict expression, and pacing control while avoiding exposition-heavy exchanges. Dialogue is probably the most difficult thing to get "just right" in novel writing. The best advice here is to learn how dialogue works through how really good dialogue writers do it. The pulp writers of the 50's and 60's were really good at writing dialogue. Read the work of great dialogue writers, some of the really great one are: Elmore Leonard, Robert Ludlum, Michael Crichton, Dan Brown, David Goodis, and Donald E. Westlake. Screenwriters like Andrew Kevin Walker, Matt Damon, and Michael Mann craft great dialogue and I suggest you read their screenplays also when studying dialogue.

Tone: Tone represents the story's emotional atmosphere and attitude toward its subject matter, created through word choice, pacing, and narrative voice. It guides readers' emotional responses while maintaining consistency with the story's themes and genre expectations. The best advice in using tone is to get inside the world of the story and feel it. The tone will emerge naturally. Having trouble with this? Watch some of your favorite movies, and read some of your favorite novels and concentrate on how you feel when you see the movie or read the novel. Can you sense the bleakness, Noir (nihilism), and dread in the world of the movie ***The Matrix***? Can you see how the writers and directors used everything from setting to atmosphere to create this tone? Can you sense the despair, claustrophobia, and psychological tension and confusion in Michael Crichton's ***Sphere***? This is tone. Explore it deeply in your brainstorming stage and explore how you can use it to make your novel come alive!

Style: Style is the author's distinctive use of language, including word choice, sentence structure, literary devices, and narrative techniques. It creates a unique voice that enhances story meaning while remaining appropriate to genre and maintaining clarity for readers. The best recommendation to develop your own style is for you make a list of your favorite authors and **read a lot** of their work and explore how different authors have different styles. After a while you'll subconsciously learn to pick up different things from different authors and eventually your own style will emerge (if it hasn't already). Another great exercise is to watch movies and with a notebook and a pen (or a laptop) attempt to write it out scene by scene (You don't have to do a whole movie, but a few scenes every once is awhile is a great exercise). Attempt to write what you see; get inside the movie, the character in that scene (become them) and write about what you see, feel, hear, taste, touch, and do. Get visceral and explore how you can use metaphor and simile to describe that scene.

Pacing: Pacing controls the story's rhythm through varying sentence structure, scene length, and narrative focus to maintain tension and reader interest. It balances action with reflection, managing information flow and emotional intensity while ensuring the story maintains forward momentum. Pacing will depend on the nature of your novel. Thriller and suspense novels tend to have a faster pace than mystery novels where the pacing can take on more of a slow burn. Some horror novels are fast paced and some like ghost stories tend to have a slower pace. One way to manage your pacing is to understand your story extremely well before you sit down to write it and to plan out how your will express each scene. You can even establish a certain average word count for certain scenes. For slow burn scenes you can go for an average of 2000 to 3000 words. And for faster paced scenes you can go for 1500-1800 words. Always minding the rhythm of your sentences because shorter more *staccato* type of sentences create a faster feel while longer descriptive, narrative, and poetic sentences tend to create a slower pace. A scene with heavy dialogue will also read and feel faster than a scene with a lot of narrative description which will feel slower. For certain sections in your novel its wise to attempt to maintain a balance of narrative to dialogue ratio for a more steady and consistent pace. Thinking of each scene as having a beginning, middle and end allows some writers to work out their pacing.

The Subconscious Power of Theme: The True Foundation of Story

While debates about the primacy of plot versus character have persisted since Aristotle first declared plot to be the soul of drama, there is a deeper truth about storytelling that often goes unrecognized: theme is the subconscious foundation from which both compelling characters and meaningful plots emerge. Rather than being merely an abstract message or moral, theme functions as the psychological bedrock that shapes every aspect of a story's development, from the protagonist's inner wounds to the narrative's climactic moments.

To understand theme's fundamental role, we must first recognize how it operates on both conscious and subconscious levels during the creative process. Consider

“The Silence of the Lambs,” where the theme of transformation through confronting fear manifests in every aspect of the story. Clarice Starling's character—her background as an orphaned daughter of a slain police officer, her drive to succeed in the male-dominated FBI, her haunting memories of screaming lambs—emerges naturally from this thematic foundation. Similarly, the plot's progression through increasingly dangerous encounters with Hannibal Lecter and Buffalo Bill represents the external manifestation of this internal journey of confronting fear. The theme doesn't just inform these elements; it generates them from the subconscious mind of the writer.

This generative power of theme becomes even more apparent when examining “The Bourne Identity.” The theme of identity being defined by present choices rather than past programming doesn't just add meaning to the story—it literally creates the story's structure. Bourne's amnesia, his discovered skills, his moral choices that differ from his training, and his relationship with Marie all emerge organically from this central thematic concern. The plot points aren't merely arranged to support the theme; they are born from it.

The subconscious development of story through theme is particularly evident in how it simultaneously shapes character and plot. In “Seven,” the theme of evil and societal apathy doesn't just inform Detective Somerset's world-weary character or Detective Mills' idealistic nature—it creates the very structure of the killer's grand design and the tragic inevitability of the ending. The theme generates both the characters' psychological makeup and the plot's inexorable progression toward its devastating conclusion.

This understanding challenges the traditional view of theme as something that emerges from or is supported by plot and character. Instead, theme operates as the primordial story soup from which both plot and character crystallize. It's the subconscious compass that guides writers toward authentic character actions and meaningful plot developments, even before they consciously understand why certain choices feel right.

Consider how this works in “Eastern Promises,” where the theme of identity and moral compromise in brutal environments generates not only Nikolai's complex character but also the very structure of the plot's revelations about his true nature. The theme doesn't just add depth to the story—it creates the story's DNA, determining how characters will act and how events will unfold in ways that feel both surprising and inevitable.

This understanding of theme's generative power has practical implications for writers. Rather than treating theme as an element to be layered onto a plot or extracted from a character's journey, writers should recognize it as the fundamental force that shapes their creative choices from the earliest stages of development. When writers deeply engage with their theme, they tap into a wellspring of subconscious material that naturally generates coherent characters and meaningful plots.

The examples we've examined demonstrate how this works in practice. In "Red Dragon," the theme of the duality of human nature doesn't just add meaning to Will Graham's struggle—it creates the very structure of his investigation and his relationship with both Hannibal Lecter and Francis Dolarhyde. The theme generates the story's events and character interactions in ways that feel organic precisely because they emerge from this deeper thematic foundation.

Understanding theme as the subconscious foundation of story also helps explain why some stories feel more cohesive and meaningful than others. When plot and character truly emerge from theme, rather than being artificially constructed to support it, the result is a story that resonates on both conscious and subconscious levels with readers or viewers. This is why the best stories feel not just well-crafted but somehow inevitable—as if they couldn't have unfolded any other way.

For writers, this means that deep engagement with theme should precede and inform character development and plot construction. Rather than starting with plot points or character sketches, writers should first explore their theme's psychological and emotional territory. From this exploration, authentic characters and meaningful plot developments will naturally emerge, guided by the subconscious understanding of the theme's implications.

The result is storytelling that transcends mere entertainment to achieve true artistic resonance. When theme operates as the generative force behind both character and plot, stories achieve a unity and power that affects audiences on both conscious and subconscious levels. This is the true magic of storytelling—not just the arrangement of events or the development of characters, but the deep exploration of universal truths that emerge organically through the interplay of all these elements, guided by the subconscious power of theme.

CHAPTER 4

Understanding Story Structure

The Three Act Structure: The most common and applicable story structure in existence. This comes from the teachings of Aristotle who established the first systematized form of storytelling. I recommend reading his famous work titled: *Poetics*. It's a very short yet substantial look at storytelling.

In it Aristotle speaks of every story having a beginning, a middle, and an end. Between the beginning and the middle there is rising action (which he calls: complications) and between the middle and the end there is falling action (an unraveling of those complications (knots)). We (writers, storytellers of all kinds, and story analysts throughout time) have interpreted this to be what we now label as a three act structure.

There are many interpretive forms to this structure. Some writers choose to divide all 3 acts equally, with each act being about 33% of the novel. Others, have chosen to follow what is now the most popular division, where the second act is twice the size of the first and third acts.

That division looks like this:

Act 1: 25%
Act 2: 50%
Act 3: 25%

I like, use, and recommend this structure to my students, however, sometimes I prefer to have my third act be slightly more fast paced and compressed. This is because I usually write in the suspense, thriller and horror genres, which the majority tend to have a more compressed third act.

This more refined structure division looks like this:

Act 1: 25%
Act 2: 55%
Act 3: 20%

***Please keep in mind that you can use either model, intuitively. It's just a 5% difference that can give your ending a bit of a faster feel to the pacing; because I prefer the later model I will be using it to illustrate the three act structure.**

The Three Act Synopsis: An act by act summary of the story. If you feel overwhelmed, you can start with a simple one paragraph summary for each of the acts. Then after reading what you wrote and thinking about the story, continue with the narrative format and extend each single paragraph into a one page summary for each act. Then you can extend each act into two or three pages. Each time you extend the synopsis you are discovering more of your story as well as understanding what your subconscious mind wants to do with this story. This then will allow you to visualize the story's structure and allow you to break it down into the twelve universal beats.

12 Universal Story Beats

1. Set up (introduce the status quo world and express the theme of the story)
2. Inciting Incident (something external happens to the hero which sets the story's main plot in motion)
3. Internal wrestling/Preparation (the hero either debates the unavoidable decision he will have to make or he prepares for it)
4. Welcome to the Jungle (the first plot point of the story that propels the hero into the act 2 world)
5. Subplot (here's where the hero meets his allies/mentor/love interest and

the subplot is introduce by way of this)

6. Trials and Tribulations (this is commonly known as the fun and games beat or the promise of the premise, or the "trailer moments" in the screenwriting world and its where all the cool ups and down action of the story occurs. It's the main reason why the reader picks up your novel, for it's premise)
7. Midpoint (the hero commonly either discovers something here or something dramatic happens to him and this creates another point of no return pushing him into the second part of act 2)
8. Complications (the stakes get higher)
9. Crisis (all seems lost at this moment in time)
10. Critical choice (also known as the dark night of the soul, where the hero eventually reaches a special revelation for good or for ill)
11. Welcome to the end (the second plot point event that propels the hero into act 3)
12. Denouement/Theme Triumphant (The resolution beat of the story)

12 Universal Story Beats by Acts

ACT 1:

1. Set up
2. Inciting Incident
3. Internal wrestling/Preparation

ACT 2:

4. Welcome to the Jungle (plot point 1)
5. Subplot
6. Trials and Tribulations
7. Midpoint
8. Complications
9. Crisis

10. Critical choice

ACT 3:

11. Welcome to the end (plot point 2)
12. Denouement/Theme Triumphant

Here's a detailed breakdown of the 12 universal story beats:

ACT 1:

Set up:

In this multiple scene beat you introduce your main character, the protagonist, or as I like to call him the hero of your story. You also introduce their status quo world, and any secondary characters that may be part of this act 1 world. You should also express the theme of the story in this beat.

Inciting Incident:

In this single scene beat, something happens to the hero that will turn their life upside down. This is inciting incident must be external. It must be something that happens to the hero externally pushing them into a situation where there is no going back to their status quo world and they are forced to take some kind of action. Usually what occurs is that the hero begins to take action starting in act 2 and the actions they take are all the wrong ones, but nevertheless its action and that's what moves the story forward. We want the hero to take wrong actions so that he can eventually learn the theme of the story and make the right right. Of course this revelation and learning of the theme will happen by the beginning of the 3rd act because we need a story for him to get there. That's the fun part. But it all begins with this beat, the inciting incident.

Internal wrestling/Preparation:

In this multiple scene beat the hero usually wrestles with the problem the inciting incident brought them, they contemplate what to do, what decision to make and or they prepare for the inevitable journey they will need to take in act 2.

ACT 2:

Welcome to the Jungle:

In this beat the hero enters the act 2 world. In this beat the hero does something that is different to his daily or normal routines, through the inciting incident they are forced into doing something different in hopes of solving the problem the inciting incident brought them. The act 2 world is usually the complete opposite to the act 1 world and it's usually a single scene beat. However, like most single scene beats, it can be extended to a couple of scenes if the whole beat doesn't fit into a single scene. My advice is the same as with every single scene beat: try to keep single scene beats single but if your story doesn't allow it, for whatever reason, don't get too bogged down, its okay, its not a big deal, allow the story's unique structure to accommodate itself into the structure. Story first, structure second. But remember story is structure and structure is story.

Subplot:

In this single scene beat, its common to see a subplot being introduced and its usually in the form of a new character being introduced which will usually function as a mentor, if not at the moment they will later on. This mentor usually plays a key role in helping the hero learn the theme. This mentor could be a love interest as well, or you could introduce both a love interest and a mentor. Keep in mind that these characters are preferably introduced here in this beat but technically they could be introduced prior in act 1, but of they are, they shouldn't seem to be important at that moment in time, they should gain importance in act 2 and if such is the case then in this beat they begin their function of reminding your hero and the reader about what this novel is really about. However, like most single scene beats, it can be extended to a couple of scenes if the whole beat doesn't fit into a single scene. My advice is the same as with every single scene beat: try to keep single scene beats single but if your story doesn't allow it, for whatever reason, don't get too bogged down, its okay, its not a big deal, allow the story's unique structure to accommodate itself into the structure. Story first, structure second. But remember story is structure and structure is story.

Trials and Tribulations:

This is the longest multiple scene beat in the whole story and will require the most scenes out of all the beats of your novel. This beat allows your to have a lot of fun putting in your hero through ups and downs. This beat is what makes your audience and readers want to pick up your novel. This is usually where the heavy action scenes are. This beat is commonly where most of the secondary characters get killed off and where meaningful discoveries are made. Take your time and plan ahead or brainstorm theses scenes using the ideas section of the workbook first or you can use a separate document file on your PC.

Midpoint:

This single scene beat is one of the most important beats in the story because it pushes the hero off into the second half of act 2. In this beat the hero usually discovers something new (usually something that pushes the plot forward), or he finds something he was looking for but it doesn't turn out exactly as he hoped for, or something happens to the hero that creates the first real meaningful change (not the full change he'll obtain at the end of the novel but a substantial change that pushes him to seek the real change he needs). However, like most single scene beats, it can be extended to a couple of scenes if the whole beat doesn't fit into a single scene. My advice is the same as with every single scene beat: try to keep single scene beats single but if your story doesn't allow it, for whatever reason, don't get too bogged down, its okay, its not a big deal, allow the story's unique structure to accommodate itself into the structure. Story first, structure second. But remember story is structure and structure is story.

Complications:

In this multiple scene beat there should be more complications stacked upon your hero, tension should rise and should push them into the *crisis* beat (also known as the all is lost moment or climax). In other words this beat should push the hero into their lowest point.

Crisis:

This is commonly a single scene beat that marks the lowest point for the hero, the all is lost moment, their worst nightmare coming true, or at least their worst nightmare about to come true if they don't do something about it. However, although a single scene is preferred and most common, this beat can also be a couple of scenes if needed. This is done easily if they are short scenes and connected linearly to convey the low point. My advice is the same as with every single scene beat: try to keep single scene beats single but if your story doesn't allow it, for whatever reason, don't get too bogged down, its okay, its not a big deal, allow the story's unique structure to accommodate itself into the structure. Story first, structure second. But remember story is structure and structure is story.

Critical Choice:

In this multiple scene beat, the hero is in the reaction stage of their low point. Its a beat that lends itself to contemplation. Its a moment in time where the hero will usually go through deep processing, they'll reflect and look at their own past, analyze things from a soul level, and most importantly they'll reach an important revelation that will force them to make a critical choice.

ACT 3:

Welcome to the end:

This is usually a single scene beat that ushers your hero into act 3. It's also commonly known universally as plot point 2, or break into 2. However, like most single scene beats, it can be extended to a couple of scenes if the whole beat doesn't fit into a single scene. My advice is the same as with every single scene beat: try to keep single scene beats single but if your story doesn't allow it, for whatever reason, don't get too bogged down, its okay, its not a big deal, allow the story's unique structure to accommodate itself into the structure. Story first, structure second. But remember story is structure and structure is story.

Denouement/Resolution/Theme Triumphant:

This beat is known as the Theme Triumphant, The Resolution, or The Denouement beat. Denouement means unraveling and as such this beat unravels any confusion or knots in the story. It ties up loose ends and allows the theme of the story to triumph (which brings resolution to the story). Whether your story is a comedy or a tragedy, the theme will be triumphant in this beat and should bring the story into full resolution. Everyone should understand or learn the lesson your novel at this moment in time. If they hadn't caught the lesson prior to this they should catch it now.

As part of the 3 act structure and the 12 universal story beats there exists the optional prologue and the epilogue. Below I provide a clear explanation of both, advice on when to use them, and effective techniques for both, as well as advice on when to avoid using them.

Prologue (Optional)

A prologue serves as an introductory segment that appears before the first chapter of your novel. A prologue should only be used if it provides crucial information that can't be naturally woven into the main narrative. This might be a historical event that shapes the main conflict, a threat from an antagonist's perspective, or a future scene that creates immediate intrigue. The key is to make it short but impactful, offering information that will make the main story more meaningful. A prologue commonly ends with a hook that connects directly to the main narrative, creating questions the reader needs answered.

When to Use a Prologue

Consider including a prologue when you want to:

- Establish crucial historical context that shapes the main conflict
- Introduce a significant event that occurred before the main timeline
- Present information from a perspective different from the main narrative
- Create immediate intrigue or tension that pulls readers into the story
- Set the tone or atmosphere for the entire work
- Reveal information that main characters don't yet know but readers should

Effective Prologue Techniques

Keep your prologue focused and compelling—typically shorter than a standard chapter. It should serve as an engaging entry point that enriches the reader's experience rather than delaying their access to the main story. A prologue may differ from the main narrative in time period, setting, perspective, or even writing style, providing a distinct frame for the story to follow.

The most effective prologues create questions or expectations that drive readers forward into chapter one. End with a hook that connects directly to your main narrative, establishing a thread that readers will follow throughout the book. The information revealed should become increasingly relevant as the story progresses.

When to Skip the Prologue

Omit a prologue if:

- The information can be naturally woven into the main narrative
- It merely delays getting to the heart of your story
- It feels disconnected from the core narrative
- Your first chapter already establishes a strong opening
- You're including it primarily for world-building that could be revealed

gradually

Remember that many readers and industry professionals approach prologues with skepticism, as poorly executed ones can feel unnecessary or disengaging. Your first chapter should always be strong enough to stand on its own, regardless of whether you include a prologue.

Epilogue (Optional)

An epilogue serves as the closing segment of your novel, occurring after the main story has concluded and all major plot points have been resolved. Like a prologue, an epilogue is entirely optional and should only be included when it adds meaningful value to the reader's experience.

When to Use an Epilogue

Consider including an epilogue when you want to:

- Provide a glimpse into the characters' futures beyond the main story's resolution
- Tie up minor loose ends that weren't essential to the main plot
- Show the longer-term consequences of the story's events
- Create a sense of closure or satisfaction for readers invested in the characters
- Plant seeds for a potential sequel or series continuation
- Offer a different perspective that frames the entire story in a new light

Effective Epilogue Techniques

Keep your epilogue concise but meaningful, typically shorter than a standard chapter. It should feel like a gift to readers who have invested in your story—a final moment of connection rather than an essential component of the plot. Consider setting it weeks, months, or even years after the main story to show character growth and the lasting impact of the narrative events.

The epilogue may shift in tone, perspective, or even tense from the main narrative, creating a sense of reflection or looking forward. End on a note that reinforces your story's themes or provides emotional resonance, leaving readers with a sense of completion while possibly hinting at new beginnings.

When to Skip the Epilogue

Omit an epilogue if:

- Your story already has a satisfying conclusion
- The main narrative resolves all necessary elements
- Adding more would dilute the impact of your ending
- The story is intentionally left open-ended

Remember that a well-crafted final chapter can often accomplish everything an epilogue might without the additional section. When in doubt, consider whether the epilogue truly enhances the reader's experience or if it's simply extending the story past its natural endpoint.

Understanding Story through the Three-Act Structure & the 12 Universal Story Beats examples

The three-act structure is a fundamental storytelling framework that traces its roots back to Aristotle's Poetics, in which he observed that well-constructed stories have a beginning, middle, and end. This basic structure has evolved over time into the three-act paradigm widely used today in novels, films, and plays. This guide provides an in-depth exploration of narrative structure, breaking down each act's essential components and illustrating them through carefully chosen examples. I've done this in two parts, firstly by giving you the macro version, which is the three act structure filtered through several three act synopsis examples, which will help you build your own three act synopsis, when the time comes for that. These examples will help you understand the big picture of the three acts in action. Secondly, I've broken down these same stories and several others into the 12 universal story beats. Act by act and beat by beat I give you examples of how story works at the micro level. This will help you not only understand the intricate nature of story but how it can be built from the scene level. From Macro to micro and from micro to macro, outside in and inside to out, you will understand story and be able to use these examples to not only deeply understand your story but to be able to craft it through ***The Subconscious Novelist*** program almost effortlessly.

A Note on Examples: This guidebook teaches novel writing through both the power of the subconscious mind and systematic outlining. To support this approach, I've chosen examples from both original screenplays and masterfully adapted novels, such as Thomas Harris's "Red Dragon" and "The Silence of the Lambs," Robert Ludlum's "The Bourne Identity," and Anne Rice's "Interview with the Vampire."

These authors write with such cinematic style that their work translates beautifully to film while maintaining powerful narrative craft on the page. For the deepest understanding of story structure, I strongly recommend studying these works in all their forms—reading the novels, examining the screenplays, and watching the film adaptations. The visual nature of film helps us internalize storytelling principles on both a conscious and subconscious level, informing our own novel writing process.

However, I understand that time can be a constraint. If you're pressed for time, watching the films is an efficient way to study these story principles, as each movie takes only about two hours to view. This makes the examples more accessible while still allowing you to observe how strong narrative structure works across mediums.

Lets begin with a brief explanation of the three act structure and the three act synopsis of several well known movies and novels.

In the first act, we are introduced to the main character, their world, and the inciting incident that disrupts their status quo and sets the story in motion. The second act, which comprises the bulk of the story, sees the protagonist facing a series of escalating challenges and obstacles as they pursue their goal, often leading to a crisis or low point. The third act brings the story to a climax and resolution, with the main character applying the lessons they've learned to overcome the final obstacle and achieve (or fail to achieve) their ultimate objective.

By studying the detailed three-act breakdowns of successful films and novels, you can internalize the rhythms and patterns of effective storytelling. The 12 universal story beats, which include the setup, inciting incident, midpoint, crisis, and resolution, among others, provide a roadmap for structuring a compelling narrative. Seeing how these beats are executed in practice, through the experiences of iconic characters like Will Hunting, Clarice Starling, or Neo, will help you understand how to craft meaningful character arcs, build and release tension, and weave thematic elements into the fabric of your own story. These synopses also illustrate important principles like the relationship between the protagonist's inner and outer journeys, the role of subplots and supporting characters, and the use of contrast and juxtaposition to create interest and momentum.

However, it's important to recognize that the three-act structure and its associated story beats are tools, not rigid formulas. Every story is unique, and the structure must serve the needs of the narrative, not vice versa. This is why the process outlined in "***The Subconscious Novelist***" focuses first on intuitive brainstorming, where you discover the story your subconscious wants you to tell, and then on telling the story to yourself (verbally and in writing), allowing your subconscious mind to guide the initial flow of the story. By progressively refining and expanding the story through multiple tellings and synopses, and eventually aligning it with the 12 key beats, you can achieve a balance between organic creativity and purposeful structure. The goal of this process and of studying the three-act structure and the 12 universal beats is not to force the story into a predetermined mold, but to use the insights gained from studying these masterful examples to craft a narrative that is both emotionally resonant and structurally sound. Ultimately, understanding the three-act structure and its component beats (both consciously and subconsciously) empowers writers like us to make intentional choices about how to shape our stories for maximum impact.

The 3 Act Structure in Action: Examples of the basic 3 act synopsis, the extended 3 act synopsis, the basic narrative beat sheet, and the extended narrative beat sheet

The following examples depict a basic 3-act synopsis approach that serves as a crucial roadmap during story development. A well-crafted synopsis allows you to visualize the complete narrative arc before diving into your novel, ensuring that the central theme, character development, and plot progression remain cohesive throughout. Think of this as the macro view of your story—a progression from general to specific.

The basic three-act synopsis condenses your story into its essential components: a clear beginning that establishes the protagonist's world and inciting incident, a middle that escalates conflict through progressive complications, and an end that delivers resolution through climactic action. This creates a structural foundation that guides your writing process while helping identify potential plot holes early, maintaining proper pacing, and ensuring character transformations feel earned rather than forced.

While the actual writing process may introduce new elements or refinements, a thoughtful synopsis provides the necessary framework to keep your story on track, balancing creative flexibility with narrative purpose. Throughout the subconscious novelist process, you'll allow your mind to reveal the story organically, gradually discovering its theme—the most crucial element. As you "tell yourself the story" repeatedly, you'll organize it into a cohesive beginning, middle, and end, first through a basic 3-act synopsis, then expanding into a detailed one.

The detailed or extended narrative 3-act synopsis that immediately follow the basic 3 act synopsis examples essentially expand each act with greater depth and nuance. While providing expanded versions of all these examples would make this book unnecessarily lengthy, these basic three-act synopses will sufficiently demonstrate how to craft an effective synopsis. To illustrate the difference between basic and detailed approaches, I'll provide only three extended narrative 3 act synopsis examples as well as three extended narrative beat sheet examples.

All the examples demonstrate how complex narratives can be effectively mapped through this method, capturing both the external plot mechanics and the essential emotional journeys that give stories their lasting impact. They'll help illustrate the progression from basic to detailed synopsis, showing how to structure your story while maintaining its thematic resonance.

8MM (Film 1999, Directed by Joel Schumacher, Screenplay by Andrew Kevin Walker)

Basic 3 Act Synopsis

Prologue

Private investigator Tom Welles works surveillance cases with clinical detachment, photographing a cheating husband at a Miami motel before delivering the evidence to his wealthy client. This establishes Welles' professional methodology and the compartmentalization between his work life and his home life in Harrisburg with his wife Amy and newborn daughter.

Act One

Welles is hired by Mrs. Christian, the widow of a powerful industrialist, to investigate an 8mm film found in her late husband's private safe. The film appears to show the actual murder of a teenage girl by a man in a leather mask. Mrs. Christian wants to know if the film is real or staged.

Despite his initial reluctance, Welles accepts the case. He methodically analyzes the film and identifies the missing girl as Mary Ann Mathews, a 16-year-old who disappeared from Cleveland three years earlier. A visit to Mary Ann's mother reveals a bright teenager who dreamed of becoming an actress in Hollywood. Welles promises to discover the truth, becoming personally invested in the case.

Act Two

Welles follows Mary Ann's trail to Los Angeles, where he discovers she briefly worked in the adult film industry under the name "Raquel" before disappearing. He meets Max California, a clerk at an adult bookstore who becomes his guide through the underground porn industry.

Posing as a wealthy collector, Welles infiltrates deeper into this world and discovers Dino Velvet, a director of violent films whose star performer "Machine" wears the same distinctive mask from the 8mm film. Welles arranges a meeting with Dino and Machine, supposedly to commission a custom film.

The meeting turns into a trap when Eddie Poole, a pornographer connected to Mary Ann, recognizes Welles. Daniel Longdale, Mrs. Christian's lawyer, appears, revealing that the 8mm film was real and commissioned by Mr. Christian for $1 million. A violent confrontation erupts when it becomes clear Longdale didn't share the full amount with his accomplices. In the chaos, Max is killed, and Welles barely escapes.

When Welles reports his findings to Mrs. Christian, she commits suicide, leaving him with no legal recourse for justice. Welles decides to take matters into his own hands.

Act Three

Welles tracks down Eddie Poole and, after confirming his involvement in Mary Ann's murder, executes him. He then confronts Machine at his home. When Machine removes his mask, the face beneath is disturbingly ordinary. Machine admits he commits atrocities simply because he enjoys them, forcing Welles to confront the nature of evil. After a brutal fight, Welles kills Machine.

Epilogue

Welles returns home physically and psychologically scarred. He breaks down in Amy's arms, finally allowing himself to feel the full weight of his experiences. As he holds his infant daughter, it's clear that while he has achieved justice for Mary Ann, the cost to his soul has been profound.

The story closes with Welles reading a letter from Mrs. Matthews. He now understands that innocence, once lost, can never be fully regained. His journey has taught him that evil exists not just in the shadows but in ordinary people living ordinary lives. This knowledge becomes both his burden and his motivation to protect his daughter from the darkness he has witnessed.

The Bourne Identity (Novel by Robert Ludlum, 1980; Film adaptation 2002, Screenplay by Tony Gilroy and William Blake Herron, Directed by Doug Liman)

Basic 3 Act Synopsis

Act 1

In the cold, dark waters of the Mediterranean Sea, a fishing boat crew makes a shocking discovery—a man's body, riddled with bullets, floating in the waves. As they pull him aboard, they find he's barely alive, but suffers from near-total amnesia, unable to recall even his own name. The only clue to his identity is a tiny laser capsule embedded in his hip, bearing the number of a Swiss bank account. This mystery man, soon to be known as Jason Bourne, is about to embark on a perilous journey to uncover his true identity and confront the shadowy forces that want him dead. Haunted by fragmented memories and possessing skills he can't explain, the man assumes the name Jason Bourne based on a passport found in the Swiss bank's safety deposit box. The box also contains a large sum of money, multiple passports with different names, and a gun—clues that point to a dangerous and mysterious past. Desperate for answers, Bourne travels to the American embassy in Zurich, where a chance encounter with Marie Kreutz, a young woman struggling with her own issues, leads to an unlikely partnership. With the authorities closing in and unknown assailants hot on his trail, Bourne convinces Marie to help him escape, plunging them both into a high-stakes game of cat and mouse across Europe.

Act 2

As Bourne and Marie race from country to country, piecing together the fragments of Bourne's shattered memories, they uncover a chilling truth: Bourne was a highly skilled assassin, part of a top-secret CIA black ops program called Treadstone. The program's ruthless handler, Alexander Conklin, is determined to eliminate Bourne to prevent the exposure of their covert operations. Bourne's extraordinary abilities in combat, espionage, and quick thinking become increasingly apparent as he outmaneuvers trained killers and navigates a complex web of government conspiracies. But with each new revelation, Bourne grows more disillusioned with his past life and begins to question the morality of his actions. As Marie becomes more deeply entangled in his dangerous world, Bourne must confront not only external threats but also his own inner demons.

Act 3

The hunt for answers leads Bourne and Marie to Paris, where a climactic confrontation with another Treadstone assassin, the Professor, forces Bourne to face the truth about his past. In a moment of clarity, Bourne's memories come flooding back, revealing the tragic mission that led to his being shot and left for dead in the Mediterranean. Disillusioned and seeking redemption, Bourne makes a fateful decision to expose Treadstone to the media, blowing the lid off the CIA's covert operations and forcing the agency to shut down the program. In the aftermath, Bourne must confront the weight of his actions and the realization that he can never fully escape his past. The story concludes with Bourne and Marie reuniting in Greece, both forever changed by their experiences. For Bourne, it's a chance to forge a new identity, free from the shadows of his former life as a government assassin. But as he looks to the future, he knows that the scars of his past will always be a part of him, shaping the man he has become and the battles he will face in the days to come.

Rounders (1998, original screenplay by David Levien and Brian Koppelman)

Basic 3 Act Synopsis

Act 1

Mike McDermott, a young, talented poker player, loses his entire bankroll of $30,000 in a single hand against the ruthless Russian mobster Teddy KGB. Shaken and disillusioned, Mike makes a solemn promise to his girlfriend Jo that he will quit poker forever and focus on his law school studies. However, this vow is put to the test when his childhood friend Lester “Worm” Murphy is released from prison. Worm, a charismatic but reckless hustler, immediately draws Mike back into the seductive world of underground poker, convincing him to help pay off his old debts.

Act 2

As Mike and Worm navigate the treacherous waters of New York City's poker underworld, they find themselves in a series of increasingly high-stakes games. Mike's natural talent and Worm's clever cheating techniques prove to be a potent combination, but also attract the attention of dangerous players. From the smoky backrooms of seedy clubs to the luxurious penthouse suites of the city's elite, Mike and Worm face challenges from all sides—seasoned pros, corrupt cops, and vicious mobsters. As the stakes rise, so do the risks, and Mike finds himself torn between his loyalty to Worm and his responsibility to Jo and his own future. When Worm's reckless behavior and mounting debts to the menacing Grama, KGB's enforcer, put both their lives on the line, Mike must confront the harsh realities of the path he's chosen and the true cost of his friendship.

Act 3

In a shocking twist, Worm abandons Mike, fleeing town and leaving him to face KGB's wrath and a staggering $15,000 debt alone. Stripped of his allies and his illusions, Mike is forced to confront the harsh truth about himself and his place in the world of poker. Guided by the wisdom of his mentor, Professor Petrovsky, who teaches him that "we can't run from who we are," Mike makes the decision to embrace his identity as a poker player fully. In a final, all-or-nothing showdown with KGB, Mike puts his skills, his heart, and his entire future on the line. In a game that's as much about psychology as it is about the cards, Mike's unwavering determination and hard-earned self-knowledge prove to be his ultimate trump cards. With a deft final play, he not only wins back his money but also his sense of self. The film concludes with Mike setting off for Las Vegas, no longer running from his destiny but running towards it, ready to take his place among the world's greatest poker players.

The Matrix (1999, original screenplay by The Wachowskis)

Basic 3 Act Synopsis

Act 1

In a world where the line between reality and illusion is blurred, Thomas Anderson, a computer programmer by day and a hacker known as "Neo" by night, finds himself plagued by a single, haunting question: "What is the Matrix?" His search for the truth leads him to the enigmatic Morpheus and his crew of rebel operatives, who reveal to Neo the shocking truth behind his existence. The world as he knows it is a lie, a complex simulation called the Matrix, designed by machines to keep humanity enslaved while using their bodies as an energy source. Faced with this shattering revelation, Neo is given a choice: take the blue pill and return to his ordinary life, blissfully unaware, or take the red pill and see how deep the rabbit hole goes.

Act 2

Neo chooses the red pill and awakens to the harsh, dystopian reality of the 22nd century, where humanity is locked in a desperate war against the machines. As he grapples with his new existence and his potential role in the resistance, Neo undergoes a grueling training regimen within the Matrix, learning to bend the rules of the simulated world and unlock his untapped potential. Under the guidance of Morpheus, who believes Neo to be "The One" prophesied to bring an end to the war, Neo begins to embrace his newfound abilities. But as he delves deeper into the mysteries of the Matrix, he encounters new allies and enemies, each with their own agendas. From the sleek and deadly Agent Smith to the treacherous Cypher, who dreams of returning to the comfort of ignorance, the dangers within the Matrix prove to be as formidable as those in the bleak real world.

Act 3

As the conflict between the rebels and the machines intensifies, Neo faces his ultimate test. In a shocking betrayal, Morpheus is captured by Agent Smith, forcing Neo and his crewmate Trinity to mount a desperate rescue mission. But the path to victory is fraught with peril, and Neo must confront not only the might of the machines but also his own doubts and limitations. In a climactic battle within the Matrix, Neo transcends his perceived boundaries, becoming the embodiment of the human will to survive and the catalyst for change. Through an act of profound sacrifice and an unwavering commitment to the truth, Neo sets in motion a chain of events that will forever alter the balance of power between man and machine. The film concludes with Neo, now fully awakened to his role as "The One," challenging the machines and offering a glimmer of hope to the embattled remnants of humanity. As he looks to the future, he knows that the road ahead will be long and hard, but with his newfound understanding and the support of those who believe in him, anything is possible. For in the Matrix, as in life, the only limits are those we place on ourselves.

Heat (1995, original screenplay by Michael Mann)

Basic 3 Act Synopsis

Act 1

In the sprawling, neon-lit expanse of Los Angeles, two men on opposite sides of the law are locked in a deadly game of cat and mouse. Neil McCauley, a meticulous and disciplined professional thief, leads a tight-knit crew of skilled criminals, planning and executing high-stakes heists with precision and finesse. On the other side, Vincent Hanna, a tenacious and driven homicide detective, is determined to track down McCauley and bring him to justice. As the film delves into their parallel lives, it reveals the striking similarities between the two men – their uncompromising dedication to their respective crafts, their strained personal relationships, and their unwavering codes of honor. When McCauley's crew pulls off a daring armored car heist, leaving three guards dead, Hanna's pursuit kicks into high gear, setting the stage for an epic confrontation between two formidable adversaries.

Act 2

As McCauley meticulously plans his final score – a lucrative bank heist that promises to set him and his crew up for life – Hanna and his team of detectives close in, using every resource and tactic at their disposal to unravel the complex web of McCauley's criminal enterprise. The pressure mounts on both sides as McCauley navigates the treacherous waters of his personal life, juggling his relationships with his crew, his new lover Eady, and his estranged family, all while staying one step ahead of Hanna's relentless pursuit. Hanna, meanwhile, becomes increasingly consumed by the hunt, pushing himself to the brink of physical and mental exhaustion, even as his single-minded devotion threatens to unravel his already strained marriage. In a pivotal moment, McCauley and Hanna find themselves face to face in a simple everyday setting—a coffee shop—engaging in a charged dialogue that lays bare their mutual respect and understanding, even as they acknowledge the inevitability of their roles as hunter and prey.

Act 3

The simmering tension between McCauley and Hanna reaches a boiling point as the day of the bank heist arrives. In a heart-pounding sequence that showcases Mann's masterful command of action and suspense, McCauley's crew engages in a brutal shootout with Hanna's team, turning the streets of downtown Los Angeles into a war zone. In the chaotic aftermath, McCauley finds himself alone, his crew dead or captured, his money gone, and his dreams of a new life shattered. With nothing left to lose, he embarks on a relentless quest for vengeance against those who betrayed him, even as Hanna and his team close in for the final confrontation. In a haunting, atmospheric finale, McCauley and Hanna face each other one last time, two warriors bound by their shared code of honor, each knowing that only one of them will walk away. As the gunfire echoes through the eerie, blue-lit darkness of the LAX airfield, the film reaches its shattering conclusion – a testament to the inescapable consequences of the paths we choose and the codes we live by. In the end, both men, for all their differences, are revealed to be two sides of the same coin – each driven by an unshakable dedication to their own sense of justice, each paying the ultimate price for their unwavering commitment to their respective worlds.

Interview with the Vampire (Novel by Anne Rice, 1976; Film adaptation 1994, Screenplay by Anne Rice, Directed by Neil Jordan)

Basic 3 Act Synopsis

Prologue

In modern-day San Francisco, a young reporter sits down with a mysterious man for what he believes will be a standard interview. But as the pale figure before him begins to speak, the reporter realizes he's in the presence of something extraordinary—a vampire named Louis de Pointe du Lac, who promises to share his life story and reveal "what it means to be a vampire."

Act 1

Louis begins his tale in 1791 Louisiana, where, as a young plantation owner grief-stricken over the death of his wife and child, he actively seeks death. His wish is granted—sort of—when the vampire Lestat de Lioncourt transforms him into a creature of the night. Lestat becomes Louis's mentor in his new immortal existence, teaching him to kill and feed, though Louis struggles with taking human life. Their uneasy partnership is complicated when Lestat transforms a young orphan girl, Claudia, into a vampire to keep Louis from leaving him. The three form a dark family unit, with Claudia growing mentally into a woman while forever trapped in a child's body.

Act 2

As decades pass, Claudia becomes increasingly resentful of her eternal childhood and the men who condemned her to it. She manipulates Louis into helping her attempt to kill Lestat, poisoning him with dead blood and slashing his throat before dumping his body in the swamps. Louis and Claudia flee to Europe in search of others of their kind, eventually finding a theater troupe of vampires in Paris led by the ancient Armand. However, their peace is shattered when a vengeful Lestat appears and accuses them of attempting to murder him. The vampire coven punishes Claudia for this crime by exposing her to the sun, killing her and her human companion. Louis retaliates by burning down the theater with the vampires trapped inside.

Act 3

Devastated by Claudia's death, Louis spends the following decades wandering the world, eventually returning to New Orleans where he finds Lestat living in squalor, afraid of the modern world. In the present day, Louis concludes his interview with the reporter, who is fascinated by the tale and begs to be made a vampire. Louis reacts with rage at the reporter's failure to understand the moral of his story about the pain and loneliness of immortal existence. After Louis vanishes, the reporter finds his recorded interview and sets out to track down Lestat, demonstrating he hasn't heeded Louis's warning about the true nature of the vampire's curse.

The Silence of the Lambs (Novel by Thomas Harris, 1988; Film adaptation 1991, Screenplay by Ted Tally Directed by Jonathan Demme)

Basic 3 Act Synopsis

Act 1

The opening scene introduces the story's heroine, Clarice Starling, a young FBI trainee with a fierce determination to succeed in the male-dominated world of law enforcement. As she navigates the grueling physical and mental challenges of the FBI Academy at Quantico, Starling's raw talent and unwavering dedication catch the eye of her superiors, setting the stage for her fateful encounter with one of the most brilliant and terrifying minds in the history of crime. Starling's life takes an unexpected turn when she is summoned by Jack Crawford, the head of the FBI's Behavioral Science Unit, and given a daunting assignment: to interview the infamous Dr. Hannibal Lecter, a brilliant psychiatrist turned cannibalistic serial killer, in the hopes of gaining insight into the mind of a new killer on the loose, known only as "Buffalo Bill." As Starling delves into the twisted world of Lecter's psyche, she finds herself drawn into a deadly game of cat and mouse, pitting her wits and her will against one of the most cunning and manipulative predators she has ever encountered. With each meeting, Lecter probes deeper into Starling's own haunted past, unearthing painful memories and long-buried secrets, even as he tantalizingly offers cryptic clues to the identity of Buffalo Bill.

Act 2

As the pressure mounts and the body count rises, Starling's hunt for Buffalo Bill takes on a new urgency. Navigating the treacherous waters of inter-agency politics, media scrutiny, and her own inner demons, Starling follows the trail of clues left by Lecter, piecing together a chilling portrait of a killer whose twisted desires and grotesque rituals are rooted in a tragic past. But even as she closes in on her prey, Starling finds herself haunted by her own troubled history, particularly the traumatic memory of her father's violent death and her desperate attempt to rescue a herd of lambs from slaughter. As her relationship with Lecter deepens and darkens, becoming a twisted mirror of her own psyche, Starling must confront the question of whether she is willing to pay the ultimate price for justice – to stare into the abyss and risk being consumed by it.

Act 3

In a shocking turn of events, Lecter stages a bloody and brilliant escape from custody, leaving a trail of carnage in his wake and throwing the FBI into chaos. With time running out and Buffalo Bill's latest victim, the daughter of a prominent senator, hanging in the balance, Starling must put aside her doubts and fears and trust her own instincts to unravel the final pieces of the puzzle. Armed with Lecter's cryptic clues and her own hard-earned knowledge of the criminal mind, Starling follows a trail that leads her to a remote farmhouse, where she must confront Buffalo Bill in a terrifying underground labyrinth filled with the bones of his victims. In a heart-stopping climax, Starling must summon all her strength and cunning to outwit the killer, rescuing his intended victim and putting an end to his reign of terror, even as she comes face to face with the darkest depths of human evil.

In the denouement, Starling emerges triumphant but forever changed, having faced her own demons and emerged stronger for it. As she graduates from the FBI Academy and takes her place among the ranks of the elite, she carries with her the scars and the hard-won wisdom of her ordeal – a testament to the strength of the human spirit in the face of unimaginable horror. And yet, even as she looks to the future with hope and determination, she knows that the specter of Hannibal Lecter will always be with her, a dark and twisted reflection of her own deepest fears and desires, forever lurking in the shadows of her mind.

Red Dragon (Novel by Thomas Harris, 1981; Film adaptation 2002, directed by Brett Ratner)

Basic 3 Act Synopsis

Note *The film adaptation of "Red Dragon" (the 2002 version directed by Brett Ratner) begins with a prologue that isn't in the book.

The movie opens with a sequence showing Hannibal Lecter at a symphony performance, where Will Graham realizes Lecter is the serial killer he's been hunting. This is followed by their violent confrontation where Lecter stabs Graham before being captured. This entire sequence serves as a prologue to the main story, showing the history between Graham and Lecter before jumping forward in time to Graham's retirement in Florida.

This prologue was added for the film to establish the backstory of how Lecter was caught and why Graham is so traumatized, which in the novel is instead revealed gradually through flashbacks and references throughout the text.

Prologue

The story opens with a chilling glimpse into the mind of a killer. FBI profiler Will Graham, haunted by his own dark past and struggling with the weight of his unique gift – the ability to empathize with even the most twisted of killers – visits his former colleague and mentor, the brilliant psychiatrist Dr. Hannibal Lecter, seeking insight into a particularly gruesome case. But as Graham probes deeper into Lecter's psyche, he makes a terrifying realization – that the man he once trusted and admired is himself a monster, the very embodiment of the evil he has spent his life hunting. In a brutal confrontation that leaves both men scarred both physically and emotionally, Graham manages to overpower Lecter and bring him to justice, but at a terrible cost to his own sanity and sense of self.

Act 1

Years later, a retired and deeply traumatized Graham is living a quiet life with his family, having turned his back on the world of serial killers and criminal profiling. But his fragile peace is shattered when his former boss, Jack Crawford, comes calling with a desperate plea for help. A new killer, dubbed the "Tooth Fairy" by the media, has emerged, his brutal murders marked by a grotesque signature – the biting and tearing of his victims' flesh. Despite his deep reluctance and the terror that grips him at the thought of returning to the darkness he thought he had left behind, Graham agrees to join the hunt, knowing that his unique skills may be the only hope of stopping the killer before he strikes again. But to do so, he must once again confront his own worst nightmare – the brilliant and twisted mind of Hannibal Lecter, now imprisoned but still wielding immense psychological power.

Act 2

As Graham delves deeper into the Tooth Fairy case, he finds himself drawn into a deadly game of cat and mouse, not just with the killer but with his own inner demons. Tormented by his past and struggling to maintain his grip on reality, Graham must navigate the treacherous waters of his own psyche, even as he probes the depths of a killer's twisted desires. With each new revelation, each new horror, Graham feels himself slipping further into the abyss, his own sanity and his relationships with his family and colleagues fraying under the immense strain. Meanwhile, the Tooth Fairy himself, a tormented and deeply disturbed man named Francis Dolarhyde, begins a strange and unsettling relationship with a blind woman named Reba, his fragile grasp on humanity threatened by his own monstrous urges and the manipulative influence of Hannibal Lecter, with whom he has begun a dangerous correspondence.

Act 3

As the Tooth Fairy's crimes escalate and the body count rises, Graham and his team find themselves in a desperate race against time to uncover the killer's identity and stop him before he can claim more innocent lives. In a series of tense and emotionally charged confrontations, Graham must confront not only the monster he hunts but also the monsters within himself – the guilt, the fear, and the terrible knowledge that he is more like his prey than he cares to admit. In a climactic showdown that pushes him to the very brink of madness, Graham must face the Tooth Fairy in a brutal battle that leaves both men bloodied and broken, their fates forever entwined in a twisted dance of death and redemption.

In the aftermath of the case, Graham emerges victorious but deeply scarred, his psyche forever altered by his journey into the heart of darkness. As he begins the long and painful process of healing, both physically and emotionally, he must come to terms with the terrible knowledge that his gift, the very thing that makes him so uniquely suited to hunting monsters, is also the thing that threatens to destroy him, to drag him down into the same abyss he has spent his life fighting against. And yet, even as he struggles to find his way back to the light, he knows that he will always carry a piece of that darkness with him, a reminder of the terrible price he has paid for his calling.

Good Will Hunting (1997, original screenplay by Matt Damon and Ben Affleck)

Basic 3 Act Synopsis

Act 1

Will Hunting, a young, unassuming janitor at MIT, leads a double life. By day, he mops floors and keeps to himself, but by night, he indulges his brilliant mind, devouring books on advanced mathematics, history, and philosophy. His extraordinary gift for mathematics is discovered when he anonymously solves a complex equation left on a chalkboard by the renowned Professor Gerald Lambeau. Intrigued and determined to nurture this raw talent, Lambeau tracks down the elusive genius, only to find that Will's intellect is matched by his troubled past and rebellious nature. When Will's run-ins with the law finally catch up with him, Lambeau sees an opportunity to make a deal: in exchange for leniency, Will must put his mind to work under Lambeau's guidance and, more importantly, confront his inner demons with the help of therapy. Reluctant but left with no choice, Will agrees, setting the stage for a journey of self-discovery that will challenge everything he believes about himself and his place in the world.

Act 2

As Will begins his sessions with a succession of therapists, his quick wit, encyclopedic knowledge, and biting sarcasm prove too much for each one. He runs circles around them intellectually, using his genius as a weapon to keep the world at bay. But when Lambeau introduces him to Sean Maguire, a fellow South Boston native with a similarly rough-hewn background, Will finds himself facing a different kind of challenge. Sean, played with disarming honesty by Robin Williams, sees through Will's intellectual defenses and refuses to back down, forcing the young man to confront the painful truths he's been running from his entire life. As their sessions become more intense and emotionally charged, Will begins to open up, revealing the depths of his fear, anger, and self-doubt. Parallel to his journey of self-discovery, Will navigates the challenges of his relationships with his best friend Chuckie, his new girlfriend Skylar, and his own sense of loyalty to his working-class roots. Each relationship brings new challenges and opportunities for growth, as Will struggles to reconcile his extraordinary potential with his deep-seated fear of abandonment and betrayal.

Act 3

As Will's breakthroughs in therapy begin to chip away at his emotional walls, he finds himself at a crossroads. When Skylar asks him to move to California with her, he panics, reverting to his old pattern of pushing people away. He lashes out at Sean, at Lambeau, and at anyone who tries to get close to him, convinced that he's unworthy of love and destined to be alone. But Sean refuses to give up on him, pushing him to confront the abuse and abandonment that have shaped his life. In a cathartic scene that has become one of the most memorable in modern cinema, Sean repeats the words "It's not your fault" over and over again, until Will finally breaks down, accepting the love and forgiveness he's been denying himself for so long. With this breakthrough, Will is finally able to see himself in a new light. He makes peace with Lambeau, acknowledging the professor's role in his growth, and he says goodbye to Sean, knowing that he'll always carry the therapist's wisdom and compassion with him. In the end, Will makes the decision to take a leap of faith, to leave behind the familiar streets of South Boston and embrace the possibility of a new life. He sets out to follow Skylar to California, ready to face whatever challenges lie ahead, armed with a newfound sense of self-acceptance and the knowledge that he is worthy of love and happiness. The final scene, with Will driving into the sunset, is a testament to the power of the human spirit to overcome even the darkest of pasts and the most daunting of obstacles.

Throughout the film, the central theme of the power of human connection and the importance of facing one's demons is woven seamlessly into the narrative.

Will's journey is not just one of intellectual growth, but of emotional healing, as he learns to trust, to love, and to accept himself for who he is. The relationships he forms along the way—with Sean, with Skylar, with Lambeau, and with his lifelong friends—serve as a testament to the transformative power of human bonds, and the idea that even the most brilliant mind is nothing without the heart to guide it. In the end, Good Will Hunting is a story about the triumph of the human spirit, about the power of love, friendship, and self-discovery to heal even the deepest wounds and unlock the most hidden potential. It is a film that reminds us that greatness lies not just in the mind, but in the courage to face one's fears, to open one's heart, and to embrace the endless possibilities of life.

Seven (1995, directed by David Fincher, screenplay by Andrew Kevin Walker)

Basic 3 Act Synopsis

Prologue

The opening credit sequence unfolds as a series of disjointed, haunting fragments: A metronome ticks with mechanical precision. In a dimly lit room, a man's hands—steady, methodical—trim his fingertips with a razor blade, filing down the ridges to erase his identity. Journals fill with cramped, immaculate handwriting—countless pages documenting twisted thoughts and meticulous plans. Photographs are defaced—black marker scratching through eyes, then violently crossing out entire faces. Thread is pulled through needle, binding book pages. Razor blades cut newspaper clippings. All performed with ritualistic care by someone preparing his life's work: a series of elaborately staged murders based on the seven deadly sins. Not random acts of violence, but a calculated sermon designed to force a morally blind world to see its own corruption.

Act 1

Detective William Somerset (Morgan Freeman), a methodical, world-weary veteran just one week from retirement, is reluctantly paired with Detective David

Mills (Brad Pitt), an eager, hot-headed transfer who has moved to the city with his wife Tracy (Gwyneth Paltrow) to advance his career. Their partnership begins with tension when they investigate a disturbing murder scene—a morbidly obese man forced to eat until his stomach ruptured, with the word "GLUTTONY" written behind the refrigerator. The next day, they discover a second victim, a wealthy attorney who was made to cut off a pound of his own flesh, with "GREED" written in blood at the scene. Somerset, recognizing the pattern of the seven deadly sins, heads to the library to research medieval literature on sin, while Mills scoffs at his intellectual approach. As Somerset immerses himself in Dante's "Inferno" and Chaucer's "Canterbury Tales," he realizes they're hunting a killer of extraordinary intelligence and commitment—someone who has likely been planning these murders for years. Meanwhile, Somerset forms a quiet bond with Tracy during a dinner at the Mills' apartment, where she privately confides her unhappiness with city life and her unannounced pregnancy, unsure if she wants to raise a child in such a hellish environment.

Act 2

The investigation accelerates as more elaborately staged murders are discovered. A drug dealer and pedophile labeled "SLOTH" has been kept barely alive, strapped to a bed for an entire year, his body and mind wasting away. A model whose face was mutilated before being given the choice between suicide or calling for help, representing "PRIDE." With each new crime scene, the detectives find carefully placed evidence—fingerprints and library records—leading them to a man using the alias "John Doe." When they track Doe to his apartment, he unexpectedly emerges from the hallway, firing at the detectives before fleeing. During the ensuing chase through rain-soaked alleyways and buildings, Doe nearly kills Mills but spares him, saying it's "not time yet." Inside Doe's apartment, they discover a disturbing shrine to his work—thousands of notebooks filled with his deranged manifestos, photographs of victims during surveillance, and religious iconography. As Somerset and Mills delve deeper into the killer's psyche, their own philosophical differences about justice and morality come to the surface. Somerset believes the world is already hell; Mills clings to the idea that good can triumph.

Act 3

In a shocking turn, John Doe (Kevin Spacey) surrenders himself at the police station, covered in blood—but it isn't his. He offers a chilling ultimatum: he will confess to all murders and lead them to the final two victims, representing "ENVY" and "WRATH," but only if both Somerset and Mills accompany him, alone. With no legal leverage, the detectives agree, and Doe directs them to drive far into the desert outside the city. During the drive, Doe sermonizes about his mission to punish the world for its indifference to sin. As they reach the designated location, a delivery van approaches on the horizon. Doe reveals that he envied Mills' normal life, and so he "took" his wife. The delivery contains Tracy's severed head—Doe's embodiment of "ENVY." In an act of calculated manipulation, Doe goads the devastated Mills into becoming "WRATH" by executing him in a hail of bullets, thereby completing Doe's perverse masterpiece. As Mills is taken away, destroyed by Doe's design, Somerset decides not to retire after all. In the film's closing moments, Somerset quotes Ernest Hemingway: "The world is a fine place and worth fighting for." He adds, "I agree with the second part," acknowledging the darkness he's witnessed while refusing to surrender to it completely.

The Machinist (2004, directed by Brad Anderson, screenplay by Scott Kosar)

Basic 3 Act Synopsis

Prologue

The film opens with Trevor Reznik (Christian Bale), a gaunt, skeletal figure, attempting to dispose of a body wrapped in a carpet by dumping it into the ocean at night. As headlights appear in the distance, Trevor abandons his efforts and flees. The scene creates immediate tension and mystery—who is this emaciated man, and whose body is he trying to hide? The film then moves backward to show Trevor's daily existence: he hasn't slept in a year, his body has wasted away to skin and bones, and he lives in a sparse apartment where he obsessively cleans with bleach and leaves Post-it notes to remind himself of basic tasks. The haunting, desaturated blue-gray color palette reflects Trevor's hollow emotional state as he moves through his isolated life like a ghost.

Act 1

Trevor works as a machinist in a noisy, industrial factory where coworkers whisper about his alarming appearance. His lonely routine consists of visiting Stevie (Jennifer Jason Leigh), a kind-hearted prostitute with whom he's formed an unusual bond, and spending his sleepless nights at an airport café where he's served by Marie (Aitana Sánchez-Gijón), a friendly waitress. Trevor's fragile equilibrium is shattered when he's distracted by the appearance of a mysterious co-worker named Ivan (John Sharian)—a bald, imposing man with a disfigured hand who seems to appear and disappear without warning. During this moment of distraction, Trevor causes an industrial accident that severs his colleague Miller's (Michael Ironside) arm. In the aftermath, Trevor finds a cryptic sticky note on his refrigerator—a game of hangman with several letters missing. Though he reports the accident, his coworkers grow increasingly hostile, believing Trevor is dangerous. When Trevor attempts to discuss Ivan with his colleagues, they insist no such person exists at the factory, deepening the mystery and Trevor's paranoia.

Act 2

As Trevor's grip on reality weakens, he begins to see Ivan everywhere, following him across the city's bleak industrial landscape. He discovers blood inexplicably dripping from his refrigerator, only to find it gone moments later. The hangman game on his fridge slowly gains new letters with each passing day. Trevor's relationship with Stevie deteriorates after he invites her to his apartment for a proper date on Mother's Day, only to become irrationally suspicious when she explores his apartment. Meanwhile, he forms a tentative connection with Marie and her son Nicholas at the airport café, offering glimpses of the normal life he desperately craves. In a disturbing scene at a carnival, Trevor accompanies Nicholas on a haunted house ride called "Route 666," where Nicholas suffers a seizure that triggers disjointed flashes of memory in Trevor. When Trevor discovers a photo in Ivan's wallet showing himself with Nicholas fishing—an event he has no recollection of—his paranoia reaches new heights. After confronting his coworkers about Ivan's existence and being met with confusion and anger, Trevor begins tracking Ivan's car, discovering that its license plate is registered in Trevor's own name.

Act 3

Trevor's investigation leads him back to Highway 152, the real location corresponding to the "Route 666" ride. Arriving at the scene at night, Trevor experiences a breakthrough when headlights illuminate the road, triggering the repressed memory of hitting a young boy with his car and fleeing the scene a year ago. In a series of devastating flashbacks shown with brutal clarity, Trevor finally remembers what happened: there is no Ivan—he's a manifestation of Trevor's guilt, a physical representation of the person Trevor was before the accident. One year ago, while driving along Highway 152, Trevor accidentally hit and killed a young boy who was standing by the roadside with his mother after their car broke down. Instead of stopping to help, Trevor panicked and fled the scene. The boy was Nicholas, the same child he imagines at the airport café. Marie is not real either, but a projection of the mother whose son he killed. The hangman game spelling out "KILLER" was Trevor's subconscious forcing him to confront his crime. Every aspect of his deteriorating existence—the insomnia, the weight loss, the paranoia—stems from this repressed trauma. In the film's final sequence, Trevor turns himself in to the police, confessing his crime. The final scene shows Trevor in what appears to be a prison cell. He lies down on the bed and closes his eyes. For the first time in a year, Trevor falls into a peaceful sleep as the screen fades into a scene of him driving through a tunnel into white light. This concluding moment suggests that by confronting his guilt and taking responsibility for his actions, Trevor has finally found the peace that had eluded him since the accident.

Eastern Promises (2007, directed by David Cronenberg, screenplay by Steven Knight)

Basic 3 Act Synopsis

Prologue

On a rainy night in London, a desperate, heavily pregnant Russian teenager named Tatiana stumbles into a pharmacy, bleeding profusely. As she collapses, the pharmacist rushes her to a nearby hospital where, despite the medical staff's best efforts, she dies during childbirth. Her newborn daughter survives, but with no family to claim her. The only clues to the girl's identity and heritage are Tatiana's diary—written entirely in Russian—and a business card for the Trans-Siberian restaurant tucked within its pages. These fragments of a life cut short will soon draw an innocent midwife into the heart of London's most dangerous criminal underworld, where secrets are buried as deep as the bodies that keep them.

Act 1

Anna Khitrova (Naomi Watts), a half-Russian midwife at the hospital, is haunted by Tatiana's death and the orphaned baby girl left behind. Determined to find the child's family, Anna takes possession of Tatiana's diary, despite hospital protocol. Unable to read Russian herself, she brings the diary to her Russian uncle Stepan (Jerzy Skolimowski), who refuses to translate it when he glimpses its disturbing contents. Undeterred, Anna follows the lead of the business card to the Trans-Siberian restaurant, an elegant establishment owned by Semyon (Armin Mueller-Stahl), a charming, grandfatherly Russian émigré who offers to translate the diary for her. At the restaurant, Anna also encounters Semyon's volatile son Kirill (Vincent Cassel) and their enigmatic driver, Nikolai Luzhin (Viggo Mortensen)—a man of few words whose cold demeanor barely conceals a capacity for brutal violence. What Anna doesn't realize is that Semyon is actually the ruthless leader of the vory v zakone, a branch of the Russian mafia, and her innocent quest has placed her in grave danger.

Act 2

As Semyon stalls Anna with his translation of the diary, the truth gradually emerges: Tatiana was sex-trafficked to London by Semyon's organization, repeatedly raped by his son Kirill, and impregnated in the process. The diary contains enough evidence to destroy Semyon's criminal empire and send him to prison. Meanwhile, Nikolai, who serves as Semyon's "cleaner" and enforcer, is steadily rising through the ranks of the vory hierarchy. In a shocking display of loyalty and commitment to the organization, Nikolai is formally inducted into the vory through an elaborate ceremony involving prison tattoos that tell the story of his criminal life—most of which are fabricated. As Anna grows increasingly suspicious of Semyon's intentions, she discovers that the baby girl is actually Kirill's daughter, making Semyon the grandfather. Rather than embracing his grandchild, Semyon orders Nikolai to dispose of both the diary and the baby to protect his family's reputation within the criminal underworld. Caught between his duty to the vory and his growing connection to Anna, Nikolai must navigate a treacherous path where a single misstep could cost him everything.

Act 3

The deadly game reaches its climax when Anna learns the full extent of Semyon's plans and races to protect the baby. In a stunning twist, Nikolai reveals himself to be an undercover agent for the British government, infiltrating the vory to gather evidence against their operations. When Semyon and Kirill dispatch Nikolai to kill a rival Chechen gangster, he finds himself ambushed in a brutal bathhouse confrontation—naked, vulnerable, armed with only his wits and fighting skill against two knife-wielding assassins. The bloody, visceral struggle leaves Nikolai gravely wounded but victorious. In the aftermath, Nikolai orchestrates an elaborate plan to protect Anna and the baby while simultaneously bringing down Semyon's empire. He collects Tatiana's diary, which contains the damning evidence needed to arrest Semyon, while manipulating events to position himself as the new pakhan (leader) of the London vory branch, with the self-destructive Kirill as his puppet. As the film closes, Anna and the baby are safe, Semyon is arrested, and Nikolai sits in the Trans-Siberian restaurant, now adorned with the stars of a vory captain on his shoulders—his true allegiances known only to himself. His face, once merely a mask of controlled emotion, now reveals the weight of living between two worlds, neither of which can ever truly be home.

EXTENDED 3 ACT SYNOPSIS EXAMPLES

8MM (1999, directed by Joel Schumacher, written by Andrew Kevin Walker)

Extended 3 Act Synopsis

Prologue

In the bustling Miami International Airport, private investigator Tom Welles moves with the practiced ease of someone accustomed to remaining invisible. His target—a middle-aged businessman suspected of infidelity—moves through the terminal unaware of Welles' constant surveillance. The investigator's methods are precise and professional; his camera carefully documents each compromising moment without judgment or emotional investment.

The chase leads through Miami's affluent neighborhoods to a run-down motel, where Welles captures irrefutable evidence of the man's extramarital affair. Later, in a wealthy client's home, he delivers the photographs with clinical detachment.

The client's bitter response—"I never liked him anyway"—barely registers. For Welles, this is simply another case closed, another check to be collected.

This opening sequence establishes not just Welles' professional methodology, but the careful compartmentalization of his life. In his modest Harrisburg home, he maintains a separate existence with his wife Amy and their newborn daughter. The contrast between his work investigating human depravity and his attempts to build a normal family life creates a tension that will eventually become unsustainable.

Act 1

Everything changes for Welles when he receives a call from Daniel Longdale, the personal attorney to Mrs. Christian, widow of a wealthy and powerful industrialist. The lawyer's carefully chosen words hint at something unusual, beyond the routine cases of infidelity and insurance fraud that typically occupy Welles' time.

Arriving at the Christian estate, Welles is struck by its oppressive grandeur. The mansion looms over him, a monument to wealth and privilege that holds darker secrets than its manicured exterior suggests. Mrs. Christian, elderly and dignified, receives him in a study filled with the artifacts of her late husband's success. She explains that while executing her husband's estate, she discovered something disturbing in his private safe - something that has shaken her understanding of the man she thought she knew.

From a small metal canister, she produces an 8mm film reel. Her hands tremble slightly as she handles it, as if the physical object itself carries a contaminating power. Welles notes her distress with professional detachment, not yet understanding how this simple reel of film will shatter his own carefully maintained boundaries.

In the mansion's darkened study, Welles threads the projector with methodical precision. The mechanical whir of the machine fills the room as the first frames flicker to life on the screen. The footage is grainy, black and white, amateur in its composition but horrifyingly clear in its content. A teenage girl, clearly terrified, alone in a sparse room. A man wearing a leather mask enters the frame. What follows unfolds with nightmare logic - brutal, methodical violence captured with cold detachment by another unseen figure behind the camera.

Welles watches the footage with growing horror, his professional mask slipping for the first time. His latex-gloved hands grip the projector tightly, knuckles white with tension. The girl's fear, her final moments, burn themselves into his consciousness. When the film ends, the room falls into a silence heavy with the weight of what they've witnessed.

Mrs. Christian's voice trembles as she voices the question that will launch Welles' investigation: “I want you to find out if this is real... if he killed that girl.” The possibility that her late husband, a pillar of society, might have paid to have an innocent young woman murdered for his entertainment represents a horror almost too great to contemplate. Yet the evidence exists, projected on the wall of his private study, a testament to depths of depravity that Welles has only begun to understand.

Despite his initial instinct to refuse the case, Welles finds himself drawn in by Mrs. Christian's desperate need to know the truth - was the film real or staged? Did her late husband, a powerful industrialist, pay to have an innocent girl murdered for his entertainment? The possibility that the girl might still be alive, that the film might be an elaborate fake, provides Welles with the moral justification to accept the case.

His investigation begins methodically. In his home office, wearing latex gloves that symbolize his attempt to maintain professional distance, Welles analyzes the film frame by frame. He notes every detail: the girl's appearance, the room's layout, the masked man's movements. His search through missing persons records leads him to Mary Ann Mathews, a 16-year-old who vanished from Cleveland three years earlier.

The visit to Cleveland introduces Welles to Janet Mathews, Mary Ann's mother, who lives in a modest home filled with memories of her daughter. Mrs. Mathews shares Mary Ann's story—a bright, ambitious teenager who dreamed of becoming an actress in Hollywood. Among her belongings, Welles finds head shots, acting class receipts, and diary entries full of hope and determination. The reality of Mary Ann as a person, not just a victim in a grainy film, begins to affect Welles on a deeper level. His promise to Mrs. Mathews to discover the truth marks the beginning of his personal investment in the case.

Act 2

Welles' investigation takes him to Los Angeles, where the garish brightness of Hollywood Boulevard masks a thriving underground of exploitation and depravity. His search for information about Mary Ann leads him through a series of increasingly disturbing encounters with figures from the adult film industry. He discovers that Mary Ann, like countless other hopefuls, was quickly drawn into the porn industry, where she worked briefly under the name "Raquel" before disappearing completely.

A breakthrough comes when Welles meets Max California, a clerk at an adult bookstore whose punk rock exterior conceals extensive knowledge of the industry's darkest corners. Max becomes Welles' guide through this moral labyrinth, helping him navigate through layers of the underground porn industry, from legitimate operations to producers of extremely violent content.

Posing as a wealthy collector interested in acquiring custom-made extreme films, Welles infiltrates deeper into this shadow world. He encounters various figures, each more disturbing than the last: sleazy producers, violent criminals, and men who commission unspeakable content for private collections. His professional detachment begins to crack as he witnesses the systematic exploitation of vulnerable young women and the casual cruelty of those who profit from their destruction.

The investigation reaches a crucial turning point when they discover Dino

Velvet, a notorious director of violent fetish films who takes obvious pleasure in pushing boundaries of depravity. Velvet's star performer, known only as "Machine," appears in his films wearing a distinctive chrome-plated mask - the same mask Welles recognized from the 8mm film. Through careful manipulation, Welles arranges a meeting with Dino and Machine, supposedly to commission a custom film.

After setting up the meeting, Welles pays Max for his help and urges him to get out of the situation, believing he's protecting his guide from further danger. However, events take a dark turn when Eddie Poole, a pornographer connected to Mary Ann's disappearance, recognizes Welles as an investigator. Unknown to Welles, Max is kidnapped by Dino's crew.

The situation reaches its crisis point at Dino Velvet's remote production facility, a grotesque space filled with implements of torture and death. What should have been a simple meeting becomes a trap when Eddie Poole appears with Daniel Longdale, Mrs. Christian's lawyer. Machine and Dino quickly disarm Welles, and to his horror, they bring out a captive Max, tied to a cross.

Machine then kills Max by slashing his throat—a moment that marks the true point of no return for Welles.Through an intense confrontation with Longdale, the terrible truth emerges: the 8mm film was real, commissioned by Mr. Christian for $1 million. However, this revelation sparks a deadly argument when Welles mentions the payment amount - it becomes clear that Longdale never shared the full sum with Dino Velvet and Eddie Poole. The tension explodes into violence, with Dino shooting Longdale with a crossbow, Longdale fatally shooting Dino, and Welles managing to stab Machine and escape, despite Eddie Poole's pursuit.

When Welles reports his findings to Mrs. Christian, the revelation of her husband's monstrous actions proves too much to bear. She commits suicide, leaving Welles with the burden of knowledge and no legal recourse for justice. The police cannot act without evidence, and the film itself would be inadmissible in court. In this dark moment, Welles makes his critical choice, declaring to his wife, “There's no one left to finish this but me.”

Act 3

With traditional justice out of reach and Max's death weighing heavily on his conscience, Welles embarks on a path of vengeance. He tracks down Eddie Poole, taking him to an abandoned house on the outskirts of Los Angeles. The confrontation reveals Eddie's true nature - his complete lack of remorse for Mary Ann's fate only reinforces Welles' conviction that these men must be stopped. After extracting what information he can, Welles executes Eddie, marking his complete break from his former ethical boundaries.

The final confrontation comes when Welles tracks down Machine at his home. Through his investigation, he's discovered the man behind the chrome mask, leading to a devastating psychological and physical showdown. When Machine finally removes his iconic mask, the face beneath is disturbingly ordinary - a stark reminder that true evil often wears the most mundane disguises.

Machine's chilling words cut to the heart of Welles' journey: “There's no mystery. The things I do, I do them because I like them. Because I want to.” This simple, horrible truth - that some evil exists without deeper meaning or justification - forces Welles to confront the darkness he's been investigating. The ensuing fight is brutal and primitive, ending with Welles killing Machine in a manner that mirrors the violence he has been investigating. In this moment, the line between investigator and subject, between justice and revenge, becomes irreparably blurred.

Epilogue

The film's conclusion finds Welles returning home, bearing both physical and psychological scars from his journey into darkness. In a powerful scene, he breaks down in Amy's arms, finally allowing himself to feel the full weight of his experiences. While he has eliminated specific evil-doers and achieved a form of justice for Mary Ann, the cost to his soul has been profound.

As he holds his infant daughter, Welles embodies the film's central theme about the price of confronting evil. He has not become like the monsters he hunted, but his exposure to their world has irrevocably altered him. His experience validates the film's underlying message: when you stare into the abyss, the abyss stares back, and no one emerges unchanged from such an encounter.

The final scenes show Welles attempting to reconnect with his family life, but the shadow of his experience lingers. Every tender moment with his daughter is now colored by his knowledge of the world's capacity for evil. He has succeeded in his mission to bring some form of justice for Mary Ann Mathews, but the cost of that justice - in terms of his own humanity and psychological well-being - will haunt him forever.

The story closes with Welles reading a letter from Mrs. Matthews, a scene that perfectly encapsulates his transformation. He now understands that innocence, once lost, can never be fully regained. His journey has taught him that evil exists not just in the shadows but in broad daylight, wearing ordinary faces and living ordinary lives. This knowledge becomes both his burden and his curse - the price paid for venturing into darkness and returning changed but not conquered.

The film leaves us with the understanding that some truths, once uncovered, can never be buried again. Welles' investigation into the depths of human depravity has left permanent scars on his psyche, but it has also reinforced his determination to protect the innocence of others, particularly his daughter, from the darkness he has witnessed. In this way, his transformation becomes not just a descent into violence and revenge, but also a brutal awakening to the responsibility of confronting evil in all its forms.

The Machinist (2004, directed by Brad Anderson, screenplay by Scott Kosar)

Extended 3 Act Synopsis

Prologue

The film opens with Trevor Reznik—a man so severely emaciated that every bone in his body protrudes through his sallow skin—carefully rolling a body wrapped in carpet toward the edge of a rocky shoreline. The night is dark, the sea black and forbidding. As he struggles with his grim task, headlights appear in the distance. Trevor freezes momentarily before abandoning his efforts, fleeing into the shadows as a security guard's pickup truck pulls into view. The guard exits his vehicle, flashlight in hand, and begins to investigate the suspicious activity.

The film then cuts to a scene of Trevor in his apartment bathroom, staring at his gaunt reflection in the mirror. His skeletal frame is shocking—hollow cheeks, protruding collarbones, with ribs and shoulder blades that jut out unnaturally from his skin. He looks like a walking corpse, his body visibly consumed by whatever torment has afflicted him.

In a silent sequence, we see Trevor methodically cleaning his hands with bleach, scrubbing with the precision of someone trying to remove invisible stains. There is no hint of emotion in his movements, just mechanical thoroughness. This brief, stark introduction immediately establishes Trevor's physical deterioration and suggests a man haunted by something he cannot wash away.

The film's desaturated palette of blues and grays renders a world as drained of vitality as Trevor himself. As the prologue concludes, Trevor notices a Post-it note on his wall. He turns toward it, his expression shifting to one of bewilderment and disorientation. The camera closes in on the note, revealing its cryptic message: "Who are you?" This question—seemingly addressed to Trevor by Trevor—lingers hauntingly as the film transitions to his daily existence, establishing the central paradox of a man who has become an enigma to himself.

Act 1

In the industrial gloom of the factory where he works as a machinist, Trevor Reznik moves with the careful precision of someone conserving every ounce of energy. His skeletal appearance draws concerned whispers from coworkers as he operates heavy machinery with a focus that borders on obsession. When fellow machinist Tucker asks if he's sick, Trevor responds with unsettling calm: "I've never felt better in my life." The dark irony of this statement is written on his starving body—skin stretched over bone with virtually no muscle mass remaining.

Trevor's existence follows rigid patterns: work at the factory during the day, coffee at an airport café during his sleepless nights, and occasional visits to Stevie, a prostitute who has developed genuine affection for him. At the airport café, waitress Marie serves him with a friendly warmth that briefly illuminates his isolated life. Trevor leaves excessive tips and makes awkward conversation, hungry for human connection. With Stevie, he sometimes merely pays to sleep beside her—not for sex, but for the simple comfort of human proximity. These ritualized interactions represent his only tethers to the human world.

In his apartment, Trevor's insomnia drives him to clean obsessively, play solitary games of Hangman on Post-it notes, and stare at the clock as hours pass without relief. His refrigerator contains nothing but condiments—his body surviving on coffee and cigarettes. The physical toll of his condition is evident in every movement, yet Trevor seems disconnected from his own deterioration, as though observing someone else's decay.

The fragile equilibrium of Trevor's existence shatters one day at the factory when he notices someone unfamiliar—a bald, muscular man whose presence creates an immediate sense of unease. This stranger, who introduces himself as Ivan, engages Trevor in conversation near a mill machine. Their brief interaction distracts Trevor at a crucial moment. His attention diverts from the task at hand,

and in that split second of inattention, his coworker Miller's arm is caught in the machine. The industrial accident unfolds with horrifying speed—Miller's screams, the spray of blood, coworkers rushing to shut down the machine. By the time they free Miller, his arm has been severed below the elbow.

In the chaotic aftermath, Trevor looks for Ivan, but the mysterious man has vanished. When Trevor mentions Ivan to his supervisor and coworkers, they respond with confusion—no one else saw this person, and there's no Ivan employed at the factory. This discrepancy creates the first explicit crack in the facade of Trevor's reality. Was Ivan real, or a hallucination born from Trevor's sleep-deprived mind?

Back at his apartment that night, Trevor discovers something new on his refrigerator—a game of Hangman drawn on a Post-it note with several letters missing. The incomplete word becomes another puzzle in his increasingly fractured existence. Trevor stares at the note, trying to remember if he created it himself, but his memory offers no clarity. The boundaries between what Trevor experiences and what he might be imagining begin to blur.

Trevor's search for answers about Ivan drives him to check employment records, question coworkers, and scan the factory floor during his shifts. Each inquiry meets with the same response—there is no Ivan. Yet Trevor continues to glimpse this mysterious figure around the factory and later, throughout the city—watching, always watching. These encounters intensify Trevor's paranoia and confusion. Is he being targeted, or is his mind creating this phantom?

As his grip on reality weakens, Trevor clings more desperately to his routines. He continues visiting the airport café, where his connection with Marie deepens. He meets her son Nicholas, a bright boy who suffers from epilepsy. These interactions represent Trevor's attempts to maintain a connection to normalcy even as his world fractures around him. Similarly, his relationship with Stevie offers moments of tenderness in his increasingly cold and paranoid existence. During one visit, Stevie notices scars on Trevor's body that he can't explain—another piece of his missing history.

Act 2

Trevor's paranoia escalates when he follows Ivan to a local bar after spotting him driving a distinctive red Firebird. Inside the dingy establishment, Trevor confronts Ivan, demanding to know why he's following him. Their tense conversation reveals little, but as Trevor leaves, he glimpses a photo in Ivan's wallet—an image of Ivan fishing with Nicholas, the boy from the airport café. This impossibility confirms that something is profoundly wrong with either Trevor's perception or reality itself. When Trevor demands answers, Ivan responds cryptically: "You know so little about yourself."

The Hangman game on Trevor's refrigerator gradually gains new letters, spelling out "K-I-L-L-E-R" one character at a time, like a message from his subconscious. Trevor begins experiencing increasingly disturbing hallucinations. His refrigerator leaks what appears to be blood, but when he opens it, he finds only condiments. He sees a mysterious figure in his apartment, only to discover no one is there. These episodes blur the line between external reality and Trevor's deteriorating mental state.

Trevor's relationship with Marie and Nicholas deepens when he joins them for an outing to a local carnival. Nicholas is drawn to a ride called "Route 666," despite his mother's concerns about his epilepsy. Trevor supports the boy's desire to experience the ride, forming a bond that momentarily makes him feel human again. On the ride, Nicholas suffers a seizure—the flashing lights and mechanical horrors triggering his condition. As Trevor helps the convulsing boy, fragmented images flash through his own mind: headlights on a dark highway, a car interior, a moment of impact. These disjointed memories appear and vanish too quickly to grasp, yet leave Trevor deeply disturbed.

As his physical condition deteriorates further, Trevor's work life becomes increasingly untenable. His paranoia about his coworkers' attitudes toward him escalates into confrontation. He accuses them of conspiring with Ivan, leading to physical altercations that further isolate him. When he attempts to prove Ivan's existence by pointing him out to coworker Reynolds, Ivan is nowhere to be seen, making Trevor appear delusional.

Trevor's connection with Stevie provides a parallel story that illuminates his disintegration. In a rare moment of reaching out, Trevor invites Stevie to his apartment for a proper date on Mother's Day. The evening begins with promise—Stevie brings food, they connect on a human level beyond their professional relationship. But the fragile normalcy shatters when Trevor becomes irrationally suspicious after Stevie explores his apartment. His paranoid accusations—that she's searching for something, conspiring against him—reveal how deeply his trust has been eroded. Stevie leaves hurt and confused, removing one of Trevor's few stabilizing human connections.

The investigation into Ivan's identity takes a dramatic turn when Trevor discovers the license plate from Ivan's red Firebird is registered in his own name—to a vehicle he has no memory of owning. This revelation creates the first explicit suggestion that Ivan might not be an external tormentor but a part of Trevor himself—perhaps a dissociated personality or a projection of his guilt. The discovery transforms the narrative from an external mystery to an internal psychological journey, as Trevor begins the painful process of excavating his buried memories.

As Trevor grapples with the implications of the DMV revelation, his grasp on reality deteriorates more rapidly. After another confrontation at work, Trevor is dismissed from the factory. This removes another stabilizing element from his life, leaving him even more isolated with his increasingly disturbing thoughts. His physical condition reaches a crisis point—his body is literally consuming itself. The extreme emaciation affects his coordination and strength, making even simple tasks difficult as his body fails him.

Trevor attempts to verify other aspects of his reality, beginning with his relationship with Marie and Nicholas. At the airport, he discovers that the café where he believed he met them nightly doesn't employ a waitress named Marie. This devastating revelation suggests that significant portions of his experienced reality are fabrications—elaborate constructions of his mind designed to protect him from some terrible truth.

When Trevor returns to his apartment, the hangman game on his refrigerator now clearly spells "KILLER," confronting him with an accusation he can no longer avoid. In a desperate attempt to find any anchor to reality, Trevor calls Stevie, only to have her reject him after his previous paranoid behavior. This removes his last human connection, leaving him completely isolated with his fracturing mind.

The crisis intensifies when Trevor realizes that the mysterious "Route 666" attraction from the carnival corresponds to an actual location—Highway 152. Something about this connection triggers partial memories that Trevor still cannot fully access. After discovering that significant portions of his perceived reality are delusions, Trevor makes the critical choice to return to Highway 152 —the real-world location corresponding to the carnival ride that triggered Nicholas's seizure. Rather than continuing to flee from whatever truth he's been avoiding, Trevor chooses to confront it directly, no matter how devastating it might be.

Act 3

Driving through the night to Highway 152, Trevor arrives at a desolate stretch of road that feels eerily familiar. As he stands at the roadside, the headlights of an approaching car illuminate the asphalt. This specific combination—the road, the darkness, the approaching lights—triggers a cascade of suppressed memories. In a series of vivid flashbacks, the truth finally erupts into consciousness: one year earlier, while driving along this same highway, Trevor accidentally hit and killed a young boy who was standing by the roadside with his mother after their car broke down. Instead of stopping to help, Trevor panicked and fled the scene.

The memories flood back with brutal clarity: the impact, the child's body flying across his hood, the windshield shattering, the mother's screams fading in his rearview mirror as he sped away. In that moment of cowardice—choosing to flee rather than face what he had done—Trevor's mind fractured. The insomnia began that very night, his body refusing the peace of sleep as penance for his failure to take responsibility.

This revelation instantly clarifies every element of Trevor's year-long psychological torment. Ivan is not a real person but a manifestation of Trevor's guilt and self-loathing—a projection of what Trevor was before the accident: strong, confident, whole. The fishing photo showed not Ivan with Nicholas, but Trevor himself before his physical deterioration. Marie and Nicholas were never real; they were Trevor's mind's way of processing his guilt by creating a relationship with the mother and child he hurt. The hangman game spelling "KILLER" was Trevor's subconscious forcing him to confront his crime.

The physical toll—his extreme emaciation, the insomnia, the hallucinations—all represent Trevor's unconscious self-punishment. Unable to consciously face what he had done, Trevor's mind created an elaborate psychological mechanism to both punish and eventually heal itself. Every element of his experience over the past year suddenly aligns into a terrible logic: Trevor has been both prisoner and jailer, victim and perpetrator, in his self-created purgatory.

In the aftermath of his remembrance, Trevor makes the decision to turn himself in to the police. This act of taking responsibility represents Trevor's moral redemption—he chooses to face the consequences of his actions rather than continuing to run. At the police station, he confesses to the hit-and-run that killed the child, providing details that only the perpetrator could know. The officers, seeing his physical condition and hearing his story of year-long insomnia, exchange glances that suggest they're unsure whether they're dealing with a criminal or a madman. In truth, Trevor has become both.

The film's final scene shows Trevor in what appears to be a prison cell. The space is sparse, institutional—not unlike the apartment where he's imprisoned himself for the past year. Trevor lies down on the bed and closes his eyes. For the first time in a year, his body surrenders to sleep. As consciousness fades, the scene transitions to Trevor driving through a tunnel with his car's broken windshield from the hit-and-run accident. He moves steadily toward a bright white light at the tunnel's end, and the image fades completely to white.

This final sequence creates a perfect visual metaphor for Trevor's journey. The tunnel represents both literal passage and spiritual transition—moving from darkness into light, from denial into acceptance, from guilt into atonement. The broken windshield acknowledges the reality of what he did, while the movement toward light suggests the possibility of redemption through honesty and responsibility.

The white fade that concludes the film emphasizes this theme of redemption through confession. It's not a happy ending in conventional terms—Trevor has lost a year of his life to self-torture and now faces legal consequences—but it represents a spiritual and psychological resolution. The weight of unacknowledged guilt had proven far more devastating than the consequences of confession could ever be.

The film leaves us with the understanding that guilt, when unacknowledged, becomes a consuming force that destroys both body and mind. Trevor's journey illustrates how the psyche will create increasingly elaborate mechanisms to process trauma when conscious acknowledgment is too painful. His physical emaciation throughout the film visually manifests his guilt consuming him from within; his final sleep represents the spiritual nourishment that comes with truth and responsibility.

In its conclusion, "The Machinist" suggests that we cannot outrun responsibility; eventually, the mind will force us to confront our darkest actions, even as we desperately try to escape them. Trevor's year of insomnia, weight loss, and hallucinations represents the high price of denial—a cost far greater than what he would have paid had he stopped at the accident scene and accepted responsibility immediately. In this way, the film becomes not just a psychological thriller but a moral parable about the impossibility of escaping our actions and the liberation that comes with finally confronting the truth.

The Silence of the Lambs (1991, directed by Jonathan Demme, screenplay by Ted Tally, adapting the novel by Thomas Harris)

Extended Three-Act Synopsis

Act 1

The story opens on a misty morning at the FBI Academy in Quantico, Virginia. Trainee Clarice Starling navigates a grueling obstacle course, her determination evident in every movement. This physical challenge symbolizes her broader struggle as a woman trying to prove herself in the male-dominated world of law enforcement. Clarice's training is interrupted when she's summoned to the office of Jack Crawford, head of the FBI's Behavioral Science Unit. The office walls, adorned with photographs of crime scenes and serial killer victims, foreshadow the darkness she's about to enter.

Crawford's assignment seems deceptively simple: interview imprisoned cannibalistic serial killer Dr. Hannibal Lecter. But Crawford's careful choice of words and studying of Clarice's reactions suggest ulterior motives. He's selecting her specifically because she's young, female, and likely to intrigue Lecter. The assignment represents both opportunity and danger for Clarice—a chance to prove herself, but also the risk of becoming psychologically wounded by engagement with pure evil.

The journey to Baltimore State Hospital for the Criminally Insane establishes Clarice's transition from the structured, safe world of the Academy to the shadowy realm of criminal psychology. Dr. Frederick Chilton, the hospital's administrator, immediately demonstrates the professional sexism Clarice regularly faces. His clumsy attempts at flirtation and his warning about Lecter "He's a monster, pure psychopath"—serve as an ineffective prelude to the sophisticated manipulation she's about to encounter.

The descent into the dungeon-like basement where Lecter is housed creates mounting tension. Clarice passes several inmates, including Multiple Miggs, who hurls crude comments and worse at her. The growing sense of violation and danger peaks as she finally reaches Lecter's cell. Unlike the other prisoners who live in shadow, Lecter stands in stark light, perfectly still, awaiting her arrival as if he's been expecting her all along.

Their initial interaction demonstrates the psychological chess match that will define their relationship. Lecter immediately seizes control, analyzing Clarice's appearance, accent, and ambitions with unsettling accuracy. He dismisses her FBI questionnaire as crude and obvious, instead proposing his own terms of engagement—he'll help her in exchange for personal information about herself. This "quid pro quo" arrangement establishes the central dynamic of their relationship: Lecter will provide insights into the Buffalo Bill case, but only by forcing Clarice to confront her own psychological vulnerabilities.

The interview is interrupted by the disturbing incident with Multiple Miggs, who assaults Clarice as she leaves. Lecter's reaction—orchestrating Miggs' suicide as punishment—demonstrates both his power and his complex attitude toward Clarice. It shows he's capable of influencing events even from within his cell, and suggests a peculiar form of respect for Clarice that will become crucial to the story.

Clarice's return to Quantico reveals the true nature of her assignment. Buffalo Bill, a serial killer who skins his female victims, has claimed another young woman. Crawford reveals he hopes Lecter might provide insights into the case, though he initially hid this motive from Clarice. This deception creates tension between Clarice and her mentor, suggesting that even those she trusts may not be entirely forthcoming with her.

Following Lecter's cryptic clue about "Miss Mofet," Clarice discovers a storage unit containing a severed head in a jar—evidence of a victim unknown to the FBI—and a rare death's-head moth cocoon. This discovery proves Lecter's potential value to the investigation while also demonstrating Clarice's investigative abilities. Crawford's increased trust in Clarice, marked by giving her greater involvement in the Buffalo Bill case, establishes her growing confidence and capability.

The act culminates with news of another Buffalo Bill kidnapping—this time Catherine Martin, the daughter of a U.S. Senator. The stakes escalate dramatically as a race against time begins. Catherine has at most three days to live, based on Buffalo Bill's established pattern. This countdown creates urgency that will drive the entire second act, while Catherine's status as a senator's daughter adds political pressure to the investigation.

Throughout this first act, the theme of transformation through confronting fear is subtly developed. Clarice must repeatedly face situations that would intimidate most trainees—the physical challenges of FBI training, the professional discrimination of men like Chilton, the crude violations by Miggs, and most significantly, the psychological challenge of engaging with Lecter. Each confrontation strengthens her, preparing her for the greater challenges to come.

Act 2

The second act opens with increasingly desperate efforts to save Catherine Martin. The killer's pattern is now clear—he holds his victims for three days before killing them and taking parts of their skin. Catherine's mother, Senator Ruth Martin, uses her political influence to offer Lecter a deal: if he helps find Buffalo Bill, he'll be transferred to a better facility with a view. This public negotiation threatens to derail the delicate psychological rapport Clarice has established with Lecter.

Lecter toys with the senator, offering misleading information about a "Louis Friend" (an anagram for "iron sulfide"—fool's gold). This false lead demonstrates both Lecter's brilliance and his contempt for authority figures who try to manipulate him. Meanwhile, Clarice continues her private exchanges with Lecter, delving deeper into her personal traumas in exchange for genuine insights into Buffalo Bill's psychology.

The investigation intensifies as Clarice and Crawford follow various leads. They perform the autopsy of Buffalo Bill's latest discovered victim, revealing his pattern of skinning and the significance of the death's-head moths. Clarice demonstrates both professional competence and emotional resilience during this gruesome procedure, though the experience clearly affects her. The moth chrysalis found in a victim's throat provides a crucial clue, as this rare species can be traced to specific locations.

In a pivotal sequence, Clarice returns to Lecter for additional insights. He demands she tell him about her worst childhood memory—when she tried and failed to save a spring lamb from slaughter, haunted ever since by the screaming of the lambs. This confession represents Clarice's deepest vulnerability and motivation: her drive to save others stems from her inability to save that lamb. Lecter's response provides the key breakthrough—Buffalo Bill knew his first victim personally, and he's not a true transsexual as they initially believed, but someone who thinks he is.

The tension escalates when Lecter engineers a brilliant and brutal escape during his transfer, killing two guards and mutilating one's body to use his face as a disguise. This shocking display of violence reminds both Clarice and the audience of Lecter's true nature, despite his genteel manner. His escape also means Clarice has lost her source of insights just as the investigation reaches its critical phase.

Catherine Martin's captivity scenes interweave throughout the act, showing her desperate attempts to survive in Buffalo Bill's basement pit. Her discovery that she's not the first victim held there, and her psychological manipulation of Bill by using his pet poodle Precious, demonstrate her resourcefulness while maintaining tension about her fate.

Clarice follows leads about Buffalo Bill's first victim, travelling alone to small towns in Ohio. This investigation leads her to a dress-making shop run by Jame Gumb (Buffalo Bill's real name), though she doesn't initially recognize him. The seemingly mundane encounter turns sinister as Clarice gradually notices details that reveal Gumb's true identity—most notably, a death's-head moth that flutters through the room.

The act reaches its crisis point as Clarice realizes she's alone in the killer's house. Her backup is racing to the wrong location based on Lecter's misleading information, and she must decide whether to maintain her cover or confront Gumb immediately. When Gumb disappears into his basement, Clarice follows, knowing Catherine Martin must be down there but also recognizing she's walking into a trap.

Throughout this second act, the theme of transformation intensifies as Clarice repeatedly faces her fears. Each challenge—from the autopsy to her deepest childhood confession to Lecter—requires her to confront something frightening and emerge stronger. The act ends with her greatest test yet: descending alone into darkness to face a killer, much as she once descended into a barn to try to save a lamb.

Act 3

The final act begins in complete darkness as Buffalo Bill cuts the power in his basement. Through the killer's night-vision goggles, we watch Clarice stumble through the pitch-black maze of rooms, her vulnerability emphasized by his predatory perspective. This sequence masterfully brings together all of Clarice's previous challenges—she must overcome her fears, use her training, and rely on her instincts all at once.

The basement becomes a psychological landscape representing Clarice's confrontation with evil. Each room reveals more about Buffalo Bill's depravity—his workshop where he sews his “woman suit” from victims' skin, his collection of death's-head moths, and finally the pit where Catherine Martin remains trapped. The killer toys with Clarice in the darkness, watching her through his goggles as she tries to both find him and protect Catherine.

In a moment that demonstrates her growth from trainee to agent, Clarice maintains her composure despite her terror. When she hears the distinctive sound of Buffalo Bill cocking his gun in the darkness, she spins and fires repeatedly, killing him. This action represents her transformation—she's no longer the helpless child who couldn't save the lamb, but a capable agent who can face darkness and triumph.

The aftermath shows Clarice helping Catherine Martin out of the pit, fulfilling her deep-seated need to save someone vulnerable. This rescue symbolically redeems her childhood failure with the lamb, though Lecter's later question suggests the psychological wounds may never fully heal.

The film's denouement begins with Clarice's graduation from the FBI Academy. Her success in the Buffalo Bill case has earned her full agent status and the respect of her colleagues. This ceremony represents her professional transformation, but a phone call from Lecter provides the story's final psychological twist.

Lecter, calling from a tropical location where he's preparing to "have an old friend for dinner" (suggesting he'll eat Dr. Chilton), asks Clarice if the lambs have stopped screaming. This question brings the story's theme full circle—Clarice has faced her fears and grown stronger, but some childhood traumas never completely resolve. Lecter's continuing freedom suggests that evil cannot be fully conquered, only confronted and survived.

The final scene shows Lecter hanging up and disappearing into a crowd, a reminder that darkness always exists in the world. But Clarice's transformation is complete—she's no longer a trainee haunted by helplessness, but a full FBI agent who has proven she can face evil and triumph, even if the lambs never completely stop screaming.

This extended ending emphasizes the story's central theme: true strength comes not from eliminating our fears but from having the courage to face them. Clarice's journey from ambitious trainee to proven agent shows how confronting our darkest fears, rather than avoiding them, leads to both professional and personal transformation. The ambiguous note about the lambs still screaming suggests that while we can learn to function despite our fears, some wounds remain with us, shaping who we become.

The 12 Universal Story Beats in Action

Following the extensive narrative 3-act synopsis, we transition to exploring the beat sheet method—first through the basic narrative beat sheet, then advancing to the extended narrative beat sheet. These progressively detailed structural tools provide increasingly granular control over story development while preserving thematic integrity.

Before examining specific examples, we first look into the basics of the 12 universal beats—the fundamental narrative moments that form the backbone of virtually any compelling story. These universal beats represent the key inflection points in your protagonist's journey: from establishing their ordinary world, through the inciting incident that disrupts it, the trials and challenges that test them, the dark night of the soul where all seems lost, to the climactic resolution and return with new wisdom. Understanding these universal beats provides the essential framework upon which your unique story will be built.

We then move into a detailed explanation of these beats in action—how they manifest across different genres, using examples from different movies and novels, and how they can be adapted to serve various narrative purposes, and how they operate together to create a cohesive emotional experience for the reader. This examination of the beats in practice creates a bridge between abstract structural concepts and their application in storytelling, preparing you to implement them effectively in your own work.

The beat sheet represents a critical evolution in the outlining process, breaking down each act into specific narrative moments or "beats" that serve as structural pillars for your story. Where the 3-act synopsis provides the architectural blueprint, the beat sheet details the specific rooms, corridors, and spaces within that structure—each with its distinct purpose in the overall narrative journey.

The basic narrative beat sheet identifies essential plot points that propel the story forward—the protagonist's initial state, the inciting incident, key decision points, and the ultimate transformation that completes their arc. This level of detail permits writers to track their protagonist's external actions alongside the crucial internal shifts that create meaningful character development. By condensing each significant moment to its essence, the basic beat sheet ensures your narrative maintains proper momentum while hitting necessary emotional notes.

When we expand to the extended narrative beat sheet, we witness how each beat can be enriched with sensory details, psychological nuance, and thematic resonance. The extended version transforms clinical plot descriptions into vivid scenes with atmospheric elements, character gestures, and symbolic imagery. It elaborates on crucial emotional moments, capturing subtle character reactions that reveal internal states and conflicts. These details transcend mere plot mechanics to evoke the story's emotional truth and immerse readers in the protagonist's experience.

The progression from basic to extended beat sheet perfectly embodies ***The Subconscious Novelist*** *approach of telling yourself the story repeatedly, with each iteration revealing deeper layers of narrative truth. This isn't merely a mechanical exercise in adding detail—it's a systematic process designed to access the rich storytelling resources of your subconscious mind. Each time you revisit your narrative through these increasingly detailed frameworks, your subconscious reveals new connections, emotional nuances, and thematic resonances that weren't accessible during initial iterations.*

This 12-day subconscious story development and systematic outlining process creates the ideal conditions for your creative mind to work its magic. The basic beat sheet establishes the essential narrative framework, while the extended version provides the space and structure for your subconscious to populate that framework with vivid imagery, meaningful symbolism, and authentic emotional dynamics. With each pass, you're essentially inviting your subconscious to contribute more to the collaborative act of creation.

Perhaps most significantly, the extended beat sheet creates space for thematic development throughout the narrative. We see how central themes manifest in increasingly sophisticated ways—from initial setup, through progressive complications, to resolution. The extended format allows thematic threads to be woven consistently throughout every beat rather than appearing only at beginning and end, creating a richer tapestry of meaning.

By studying both basic and extended beat sheets, writers can observe how the expansion process doesn't simply add words but deepens meaning. Each basic beat contains the essential narrative DNA, while the extended version cultivates those seeds into fully realized dramatic moments. This progression demonstrates how complex emotional journeys can be methodically constructed while maintaining narrative coherence and thematic resonance.

The beat sheet method ultimately serves the subconscious novelist process by providing a framework detailed enough to guide consistent writing while remaining flexible enough to accommodate the organic revelations that emerge during the creative journey. It balances structural discipline with creative discovery, ensuring your novel remains both cohesive and authentic to the deeper truths your subconscious mind is working to express. Through this iterative process, your story becomes not just a product of conscious crafting, but a profound expression of your complete creative self.

Understanding The 12 Universal Beats through examples

The Prologue (Optional Pre-Act 1 Element)

Understanding the Beat: While technically part of Act 1's setup, the prologue functions as a separate entity that establishes crucial backstory or high stakes before the main story begins. This optional storytelling tool is particularly effective in novels and films that require significant context or need to establish dramatic stakes immediately.

Masterful Examples:

"Interview with the Vampire" (Novel by Anne Rice, 1976; Film adaptation 1994, directed by Neil Jordan): The prologue opens in modern-day San Francisco with vampire Louis (Brad Pitt) agreeing to tell his life story to reporter Daniel Molloy (Christian Slater). This frame narrative accomplishes several crucial goals:

- Establishes supernatural elements credibly by showing their existence in our modern world
- Creates immediate intrigue by revealing Louis's immortal nature
- Sets up the story's themes of loneliness, immortality, and the burden of eternal life
- Provides a relatable entry point for the audience through Molloy's skepticism

The scene begins with Molloy setting up his recording equipment, treating this as just another interview, until Louis's supernatural speed and presence reveal something far more extraordinary. Louis's opening line, "I was 24 years old when I became a vampire," immediately hooks both Molloy and the audience, promising a story that will span centuries.

"Terminator 2: Judgment Day" (1991, original screenplay by James Cameron and William Wisher): The prologue opens with Sarah Connor's narration explaining Judgment Day, establishing both crucial backstory and apocalyptic stakes. The sequence provides:

- Essential exposition about Skynet and the human resistance
- Visual evidence of the catastrophic future that must be prevented
- Context for Sarah Connor's seemingly paranoid behavior in the present
- Immediate tension by showing the consequences of failure

The prologue begins with a peaceful playground scene that transforms into nuclear devastation, creating an emotional impact that resonates throughout the film. This contrast between present peace and future destruction establishes the urgent stakes driving the story's action.

“Red Dragon” (Novel by Thomas Harris, 1981; Film adaptation 2002, directed by Brett Ratner): The prologue depicts FBI profiler Will Graham's fateful discovery that his mentor, Dr. Hannibal Lecter, is the serial killer he's been hunting. This sequence:

- Establishes the complex relationship between Graham and Lecter
- Demonstrates Graham's exceptional ability to understand killers
- Shows the devastating personal cost of his gift
- Sets up the psychological trauma that will affect Graham throughout the main story

The scene unfolds through Graham's gradual realization, as small details in Lecter's office lead him to the horrible truth about his mentor. Their final confrontation establishes both characters' brilliance while showing how Graham's ability to think like a killer nearly costs him his life.

Act One: The Setup

Act 1 is all about establishing the story's foundation—introducing the protagonist, their status quo world, and the central themes that will drive the narrative. This act typically includes the inciting incident, an external event that disrupts the hero's ordinary life and sets the story in motion. The hero then wrestles with this problem, contemplating the inevitable journey they must take. Act 1 ends with the hero's decision to step into the unknown world of Act 2, leaving their comfort zone behind.

Beat 1: Setup (Multiple Scenes)

In this multiple scene beat, we introduce the protagonist, their status quo world, and any secondary characters that may be part of their Act 1 world. While this beat typically expresses the theme that will drive the story, it's important to note that theme placement can be flexible.

A Note on Theme Placement: While the Setup beat is the ideal place to introduce your story's theme, some narratives effectively introduce or clarify their themes early in Act 2 (usually around the Welcome to the Jungle or Subplot beat). If the theme wasn't stated, expressed, implied, or made obvious in Act 1, it may appear for the first time in early Act 2. Additionally, if the theme was expressed in Act 1, you can add a reinforcement or reminder of the theme in Act 2, provided it's not overdone and serves the character's growth.

A masterful example of Act 2 theme introduction appears in "Rounders" (1998, written by David Levien and Brian Koppelman, directed by John Dahl). The film's theme—"we can't run away from who we are, our destiny chooses us"—is expressed beautifully in an intimate scene between Mike McDermott (Matt Damon) and his law professor, Petrovsky (Martin Landau). Set in a quiet bar/restaurant early in Act 2, Petrovsky shares his personal journey with Mike. He reveals how he broke from his family's long lineage of rabbis because he "couldn't see God in the Talmud or Midrash." Despite devastating consequences, including his father never speaking to him again, Petrovsky followed his true calling to become a lawyer. His powerful line encapsulates the film's theme: "The last thing I took away from the yeshivas is: 'we can't run away from who we are, our destiny chooses us'." This scene not only expresses the theme but directly connects to Mike's central conflict between his natural talent for poker and his attempts to pursue a "respectable" legal career.

Masterful Set Up Beat Examples:

"The Silence of the Lambs" (Novel by Thomas Harris, 1988; Film adaptation 1991, directed by Jonathan Demme): The setup introduces FBI trainee Clarice Starling at Quantico's training academy. We first meet her on the obstacle course, immediately establishing her as someone pushing against boundaries. The physical challenge of the course represents her larger struggle to prove herself in a male-dominated field.

Key elements of the setup include:

- Starling's determination shown through her solitary training

- Her status as an outsider emphasized when she's the only woman in an elevator full of male trainees
- Her composure when summoned by Jack Crawford (Scott Glenn)
- The contrast between her youth and the experienced agents around her

The setup establishes themes about gender power dynamics and psychological complexity through Starling's careful navigation of professional spaces dominated by men. Her background as a cop's daughter who went to UVA on a scholarship reveals both her ambition and her working-class roots, which will become crucial to her character arc.

"Rounders" (1998, original screenplay by David Levien and Brian Koppelman, directed by John Dahl): The story opens by introducing Mike McDermott (Matt Damon) in an underground poker club. Through his internal monologue analyzing tells and betting patterns, we immediately understand his exceptional talent: "If you can't spot the sucker in your first half hour at the table, then you are the sucker."

The setup establishes several crucial elements:

- Mike's extraordinary ability to read opponents
- The high-stakes world of underground poker
- His relationship with girlfriend Jo (Gretchen Mol)
- His attempt to leave poker behind for law school

The opening sequence culminates in Mike losing his entire bankroll ($30,000) to Russian mobster Teddy KGB (John Malkovich), establishing both his skill and his fatal flaw of overreaching. The story then shifts to show Mike attempting to rebuild his life at law school, establishing the central conflict between natural talent and societal expectations.

"Heat" (1995, original screenplay by Michael Mann): The setup introduces two protagonists in parallel —professional thief Neil McCauley (Robert De Niro) and homicide detective Vincent Hanna (Al Pacino). We first see McCauley executing a precisely planned hospital heist, demonstrating his methodical approach and strict professional discipline.

Key elements include:

- McCauley's precise planning and execution
- Hanna's equally methodical approach to investigation
- The professional worlds of both men
- Their shared dedication to their opposing crafts

This parallel introduction establishes the film's central theme about the thin line between cop and criminal, showing two men whose dedication to their professions makes them more similar than different. The setup raises questions about the nature of obsession and the cost of total commitment to one's calling.

"Good Will Hunting" (1997, original screenplay by Matt Damon and Ben Affleck): The setup establishes Will Hunting's two contrasting worlds—his working-class South Boston life and his hidden mathematical genius. We see him first as a janitor at MIT, then solving an impossibly complex math problem anonymously.

Key elements include:

- Will's everyday life with his friends, particularly Chuckie (Ben Affleck)
- His job as a janitor at MIT
- His extraordinary mathematical ability
- His resistance to recognition or advancement

The setup carefully establishes themes about potential versus fear, authenticity versus pretense, and the conflict between loyalty to one's roots and personal growth. Will's reluctance to acknowledge his gift suggests deeper emotional wounds that will drive the story's central conflict.

Beat 2: Inciting Incident (Single Scene)

Understanding the Beat: In this single scene beat, something happens to the hero that will turn their life upside down. This must be an external event that forces the hero into action—it cannot be an internal decision. This event pushes them into a situation where there's no going back to their status quo world. Usually, the actions they take in response will be wrong ones, allowing them to eventually learn the theme through their mistakes. Though ideally a single scene, this beat can occasionally extend to a small sequence if necessary for proper establishment of the incident.

Masterful Examples:

"The Bourne Identity" (Novel by Robert Ludlum, 1980; Film adaptation 2002, directed by Doug Liman): The inciting incident occurs when Jason Bourne discovers a safe deposit box in Zurich containing multiple passports, large sums of money in different currencies, and a gun. Having spent the story's opening dealing passively with his amnesia, this discovery forces him into active pursuit of his identity. The scene unfolds methodically as Bourne examines each item:

- First, the passports with his photo but different names
- Then, stacks of various international currencies
- Finally, a gun and bank account information

Each item raises new questions while suggesting disturbing answers. The various nationalities of the passports indicate a sophisticated operation. The money suggests resources and preparation. The weapon forces him to confront the possibility that his past involves violence. This moment transforms him from a passive victim of circumstances into an active protagonist who must uncover the truth, even if he might not like what he finds.

"Red Dragon" (Novel by Thomas Harris, 1981; Film adaptation 2002, directed by Brett Ratner): The inciting incident arrives when FBI Section Chief Jack Crawford (Harvey Keitel) visits Will Graham (Edward Norton) at his remote Florida home. Graham has built a peaceful life away from profiling after his traumatic capture of Hannibal Lecter. Crawford's arrival with crime scene photos from the "Tooth Fairy" killer forces Graham to confront his greatest fear—losing himself in the mind of another murderer.

The scene's power comes from Graham's clear reluctance: "I don't want to start doing that again, looking at families in their houses while they..." To which Crawford responds, "We have two families dead, Will. Two families, two months." This exchange establishes both the external conflict (catching a serial killer) and the internal conflict (Graham's fear of his own gift for understanding evil).

"Rounders" (1998, original screenplay by David Levien and Brian Koppelman, directed by John Dahl): The inciting incident occurs when Lester "Worm" Murphy (Edward Norton) is released from prison and immediately seeks out Mike McDermott (Matt Damon). Their reunion in a diner shows how Worm's charismatic but dangerous presence immediately threatens Mike's carefully constructed new life. The scene reveals their complex history through dialogue:

Worm: "You still know your way around a deck of cards?" Mike: "I'm not playing right now." Worm: "What are you doing then?" Mike: "Going to law school." Worm: "Law school? You're kidding me, right?"

This exchange perfectly captures their divergent paths while establishing the threat Worm represents to Mike's attempted reformation. The scene forces Mike to confront both his past literally and figuratively —Worm represents both Mike's former life and a debt of loyalty that can't be ignored.

"The Matrix" (1999, original screenplay by The Wachowskis): The inciting incident builds through a sequence where Neo receives mysterious messages on his computer that lead him to meet Trinity (Carrie-Anne Moss) at a nightclub. The messages culminate in the cryptic instruction to "follow the white rabbit," setting up the film's Alice in Wonderland motif. When Trinity tells him, "I know why you hardly sleep, why you live alone, and why night after night you sit at your computer. You're looking for him... I know because I was once looking for the same thing," she presents the first tangible evidence that Neo's suspicions about reality might be justified.

This sequence effectively establishes the film's central themes about questioning reality and the nature of choice, while setting up the larger conflict between human perception and hidden truth. Trinity's words force Neo to make a choice —he can either dismiss this as a strange encounter or follow the path that will lead him to Morpheus and the truth about the Matrix.

Beat 3: Internal Wrestling/Preparation (Multiple Scenes)

Understanding the Beat: In this multiple scene beat, the hero wrestles with the problem presented by the inciting incident. They contemplate their decisions and/or prepare for the inevitable journey they'll need to take in Act 2. This beat showcases the protagonist's reluctance to change while establishing the stakes of their upcoming journey.

Masterful Examples:

"Good Will Hunting" (1997, original screenplay by Matt Damon and Ben Affleck): Will Hunting's internal wrestling unfolds across several therapy sessions after Professor Lambeau discovers his mathematical genius. The sequence begins with Will's defiant resistance, shown through a series of failed therapy appointments where he systematically destroys each therapist's attempts to reach him.

In one particularly revealing scene, Will verbally spars with a therapist by pointing out a watercolor painting in the office: "The trick is to look at the painting and really concentrate on it. Really focus on it. The painting was painted by Vincent Van Gogh, and he looked out the window of the sanitarium where he was staying, and this is what he saw. And this painting is worth millions, and if I could have one wish in the world, I would wish for the money that this painting is worth... See, to me, this is just a piece of shit. And I see from your docket that you spent some time in the Mayo Clinic. The Mind is an extraordinary thing. Ever read any Noam Chomsky?"

This monologue reveals Will's sophisticated defense mechanisms—using his intelligence to keep people at a distance while simultaneously demonstrating his fear of genuine connection. The wrestling continues through his initial meetings with Sean Maguire, where his usual intellectual weapons begin to fail him. When Sean shares his own experience of abuse, we see Will's first moment of genuine discomfort—he's met someone who can see through his defenses.

"The Matrix" (1999, original screenplay by The Wachowskis): Neo's wrestling period builds through increasingly strange experiences that challenge his perception of reality. At his corporate job, reality begins to fray around the edges—his computer speaks to him, Trinity reveals knowledge about his private thoughts, and the world itself seems to glitch.

The wrestling culminates in the famous "red pill/blue pill" scene with Morpheus: "You take the blue pill, the story ends, you wake up in your bed and believe whatever you want to believe. You take the red pill, you stay in Wonderland, and I show you how deep the rabbit hole goes." This moment represents the pinnacle of Neo's internal struggle—choosing between comfortable ignorance and difficult truth.

Even after choosing the red pill, Neo's wrestling continues through his physical and psychological adjustment to the real world. When he first learns about the Matrix, he rejects the reality: "No. I don't believe it. It's not possible." This denial showcases the depth of his internal struggle with accepting a completely new reality.

"The Silence of the Lambs" (Novel by Thomas Harris, 1988; Film adaptation 1991, directed by Jonathan Demme): Clarice Starling's wrestling period occurs after her initial assignment to interview Dr. Lecter. Through conversations with her friend Ardelia and quiet moments alone, we see her struggling with the professional risks of engaging with Lecter versus her determination to prove herself in the FBI.

A key scene shows Starling reviewing Lecter's case file late at night, looking at photos of his victims while contemplating Crawford's warning: "Believe me, you don't want Hannibal Lecter inside your head." Her decision to proceed despite the warnings reveals both her ambition and her genuine desire to save Buffalo Bill's potential victims.

“Red Dragon” (Novel by Thomas Harris, 1981; Film adaptation 2002, directed by Brett Ratner): Will Graham's wrestling period takes place after Crawford's request for help with the “Tooth Fairy” killer. We see him torn between his moral obligation to stop a killer and his fear of losing himself in another murderer's mind. The scenes with his wife Molly reveal both his deep fear of returning to profiling and his inability to ignore the mounting death toll.

A crucial moment comes when Graham revisits the case files: “I know I can catch this guy, Molly. But I don't know if I can do it and stay the same person I am right now.” This dialogue perfectly encapsulates the internal wrestling—he knows what he needs to do but fears the cost to his psyche and his family.

Act Two: The Confrontation

Act 2 is the longest and most complex part of the story, where the hero faces a series of escalating challenges that test their resolve and force them to grow. This act begins with the hero entering a new, unfamiliar world that often functions as a mirror to their inner journey. Subplots and new characters are introduced, adding depth and complexity to the main storyline. The hero's trials and tribulations build toward a midpoint crisis—a major revelation or reversal that raises the stakes and pushes the story in a new direction. Further complications lead to a “crisis” moment, where the hero faces their darkest hour and must make a critical choice that will define their path forward.

Beat 4: Welcome to the Jungle / Plot Point 1 (Single Scene)

Understanding the Beat: This crucial single scene beat marks the hero's entry into the Act 2 world. Here, the protagonist takes action different from their normal routines, often entering an environment that sharply contrasts with their Act 1 world. While ideally contained in a single scene, this beat can occasionally extend to a small sequence if necessary for a proper transition into the new world.

Masterful Examples:

"The Silence of the Lambs" (Novel by Thomas Harris, 1988; Film adaptation 1991, directed by Jonathan Demme): Clarice Starling's "Welcome to the Jungle" moment occurs during her first meeting with Dr. Hannibal Lecter in the Baltimore State Hospital for the Criminally Insane. This scene marks a dramatic shift from the structured, academic world of Quantico into the psychological labyrinth of Lecter's domain. The contrast couldn't be more stark—from the orderly FBI training facility to the dungeon-like basement where society's most dangerous criminals are kept.

The scene begins with Dr. Chilton's warning about Lecter: "Do not touch the glass. Do not approach the glass. You pass him nothing but soft paper—no pencils or pens. No staples or paperclips in his paper. Use the sliding food carrier only. If he attempts to pass you anything, do not accept it." This extensive list of precautions immediately establishes the dangerous new world Starling is entering.

The actual meeting showcases the complete shift in power dynamics. Despite Lecter being physically imprisoned, he demonstrates immediate psychological dominance: "A census taker once tried to test me. I ate his liver with some fava beans and a nice Chianti." This scene establishes the complex relationship that will define the story—Lecter as both mentor and monster, Starling as both student and potential prey.

"Rounders" (1998, original screenplay by David Levien and Brian Koppelman, directed by John Dahl): Mike McDermott's entry into Act 2 occurs when he returns to the underground poker world to help Worm pay off his debts. The scene takes place in a high-stakes underground club, marking his first serious game since losing to KGB. This represents a complete departure from his recent law school life and his promises to Jo about leaving poker behind.

Mike's voiceover captures the significance of this transition: "First time at the table since Worm got out. First time in a long while I thought about what I was gonna do." The scene shows Mike immediately falling back into his element, reading tells and calculating odds, demonstrating that despite his attempts to leave this world behind, it's where he truly belongs.

This moment is particularly powerful because it represents Mike doing exactly what he promised Jo he wouldn't do—returning to poker. When he sits down at the table, the familiar click of chips and shuffle of cards signal his return to his true world, contrasting sharply with the sterile law school environment we've seen in Act 1.

"The Matrix" (1999, original screenplay by The Wachowskis): Neo's "Welcome to the Jungle" moment occurs when he takes the red pill and awakens to the real world. This scene represents the most dramatic possible transition—from the familiar digital world of the Matrix to the horrifying reality of human batteries being harvested by machines. The scene begins with Neo awakening in his pod, covered in goo, seeing the vast human farms for the first time.

This moment perfectly exemplifies the beat's purpose—showing the hero entering a world completely opposite to their Act 1 reality. Neo's famous line upon awakening in the real world, "Why do my eyes hurt?" receives Morpheus's reply: "Because you've never used them before." This dialogue perfectly captures the profound nature of this transition.

"Good Will Hunting" (1997, original screenplay by Matt Damon and Ben Affleck): Will's entry into Act 2 occurs during his first real therapy session with Sean Maguire. While Will has been to other therapists, this scene marks his entry into a new world of genuine emotional engagement. The scene begins with Will attempting his usual intellectual dominance, criticizing Sean's painting and trying to psychoanalyze him.

The dynamic shifts dramatically when Sean responds not with clinical detachment but with raw authenticity: "You're just a kid. You don't have the faintest idea what you're talking about... you presume to know everything about me because you saw a painting of mine." This marks Will's entry into a world where his intellectual defenses won't protect him—a complete contrast to his Act 1 world where his genius allowed him to maintain emotional distance.

Beat 5: Subplot (Single Scene)

Understanding the Beat: In this single scene beat, a subplot is typically introduced through a new character who will function as a mentor, love interest, or both. While this character might have appeared briefly in Act 1, it's here in early Act 2 that they begin their crucial function of helping the hero learn the theme. Though ideally a single scene, this beat can occasionally extend to a small sequence if necessary for proper character establishment.

Masterful Examples:

"Rounders" (1998, original screenplay by David Levien and Brian Koppelman, directed by John Dahl): The subplot emerges through Mike's relationship with Professor Petrovsky (Martin Landau), introduced in a pivotal scene at a bar/restaurant. While Petrovsky appeared briefly in Act 1 as Mike's law professor, it's here that he transforms into a crucial mentor figure. The scene begins with casual conversation but deepens when Petrovsky shares his personal story about choosing between family tradition and his true calling.

Petrovsky reveals how he broke from his family's generations of rabbis because he "couldn't see God in the Talmud or Midrash." Despite devastating consequences—his father never speaking to him again— he followed his calling to become a lawyer. His powerful revelation of the film's theme, "We can't run away from who we are, our destiny chooses us," serves as both personal confession and prophecy for Mike's journey. This subplot directly parallels Mike's struggle between his natural talent for poker and his attempt to pursue a "respectable" legal career.

"The Silence of the Lambs" (Novel by Thomas Harris, 1988; Film adaptation 1991, directed by Jonathan Demme): The subplot develops through Dr. Hannibal

Lecter's evolution from interview subject to dark mentor. Though introduced earlier, it's in this beat that their relationship transforms into something more complex. During a crucial interview session, Lecter shifts from hostile witness to engaged teacher, offering Clarice insight into Buffalo Bill's psychology while demanding personal truths in return.

Their famous “quid pro quo” arrangement begins here, with Lecter stating, “What became of your lamb, Clarice? Did you save it? Did you keep it from harm?” This question initiates their deeper relationship, where Lecter serves as both mentor and tormentor, helping Clarice understand not just Buffalo Bill but her own psychological drives. The subplot enriches the main plot by connecting Clarice's pursuit of Buffalo Bill with her deeper mission to silence her own psychological demons.

“Good Will Hunting” (1997, original screenplay by Matt Damon and Ben Affleck): The subplot emerges through Sean Maguire's (Robin Williams) transformation from assigned therapist to true mentor. While we've seen failed therapy sessions before, this beat shows their first real connection. The scene begins with Sean breaking protocol by holding their session outside his office, challenging Will's expectations and defense mechanisms.

Sean shares his own experience of abuse, creating a bridge to Will's trauma: “It's not your fault.” This simple statement, though rejected initially, plants the seed for Will's eventual healing. The subplot introduces both love and warfare—Sean genuinely cares for Will but isn't afraid to engage in psychological combat with him. Their relationship becomes the vehicle through which the film explores its themes of authentic connection and the courage to risk being hurt by loving others.

“The Matrix” (1999, original screenplay by The Wachowskis): The subplot develops through Trinity's (Carrie-Anne Moss) shift from mysterious guide to essential partner in Neo's journey. Though present earlier, it's in this beat that their relationship deepens beyond the professional. During a quiet moment on the Nebuchadnezzar, Trinity explains why she believes in Neo: “I felt exactly what you're feeling now. I denied it too."

Their connection adds emotional stakes to Neo's journey of self-discovery. Trinity becomes both love interest and spiritual guide, her faith in Neo helping to awaken his belief in himself. This subplot enriches the main plot by adding a human, emotional dimension to the philosophical questions about reality and choice. Her statement, "The Matrix cannot tell you who you are," connects directly to the film's themes about self-discovery and authentic identity.

Beat 6: Trials and Tribulations (Multiple Scenes)

Understanding the Beat: This is the longest multiple scene beat in your story, where you can explore your protagonist's journey through a series of escalating challenges. This beat allows for extensive character development through action and conflict, showing how your hero handles increasingly difficult situations.

Masterful Examples:

"Rounders" (1998, original screenplay by David Levien and Brian Koppelman, directed by John Dahl): Mike McDermott's trials unfold through a series of increasingly dangerous poker games as he attempts to help Worm pay off his debt to dangerous criminals. The sequence begins in relatively safe territory — college games where Mike and Worm can easily win—but escalates dramatically when Worm starts cheating at higher-stakes venues.

A pivotal sequence occurs at a game populated by off-duty police officers. Here, Mike must demonstrate both his poker expertise and his ability to navigate treacherous social waters. The scene builds tension through Mike's internal monologue as he spots Worm's cheating: "I should have known Worm would be mechanic enough to deal off the bottom of the deck... but I was too busy keeping him from getting bounced out of the game to notice." This realization forces Mike to choose between loyalty to his friend and his own moral code.

The games grow progressively more dangerous, culminating in a violent confrontation with KGB's enforcers. Each game tests not just Mike's poker skills but his understanding of himself. We see this through his voiceover: "In "life", we get no say in the cards we're dealt. But in poker, we're forced to play them... it's about making the best of what you've got." This directly connects to the film's theme about accepting who we truly are versus who society wants us to be.

"The Silence of the Lambs" (Novel by Thomas Harris, 1988; Film adaptation 1991, directed by Jonathan Demme): Clarice Starling's trials manifest through parallel challenges: her psychological chess match with Dr. Lecter and her pursuit of Buffalo Bill. Each interaction with Lecter demands a piece of her soul in exchange for insights about the killer. The quid pro quo arrangement forces Starling to confront her deepest traumas, particularly her childhood memory of trying to save spring lambs from slaughter.

A crucial sequence unfolds during the autopsy of Buffalo Bill's latest victim. Starling must overcome her personal discomfort to discover vital evidence—a moth cocoon in the victim's throat. This leads to investigating a storage unit where she finds a severed head preserved in a jar, each discovery pushing her further from the structured world of FBI training into the grotesque reality of actual investigation.

The trials culminate in a powerful exchange with Lecter about her childhood trauma: "And you think if you save Catherine, you could make them stop, don't you? You think if Catherine lives, you won't wake up in the dark ever again to that awful screaming of the lambs." This dialogue directly connects to the film's central theme about whether saving others can heal our own wounds.

"The Matrix" (1999, original screenplay by The Wachowskis): Neo's trials are structured as a series of training programs that systematically challenge his understanding of reality. These begin with basic combat training but quickly escalate to tests that require him to fundamentally alter his perception of what's possible.

The famous jump program sequence serves as a perfect example. Morpheus's instruction becomes central to the film's philosophy: “You have to let it all go, Neo—fear, doubt, and disbelief. Free your mind.” When Neo fails his first jump, the impact teaches him that while the Matrix isn't real, the consequences of believing in its limitations are.

This culminates in the sparring match with Morpheus where Neo begins to transcend his mental barriers. The sequence ends with Morpheus's crucial observation: “I'm trying to free your mind, Neo. But I can only show you the door. You're the one that has to walk through it.” Each trial reinforces the film's central theme about the relationship between belief and reality.

Beat 7: Midpoint (Single Scene)

Understanding the Beat: This single scene beat is one of the most important in the story because it pushes the hero into the second half of Act 2. At the midpoint, the hero typically makes a crucial discovery, finds something they were seeking (though it may not be what they expected), or experiences their first meaningful change. While ideally a single scene, this beat can occasionally extend to a small sequence if necessary for proper establishment of the pivot point.

Masterful Examples:

“The Silence of the Lambs” (Novel by Thomas Harris, 1988; Film adaptation 1991, directed by Jonathan Demme): The midpoint occurs when Clarice makes a breakthrough in the investigation through Dr. Lecter's cryptic clue about Buffalo Bill: “We begin by coveting what we see every day.” This leads her to discover crucial information about Bill's first victim, Benjamin Raspail.

The scene unfolds in layers:

- Starling connects Lecter's hint to the possibility that Bill knew his first victim personally
- She uncovers evidence in a storage unit containing a preserved head
- The discovery proves Lecter's value as an informant while revealing the

true horror of what she's pursuing

- The scene forces Starling to confront both the physical horror of her investigation and her growing dependence on Lecter's insights

This midpoint raises the stakes by:

- Revealing the extent of Buffalo Bill's pathology
- Deepening Starling's psychological entanglement with Lecter
- Proving her investigative abilities while showing the personal cost of success
- Setting up the complex psychological dynamics that will drive the story's second half

"Rounders" (1998, original screenplay by David Levien and Brian Koppelman, directed by John Dahl): The midpoint arrives when Mike discovers the true extent of Worm's debt to dangerous criminals. During a tense scene at a diner, Worm finally reveals that he owes money to Grama, who works for KGB.

Key dialogue reveals the stakes: Worm: "It's worse than you think. The debt's to Grama." Mike: "Grama? You owe money to Grama?" Worm: "And he works for KGB now."

This revelation:

- Forces Mike to confront the reality that his friend's recklessness has put them both in mortal danger
- Connects back to Mike's devastating loss to KGB in the opening
- Sets up the inevitable confrontation that will drive the story's second half
- Creates urgency by establishing a deadline for repayment

"The Matrix" (1999, original screenplay by The Wachowskis): The midpoint occurs during Neo's first jump program test. His failure to make the jump represents both his continued attachment to the rules of the Matrix and his first real understanding of what breaking those rules might mean.

The scene pivots on Morpheus's crucial teaching: "You have to let it all go, Neo.

Fear, doubt, and disbelief. Free your mind."

This moment:

- Shows Neo's first real comprehension of what "freeing his mind" actually means
- Demonstrates both his potential and his limitations
- Sets up his journey toward truly believing in his abilities
- Creates a clear marker between his training and the real challenges to come

"Good Will Hunting" (1997, original screenplay by Matt Damon and Ben Affleck): The midpoint comes during a crucial therapy session where Sean breaks through Will's intellectual defenses by sharing his own experience of abuse. This represents Will's first moment of genuine vulnerability.

The scene centers on Sean's revelation: "I used to get beaten too... There's nothing you can tell me that I haven't heard before. Nothing you can show me that I haven't seen. So if you're thinking about tanking another session..."

This pivotal moment:

- Forces Will to see Sean as someone who truly understands his pain
- Marks Will's first inability to hide behind his intelligence
- Shows the beginning of genuine therapeutic progress
- Sets up the deeper emotional work that will follow

Beat 8: Complications (Multiple Scenes)

Understanding the Beat: In this multiple scene beat, complications stack upon your hero, tension rises, and events push them toward their crisis point (the "all is lost" moment). These scenes should progressively increase pressure on the protagonist while revealing the true depth of their challenges.

Masterful Examples:

"Rounders" (1998, original screenplay by David Levien and Brian Koppelman, directed by John Dahl): The complications escalate through a series of increasingly dangerous situations after Mike discovers Worm's debt to Grama. Each scene builds upon the previous one:

1. Mike and Worm attempt to earn money legitimately through poker, but Worm can't resist cheating: “Just play straight with me,” Mike pleads. “You know I can't play straight! That's not me!” Worm responds, revealing the fundamental conflict in their partnership.
2. They get caught cheating at a game with state troopers, leading to a violent confrontation: “In my club, I catch someone cheating, they're lucky if they get out with their legs still attached to their body.” This raises the stakes from financial to physical danger.
3. Jo discovers Mike has returned to poker, ending their relationship: “I can't watch you go like this... I'm not going to sit here and watch you lose it all.” This costs Mike his stability and support system.
4. Grama ups the pressure by beating Worm and threatening both their lives: “Five days. Five thousand dollars a day. Or maybe I take it out in flesh.”

These complications:

- Strip away Mike's safety nets one by one
- Force him to confront the consequences of his choices
- Push him toward the inevitable confrontation with KGB
- Demonstrate the mounting cost of his loyalty to Worm

“The Silence of the Lambs” (Novel by Thomas Harris, 1988; Film adaptation 1991, directed by Jonathan Demme): The complications intensify through multiple developments:

1. Buffalo Bill kidnaps Senator Martin's daughter Catherine, raising the political stakes: “Now the FBI is involved in a real way... and they're going to be watching every move we make.”
2. Dr. Chilton interferes with Starling's investigations by revealing her deception to Lecter: “I erased the tapes. But I can't erase what's in

Lecter's mind."

3. Lecter negotiates a false deal with Senator Martin, wasting precious time: "Quid pro quo, Clarice. I tell you things, you tell me things."
4. Lecter escapes custody in a brutally sophisticated way, creating a second major threat: "He's in an ambulance, Clarice. He's already killed one person that we know of."

These complications:

- Add time pressure to find Catherine Martin before she's killed
- Threaten Starling's relationship with her key source (Lecter)
- Create competing threats that divide the FBI's resources
- Force Starling to work increasingly alone

"Good Will Hunting" (1997, original screenplay by Matt Damon and Ben Affleck): The complications build through several emotional challenges:

1. Skylar asks Will to come to California with her: "I want you to come with me." "I can't." This forces Will to confront his fear of intimacy.
2. Sean pushes Will to confront his abuse: "It's not your fault." "Don't fuck with me." Will's resistance to healing intensifies.
3. Lambeau increases pressure about the job interviews: "You don't have to prove anything to anyone except yourself." This adds professional pressure to Will's emotional struggles.
4. Chuckie confronts Will about wasting his potential: "You're sitting on a winning lottery ticket, and you're too much of a pussy to cash it in."

These complications:

- Force Will to face all his defense mechanisms
- Increase tension between his different possible futures
- Push him toward emotional breaking point
- Set up his eventual crisis decision

"The Matrix" (1999, original screenplay by The Wachowskis): The complications escalate through mounting challenges:

1. Morpheus reveals the overwhelming scope of their enemy: "The Matrix is a system, Neo. That system is our enemy."
2. Mouse is killed, showing the real cost of their fight: "Only the One can end the war."
3. Cypher betrays the team: "I'm tired of this war... I'm tired of fighting."
4. Morpheus is captured, forcing Neo to potentially sacrifice his mentor: "He's going to crack, and Zion's going to fall."

These complications:

- Reveal the true scale of what they're fighting
- Show the human cost of resistance
- Test loyalties and beliefs
- Push Neo toward his moment of choice

Beat 9: Crisis (Single Scene)

Understanding the Beat: This commonly single scene beat marks the lowest point for the hero—their "crisis" moment or worst nightmare coming true. While ideally contained in a single powerful scene, it can occasionally extend to a small sequence of connected scenes if needed to fully convey the depth of the crisis. This is the moment that will force the hero toward their ultimate transformation.

Masterful Examples:

"Rounders" (1998, original screenplay by David Levien and Brian Koppelman, directed by John Dahl): The crisis arrives when Mike discovers that Worm has fled, leaving him alone to face a $15,000 debt to KGB's men. The scene unfolds in Mike's apartment after Grama's thugs have ransacked it:

Mike finds a note from Worm: "I'm sorry. They're gonna come after you now. I would have paid them myself, but I can't generate that kind of cash in time. I've got to get out of town. You're gonna have to get out too. If I were you, I'd get out of town. At least for a while. Sorry, Mike. This is just the way it is. —Worm."

This crisis point works on multiple levels:

- Financial disaster: Mike now owes an impossible sum
- Personal betrayal: His loyalty to Worm has been repaid with abandonment
- Physical danger: KGB's enforcers will come for him
- Complete isolation: He's lost Jo, his law school future, and now Worm

Mike's voiceover captures the totality of his crisis: "Some people, they just don't have what it takes to play cards. Like my father... But me? I'm making moves to avoid coming home and having him find out that I've blown it all. That I've lost everything he worked for because I can't stand to play it safe with his money. Because I can't stand to look at the safe road ahead. I know it's not what he had in mind for me."

"The Silence of the Lambs" (Novel by Thomas Harris, 1988; Film adaptation 1991, directed by Jonathan Demme): The crisis occurs when Clarice realizes she's been pursuing the wrong lead while Catherine Martin remains trapped in Buffalo Bill's pit. The scene takes place in the FBI offices as Clarice watches Catherine's mother plead on television:

Senator Martin: "Catherine is very gentle and kind. Talk to her and you'll see. You have the power to save Catherine. Please... please."

This moment crystallizes Clarice's failure on multiple levels:

- Professional failure: She's no closer to finding Buffalo Bill
- Personal failure: She's unable to save another innocent
- Psychological crisis: The parallel to her childhood trauma with the lambs becomes overwhelming
- Complete isolation: With Lecter escaped, she's lost her primary source of insight

The scene ends with Crawford telling her: "We're pulling you off the case. We can't afford any more mistakes." This removes her last chance at redemption.

"Good Will Hunting" (1997, original screenplay by Matt Damon and Ben Affleck): Will's crisis comes when he sabotages his relationship with Skylar, deliberately pushing her away when she expresses her love for him. The scene takes place in her dorm room:

Skylar: "I love you." Will: "You don't love me. You don't know me... You want to pretend I'm some character in your little story? Some troubled genius you want to save?" Skylar: "Is that what you think this is?" Will: "That's what I know it is."

This crisis represents:

- Emotional breakdown: Will chooses isolation over vulnerability
- Self-sabotage: He destroys his chance at real connection
- Pattern repetition: He proves his deepest fears about being unlovable
- Complete isolation: He's pushing away the person who truly sees him

The scene ends with Will's devastating line: "I don't love you." The lie in these words makes his crisis complete.

"The Matrix" (1999, original screenplay by The Wachowskis): The crisis arrives when Neo apparently dies at the hands of Agent Smith in the Matrix. This moment represents:

- Physical death: Neo is actually flatlined in the real world
- Faith crisis: The prophecy seems false
- Group crisis: The resistance loses their potential savior
- Complete defeat: The machines appear to have won

Trinity's words over his body capture the depth of the crisis: "Neo, I'm not afraid anymore. The Oracle told me that I would fall in love and that that man... the man that I loved would be The One. So you see, you can't be dead. You can't be... because I love you."

Beat 10: Critical Choice (Multiple Scenes)

Understanding the Beat: In this multiple scene beat, the hero is in the reaction stage of their low point. This moment lends itself to deep contemplation where the hero processes their crisis, reflects on their past, analyzes things at a soul level, and reaches an important revelation that forces them to make a critical choice that will define their path forward.

Masterful Examples:

"Rounders" (1998, original screenplay by David Levien and Brian Koppelman, directed by John Dahl): Mike's critical choice unfolds through a sequence of reflection and decision after Worm's betrayal leaves him owing $15,000 to KGB. The sequence builds through several key moments:

1. Mike visits his old professor Petrovsky, reconnecting with the theme established earlier: "We can't run away from who we are. Our destiny chooses us."
2. Mike reflects on his options through voiceover: "I could go back to the office. Back to grinding out mindless hours. Or I could play. Play for all the money Grama wants to take from me. Play for Worm, for me, for the girl I lost, for time I can't get back."
3. The crucial moment comes when Mike realizes he must embrace who he truly is: "I've made a lot of mistakes, and in my life I've made all of them twice. But now I know what I'm meant to do. I'm like my old man. I'm a card player."

This choice represents:

- Acceptance of his true nature
- Rejection of society's expectations
- Commitment to authenticity
- Willingness to risk everything on his talent

"The Silence of the Lambs" (Novel by Thomas Harris, 1988; Film adaptation 1991, directed by Jonathan Demme): Clarice's critical choice develops through her processing of multiple revelations about the case and herself:

1. She revisits Lecter's clues in solitude: “We begin by coveting what we see every day... He coveted that girl's skin... He's making himself a woman suit out of real women!”
2. She connects her personal trauma to her motivation: “I hear the lambs screaming, Dr. Lecter... I wake up sometimes in the dark and hear the lambs screaming.”
3. Her critical choice crystallizes in her decision to pursue the case alone, even without FBI backing: “Catherine Martin is alive. She's right there, right now, waiting. She's worth saving. She's all I have.”

This represents:

- Choosing personal mission over institutional approval
- Accepting her past trauma as driving force
- Committing to saving others to save herself
- Taking full responsibility for the outcome

“Good Will Hunting” (1997, original screenplay by Matt Damon and Ben Affleck): Will's critical choice emerges through several emotional revelations after pushing Skylar away:

1. A breakthrough session with Sean where the repetition of “It's not your fault” finally breaks Will's defenses: “I know... Oh God, I'm so sorry! I'm so sorry Sean!”
2. Chuckie's brutal honesty about Will's potential: “You're sitting on a winning lottery ticket, and you're too much of a pussy to cash it in... If you're still here tomorrow, I'll f***ing kill you.”
3. Will's final realization comes through reading Sean's note: “Your move, chief.”

This choice involves:

- Accepting love as worth the risk of pain
- Taking responsibility for his own future

- Honoring his gifts rather than hiding them
- Choosing growth over safety

"The Matrix" (1999, original screenplay by The Wachowskis): Neo's critical choice comes after his apparent death, through a sequence of realizations:

1. Trinity's declaration of love connects to the Oracle's prophecy: "The Oracle told me I would fall in love and that man would be The One."
2. Neo's understanding that death itself is part of the Matrix: "There is no spoon."
3. The final choice to reject the system's rules entirely: "No... I don't believe it!"

This represents:

- Choosing belief in himself over system limitations
- Accepting his role as The One
- Rejecting all imposed restrictions
- Embracing full potential despite risks

Act 3: The Resolution

Act 3 is the climax of the story, where all the threads come together, and the hero must confront their ultimate test. This act begins with a clear turning point, showing the hero's transformation and readiness for the final battle. The story builds to a crescendo, with the hero drawing upon all they've learned to overcome both external and internal obstacles. Whether the ending is happy or tragic, Act 3 must deliver a satisfying conclusion that brings the theme to its most powerful expression. The denouement ties up loose ends and shows how the hero's journey has fundamentally changed them and their world.

Beat 11: Welcome to the End / Plot Point 2 (Single Scene)

Understanding the Beat: This single scene beat marks the hero's entry into Act 3. It shows their preparation for the final confrontation and demonstrates how their journey has transformed them. While ideally a single scene, it can occasionally extend to a small sequence if necessary to properly establish the transition into the final act.

Masterful Examples:

"Rounders" (1998, original screenplay by David Levien and Brian Koppelman, directed by John Dahl): The break into Act 3 occurs when Mike enters KGB's club for the final confrontation. This moment shows his transformation from the person who lost everything in the same club at the beginning of the film.

Mike's entrance demonstrates his change:

- He walks in with confidence rather than desperation
- He has accepted his true identity as a poker player
- He's there by choice rather than necessity
- He understands both himself and his opponent

The scene establishes:

- The stakes: His entire bankroll plus the debt
- The opponent: KGB waiting for him
- The transformation: Mike's new self-awareness
- The theme: Embracing one's true nature

Mike's inner monologue reveals his clarity: "This is it. This is what I do." He has finally embraced who he is rather than who others want him to be.

"The Silence of the Lambs" (Novel by Thomas Harris, 1988; Film adaptation 1991, directed by Jonathan Demme): The transition into Act 3 occurs when Clarice follows her instincts to Buffalo Bill's house in Belvedere, Ohio. This moment shows her evolution from trainee to full agent, willing to trust her own judgment.

The scene establishes:

- Her independence from institutional support
- Her willingness to act on her insights
- The culmination of her training

- The parallel to her childhood trauma with the lambs

Clarice's approach to the house demonstrates her transformation from student to agent, showing how she's integrated everything she's learned from both her FBI training and her conversations with Lecter.

"Good Will Hunting" (1997, original screenplay by Matt Damon and Ben Affleck): Will's break into Act 3 comes when he finds and reads Sean's note after their final session. This moment represents his readiness to make a genuine change in his life.

The scene shows:

- Will's emotional preparation for growth
- His acceptance of the risk of change
- The integration of his therapy insights
- His readiness to choose a different path

Sean's simple note ("Your move, chief") encapsulates the choice Will must make —stay safe in his familiar world or risk everything for growth and love.

"The Matrix" (1999, original screenplay by The Wachowskis): Neo's entry into Act 3 occurs when he fully accepts his identity as The One and returns to the Matrix to save Morpheus. This moment shows his complete transformation from doubtful newcomer to empowered hero.

The scene demonstrates:

- His mastery over the Matrix
- His acceptance of his role
- His willingness to risk everything
- His transcendence of systemic limitations

The moment establishes Neo's readiness for the final confrontation, showing how far he's come from his initial confusion about the nature of reality.

Beat 12: Theme Triumphant / Denouement (Multiple Scenes)

Understanding the Beat: This final beat brings resolution to the story, unraveling any remaining confusion or knots. Whether the ending is happy or tragic, the theme must triumph, and all audiences should understand the story's central message. This beat ties together both external and internal conflicts while demonstrating how the hero's journey has served the theme.

Masterful Examples:

"Rounders" (1998, original screenplay by David Levien and Brian Koppelman, directed by John Dahl): The theme triumphant unfolds through Mike's final poker game against KGB and its aftermath. The sequence demonstrates the triumph of the film's theme: "We can't run away from who we are, our destiny chooses us."

The resolution comes in layers:

1. The poker game itself shows Mike's complete acceptance of his nature: "You can't lose what you don't put in the middle... but you can't win much either."
2. Mike's victory comes through understanding both himself and his opponent: "In my hand, I'm representing the nuts. But the key is, I got KGB believing I'm weak... He's trying to bully me like he did last time. But this time, I know what he's holding."
3. After winning, Mike makes peace with his true identity: "We're always looking for that big score, the royal flush. But success is about grinding it out, just like Grandma always said— grind it out, honey, grind it out."
4. The final scene shows Mike heading to Las Vegas: "Some people insist that poker is all about luck. They're wrong. I've gambled with my life before—this is no different."

The theme triumphs because:

- Mike embraces his true nature as a poker player
- He succeeds by being authentic rather than trying to be "respectable"

- His victory comes through self-knowledge
- He chooses his destiny rather than having it chosen for him

"The Silence of the Lambs" (Novel by Thomas Harris, 1988; Film adaptation 1991, directed by Jonathan Demme): The theme triumphant emerges through Clarice's confrontation with Buffalo Bill and its aftermath. The resolution demonstrates the power of facing one's deepest fears.

Key moments include:

1. The basement confrontation where Clarice must face her fears in total darkness: "I can smell your cunt!"—Bill taunts, but Clarice maintains her composure.
2. The parallel between saving Catherine and the lambs: "Get me out of here!" Catherine screams, echoing the lambs from Clarice's childhood.
3. Graduation ceremony showing Clarice's professional triumph: "Congratulations, Agent Starling."—her new title representing her transformation.
4. Lecter's final call, connecting past to future: "I do wish we could chat longer, but... I'm having an old friend for dinner."

The theme triumphs because:

- Clarice faces her childhood trauma
- She saves Catherine where she couldn't save the lamb
- She proves herself in a male-dominated field
- She maintains her integrity throughout

"Good Will Hunting" (1997, original screenplay by Matt Damon and Ben Affleck): The theme triumphant comes through Will's decision to "go see about a girl" and its implications for his growth. The resolution shows the triumph of authentic connection over intellectual defense mechanisms.

The sequence includes:

1. Chuckie arriving at Will's empty house: "Son of a bitch stole my line."—

showing pride rather than disappointment.

2. Will's drive to California, demonstrating his choice to risk love: "I had to go see about a girl."
3. The letter to Sean explaining his choice: "Thank you for everything. I'll be seeing you."

The theme triumphs because:

- Will chooses emotional truth over intellectual safety
- He risks vulnerability for authentic connection
- He honors his potential rather than hiding from it
- He breaks the cycle of self-sabotage

"The Matrix" (1999, original screenplay by The Wachowskis): The theme triumphant occurs through Neo's final confrontation with Agent Smith and his message to the machines. The resolution demonstrates the power of choosing one's own reality.

Key elements include:

1. Neo's complete mastery over the Matrix: "I know you're out there. I can feel you now."
2. His message to the machines: "I'm going to show these people what you don't want them to see. I'm going to show them a world without you."
3. The final phone call: "Where we go from there is a choice I leave to you."

The theme triumphs because:

- Neo fully embraces his role as The One
- He demonstrates the power of belief over systemic control
- He offers others the same choice he was given
- He transforms from doubter to liberator

Basic Narrative Beat Sheet Examples

Seven

Basic Narrative Beat Sheet

THEME

The central theme of "Seven" revolves around the nature of evil and apathy in modern society. The film explores how people have become desensitized to sin and human suffering in an increasingly corrupt world. The theme is captured in Somerset's quote: "Ernest Hemingway once wrote, 'The world is a fine place and worth fighting for.' I agree with the second part."

ACT 1

Prologue

The opening credit sequence unfolds as a series of disjointed, haunting fragments: A metronome ticks with mechanical precision. In a dimly lit room, a man's hands—steady, methodical—trim his fingertips with a razor blade, filing down the ridges to erase his identity. Journals fill with cramped, immaculate handwriting—countless pages documenting twisted thoughts and meticulous plans. Photographs are defaced—black marker scratching through eyes, then violently crossing out entire faces. Thread is pulled through needle, binding book pages. Razor blades cut newspaper clippings. All performed with ritualistic care by someone preparing his life's work: a series of elaborately staged murders based on the seven deadly sins. Not random acts of violence, but a calculated sermon designed to force a morally blind world to see its own corruption.

1. Set Up

Detective William Somerset (Morgan Freeman) is a weary, soon-to-retire detective who has seen too much of the world's evil. He's paired with Detective

David Mills (Brad Pitt), a young, idealistic, and hot-headed cop who has recently transferred to the precinct with his wife Tracy (Gwyneth Paltrow). Somerset is disillusioned with the city and its violence, representing wisdom acquired through painful experience, while Mills represents naive optimism and belief in justice.

The status quo world is established as a nameless, rain-soaked city drowning in crime and moral decay. Somerset's apartment reflects his methodical, intellectual nature, while Mills' half-unpacked apartment shows his impulsiveness and transitional state. Tracy feels uncomfortable in the city but tries to make it work for her husband's career.

The theme is subtly introduced through Somerset's weariness with the world's evil and his resignation that things won't change, contrasted with Mills' belief that he can make a difference.

2. Inciting Incident

The discovery of an extremely obese man forced to eat until his stomach ruptured (representing the sin of Gluttony). What makes this murder stand out is the meticulous planning and symbolism behind it. Somerset immediately recognizes this isn't a typical homicide but something designed to make a statement. This external event forces both detectives into a case that will change their lives forever.

3. Internal Wrestling/Preparation

Somerset initially tries to distance himself from the case, knowing he's retiring in seven days. He visits the library to research the seven deadly sins, suspecting the killer is using them as inspiration. Meanwhile, Mills eagerly pursues the investigation, dismissing Somerset's methodical approach. Their conflicting methods create tension.

Somerset considers dropping the case but reconsiders after connecting with

Tracy, who confides her unhappiness in the city and her undisclosed pregnancy. Somerset recognizes in Tracy an innocence worth protecting in this corrupt world, which renews his sense of responsibility.

Somerset prepares by researching Dante's "Divine Comedy," Milton's "Paradise Lost," and other works dealing with the seven deadly sins, anticipating the killer's next moves based on the remaining sins.

ACT 2

4. Welcome to the Jungle (Plot Point 1)

The discovery of a second elaborately staged murder scene—a wealthy attorney forced to cut off a pound of his own flesh (representing Greed). This confirms Somerset's theory about the seven deadly sins and fully establishes the pattern of the killer's design. The detectives now understand they're dealing with a methodical serial killer with a specific message. This completely disrupts their normal police work and plunges them into a much darker investigation than either anticipated.

Somerset and Mills now commit to working together despite their differences. The world of Act 2 is the twisted moral landscape created by the killer John Doe, a dark mirror reflection of the already corrupt city.

5. Subplot

As they work together more closely, Somerset develops a mentoring relationship with Mills, trying to temper the younger detective's impulsiveness. More significantly, Somerset forms a connection with Tracy during a dinner at the Mills' apartment. Tracy privately reveals her pregnancy to Somerset and her fears about raising a child in the city. She asks for his advice, creating a triangle of trust and concern that extends beyond the main murder investigation.

This subplot humanizes both detectives and raises the emotional stakes of the case. Somerset becomes invested not just in solving the case but in protecting what Mills' family represents—hope and innocence in a corrupt world. This reinforces the theme as Somerset finds something "worth fighting for" despite his disillusionment.

6. Trials and Tribulations

The investigation intensifies as they discover more elaborate murder scenes:

- The victim of Sloth: a drug dealer and child molester kept alive but physically and mentally tortured for a full year
- The victim of Lust: a prostitute forced to death by a customer using a bladed sex device
- The victim of Pride: a beautiful model whose face was disfigured before being given the choice between suicide or calling for help and living disfigured

Each crime scene is more disturbing than the last, revealing the killer's meticulous planning and theological justifications. The detectives follow leads through fingerprint analysis, library records, and witness statements, but are constantly one step behind.

Mills becomes increasingly frustrated and emotionally involved, while Somerset tries to maintain professional distance while recognizing the killer's intelligence. They debate the nature of evil and whether their work makes any difference in such a corrupt world, highlighting their philosophical differences and further developing the theme.

7. Midpoint

The dramatic shift occurs when the detectives discover John Doe's apartment. The place is a treasure trove of disturbing journals, photographs, and religious iconography that reveals the depth of Doe's twisted obsession and meticulous planning. The thousands of notebooks document his deteriorating mental state and theological justifications.

Just as they're exploring the apartment, John Doe returns, sees them, and flees. This leads to a rain-soaked chase sequence where Mills almost catches Doe but is outsmarted. Doe could have killed Mills but instead holds a gun to his head before leaving him alive—suggesting a specific plan for Mills that hasn't yet been revealed.

This midpoint escalates the cat-and-mouse game and shifts the power dynamic. The detectives now know who their killer is, but Doe is still controlling the narrative.

8. Complications

The stakes rise dramatically as:

- The police attempt to build a case against Doe with the evidence from his apartment
- The killer's methodical nature becomes more apparent, suggesting everything is happening according to his plan
- Mills becomes increasingly obsessed with catching Doe, putting strain on his personal life
- Somerset tries to keep Mills from spiraling emotionally, worried about his volcanic temper
- Pressure from police superiors mounts as the murders gain public attention

The city lives in fear as they wait for the next deadly sin murder to occur. Mills begins taking the case personally, especially after Doe directly confronts him during the chase. Somerset worries that Mills is falling into a trap set by the killer.

9. Crisis

In a shocking turn, John Doe walks into the police station covered in blood and turns himself in. This is the "crisis" moment because it completely disrupts the investigators' expectations. Doe offers to confess to all murders and lead them to the final two victims (representing Envy and Wrath), but only if Mills and Somerset accompany him alone to a remote location. If they don't comply, they'll never find the bodies.

The decision to comply with Doe's demands feels like a defeat—the killer is dictating terms even in custody. This creates the ultimate crisis point as the detectives must decide whether to play by Doe's rules, knowing they're walking into some kind of trap.

10. Critical Choice

Somerset recognizes the danger of following Doe's plan but Mills is determined to see the case through to the end. After intense contemplation, Somerset chooses to accompany them rather than let Mills go alone, recognizing that the younger detective needs his steady influence.

Mills struggles with his growing rage toward Doe, who subtly taunts him during this period. Mills must decide what kind of detective and man he wants to be—one who upholds justice at all costs, or one who might bend under extreme circumstances.

The district attorney and police captain make the administrative decision to accept Doe's terms, setting the stage for the climax. Somerset almost walks away but chooses to stay, demonstrating his character growth and commitment to see things through despite his initial desire to remain detached.

ACT 3

11. Welcome to the End (Plot Point 2)

A police convoy takes Doe, Mills, and Somerset to a remote desert location. Doe calmly directs them where to go, maintaining control even in custody. As they reach the designated spot, a delivery van approaches on the horizon, which Doe explains contains his final "project."

This moment transitions the story into its final phase, where Doe's master plan will be revealed. The setting shifts from the dark, rain-soaked city to an exposed, sunlit desert—nowhere to hide, suggesting the final confrontation with evil will happen in broad daylight.

12. Denouement/Theme Triumphant

In the devastating climax, the delivery van driver brings a box addressed to Mills. Despite Somerset's attempt to intervene, Mills demands to know what's in the box. Somerset looks inside first and is horrified, trying to prevent Mills from seeing the contents. Doe then reveals he represents the sin of Envy—he was envious of Mills' normal life and wife. He confesses to beheading Tracy (Mills' pregnant wife) and putting her head in the box.

Mills is faced with an impossible moral choice that embodies the theme: in a world of unspeakable evil, how does one respond? Doe's plan is to provoke Mills into killing him in rage, thus making Mills embody the sin of Wrath and completing his "masterpiece."

Despite Somerset's desperate pleas, Mills succumbs to his grief and rage, shooting Doe repeatedly—exactly as the killer planned. In this moment, Mills becomes the final sin (Wrath), completing Doe's twisted sermon about the sins of modern society.

The theme triumphs as the story reveals there are no easy answers or clean resolutions when confronting true evil. Mills, who represented hope and idealism, is destroyed by his encounter with evil. Somerset, who was ready to give up, witnesses the full tragedy of human nature but recommits to fighting despite knowing the battle may be futile.

The film ends with Somerset quoting Hemingway: "Ernest Hemingway once wrote, 'The world is a fine place and worth fighting for.' I agree with the second part." This perfectly encapsulates the theme—the world may be irredeemably corrupt, but the struggle against that corruption still has meaning. Somerset, who was ready to retire, will now stay to fight, having experienced firsthand both the depths of human evil and the necessity of standing against it.

John Doe achieves his goal of delivering his "sermon" about society's apathy toward sin, but Somerset's final words suggest that evil hasn't completely triumphed. The theme resonates in the moral ambiguity of the ending—evil has been punished, but at terrible cost, leaving the audience to reflect on the nature of justice, vengeance, and moral compromise in an imperfect world.

Rounders

Basic Narrative Beat Sheet

THEME

The central theme of "Rounders" revolves around identity and authenticity—specifically, accepting who you truly are versus who society expects you to be. The film explores how denying one's true nature leads to failure, while embracing it (even if it's unconventional) is the path to fulfillment. This is captured in the film's famous line: "You can't lose what you don't put in the middle... but you can't win much either."

ACT 1

1. Set Up

Mike McDermott (Matt Damon) is a gifted poker player and law student who has seemingly given up his gambling life after losing his entire bankroll ($30,000) to Russian mobster Teddy "KGB" (John Malkovich) nine months earlier. His status quo world is one of restraint and compromise—attending law school to please his girlfriend Jo (Gretchen Mol), working a delivery job to make ends meet, and suppressing his natural talent and passion for poker.

We see Mike's internal conflict immediately as he narrates about the poker world with obvious love and knowledge, despite claiming to have left it behind. His relationship with Jo represents the conventional path he's trying to follow, while his mentor Joey Knish (John Turturro) represents the professional grinder who plays it safe. Professor Petrovsky (Martin Landau) symbolizes wisdom and perspective.

The theme is introduced through Mike's opening narration: "Listen, here's the thing. If you can't spot the sucker in your first half hour at the table, then you are the sucker." This applies not just to poker but to life—Mike is being a "sucker" by denying his true nature and trying to be someone he's not. His encyclopedic knowledge and obvious passion for poker betray his authentic identity despite his attempts to suppress it.

2. Inciting Incident

Lester "Worm" Murphy (Edward Norton), Mike's childhood friend, is released from prison and immediately reenters Mike's life. Worm embodies the chaotic, reckless side of the gambling lifestyle and serves as the catalyst that will pull Mike back into the poker world. This external event disrupts Mike's carefully constructed "reformed" life and sets the main plot in motion.

Thematically, Worm represents the part of Mike's identity he's trying to suppress—the risk-taker, the gambler. Worm's return forces Mike to confront aspects of himself he's been denying.

3. Internal Wrestling/Preparation

Mike struggles with Worm's reappearance, torn between loyalty to his old friend and his promise to Jo to stay away from gambling. While he initially resists returning to poker, he soon finds himself drawn back to the underground clubs where he once thrived.

In a key scene, Mike watches other players and mentally corrects their strategy, showing how poker thinking is intrinsic to his nature. His narration during these scenes reveals his true self bleeding through the façade he's created.

Jo senses Mike's internal conflict and confronts him about spending time with Worm. Mike reassures her he's not gambling again, though he's clearly tempted—representing his continued attempt to deny his authentic self to maintain his relationship and conventional life path.

The theme manifests here as Mike's growing discomfort with living a life that doesn't align with his true nature—like a fish trying to live on land.

ACT 2

4. Welcome to the Jungle (Plot Point 1)

Mike's resolve finally breaks when he and Worm visit an underground poker club run by state troopers. After observing a session where he recognizes a player's tell, Mike cannot resist sitting down to play. He wins $4,000 in this session—his triumphant return to the poker world.

This moment marks Mike's first step back toward his authentic self. As he plays, we see him come alive, utilizing skills that define his true identity. His narration becomes more passionate and confident. The contrast between the constrained law student and the natural poker player becomes stark—from the structured, conventional world of legal education to the high-risk, adrenaline-fueled poker underground where he truly belongs.

Thematically, this represents the beginning of Mike's journey back to authenticity, though he still sees it as a temporary deviation rather than an acceptance of his true nature.

5. Subplot

Mike develops a deeper connection with Professor Petrovsky, who recognizes

Mike's distraction in class but also sees his exceptional talent. After Mike wins a moot court competition through skillful reading of his opponent (using poker instincts), Petrovsky pulls him aside and shares his own story of a dual life—how he abandoned his true passion (literature) to escape persecution in Russia.

Petrovsky tells Mike: "We can't run from who we are. Our destiny chooses us." This directly addresses the theme of authenticity and foreshadows Mike's eventual acceptance of his true identity.

Additionally, Mike's relationship with Jo intensifies as she discovers he's been playing poker again. Their arguments center around identity—Jo wants Mike to be someone he's not (a conventional lawyer), while Mike struggles to articulate that poker isn't just gambling for him; it's who he is at his core.

These subplots create thematic tension around the central question: Is it better to be true to yourself or to conform to societal expectations?

6. Trials and Tribulations

This extended sequence follows Mike as he navigates various poker challenges and obstacles:

- Mike enters a high-stakes game with Worm, who gets caught cheating, forcing Mike to use his people-reading skills to talk their way out
- Mike begins playing regularly to help Worm pay off his debt, pulling him deeper into his authentic world
- Worm continues to cheat while playing under Mike's name, creating a conflict between different aspects of the poker identity—the honest, skilled player versus the hustler
- Jo discovers Mike has fully returned to poker and gives him an ultimatum that forces him to choose between authentic happiness and a safe, expected path
- Mike tries to balance law school and poker, with his true passion increasingly winning out

Throughout these trials, Mike's narration reveals his deep understanding of the poker world—not just the rules but the psychology and philosophy behind it. These insights show how completely poker is interwoven with his identity, making his attempts to abandon it equivalent to self-denial.

The theme develops as Mike becomes increasingly comfortable in the poker world while growing more distant from his law school life, showing how returning to authenticity feels natural despite its complications.

7. Midpoint

In Atlantic City, Mike discovers that Worm has been cheating while playing under Mike's name, damaging the reputation Mike values deeply. This betrayal leads to a confrontation where Worm reveals the full extent of his debt—$15,000 owed to Grama, who will severely hurt or kill Worm if it's not paid in five days.

This pivotal revelation creates an identity crisis for Mike: Does he embrace the responsible, loyal friend identity and help Worm despite his betrayal? Or does he protect his reputation as an honest poker player by cutting Worm loose?

Mike chooses loyalty, deciding to help Worm despite the betrayal, but this decision forces him to fully commit to his poker identity, as only by embracing his true skills can he earn enough money in time. This represents a significant step toward accepting his authentic self, though still motivated by external pressure rather than internal acceptance.

Thematically, this midpoint forces Mike to rely on his true nature rather than his constructed identity to solve a crisis.

8. Complications

The stakes escalate dramatically as:

- Jo learns that Mike has chosen poker over law school and ends their relationship, saying: "I don't think this is just a phase anymore...this is who you are"—directly addressing the theme

- Mike must now earn $15,000 in just five days, requiring him to fully utilize his poker talents
- Mike takes increasingly larger risks at higher stakes games, relying more on his natural abilities
- Mike risks his tuition money, symbolically choosing his poker identity over his law student identity

During this sequence, Mike has a key conversation with Knish about different types of poker players. Knish describes himself as a grinder who makes a living but “doesn't have the stones to go for it.” This contrasts with Mike, who has the talent and courage to pursue greatness but must accept the higher risks that come with it—another reflection of the theme of being true to one's authentic self despite the consequences.

Thematically, these complications force Mike to confront what matters most to him and what kind of person he truly is, pushing him toward acceptance of his authentic identity.

9. Crisis

The “crisis” moment occurs when Mike and Worm sit down in a game run by state troopers who recognize Worm from his previous cheating. A fight breaks out, they lose all their money, and their car is impounded with their remaining bankroll inside.

When they return to the city, Grama and his thugs catch up to them, severely beating Worm. Mike offers to take on Worm's debt, now increased to $25,000, with only 48 hours to pay. Worm decides to flee town, abandoning Mike to deal with the consequences alone.

This crisis represents the complete collapse of Mike's plans—he's lost his girlfriend, his law school career is in jeopardy, his poker bankroll is gone, his reputation is damaged, his friend has betrayed and abandoned him, and he now faces a potentially deadly debt to dangerous criminals.

Thematically, this represents the consequences of living in the limbo between identities—neither fully embracing his authentic poker self nor fully committing to the conventional path. This crisis forces Mike to make a definitive choice about who he truly is.

10. Critical Choice

In this dark night of the soul, Mike visits Petrovsky and confesses everything. Petrovsky offers him money to escape town, but after deep reflection, Mike makes the critical choice to stay and face his problems directly.

During this pivotal conversation, Petrovsky says: "We cannot run from who we are. Our destiny chooses us." This crystallizes the theme and helps Mike reach the revelation that he must embrace his true identity as a poker player rather than running away.

Mike decides to confront Teddy KGB—the source of his original down fall—in a heads-up poker match to win the money he needs. This choice represents Mike's complete acceptance of who he really is and his willingness to risk everything on his true skills.

Mike borrows $10,000 from Knish, who warns him against playing KGB but ultimately supports his decision. When Knish asks why Mike would risk everything against KGB again, Mike simply replies, I'm not playing for the money...I'm playing for me." This line directly expresses Mike's acceptance of his authentic self, marking the completion of his character journey from denial to acceptance.

ACT 3

11. Welcome to the End (Plot Point 2)

Mike enters KGB's club and proposes a heads-up match for his remaining $10,000. KGB agrees but insists that if Mike loses, he'll have to answer to

Grama for the rest of the debt. Mike accepts these terms, fully committing to his path.

The high-stakes poker showdown begins, representing the final confrontation not just with KGB but with Mike's own past failures and self-deception. This transition into Act 3 brings Mike full circle to the location of his initial defeat, but now he enters as his authentic self rather than the overconfident player who lost everything nine months earlier.

Mike's narration during this sequence reveals a new level of self-awareness and acceptance of his poker identity. He's no longer fighting against who he is but embracing it fully, which gives him a clarity and focus he lacked in their first confrontation.

Thematically, this represents Mike putting his authentic self "in the middle"—risking everything on being who he truly is rather than who others want him to be.

12. Denouement/Theme Triumphant

The final poker match between Mike and KGB unfolds as a battle of identities—KGB's intimidating persona versus Mike's authentic poker self. In the first round, Mike wins $20,000 by recognizing KGB's tell (the Oreo cookie ritual) and strategically allowing him to win smaller pots while setting up a major victory.

KGB, enraged by his loss, demands to continue playing. Against Knish's advice to walk away with enough money to pay the debt, Mike agrees to keep playing because he recognizes KGB is now on tilt (playing emotionally rather than rationally). This decision represents Mike's complete confidence in his abilities and acceptance of his identity as a master poker player.

In the second round, Mike deliberately loses a hand to reinforce KGB's false confidence, then wins everything by catching KGB's bluff at the crucial moment. Mike walks away with $60,000—enough to pay off Worm's debt, restart his poker career, and consider his future on his own terms.

In the final scenes, Mike pays off Grama, ensuring Worm's safety despite his betrayal (showing growth and compassion). He then leaves New York for Las Vegas to pursue his dream of playing in the World Series of Poker, fully embracing his true identity.

The theme triumphs as Mike narrates his philosophy: “You can't lose what you don't put in the middle. But you can't win much either.” This perfectly encapsulates the film's message about authenticity—you must risk being your true self to find fulfillment, even if society values a different path. Mike has rejected the safe conventional life that wasn't true to his nature and embraced the uncertainty and authenticity of the poker life that is.

The film ends with Mike heading to Las Vegas, not with naive dreams of easy riches, but with clear-eyed acceptance of both the risks and rewards of living authentically. His journey from denial to acceptance demonstrates that true failure comes not from losing at what you love, but from never allowing yourself to fully pursue it.

8MM

Basic Narrative Beat Sheet

THEME

The central theme of “8MM” revolves around the corrupting influence of confronting evil. The film explores how witnessing depravity changes a person, even when their intentions are noble. This theme is captured in the transformation of Tom Welles from a detached professional to someone capable of vigilante justice after staring into the abyss of human cruelty.

ACT 1

Prologue

In the bustling Miami International Airport, private investigator Tom Welles moves with the practiced ease of someone accustomed to remaining invisible. His target - a middle-aged businessman suspected of infidelity - moves through the terminal unaware of Welles' constant surveillance. The investigator's methods are precise and professional; his camera carefully documents each compromising moment without judgment or emotional investment.

The chase leads through Miami's affluent neighborhoods to a run-down motel, where Welles captures irrefutable evidence of the man's extramarital affair. Later, in a wealthy client's home, he delivers the photographs with clinical detachment. The client's bitter response—"I never liked him anyway"—barely registers. For Welles, this is simply another case closed, another check to be collected.

This opening sequence establishes not just Welles' professional methodology, but the careful compartmentalization of his life. In his modest Harrisburg home, he maintains a separate existence with his wife Amy and their newborn daughter. The contrast between his work investigating human depravity and his attempts to build a normal family life creates a tension that will eventually become unsustainable.

1. Set Up

Private investigator Tom Welles works with clinical detachment, maintaining strict boundaries between his professional life investigating human depravity and his personal life with his wife Amy and their newborn daughter. The film establishes his methodical approach as he conducts surveillance on a cheating husband in Miami, delivering the evidence to a wealthy client without emotional investment. His compartmentalized existence creates a tension that foreshadows his eventual transformation.

2. Inciting Incident

Mrs. Christian, widow of a powerful industrialist, hires Welles to investigate an 8mm film found in her late husband's private safe. The film appears to show the actual murder of a teenage girl by a man wearing a leather mask. Mrs. Christian needs to know if the film is real or staged. This discovery forces Welles to confront a level of evil beyond his usual cases of infidelity and insurance fraud.

3. Internal Wrestling/Preparation

Welles initially hesitates to accept the case but is drawn in by Mrs. Christian's desperation and the possibility that the film might be fake. He methodically analyzes the film frame by frame in his home office, wearing latex gloves that symbolize his attempt to maintain professional distance. His search through missing persons records leads him to Mary Ann Mathews, a 16-year-old who disappeared from Cleveland. Welles visits Mary Ann's mother, sees the girl as a real person with dreams and ambitions, and becomes personally invested in discovering the truth.

ACT 2

4. Welcome to the Jungle (Plot Point 1)

Welles' investigation takes him to Los Angeles, plunging him into the underground world of pornography as he follows Mary Ann's trail. This marks his entry into a moral wilderness far removed from his controlled professional life. He discovers that Mary Ann briefly worked in the adult film industry under the name “Raquel” before disappearing completely. This confirms his worst fears about the film's authenticity and commits him fully to the investigation.

5. Subplot

Welles meets Max California, a clerk at an adult bookstore whose punk exterior hides extensive knowledge of the industry's darkest corners. Max becomes

Welles' guide through this moral labyrinth, establishing a mentor/ally relationship that humanizes Welles' journey. This connection represents a lifeline of relative innocence in a corrupt world, paralleling Welles' distant relationship with his family, who represent what he's fighting to protect.

6. Trials and Tribulations

Posing as a wealthy collector interested in custom-made extreme films, Welles and Max infiltrate deeper into the shadow world of underground pornography. They encounter increasingly disturbing figures in this industry, from sleazy producers to men who commission unspeakable content. Welles' professional detachment begins to crack as he witnesses systematic exploitation. The investigation leads them to Dino Velvet, a notorious director of violent fetish films whose star performer, "Machine," wears the same distinctive mask from the 8mm film.

7. Midpoint

Welles discovers Dino Velvet's connection to the film and arranges a meeting to commission a custom film, hoping to confirm Machine's identity. At this pivotal moment, he pays Max for his help and urges him to leave, believing he's protecting his guide from danger. This decision to continue alone marks Welles' deeper commitment to the case and foreshadows the personal price he will pay for pursuing justice.

8. Complications

The situation escalates when Eddie Poole, a pornographer connected to Mary Ann's disappearance, recognizes Welles as an investigator. Unknown to Welles, Max is kidnapped by Dino's crew. The stakes rise dramatically as Welles realizes he's been identified and his cover is blown, putting both himself and Max in grave danger.

9. Crisis

The "all is lost" moment occurs at Dino Velvet's remote production facility when what should have been a simple meeting becomes a deadly trap. Daniel Longdale, Mrs. Christian's lawyer, appears, revealing his complicity in the crime. Machine and Dino quickly disarm Welles, and bring out a captive Max. Welles learns the terrible truth: the 8mm film was real, commissioned by Mr. Christian for $1 million. The confrontation explodes into violence, with Max being killed in the chaos—a moment that marks the true point of no return for Welles.

10. Critical Choice

When Welles reports his findings to Mrs. Christian, she commits suicide, leaving him with no legal recourse for justice. The police cannot act without evidence, and the film itself would be inadmissible in court. In this dark moment of reflection, Welles makes his critical choice, declaring to his wife, "There's no one left to finish this but me." He decides to abandon legal channels and pursue vigilante justice, marking his complete transformation from detached observer to active participant.

ACT 3

11. Welcome to the End (Plot Point 2)

With traditional justice out of reach and Max's death weighing on his conscience, Welles tracks down Eddie Poole. He takes him to an abandoned house and extracts a confession, confirming Eddie's role in Mary Ann's murder. Eddie's complete lack of remorse solidifies Welles' conviction that these men must be stopped, and he executes Eddie. This action marks Welles' irreversible break from his former ethical boundaries and propels him toward the final confrontation.

12. Denouement/Theme Triumphant

In the final confrontation, Welles tracks down Machine at his home. The face behind the chrome mask is disturbingly ordinary—a stark reminder that true evil often wears the most mundane disguises. Machine's chilling words, "The things I do, I do them because I like them. Because I want to," force Welles to confront the senseless nature of evil. After a brutal fight, Welles kills Machine, completing his transformation.

The film concludes with Welles returning home, bearing physical and psychological scars from his journey into darkness. He breaks down in his wife's arms, finally allowing himself to feel the full weight of his experiences. As he holds his infant daughter, we see that while he has achieved a form of justice for Mary Ann, the cost to his soul has been profound. The film's theme triumphs as Welles now understands that innocence, once lost, can never be fully regained, and that confronting evil changes you irrevocably. His experience validates the film's central message: when you stare into the abyss, the abyss stares back at you; when you dance with the devil the devil changes you.

Good Will Hunting

Basic Narrative Beat Sheet

THEME

The central theme of "Good Will Hunting" revolves around self-worth and the courage to embrace vulnerability—specifically, how fear of abandonment and failure can prevent a person from realizing their full potential. The film explores how emotional walls built for self-protection ultimately become prisons that prevent authentic connection and growth. This is captured in Sean's pivotal line to Will: "You'll have bad times, but it'll always wake you up to the good stuff you weren't paying attention to."

ACT 1

1. Set Up

Will Hunting (Matt Damon) is a 20-year-old janitor at MIT with extraordinary mathematical abilities that he keeps hidden from the world. His status quo world is one of deliberate limitation—working menial jobs, hanging out with his South Boston friends Chuckie (Ben Affleck), Billy, and Morgan, and engaging in occasional violence and petty crime. Will is brilliant but emotionally closed off, using his intelligence as a weapon rather than a gift.

We see Will's conflicted nature immediately—he can solve complex mathematical problems that stump MIT professors, yet he mops floors and pushes this ability away. His childhood friend Chuckie represents his roots and comfort zone, while Professor Gerald Lambeau (Stellan Skarsgård) represents the academic world that could be Will's future if he chose it. The neighborhood bar, construction site, and streets of South Boston represent his safe but limiting environment.

The theme is introduced through Will's contradictory behaviors—his extraordinary mind trapped in a deliberately ordinary life, his fierce loyalty to friends contrasted with his inability to form deeper connections. His verbal abilities allow him to keep people at arm's length, revealing a fear of true intimacy and vulnerability that defines his character.

2. Inciting Incident

Professor Lambeau posts an extremely difficult mathematical proof on a hallway blackboard as a challenge for his graduate students. Will, while cleaning the halls at night, not only solves the problem but does so with remarkable elegance and insight. When Lambeau posts a far more difficult second problem, Will solves it anonymously again. Lambeau sets a trap to catch the mysterious solver, but before he can confront Will, Will is arrested for assaulting a police officer—a former childhood bully.

This external event—Will's mathematical genius being discovered—disrupts his carefully maintained anonymity and sets the main plot in motion. It represents the collision of the two worlds Will has tried to keep separate.

3. Internal Wrestling/Preparation

Will faces a jail sentence for his assault charge. Professor Lambeau, recognizing Will's extraordinary potential, intervenes and arranges a deal with the judge: Will can avoid jail if he studies mathematics with Lambeau and agrees to see a therapist. Will reluctantly accepts this arrangement to stay out of jail, though he has no intention of genuinely participating.

Will wrestles internally with this forced change to his comfortable routine. He prepares by reading psychology books to intellectually arm himself against therapy, planning to use his intelligence to manipulate and dismiss any therapist he meets. This represents his fear of vulnerability and emotional exposure—he would rather go to jail than risk someone getting close enough to see his pain.

The theme manifests here as Will builds his defenses higher in preparation for therapy, showing how his fear of vulnerability has become both a shield and a prison. His resistance foreshadows the central struggle he will face: maintaining his walls versus allowing himself to be truly seen.

ACT 2

4. Welcome to the Jungle (Plot Point 1)

Will begins his therapy sessions, quickly defeating five therapists with his psychological knowledge and verbal attacks. Lambeau, desperate and running out of options, turns to his former college roommate and estranged friend, Sean Maguire (Robin Williams), a community college psychology professor with his own troubled past.

In their first session, Will analyzes a painting in Sean's office and then proceeds to psychoanalyze Sean himself, attacking him personally to establish dominance. Sean responds unexpectedly by physically threatening Will and telling him, “You don't know about real loss.” This confrontation marks Will's entry into a completely different therapeutic relationship—one he cannot control through intellect alone.

This moment propels Will into the Act 2 world where his usual defense mechanisms no longer work. Sean isn't impressed by Will's intelligence and refuses to be manipulated or intimidated. This forces Will to either find new ways to resist therapy or begin to engage authentically—a direct challenge to his fear of vulnerability.

5. Subplot

Will meets Skylar (Minnie Driver), a Harvard pre-med student, at a Harvard bar where he impresses her by demolishing an arrogant graduate student in a battle of wits. Their immediate attraction forms the romantic subplot that will test Will's ability to be vulnerable in a relationship.

Simultaneously, a substantial subplot develops between Sean and Lambeau, whose friendship fractured years earlier. Their differing approaches to helping Will—Lambeau focused on his mathematical genius, Sean on his emotional health—creates tension that mirrors Will's internal conflict between intellectual achievement and emotional authenticity.

Additionally, Will's relationship with Chuckie deepens as a subplot when Chuckie admits he prays that Will will use his abilities to escape South Boston, even though it would mean losing his best friend. This conversation reveals the theme from another angle—Chuckie understands Will's worth better than Will does himself.

These subplots all reflect the central theme by presenting Will with models of genuine connection (Skylar), the consequences of emotional avoidance (Lambeau), and the possibility of love that doesn't abandon (Chuckie and Sean).

6. Trials and Tribulations

Will begins working on advanced mathematics with Lambeau while continuing therapy sessions with Sean. The contrast between these worlds creates numerous challenges:

- Will excels mathematically but resists job interviews Lambeau arranges with prestigious research firms and the NSA
- In therapy, Sean gradually breaks through Will's defenses by sharing his own experiences and meeting Will on his own terms
- Will's relationship with Skylar develops, but he keeps parts of himself hidden from her, lying about having brothers and being an orphan
- Will struggles to reconcile his loyalty to his South Boston friends with the new opportunities opening to him
- Lambeau becomes increasingly frustrated with what he sees as Will squandering his gift

Throughout these trials, Will begins to open up slightly to Sean during their park bench sessions, discussing philosophy and sharing bits of his experience, though still avoiding his deepest trauma. His defenses start to crack, but whenever emotional intimacy approaches—with Sean or Skylar—Will retreats or deflects with humor or intellect.

The theme develops as Will experiences the tension between the safety of emotional isolation and the potential rewards of connection. His mathematical ability provides no answers for these emotional challenges, forcing him to confront the limitations of intellect as a defense mechanism.

7. Midpoint

The pivotal shift occurs during a therapy session when Sean puts Will's juvenile court records on the table—documentation of the severe abuse Will suffered as a child. When Will makes a joke about his abuse, Sean repeatedly tells him, "It's not your fault," breaking through Will's intellectual defenses and touching the emotional core of his trauma.

For the first time, Will cannot maintain his emotional walls. He initially resists Sean's words but eventually breaks down sobbing as he begins to accept that he didn't deserve the abuse he suffered. This emotional breakthrough represents Will's first step toward authentic vulnerability and self-acceptance.

This midpoint fundamentally changes the dynamic between Will and Sean, moving their relationship from adversarial to genuine therapeutic alliance. It also shifts Will's internal journey from resistance to gradual acceptance of his need for emotional healing.

8. Complications

The stakes escalate dramatically as:

- Will's relationship with Skylar deepens, but when she says she loves him and asks him to come to California with her, he panics
- During a fight with Skylar, Will reveals his abusive past but cannot accept her love, telling her he doesn't love her to push her away
- Lambeau arranges more job interviews and becomes increasingly impatient with Will's resistance to pursuing mathematical opportunities
- Tension between Sean and Lambeau escalates as they argue about what's best for Will
- Will must choose between the comfort of his limited existing life and the frightening possibilities of love and achievement

Will's sabotage of his relationship with Skylar represents the theme in action—his fear of abandonment causes him to reject love before it can reject him. When Skylar asks him to come to California, he responds, “What do I have here that's so terrific that I want to leave? I got a best friend, I got a job, I live in a great place...” revealing how his fear has led him to settle for a safe but limited existence.

These complications force Will to confront the consequences of his emotional walls—he's losing Skylar and potentially his chance at a fulfilling future.

9. Crisis

The "crisis" moment occurs when Will has a brutal fight with Lambeau, who is pushing him to take a job at a prestigious firm. Will rejects the opportunity, and Lambeau accuses him of being afraid to fail. Will responds by cruelly mocking Lambeau's life achievements, destroying the relationship.

Simultaneously, Skylar leaves for Stanford medical school after Will refuses to go with her or even tell her he loves her. Will has now alienated both Skylar and Lambeau, leaving only Sean and his neighborhood friends in his life.

This crisis represents the consequences of Will's fear-based choices—his terror of vulnerability and failure has led him to push away people who recognize his worth and the opportunities that could give his life meaning. He's succeeding at staying "safe" but at the cost of any chance at fulfillment or genuine connection.

10. Critical Choice

In this dark night of the soul, Will has a breakthrough session with Sean, who shares the story of missing Game 6 of the 1975 World Series to meet his future wife, illustrating how life's most meaningful experiences often come from taking risks on people rather than achievements. Sean shows Will his own scrapbook of abuse similar to Will's, creating a profound moment of connection.

Sean challenges Will directly about his choices: "You'll have bad times, but it'll always wake you up to the good stuff you weren't paying attention to. You don't want to be 50 years old and think about what you coulda done."

This leads to Will's critical realization that he's been hiding from life rather than living it. In a pivotal scene with Chuckie at the construction site, Chuckie tells Will that the worst part of his day is the walk to Will's door each morning, hoping he won't be there—hoping Will will have finally moved on to something better.

These conversations force Will to make the critical choice between the safety of his limited life and the risk of pursuing love and his potential. Will chooses courage over fear, deciding to "go see about a girl" and follow Skylar to California—embracing both vulnerability in love and the uncertainty of leaving his safe environment.

ACT 3

11. Welcome to the End (Plot Point 2)

Will takes decisive action by giving Lambeau the solutions to the next series of mathematical problems, effectively completing their arrangement and closing that chapter. He then goes to Sean's office for a final session, where they achieve mutual respect and genuine connection.

Sean announces he's taking a sabbatical to travel the world—inspired by his work with Will to take his own advice about living life fully. When Will asks if Sean would be willing to meet again in the future for therapy, Sean agrees, saying, "We'll have our talks, you know, you'll justify your Lord of the Rings obsession..." Their relationship has transformed from therapist/patient to a genuine friendship.

This transition into Act 3 represents Will's acceptance of change and his willingness to leave behind the safety of his limited existence. By reaching out to maintain his connection with Sean, Will demonstrates his new capacity for authentic relationships.

12. Denouement/Theme Triumphant

On Will's 21st birthday, Chuckie and the guys arrive at his apartment to take him out, but he isn't there. Chuckie's wish has come true—Will has moved on. In the final scenes, we see Chuckie arrive at Will's apartment to find it empty, bringing full circle his earlier statement about hoping Will would be gone someday.

Meanwhile, Will writes a letter to Sean explaining his decision to pass on the job offers and instead "go see about a girl," using Sean's own story of sacrificing the World Series for love as inspiration. Will drives across the country toward California and Skylar, choosing love and uncertainty over safety and limitation.

The theme triumphs as Will finally embraces vulnerability and his own worth. He chooses connection over isolation, possibility over safety, and love over fear. His journey from self-protective isolation to the courage to be vulnerable is complete.

The film ends with the image of Will's car on the open road—a visual metaphor for the unlimited possibilities now available to him. The ending affirms the film's central message that true self-worth comes not just from recognizing one's talents but from having the courage to risk emotional vulnerability and connection. Will has finally understood that his worth isn't defined by his mathematical genius or his traumatic past, but by his capacity to love and be loved, and his courage to embrace an uncertain future.

The Machinist

Basic Narrative Beat Sheet

THEME

The central theme of "The Machinist" revolves around guilt, self-punishment, and the destructive power of denial. The film explores how the human mind can create elaborate mechanisms to avoid confronting unbearable truths, and how guilt literally and figuratively consumes us when we refuse to face our actions. The theme is embodied in Trevor's physical deterioration and hallucinations—his body and mind destroying themselves because he cannot acknowledge what he has done.

ACT 1

1. Set Up

Trevor Reznik (Christian Bale) is introduced as an emaciated insomniac who hasn't slept in a year. His gaunt, skeletal appearance immediately signals something is severely wrong. We see his lonely routine: working as a machinist in a grimy industrial factory, visiting a kind prostitute named Stevie (Jennifer Jason Leigh), and spending his sleepless nights at an airport café where he's served by Marie (Aitana Sánchez-Gijón). Trevor's apartment is sparse and obsessively clean—he constantly scrubs with bleach and leaves Post-it notes to remind himself of basic tasks.

The status quo world is established as one of isolation, ritual, and deterioration. Trevor exists rather than lives, going through mechanical motions with an increasingly unreliable grasp on reality. His coworkers whisper about his alarming appearance, creating further distance between Trevor and normal human connection.

The theme is subtly introduced through Trevor's physical wasting away—a visual manifestation of guilt literally consuming him from the inside out. His need for control (through cleaning rituals and notes) suggests he's compensating for something he can't control or face.

2. Inciting Incident

Trevor is momentarily distracted at work by the appearance of a mysterious new coworker named Ivan (John Sharian)—a bald, imposing man with a disfigured hand. During this distraction, Trevor causes an industrial accident that severs his colleague Miller's (Michael Ironside) arm. This accident disrupts Trevor's already fragile routine and marks the beginning of his descent into deeper paranoia. What makes this incident significant is that no one else seems to see or know Ivan, raising the first major question about Trevor's perception of reality.

3. Internal Wrestling/Preparation

Trevor struggles to make sense of what happened with Ivan and the accident. He attempts to report the incident properly but finds his coworkers growing increasingly hostile, believing he's dangerous. A cryptic sticky note appears on his refrigerator with a game of hangman missing several letters, further unsettling him. Trevor begins investigating who Ivan might be, checking with HR and colleagues, all of whom deny the man exists.

As paranoia grows, Trevor becomes increasingly vigilant—checking his apartment for intruders, trying to catch glimpses of Ivan, and becoming more obsessively clean as his external world becomes more chaotic. This preparation focuses on Trevor attempting to gather evidence about Ivan's existence while simultaneously trying to maintain the few stable elements of his life, though both efforts are increasingly futile.

ACT 2

4. Welcome to the Jungle (Plot Point 1)

Trevor's paranoia escalates when he discovers a photo in Ivan's wallet showing Trevor himself with Nicholas (Marie's son) fishing—an event he has no recollection of. This impossibility confirms something is severely wrong with either his reality or his memory. Trevor now fully commits to discovering who Ivan is and why he seems to be targeting him.

This plot point propels Trevor into the Act 2 world of active investigation and deteriorating sanity. The normal world of routine is completely disrupted as Trevor becomes obsessed with uncovering the truth about Ivan. The hangman game on his refrigerator gradually gains new letters, spelling out "K-I-L-L-E-R," adding urgency to his quest.

5. Subplot

Trevor develops a relationship with Marie, the waitress at the airport café, and her son Nicholas. This provides Trevor with a glimpse of the normal life he craves—a connection to warmth and normalcy that contrasts with his isolated existence. He takes them to a carnival, spending time with Nicholas on rides and appearing momentarily at peace.

This subplot serves as both respite and catalyst—these scenes appear to be the only moments where Trevor experiences human connection and joy, yet they're also riddled with disquieting elements that push the story forward. Nicholas suffers a seizure on the "Route 666" carnival ride, triggering disjointed flashes of memory in Trevor and deepening the mystery of his connection to the boy.

6. Trials and Tribulations

Trevor's investigation into Ivan leads him across the city through industrial wastelands and shadowy locations. He follows Ivan's car, only to discover the license plate is registered in Trevor's own name. Blood mysteriously appears dripping from his refrigerator, only to vanish moments later. Trevor brings Stevie to his apartment for a proper date, but becomes irrationally suspicious and accusatory, damaging one of his few human connections.

Trevor confronts his coworkers about Ivan again, leading to an aggressive altercation that leaves him further isolated. He finds himself doubting his own sanity as evidence mounts that Ivan may be a projection of his own mind. Each attempt to verify reality leaves Trevor more confused and desperate.

Trevor begins losing weight even more dramatically, his body becoming a living skeleton as his mental state deteriorates in parallel. The hangman game on his refrigerator continues to form the word "KILLER," heightening his paranoia about what he might have done.

7. Midpoint

In a pivotal scene, Trevor discovers what appears to be Ivan's car—the same one from earlier encounters. Following the discovery that the car is registered in his own name, Trevor begins to suspect that Ivan might be a part of himself that he's dissociated from. This represents the first moment where Trevor considers that his perception of reality might be fundamentally flawed.

This revelation creates a dramatic shift in the story—from Trevor pursuing an external tormentor to questioning whether the enemy is within his own fractured psyche. The mystery deepens but also begins to take a more introspective turn as Trevor must now confront the possibility that he is not a victim but possibly the perpetrator of something terrible he can't remember.

8. Complications

Trevor's physical and mental state continues to deteriorate more rapidly. His hallucinations become more vivid and disorienting, blurring the line between reality and delusion. The workplace becomes increasingly hostile as Trevor's behavior grows more erratic. His relationship with Stevie collapses completely after his paranoid accusations.

Trevor becomes fixated on the growing hangman puzzle spelling "KILLER" and begins experiencing more intense flashbacks triggered by mundane events—headlights on the road, the sound of tires screeching. The stakes escalate as Trevor realizes he might be responsible for something terrible, yet still cannot access the memory directly.

The police begin investigating Trevor's erratic behavior, adding external pressure to his internal crisis. Trevor starts to feel trapped between his deteriorating body, fractured mind, and the suspicions of those around him.

9. Crisis

Trevor reaches his lowest point when he can no longer distinguish between hallucination and reality. He violently confronts a coworker who he believes is conspiring with Ivan, only to be thrown out of the factory for good. His physical condition has become life-threatening, yet he still cannot sleep.

In a desperate moment, Trevor discovers that the airport café he's been visiting doesn't have a waitress named Marie, nor does she have a son named Nicholas. The realization that significant portions of his reality are fabricated creates a crisis of identity and sanity. Trevor now must face the possibility that his entire perception of the past year has been a complex delusion.

10. Critical Choice

After discovering that Marie and Nicholas aren't real, Trevor makes the critical choice to return to Highway 152—the location corresponding to the "Route 666" ride that triggered Nicholas's seizure. Rather than continuing to run from whatever truth he's been avoiding, Trevor chooses to confront it directly, no matter how devastating it might be.

This choice represents Trevor's spiritual and psychological turning point—the decision to stop running and face whatever he's been punishing himself for. It's a moment of tragic courage as Trevor chooses truth over the elaborate protective delusions his mind has created.

ACT 3

11. Welcome to the End (Plot Point 2)

Arriving at Highway 152 at night, Trevor experiences a complete breakthrough when approaching headlights illuminate the road—the same conditions as a year ago. The truth finally erupts into his consciousness: one year earlier, Trevor hit and killed a young boy who was standing by the roadside with his mother after their car broke down. Instead of stopping to help, Trevor panicked and fled the scene.

This revelation propels the story into its final phase of recognition and reckoning. The truth that Trevor's mind has been protecting him from is finally fully exposed, explaining everything: his insomnia, his extreme weight loss, the hallucinations of Ivan (a manifestation of his guilt and his pre-accident self), and the imagined relationships with Marie (the mother) and Nicholas (the boy he killed).

12. Denouement/Theme Triumphant

Trevor turns himself in to the police, confessing his crime. The final scene shows Trevor in what appears to be a prison cell. He lies down on the bed and, for the first time in a year, falls into a peaceful sleep as the screen fades to white.

The theme triumphs as Trevor's acceptance of responsibility finally allows him the peace that had eluded him. His body and mind had been punishing him relentlessly for a year—his guilt manifested as insomnia, extreme weight loss, and elaborate hallucinations. Only by confronting and accepting his responsibility for the hit-and-run does Trevor find release from this self-imposed torment.

The film concludes with the visual metaphor of sleep finally coming to Trevor, suggesting that only through acceptance of our darkest truths can we find peace. The white fade emphasizes the theme of redemption through confession—not a happy ending, but a truthful one that offers release from denial's prison.

Eastern Promises

Basic Narrative Beat Sheet

THEME

The central theme of "Eastern Promises" revolves around identity and moral compromise—specifically, how people adopt false identities or corrupt their true selves to survive in brutal environments, and the possibility of redemption through decisive moral action. The film explores how environment shapes identity, the price of living a lie, and whether one can maintain one's humanity while immersed in a world of violence. This is captured in Nikolai's statement: "I am dead already. Now I live in the zone all the time."

ACT 1

1. Set Up

Anna Khitrova (Naomi Watts) is a midwife at a London hospital who delivers the baby of a 14-year-old Russian girl who dies in childbirth. Her status quo world is one of compassion, ethics, and structure—working in a hospital to bring life into the world, living with her Russian mother and opinionated uncle, and grieving the recent loss of her own baby. Anna finds a diary written in Russian among the dead girl's possessions and becomes determined to find the baby's family.

We see Anna's compassionate nature immediately—she refuses to let the anonymous girl and her baby become just another statistic. Her Russian heritage connects her to the mystery while her professional ethics drive her to find the baby's relatives. Her mother Helen represents a link to Russian culture, while her uncle Stepan represents suspicion of the Russian criminal underworld.

The theme is introduced subtly through the contrast between Anna's ordered, ethical world and the criminal underworld she's about to encounter. The diary—written in a language she understands culturally but cannot read—symbolizes the hidden truths and dual identities that will define the story. The dead girl's butterfly tattoo hints at forced transformation, another key thematic element.

2. Inciting Incident

Anna discovers a business card for the Trans-Siberian Restaurant in the diary and visits the establishment seeking help in translating the diary and finding the baby's family. There she meets Semyon (Armin Mueller-Stahl), the seemingly avuncular owner who offers to translate the diary for her. This encounter, which appears helpful on the surface, is actually Anna's first step into a dangerous world, as Semyon is the head of the vory v zakone (Russian mafia) in London. This external event disrupts Anna's safe, ethical world and sets the main plot in motion.

Unknown to Anna, her pursuit of the baby's family has put her in contact with the very criminal organization responsible for the girl's tragic circumstances. This ironic collision of worlds introduces the film's exploration of hidden identities and moral compromise.

3. Internal Wrestling/Preparation

Anna begins to realize the danger she's courting when her uncle Stepan translates part of the diary, revealing that the girl, Tatiana, was forced into sex slavery by Russian gangsters. Stepan warns Anna to stay away from the restaurant and the Russians, but her concern for the baby's welfare drives her forward despite growing unease.

Meanwhile, we are introduced to Nikolai Luzhin (Viggo Mortensen), the driver and "undertaker" for the Vory crime family, who works closely with Semyon's volatile son Kirill (Vincent Cassel). Nikolai projects cool professionalism as he disposes of a body, displaying efficiency without emotion—a man who appears to have fully embraced the criminal identity required to survive in this world.

The theme manifests here through the contrast between Anna's transparent motivation and growing fear, and Nikolai's opaque, controlled exterior that gives no hint of his true nature or feelings. Both are preparing to navigate a dangerous intersection of worlds—Anna reluctantly, Nikolai with practiced precision.

ACT 2

4. Welcome to the Jungle (Plot Point 1)

Anna returns to the restaurant with the diary despite warnings. She meets Nikolai, who watches her with inscrutable interest. Semyon's seemingly helpful demeanor shifts subtly to menace as he questions Anna about who else has seen the diary and suggests she leave it with him. When Anna refuses, Semyon applies pressure, mentioning her address—revealing he knows where she lives and implicitly threatening her.

This moment marks Anna's entry into the criminal world where nothing is as it seems. The restaurant transforms from a quaint ethnic establishment to a criminal front, just as Semyon shifts from charming host to threatening mafia boss. The contrast between Anna's transparent world of hospital protocols and family dinners and the opaque world of criminal codes and hidden threats creates tension that will drive the second act.

Thematically, this represents the collision of Anna's authentic identity with a world built on deception, setting up the central conflict between truth and survival that defines the story.

5. Subplot

Several crucial subplots develop to enrich the main narrative:

Nikolai's relationship with Kirill forms a significant subplot, revealing layers of complexity in both men. Kirill is desperate for his father's approval and driven by insecurity, while Nikolai carefully manages Kirill's volatile emotions. Their relationship is both professional and personal, with homoerotic undertones that Kirill both displays and violently denies.

Another subplot involves Nikolai's ambition to advance within the Vory, seeking to become a "made" member through proving his loyalty and capability. This process requires him to receive the distinctive criminal tattoos that tell his "story" and mark his status within the organization.

Additionally, Anna's family dynamics create a subplot that contrasts with the criminal "family" of the Vory. Her mother Helen tries to protect her while understanding her determination, while her uncle Stepan provides historical context about Russian criminals and disapproves of Anna's involvement.

These subplots reflect the central theme by presenting different aspects of identity—Kirill's insecure performance of masculinity, Nikolai's calculated criminal persona, and Anna's struggle between professional ethics and personal safety.

6. Trials and Tribulations

As Anna and Nikolai navigate their respective worlds, they face mounting challenges:

- Anna discovers that Semyon is likely Tatiana's rapist and the father of the baby
- Nikolai must manage Kirill's volatility after Kirill orders the murder of a Chechen rival
- Anna's family faces escalating danger as Semyon learns they have the diary
- Nikolai undergoes a painful tattoo ceremony to advance in the Vory hierarchy
- Anna learns more horrors from the diary about sex trafficking
- Nikolai is forced to participate in increasingly disturbing activities to maintain his cover

Throughout these trials, Anna's determination to protect the baby brings her deeper into the criminal world, while Nikolai maintains his enigmatic persona, giving few hints of his true thoughts or feelings. Their paths intersect periodically, with Anna sensing something different about Nikolai but unable to fully trust him.

The theme develops through the escalating moral compromises Nikolai makes to maintain his identity within the Vory, while Anna's ethical certainties are increasingly challenged by the complex, dangerous reality she's uncovered.

7. Midpoint

The pivotal shift occurs when Nikolai is alone with Anna and reveals a glimpse of his true nature. He warns her about the danger she's in and advises her to give the diary to Semyon to protect herself and her family. This moment of apparent honesty creates ambiguity—is Nikolai genuinely concerned for Anna, or merely doing Semyon's bidding?

This midpoint transforms the dynamics between the characters. Anna's suspicion of Nikolai becomes tinged with the possibility that he might not be fully corrupted. For Nikolai, this interaction with Anna represents a rare moment when his carefully maintained criminal persona might be slipping, revealing something more beneath.

Simultaneously, Semyon confirms through DNA testing that he is indeed the father of the baby, raising the stakes dramatically as he now has a biological motivation to eliminate evidence of his crime of raping a minor.

This midpoint creates another layer of tension as we begin to question Nikolai's true allegiance and whether his identity as a loyal Vory member is as solid as it appears.

8. Complications

The stakes escalate dramatically as:

- Semyon orders Kirill and Nikolai to get rid of the baby
- Anna is attacked by thugs looking for the diary
- Nikolai is approached for a “stars” tattoo ceremony, marking his promotion to captain
- The diary is stolen from Anna's family home

- Anna discovers that Tatiana was forced to work as a prostitute by Semyon's organization
- Semyon pressures Nikolai to kill a rival and dispose of the body

The pressure builds on both Anna and Nikolai as Semyon moves to eliminate all evidence of his crimes. Anna's family is now directly endangered, while Nikolai must carefully navigate between maintaining his cover and preventing further harm.

The theme intensifies as Nikolai is forced deeper into his criminal identity through the tattoo ceremony, literally inscribing the false self onto his body permanently. Meanwhile, Anna confronts the reality that her ethical quest has put those she loves in danger, challenging her self-image as a protector.

9. Crisis

The "crisis" moment occurs in two parts. First, Anna confronts Semyon about raping Tatiana and threatening her family. Semyon responds with calculated menace, effectively telling Anna she is powerless against him and implying her family will suffer if she continues her quest.

Second, Nikolai is ambushed in a bathhouse by Chechen assassins seeking revenge for the murder Kirill ordered. Nearly naked, with only his tattoos as "armor," Nikolai fights for his life in a brutal, extended combat sequence that strips away all pretense and protection.

This crisis represents the complete collapse of safety for both protagonists—Anna faces the terrifying power of the criminal organization she's challenged, while Nikolai's carefully maintained cover is at risk as he fights for survival. The bathhouse setting, with Nikolai vulnerable and exposed, symbolically represents the stripping away of false identities when survival is at stake.

10. Critical Choice

In this dark night of the soul, Nikolai survives the assassination attempt but is severely wounded. Hospitalized, he is visited by a British intelligence handler, revealing the film's major twist—Nikolai is actually an undercover FSB agent (Russian intelligence) who has infiltrated the Vory to gather evidence against Semyon and other criminals.

Despite his injuries, Nikolai makes the critical choice to maintain his undercover operation rather than retreat to safety. He chooses to leverage his new status as a Vory captain to finally bring down Semyon and protect Anna and the baby, even though continuing his mission means remaining in constant danger.

For Anna, the critical choice comes when she decides to directly confront Semyon again, meeting him with the baby at the Trans-Siberian Restaurant in a desperate attempt to resolve the situation. She chooses to face the danger directly rather than flee, demonstrating moral courage that parallels Nikolai's decision.

The theme crystallizes in these moments of choice—both Anna and Nikolai choose authentic moral action over self-preservation, revealing their true identities through decisive ethical choices despite the personal cost.

ACT 3

11. Welcome to the End (Plot Point 2)

Nikolai intervenes in Semyon's plan by substituting himself for Kirill in the mission to dispose of the baby. He colludes with Anna, helping her escape with the infant. He then manipulates evidence to implicate Semyon in Tatiana's rape through the DNA samples, ensuring Semyon will be arrested and his criminal organization disrupted.

This moment transitions the story into its final phase as the true allegiances and identities are revealed. The setting shifts from the dangerous criminal world to places of resolution—the hospital where Anna works, representing healing, and the riverside where Semyon is arrested, representing justice.

Nikolai's crossing into Act 3 represents the alignment of his actions with his true moral identity, after long submersion in a false criminal persona. He can finally take direct action to protect the innocent and bring down the guilty, though still maintaining his cover for the future.

12. Denouement/Theme Triumphant

In the aftermath, Semyon is arrested for statutory rape based on the DNA evidence connecting him to Tatiana's baby. Kirill, devastated by his father's downfall, attempts suicide but is saved by Nikolai. Nikolai assumes leadership of the Vory family, now positioned to continue his undercover work at an even higher level.

Anna adopts Tatiana's baby, Christine, providing her with the family and protection that Tatiana sought in coming to London. Before the final resolution, Nikolai meets with Anna one last time, maintaining his criminal persona but with a subtle acknowledgment of their shared secret. Anna recognizes that despite his appearance as a Vory captain, Nikolai acted to protect her and the baby when it mattered most.

The theme triumphs as the story reveals the complex truth about identity—that a person's true self is revealed not through appearances or affiliations but through decisive moral action. Nikolai, despite being covered in criminal tattoos and embedded in a violent organization, maintains his moral core and uses his false identity to serve justice. Anna, despite her naïveté about the criminal world, maintains her courage and compassion even when facing its darkest aspects.

The film ends with Nikolai fully established in his role as the new Vory leader, but with the audience now aware of his true identity and purpose. This ambiguous ending affirms the central message about the complexity of identity and moral compromise—Nikolai has "won" but remains trapped in his criminal persona indefinitely, having saved others at the cost of his own freedom to live authentically.

The final image of Nikolai sitting alone in the restaurant, surrounded by the trappings of his criminal success but isolated by his secret identity, reminds us of his earlier statement: “I am dead already. Now I live in the zone all the time.” His triumph is bittersweet—he has maintained his moral purpose but at the cost of living permanently as someone else, raising the question of whether one can maintain a false identity indefinitely without it becoming, in some sense, real.

The Bourne Identity

Basic Narrative Beat Sheet (Novel and Film)

THEME

The central theme of “The Bourne Identity” revolves around the search for self-knowledge and the question of whether identity is defined by past actions or present choices—specifically, whether a person can transcend their programming and create a new moral self when faced with the truth of who they were. The story explores how memory, though crucial to identity, is not its sole determinant, and how authentic connection to others can anchor one's humanity even when past certainties dissolve. This is captured in Bourne's pivotal realization: “I can feel it. This isn't me. This isn't who I am.”

ACT 1

1. Set Up

Jason Bourne (Matt Damon in the film, unnamed in the early chapters of the novel) is pulled from the Mediterranean Sea by fishermen, suffering from gunshot wounds and complete amnesia. His status quo world is one of confusion and vulnerability—he has exceptional skills but no understanding of who he is or why people are trying to kill him. The only clue to his identity is a laser-projected bank account number embedded in his hip.

We see Bourne's conflicted nature immediately—his body reacts with trained violence before his conscious mind can intervene, suggesting a dangerous past at odds with his present confusion and moral instincts. The fishing boat represents temporary sanctuary, while his injuries and amnesia represent his disconnection from his former self.

The theme is introduced through Bourne's first experience of identity conflict—his body knows how to fight and his mind automatically speaks multiple languages, yet he has no conscious access to who he is or how he acquired these abilities. This duality between training and conscious identity establishes the central thematic question of whether Bourne is defined by his forgotten past or his present choices.

In the novel by Robert Ludlum, this setup is more elaborate, with Bourne spending significant time recovering under the care of an alcoholic British doctor on the Mediterranean island of Port Noir before beginning his quest. The film streamlines this opening, bringing Bourne more quickly into action.

2. Inciting Incident

Bourne travels to Zurich, following the bank account lead, and discovers a safety deposit box containing money, passports with his photo but different names, and a gun. Most importantly, he finds the name "Jason Bourne" and an address in Paris. This external discovery disrupts his passive state of questioning and sets the main plot in motion, giving him a concrete path to follow toward his identity.

The safety deposit box contents represent the first tangible connection to his past, but also deepen the mystery—why would one man need multiple identities? The presence of the gun suggests a violent profession, creating immediate tension between Bourne's apparent skills and his current moral instincts.

In the film, this scene is more action-oriented, with Bourne almost immediately confronted by police officers whom he neutralizes with surprising combat skills. The novel spends more time on Bourne's internal process as he begins piecing together clues about his identity.

3. Internal Wrestling/Preparation

Bourne struggles to reconcile the evidence of his past with his present experience. He feels revulsion at the gun and discomfort with his violent capabilities, suggesting a disconnect between his former and current selves. When the US Embassy proves hostile rather than helpful, Bourne offers Marie Kreutz (Franka Potente in the film/Marie St. Jacques in the novel) money to drive him to Paris.

Bourne prepares by testing his abilities, discovering he knows advanced combat techniques, speaks multiple languages, and notices tactical details automatically. He also begins forming a tenuous connection with Marie, who initially fears him but gradually becomes intrigued by his situation.

The theme manifests here as Bourne begins actively searching for his identity while simultaneously demonstrating values and choices that may contradict his past. His decision to pay Marie rather than force her to help him represents an early moral choice that may diverge from his trained responses.

In the novel, Marie is a Canadian economist whom Bourne initially takes hostage during a confusing confrontation with assassins. Their relationship develops from Stockholm Syndrome into genuine connection. The film transforms this problematic dynamic into a more mutual arrangement where Marie accepts payment to drive Bourne to Paris.

ACT 2

4. Welcome to the Jungle (Plot Point 1)

Bourne and Marie arrive at the Paris address only to discover it's an apartment maintained for "Jason Bourne"—a cover identity rather than his true self. While there, Bourne is attacked by another assassin (Castel) whom he defeats but fails to interrogate when the man commits suicide rather than be captured. This confirms that powerful forces want Bourne dead and propels him into an active fight for survival.

This moment marks Bourne's entry into a world of professional killers and intelligence operations. The apartment transforms from a potential answer to his questions into another layer of mystery and danger. The contrast between Bourne's hope for resolution and the violent reality he encounters creates tension that drives the second act.

Thematically, this represents the collapse of Bourne's hope for a simple answer to his identity. The apartment reveals that "Jason Bourne" is itself a construct, deepening the question of who he really is beneath the layers of deception.

The film and novel handle this turning point similarly, though the novel provides more complex background on the Jason Bourne identity as part of "Treadstone," a top-secret government operation.

5. Subplot

Several crucial subplots develop to enrich the main narrative:

The "Treadstone" subplot reveals that CIA Deputy Director Ward Abbott (Brian Cox in the film/different characters with similar functions in the novel) and Operation Chief Alexander Conklin (Chris Cooper in the film) are working to eliminate Bourne to cover up a failed assassination operation. This subplot provides context for Bourne's skills and amnesia while creating an organizational antagonist.

Bourne's developing relationship with Marie forms a significant emotional subplot, showing his capacity for connection and protection despite his violent programming. Marie becomes not just a companion but a moral anchor who sees Bourne as a person distinct from his past actions.

Additionally, a subplot involves "The Professor" (Clive Owen in the film), another Treadstone assassin sent to eliminate Bourne, setting up a mirror character who represents what Bourne was and could still become.

In the novel, a major subplot concerns Carlos the Jackal, a real-life terrorist against whom the Jason Bourne identity was created as bait. This element is removed from the film adaptation, which focuses more on the internal corruption of American intelligence agencies.

These subplots reflect the central theme by presenting different aspects of identity—the organizational view of Bourne as an asset or liability, Marie's view of him as a person worthy of compassion, and the Professor's reflection of Bourne's professional identity.

6. Trials and Tribulations

As Bourne seeks answers while evading capture, he faces numerous challenges:

- He discovers his involvement in an assassination attempt on exiled African leader Nykwana Wombosi (the film's replacement for the novel's Carlos plot)
- He uses creative tactics to evade police surveillance in Paris
- He confronts the lingering effects of his training, including nightmares and flashbacks
- He and Marie constantly relocate to stay ahead of pursuers
- He gradually pieces together fragments of memory that suggest a troubling past
- Marie struggles with the danger that follows Bourne

Throughout these trials, Bourne demonstrates exceptional capabilities while questioning their origin and purpose. His relationship with Marie deepens, humanizing him and creating stakes beyond his own survival. Their developing bond contrasts with the cold, mechanical efficiency of the Treadstone operatives pursuing them.

The theme develops through Bourne's increasing awareness of his likely past as an assassin, juxtaposed with his present desire to protect Marie and discover the truth. This tension between what he was trained to be and what he chooses to be drives the narrative forward.

The film condenses and alters many of the novel's plot points while maintaining the essential emotional journey. The novel's complex Carlos conspiracy is replaced with a straightforward failed assassination mission, making the story more focused on Bourne's personal journey rather than international intrigue.

7. Midpoint

The pivotal shift occurs when Bourne, following a lead about Wombosi, remembers his failed assassination attempt. He recalls boarding Wombosi's yacht to kill him but finding himself unable to shoot when he saw Wombosi's children present. This moral hesitation led to Wombosi shooting Bourne, who fell into the sea with bullet wounds that caused his amnesia.

This revelation transforms Bourne's understanding of himself—he wasn't a victim of violence but its perpetrator, yet his failure to complete his mission stemmed from a moral choice that contradicted his training. This suggests his true self might have been asserting itself even before his amnesia, creating a thread of moral continuity between his past and present.

For Marie, this midpoint creates a crisis as she must decide whether to continue helping a man she now knows was an assassin. Her choice to stay with Bourne despite this revelation deepens their relationship and reinforces the theme that present choices can matter more than past actions.

This midpoint sequence in the film is a significant departure from the novel, where Bourne's amnesia stems from a different traumatic event. The film creates a more direct moral knot by tying Bourne's amnesia specifically to a moment of conscience overriding his programming.

8. Complications

The stakes escalate dramatically as:

- Wombosi is assassinated by the Professor, removing a potential source of answers

- Conklin intensifies the manhunt for Bourne
- Marie becomes a target alongside Bourne
- Bourne sends Marie away to protect her, facing his pursuers alone
- The emotional distance between Bourne's current self and his past actions widens as he learns more about Treadstone
- Bourne sets a trap to confront Conklin directly

The pressure builds on both the external level (the manhunt) and the internal level (Bourne's moral reckoning with his past). Bourne must not only survive the pursuers but reconcile the trained killer he was with the person he wants to be.

The theme intensifies as Bourne begins to define himself by his present choices rather than his past programming. His decision to protect Marie by separating from her demonstrates his prioritization of her safety over his own need for emotional support—a choice the old Bourne might not have made.

The film and novel handle these complications differently in their details, but both maintain the core tension between Bourne's former identity as a government assassin and his emerging identity as someone seeking truth and moral clarity.

9. Crisis

The "crisis" moment occurs when Bourne confronts Conklin, who reveals that Treadstone created Jason Bourne as a highly trained assassin. Conklin tells Bourne that being an assassin is not something he was recruited for—it's who he is at his core. He attempts to reactivate Bourne's programming by speaking coded phrases, trying to short-circuit Bourne's emerging identity and return him to his role as an obedient operative.

This crisis represents the complete collapse of Bourne's hope for a moral past. He must face the possibility that his entire identity was constructed for killing, that his skills exist solely for elimination and not protection, and that any moral qualms he feels are merely a side effect of his amnesia rather than his true nature.

In the film, this confrontation takes place in Bourne's former Paris safe house, bringing the story full circle to the place where he first sought answers. The novel structures this crisis differently but maintains the essential question of whether Bourne can transcend his programming.

10. Critical Choice

In this dark night of the soul, Bourne rejects Conklin's attempt to reactivate him, delivering the film's thematic statement: “I don't want to do this anymore.” Despite remembering his training and being physically capable of returning to his former life, Bourne chooses to walk away from Treadstone and the identity they created for him.

Bourne makes the critical choice to define himself by his present moral compass rather than his past actions or programming. He refuses to kill Conklin despite his anger, demonstrating that his emergent identity has truly broken from his conditioning.

The theme crystallizes in this moment of choice—Bourne asserts that identity is not fixed by past actions or training but can evolve through conscious moral choices in the present. His decision represents the triumph of his human autonomy over his programming as a “weapon.”

The novel handles this pivotal moment differently, with Bourne's ultimate goal being to clear his name rather than simply escape his past. However, both versions emphasize Bourne's choice to forge an identity based on his present values rather than his constructed past.

ACT 3

11. Welcome to the End (Plot Point 2)

After Bourne spares Conklin and leaves, Abbott arranges for Conklin's assassination to tie up loose ends, demonstrating the ruthless calculus of the organization Bourne has rejected. Bourne, meanwhile, evades the last Treadstone assassin (the Professor) and, in the film's most emotionally resonant scene, holds the dying man who tells him, "Look at what they make you give." This moment transitions the story into its final phase.

The setting shifts from urban Paris to the rural countryside, symbolizing Bourne's movement away from his constructed identity toward something more authentic. The narrative shifts from Bourne being hunted to Bourne actively seeking closure and a new beginning.

Bourne's crossing into Act 3 represents his commitment to creating a new identity separate from Treadstone, one based on his connection with Marie and his emerging moral framework rather than his programmed skills.

The novel's third act is significantly different, involving complex machinations to draw out Carlos the Jackal. The film simplifies this conclusion to focus more directly on Bourne's personal journey toward a new identity.

12. Denouement/Theme Triumphant

The film ends with Bourne reuniting with Marie in Greece, where she has established a new life running a scooter rental shop. Despite not recovering all his memories, Bourne has found peace in choosing who he wants to be rather than obsessing over who he was. When Marie asks if he's disappointed that he hasn't remembered everything, Bourne responds that how they move forward together matters more than his past.

In a scene that closes the CIA narrative thread, Abbott testifies before Congress that Treadstone has been shut down, covering up the organization's illegal activities while Bourne remains officially "missing." This epilogue suggests that while individual morality can evolve, institutional corruption often remains entrenched.

The theme triumphs as the story reveals the complete arc of Bourne's transformation from a programmed assassin to a man who defines himself through present choices and human connection. Though his memories remain incomplete, Bourne has achieved something more important—the freedom to choose who he becomes rather than being defined by who he was designed to be.

The film's ending differs significantly from the novel, which concludes with a complex confrontation with Carlos and Bourne's eventual return to government service. The film's simpler, more emotionally resonant conclusion emphasizes personal redemption and escape from the cycle of violence rather than continued engagement with the espionage world.

The final image of Bourne and Marie together represents the triumph of authentic human connection over programmed isolation. Bourne has not only survived physically but has managed to preserve and develop his humanity despite the dehumanizing training he underwent. His journey affirms the central message that identity is not fixed by past actions or external definitions but can be reclaimed through conscious moral choice and genuine connection with others.

Key Differences Between Novel and Film Adaptation

Robert Ludlum's 1980 novel and Doug Liman's 2002 film differ substantially in several key areas:

Novel

- Set during the Cold War era of the late 1970s/early 1980s
- Features Carlos the Jackal as the primary antagonist, with Bourne created as bait to draw him out
- Marie St. Jacques is a Canadian economist initially taken hostage by

Bourne

- More complex plot involving multiple international conspiracies
- Bourne's amnesia stems from a trauma different than the failed assassination
- Ends with Bourne returning to government service to continue the fight against Carlos
- More focused on international espionage and terrorism
- Longer timeframe with more detailed development of Bourne's skills and memories

Film

- Updated to a post-Cold War, early 2000s setting
- Focuses on internal CIA corruption rather than an external terrorist threat
- Marie Kreutz is a German drifter who helps Bourne voluntarily
- Streamlined narrative focusing on Bourne's personal journey
- Bourne's amnesia directly results from his moral choice not to kill Wombosi
- Ends with Bourne rejecting government service to build a new life with Marie
- More focused on personal identity and moral choice
- Compressed timeframe with faster-paced action sequences
- Features more intimate, realistic combat scenes that would influence action filmmaking

Despite these significant differences, both the novel and film maintain the central thematic exploration of identity and self-determination. The story resonates because it examines the universal question of whether we are defined by our past actions or our present choices, and whether redemption is possible for someone trained to do harm.

The film's success spawned a franchise that would further explore Bourne's journey to uncover his past, while maintaining the core theme that identity is ultimately determined not by memory or programming but by the moral choices we make in the present moment.

Red Dragon

Basic Narrative Beat Sheet (Novel and Film Adaptations)

THEME

The central theme of "Red Dragon" revolves around the duality of human nature—specifically, how the line between monster and man is often blurred, and how confronting one's own darkness is necessary to understand and defeat external evil. The story explores how trauma and empathy can lead down divergent paths: toward destructive transformation or compassionate insight. This is captured in Will Graham's realization that to catch the Tooth Fairy, he must not only think like him but acknowledge the darkness within himself: "Fear is the price of imagination."

ACT 1

1. Set Up

Will Graham (William Petersen/Edward Norton) is a retired FBI profiler living in Marathon, Florida with his wife Molly and stepson Kevin. His status quo world is one of retreat and recovery—having left the Bureau after being nearly killed while capturing Dr. Hannibal Lecter (Brian Cox/Anthony Hopkins), a cannibalistic serial killer whose mind is disturbingly similar to Graham's own. Will bears both physical scars (a knife wound across his abdomen) and psychological scars from his previous cases.

We see Will's conflicted nature immediately—he possesses an extraordinary ability to empathize with killers, to "think like them," but this gift comes at great personal cost. His beachfront home represents safety and distance from the darkness he previously immersed himself in, while his family represents the normal life he's trying to maintain.

The theme is introduced through Will's troubled past and his intuitive methods—his ability to solve cases stems from recognizing the humanness of monsters and the potential for monstrosity in humans, including himself. This uncomfortable blurring of boundaries between hunter and hunted establishes the central thematic tension of the story.

2. Inciting Incident

Jack Crawford (Dennis Farina/Harvey Keitel), head of the FBI's Behavioral Science Unit, visits Will's home in Florida to ask for his help on the "Tooth Fairy" case—a killer who has murdered two families during full moons. Crawford shows Will crime scene photos, appealing to his sense of duty and unique abilities. Despite initial resistance, Will agrees to examine just the crime scenes, already sensing his inevitable deeper involvement. This external request disrupts Will's carefully constructed refuge and sets the main plot in motion.

In the film adaptations, the horrific nature of the crimes is emphasized visually, highlighting both the urgency of stopping the killer before the next full moon and the psychological burden Will is taking on by returning to this work.

3. Internal Wrestling/Preparation

Will struggles with his decision to rejoin the investigation, knowing the toll it will take on his mental health and his family. He visits the crime scenes in Birmingham and Atlanta, immediately falling back into his unique method of empathic reconstruction—walking through the houses, touching objects, speaking aloud as if he were the killer to understand his motivations and methods.

Will's wife Molly expresses concern but ultimately supports his decision, understanding both his need to help and his guilt over potential future victims. Will prepares mentally by immersing himself in the case files and evidence, but knows he needs more insight to catch this killer before the next full moon brings another family's slaughter.

The theme manifests here as Will begins to open himself to the darkness he had sealed away, recognizing that his ability to catch monsters stems from his uncomfortable similarity to them. His process of walking through crime scenes and speaking as the killer physically demonstrates the thematic idea of inhabiting the space between hunter and hunted.

ACT 2

4. Welcome to the Jungle (Plot Point 1)

Recognizing he needs more insight, Will makes the difficult decision to visit Hannibal Lecter in prison. This confrontation with his former adversary—the man who nearly killed him and who recognized the darkness within Will—marks his full commitment to the case and his willingness to risk his psychological well-being.

Lecter taunts Will with personal insights and offers cryptic assistance regarding the Tooth Fairy case. Their interaction reawakens Will's fears about his own nature—Lecter suggests they are alike, telling Will, “You caught me because we're just alike,” emphasizing the thematic question of what separates the monster-catcher from the monster.

This moment propels Will into the Act 2 world of active investigation, where he must balance maintaining his sanity with opening his mind to understand the killer. The contrast between Will's beachfront refuge and the institutional settings of the FBI, with their crime photos and evidence boards, creates visual tension that mirrors his internal struggle.

5. Subplot

The narrative introduces Francis Dolarhyde (Tom Noonan/Ralph Fiennes), the man behind the "Tooth Fairy" murders, revealing his tortured psychology, physical insecurity about his cleft palate, and obsession with William Blake's painting "The Great Red Dragon and the Woman Clothed in Sun." This substantial subplot humanizes the antagonist by showing his own trauma and transformation.

Another crucial subplot develops when Dolarhyde begins a relationship with a blind woman named Reba McClane (Joan Allen/Emily Watson). This relationship presents Dolarhyde with the possibility of human connection and redemption, creating tension between his monstrous "becoming" and his human desire for acceptance and love.

Additionally, ambitious tabloid reporter Freddy Lounds (Stephen Lang/Philip Seymour Hoffman) pursues the story, creating complications for the investigation and ultimately becoming a target for Dolarhyde.

These subplots reflect the central theme by presenting different aspects of duality and transformation—Dolarhyde's struggle between monster and man, Reba's ability to "see" humanity where others see only monstrosity, and Lounds' exploitation of tragedy for personal gain.

6. Trials and Tribulations

Will delves deeper into the investigation, facing numerous challenges:

- He battles insomnia and nightmares as he immerses himself in the killer's psychology
- He consults with forensic experts and discovers bite mark evidence that provides insights
- He develops a theory about the killer watching home movies to select victims
- He deals with pressure from Crawford and the FBI as the next full moon approaches
- He coordinates with local police who are skeptical of his psychological

profiling methods

- He worries about his family's safety as he becomes more visible in the investigation

Meanwhile, Dolarhyde's story advances through parallel trials:

- He struggles with his growing feelings for Reba, which conflict with his transformation into the "Red Dragon"
- He becomes agitated after seeing Will's profile of him in Lounds' tabloid, which calls him impotent and insane
- He kidnaps Lounds, forces him to recant the profile on tape, and kills him in a fiery spectacle
- He experiences moments of tenderness with Reba that temporarily suppress his murderous urges
- He visits the original Blake painting, literally consuming it in an attempt to internalize its power

Throughout these trials, Will becomes increasingly immersed in the case, risking his psychological stability as he tries to understand the killer's motivations and predict his next move. His methods continue to blur the line between empathy and disturbing similarity.

The theme develops through Will's increasing isolation and his growing awareness that to catch this killer, he must acknowledge rather than deny the darkness within himself. Similarly, Dolarhyde's relationship with Reba reveals that the monster is also a man capable of tenderness and connection.

7. Midpoint

The pivotal shift occurs when Will has a breakthrough in understanding the killer's selection process. He realizes the Tooth Fairy is choosing families through their home movies processed at the film lab where Dolarhyde works. Simultaneously, Will recognizes that Lecter has been corresponding with the killer through coded personal ads in the tabloid.

This revelation dramatically changes the investigation, giving the FBI their first concrete lead while also revealing Lecter's continued dangerous influence despite his imprisonment. It transforms the investigation from reactive to proactive, as they now have a potential way to identify and stop the killer before he strikes again.

For Dolarhyde, the midpoint comes when he experiences a night of genuine connection with Reba, making love with her and experiencing momentary freedom from his murderous compulsions. This creates a war within Dolarhyde between his desire to "become" the Red Dragon and his human longing for connection with Reba.

This midpoint creates another point of no return as both protagonist and antagonist confront the duality at the core of their natures—Will's uncomfortable recognition of how well he understands the killer, and Dolarhyde's conflict between monster and man.

8. Complications

The stakes escalate dramatically as:

- Will's family is moved to a safehouse after Lecter learns their address and shares it with Dolarhyde
- The FBI sets a trap using the film lab lead, but Dolarhyde evades capture
- Dolarhyde mistakenly believes Reba is betraying him when he sees her with a coworker
- The Dragon persona becomes more dominant as Dolarhyde feels betrayed by Reba
- Will comes to believe that Dolarhyde will kill Reba as his final transformation

- The full moon approaches, signaling imminent danger for another family

Will becomes increasingly isolated as he goes deeper into the killer's psychology, straining his relationship with his family and colleagues. His growing obsession with the case mirrors Dolarhyde's obsession with becoming the Dragon, creating a thematic parallel between hunter and hunted.

The theme intensifies as both Will and Dolarhyde struggle with their dual natures—Will using his darkness as a tool while trying not to be consumed by it, Dolarhyde increasingly losing his battle against the Dragon persona.

9. Crisis

The "crisis" moment occurs when Dolarhyde, believing Reba has betrayed him, brings her to his house and appears ready to kill her as part of his transformation. He sets his house on fire with Reba inside, leading her to believe he has committed suicide with a shotgun blast (though he has actually shot someone else's body to fake his death).

Meanwhile, Will reaches a psychological breaking point, having immersed himself so deeply in the killer's mindset that he risks losing himself. When he believes Dolarhyde is dead, Will experiences both relief and a disturbing sense of incompletion—his prey has escaped him by escaping justice.

This crisis represents the apparent failure of both Will's investigation (the killer has escaped formal justice) and Dolarhyde's humanity (he has chosen the Dragon over his connection with Reba, though he spared her life). Both men appear to have lost their respective battles with duality.

10. Critical Choice

In this dark night of the soul, Will returns to his hotel room and receives a call from his wife Molly. Their conversation leads Will to a crucial realization—the body in Dolarhyde's house was not his own. Empathizing once more with the killer, Will understands that Dolarhyde faked his death to be free to come after Will and his family, whom he sees as his ultimate adversaries.

Will makes the critical choice to face Dolarhyde directly rather than remaining in the investigative role. He recognizes that this confrontation is not just about catching a killer but about facing the darkness that connects them. Will chooses to use his understanding of Dolarhyde not just to predict him but to draw him out and end the threat permanently.

For Dolarhyde, the critical choice came in sparing Reba—a decision that preserved some small part of his humanity even as he surrendered to the Dragon. This choice reveals the thematic truth that even in the most monstrous, some humanity remains, just as in the most empathic (like Will), some capacity for darkness exists.

ACT 3

11. Welcome to the End (Plot Point 2)

Will returns to his family home in Florida, knowing Dolarhyde will follow. He prepares for a final confrontation, setting a trap with the cooperation of local law enforcement. This moment transitions the story into its final phase as Will moves from hunter to hunted and back again.

The setting returns to Will's home—the place of safety that opened the story—now transformed into a battleground, symbolizing that there is no true escape from the darkness Will tried to leave behind. The narrative shifts from investigation to confrontation, from understanding evil to facing it directly.

Will's crossing into Act 3 represents his complete acceptance of his dual nature—he embraces his ability to think like the killer while maintaining his moral compass, using his darkness as a weapon against greater darkness.

12. Denouement/Theme Triumphant

In the final confrontation, Dolarhyde attacks Will at his home (in the novel and 2002 film) or at Lecter's lake house (in the 1986 film). A violent struggle ensues, with Will severely wounded. In the novel and 2002 film, Molly saves Will by shooting Dolarhyde multiple times, while in the 1986 film, Will defeats Dolarhyde himself.

The aftermath shows Will recovering from his physical wounds while beginning to heal psychologically as well. He returns to his family, damaged but alive, having confronted both the external monster and his own internal darkness.

For Dolarhyde, death represents a tragic end to a life shaped by childhood trauma and mental illness. His humanity, briefly glimpsed in his relationship with Reba, was ultimately consumed by the Dragon he believed he was becoming.

The theme triumphs as the story reveals the complex truth about human nature—that understanding monsters requires acknowledging our own capacity for darkness, and that the line between monster and man is thinner than we wish to believe. Will's journey demonstrates that confronting rather than denying one's shadow self is necessary to defeat external evil.

The story ends with Will scarred but intact, his family restored, and the immediate threat eliminated. Yet the larger thematic question remains unresolved: how much can we understand evil without becoming what we hunt? Will's uneasy peace suggests that this balance requires constant vigilance, as the potential for darkness exists in all of us.

In both the novel and films, the ending affirms the central message about the duality of human nature and the price of empathy. Will's ability to "think like them" makes him an effective hunter of killers but comes at great personal cost. His journey embodies the core thematic idea that to understand and defeat monsters, we must first acknowledge the monster within ourselves.

Key Differences Between Novel and Film Adaptations

The novel by Thomas Harris provides more detailed exploration of Dolarhyde's traumatic childhood and psychological development, creating a more nuanced portrayal of the antagonist.

"Manhunter" (1986)

- Directed by Michael Mann with a stylized 1980s aesthetic
- Will Graham portrayed by William Petersen
- Retitled from "Red Dragon" to avoid confusion with a Hong Kong film
- More focused on Will's psychological journey than Dolarhyde's background
- Changed Dolarhyde's death scene to a confrontation at Lecter's lake house
- Less emphasis on the Lecter character (played by Brian Cox)

"Red Dragon" (2002)

- Directed by Brett Ratner as a companion piece to "The Silence of the Lambs" and "Hannibal"
- Will Graham portrayed by Edward Norton
- More faithful to the novel's plot and themes
- Features Anthony Hopkins reprising his iconic role as Hannibal Lecter
- Added a prologue showing Lecter's capture by Graham
- Greater balance between Will's story and Dolarhyde's development
- Ending closer to the novel with Molly shooting Dolarhyde

Despite these differences, all versions maintain the central thematic exploration of duality, empathy, and the thin line between man and monster that makes "Red Dragon" a compelling psychological thriller.

8MM

Extended Narrative Beat Sheet

THEME

The central theme of "8MM" revolves around the corrupting influence of confronting evil and the cost of venturing into darkness. The film explores how witnessing depravity irrevocably changes a person, even when their intentions are noble. This theme is embodied in Tom Welles' transformation from detached professional to vengeful executioner, demonstrating that once you stare into the abyss, it stares back, and no one emerges unchanged.

ACT 1

Prologue

In the bustling Miami International Airport, private investigator Tom Welles moves with the practiced ease of someone accustomed to remaining invisible. His target—a middle-aged businessman suspected of infidelity—moves through the terminal unaware of Welles' constant surveillance. The investigator's methods are precise and professional; his camera carefully documents each compromising moment without judgment or emotional investment.

The chase leads through Miami's affluent neighborhoods to a run-down motel, where Welles captures irrefutable evidence of the man's extramarital affair. Later, in a wealthy client's home, he delivers the photographs with clinical detachment. The client's bitter response—"I never liked him anyway"—barely registers. For Welles, this is simply another case closed, another check to be collected.

This opening sequence establishes not just Welles' professional methodology, but the careful compartmentalization of his life. In his modest Harrisburg home, he maintains a separate existence with his wife Amy and their newborn daughter. The contrast between his work investigating human depravity and his attempts to build a normal family life creates a tension that will eventually become unsustainable.

1. Set Up

In Miami International Airport, private investigator Tom Welles moves with practiced invisibility, surveilling a middle-aged businessman suspected of infidelity. His methodology is precise and professional—he documents each compromising moment without judgment or emotional investment. The chase leads to a run-down motel where Welles captures irrefutable evidence of the man's affair.

Later, in a wealthy client's home, he delivers the photographs with clinical detachment. The client's bitter response—"I never liked him anyway"—barely registers with Welles. This is simply another case closed, another check to be collected.

This opening sequence establishes Welles' professional methodology and the careful compartmentalization of his life. In his modest Harrisburg home, he maintains a separate existence with his wife Amy and their newborn daughter. The contrast between his work investigating human depravity and his attempts to build a normal family life creates a tension that will eventually become unsustainable.

The theme is subtly introduced through this compartmentalization—Welles believes he can witness depravity without being affected by it, maintaining a clear boundary between his professional and personal lives. This illusion of detachment will be systematically destroyed throughout the story.

2. Inciting Incident

Everything changes for Welles when he receives a call from Daniel Longdale, the personal attorney to Mrs. Christian, widow of a wealthy and powerful industrialist. The carefully chosen words hint at something unusual, beyond the routine cases of infidelity and insurance fraud that typically occupy Welles' time.

Arriving at the Christian estate, Welles is struck by its oppressive grandeur. Mrs. Christian, elderly and dignified, receives him in a study filled with artifacts of her late husband's success. She explains that while executing her husband's estate, she discovered something disturbing in his private safe—something that has shaken her understanding of the man she thought she knew.

From a small metal canister, she produces an 8mm film reel. Her hands tremble slightly as she handles it, suggesting the object itself carries a contaminating power. When Welles views the footage, he witnesses what appears to be the actual murder of a teenage girl by a man in a leather mask. Mrs. Christian's request—"I want you to find out if this is real... if he killed that girl"—launches Welles' investigation into whether her late husband paid to have an innocent girl murdered for his entertainment.

This external event disrupts Welles' carefully ordered existence and presents a case far darker than his usual work. Unlike routine surveillance, this investigation will force him to confront pure evil directly rather than merely documenting others' moral failures from a safe distance.

3. Internal Wrestling/Preparation

Despite his initial instinct to refuse the case, Welles finds himself drawn in by Mrs. Christian's desperate need to know the truth. The possibility that the girl might still be alive, that the film might be an elaborate fake, provides Welles with the moral justification to accept the case.

His investigation begins methodically. In his home office, wearing latex gloves that symbolize his attempt to maintain professional distance, Welles analyzes the film frame by frame. He notes every detail: the girl's appearance, the room's layout, the masked man's movements. His search through missing persons records leads him to Mary Ann Mathews, a 16-year-old who vanished from Cleveland three years earlier.

The visit to Cleveland introduces Welles to Janet Mathews, Mary Ann's mother, who lives in a modest home filled with memories of her daughter. Mrs. Mathews shares Mary Ann's story—a bright, ambitious teenager who dreamed of becoming an actress in Hollywood. Among her belongings, Welles finds head shots, acting class receipts, and diary entries full of hope and determination.

The reality of Mary Ann as a person, not just a victim in a grainy film, begins to affect Welles on a deeper level. His promise to Mrs. Mathews to discover the truth marks the beginning of his personal investment in the case. This emotional connection represents a departure from his usual professional detachment, setting the stage for his deeper transformation.

ACT 2

4. Welcome to the Jungle (Plot Point 1)

Welles' investigation takes him to Los Angeles, where the garish brightness of Hollywood Boulevard masks a thriving underground of exploitation and depravity. This geographical transition represents his entry into a moral wilderness far removed from his controlled professional life and sheltered family existence.

His search for information about Mary Ann leads him through a series of increasingly disturbing encounters with figures from the adult film industry. He discovers that Mary Ann, like countless other hopefuls, was quickly drawn into the porn industry, where she worked briefly under the name "Raquel" before disappearing completely.

This confirmation that Mary Ann was a real person who fell into the exploitation machine marks the point of no return for Welles. The investigation is no longer abstract—he's following the trail of a specific young woman whose dreams were corrupted and whose life was likely ended for someone's entertainment. The reality of this underground world, where vulnerable people are routinely exploited and discarded, represents the "jungle" Welles must navigate to find the truth.

5. Subplot

A breakthrough comes when Welles meets Max California, a clerk at an adult bookstore whose punk rock exterior conceals extensive knowledge of the industry's darkest corners. Max becomes Welles' guide through this moral labyrinth, helping him navigate through layers of the underground porn industry, from legitimate operations to producers of extremely violent content.

Their developing relationship creates a subplot that humanizes Welles' journey. Max represents a figure who has maintained his humanity despite prolonged exposure to this dark world. His experiences provide a contrast to Welles' naivety about the depths of depravity they're investigating, while his reluctant moral code offers a model for how one might survive such exposure without complete corruption.

This mentor/ally relationship parallels Welles' distant connection to his family, who represent what he's ostensibly fighting to protect. The contrast between Max's worldliness and Amy's innocence highlights the widening gap between Welles' compartmentalized worlds.

6. Trials and Tribulations

Posing as a wealthy collector interested in acquiring custom-made extreme films, Welles infiltrates deeper into the shadow world of pornography. He encounters various figures, each more disturbing than the last: sleazy producers, violent criminals, and men who commission unspeakable content for private collections.

His professional detachment begins to crack as he witnesses the systematic exploitation of vulnerable young women and the casual cruelty of those who profit from their destruction. Each encounter forces Welles to participate more actively in the deception, requiring him to express interest in extreme content and to present himself as someone who might commission such material.

The investigation reaches a crucial turning point when they discover Dino Velvet, a notorious director of violent fetish films who takes obvious pleasure in pushing boundaries of depravity. Velvet's star performer, known only as "Machine," appears in his films wearing a distinctive chrome-plated mask—the same mask Welles recognized from the 8mm film.

Through careful manipulation, Welles arranges a meeting with Dino and

Machine, supposedly to commission a custom film. After setting up the meeting, Welles pays Max for his help and urges him to get out of the situation, believing he's protecting his guide from further danger. This decision to continue alone marks Welles' deeper commitment to the case and foreshadows the personal price he will pay for pursuing justice.

7. Midpoint

The dramatic shift occurs when Eddie Poole, a pornographer connected to Mary Ann's disappearance, recognizes Welles as an investigator. Unknown to Welles, Max is kidnapped by Dino's crew, transforming what should have been a controlled undercover operation into a life-threatening situation.

The meeting at Dino Velvet's remote production facility—a grotesque space filled with implements of torture and death—becomes a trap when Eddie Poole appears with Daniel Longdale, Mrs. Christian's lawyer. Machine and Dino quickly disarm Welles, and to his horror, they bring out a captive Max, tied to a cross.

Through an intense confrontation with Longdale, the terrible truth emerges: the 8mm film was real, commissioned by Mr. Christian for $1 million. However, this revelation sparks a deadly argument when Welles mentions the payment amount—it becomes clear that Longdale never shared the full sum with Dino Velvet and Eddie Poole.

The tension explodes into violence, with Dino shooting Longdale with a crossbow, Longdale fatally shooting Dino, and Welles managing to stab Machine and escape, despite Eddie Poole's pursuit. In the chaos, Machine kills Max by slashing his throat—a moment that marks the true point of no return for Welles.

This midpoint completely changes the nature of the investigation. What began as a search for truth becomes a matter of personal vengeance for Welles. Max's death represents the first real consequence of Welles' decision to pursue this case, shattering the illusion that he can investigate evil without being touched by it.

8. Complications

When Welles reports his findings to Mrs. Christian, the revelation of her husband's monstrous actions proves too much to bear. She commits suicide, leaving Welles with the burden of knowledge and no legal recourse for justice. The police cannot act without evidence, and the film itself would be inadmissible in court.

The stakes rise dramatically as Welles realizes that conventional justice is impossible. The powerful men behind Mary Ann's murder will never face legal consequences for their actions. The legal system that Welles has operated within throughout his career is revealed as inadequate when confronted with evil of this magnitude.

Welles faces a profound moral crisis: having witnessed true evil, can he simply return to his normal life? Can he compartmentalize what he's seen as just another case? The knowledge of what happened to Mary Ann and the memory of Max's death make such detachment impossible, forcing Welles to consider actions outside the boundaries of his previous ethical framework.

9. Crisis

The "all is lost" moment comes when Welles realizes that not only will the perpetrators escape justice through legal channels, but that the entire system is designed to protect people like Mr. Christian while discarding people like Mary Ann. The innocents are already dead, the witnesses silenced, and the evidence inadmissible.

Welles faces a profound existential crisis: having stared into the abyss of human depravity, he cannot unsee what he has witnessed. The protective barriers between his professional and personal lives have completely collapsed. He can no longer pretend to be merely an observer of human wickedness—he must either accept his helplessness or take action outside the system.

This crisis is intensified by his growing alienation from his family. The gap between his experiences in the underground world and his domestic life has become unbridgeable. His wife Amy cannot comprehend what he's seen, and his desire to protect his infant daughter from such knowledge only highlights his isolation.

10. Critical Choice

In this dark moment of reflection, Welles makes his critical choice, declaring to his wife, "There's no one left to finish this but me." This decision to pursue vigilante justice marks his complete break from his former identity as a detached professional who works within the system.

Welles struggles with the knowledge that becoming an executioner means crossing a moral line from which there is no return. Yet the faces of Mary Ann, Max, and all the other victims he's encountered compel him forward. His choice is not merely about punishing the guilty but about affirming that some actions demand response, even when the system fails.

This critical choice reflects the story's central theme—confronting evil changes you irrevocably. By choosing to execute those responsible, Welles is consciously sacrificing his former self, acknowledging that he cannot return to his compartmentalized existence after what he's witnessed.

ACT 3

11. Welcome to the End (Plot Point 2)

With traditional justice out of reach and Max's death weighing heavily on his conscience, Welles embarks on a path of vengeance. He tracks down Eddie Poole, taking him to an abandoned house on the outskirts of Los Angeles. The confrontation reveals Eddie's true nature—his complete lack of remorse for

Mary Ann's fate only reinforces Welles' conviction that these men must be stopped.

After extracting what information he can, Welles executes Eddie, marking his complete break from his former ethical boundaries. This action irrevocably transforms Welles from observer to participant, from detective to executioner. There is no possibility of compartmentalization or professional detachment in this act—Welles has fully entered the moral darkness he once merely documented.

This plot point transitions the story into its final phase, where Welles will confront not just Machine but also the nature of evil itself and his own capacity for violence. The abandoned house symbolizes the moral wasteland Welles now inhabits—far from the structured world of professional ethics and legal boundaries.

12. Denouement/Theme Triumphant

The final confrontation comes when Welles tracks down Machine at his home. Through his investigation, he's discovered the man behind the chrome mask, leading to a devastating psychological and physical showdown. When Machine finally removes his iconic mask, the face beneath is disturbingly ordinary—a stark reminder that true evil often wears the most mundane disguises.

Machine's chilling words cut to the heart of Welles' journey: "There's no mystery. The things I do, I do them because I like them. Because I want to." This simple, horrible truth—that some evil exists without deeper meaning or justification—forces Welles to confront the darkness he's been investigating. The ensuing fight is brutal and primitive, ending with Welles killing Machine in a manner that mirrors the violence he has been investigating.

The film's conclusion finds Welles returning home, bearing both physical and psychological scars from his journey into darkness. In a powerful scene, he breaks down in Amy's arms, finally allowing himself to feel the full weight of his experiences. While he has eliminated specific evil-doers and achieved a form of justice for Mary Ann, the cost to his soul has been profound.

As he holds his infant daughter, Welles embodies the film's central theme about the price of confronting evil. He has not become completely like the monsters he hunted, but his exposure to their world has irrevocably altered him. His experience validates the film's underlying message: when you stare into the abyss, the abyss stares back, and no one emerges unchanged from such an encounter.

The story closes with Welles reading a letter from Mrs. Matthews, a scene that perfectly encapsulates his transformation. He now understands that innocence, once lost, can never be fully regained. His journey has taught him that evil exists not just in the shadows but in broad daylight, wearing ordinary faces and living ordinary lives. This knowledge becomes both his burden and his curse—the price paid for venturing into darkness and returning changed but not conquered.

The theme triumphs as we understand that some truths, once uncovered, can never be buried again. Welles' investigation into the depths of human depravity has left permanent scars on his psyche, but it has also reinforced his determination to protect the innocence of others, particularly his daughter, from the darkness he has witnessed. In this way, his transformation becomes not just a descent into violence and revenge, but also a brutal awakening to the responsibility of confronting evil in all its forms.

The Machinist

Extended Narrative Beat Sheet

THEME

The central theme of "The Machinist" revolves around the corrosive power of guilt and the mind's capacity for self-punishment. The film explores how unresolved trauma creates elaborate defense mechanisms that ultimately destroy both body and mind. This theme is embodied in Trevor Reznik's physical deterioration and psychological fracturing—his body wasting away while his mind constructs an intricate delusion to both hide and process his guilt. The film suggests that we cannot outrun responsibility; eventually, the mind will force us to confront our darkest actions, even as we desperately try to escape them.

ACT 1

Prologue

The film opens with Trevor Reznik—a man so severely emaciated that every bone in his body protrudes through his sallow skin—carefully rolling a body wrapped in carpet toward the edge of a rocky shoreline. The night is dark, the sea black and forbidding. As he struggles with his grim task, headlights appear in the distance. Trevor freezes momentarily before abandoning his efforts, fleeing into the shadows as a security guard's pickup truck pulls into view. The guard exits his vehicle, flashlight in hand, and begins to investigate the suspicious activity.

The film then cuts to a scene of Trevor in his apartment bathroom, staring at his gaunt reflection in the mirror. His skeletal frame is shocking—hollow cheeks, protruding collarbones, with ribs and shoulder blades that jut out unnaturally from his skin. He looks like a walking corpse, his body visibly consumed by whatever torment has afflicted him.

In a silent sequence, we see Trevor methodically cleaning his hands with bleach, scrubbing with the precision of someone trying to remove invisible stains. There is no hint of emotion in his movements, just mechanical thoroughness. This brief, stark introduction immediately establishes Trevor's physical deterioration and suggests a man haunted by something he cannot wash away.

The muted color palette of blues and grays creates a world drained of vitality, matching Trevor's depleted physical state. The prologue concludes with Trevor noticing a post-it note on the wall, he turns to see it, his face in shock and lost, we then see a close-up of the Post-it note stuck to a surface in Trevor's apartment that reads simply: “Who are you?” This cryptic question lingers as the film transitions to Trevor's daily life, setting up the central mystery of a man who has become a stranger even to himself.

1. Set Up

In the industrial gloom of the factory where he works as a machinist, Trevor Reznik moves mechanically through his shift. His cadaverous appearance—skin stretched over bone with virtually no muscle mass—draws concerned whispers from coworkers. When asked if he's sick, Trevor responds with unsettling calm: “I've never felt better in my life.” The dark irony of this statement is written on his starving body.

Trevor's life operates on a mechanical schedule: work at the factory, coffee at an airport café where waitress Marie (Aitana Sánchez-Gijón) serves him, and occasional visits to Stevie (Jennifer Jason Leigh), a prostitute who has developed genuine affection for him. These ritualized interactions represent his only human connections. At the café, he leaves excessive tips and makes awkward conversation, while with Stevie, he sometimes merely sleeps beside her—paying for human contact rather than sex.

In his apartment, Trevor's insomnia drives him to clean obsessively and play solitary Hangman games on Post-it notes. He hasn't slept in a year—a fact he states without emotion, as though describing someone else's condition. His refrigerator contains nothing but condiments, his body seemingly surviving on coffee and cigarettes. Trevor's status quo is a half-life of insomnia and isolation, sustained by rigid routine and compartmentalization.

The theme is introduced through Trevor's physical wasting—his body literally consuming itself—and his fragmented consciousness, which drops cryptic notes to itself like breadcrumbs toward a truth he cannot face. His attempts to maintain normalcy through routine only emphasize the profound abnormality of his existence. The blue-green color palette and industrial settings reflect Trevor's internal landscape: cold, mechanical, and stripped of vitality.

2. Inciting Incident

While operating a mill machine at the factory, Trevor notices someone unfamiliar—a bald, muscular man whose presence creates an immediate sense of unease. When this stranger, who introduces himself as Ivan (John Sharian), engages Trevor in conversation, Trevor becomes momentarily distracted. In this split second of inattention, the machine malfunctions, and Trevor's coworker Miller (Michael Ironside) loses his arm in a horrific industrial accident.

The accident creates a dual disruption: externally, it fractures Trevor's carefully maintained work routine and makes him a pariah among his coworkers; internally, it triggers a psychological break that allows repressed elements to surface. Ivan's appearance at this precise moment suggests a connection between Trevor's fragmenting psyche and the physical accident—as though his guilt has materialized to force a confrontation.

What makes this incident significant is not just the accident itself, but the mysterious Ivan, whom no one else at the factory acknowledges. When Trevor tries to discuss Ivan with coworkers and management, they respond with confusion and suspicion. This raises the first explicit question about the reliability of Trevor's perception, creating the central mystery that drives the narrative: Is Ivan real, or is he a manifestation of Trevor's deteriorating mental state?

3. Internal Wrestling/Preparation

The aftermath of Miller's accident leaves Trevor increasingly isolated at work. His coworkers avoid him, viewing his skeletal appearance and erratic behavior as dangerous. Meanwhile, a new element appears in Trevor's apartment—a cryptic game of Hangman on a Post-it note with several letters missing. The incomplete word becomes another puzzle in Trevor's fragmenting reality.

Trevor attempts to verify Ivan's existence. He checks with human resources, who have no record of such an employee. He questions coworkers, who deny having seen the man. Yet Trevor continues to glimpse Ivan around the factory and later, throughout the city—watching, always watching. These encounters intensify Trevor's paranoia and confusion. Is he being targeted, or is his mind creating this mysterious figure?

As his external world becomes more chaotic, Trevor clings even more desperately to his routines. He continues his visits to the airport café, where his connection with Marie deepens. He meets her son Nicholas, a bright boy who suffers from epilepsy. These interactions represent Trevor's attempts to maintain a connection to normalcy even as his reality fractures. Similarly, his relationship with Stevie offers moments of human warmth in his increasingly cold and paranoid existence.

Trevor's preparation for confronting the mystery manifests in his growing vigilance. He carefully inspects his apartment for signs of intrusion, checks and rechecks doors, and becomes hyperaware of patterns and coincidences. Metaphorically, he is preparing for a confrontation not with an external enemy, but with the truth his mind has been hiding from itself—though he doesn't yet recognize this distinction.

ACT 2

4. Welcome to the Jungle (Plot Point 1)

Trevor's paranoia escalates when he follows Ivan to a local bar and confronts him. During their tense conversation, he glimpses a photo in Ivan's wallet—an image of Ivan fishing with Nicholas, the boy from the airport café. This impossibility confirms that something is profoundly wrong with either his perception or reality itself. When Trevor demands answers, Ivan responds cryptically: "You know so little about yourself."

This encounter represents Trevor's full entry into the psychological wilderness—the "jungle" of his own fractured mind where reality, memory, and delusion intertwine indistinguishably. The normal rules of logic no longer apply as Trevor commits fully to uncovering who Ivan is and why he seems to be targeting him. The hangman game on his refrigerator gradually gains new letters, spelling out "K-I-L-L-E-R," adding urgency to his quest.

This plot point propels Trevor from passive victim to active investigator. He can no longer dismiss Ivan as a strange coincidence or hallucination; the photo creates a direct connection between two separate parts of Trevor's life that should not intersect. If Ivan knows Nicholas, then either Trevor's relationship with Marie and her son is not what it seems, or Ivan has been following Trevor more closely than he realized. Either possibility drives Trevor deeper into the psychological labyrinth.

5. Subplot

As Trevor's work life disintegrates, his relationship with Marie and Nicholas becomes increasingly important. He joins them for an outing to a local carnival, where Nicholas wants to ride the Route 666 attraction despite his mother's concerns about his epilepsy. Trevor supports the boy, forming a bond that momentarily makes him feel human again.

This developing connection provides Trevor with glimpses of the normal life he craves—warmth, affection, and purpose that stand in stark contrast to his isolated existence. Marie's single motherhood and struggle to balance work with caring for Nicholas creates a natural space for Trevor to offer support and connection. When Nicholas suffers a seizure on the Route 666 ride, Trevor helps care for him, demonstrating genuine concern that surprises both himself and Marie.

This subplot serves as both respite and catalyst. The scenes with Marie and Nicholas represent the only moments where Trevor appears genuinely at peace, yet they're interwoven with disquieting elements that push the story forward. Nicholas's seizure on Route 666 triggers disjointed flashes of memory in Trevor—images of highway lights and a car's interior—that connect subtly to the truth he's repressing. Likewise, Ivan's appearance in photos with Nicholas creates unsettling questions about the reality of Trevor's experiences.

The relationship with Stevie provides a parallel subplot that further illuminates Trevor's disintegration. When Trevor invites Stevie to his apartment for a proper date on Mother's Day, the evening quickly unravels as his paranoia surfaces. Her innocent exploration of his apartment triggers disproportionate suspicion and anger, fracturing one of his few human connections. This scene contrasts sharply with his interaction with Marie, highlighting how Trevor's ability to maintain normal relationships is deteriorating alongside his mental state.

6. Trials and Tribulations

Trevor's investigation into Ivan leads him through a series of increasingly disorienting encounters. He follows Ivan's distinctive car through the city's industrial areas, only to discover the vehicle is registered in his own name. This revelation suggests a connection between himself and Ivan that defies Trevor's understanding of his own identity.

Trevor's physical deterioration accelerates in parallel with his mental disintegration. His body becomes even more skeletal, his movements more mechanical and uncertain. The insomnia reaches its 13th month with no relief in sight. Trevor's apartment begins to reflect his psychological state—blood mysteriously drips from his refrigerator, only to vanish when he looks again. The hangman game continues to form the word "KILLER," letter by letter, like a message from his subconscious.

At work, Trevor's paranoia about his coworkers' attitudes toward him escalates into confrontation. He accuses them of conspiring with Ivan, leading to physical altercations that further isolate him. When he attempts to prove Ivan's existence by pointing him out to a coworker, Ivan is nowhere to be seen, making Trevor appear delusional.

In a particularly disturbing scene, Trevor's refrigerator begins leaking what appears to be blood. He opens it to find a severed human finger, only to blink and see nothing but condiments. These hallucinations occur with increasing frequency, blurring the line between external reality and Trevor's internal psychological landscape.

Trevor's relationship with Stevie deteriorates completely after he invites her to his apartment and becomes irrationally suspicious when she explores it. His paranoid accusations—that she's searching for something, conspiring against him—reveal how deeply his trust has been eroded. Stevie leaves hurt and confused, removing one of Trevor's few stabilizing human connections.

Each of these trials pushes Trevor closer to a truth his mind is simultaneously revealing and concealing. The inconsistencies in reality, the cryptic clues, and the deterioration of his relationships all serve as pressure points forcing Trevor toward the inevitable confrontation with what he has done.

7. Midpoint

In a pivotal scene at the DMV, Trevor discovers that the license plate from Ivan's car is registered in his own name—to a red 1969 Pontiac Firebird he has no memory of owning. This revelation creates the first explicit suggestion that Ivan might not be an external tormentor but a part of Trevor himself—perhaps a dissociated personality or a projection of his guilt.

This discovery represents a dramatic shift in the story's direction. Until this point, Trevor has been pursuing Ivan as an external threat; now, he must consider the possibility that the enemy exists within his own fractured psyche. The midpoint transforms the narrative from an external mystery to an internal psychological journey, as Trevor begins the painful process of excavating his own buried memories.

Trevor's response to this revelation is complex—denial, confusion, and a desperate attempt to maintain his perception of reality even as it crumbles. When he returns to his apartment, he finds the hangman game has progressed further toward spelling "KILLER," suggesting his subconscious knows a truth his conscious mind cannot yet face.

This midpoint forces Trevor to question everything he's experienced over the past year. If Ivan's car is registered to him, what else might be a creation of his own mind? Are Marie and Nicholas real? Is Stevie? The boundaries between external reality and internal projection begin to dissolve, creating a psychological maze from which Trevor must find his way out.

8. Complications

As Trevor grapples with the implications of the DMV revelation, his grasp on reality deteriorates more rapidly. His coworkers' hostility intensifies after another confrontation, leading to Trevor's dismissal from the factory. This removes another stabilizing element from his life, leaving him even more isolated with his increasingly disturbing thoughts.

Trevor attempts to verify other aspects of his reality, beginning with his relationship with Marie and Nicholas. At the airport, he discovers that the café where he believed he met them nightly doesn't employ a waitress named Marie. This devastating revelation suggests that significant portions of his experienced reality are fabrications—elaborate constructions of his mind designed to protect him from some terrible truth.

The hangman game on Trevor's refrigerator continues to gain letters, now clearly spelling “KILLER.” The implication that Trevor himself might be a killer creates a new level of urgency and horror. If Ivan is a projection and Marie doesn't exist, what other fictions has his mind created? And what truth lies beneath these elaborate defenses?

Trevor's physical condition reaches a crisis point—his body is literally consuming itself. The extreme emaciation has begun affecting his coordination and strength. Even simple tasks become difficult as his body fails him. This physical deterioration parallels his psychological disintegration, both representing the unsustainable cost of his year-long denial.

These complications raise the stakes dramatically. Trevor is no longer simply seeking answers about Ivan; he's desperately trying to distinguish reality from delusion before his mind and body collapse completely. The boundaries between past and present, real and imagined, self and other, have become so blurred that Trevor can no longer navigate with any certainty.

9. Crisis

Trevor reaches his lowest point when he can no longer distinguish between hallucination and reality. After discovering Marie doesn't exist at the airport café, he returns to his apartment in a state of complete disorientation. The hangman game on his refrigerator now clearly spells "KILLER," confronting Trevor with an accusation he can no longer avoid.

In a desperate attempt to find any anchor to reality, Trevor calls Stevie, only to have her reject him after his previous paranoid behavior. This removes his last human connection, leaving him completely isolated with his fracturing mind. Trevor's physical condition has become life-threatening—skeletal, weak, and still unable to sleep after more than a year.

The crisis intensifies when Trevor realizes that the mysterious "Route 666" highway from the carnival ride corresponds to an actual location—Highway 152. Something about this connection triggers partial memories that Trevor still cannot fully access. The crisis represents the complete collapse of Trevor's elaborate psychological defenses—the delusions that have protected him from the truth can no longer be maintained.

This "all is lost" moment focuses on Trevor's absolute isolation and disorientation. He has lost his job, his connections to Stevie, Marie, and Nicholas (whether real or imagined), and most critically, his ability to distinguish between reality and delusion. Without these anchors, Trevor faces the terrifying prospect that he may have done something unforgivable that his mind has been hiding from itself.

10. Critical Choice

After discovering that significant portions of his perceived reality are delusions, Trevor makes the critical choice to return to Highway 152—the real-world location corresponding to the "Route 666" ride that triggered Nicholas's seizure. Rather than continuing to flee from whatever truth he's been avoiding, Trevor chooses to confront it directly, no matter how devastating it might be.

This choice represents Trevor's spiritual and psychological turning point. He recognizes, at some level, that the only way out of his self-created labyrinth is to face its center—to confront the event that triggered his year-long insomnia, weight loss, and psychological fracturing. It's a moment of tragic courage as Trevor chooses truth over the elaborate protective delusions his mind has created.

The decision to drive to Highway 152 symbolizes Trevor's willingness to finally face responsibility for whatever he has done. After a year of running—physically through insomnia and psychologically through elaborate delusions—Trevor turns and faces his pursuer, recognizing that it has been himself all along. This critical choice transitions the narrative toward its inevitable revelation and resolution.

ACT 3

11. Welcome to the End (Plot Point 2)

Arriving at Highway 152 at night, Trevor experiences a complete breakthrough when approaching headlights illuminate the road—creating the same conditions as a year ago. In a series of vivid flashbacks, the truth finally erupts into consciousness: one year earlier, while driving along this same highway, Trevor accidentally hit and killed a young boy who was standing by the roadside with his mother after their car broke down. Instead of stopping to help, Trevor panicked and fled the scene.

This revelation instantly clarifies every element of Trevor's year-long psychological turmoil. Ivan is not a real person but a manifestation of Trevor's guilt and self-loathing—a projection of what Trevor was before the accident: strong, confident, whole. Marie and Nicholas were never real; they were Trevor's mind's way of processing his guilt by creating a relationship with the mother and child he hurt. The hangman game spelling "KILLER" was Trevor's subconscious forcing him to confront his crime.

The physical toll—his extreme emaciation, the insomnia, the hallucinations—all represent Trevor's unconscious self-punishment. Unable to consciously face what he had done, Trevor's mind created an elaborate psychological mechanism to both punish and eventually heal itself. The insomnia began the night of the hit-and-run, his body refusing the peace of sleep as atonement for his failure to take responsibility.

This plot point propels the story into its final phase of recognition and reckoning. With the truth fully exposed, Trevor must decide how to respond to his responsibility for the boy's death. The revelation doesn't just explain the mystery; it transforms Trevor's understanding of himself and forces him to make a final moral choice.

12. Denouement/Theme Triumphant

In the aftermath of his remembrance, Trevor makes the decision to turn himself in to the police. This act of taking responsibility represents Trevor's moral redemption—he chooses to face the consequences of his actions rather than continuing to run. The confession provides the resolution that his psyche has been demanding through a year of self-torture.

The film's final scene shows Trevor in what appears to be a prison cell. He lies down on the bed and closes his eyes. As he finally surrenders to sleep, the scene transitions to Trevor driving through a tunnel with his broken windshield from the hit-and-run accident, moving toward a bright white light at the tunnel's end. This final image then fades completely to white.

This concluding sequence brilliantly completes Trevor's psychological journey. The tunnel imagery functions as both literal and metaphorical—it represents Trevor finally confronting and passing through the trauma that has defined his existence for the past year. The broken windshield acknowledges his responsibility, while the white light suggests a form of redemption or release that comes from facing the truth. By bookending the film with the accident's aftermath and then returning to the moment that triggered everything, the narrative comes full circle.

The theme triumphs as Trevor's acceptance of responsibility finally releases him from self-punishment. His body and mind had been executing a punitive sentence of their own making—his guilt manifested as insomnia, extreme weight loss, and elaborate hallucinations. These symptoms were both punishment and path toward truth, his psyche's elaborate mechanism for eventually forcing him to face what he had done.

The driving-through-tunnel sequence emphasizes the theme of redemption through confession. It's not a happy ending in conventional terms—Trevor will face legal consequences for the hit-and-run—but it represents a spiritual and psychological resolution. The weight of unacknowledged guilt was far more devastating than the consequences of confession could ever be.

The denouement reinforces the film's central message about the impossibility of escaping responsibility for our actions. No matter how elaborate our psychological defenses, the mind will eventually force a confrontation with the truth. Trevor's journey illustrates how guilt, when unacknowledged, becomes a consuming force that destroys both body and mind. His ultimate confession and the peace it brings suggest that facing consequences, however painful, is less destructive than the psychological burden of denial.

This final image of Trevor driving through the tunnel toward the light provides perfect visual closure to a story centered on running from truth. The broken windshield acknowledges his guilt while the movement forward through the tunnel suggests progression rather than stasis. His physical emaciation throughout the film visually manifests his guilt consuming him from within; his final journey toward the light represents the spiritual restoration that comes with truth and responsibility, completing the film's psychological journey with elegant visual symmetry.

The Silence of the Lambs

Extended Narrative Beat Sheet (Novel and Film Adaptation)

THEME

The central theme of "The Silence of the Lambs" revolves around transformation through confronting fear—specifically, how facing one's deepest psychological terrors is necessary for personal and professional evolution. The story explores how denial and avoidance perpetuate victimhood, while confrontation of darkness (both external and internal) leads to empowerment. This is captured in Hannibal Lecter's pivotal question to Clarice: "Have the lambs stopped screaming?"

ACT 1

1. Set Up

Clarice Starling (Jodie Foster in the film) is an FBI trainee at the Academy in Quantico, Virginia, striving to prove herself in the male-dominated world of law enforcement. Her status quo world is one of constant effort and compensation—running obstacle courses, studying forensics, and enduring the evaluating gazes of her male counterparts. Though competent, she's not yet seen as an equal by the FBI establishment.

We see Clarice's determination immediately as she runs through the woods, pushing herself physically despite being summoned to meet FBI Chief Jack Crawford (Scott Glenn in the film). Her modest background is evident in her accent and demeanor, which she tries to polish but can't completely disguise. Crawford represents both authority and opportunity, while the Academy represents the structured, rule-bound world she's trying to succeed within.

The theme is introduced subtly through Clarice's fierce ambition and her willingness to take on difficult assignments that others might avoid. Her determination suggests she's running from something as much as toward something, hinting at deeper motivations that drive her pursuit of justice.

In the novel, Thomas Harris provides more detailed background on Clarice's childhood in West Virginia, her father's death while serving as a town marshal, and her subsequent time in an orphanage—establishing more explicitly the origins of her drive to protect others and her sensitivity to the vulnerable.

2. Inciting Incident

FBI Chief Jack Crawford assigns Clarice to interview Dr. Hannibal Lecter (Anthony Hopkins in the film), a brilliant psychiatrist and cannibalistic serial killer, in hopes that he might provide insight into an active case involving a serial killer known as "Buffalo Bill" who is abducting and skinning women. This external assignment disrupts Clarice's training routine and thrusts her into direct contact with extraordinary evil, setting the main plot in motion.

The novel provides more context for this assignment, with Crawford more explicitly using Clarice as a tool to manipulate Lecter—something she gradually becomes aware of. The novel presents Crawford as more calculating in his decision to send an inexperienced female trainee to interview Lecter, knowing the doctor's fascination with psychological vulnerability.

3. Internal Wrestling/Preparation

Clarice studies Lecter's case file and prepares for the interview, wrestling with anxiety but determined to prove herself. She's warned about Lecter's manipulative brilliance and the strict protocols for interacting with him. Dr.

Frederick Chilton (Anthony Heald in the film), the hospital administrator, attempts to flirt with and undermine Clarice, offering the first glimpse of the professional sexism she regularly endures.

The novel delves deeper into Clarice's preparation and anxieties, providing more of her internal monologue as she rehearses professional language and demeanor, knowing she'll be scrutinized not just by Lecter but by her superiors evaluating her performance.

The theme develops as Clarice steels herself to confront a monster, not yet realizing that this encounter will force her to face her own inner demons as well. Her preparation reveals a pattern of using structure and protocol as armor against vulnerability, which Lecter will later penetrate with ruthless precision.

ACT 2

4. Welcome to the Jungle (Plot Point 1)

Clarice meets Hannibal Lecter in the basement of the Baltimore State Hospital for the Criminally Insane. Despite her preparation, Lecter immediately seizes control of the interaction, analyzing her from her shoes to her accent, and dismissing the questionnaire she's brought. When Clarice adapts and speaks more authentically, Lecter offers a cryptic clue about a former patient named "Miss Mofet."

This encounter marks Clarice's entry into a psychological landscape far more treacherous than the structured world of the Academy. Lecter establishes the terms of their rclationship: he will help with Buffalo Bill, but only in exchange for personal information about Clarice. This quid pro quo arrangement sets up the central dynamic of their relationship.

The film adaptation captures this scene almost verbatim from the novel, recognizing its crucial importance to establishing the psychological chess match between Clarice and Lecter. Both versions emphasize Lecter's supernatural ability to see through Clarice's professional veneer to the vulnerable human beneath.

5. Subplot

Following Lecter's clue about "Miss Mofet," Clarice discovers a storage unit containing a severed head in a jar and a rare death's-head moth cocoon. This discovery earns her Crawford's increased trust and a more official role in the Buffalo Bill investigation, establishing the professional advancement subplot that runs parallel to her psychological journey.

Meanwhile, a more personal subplot develops through Clarice's growing relationship with Lecter, who demands personal truths in exchange for his insights. Additionally, the plight of Catherine Martin (Brooke Smith in the film), Buffalo Bill's latest kidnapping victim whose time is running out, creates urgency and raises the emotional stakes of the investigation.

The novel expands these subplots significantly, particularly:

- More detailed interactions with Crawford and the forensic team, highlighting the scientific aspects of the investigation
- A deeper exploration of Clarice's friendship with fellow trainee Ardelia Mapp, providing context for Clarice's isolation and determination
- More extensive background on Buffalo Bill (Jame Gumb) and his psychological development
- Greater development of Catherine Martin's captivity and her desperate attempts to survive

These subplots all reflect the central theme by presenting Clarice with escalating challenges that force her to confront fears—professional inadequacy, personal vulnerability, and the possibility of failure with life-or-death consequences.

6. Trials and Tribulations

Clarice navigates a series of increasingly challenging obstacles as the Buffalo

Bill investigation intensifies:

- She performs her first autopsy on a victim in West Virginia, steeling herself against the horror while extracting crucial evidence
- She endures another manipulative encounter with Lecter, who demands more personal information about her childhood
- She discovers a pattern in Buffalo Bill's victims and realizes he's making a "woman suit" from their skin
- She interviews people connected to the first victim, facing skepticism about her authority as a female trainee
- She returns to Lecter for more insights, this time sharing the traumatic story of hearing spring lambs being slaughtered as a child
- She earns a crucial breakthrough when Lecter provides information about Buffalo Bill's physical appearance and psychology

The novel provides more extensive forensic details of the investigation and more nuanced development of Clarice's growing confidence in her abilities. It also offers deeper insights into the psychological strategies Clarice employs when dealing with Lecter, showing her growing awareness of how to navigate his dangerous brilliance.

The film condenses many of these trials for pacing but maintains the essential emotional beats of Clarice's growing confidence contrasted with her necessary vulnerability with Lecter. Both versions highlight how each confrontation with horror strengthens rather than weakens Clarice, building toward her ultimate transformation.

7. Midpoint

The pivotal shift occurs when Senator Ruth Martin offers Lecter a transfer to a federal institution with better conditions in exchange for helping save her daughter Catherine. Lecter provides case information but deliberately misleads the FBI about Buffalo Bill's identity, claiming his name is "Louis Friend" (an anagram for "iron sulfide"—fool's gold).

Clarice recognizes something is wrong with Lecter's information and returns to him one last time. In their most intense exchange, Clarice shares her deepest childhood trauma—her failed attempt to save a spring lamb from slaughter, and the nightmares about the lambs' screaming that have haunted her since. In return, Lecter gives her the breakthrough insight that Buffalo Bill knew his first victim personally.

This profound exchange transforms their relationship and provides Clarice with the crucial insight needed to solve the case. Both the novel and film treat this scene as the emotional core of the story, recognizing its thematic significance in Clarice's willingness to be completely vulnerable with Lecter in exchange for the truth she needs.

8. Complications

The stakes escalate dramatically as:

- Lecter brutally murders two guards during his transfer, escaping custody in a scene of shocking violence
- Catherine Martin remains captive in Buffalo Bill's basement, with time running out as he prepares to kill her
- Crawford and the FBI pursue the false lead about "Louis Friend" while Clarice follows her own theory about the first victim
- Clarice is removed from the case after Lecter's escape, but continues investigating on her own
- Lecter remains at large, a lingering threat and ambiguous ally to Clarice

The novel provides more graphic detail of Lecter's escape, particularly the horrific fate of his guards, intensifying the sense of menace that follows his disappearance. The novel also gives more insight into Catherine's psychological strategies for survival and her interactions with Buffalo Bill/Jame Gumb.

The film emphasizes the isolation of Clarice as she operates increasingly independently, relying on her own judgment rather than institutional support.

Both versions heighten tension as Clarice must now rely entirely on her own courage and insight, without the safety net of institutional support or even Lecter's twisted guidance.

9. Crisis

The “crisis” moment occurs when Clarice's investigation leads her to the house of Jame Gumb (Ted Levine in the film), whom she believes may have known Buffalo Bill's first victim. During their conversation, she spots a death's-head moth like the one found in the storage unit, realizing too late that Gumb himself is Buffalo Bill. Alone and without backup, Clarice finds herself in the killer's house as he disappears from view.

This crisis represents Clarice's most extreme vulnerability—she's isolated, outmatched physically, and in the literal darkest environment of the film when Gumb cuts the power and observes her through night-vision goggles. The tables have completely turned; the investigator has become potential prey.

The novel and film handle this scene similarly, though the novel provides more of Clarice's internal thought process as she realizes the danger she's in and formulates her response. Both versions create intense claustrophobia and dread as Clarice navigates the killer's lair.

10. Critical Choice

In the darkness of Buffalo Bill's basement, Clarice faces her moment of truth. Despite her terror, she doesn't panic or freeze. Instead, she draws her weapon and moves methodically through the darkness, using her training and senses to track Gumb. When she hears the sound of his gun being cocked, she fires rapidly in that direction, killing him.

This critical choice to confront rather than flee from mortal danger represents Clarice's complete transformation from student to agent, from theoretical knowledge to lived experience. In this moment, she chooses courage over fear, action over paralysis, and responsibility over self-preservation.

The novel provides more detail about Clarice's thought process during this confrontation, particularly her awareness that failure means not only her death but Catherine Martin's as well. The film creates a more visceral experience of the showdown through its use of the night-vision perspective, showing viewers what Gumb sees as he stalks Clarice.

Both versions emphasize that Clarice's triumph comes not from superior physical strength but from training, courage, and her willingness to face darkness—both literal and metaphorical.

ACT 3

11. Welcome to the End (Plot Point 2)

Clarice rescues Catherine Martin from the pit in Buffalo Bill's basement. The FBI arrives belatedly, finding Clarice has already resolved the situation. This moment transitions the story from the intense manhunt to its denouement, as Clarice emerges from the killer's den transformed by her ordeal.

This transition into Act 3 represents Clarice's emergence from darkness—both literally from the basement and figuratively from her trial by fire. She has accomplished what the entire FBI apparatus could not, through a combination of intellectual insight, emotional intelligence, and raw courage.

The novel provides a more extended aftermath of the rescue, including Clarice's interactions with Catherine and the arriving FBI agents. The film streamlines this section to maintain momentum, but both versions emphasize how this experience has fundamentally changed Clarice.

12. Denouement/Theme Triumphant

Clarice graduates from the FBI Academy with honors, her accomplishment in solving the Buffalo Bill case earning her the respect of her peers and superiors.

During the graduation celebration, she receives a phone call from Hannibal Lecter, who is now in the Bahamas, preparing to "have an old friend for dinner" (his former hospital nemesis, Dr. Chilton).

Lecter congratulates Clarice and asks, "Have the lambs stopped screaming?" Before she can fully answer, he hangs up, saying, "Goodbye, Clarice," and disappears into the crowd.

The theme triumphs as the story reveals the complete arc of Clarice's transformation. She has faced her deepest fears—both the external horror of Buffalo Bill and the internal trauma symbolized by the screaming lambs—and emerged stronger. While Lecter's question suggests her nightmares may not be entirely silenced, Clarice has proven she can function powerfully despite her fears rather than being paralyzed by them.

The novel and film handle this conclusion similarly, though the novel provides more detail about Clarice's new status in the FBI and her reflections on her experiences. Both versions leave Lecter at large, creating an ambiguous note to the resolution—evil has not been eliminated from the world, merely one manifestation of it.

Key Differences Between Novel and Film Adaptation

Thomas Harris's 1988 novel provides deeper psychological explorations and more extensive background on several key characters:

Novel

- More detailed background on Clarice's childhood and psychological motivations
- Greater development of secondary characters like Ardelia Mapp and Jack Crawford
- More extensive forensic details and procedural aspects of the investigation
- Deeper exploration of Jame Gumb's psychology and development into

Buffalo Bill

- More detailed description of Lecter's escape and its aftermath
- Extended epilogue showing Clarice's new status within the FBI

Film (1991)

- Directed by Jonathan Demme with a focus on psychological tension
- Jodie Foster brings vulnerability and determination to Clarice
- Anthony Hopkins creates an iconic portrayal of Lecter with less screen time
- Visual storytelling emphasizes Clarice's isolation in male-dominated environments
- Uses subjective camera techniques to heighten identification with Clarice
- More streamlined narrative focusing on the Clarice-Lecter dynamic
- The night-vision sequence creates one of cinema's most memorable climactic confrontations

Despite these differences, both the novel and film maintain the central thematic exploration of transformation through confronting fear. The story resonates because it shows that facing our fears—rather than being consumed by them—is the path to personal growth and empowerment.

The success of both versions of "The Silence of the Lambs" stems from their unflinching examination of how confronting darkness, both external and internal, can lead to transformation. As Lecter tells Clarice: "Our scars have the power to remind us that the past was real." It is by acknowledging rather than denying these scars that Clarice finds her strength and ultimately silences the lambs.

CHAPTER 5

12-Day Subconscious Novelist Outline System

Overview

Day 1: Subconscious Exploration

- Enter meditative/hypnotic state
- Free association writing session
- Record all ideas, characters, scenes, themes
- Review emergent patterns
- Use "what if" scenarios
- Draw connections between elements
- Mark recurring themes/ideas

Day 2: Initial Research & Concept Development

- Enter meditative/hypnotic state
- Categorize research needs:
    - Technical requirements
    - Historical context
    - Location specifics
    - Professional procedures
- Identify expert sources
- Begin preliminary research
- Document key findings
- Connect research to story elements

Day 3: Character Development - Protagonist & Antagonist

- Enter meditative/hypnotic state
- Hero development:
    - External profile

    - Internal profile
    - Psychological wounds
    - Greatest fears
    - Core desires
    - Daily routines
    - Transformation arc
- Villain development:
    - Mirror profile
    - Psychological makeup
    - Master plan
    - Resources/capabilities
    - Impact on hero

Day 4: Theme Integration & Basic Three-Act Synopsis

- Enter meditative/hypnotic state
- Theme development:
    - Core message identification
    - Character-theme connections
    - World-theme integration
    - Symbolic elements
- Develop initial synopsis for each act:
    - Act 1 (25%): Opening world, character introductions, conflict setup, core incident
    - Act 2 (55%): Primary challenges, key plot points, relationship developments, crisis structure
    - Act 3 (20%): Climax outline, resolution approach, theme completion

Day 5: Secondary Characters & World Building

- Enter meditative/hypnotic state

- Support cast development:
    - Allies
    - Mentors
    - Love interests
    - Family members
- World construction:
    - Physical locations
    - Social structures
    - Power dynamics
    - Cultural elements
    - Technology level
    - Time period details

Day 6: Research Material Organization & Story Integration

- Enter meditative/hypnotic state
- Compile all research materials
- Organize by topic/relevance
- Map research to specific story elements:
    - Character backgrounds
    - Plot authenticity
    - Setting details
    - Technical accuracy
- Identify research gaps
- Plan for additional research needs
- Create reference system for writing phase

Day 7: Expanded Three-Act Synopsis

- Enter meditative/hypnotic state
- Review and adjust basic synopsis
- Expand into detailed narrative:

    - Act 1: Full setup and inciting incident
    - Act 2: New world & rising conflict
    - Act 3: Detailed climax and resolution
- Add character arc progressions
- Enhance thematic elements
- Deepen conflict descriptions

Day 8: Basic Beat Sheet Development

- Enter meditative/hypnotic state
- Convert narrative synopsis into 12 universal beats:
    - Act 1:
        - Setup
        - Inciting Incident
        - Internal Wrestling/Preparation
    - Act 2:
        - Welcome to the Jungle
        - Subplot Introduction
        - Trials and Tribulations
        - Midpoint
        - Complications
        - Crisis
        - Critical Choice
    - Act 3:
        - Welcome to the End
        - Theme Triumphant

Day 9: Detailed Beat Sheet

- Enter meditative/hypnotic state
- Expand each beat with:
    - Complete scene requirements

- Character development moments
- Theme integration points
- Emotional progressions
- Detailed plot points
- Conflict escalations
- Setting descriptions
- Key dialogue concepts

Day 10: Basic Chapter Outline

- Enter meditative/hypnotic state
- Basic scene breakdown of each beat
- Map beats to 30-chapter structure
- Initial pacing structure
- Primary subplot tracking
- Key character moments
- Core theme developments
- Basic transitions

Day 11: Detailed Chapter Outline (Scene by Scene Breakdown) - Part 1

- Enter meditative/hypnotic state
- For chapters 1-15, detail:
    - Detailed scene-by-scene breakdown
    - Opening hooks
    - Character objectives
    - Specific conflicts
    - Detailed settings
    - Key dialogue points
    - Scene outcomes
    - Emotional impacts

    - Thematic elements
    - Transition details

Day 12: Detailed Chapter Outline (Scene by Scene Breakdown) - Part 2

- Enter meditative/hypnotic state
- For chapters 16-30, detail:
    - Detailed scene-by-scene breakdown
    - Opening hooks
    - Character objectives
    - Specific conflicts
    - Detailed settings
    - Key dialogue points
    - Scene outcomes
    - Emotional impacts
    - Thematic elements
    - Transition details

Post-Outline Writing Process

1. Master Outline Assembly & Writing Plan:
    - Review and adjust detailed outline
    - Create comprehensive character sheets
    - Compile research references
    - Organize setting bible
    - Establish writing schedule:
        - Daily word count goals
        - Chapter completion timeline
        - Progress tracking method
    - Create master folder containing:
        - All development documents

- Research materials
- Character profiles
- World-building details
- Chapter outlines
- Writing timeline

2. First Draft (30-60 days):
   - Follow chapter outline
   - 2,000-3,000 words per chapter
   - One chapter per day goal
   - Maintain momentum over perfection
3. Revision Process:
   - Initial read-through
   - Content editing
   - Structure verification
   - Character arc review
   - Theme consistency check
   - Line editing
   - Final polish
4. Final Review:
   - Complete read-through
   - Last adjustments
   - Formatting check
   - Submission preparation

The 12 Day Subconscious Novelist Outline Hypnotic Meditations & Affirmations Program

Day 1: Subconscious Exploration

At this stage of the process, you are focusing on opening your creative mind and allowing your subconscious to freely express ideas. You will enter a hypnotic state and engage in free association writing (automatic writing), recording all ideas, words, images, characters, scenes, and themes that emerge. You'll then review these elements for patterns and make connections between different components, marking recurring themes and exploring "what if" scenarios. Make sure you write and or draw everything that comes to mind down (in the ***free association play sheets***). Do not question it, just write it down and intuitively follow whatever idea, word, images, characters, scenes, themes you feel guided to follow and explore whatever you feel compelled to explore. Most importantly have fun and enjoy the process.

Meditative/Hypnotic State

Pre-Reading Hypnotic Suggestion

As you begin to read these words, you'll notice something interesting happening. The very act of reading this script will naturally and effortlessly guide you into a peaceful, relaxed state. You may notice your breathing becoming slower and deeper as you read. Your eyes might begin to feel heavy, and that's perfectly natural. Every word you read will deepen this relaxation. Trust that your subconscious mind will absorb and respond to these suggestions even as you consciously read them. When you're ready, begin reading the induction below.

Base Induction (Self-Guided)

Find a comfortable position where you won't be disturbed. Take a moment to settle in, knowing that simply reading these words begins the process of relaxation.

Take a deep breath now and hold it. As your eyes move across these words, you can begin to feel their weight. Exhale slowly, and as you do, notice how your eyelids are already becoming heavier, more relaxed. So relaxed that they're beginning to feel as though they just won't work properly. You might want to test this sensation, knowing they're becoming too relaxed to open easily... that's right.

And now, as you continue reading, become aware of your breathing. Notice how each breath naturally brings you deeper into this relaxed state. Allow this peaceful feeling to flow through your body like a gentle wave.

Starting with your toes, you can begin to feel them becoming completely relaxed. This soothing wave of relaxation flows upward, melting away any tension as it moves. It flows into your feet, warming and relaxing every muscle. It seeps into your ankles, making them feel heavy and comfortable. This peaceful feeling continues up through your calves, softening them completely. It reaches your knees, dissolving any remaining tension. The relaxation flows through your thighs, and with each word you read, you can feel this relaxation deepening, becoming more profound.

As your eyes follow these words, this wave of relaxation continues its journey, flowing into your hips, releasing any tension stored there. It spreads through your lower back, soothing and relaxing every muscle. The relaxation seeps into your abdomen, and you might notice your breathing becoming even slower, even deeper. This peaceful feeling fills your entire torso, flowing through your chest, releasing any tension there. It spreads across your shoulders, and you might notice them dropping slightly as they relax completely. This wave of tranquility flows down your upper back, releasing any remaining tension.

The relaxation now flows down your arms like warm honey, moving slowly and sweetly. It seeps into your elbows, making them feel heavy and comfortable. It continues along your forearms, dissolving any tension it finds. It flows into your wrists, making them feel loose and relaxed. This peaceful feeling spreads through your hands, and you might notice them becoming warmer as it does. Finally, it reaches your fingertips, and you can feel a pleasant tingling sensation there.

As you continue reading, allow this wave of relaxation to flow upward once more, moving through your neck, releasing any tension it finds there. It seeps into your jaw, and you might notice your teeth separating slightly as those muscles relax. This peaceful feeling spreads across your face, softening every muscle it touches. Finally, it flows throughout your scalp, and you might notice a pleasant heaviness in your head.

Your entire body is now resting in perfect relaxation, and with each word you read, you drift deeper into this peaceful state. You can now begin a countdown in your mind, knowing that each number will take you twice as deep as before.

Begin counting now:

One... feeling yourself drifting twice as deep...

Two... doubling that relaxation once again...

Three... allowing yourself to sink even deeper still...

You have now reached a perfect state of relaxation and receptivity. Your creative mind is open and ready. As you continue reading, each word will deepen this state while awakening your creative powers.

Day 1: Subconscious Exploration – Affirmation

My creative mind is vast and endless, like an ocean of possibilities. As I relax deeper and deeper, I become aware of the incredible creative power within me.

My subconscious mind is a treasure chest of ideas, characters, and stories, all waiting to be discovered. With each breath, I'm opening this treasure chest wider and wider.

Ideas flow freely through my mind like a gentle stream. Each thought, each image, each possibility is clear and vivid. I capture these ideas effortlessly, knowing they are valuable gifts from my creative mind.

My imagination is limitless. Characters, scenes, and stories emerge naturally and easily. I recognize patterns and connections between ideas, seeing how they weave together into a tapestry of story.

When I return to normal wakefulness, I find it easy to record these ideas. My hand moves across the page smoothly, capturing every precious thought and inspiration.

My creative mind remains open and receptive throughout the day, continuing to provide me with rich, vivid ideas for my story.

I am a great writer and I trust the power of my subconscious mind to reveal the right story for me to tell at this moment in time and point of space. I trust, both consciously and subconsciously that I will discover this story now.

I love writing and I love how I can write effortlessly through the perfect storytelling power of my subconscious mind. Thank you, thank you, thank you.

Day 2: Initial Research & Concept Development

At this stage of the process you should have a better idea of your story and the possible elements you might need to incorporate and research deeper to be able to organize, structure, outline and eventually write your novel. Take a moment (after the hypnotic meditation process) to go through everything you've written up to now and analyze what research categories you may need to explore. Write everything that comes to mind down. Whatever you feel may be necessary to research write it down. You can explore these areas today, make notes and get really specific about what you really need to research. Then take some time to explore this research. If you feel like you'll need more research later on, you can do it at the end of the 12 day outline before starting to write your novel. This may or may not require you to rework your outline one final time. From my experience I find it useful to do research but it's important to be conscious of not getting too carried away, which is why I recommend just one day of research to develop the outline and at this stage you can make notes if feel you'll need to do a bit more research later. You could technically take a couple of days or a week to do research before continuing with the outline but I really do encourage you to avoid doing this at first because research can potentially take you out of the story. So for now, just stick to the plan. One day of good research and make lots of notes. Write everything down. If you are working more digitally, then you can copy and print visuals related to the research as well. If you find articles or lots of written material with topics related to your research, make sure you print those out and then go over them in more detail later. Do just the basic research now. Don't allow research to take you away from your story. Keep in mind that your research right now should be though of as fuel for your story so do not get deviated by going down rabbits holes of research (at least not yet). In the following pages write down some important notes on your research. I created some sub-categories of research to engage your subconscious mind a bit as you research. These are: technical requirements, historical context, location specifics, professional procedures, expert sources/people/resources to consult, important discoveries, and how research connects to plot.

Pre-Reading Hypnotic Suggestion

As you begin to read these words, you'll notice something interesting happening. The very act of reading this script will naturally and effortlessly guide you into a peaceful, relaxed state. You may notice your breathing becoming slower and deeper as you read. Your eyes might begin to feel heavy, and that's perfectly natural. Every word you read will deepen this relaxation. Trust that your subconscious mind will absorb and respond to these suggestions even as you consciously read them. When you're ready, begin reading the induction below.

Base Induction (Self-Guided)

Find a comfortable position where you won't be disturbed. Take a moment to settle in, knowing that simply reading these words begins the process of relaxation.

Take a deep breath now and hold it. As your eyes move across these words, you can begin to feel their weight. Exhale slowly, and as you do, notice how your eyelids are already becoming heavier, more relaxed. So relaxed that they're beginning to feel as though they just won't work properly. You might want to test this sensation, knowing they're becoming too relaxed to open easily... that's right.

And now, as you continue reading, become aware of your breathing. Notice how each breath naturally brings you deeper into this relaxed state. Allow this peaceful feeling to flow through your body like a gentle wave.

Starting with your toes, you can begin to feel them becoming completely relaxed. This soothing wave of relaxation flows upward, melting away any tension as it moves. It flows into your feet, warming and relaxing every muscle. It seeps into your ankles, making them feel heavy and comfortable. This peaceful feeling continues up through your calves, softening them completely. It reaches your knees, dissolving any remaining tension. The relaxation flows through your thighs, and with each word you read, you can feel this relaxation deepening, becoming more profound.

As your eyes follow these words, this wave of relaxation continues its journey, flowing into your hips, releasing any tension stored there. It spreads through your lower back, soothing and relaxing every muscle. The relaxation seeps into your abdomen, and you might notice your breathing becoming even slower, even deeper. This peaceful feeling fills your entire torso, flowing through your chest, releasing any tension there. It spreads across your shoulders, and you might notice them dropping slightly as they relax completely. This wave of tranquility flows down your upper back, releasing any remaining tension.

The relaxation now flows down your arms like warm honey, moving slowly and sweetly. It seeps into your elbows, making them feel heavy and comfortable. It continues along your forearms, dissolving any tension it finds. It flows into your wrists, making them feel loose and relaxed. This peaceful feeling spreads through your hands, and you might notice them becoming warmer as it does. Finally, it reaches your fingertips, and you can feel a pleasant tingling sensation there.

As you continue reading, allow this wave of relaxation to flow upward once more, moving through your neck, releasing any tension it finds there. It seeps into your jaw, and you might notice your teeth separating slightly as those muscles relax. This peaceful feeling spreads across your face, softening every muscle it touches. Finally, it flows throughout your scalp, and you might notice a pleasant heaviness in your head.

Your entire body is now resting in perfect relaxation, and with each word you read, you drift deeper into this peaceful state. You can now begin a countdown in your mind, knowing that each number will take you twice as deep as before.

Begin counting now:

One... feeling yourself drifting twice as deep...

Two... doubling that relaxation once again...

Three... allowing yourself to sink even deeper still...

You have now reached a perfect state of relaxation and receptivity. Your creative mind is open and ready. As you continue reading, each word will deepen this state while awakening your creative powers.

Day 2: Research & Concept Development - Affirmation

My mind is a powerful research tool, naturally drawing me to the information my story needs. I notice relevant details everywhere, easily connecting them to my developing story.

My concept grows stronger and clearer with each piece of research I discover. I instinctively know which information will enrich my story and which to set aside.

My mind organizes information effortlessly, creating clear connections between research and story elements. These connections deepen my understanding and strengthen my narrative.

I find joy in the discovery process, each new piece of information sparking fresh ideas and possibilities for my story. My curiosity is alive and active, guiding me to exactly what my story needs.

My subconscious mind continues working even when I'm not actively researching, making connections and uncovering insights that serve my story. I am a great writer and I deeply understand all the research I need for the story I am currently writing.

All research information I need for my story comes alive in my mind's eye as I discover the story my subconscious mind wants to tell and I can effortlessly express whatever research information is needed to make the story believable and truly entertaining and impactful to my readers.

I am a great writer and I understand all the elements of story effortlessly.

I love writing and I love how I can write effortlessly through the perfect storytelling power of my subconscious mind. Thank you, thank you, thank you.

Day 3: Character Development - Protagonist & Antagonist

At this stage of the process you are focusing on exploring and developing your hero (protagonist) and villain (antagonist). You will explore their physical characteristics, names, ages, personalities, occupations, values, core beliefs, core desires, habits, motivations, psychological wounds, fears, and their transformational arcs.

Pre-Reading Hypnotic Suggestion

As you begin to read these words, you'll notice something interesting happening. The very act of reading this script will naturally and effortlessly guide you into a peaceful, relaxed state. You may notice your breathing becoming slower and deeper as you read. Your eyes might begin to feel heavy, and that's perfectly natural. Every word you read will deepen this relaxation. Trust that your subconscious mind will absorb and respond to these suggestions even as you consciously read them. When you're ready, begin reading the induction below.

Base Induction (Self-Guided)

Find a comfortable position where you won't be disturbed. Take a moment to settle in, knowing that simply reading these words begins the process of relaxation.

Take a deep breath now and hold it. As your eyes move across these words, you can begin to feel their weight. Exhale slowly, and as you do, notice how your eyelids are already becoming heavier, more relaxed. So relaxed that they're beginning to feel as though they just won't work properly. You might want to test this sensation, knowing they're becoming too relaxed to open easily... that's right.

And now, as you continue reading, become aware of your breathing. Notice how each breath naturally brings you deeper into this relaxed state. Allow this peaceful feeling to flow through your body like a gentle wave.

Starting with your toes, you can begin to feel them becoming completely relaxed. This soothing wave of relaxation flows upward, melting away any tension as it moves. It flows into your feet, warming and relaxing every muscle. It seeps into your ankles, making them feel heavy and comfortable. This peaceful feeling continues up through your calves, softening them completely. It reaches your knees, dissolving any remaining tension. The relaxation flows through your thighs, and with each word you read, you can feel this relaxation deepening, becoming more profound.

As your eyes follow these words, this wave of relaxation continues its journey, flowing into your hips, releasing any tension stored there. It spreads through your lower back, soothing and relaxing every muscle. The relaxation seeps into your abdomen, and you might notice your breathing becoming even slower, even deeper. This peaceful feeling fills your entire torso, flowing through your chest, releasing any tension there. It spreads across your shoulders, and you might notice them dropping slightly as they relax completely. This wave of tranquility flows down your upper back, releasing any remaining tension.

The relaxation now flows down your arms like warm honey, moving slowly and sweetly. It seeps into your elbows, making them feel heavy and comfortable. It continues along your forearms, dissolving any tension it finds. It flows into your wrists, making them feel loose and relaxed. This peaceful feeling spreads through your hands, and you might notice them becoming warmer as it does. Finally, it reaches your fingertips, and you can feel a pleasant tingling sensation there.

As you continue reading, allow this wave of relaxation to flow upward once more, moving through your neck, releasing any tension it finds there. It seeps into your jaw, and you might notice your teeth separating slightly as those muscles relax. This peaceful feeling spreads across your face, softening every muscle it touches. Finally, it flows throughout your scalp, and you might notice a pleasant heaviness in your head.

Your entire body is now resting in perfect relaxation, and with each word you read, you drift deeper into this peaceful state. You can now begin a countdown in your mind, knowing that each number will take you twice as deep as before.

Begin counting now:

One... feeling yourself drifting twice as deep...

Two... doubling that relaxation once again...

Three... allowing yourself to sink even deeper still...

You have now reached a perfect state of relaxation and receptivity. Your creative mind is open and ready. As you continue reading, each word will deepen this state while awakening your creative powers.

Day 3: Character Development - Affirmation

The characters in my story are becoming real, living beings in my mind. I can see them clearly, understand their thoughts, feel their emotions.

My protagonist's journey is clear to me now. I understand their deepest fears, their greatest desires, their most profound wounds. These elements come together to create a complex, compelling character.

My antagonist's motivations are equally clear. I understand what drives them, what they believe, why they must oppose my protagonist. Their conflict feels real and necessary.

The relationship between my characters is rich with tension and meaning. I see how they challenge each other, how they force growth and change.

My characters' voices are distinct and authentic. When I write their dialogue, their words flow naturally and true to who they are.

I am a great writer and I deeply understand the hero and villain of the story I am currently writing. My characters come alive in my mind's eye, and I can express their actions, senses, thoughts and emotions effortlessly.

I love writing and I love how I can write effortlessly through the perfect storytelling power of my subconscious mind. Thank you, thank you, thank you.

Day 4: Theme Integration & Basic Three-Act Synopsis

At this stage of the process, you're focusing on identifying the core theme of your story and creating the basic structure for your three-act narrative. Themes are the universal truths that your story explores, the deeper message beneath the plot and characters. Today, you'll identify your primary theme and explore how it manifests through your characters, world, and symbolic elements. You'll then develop an initial synopsis for each act of your story, establishing the framework that will support your entire narrative.

After the hypnotic meditation process, spend time exploring what your story is truly about at its core. What statement about life or human nature does it make? How do your characters embody or challenge this theme? Look for opportunities to weave your theme throughout your story world, creating a cohesive narrative experience. Then, using the basic three-act structure (Act 1: 25%, Act 2: 55%, Act 3: 20%), sketch the broad strokes of your story's beginning, middle, and end. Make sure you write everything down, allowing your intuition to guide you through this process without judgment. Most importantly, have fun and enjoy witnessing your story take shape.

Meditative/Hypnotic State

Pre-Reading Hypnotic Suggestion

As you begin to read these words, you'll notice something interesting happening.

The very act of reading this script will naturally and effortlessly guide you into a peaceful, relaxed state. You may notice your breathing becoming slower and deeper as you read. Your eyes might begin to feel heavy, and that's perfectly natural. Every word you read will deepen this relaxation. Trust that your subconscious mind will absorb and respond to these suggestions even as you consciously read them. When you're ready, begin reading the induction below.

Base Induction (Self-Guided)

Find a comfortable position where you won't be disturbed. Take a moment to settle in, knowing that simply reading these words begins the process of relaxation.

Take a deep breath now and hold it. As your eyes move across these words, you can begin to feel their weight. Exhale slowly, and as you do, notice how your eyelids are already becoming heavier, more relaxed. So relaxed that they're beginning to feel as though they just won't work properly. You might want to test this sensation, knowing they're becoming too relaxed to open easily... that's right.

And now, as you continue reading, become aware of your breathing. Notice how each breath naturally brings you deeper into this relaxed state. Allow this peaceful feeling to flow through your body like a gentle wave.

Starting with your toes, you can begin to feel them becoming completely relaxed. This soothing wave of relaxation flows upward, melting away any tension as it moves. It flows into your feet, warming and relaxing every muscle. It seeps into your ankles, making them feel heavy and comfortable. This peaceful feeling continues up through your calves, softening them completely. It reaches your knees, dissolving any remaining tension. The relaxation flows through your thighs, and with each word you read, you can feel this relaxation deepening, becoming more profound.

As your eyes follow these words, this wave of relaxation continues its journey, flowing into your hips, releasing any tension stored there. It spreads through your lower back, soothing and relaxing every muscle. The relaxation seeps into your abdomen, and you might notice your breathing becoming even slower, even deeper. This peaceful feeling fills your entire torso, flowing through your chest, releasing any tension there. It spreads across your shoulders, and you might notice them dropping slightly as they relax completely. This wave of tranquility flows down your upper back, releasing any remaining tension.

The relaxation now flows down your arms like warm honey, moving slowly and sweetly. It seeps into your elbows, making them feel heavy and comfortable. It continues along your forearms, dissolving any tension it finds. It flows into your wrists, making them feel loose and relaxed. This peaceful feeling spreads through your hands, and you might notice them becoming warmer as it does. Finally, it reaches your fingertips, and you can feel a pleasant tingling sensation there.

As you continue reading, allow this wave of relaxation to flow upward once more, moving through your neck, releasing any tension it finds there. It seeps into your jaw, and you might notice your teeth separating slightly as those muscles relax. This peaceful feeling spreads across your face, softening every muscle it touches. Finally, it flows throughout your scalp, and you might notice a pleasant heaviness in your head.

Your entire body is now resting in perfect relaxation, and with each word you read, you drift deeper into this peaceful state. You can now begin a countdown in your mind, knowing that each number will take you twice as deep as before.

Begin counting now: One... feeling yourself drifting twice as deep... Two... doubling that relaxation once again... Three... allowing yourself to sink even deeper still...

You have now reached a perfect state of relaxation and receptivity. Your creative mind is open and ready. As you continue reading, each word will deepen this state while awakening your creative powers.

Day 4: Theme Integration & Basic Three-Act Synopsis - Affirmation

My story's theme is emerging clearly now, like a lighthouse beacon cutting through fog. With each breath, this core truth becomes more evident to me.

I now recognize the deeper meaning of my story, the universal truth it explores. This theme resonates with me personally and will resonate with my readers on a profound level.

I see how my characters embody different aspects of this theme—some embracing it, others resisting it, all transformed by it. Their journeys illustrate the theme naturally and powerfully.

The world of my story reflects this theme in its structures, conflicts, and environments. Every element of my setting can be aligned to support and illuminate this central truth.

Symbolic elements appear in my mind's eye—objects, places, weather, colors - all representing aspects of my theme in subtle but meaningful ways. These symbols weave naturally throughout my narrative.

My three-act structure now unfolds with perfect clarity. Act One introduces my world, my characters, and establishes the central conflict with an inciting incident that sets everything in motion.

Act Two expands this world, developing relationships, intensifying challenges, and building toward a powerful midpoint that shifts the trajectory of the story. The stakes continue to rise as my protagonist faces increasingly difficult obstacles.

Act Three brings all elements together in a satisfying climax that resolves the external conflict while completing my protagonist's inner journey. The theme is fully realized through this resolution.

I trust the natural flow of this structure, knowing that my subconscious mind is guiding me toward the perfect arrangement of scenes and sequences. The complete three-act journey is clear to me now.

When I return to full wakefulness, my hand moves effortlessly across the page, capturing this theme and structure in perfect detail. My mind remains open to refinements and inspirations throughout the day.

I am a great writer and I deeply understand the power of theme to unite and elevate my story. I see how theme strengthens character, plot, and setting, creating a cohesive and meaningful narrative. I love writing and I love how I can write effortlessly through the perfect storytelling power of my subconscious mind. Thank you, thank you, thank you.

Day 5: Secondary Characters & World Building

At this stage of the process, you're focusing on developing the supporting cast and constructing the world of your story. Secondary characters are vital to your narrative—they challenge, support, and reflect aspects of your protagonist while adding depth and dimension to your story. Simultaneously, world building creates the environment where your story unfolds, establishing the rules, structures, and atmosphere that shape your characters' experiences.

After the hypnotic meditation process, take time to develop each supporting character with intention, considering how they serve the story and interact with your protagonist. Think about allies who support your hero, mentors who guide them, love interests who challenge them emotionally, and family members who complicate their journey. Then, explore the physical, social, and cultural dimensions of your story world. Consider the locations where scenes will unfold, the power structures that govern your world, the cultural norms that influence behavior, and the technological or historical elements that define the setting. Make sure you write everything down, allowing your intuition to guide you without judgment or censorship. Most importantly, have fun and enjoy watching your story world come alive with rich characters and vivid settings.

Meditative/Hypnotic State

Pre-Reading Hypnotic Suggestion

As you begin to read these words, you'll notice something interesting happening. The very act of reading this script will naturally and effortlessly guide you into a peaceful, relaxed state. You may notice your breathing becoming slower and deeper as you read. Your eyes might begin to feel heavy, and that's perfectly natural. Every word you read will deepen this relaxation. Trust that your subconscious mind will absorb and respond to these suggestions even as you consciously read them. When you're ready, begin reading the induction below.

Base Induction (Self-Guided)

Find a comfortable position where you won't be disturbed. Take a moment to settle in, knowing that simply reading these words begins the process of relaxation.

Take a deep breath now and hold it. As your eyes move across these words, you can begin to feel their weight. Exhale slowly, and as you do, notice how your eyelids are already becoming heavier, more relaxed. So relaxed that they're beginning to feel as though they just won't work properly. You might want to test this sensation, knowing they're becoming too relaxed to open easily... that's right.

And now, as you continue reading, become aware of your breathing. Notice how each breath naturally brings you deeper into this relaxed state. Allow this peaceful feeling to flow through your body like a gentle wave.

Starting with your toes, you can begin to feel them becoming completely relaxed. This soothing wave of relaxation flows upward, melting away any tension as it moves. It flows into your feet, warming and relaxing every muscle. It seeps into your ankles, making them feel heavy and comfortable. This peaceful feeling continues up through your calves, softening them completely. It reaches your knees, dissolving any remaining tension. The relaxation flows through your thighs, and with each word you read, you can feel this relaxation deepening, becoming more profound.

As your eyes follow these words, this wave of relaxation continues its journey, flowing into your hips, releasing any tension stored there. It spreads through your lower back, soothing and relaxing every muscle. The relaxation seeps into your abdomen, and you might notice your breathing becoming even slower, even deeper. This peaceful feeling fills your entire torso, flowing through your chest, releasing any tension there. It spreads across your shoulders, and you might notice them dropping slightly as they relax completely. This wave of tranquility flows down your upper back, releasing any remaining tension.

The relaxation now flows down your arms like warm honey, moving slowly and sweetly. It seeps into your elbows, making them feel heavy and comfortable. It continues along your forearms, dissolving any tension it finds. It flows into your wrists, making them feel loose and relaxed. This peaceful feeling spreads through your hands, and you might notice them becoming warmer as it does. Finally, it reaches your fingertips, and you can feel a pleasant tingling sensation there.

As you continue reading, allow this wave of relaxation to flow upward once more, moving through your neck, releasing any tension it finds there. It seeps into your jaw, and you might notice your teeth separating slightly as those muscles relax. This peaceful feeling spreads across your face, softening every muscle it touches. Finally, it flows throughout your scalp, and you might notice a pleasant heaviness in your head.

Your entire body is now resting in perfect relaxation, and with each word you read, you drift deeper into this peaceful state. You can now begin a countdown in your mind, knowing that each number will take you twice as deep as before.

Begin counting now: One... feeling yourself drifting twice as deep... Two... doubling that relaxation once again... Three... allowing yourself to sink even deeper still...

You have now reached a perfect state of relaxation and receptivity. Your creative mind is open and ready. As you continue reading, each word will deepen this state while awakening your creative powers.

Day 5: Secondary Characters & World Building - Affirmation

My mind now effortlessly brings forth the supporting characters who will populate my story. I see them clearly—their faces, their mannerisms, their unique voices and perspectives.

I understand how each secondary character serves my narrative. Some will challenge my protagonist, others will support and guide them. Each has their own desires, fears, and motivations that make them feel real and three-dimensional.

The allies in my story now come into focus. I see how they complement my protagonist, providing skills, perspectives, or emotional support that my hero needs on their journey. These relationships feel authentic and meaningful.

The mentors in my story emerge with wisdom and purpose. I understand what knowledge or guidance they offer, and how their own backstories inform their relationship with my protagonist. They have their own flaws and complexities.

Any love interests in my story now reveal themselves fully. I see how these relationships create emotional depth and complexity, challenging my protagonist to grow and change. These connections feel genuine and compelling.

The family members in my story now appear with all their complications and contradictions. I understand the history they share with my protagonist and how these bonds shape my hero's choices and reactions throughout the story.

The world of my story now unfolds before me in vivid detail. I can see the physical locations where scenes will take place—the architecture, the natural environment, the atmosphere and mood of each setting.

The social structures of my world are clear to me. I understand the power dynamics at play, who holds authority and why, and how my characters navigate these systems. These structures create natural sources of conflict and tension.

The cultural elements of my world are rich and textured. I see the customs, beliefs, arts, and traditions that shape how people in this world think and behave. These details make my story world feel authentic and lived-in.

The technological level or time period of my world is perfectly clear. I understand what is possible and impossible within this setting, creating natural boundaries and opportunities for my characters and plot.

All these elements—characters and world—weave together seamlessly in my mind. I see how they interact, influence each other, and create a rich, complex environment for my story to unfold.

When I return to full wakefulness, my hand moves effortlessly across the page, capturing these characters and settings in perfect detail. My mind remains open to refinements and inspirations throughout the day.

I am a great writer and I deeply understand how secondary characters and world building enrich and strengthen my narrative. I see how these elements support my theme, advance my plot, and deepen my protagonist's journey.

I love writing and I love how I can write effortlessly through the perfect storytelling power of my subconscious mind. Thank you, thank you, thank you.

Day 6: Research Material Organization & Story Integration

At this stage of the process, you're focusing on organizing all the research you've gathered and integrating it seamlessly into your story. Effective research adds authenticity and depth to your narrative, but it must serve the story rather than overshadow it. Today, you'll compile and organize all your research materials, mapping them to specific elements of your story, identifying any gaps that require further exploration, and creating a reference system that will support you during the writing phase.

After the hypnotic meditation process, take time to gather all your research notes, articles, images, and references. Sort them by topic and relevance, creating categories that align with your story elements—character backgrounds, plot authenticity, setting details, and technical accuracy. Notice where you might need additional information and make note of those areas. Create a simple but effective reference system that will allow you to quickly access the information you need when writing. Remember, research should enrich your story without distracting from the narrative. Write everything down, allowing your intuition to guide you through this organizational process. Most importantly, have fun and enjoy watching your story gain depth and authenticity through well-integrated research.

Meditative/Hypnotic State

Pre-Reading Hypnotic Suggestion

As you begin to read these words, you'll notice something interesting happening. The very act of reading this script will naturally and effortlessly guide you into a peaceful, relaxed state. You may notice your breathing becoming slower and deeper as you read. Your eyes might begin to feel heavy, and that's perfectly natural. Every word you read will deepen this relaxation. Trust that your subconscious mind will absorb and respond to these suggestions even as you consciously read them. When you're ready, begin reading the induction below.

Base Induction (Self-Guided)

Find a comfortable position where you won't be disturbed. Take a moment to settle in, knowing that simply reading these words begins the process of relaxation.

Take a deep breath now and hold it. As your eyes move across these words, you can begin to feel their weight. Exhale slowly, and as you do, notice how your eyelids are already becoming heavier, more relaxed. So relaxed that they're beginning to feel as though they just won't work properly. You might want to test this sensation, knowing they're becoming too relaxed to open easily... that's right.

And now, as you continue reading, become aware of your breathing. Notice how each breath naturally brings you deeper into this relaxed state. Allow this peaceful feeling to flow through your body like a gentle wave.

Starting with your toes, you can begin to feel them becoming completely relaxed. This soothing wave of relaxation flows upward, melting away any tension as it moves. It flows into your feet, warming and relaxing every muscle. It seeps into your ankles, making them feel heavy and comfortable. This peaceful feeling continues up through your calves, softening them completely. It reaches your knees, dissolving any remaining tension. The relaxation flows through your thighs, and with each word you read, you can feel this relaxation deepening, becoming more profound.

As your eyes follow these words, this wave of relaxation continues its journey, flowing into your hips, releasing any tension stored there. It spreads through your lower back, soothing and relaxing every muscle. The relaxation seeps into your abdomen, and you might notice your breathing becoming even slower, even deeper. This peaceful feeling fills your entire torso, flowing through your chest, releasing any tension there. It spreads across your shoulders, and you might notice them dropping slightly as they relax completely. This wave of tranquility flows down your upper back, releasing any remaining tension.

The relaxation now flows down your arms like warm honey, moving slowly and sweetly. It seeps into your elbows, making them feel heavy and comfortable. It continues along your forearms, dissolving any tension it finds. It flows into your wrists, making them feel loose and relaxed. This peaceful feeling spreads through your hands, and you might notice them becoming warmer as it does. Finally, it reaches your fingertips, and you can feel a pleasant tingling sensation there.

As you continue reading, allow this wave of relaxation to flow upward once more, moving through your neck, releasing any tension it finds there. It seeps into your jaw, and you might notice your teeth separating slightly as those muscles relax. This peaceful feeling spreads across your face, softening every muscle it touches. Finally, it flows throughout your scalp, and you might notice a pleasant heaviness in your head.

Your entire body is now resting in perfect relaxation, and with each word you read, you drift deeper into this peaceful state. You can now begin a countdown in your mind, knowing that each number will take you twice as deep as before.

Begin counting now: One... feeling yourself drifting twice as deep... Two... doubling that relaxation once again... Three... allowing yourself to sink even deeper still...

You have now reached a perfect state of relaxation and receptivity. Your creative mind is open and ready. As you continue reading, each word will deepen this state while awakening your creative powers.

Day 6: Research Material Organization & Story Integration - Affirmation

My mind now effortlessly organizes all the research I've gathered for my story. I see clearly how each piece of information contributes to the authenticity and richness of my narrative.

I easily categorize my research by topic and relevance. Each category aligns perfectly with specific elements of my story—character backgrounds, plot points, setting details, and technical aspects. This organization feels natural and intuitive.

For my characters, I now integrate relevant research that enriches their backgrounds, professions, skills, and challenges. I understand exactly what information each character needs to feel authentic and three-dimensional. These details flow seamlessly into their development.

For my plot, I identify the research that ensures authenticity and believability. I see where specialized knowledge supports key events, conflicts, and resolutions. These elements strengthen my story's foundation and enhance its impact.

For my settings, I incorporate research that brings locations to life with vivid, accurate details. I understand the geography, architecture, atmosphere, and cultural nuances of each place in my story. These elements create immersive, believable environments.

For technical aspects of my story, I organize specialized information that adds credibility and depth. I see how professional procedures, specialized tools, or specific terminologies enhance realism without overwhelming the narrative.

I now clearly recognize any gaps in my research. My mind intuitively identifies areas where additional information would strengthen my story. I make note of these areas for focused exploration later.

I create a simple, effective reference system for my research materials. This system allows me to access exactly what I need during the writing process, supporting my creativity without interrupting my flow.

I understand the perfect balance between research and storytelling. My research serves the narrative, adding depth and authenticity without distracting from the emotional heart of my story.

My subconscious mind continues to make connections between my research and story elements even when I'm not actively working. These connections deepen and enrich my narrative in surprising and satisfying ways.

When I return to full wakefulness, my hand moves effortlessly across the page, mapping research to story elements with perfect clarity. My mind remains receptive to new insights and connections throughout the day.

I am a great writer and I deeply understand how well-integrated research enhances the power of my storytelling. I see how these elements support my theme, advance my plot, and deepen my readers' engagement.

I love writing and I love how I can write effortlessly through the perfect storytelling power of my subconscious mind. Thank you, thank you, thank you.

Day 7: Expanded Three-Act Synopsis

At this stage of the process, you are focusing on expanding your basic synopsis into a detailed narrative. You will develop each act's events in greater detail, adding character arc progressions, enhancing thematic elements, and deepening conflict descriptions. This expanded version serves as the foundation for your beat sheet development. Using your 3 act synopsis, develop each act in richer detail. Remember you are expanding the 3 act synopsis at this point so think of this stage of the process as telling yourself the story all over again, but adding more details this time. Again, remember, the more you tell yourself the story the more you discover about it, the more you discover about it, the more you understand it and the more you understand it the better you'll write it. Remember to write down everything that comes to mind, even if you find yourself exploring a bit too much and out of the structure of the story and other ideas that pop into your mind, and need make a note of them in the ideas section in the back of the workbook or use index cards or even a separate document in your word processor. Its very important to remember to make sure you label each idea and where it might belong in the story so you don't forget what you wanted to do with it. Use a highlighter if necessary. It doesn't matter if the idea pertains to something that may require research later. Just write it down and you'll have a chance to explore it later. Write everything down. You may or may not use the idea but if you don't write it down you'll never know. Plus one idea you write down may lead you into another one, and then to another and so on and so forth. Write it all down. And please, enjoy the process. Remember what Carl Jung said: "The creative mind plays with the object it loves!"

Pre-Reading Hypnotic Suggestion

As you begin to read these words, you'll notice something interesting happening. The very act of reading this script will naturally and effortlessly guide you into a peaceful, relaxed state. You may notice your breathing becoming slower and deeper as you read. Your eyes might begin to feel heavy, and that's perfectly natural. Every word you read will deepen this relaxation. Trust that your subconscious mind will absorb and respond to these suggestions even as you consciously read them. When you're ready, begin reading the induction below.

Base Induction (Self-Guided)

Find a comfortable position where you won't be disturbed. Take a moment to settle in, knowing that simply reading these words begins the process of relaxation.

Take a deep breath now and hold it. As your eyes move across these words, you can begin to feel their weight. Exhale slowly, and as you do, notice how your eyelids are already becoming heavier, more relaxed. So relaxed that they're beginning to feel as though they just won't work properly. You might want to test this sensation, knowing they're becoming too relaxed to open easily... that's right.

And now, as you continue reading, become aware of your breathing. Notice how each breath naturally brings you deeper into this relaxed state. Allow this peaceful feeling to flow through your body like a gentle wave.

Starting with your toes, you can begin to feel them becoming completely relaxed. This soothing wave of relaxation flows upward, melting away any tension as it moves. It flows into your feet, warming and relaxing every muscle. It seeps into your ankles, making them feel heavy and comfortable. This peaceful feeling continues up through your calves, softening them completely. It reaches your knees, dissolving any remaining tension. The relaxation flows through your thighs, and with each word you read, you can feel this relaxation deepening, becoming more profound.

As your eyes follow these words, this wave of relaxation continues its journey, flowing into your hips, releasing any tension stored there. It spreads through your lower back, soothing and relaxing every muscle. The relaxation seeps into your abdomen, and you might notice your breathing becoming even slower, even deeper. This peaceful feeling fills your entire torso, flowing through your chest, releasing any tension there. It spreads across your shoulders, and you might notice them dropping slightly as they relax completely. This wave of tranquility flows down your upper back, releasing any remaining tension.

The relaxation now flows down your arms like warm honey, moving slowly and sweetly. It seeps into your elbows, making them feel heavy and comfortable. It continues along your forearms, dissolving any tension it finds. It flows into your wrists, making them feel loose and relaxed. This peaceful feeling spreads through your hands, and you might notice them becoming warmer as it does. Finally, it reaches your fingertips, and you can feel a pleasant tingling sensation there.

As you continue reading, allow this wave of relaxation to flow upward once more, moving through your neck, releasing any tension it finds there. It seeps into your jaw, and you might notice your teeth separating slightly as those muscles relax. This peaceful feeling spreads across your face, softening every muscle it touches. Finally, it flows throughout your scalp, and you might notice a pleasant heaviness in your head.

Your entire body is now resting in perfect relaxation, and with each word you read, you drift deeper into this peaceful state. You can now begin a countdown in your mind, knowing that each number will take you twice as deep as before.

Begin counting now:

One... feeling yourself drifting twice as deep...

Two... doubling that relaxation once again...

Three... allowing yourself to sink even deeper still...

You have now reached a perfect state of relaxation and receptivity. Your creative mind is open and ready. As you continue reading, each word will deepen this state while awakening your creative powers.

Day 7: Expanded Three-Act Synopsis – Affirmation

My story's complete arc is clear in my mind, from the opening scene to the final moment. I understand how each part connects to create a meaningful whole.

Details emerge naturally as I expand each act, adding depth and richness to my story. I see clearly how to develop each important moment.

The hero's journey through each act is clear and compelling. I understand exactly how he (she) changes and grows through each phase of the story.

The escalation of conflict and tension through the acts feels natural and effective. Each act builds upon the last, creating increasing momentum.

The emotional impact of my story builds steadily, reaching its peak at exactly the right moment.

I am a great writer and I understand story structure perfectly. I can expand my three act structure effortlessly.

I love writing and I love how I can write effortlessly through the perfect storytelling power of my subconscious mind. Thank you, thank you, thank you.

Day 8: Basic Beat Sheet Development

At this stage of the process, you are focusing on converting your narrative synopsis into the twelve universal story beats. You will map out your setup, inciting incident, internal wrestling, welcome to the jungle, subplot introduction, trials and tribulations, midpoint, complications, crisis, critical choice, welcome to the end, and theme triumphant beats. Using your extended 3 act synopsis, develop each act in richer detail by exploring each beat. Don't worry about getting overly detailed at this stage, just break down each act into their respective beats and explore what would happen in each beat. Write down everything that comes to mind,you'll refine this stuff later in the detailed beat sheet. Now, if you find yourself exploring a bit too much and out of the structure of the story and other ideas pop into your mind, make a note of them in the ideas section in the back of the workbook or use index cards or even a separate document in your word processor. Its very important to remember to make sure you label each idea and where it might belong in the story so you don't forget what you wanted to do with it. Use a highlighter if necessary. Write everything down. You may or may not use the idea but if you don't write it down you'll never know. Plus one idea you write down may lead you into another one, and then to another and so on and so forth. Write it all down. And please, enjoy the process. Remember what Carl Jung said: "The creative mind plays with the object it loves!"

Pre-Reading Hypnotic Suggestion

As you begin to read these words, you'll notice something interesting happening. The very act of reading this script will naturally and effortlessly guide you into a peaceful, relaxed state. You may notice your breathing becoming slower and deeper as you read. Your eyes might begin to feel heavy, and that's perfectly natural. Every word you read will deepen this relaxation. Trust that your subconscious mind will absorb and respond to these suggestions even as you consciously read them. When you're ready, begin reading the induction below.

Base Induction (Self-Guided)

Find a comfortable position where you won't be disturbed. Take a moment to settle in, knowing that simply reading these words begins the process of relaxation.

Take a deep breath now and hold it. As your eyes move across these words, you can begin to feel their weight. Exhale slowly, and as you do, notice how your eyelids are already becoming heavier, more relaxed. So relaxed that they're beginning to feel as though they just won't work properly. You might want to test this sensation, knowing they're becoming too relaxed to open easily... that's right.

And now, as you continue reading, become aware of your breathing. Notice how each breath naturally brings you deeper into this relaxed state. Allow this peaceful feeling to flow through your body like a gentle wave.

Starting with your toes, you can begin to feel them becoming completely relaxed. This soothing wave of relaxation flows upward, melting away any tension as it moves. It flows into your feet, warming and relaxing every muscle. It seeps into your ankles, making them feel heavy and comfortable. This peaceful feeling continues up through your calves, softening them completely. It reaches your knees, dissolving any remaining tension. The relaxation flows through your thighs, and with each word you read, you can feel this relaxation deepening, becoming more profound.

As your eyes follow these words, this wave of relaxation continues its journey, flowing into your hips, releasing any tension stored there. It spreads through your lower back, soothing and relaxing every muscle. The relaxation seeps into your abdomen, and you might notice your breathing becoming even slower, even deeper. This peaceful feeling fills your entire torso, flowing through your chest, releasing any tension there. It spreads across your shoulders, and you might notice them dropping slightly as they relax completely. This wave of tranquility flows down your upper back, releasing any remaining tension.

The relaxation now flows down your arms like warm honey, moving slowly and sweetly. It seeps into your elbows, making them feel heavy and comfortable. It continues along your forearms, dissolving any tension it finds. It flows into your wrists, making them feel loose and relaxed. This peaceful feeling spreads through your hands, and you might notice them becoming warmer as it does. Finally, it reaches your fingertips, and you can feel a pleasant tingling sensation there.

As you continue reading, allow this wave of relaxation to flow upward once more, moving through your neck, releasing any tension it finds there. It seeps into your jaw, and you might notice your teeth separating slightly as those muscles relax. This peaceful feeling spreads across your face, softening every muscle it touches. Finally, it flows throughout your scalp, and you might notice a pleasant heaviness in your head.

Your entire body is now resting in perfect relaxation, and with each word you read, you drift deeper into this peaceful state. You can now begin a countdown in your mind, knowing that each number will take you twice as deep as before.

Begin counting now:

One... feeling yourself drifting twice as deep...

Two... doubling that relaxation once again...

Three... allowing yourself to sink even deeper still...

You have now reached a perfect state of relaxation and receptivity. Your creative mind is open and ready. As you continue reading, each word will deepen this state while awakening your creative powers.

Day 8: Basic Beat Sheet – Affirmation

Each beat of my story is clear and distinct in my mind. I understand the purpose and impact of each one.

I see how these beats work together to create a powerful narrative rhythm. The flow from one beat to the next feels natural and compelling.

Each beat serves multiple purposes, advancing the plot while developing characters and theme. I understand how to make each beat count.

The emotional journey through these beats is clear and effective. I know how to make each beat resonate with my readers.

My confidence in structuring these beats grows stronger with each scene I plan.

I am a great writer and understand how the universal story beats function and easily use them to make my story flow better from act to act.

I love writing and I love how I can write effortlessly through the perfect storytelling power of my subconscious mind. Thank you, thank you, thank you.

Day 9: Detailed Beat Sheet

At this stage of the process, you are focusing on expanding each beat with complete scene requirements. You will develop character moments, theme integration points, emotional progressions, detailed plot points, conflict escalations, setting descriptions, and key dialogue concepts for each beat. At this stage of the process, you are refining your beat sheet, expanding it with deeper and more layered details. By now, you have told the story to yourself several times (remember *repetition is hypnotic*) and have looked at it from different internal angles. The story and it's theme should already make sense. You should feel it's structure getting tighter and more powerful with each step of the process. In this particular stage you are just refining it even more through a micro narrative form.

Pre-Reading Hypnotic Suggestion

As you begin to read these words, you'll notice something interesting happening. The very act of reading this script will naturally and effortlessly guide you into a peaceful, relaxed state. You may notice your breathing becoming slower and deeper as you read. Your eyes might begin to feel heavy, and that's perfectly natural. Every word you read will deepen this relaxation. Trust that your subconscious mind will absorb and respond to these suggestions even as you consciously read them. When you're ready, begin reading the induction below.

Base Induction (Self-Guided)

Find a comfortable position where you won't be disturbed. Take a moment to settle in, knowing that simply reading these words begins the process of relaxation.

Take a deep breath now and hold it. As your eyes move across these words, you can begin to feel their weight. Exhale slowly, and as you do, notice how your eyelids are already becoming heavier, more relaxed. So relaxed that they're beginning to feel as though they just won't work properly. You might want to test this sensation, knowing they're becoming too relaxed to open easily... that's right.

And now, as you continue reading, become aware of your breathing. Notice how each breath naturally brings you deeper into this relaxed state. Allow this peaceful feeling to flow through your body like a gentle wave.

Starting with your toes, you can begin to feel them becoming completely relaxed. This soothing wave of relaxation flows upward, melting away any tension as it moves. It flows into your feet, warming and relaxing every muscle. It seeps into your ankles, making them feel heavy and comfortable. This peaceful feeling continues up through your calves, softening them completely. It reaches your knees, dissolving any remaining tension. The relaxation flows through your thighs, and with each word you read, you can feel this relaxation deepening, becoming more profound.

As your eyes follow these words, this wave of relaxation continues its journey, flowing into your hips, releasing any tension stored there. It spreads through your lower back, soothing and relaxing every muscle. The relaxation seeps into your abdomen, and you might notice your breathing becoming even slower, even deeper. This peaceful feeling fills your entire torso, flowing through your chest, releasing any tension there. It spreads across your shoulders, and you might notice them dropping slightly as they relax completely. This wave of tranquility flows down your upper back, releasing any remaining tension.

The relaxation now flows down your arms like warm honey, moving slowly and sweetly. It seeps into your elbows, making them feel heavy and comfortable. It continues along your forearms, dissolving any tension it finds. It flows into your wrists, making them feel loose and relaxed. This peaceful feeling spreads through your hands, and you might notice them becoming warmer as it does. Finally, it reaches your fingertips, and you can feel a pleasant tingling sensation there.

As you continue reading, allow this wave of relaxation to flow upward once more, moving through your neck, releasing any tension it finds there. It seeps into your jaw, and you might notice your teeth separating slightly as those muscles relax. This peaceful feeling spreads across your face, softening every muscle it touches. Finally, it flows throughout your scalp, and you might notice a pleasant heaviness in your head.

Your entire body is now resting in perfect relaxation, and with each word you read, you drift deeper into this peaceful state. You can now begin a countdown in your mind, knowing that each number will take you twice as deep as before.

Begin counting now:

One... feeling yourself drifting twice as deep...

Two... doubling that relaxation once again...

Three... allowing yourself to sink even deeper still...

You have now reached a perfect state of relaxation and receptivity. Your creative mind is open and ready. As you continue reading, each word will deepen this state while awakening your creative powers.

Day 9: Detailed Beat Sheet - Affirmation

The details within each beat emerge clearly in my mind. I see exactly what needs to happen in each moment of my story.

Character development opportunities within each beat are clear to me. I know how to use these moments to deepen my characters.

Thematic elements naturally weave through each beat, strengthening my story's meaning. I recognize these opportunities and use them effectively to maximize the impact of my story.

The emotional progression through each beat feels natural and powerful. I understand how to make each moment count.

My creativity flows freely as me as the power of my subconscious mind helps me develop these beats, effortlessly, bringing fresh insights and powerful moments to my story.

I am a great writer and understand story structure perfectly. I know how to use the universal story beats to organize my story to flow beautifully from beginning to end. I understand how to expand my beat sheet effortlessly through the power of my subconscious mind.

I love writing and I love how I can write effortlessly through the perfect storytelling power of my subconscious mind. Thank you, thank you, thank you.

Day 10: Basic 30 Chapter Outline

At this stage of the process, you are focusing on mapping your beats to a 30-chapter structure. You will establish basic scene allocation, initial pacing structure, primary subplot tracking, key character moments, core theme developments, and basic transitions between chapters. Remember, you are refining your story even more by getting all of the information you've written thus far and getting even more refined and detailed through the micro process of doing a basic 30 chapter outline. In my experience (as an avid reader and life-long writer), I've noticed that 30 chapters are just about "right" when it comes to story structure (regardless of the novel's length). Some authors stick strictly to one scene per chapter, others have multiple scenes per chapters and others have a combination of single scene chapters and multi-scene chapters. Some authors have varied their approach with each novel they write. Others (the majority) don't have a set structure for their novels and just allow their chapters to emerge naturally as the novel is created. All of these are fine approaches and there isn't a "right" way to structure your chapters, because the reality is that chapters are arbitrary divisions. However, I personally believe that it is easier to have a pre-determined chapter division because it gives us one less thing to think about and allows for there to be a "uniform" structure to each novel without it feeling formulaic. How exactly does this work? Well, for starters, for this to work correctly, we would need a set chapter division system to work with and this system must only create the chapter divisions based off each act and beat structure and not confine us to a set amount of scenes per chapter, so that our novel can self develop within this structure and still have an organic feel. Why? because the scenes will dictate the narrative flow. This means that each chapter is free to have any amount of scenes within that act and beat structure. Usually this manifests anywhere from 1 to 3 scenes per chapter. You could potentially have more scenes if needed, but the "sweet spot" is usually around that amount of scenes. I have created this structure for you and all you need to do is insert your novel's structure into it. Enjoy the process!

Pre-Reading Hypnotic Suggestion

As you begin to read these words, you'll notice something interesting happening. The very act of reading this script will naturally and effortlessly guide you into a peaceful, relaxed state. You may notice your breathing becoming slower and deeper as you read. Your eyes might begin to feel heavy, and that's perfectly natural. Every word you read will deepen this relaxation. Trust that your subconscious mind will absorb and respond to these suggestions even as you consciously read them. When you're ready, begin reading the induction below.

Base Induction (Self-Guided)

Find a comfortable position where you won't be disturbed. Take a moment to settle in, knowing that simply reading these words begins the process of relaxation.

Take a deep breath now and hold it. As your eyes move across these words, you can begin to feel their weight. Exhale slowly, and as you do, notice how your eyelids are already becoming heavier, more relaxed. So relaxed that they're beginning to feel as though they just won't work properly. You might want to test this sensation, knowing they're becoming too relaxed to open easily... that's right.

And now, as you continue reading, become aware of your breathing. Notice how each breath naturally brings you deeper into this relaxed state. Allow this peaceful feeling to flow through your body like a gentle wave.

Starting with your toes, you can begin to feel them becoming completely relaxed. This soothing wave of relaxation flows upward, melting away any tension as it moves. It flows into your feet, warming and relaxing every muscle. It seeps into your ankles, making them feel heavy and comfortable. This peaceful feeling continues up through your calves, softening them completely. It reaches your knees, dissolving any remaining tension. The relaxation flows through your thighs, and with each word you read, you can feel this relaxation deepening, becoming more profound.

As your eyes follow these words, this wave of relaxation continues its journey, flowing into your hips, releasing any tension stored there. It spreads through your lower back, soothing and relaxing every muscle. The relaxation seeps into your abdomen, and you might notice your breathing becoming even slower, even deeper. This peaceful feeling fills your entire torso, flowing through your chest, releasing any tension there. It spreads across your shoulders, and you might notice them dropping slightly as they relax completely. This wave of tranquility flows down your upper back, releasing any remaining tension.

The relaxation now flows down your arms like warm honey, moving slowly and sweetly. It seeps into your elbows, making them feel heavy and comfortable. It continues along your forearms, dissolving any tension it finds. It flows into your wrists, making them feel loose and relaxed. This peaceful feeling spreads through your hands, and you might notice them becoming warmer as it does. Finally, it reaches your fingertips, and you can feel a pleasant tingling sensation there.

As you continue reading, allow this wave of relaxation to flow upward once more, moving through your neck, releasing any tension it finds there. It seeps into your jaw, and you might notice your teeth separating slightly as those muscles relax. This peaceful feeling spreads across your face, softening every muscle it touches. Finally, it flows throughout your scalp, and you might notice a pleasant heaviness in your head.

Your entire body is now resting in perfect relaxation, and with each word you read, you drift deeper into this peaceful state. You can now begin a countdown in your mind, knowing that each number will take you twice as deep as before.

Begin counting now:

One... feeling yourself drifting twice as deep...

Two... doubling that relaxation once again...

Three... allowing yourself to sink even deeper still...

You have now reached a perfect state of relaxation and receptivity. Your creative mind is open and ready. As you continue reading, each word will deepen this state while awakening your creative powers.

Day 10: Chapter Outline - Affirmation

My chapter structure is clear and organized in my mind. I see exactly how to break my story into powerful, effective chapters.

Each chapter's purpose is distinct and meaningful. I understand what needs to happen in each one and why.The flow from one chapter to the next feels natural and compelling. I know how to end each chapter in a way that pulls readers forward.

My confidence in planning these chapters grows stronger. I trust the power of my subconscious mind to guide my to what belongs in each chapter. The overall rhythm of my chapters creates a perfect pace for my story.

I am a great writer and understand story structure perfectly. Through unwavering trust in the power of my subconscious mind I know intuitively how to use chapters to organize my story to flow beautifully from beginning to end. I am a great writer and I understand how to make great chapters for my story. They are clear, organized and each chapter perfectly moves the story forward. I love writing and I love how I can write effortlessly through the perfect storytelling power of my subconscious mind. Thank you, thank you, thank you.

Day 11: Detailed Chapter-by-Chapter Outline (Scene by Scene Breakdown) -Part 1

At this stage of the process you are refining your story by refining your chapter by chapter outline at the scene level. You are getting more detailed in each act, beat, scene and chapter. For each chapter, you will develop scene-by-scene breakdowns, opening hooks, character objectives, specific conflicts, detailed settings, key dialogue points, scene outcomes, emotional impacts, thematic elements, and transition details.

Pre-Reading Hypnotic Suggestion

As you begin to read these words, you'll notice something interesting happening. The very act of reading this script will naturally and effortlessly guide you into a peaceful, relaxed state. You may notice your breathing becoming slower and deeper as you read. Your eyes might begin to feel heavy, and that's perfectly natural. Every word you read will deepen this relaxation. Trust that your subconscious mind will absorb and respond to these suggestions even as you consciously read them. When you're ready, begin reading the induction below.

Base Induction (Self-Guided)

Find a comfortable position where you won't be disturbed. Take a moment to settle in, knowing that simply reading these words begins the process of relaxation.

Take a deep breath now and hold it. As your eyes move across these words, you can begin to feel their weight. Exhale slowly, and as you do, notice how your eyelids are already becoming heavier, more relaxed. So relaxed that they're beginning to feel as though they just won't work properly. You might want to test this sensation, knowing they're becoming too relaxed to open easily... that's right.

And now, as you continue reading, become aware of your breathing. Notice how each breath naturally brings you deeper into this relaxed state. Allow this peaceful feeling to flow through your body like a gentle wave.

Starting with your toes, you can begin to feel them becoming completely relaxed. This soothing wave of relaxation flows upward, melting away any tension as it moves. It flows into your feet, warming and relaxing every muscle. It seeps into your ankles, making them feel heavy and comfortable. This peaceful feeling continues up through your calves, softening them completely. It reaches your knees, dissolving any remaining tension. The relaxation flows through your thighs, and with each word you read, you can feel this relaxation deepening, becoming more profound.

As your eyes follow these words, this wave of relaxation continues its journey, flowing into your hips, releasing any tension stored there. It spreads through your lower back, soothing and relaxing every muscle. The relaxation seeps into your abdomen, and you might notice your breathing becoming even slower, even deeper. This peaceful feeling fills your entire torso, flowing through your chest, releasing any tension there. It spreads across your shoulders, and you might notice them dropping slightly as they relax completely. This wave of tranquility flows down your upper back, releasing any remaining tension.

The relaxation now flows down your arms like warm honey, moving slowly and sweetly. It seeps into your elbows, making them feel heavy and comfortable. It continues along your forearms, dissolving any tension it finds. It flows into your wrists, making them feel loose and relaxed. This peaceful feeling spreads through your hands, and you might notice them becoming warmer as it does. Finally, it reaches your fingertips, and you can feel a pleasant tingling sensation there.

As you continue reading, allow this wave of relaxation to flow upward once more, moving through your neck, releasing any tension it finds there. It seeps into your jaw, and you might notice your teeth separating slightly as those muscles relax. This peaceful feeling spreads across your face, softening every muscle it touches. Finally, it flows throughout your scalp, and you might notice a pleasant heaviness in your head.

Your entire body is now resting in perfect relaxation, and with each word you read, you drift deeper into this peaceful state. You can now begin a countdown in your mind, knowing that each number will take you twice as deep as before.

Begin counting now:

One... feeling yourself drifting twice as deep...

Two... doubling that relaxation once again...

Three... allowing yourself to sink even deeper still...

You have now reached a perfect state of relaxation and receptivity. Your creative mind is open and ready. As you continue reading, each word will deepen this state while awakening your creative powers.

Day 11: Detailed Chapter Outline (Scene by Scene Breakdown) Part 1 - Affirmation

Every scene within my chapters is clear and vivid in my mind. I see exactly how each scene should play out.

I perfectly understand how to use scene elements. I can construct excellent dialogue, descriptions, and actions to create maximum impact in my story. Each scene serves multiple purposes in my story.

The emotional journey through each chapter is clear and effective. I know how to make readers feel exactly what I want them to feel.

The transitions between scenes feel natural and smooth. Each scene flows perfectly into the next.

My confidence in crafting powerful chapters grows stronger with each scene I plan.

I am a great writer and I understand how to make great scenes for my story. They are clear, organized and each scene perfectly moves the story forward. I love writing scenes, and I love to see them integrate into each other effortlessly through the perfect storytelling power of my subconscious mind.

Day 12: Detailed Chapter Outline (Scene by Scene Breakdown) - Part 2

At this stage of the process, you're completing the detailed outline of your novel by focusing on the second half of your story (chapters 16-30). This is where your narrative reaches its climax and resolution, bringing together all the character development, plot threads, and thematic elements you've been building. Today, you'll create a comprehensive scene-by-scene breakdown for each chapter, ensuring a powerful and satisfying conclusion to your story.

After the hypnotic meditation process, take time to detail each scene in chapters 16-30. For every scene, consider the opening hook that draws readers in, the specific objectives each character is pursuing, the conflicts that create tension, and the detailed settings that bring your world to life. Note key dialogue points that reveal character and advance the plot, the specific outcomes of each scene, and the emotional impacts these outcomes have on your characters and readers. Ensure your theme continues to develop, reaching its fullest expression in these final chapters. Pay special attention to transitions between scenes, creating a smooth flow that carries readers through to the end. Make sure you write everything down, allowing your intuition to guide you through this process without judgment. Most importantly, have fun and enjoy watching your complete story take final shape.

Meditative/Hypnotic State

Pre-Reading Hypnotic Suggestion

As you begin to read these words, you'll notice something interesting happening. The very act of reading this script will naturally and effortlessly guide you into a peaceful, relaxed state. You may notice your breathing becoming slower and deeper as you read. Your eyes might begin to feel heavy, and that's perfectly natural. Every word you read will deepen this relaxation. Trust that your subconscious mind will absorb and respond to these suggestions even as you consciously read them. When you're ready, begin reading the induction below.

Base Induction (Self-Guided)

Find a comfortable position where you won't be disturbed. Take a moment to settle in, knowing that simply reading these words begins the process of relaxation.

Take a deep breath now and hold it. As your eyes move across these words, you can begin to feel their weight. Exhale slowly, and as you do, notice how your eyelids are already becoming heavier, more relaxed. So relaxed that they're beginning to feel as though they just won't work properly. You might want to test this sensation, knowing they're becoming too relaxed to open easily... that's right.

And now, as you continue reading, become aware of your breathing. Notice how each breath naturally brings you deeper into this relaxed state. Allow this peaceful feeling to flow through your body like a gentle wave.

Starting with your toes, you can begin to feel them becoming completely relaxed. This soothing wave of relaxation flows upward, melting away any tension as it moves. It flows into your feet, warming and relaxing every muscle. It seeps into your ankles, making them feel heavy and comfortable. This peaceful feeling continues up through your calves, softening them completely. It reaches your knees, dissolving any remaining tension. The relaxation flows through your thighs, and with each word you read, you can feel this relaxation deepening, becoming more profound.

As your eyes follow these words, this wave of relaxation continues its journey, flowing into your hips, releasing any tension stored there. It spreads through your lower back, soothing and relaxing every muscle. The relaxation seeps into your abdomen, and you might notice your breathing becoming even slower, even deeper. This peaceful feeling fills your entire torso, flowing through your chest, releasing any tension there. It spreads across your shoulders, and you might notice them dropping slightly as they relax completely. This wave of tranquility flows down your upper back, releasing any remaining tension.

The relaxation now flows down your arms like warm honey, moving slowly and sweetly. It seeps into your elbows, making them feel heavy and comfortable. It continues along your forearms, dissolving any tension it finds. It flows into your wrists, making them feel loose and relaxed. This peaceful feeling spreads through your hands, and you might notice them becoming warmer as it does. Finally, it reaches your fingertips, and you can feel a pleasant tingling sensation there.

As you continue reading, allow this wave of relaxation to flow upward once more, moving through your neck, releasing any tension it finds there. It seeps into your jaw, and you might notice your teeth separating slightly as those muscles relax. This peaceful feeling spreads across your face, softening every muscle it touches. Finally, it flows throughout your scalp, and you might notice a pleasant heaviness in your head.

Your entire body is now resting in perfect relaxation, and with each word you read, you drift deeper into this peaceful state. You can now begin a countdown in your mind, knowing that each number will take you twice as deep as before.

Begin counting now: One... feeling yourself drifting twice as deep... Two... doubling that relaxation once again... Three... allowing yourself to sink even deeper still...

You have now reached a perfect state of relaxation and receptivity. Your creative mind is open and ready. As you continue reading, each word will deepen this state while awakening your creative powers.

Day 12: Detailed Chapter Outline (Scene by Scene Breakdown) Part 2 - Affirmation

My mind now effortlessly reveals the complete second half of my story. I see chapters sixteen through thirty with perfect clarity, each scene unfolding naturally and powerfully before me.

I see the opening hook for each scene—that compelling moment that immediately engages the reader's attention and pulls them deeper into the story.

These hooks flow naturally from what has come before while creating new intrigue and forward momentum.

The character objectives in each scene are crystal clear to me. I understand exactly what my protagonist and other characters want in every moment, how these desires conflict with one another, and how they drive the action forward with increasing urgency.

The specific conflicts in each scene now emerge with perfect clarity. I see how tensions escalate, complications multiply, and stakes rise as my story moves toward its climax. These conflicts feel necessary and inevitable, growing organically from my characters and their situations.

The detailed settings for each scene appear vividly in my mind's eye. I see the physical spaces where action unfolds, the sensory details that bring these places to life, and how these environments reflect and influence the emotional tone of each scene.

Key dialogue points now reveal themselves for each scene. I hear the distinctive voices of my characters, the subtext beneath their words, the revelations and deceptions that advance my plot and deepen characterization. This dialogue feels natural yet purposeful.

The specific outcome of each scene is perfectly clear to me. I understand how each scene changes the situation, reveals new information, shifts relationships, or advances my protagonist toward their ultimate goal or transformation. Each outcome creates a clear cause-and-effect chain.

The emotional impact of each scene resonates deeply within me. I feel how these moments affect my characters and will affect my readers, creating the emotional journey that is the heart of my story. These emotional beats build with perfect pacing toward my story's climax.

The thematic elements in these final chapters express my story's meaning with increasing power and clarity. I see how every scene contributes to the development of my theme, leading to its fullest expression in the story's resolution.

The transitions between scenes flow smoothly in my mind. I see how to move from one scene to the next with purpose and elegance, maintaining momentum while giving readers the necessary information and emotional beats to stay engaged.

As I approach my story's climax, I see how all plot threads, character arcs, and thematic elements converge with maximum impact. This moment feels both surprising and inevitable, the perfect culmination of everything that has come before.

The resolution of my story now unfolds with satisfying completeness. I see how my protagonist's journey concludes, how conflicts are resolved, and how my theme reaches its final, most powerful expression. This ending feels both complete and resonant.

When I return to full wakefulness, my hand moves effortlessly across the page, capturing this detailed chapter outline with perfect clarity. My mind remains open to refinements and inspirations throughout the day.

I am a great writer and I deeply understand how to create a powerful, engaging story structure. I see how these final chapters bring my narrative to a satisfying conclusion that will resonate with readers long after they finish my book.

I love writing and I love how I can write effortlessly through the perfect storytelling power of my subconscious mind. Thank you, thank you, thank you.

Post-Outline Writing Process

1. Master Outline Assembly & Writing Plan

Review and adjust detailed outline

- Perform a complete read-through of your entire 12-day outline
- Check for narrative flow and pacing issues across all chapters
- Verify that character arcs progress logically and emotionally

- Ensure all plot threads are properly introduced, developed, and resolved
- Identify any remaining plot holes or logical inconsistencies
- Make final adjustments to scene sequence and chapter divisions
- Strengthen weak transitions between scenes and chapters

Create comprehensive character sheets

- Develop detailed profiles for all major and supporting characters
- Include physical descriptions, personality traits, speech patterns, and mannerisms
- Document character backgrounds, motivations, and emotional wounds
- Map each character's transformation arc throughout the story
- Note key relationships between characters and how they evolve
- Include character-specific references (images, inspiration notes)
- Create quick-reference sheets for maintaining consistency during writing

Compile research references

- Organize all research materials by topic (historical, technical, geographical, etc.)
- Create summary sheets for frequently referenced information
- Verify critical facts that impact plot or character decisions
- Note areas where creative license is being taken versus factual accuracy
- Include visual references for important scenes, objects, or locations
- Create glossaries for specialized terminology
- Document sources for future reference or acknowledgments

Organize setting bible

- Develop detailed descriptions of all major locations
- Create maps of physical spaces when relevant
- Document cultural, social, and political aspects of your story world
- Establish rules for any fantastical or speculative elements
- Include sensory details specific to each location
- Note how settings change over time or impact characters

- Create visual references for consistent description

Establish writing schedule

- *Daily word count goals*
    - Set realistic targets based on your writing speed and available time
    - Consider varying goals for workdays versus weekend/free days
    - Build in buffer days for unexpected interruptions
    - Start with modest goals and increase as momentum builds
- *Chapter completion timeline*
    - Map specific chapters to calendar dates
    - Account for varying chapter lengths and complexity
    - Schedule more time for pivotal or challenging scenes
    - Build in review days between major story sections
- *Progress tracking method*
    - Select a word count tracker (spreadsheet, app, or physical chart)
    - Determine how to measure progress beyond raw word count
    - Establish check-in points for quality assessment
    - Create visual representation of progress for motivation

Create master folder containing

- *All development documents*
    - Organize all 12 days of outline materials
    - Include initial brainstorming and concept documents
    - Store beat sheets and synopsis versions
    - Maintain earlier draft versions for reference
- *Research materials*
    - Organize by topic and relevance to story elements
    - Include source information for all materials
    - Create easy navigation system with table of contents
    - Include both digital and physical reference locations
- *Character profiles*

    - Store detailed character sheets in order of importance
    - Group related characters together (family members, colleagues)
    - Include visual references and inspiration notes
    - Document character relationships and conflicts
- *World-building details*
    - Organize by location, culture, or chronology as appropriate
    - Include maps, diagrams, and visual references
    - Document rules of the world (magical systems, technology)
    - Store historical timeline and background events
- *Chapter outlines*
    - Maintain scene-by-scene breakdowns in sequential order
    - Include cross-references to character arcs and theme developments
    - Note research elements needed for each chapter
    - Document emotional beats and key moments
- *Writing timeline*
    - Create calendar view of entire writing schedule
    - Mark milestone dates and deadlines
    - Note planned breaks or reduced-output periods
    - Include reward system for meeting goals

2. First Draft (30-60 days)

Follow chapter outline

- Refer to your detailed outline before beginning each chapter
- Review character objectives and conflicts for each scene
- Focus on capturing the essential emotional and plot elements
- Allow for organic development while maintaining core structure
- Make brief notes on any significant deviations for outline adjustment
- Refer to research materials only as needed during writing
- Use your outline as a roadmap, not a constraint

2,000-3,000 words per chapter

- Aim for consistency in chapter length for reading rhythm
- Allow for natural variations based on scene importance
- Focus on scene completeness rather than exact word count
- Monitor overall manuscript length against genre expectations
- Adjust pacing if chapters consistently run too short or long
- Use chapter word count as a general guideline, not a strict rule
- Prioritize effective storytelling over meeting word count targets

One chapter per day goal

- Begin each day by reviewing your outline for the current chapter
- Visualize the chapter's key scenes before writing
- Create a distraction-free environment for focused writing
- Break chapter into manageable scene blocks if needed
- Write continuously to maintain flow and momentum
- Complete each chapter before evaluating or editing
- Celebrate completion of each chapter as a significant milestone

Maintain momentum over perfection

- Resist the urge to edit while writing first draft
- Accept that first drafts are inherently imperfect
- Use placeholders (TK, XXX) for missing research or details
- Keep writing even through difficult scenes
- Address critical plot problems but defer minor issues
- Focus on forward progress every day
- Remember that all elements can be refined during revision

3. Revision Process

Initial read-through

- Complete entire manuscript reading without making changes
- Take notes on overall impressions and major issues

- Identify structural problems, character inconsistencies, and plot holes
- Note pacing issues and emotional high/low points
- Mark sections that need expansion or reduction
- Create a revision plan based on prioritized issues
- Allow time between completion and read-through for perspective

Content editing

- Address major plot issues and narrative inconsistencies
- Ensure character motivations are clear and consistent
- Strengthen scenes that lack tension or purpose
- Develop underdeveloped relationships or conflicts
- Add missing sensory and emotional details
- Cut redundant scenes or combine similar ones
- Ensure satisfying payoffs for all setups

Structure verification

- Confirm effective three-act structure implementation
- Verify proper placement of major plot points
- Check scene and chapter transitions for smoothness
- Ensure appropriate pacing throughout the manuscript
- Confirm that tension builds appropriately toward climax
- Verify that all subplots are properly resolved
- Ensure balanced distribution of action and reflection

Character arc review

- Verify consistent character voices and behaviors
- Ensure protagonist shows clear growth and transformation
- Check that character decisions align with established motivations
- Verify that relationships develop naturally
- Ensure antagonist has depth and clear motivation
- Confirm that supporting characters serve clear purposes
- Strengthen character moments that feel flat or predictable

Theme consistency check

- Identify all expressions of your core theme
- Ensure theme develops progressively throughout the story
- Verify that theme is expressed through action, not just dialogue
- Check for contradictory thematic messages
- Strengthen symbolic elements that support theme
- Ensure theme reaches satisfying completion
- Avoid heavy-handed thematic statements

Line editing

- Improve sentence structure and flow
- Eliminate redundant words and phrases
- Replace vague language with specific details
- Strengthen dialogue and dialogue tags
- Improve paragraph transitions
- Ensure consistent point of view
- Vary sentence length and structure for rhythm
- Convert telling to showing where appropriate

Final polish

- Check grammar, spelling, and punctuation
- Verify consistent formatting throughout
- Ensure proper use of specialized terminology
- Check for overused words and phrases
- Verify consistent use of names and terms
- Read dialogue aloud to ensure naturalness
- Implement feedback from beta readers if available

4. Final Review

Complete read-through

- Read entire manuscript out loud if possible

- Focus on reader experience rather than technical aspects
- Note any remaining issues that affect enjoyment or clarity
- Verify emotional impact of key scenes
- Check overall pacing and reading experience
- Ensure opening hooks and chapter endings are strong
- Confirm satisfying resolution of all story elements

Last adjustments

- Make final minor corrections
- Address any lingering inconsistencies
- Strengthen any remaining weak points
- Ensure all placeholder text has been replaced
- Verify all research elements are accurately incorporated
- Make final word choice improvements
- Trust your instincts on final creative decisions

Formatting check

- Ensure consistent chapter headings and breaks
- Verify proper paragraph formatting and indentation
- Check spacing between scenes
- Ensure consistent use of italics, bold, and other formatting
- Format according to industry standards or submission guidelines
- Check page numbering and header/footer formatting
- Verify proper formatting of any special elements (letters, texts, etc.)

Submission preparation

- Prepare title page according to industry standards
- Write compelling synopsis if required for submission
- Develop author bio appropriate for submission purpose
- Research appropriate agents or publishers for your genre
- Prepare submission packages according to specific guidelines
- Create tracking system for submissions

- Prepare elevator pitch and marketing materials
- Celebrate completing your novel!

Self-publishing preparation

- Select appropriate self-publishing platforms (Amazon KDP, IngramSpark, Draft2Digital, etc.)
- Format manuscript for both e-book and print specifications
- Commission professional cover design or create your own using design tools
- Obtain ISBN numbers if not using platform-provided options
- Write compelling book description for online retailers
- Select appropriate categories and keywords for maximum discoverability
- Determine pricing strategy across different formats and platforms
- Create author accounts on all chosen publishing platforms
- Prepare marketing assets (author website, social media graphics, email newsletter)
- Plan launch strategy with pre-orders, announcements, and promotional activities
- Research advertising options on retail platforms and social media
- Consider audiobook production options if applicable
- Develop a post-launch marketing calendar for sustained visibility
- Create a system for collecting and responding to reader reviews

Going Deeper: Accessing Your Creative Subconscious Through Hypnosis

As writers, we often sense there are stories within us waiting to be told – narratives that our deeper mind holds but our conscious awareness hasn't yet grasped. Hypnosis offers a powerful gateway to access these hidden stories.

The beauty of hypnosis lies in its multifaceted nature. In the creative writing context, we can understand it as:

- A doorway to altered consciousness where your inner storyteller can speak freely, uninhibited by your conscious mind's tendency to edit and judge. This state allows characters, plots, and entire worlds to emerge organically from your deeper imagination.
- A state of heightened creative suggestibility where your mind becomes more receptive to images, sensations, and narrative possibilities that might otherwise remain buried beneath everyday thoughts.
- A bridge across the gap between your analytical writing mind and your intuitive storytelling mind, allowing them to work in harmony rather than opposition.
- A sanctuary where your imagination can fully embrace the reality of your story world, bringing forth authentic details and emotional truths that resonate with readers.

At its core, hypnosis for writers is simply a state of creative receptivity. In this receptive state – which can involve physical relaxation but doesn't require it – you can:

- Discover character backgrounds and motivations that surprise even you
- Uncover plot twists that emerge from your deeper storytelling instincts
- Access emotional truths that give your writing authenticity and power
- Plant seeds for story ideas that develop naturally over time

- Amplify and sustain your creative flow state

The techniques we'll explore in this section are designed specifically for writers, embedding various hypnotic tools like imagery, indirect suggestion, and creative presupposition into exercises that will help you access and channel your subconscious storytelling wisdom.

While we won't delve into the technical aspects of hypnotic practice, rest assured that the guided meditations and exercises provided here incorporate proven approaches to accessing your creative subconscious mind. These tools will help you tap into the stories that are uniquely yours to tell—the ones your deeper self is eager to share with the world.

The Four States of Mind in the Creative Writing Process

As writers, understanding the different states of consciousness can help us access various levels of creativity and storytelling ability. These states are characterized by different brainwave patterns, each offering unique benefits to our writing process.

Beta State (14-40 Hz): The Active Writer's Mind

- This is our normal waking state—where we edit, revise, and critically analyze our work
- Here we organize plot structures, plan character arcs, and make logical decisions about our story
- While excellent for technical editing and structural planning, this state can sometimes inhibit raw creativity due to its analytical nature
- Many writers experience writer's block in this state due to overcritical thinking and self-judgment

Alpha State (8-13 Hz): The Creative Flow State

- This is where initial creative (subconscious) writing often flows most naturally
- Writers enter this state when they're "in the zone" but still aware of their

surroundings

- Perfect for:
    - Free writing and brainstorming sessions
    - Developing character backgrounds
    - Discovering plot possibilities
    - Subconscious Outline Development
    - First draft writing where inner critic needs to stay quiet
- Many writers naturally slip into this state during their long writing sessions or when they're deeply absorbed in creating their first draft

Theta State (4-7 Hz): The Deep Creative Well

- This is where many breakthrough story ideas originate
- Writers often access this state just before falling asleep or upon waking
- Characterized by:
    - Deep access to subconscious imagery
    - Unexpected character insights
    - Surprising plot twists that seem to "write themselves"
    - Profound thematic connections
- Keep a notebook by your bed—many writers report their best ideas come from this state

Delta State (0.5-3 Hz): The Storyteller's Rest

- The deepest state, usually experienced during sleep
- While not actively writing in this state, it's crucial for:
    - Processing story problems
    - Integrating new ideas
    - Allowing your subconscious to work on plot solutions
    - Creative regeneration and renewal

Understanding these states can help you intentionally access different levels of creativity in your writing process. The key is learning to move between these states deliberately—using beta for editing and planning, alpha for flowing creative work, theta for accessing deep creative insights, and respecting delta as the necessary regenerative phase that supports all other creative states.

As you practice accessing these different states, you'll develop the ability to call upon the most appropriate state for whatever aspect of the writing process you're engaged in, whether that's generating new ideas, writing first drafts, or polishing final work.

The 12-Day Program and the Four States of Mind

The 12-day novel outlining program is designed to take advantage of all four states of mind, strategically using each state for optimal creative output and story development. Here's how each day aligns with these mental states:

Days 1-3: Emphasizing Theta and Alpha States

Day 1: Subconscious Exploration

- **Primary State**: Theta
- **Secondary State**: Alpha
- Uses deep meditative states (Theta) for accessing subconscious material
- Transitions to Alpha for recording and free association writing
- Delta state preparation occurs the night before through intention setting

Day 2: Initial Research & Concept Development

- **Primary State**: Alpha
- **Secondary State**: Beta
- Uses Alpha state for intuitive connections and creative insights
- Shifts to Beta for organizing research materials
- Theta state moments allowed for unexpected connections

Day 3: Character Development - Protagonist & Antagonist

- **Primary State**: Theta
- **Secondary State**: Alpha
- Deep character insights accessed through Theta
- Character details recorded in Alpha state
- Beta state used for organizing character profiles

Days 4-6: Balancing Alpha and Beta States

Day 4: Theme Integration & Basic Three-Act Synopsis

- **Primary State**: Alpha
- **Secondary State**: Beta
- Theme development flows in Alpha
- Theta state accessed for deeper thematic insights
- Story structure organization in Beta
- Synopsis development combines Alpha creativity with Beta structure

Day 5: Secondary Characters & World Building

- **Primary State**: Alpha
- **Secondary State**: Beta
- Creative character and world-building flows in Alpha
- World rules and systems organized in Beta
- Theta state accessed for deeper world insights

Day 6: Research Material Organization & Story Integration

- **Primary State**: Beta
- **Secondary State**: Alpha
- Research organization primarily in Beta
- Creative connections between research and story in Alpha
- Theta moments for integrative insights

Days 7-9: Utilizing Beta with Alpha Support

Day 7: Expanded Three-Act Synopsis

- **Primary State**: Alpha
- **Secondary State**: Beta
- Story expansion flows in Alpha
- Structure maintained in Beta
- Theta accessed for deeper plot insights

Day 8: Basic Beat Sheet Development

- **Primary State**: Beta
- **Secondary State**: Alpha
- Beat organization in Beta
- Creative elements flow in Alpha
- Theta moments for beat insights

Day 9: Detailed Beat Sheet

- **Primary State**: Beta
- **Secondary State**: Alpha
- Detail organization in Beta
- Creative elaboration in Alpha
- Theta state for scene depth

Days 10-12: Maximizing Beta State

Day 10: Basic Chapter Outline

- **Primary State**: Beta
- **Secondary State**: Alpha
- Structure work in Beta
- Creative flow in Alpha for scene ideas

- Beat breakdown organization in Beta
- Theta accessed for chapter insights

Day 11: Detailed Chapter Outline (Part 1)

- **Primary State**: Beta
- **Secondary State**: Alpha
- Detailed organization in Beta
- Scene flow in Alpha
- Theta moments for deep scene work

Day 12: Detailed Chapter Outline (Part 2)

- **Primary State**: Beta
- **Secondary State**: Alpha
- Continued detailed organization in Beta
- Scene flow in Alpha
- Theta moments for completing deep scene work

Delta State Integration Throughout

- Each night during the program, the Delta state processes the day's work
- Morning insights are recorded before beginning each day's tasks
- Delta state regeneration supports continued creativity
- Program encourages adequate sleep for optimal creative function

Daily Brain State Management

To maximize the effectiveness of this program:

1. Begin each day with Theta state meditation
2. Move into Alpha state for creative work
3. Shift to Beta state for organization
4. Return to Alpha for creative elaboration

5. End with Beta for finalizing the day's work
6. Allow Delta state processing during sleep

Brain State Transitions

The program includes techniques for smoothly transitioning between states:

- Meditation techniques for accessing Theta
- Writing prompts for engaging Alpha
- Organization templates for Beta work
- Sleep preparation for Delta

By understanding and intentionally working with these different brain states throughout the 12-day process, you can:

- Access deeper creativity
- Maintain organizational clarity
- Balance structure and inspiration
- Achieve optimal creative flow
- Integrate conscious and subconscious insights
- Create a more complete and cohesive outline

This brain state integration helps ensure that the final outline benefits from both deep creative insights and careful structural planning.

The Complete Guide to Subconscious Story Development and Systematic Outlining

Forging a Creative Partnership with Your Subconscious Mind

As novelists, our greatest stories often emerge not from conscious effort alone, but from the mysterious depths of our subconscious mind. This comprehensive guide introduces a powerful 12-day system for accessing, nurturing, and sustaining a productive relationship with your creative subconscious—transforming the way you outline novels forever.

The techniques outlined here will help you tap into the wellspring of creativity that exists beneath your conscious awareness, allowing your story outlines to develop with greater authenticity, emotional resonance, and structural integrity. By establishing a consistent practice of subconscious outlining, you'll discover that your best ideas, most compelling characters, and most satisfying plot twists have been waiting for you all along—in the deeper levels of your storytelling mind.

This system draws from the principles detailed in my book, *A Hypnotic Realization of Oneness: 40 Weeks of Hypnotic Meditation for Spiritual Awakening*, adapting the four fundamental principles of hypnosis specifically for the novel outlining process.

Understanding the Foundation: The Four Principles of Subconscious Outlining

To access your deeper storytelling mind for efficient outlining, there are four key principles that create the optimal state for creative flow. These principles, drawn from my book *A Hypnotic Realization of Oneness: 40 Weeks of Hypnotic Meditation for Spiritual Awakening*, form the cornerstone of the 12-day subconscious outlining system. I've adapted the fundamental A.B.C.D. principles of hypnosis specifically for novel outlining:

1. Attention: Deep Absorption in Your Story World

Your journey into subconscious writing begins with the focused absorption of your attention into your narrative landscape. This is not merely concentration, but a total immersion in your fictional world:

- **Complete Immersion**: Allow yourself to mentally and emotionally step into your story world, experiencing it as a living, breathing place. This means seeing your settings in vivid detail, hearing the ambient sounds, feeling the textures and temperatures, and sensing the emotional atmosphere of each scene.

- **Sensory Engagement**: Activate all your senses as you write. Don't just see your character walking through a forest—feel the crunch of leaves underfoot, smell the damp earth, hear the distant call of birds, taste the crisp air. This multisensory approach strengthens your connection to the story world.
- **Present Moment Awareness**: Release thoughts about your daily life, worries about your writing career, or concerns about reader reception. Be fully present with your characters and their journey, allowing the "real world" to fade into the background during your writing sessions.
- **Sustained Focus**: Develop the ability to maintain this immersive state for increasingly longer periods. With practice, you'll find yourself able to sustain deep story absorption for your entire writing session, creating a continuous flow of authentic material.

2. Bypass the Inner Critic: Redirecting Your Analytical Mind

The analytical mind serves an essential purpose during the outlining process, but it must work in partnership with—not opposition to—your creative subconscious. Learning to temporarily redirect this critical faculty opens the channel to your creative depths while ultimately strengthening your outline:

- **Recognizing Critical Limitations**: Become aware of how your inner critic can restrict your outline's potential—through premature judgment of ideas, excessive concern about market trends, or forcing characters into predetermined paths. Recognize these limitations so you can access broader creative possibilities.
- **Creating an "Outline Sanctuary"**: Establish a mental understanding that the 12-day outlining process is a sacred space where ideas can emerge freely before being organized. Your analytical mind will have its crucial role in structuring these insights, but first, allow the raw material to surface without censorship. This sanctuary mindset creates a psychological container where your creative subconscious feels safe to

reveal the deeper elements of your story, knowing they will be respectfully integrated into your outline structure rather than dismissed through premature judgment.

- **Physical Relaxation Techniques**: Tension in the body often restricts creative flow. Consciously relaxing your shoulders, jaw, and forehead sends signals to your brain that it's safe to access deeper creative wisdom. Deep, slow breathing further enhances the state of relaxed alertness needed for effective outlining. Each deliberate breath helps transition your mind from analytical planning to receptive awareness, creating the optimal neurological state for accessing your story's blueprint.
- **Permission to Explore Possibilities**: Actively give yourself permission to consider multiple story directions, character motivations, and plot twists—even those that initially seem impractical. This exploration paradoxically leads to stronger, more cohesive outlines as you discover unexpected connections and structures.
- **Timed Subconscious Sessions**: Setting a timer for focused hypnotic exploration (15-30 minutes) before each day's outlining work creates a reservoir of creative material. This preparatory immersion enriches your subsequent analytical organization, creating a harmonious partnership between creative generation and structural development.

3. Connect with the Creative Subconscious: Accessing Your Deeper Narrative Wisdom for Outlining

Once you've absorbed your attention and redirected your inner critic, you can establish a direct line of communication with your creative subconscious—the source of your most powerful stories:

- **Receptive Character Exploration**: Develop the ability to "listen" to your characters within the hypnotic state before documenting their profiles in your outline. This receptivity reveals motivations, background details, and character arcs that feel authentic precisely because they emerge from deeper awareness rather than conscious invention.

- **Following Structural Intuition**: Pay attention to subtle intuitive nudges about your story's fundamental structure. These might manifest as sudden insights about plot sequences, unexpected connections between scenes, or a sense that certain elements belong in a different act. These intuitive signals often reveal the most effective framework for your novel.
- **Harvesting Synchronicity**: Notice meaningful coincidences in your research or daily life that connect to your developing outline. Your subconscious mind is constantly making connections that your conscious mind might miss—document these synchronistic elements in your outline where they can serve as powerful narrative anchors.
- **Integrating Emergent Elements with Traditional Structure**: The 12-day outlining system provides the essential framework, while your subconscious offers the unique content that fills this framework. This partnership creates outlines that are both structurally sound and creatively distinctive.
- **Character Independence Within Structure**: For each character profile in your outline, cultivate the feeling that your characters have their own agency while fitting within your overall narrative plan. This balanced approach creates characters who feel authentic while serving your story's structural needs.

4. Direct Experience: Channeling the Flow State into Your Outline

The culmination of the previous principles manifests as direct experience—the moment when you're no longer constructing an outline but receiving it from your deeper storytelling mind:

- **Outlining from Within**: Position your awareness inside the story world as you develop each day's outline components. This immersive perspective allows you to document scene sequences, character developments, and plot points with vivid clarity because you're experiencing them rather than abstractly planning them.

- **Emotional Blueprint Mapping**: Allow yourself to genuinely feel the emotional progression of your novel as you outline its structure. When you experience emotional responses while mapping your three-act structure or detailing your beat sheet, you're creating an outline with built-in emotional intelligence that will guide your eventual drafting.
- **Structured Revelation**: The 12-day outlining system provides the framework, while your subconscious supplies the content. This partnership often manifests as surprising elements—character decisions, plot twists, or thematic connections—that emerge within your structured outline work.
- **Productive Flow States**: The outlining process becomes remarkably efficient when you achieve this state of direct experience. What might normally take weeks of analytical planning often crystallizes in days because you're accessing your story's blueprint directly from your creative source.
- **Effortless Outline Development**: At its peak, direct experience manifests as outlining that seems to complete itself. Story elements arrange themselves naturally into the appropriate days of the 12-day system, scenes intuitively connect to create meaningful sequences, and the overall narrative structure emerges with organic coherence while fulfilling the technical requirements of effective storytelling.

The Mechanics of the 12-Day Subconscious Outlining Process

Understanding how these four principles interact creates a foundation for the 12-day outlining practice. Here's how the subconscious outlining process works in practice:

The Continuous Flow of Creative Energy

When you engage in deep creative writing, the four principles work together in a natural progression:

1. Absorption of Attention in Story

- **Intentional Initiation**: The process begins the moment you sit down with the deliberate intention to connect with your story. This intention acts as a signal to your subconscious that it's time to create.
- **Environmental Cues**: Your dedicated writing space, time, and ritual all serve as powerful triggers that help your mind transition into creative mode. Over time, these external cues become increasingly effective at initiating the creative state.
- **Progressive Deepening**: As your session continues, your absorption naturally intensifies. What might begin as conscious effort to focus gradually transforms into effortless immersion where the story world becomes more real than your physical surroundings.
- **Foundational Presence**: This attention forms the foundation upon which all other aspects of the process rest. Without this focused absorption, the remaining principles cannot fully activate.

2. Bypassing the Inner Critic

- **Early Signs of Creative Relaxation**: As your analytical mind begins to step aside, you'll notice subtle shifts—your breathing becomes deeper, your posture more relaxed, and your thoughts less evaluative and more exploratory.
- **The Quiet Mind Phenomenon**: The constant background chatter of self-doubt gradually subsides, replaced by a quieter mental space where story elements can emerge more clearly. This isn't about silencing thought entirely, but rather shifting from analytical to intuitive thinking.
- **Physical Manifestations**: Your body provides valuable feedback about

this transition—tension in your shoulders or jaw often signals that your critical mind is still active, while a sense of ease and flow indicates successful bypassing.

- **Sustaining the Bypass**: Maintaining this state requires gentle vigilance. If you notice critical thoughts returning (questioning your word choices, doubting your direction), simply acknowledge them without judgment and return your focus to your story immersion.

3. Connecting with Your Creative Subconscious for Outline Development

- **The Bridge of Structured Imagery**: Each day of the 12-day outlining system becomes a specialized bridge to your creative subconscious. As you enter the hypnotic state before working on that day's specific outline component (character profiles, beat sheets, etc.), you access precisely the creative material needed for that element.
- **Emotional Blueprint Recognition**: Your subconscious communicates the emotional architecture of your story through visceral responses. When you feel unexpectedly moved while mapping a particular plot point or character arc in your outline, your subconscious is revealing crucial emotional landmarks that should be documented in your outline.
- **Integrated Associations**: The creative subconscious works through association rather than linear logic. When seemingly unrelated elements surface during your hypnotic preparation, document them in your outline —they often create powerful narrative connections that strengthen your novel's underlying structure.
- **Character Blueprint Development**: One of the clearest signs of effective subconscious outlining is when your character profiles develop with surprising depth and consistency. This "character blueprint clarity" indicates you're accessing deeper layers of your creative mind where authentic character psychology can be mapped into your outline with precision.

4. Direct Outline Experience

- **The Emergence of Structured Flow**: All previous elements culminate in the structured flow state—a unique consciousness where you access your story's complete blueprint. In this state, outline development feels less like analytical planning and more like documenting a story architecture that already exists in your subconscious mind.
- **Markers of Direct Outline Experience**: You know you've achieved direct outline experience when:
    - You lose track of time during your daily outlining sessions
    - You find yourself emotionally responding to elements within your outline structure
    - Your outline development significantly accelerates without added effort
    - The 12-day system fills with material that feels discovered rather than invented
    - Your outline documents have a holographic quality, where each part somehow contains and reflects the whole
- **The Blueprint Perception**: At its deepest level, direct outline experience creates a temporary shift in your perception—you see your novel's complete structure with remarkable clarity. This perceptual shift produces outlines with exceptional coherence, originality, and narrative power.

The Power of the 12-Day System

The Subconscious Novelist's outlining process isn't just a technique—it's a transformative system that creates exceptional novel blueprints:

- **Progressive Skill Development**: Each day of the 12-day system builds upon previous work while developing specific outlining skills—from character development to beat sheets to scene sequencing. This systematic progression trains your subconscious to provide increasingly structured creative material.

- **Deepening Relationship**: The daily hypnotic practice within the 12-day system builds a working relationship with your creative subconscious specifically focused on narrative architecture. Like any relationship, consistency and respect are key—your subconscious responds by revealing more of your story's blueprint with each session.
- **Day-Specific Activation**: Each day's hypnotic preparation activates precisely the creative resources needed for that day's outlining task. This targeted activation becomes increasingly refined as you progress through the system, eventually allowing you to access specific creative domains (character insight, plot development, thematic connections) at will.
- **Comprehensive Blueprint Development**: The 12-day structure ensures you develop every essential element of your novel's architecture—from character psychology to scene structure to thematic resonance. This comprehensive approach prevents the plot holes and character inconsistencies that often plague less structured approaches.
- **Integration of Intuition and Structure**: By combining hypnotic subconscious activation with systematic outlining, you create the perfect partnership between creative intuition and narrative craft. Your outlines benefit from both the unexpected insights of the subconscious and the proven structural elements of effective storytelling.

Establishing Your 12-Day Outlining Sanctuary

The physical and temporal environment you create profoundly impacts your ability to access your creative subconscious during each day of your outlining process. Here's how to establish the ideal conditions for your 12-day journey:

1. Scheduling Your Sacred Writing Time

The consistency of when you write is often more important than the duration of your sessions:

- **Biorhythmic Alignment**: Identify your natural creative peaks throughout the day. Some writers access their subconscious most easily during the hypnagogic state just after waking, while others find their creative depth late at night when the analytical mind is fatigued. Experiment to discover your optimal window.

- **Consistency Creates Conditioning**: When you write at the same time consistently, your brain begins to prepare for creative immersion even before you begin. This neurological anticipation dramatically enhances your ability to access your creative subconscious quickly.
- **Protected Boundaries**: Treat this scheduled time as non-negotiable—a sacred appointment with your creative self. When you honor these boundaries consistently, both your conscious and subconscious mind recognize the seriousness of your commitment.
- **Productive Frequency**: For most writers, multiple shorter sessions (30-60 minutes) spaced throughout the week are more effective for subconscious engagement than infrequent marathon sessions. Consider starting with 3-5 sessions weekly rather than fewer, longer blocks.
- **Transition Buffers**: Schedule 5-10 minutes before and after your writing session for mental transition. The pre-writing buffer allows you to disengage from daily concerns, while the post-writing buffer gives you time to document any additional insights before fully returning to regular activities.

2. Creating Your Physical Writing Space

Your environment sends powerful signals to your subconscious about the nature of the activity you're engaging in:

- **Dedicated Territory**: Designate a specific physical location used exclusively (or primarily) for creative writing. This space becomes associated with subconscious activation through repeated use. If space limitations prevent a dedicated room, even a particular chair or corner can serve this purpose.

- **Sensory Consistency**: Consider creating consistent sensory elements that signal "story time" to your subconscious, while not absolutely necessary, it can be of benefit:
    - A specific scent (candle, essential oil, or incense)
    - Background sounds (instrumental music, nature sounds, or white noise)
    - Tactile elements (a special notebook, keyboard, or writing implement) *The Subconscious Novelist's Workbook
    - Visual cues (particular lighting, inspirational images, or a clear workspace)
- **Energetic Cleansing**: Before each session, take a moment to "clear" your space of lingering energies from other activities. This can be as simple as opening a window briefly, rearranging your materials, or taking three conscious breaths with the intention of creating a fresh creative field.
- **Threshold Objects**: Many writers benefit from "threshold objects"—items that symbolize the transition into creative space. This might be a special candle you light, a stone you hold, or even putting on a particular item of clothing that signals to your subconscious that you are crossing into story territory.
- **Digital Sanctuary**: If writing digitally, consider creating a dedicated user account or software setup exclusively for creative writing—free from email notifications, social media, or other work documents that might pull you out of your creative depth.

3. Protecting Your Creative Bubble

External intrusions can instantly shatter your connection to your creative subconscious. Implement these protective measures:

- **Communication Protocols**: Clearly communicate your writing schedule to family members, housemates, or colleagues. Consider creating a visual signal (like a door sign or colored light) that indicates you are in deep creative work and should not be disturbed except for genuine emergencies.

- **Digital Fortress**: Implement rigorous digital boundaries during your writing time:
  - Enable airplane mode on your phone
  - Use website blocking software to prevent internet distractions
  - Disable notifications on all devices
  - Consider using a dedicated writing device without internet capability
- **Expectation Management**: Train those around you to respect your creative time by consistently enforcing boundaries. Gentle but firm reinforcement of these boundaries eventually creates a protective culture around your writing practice.
- **Transitional Rituals**: Develop pre-writing rituals that signal the shift from mundane consciousness to creative consciousness. This might involve a brief meditation, a particular sequence of stretches, or even a specific beverage that you only consume during writing time.
- **Energy Protection**: I know from experience of coaching writers that some find benefit in visualizing a protective energetic bubble around themselves before writing—an imaginary barrier that keeps external concerns at bay while containing the creative energy they generate. I've taught this technique to quite a few of my students and they all say they won't sit down to write without doing this first.

4. Establishing Physical Comfort

Physical discomfort creates a constant drain on your creative energy and prevents deep subconscious access:

- **Ergonomic Optimization**: Invest in proper ergonomic support—a chair that maintains healthy posture, a desk at the appropriate height, and proper wrist support if typing. Physical alignment facilitates energetic alignment.

- **Dynamic Balance**: Find the perfect balance between comfort and alertness. Too comfortable (like writing in bed) often leads to drowsiness, while uncomfortable positions create distracting tension. Aim for a supported, aligned posture that allows both relaxation and awareness.
- **Movement Integration**: Consider incorporating gentle movement options into your writing space—a standing desk option, a balance ball chair, or simply room to stand and stretch periodically. Brief movement actually enhances creative flow rather than disrupting it.
- **Temperature Regulation**: Maintain a slightly cool environment that keeps you alert without causing discomfort. Many writers find that a temperature around 68-70°F (20-21°C) provides the optimal balance between comfort and mental clarity.
- **Hydration and Nourishment**: Keep water easily accessible during writing sessions, and consider light, energy-sustaining snacks for longer sessions. Avoid heavy meals before writing, as they can redirect blood flow from brain to digestive system.

The Daily Subconscious Outlining Process: Step-by-Step

With your outlining sanctuary established, you're ready to engage in the daily subconscious activation process that powers each day of your 12-day outlining system. While the specific focus changes each day (from character development to beat sheets to chapter breakdowns), the core process for accessing your creative subconscious remains consistent:

1. Initial Settling (5-7 minutes)

Begin by creating the optimal conditions for creative flow:

- **Postural Preparation**: Sit comfortably in your writing space with your spine naturally aligned. Place both feet flat on the floor to ground your energy, and rest your hands gently in your lap or on your writing surface.

- **Breath Calibration**: Take several deep, natural breaths—inhaling through your nose and exhaling through slightly parted lips. With each exhale, imagine releasing tension and analytical thinking. Notice how each breath naturally deepens, creating a rhythm that soothes your nervous system.
- **Conscious Decompression**: Allow the concerns of your day to gradually fall away. If persistent thoughts arise, acknowledge them without judgment and imagine placing them in a container outside your creative space, where they'll wait safely until your writing session concludes.
- **Inner Sanctuary Activation**: Direct your awareness inward, toward the space where your stories live. This might feel like turning your attention to the center of your chest, the area behind your forehead, or whatever internal location feels like home to your creative essence.
- **Story Field Engagement**: Gently bring your awareness to your current project. Without forcing specific details, simply hold the general feeling of your story world in your awareness, allowing it to gradually come into clearer focus as your session progresses.

2. Entering the Creative State (3-5 minutes)

Deepen your connection to your creative subconscious through these techniques:

- **Focal Point Concentration**: Choose a single point to rest your gaze upon—this might be an object on your desk, a mark on the wall, or even the blank page before you. This external focus paradoxically facilitates internal focus by giving your conscious mind a simple task.
- **Visual Softening**: Allow your gaze to gradually soften, letting the edges of your focal point blur slightly. This visual relaxation mirrors the mental relaxation required for creative access—a softening of the boundaries between conscious and subconscious awareness.
- **Inward Turning**: As your gaze softens, allow your awareness to turn

gently inward. Rather than actively seeking story elements, adopt a receptive attitude—creating space for your creative subconscious to communicate with you.

- **Progressive Relaxation**: Notice any remaining tension in your body—particularly in your jaw, shoulders, and hands (common storage points for creative tension). With each breath, invite these areas to release and relax, creating an unobstructed channel for creative energy.
- **Story Immersion**: Begin to feel yourself sinking into your story world as if it were a living environment you could actually enter. Notice the sensory details that emerge—the quality of light, ambient sounds, temperature, smells. Allow these details to become increasingly vivid without forcing or straining.

3. Deepening the Creative Connection (For Each Day of Your 12-Day System)

Each day of your 12-day outlining system focuses on a specific component of your novel's architecture. Here's how to access the precise creative material needed for each day:

Day 1-4: Foundational Exploration (10-20 minutes)

Perfect for the early days focusing on subconscious exploration, initial research, character development, and thematic integration:

- **Maintained Hypnotic State**: Remain in your relaxed, receptive state with eyes closed or softly focused. Your body remains still while your awareness explores the foundational elements of your story world.
- **Framework-Specific Reception**: For each day's focus (exploring story seeds, gathering research needs, developing character profiles, identifying themes), allow your subconscious to reveal precisely what you need for that day's outlining task.
- **Directed Exploration**: Allow your awareness to be drawn to whatever

aspects of the day's focus feel most energetically alive. If working on character profiles (Day 3), your awareness naturally gravitates toward character insights; if focusing on thematic elements (Day 4), thematic connections become prominent.

- **Outline-Ready Recording**: As insights emerge, mentally organize them into the specific outline component you're developing that day. Trust that your subconscious is revealing exactly what belongs in today's section of your developing outline.
- **Structural Integration**: Note how each element that emerges naturally connects to your overall novel structure. Even in these early exploratory days, your subconscious begins organizing material into a coherent narrative architecture.

Days 5-8: Structural Development (10-20 minutes)

Ideal for the middle phase focusing on secondary characters, research integration, expanded synopsis, and beat sheet development:

- **Framework-Aligned Receptivity**: Maintain your hypnotic state while introducing gentle prompts that direct your subconscious toward the specific structural elements needed for today's outlining task.
- **Structure-Focused Prompts**: Offer yourself creative suggestions framed around that day's structural focus. For example:
    - Day 5: "My supporting characters' connections to the protagonist are becoming clear..."
    - Day 6: "The perfect integration points for my research are revealing themselves..."
    - Day 7: "The expanded narrative flow across all three acts is emerging now..."
    - Day 8: "The twelve fundamental beats of my story are arranging themselves naturally..."
- **Structural Receptivity**: After offering a prompt, create mental space for

your subconscious to respond with structural insights. Avoid premature organization; allow 30-60 seconds of receptive silence for each prompt.

- **Architecture-Oriented Awareness**: Notice how insights emerge not as random fragments but as elements that already have natural positions within your story's structure. Your subconscious inherently understands narrative architecture when properly accessed.
- **Progressive Structural Building**: As one structural element becomes clear, allow your awareness to naturally progress to the next related element, building a coherent framework for that day's specific outline component.

Days 9-12: Detailed Implementation (10-20 minutes)

Essential for the final phase focusing on detailed beat sheets, chapter outlines, and scene-by-scene breakdowns:

- **Precision-Focused Trance State**: Maintain your hypnotic state with heightened attention to narrative detail. As your outline becomes increasingly specific, your subconscious reveals correspondingly precise creative material.
- **Scene-Level Intention**: Before exploring each scene or chapter, set a clear structural intention—“I'm revealing the perfect opening hook for Chapter 3” or “I'm discovering the ideal midpoint reversal.” Frame your intention as structural revelation rather than invention.
- **Detail-Rich Emergence**: As you focus on specific scenes or chapters, allow your subconscious to reveal multiple layers simultaneously—character motivations, setting details, dialogue concepts, and emotional beats that belong in that precise narrative moment.
- **Blueprint Integration**: As you document these detailed elements, maintain awareness of how each scene contributes to your overall story architecture. Your subconscious naturally presents scene-level details that strengthen your entire narrative structure.

- **Completion Verification**: For each scene or chapter you outline, briefly verify its structural completeness—does it contain a clear goal, conflict, outcome, and transition? Your subconscious will reveal any missing elements when prompted.

4. Closing the Session (3-5 minutes)

Properly concluding your writing session is as important as how you begin it:

- **Gratitude Practice**: Take a moment to appreciate whatever emerged during your session, regardless of quantity or perceived quality. This gratitude reinforces your positive relationship with your creative subconscious.
- **Insight Capture**: Before fully returning to ordinary awareness, note any additional insights, images, or directions that surface. These closing impressions often contain valuable seed ideas for your next session.
- **Gentle Transition**: Rather than abruptly ending your writing time, allow yourself a gradual return to regular awareness. Take several deep breaths, wiggle your fingers and toes, and slowly expand your awareness back to your physical environment.
- **Forward Linking**: Briefly consider where you might begin in your next session. Without rigidly planning, plant a gentle suggestion in your subconscious about what you'd like to explore next. This creates continuity between sessions.
- **Physical Grounding**: Complete your session with a physical action that symbolizes the transition back to everyday consciousness—closing your notebook, saving your file, or standing and stretching. This clear endpoint helps maintain the sanctity of your creative space.

Advanced Techniques for Enhancing Your 12-Day System

As you become familiar with the basic 12-day outlining process, you may wish to explore these advanced methods for enhancing your outline development:

1. Subconscious Story Elicitation: The Sleep Story Seeding Method

Programming Your Creative Dreams

This simple yet powerful process helps you partner with your subconscious mind during sleep to develop your stories. Whether or not you remember your dreams, this practice strengthens the connection between your conscious and subconscious storytelling minds, leading to improved writing and more natural story development.

Before Sleep Preparation

- Place a notebook and pen within easy reach of your bed
- Dim or turn off the lights to signal transition time
- Lay comfortably in bed
- Take three relaxing breaths
- Speak this creative subconscious affirmation softly to yourself:

“I'm now entering the space where stories grow. My analytical mind can rest, knowing my creative mind works best in silence.

My body relaxes completely, from my head to my toes. All tension dissolves, leaving only peaceful awareness.

I know that my subconscious mind is infinite intelligence and the storehouse of all creativity. It is a vast story library, containing all possibilities and connections. It knows my story completely and reveals it to me in perfect ways.

Tonight, as I sleep, my deeper mind works on my behalf, sorting through possibilities, making connections, and developing ideas that I could never reach through conscious effort alone. Whether I remember my dreams or not, this creative work continues.

I now ask my subconscious mind to work on: (briefly state your current story challenge or project)

I fully trust this process, knowing that my subconscious mind always responds to my faith in it. In the morning, throughout the rest of the day, and during my writing time, I will receive exactly what I need for my story's development.

I trust my creative mind completely. It knows the story that wants to emerge. This is the truth, this is working now, and I give thanks that it is so."

Morning Harvest

Upon waking, before fully alert:

- Reach for your notebook
- Write whatever comes to mind, whether it seems story-related or not
- Don't judge or analyze—just record
- If nothing specific comes, write "My story is developing" and trust the process

Trust Building

Remember:

- Your subconscious mind is always working on your story, even when you're not aware of it
- Each time you practice this process, you strengthen the bridge between your conscious and subconscious creativity
- Story elements will begin emerging more naturally during your regular writing sessions
- Even nights without memorable dreams or morning insights are valuable —your creative mind is still at work
- This practice accumulates power over time, leading to:
    - More natural story development
    - Stronger character insights
    - Unexpected plot connections
    - Deeper thematic understanding

- Improved overall writing flow

Building the Relationship

Think of this as developing a partnership with your creative subconscious. Like any relationship, it grows stronger with:

- Regular practice
- Patient trust
- Grateful acknowledgment
- Acceptance of its natural rhythm and timing

The real magic of this process isn't in immediate dream revelations (though these may come), but in the gradual strengthening of your connection to your deeper storytelling wisdom. Over time, you'll find your outlining becomes more intuitive, your writing flows more naturally, and your stories emerge with greater authenticity and power.

Practice this process nightly, even when you feel stuck or uninspired. Your subconscious mind appreciates the consistent invitation to participate in your creative work.

2. The Hypnagogic Outline Enhancement Method

The boundary between wakefulness and sleep is a particularly fertile territory for outline enhancement:

- **Pre-Sleep Outline Review**: Before bed, review the specific component of your 12-day outline you'll be working on tomorrow for 5-10 minutes, ending by formulating a specific structural question you'd like insight on overnight.
- **Bedside Capture Tools**: Keep a voice recorder or notebook within immediate reach of your bed. The insights you receive during hypnagogic states regarding your outline are often impossible to recall if not captured immediately.

- **Morning Twilight Outlining**: Set your alarm 30 minutes earlier than normal. Upon waking, begin working immediately on that day's outline component—before checking devices, speaking, or fully awakening. This liminal state provides exceptional access to subconscious material for your outline. Keep a voice recorder or notebook within arm's reach to capture ideas as they emerge, allowing you to review these insights later without losing the valuable material that surfaces during this hypnagogic state.
- **Dream Integration**: If you recall dreams that seem connected to your story, record them without attempting to immediately make them "fit" your story or the 12-day structure. The connections often become clear later in your outlining process, or the dream imagery transforms into something more applicable to your developing outline.

3. Character Channeling for Outline Development

This powerful method deepens character authenticity within your 12-day outline:

- **Character Profile Meditation**: Begin with 5 minutes of meditation focused exclusively on one character before adding them to your outline. Imagine their physical sensations, emotional state, and thought patterns until you feel a distinct shift in your awareness.
- **First-Person Character Journaling**: As part of Day 3 (Character Development) or Day 5 (Secondary Characters), write a journal entry completely in first person as this character. This helps you develop more authentic motivation profiles, psychological wounds, and transformation arcs for your outline.
- **Physical Character Embodiment**: When mapping your character's journey through your beat sheet or chapter outline, subtly adopt their physical characteristics—their posture, breathing pattern, facial expressions. This somatic component dramatically enhances your psychological connection to their arc throughout your outline.

- **Character Interview for Plot Points**: When planning critical decision points in your beat sheet or chapter outline, pause and have an actual conversation (out loud or in writing) with your character, asking them directly how they would react at this structural turning point.

4. Deep Immersion Scene Mapping

This technique creates extraordinarily vivid scene outlines for your 12-day system through progressive sensory layering:

- **Location Blueprint Meditation**: Before adding a key location to your scene breakdown in Days 9-12, visualize it as an empty stage. Spend 3-5 minutes simply absorbing the basic geography and spatial relationships that will serve as the setting for multiple scenes.
- **Sensory Layer Documentation**: Systematically add and document sensory layers for your scene outlines:
  - First, note all visual elements (lighting, colors, objects) that should appear in your scene
  - Then add sounds (ambient noise, distant conversations, natural sounds) to your outline notes
  - Follow with smells and tastes associated with the environment as scene-specific details
  - Finally, add tactile sensations (textures, temperature, air movement) to complete the sensory map
- **Emotional Location Coding**: Beyond physical sensations, document the emotional "temperature" of each key location in your outline. Every setting has an emotional quality—threatening, comforting, melancholy, energizing—that influences how characters interact within it and should be noted in your scene breakdown.
- **Temporal Location Variation**: When documenting locations that appear multiple times in your outline, note how they appear across different times—at various times of day, in different weather, or even in different

seasons. This temporal dimension adds remarkable depth to your scene sequencing.

5. Symbolic Gateway for 12-Day Progression

This method uses personal symbols to quickly access your deepest creative states at each stage of the 12-day outlining system:

- **Daily Symbol Selection**: For each day of the 12-day system, identify or create a personal symbol that represents that day's specific outlining focus—perhaps a character silhouette for Character Development day, a mountain peak for Climax plotting, or a branching path for exploring multiple plot options.
- **Progressive Conditioning**: At the beginning of each day's outlining session, bring that day's specific symbol into your awareness just as you enter your creative state. With consistent repetition, each symbol becomes neurologically linked with the specific creative resources needed for that day's outline component.
- **Rapid Access Triggers**: Once established (usually by the second week of your system), briefly engaging with the day's chosen symbol creates an immediate shift toward the specific type of creative consciousness needed for that day's outlining work.
- **Symbol System Integration**: By the end of the 12-day system, you'll have developed a complete symbol vocabulary that enables you to quickly access precisely the creative state needed for any future outlining task, greatly accelerating your work on subsequent novels.

Maintaining Your 12-Day Outlining Practice

Consistency is the key to mastering the 12-day subconscious outlining system. Here are strategies for sustaining your practice:

1. Daily Integration Within the 12-Day System

While your structured 12-day sessions form the core of your practice, integration throughout each day enhances your results:

- **Outline Insight Capture System**: The subconscious mind continues working on your outline even when you're engaged in other activities. Carry a small pocket notebook, index cards, or use a dedicated note-taking app on your phone to capture structural insights whenever they arise, noting which day of the 12-day system they apply to.
- **12-Day Momentum Micro-Sessions**: Even 5-minute bursts of focus on your current day's outline component throughout your day can maintain your connection to your developing story structure. These brief immersions keep your creative channels open between longer sessions.
- **Pre-Sleep Next-Day Preparation**: Spend the last few minutes before sleep contemplating the specific outline component you'll be working on tomorrow. Your subconscious mind will often present structural solutions upon waking that perfectly align with that day's outlining task.
- **Walking Blueprint Meditation**: A 10-15 minute walk while holding your current day's outline focus lightly in your awareness often yields surprising structural insights. The rhythmic movement and changing scenery stimulate creative connections that strengthen your developing story architecture.

2. Overcoming Resistance to the 12-Day System

Even with the structured 12-day approach, resistance occasionally emerges. These strategies help maintain momentum:

- **Daily Minimum Commitment**: On difficult days, commit to just fifteen minutes of work on that day's outline component. This minimal commitment often overcomes initial resistance, and frequently expands into productive completion of that day's outline task once begun.
- **Process Focus Within Structure**: Shift your attention from output

(completion of outline sections) to process (accessing the creative state for each day's focus). This removes performance pressure while still honoring the 12-day framework.

- **Resistance Dialogue for Specific Days**: When you feel resistant to a particular day's outlining task, have a written dialogue with your resistance. Ask it questions: "What about today's outline component feels challenging?" or "What support do you need to complete today's section?" The answers often reveal surprising insights about your story's structure.
- **12-Day System Flexibility**: If one day's outlining work feels particularly challenging, consider whether you might benefit from spending an extra day or two on it, adjusting your 12-day timeline as needed. In fact, while 12 days represents the ideal minimum timeframe for developing a robust, powerful outline, the system could expand to 20 days if necessary. What matters most is not rigid adherence to the timeline but completing a comprehensive outline that serves your novel. The structure provides essential guidance while allowing adaptations based on your unique creative process and the specific needs of your story.

3. Deepening the 12-Day System With Practice

Your relationship with the 12-day outlining system naturally evolves with continued practice across multiple novels:

- **Increasing Structural Intuition**: As you complete multiple 12-day outline cycles for different novels, your subconscious develops remarkable structural awareness. You'll find yourself intuitively knowing exactly what each day's outline component needs without conscious analysis.
- **Compressed Timeline Potential**: The 12-day process can be compressed into a shorter timeline if you're able to dedicate more hours of focused work to each day's component. By investing additional time each day—

perhaps doubling your session length or adding a second session—you can potentially complete the system in 7-10 days. This isn't about rushing through the steps, but rather about concentrating more focused attention on each component within a shorter overall timeframe. With experience, this compression becomes even more effective as your facility with subconscious outlining develops. The quality remains exceptional while the overall calendar time decreases. When I've completed an outline in fewer days, I always go back and review it thoroughly to ensure nothing was missed. In my extensive experience with this system, I've found that 12 days consistently remains the sweet spot for most writers—providing enough time for deep creative immersion while maintaining productive momentum.

- **Seamless Craft Integration**: As your practice matures, you'll discover a harmonious relationship between subconscious creativity and conscious story architecture. Rather than opposing forces, they become complementary aspects of your outlining process, creating blueprints that are both structurally sound and creatively distinctive.
- **System Personalization**: Over time, develop variations of the 12-day system that resonate with your unique creative temperament. While maintaining the essential framework, you might find certain days benefit from expanded techniques or approaches specifically tailored to your storytelling strengths.

Completing The Subconscious Novelist's 12-Day Outlining System

By completing the 12-day subconscious outlining process, you transform from someone who struggles with story structure to a true "subconscious novelist"—a writer whose outlines emerge from the deepest, most authentic levels of creative awareness while maintaining professional structural integrity.

This transformation manifests in your finished outline through:

- Character profiles with psychological depth and authenticity that will resonate with readers on a profound level
- Plot structures that balance satisfying architecture with genuine surprise and organic development
- Thematic integration that flows naturally through all narrative elements rather than feeling imposed
- Scene breakdowns that carry an energetic aliveness beyond mere technical accuracy
- A distinctive story blueprint that cannot be imitated because it springs from your unique creative depths

The 12-day system outlined in this guide provides a comprehensive method for accessing, nurturing, and sustaining your relationship with your creative subconscious throughout the entire outlining process. While individual techniques can be practiced separately with benefit, their greatest power emerges when applied within the structured 12-day framework.

Remember that this is not merely a set of techniques but a transformative outlining practice that prepares you for efficient, inspired drafting. Each day of the 12-day system is both a productive outlining session and an investment in your evolving relationship with your subconscious storytelling mind.

Trust that your deepest creative self knows the novel you need to write, and this 12-day outlining system creates the optimal conditions for that story to emerge with structural integrity, emotional authenticity, and narrative grace.

Best Practices for the Subconscious Novelist

Setting the Foundation

Time and Word Goals

- Set consistent daily writing times—this trains your subconscious to be creative on schedule

- Start with modest word count goals (500-1000 words) and build up gradually to more advanced goals (2000-2500 words)
- Focus on consistency rather than quantity
- Track your progress but don't become enslaved to numbers
- Remember: steady progress beats sporadic bursts

The Psychology of Writing

- Release the pressure of "writing a novel" —you're simply telling a story
- Let go of perfectionism your outline is a discovery process. Your first draft will be nearly perfect thanks to this precise and detailed outlining process. Relax, you got this (your subconscious mind does!)
- Trust your subconscious mind to do the heavy lifting
- Remember: you're not creating the story, you're uncovering it

Partnering With Your Subconscious

Building the Relationship

- Your subconscious mind is the real writer—you're taking dictation
- Treat it as a respected collaborator, not a servant
- Listen more than you direct
- Trust its timing and process
- Practice gratitude for its contributions

Story Development Techniques

- Tell yourself the story repeatedly throughout the day (out loud if possible/use a voice recorder)
- Let each telling reveal new details and connections (explore with free association essays on each new connection you discover)
- Notice which elements persist across tellings (these are often key)

- Pay attention to what excites you in each telling (make a note on this and explore in detail later)
- Allow the story to evolve naturally with each iteration (choose whatever impacts you the most)

Automatic Writing Practice (Optional)

- Set aside time for pure, unfiltered writing (before or after outlining or writing)
- Enter a subconscious (self hypnosis state) prior to starting your automatic writing session
- Let words flow without judgment or direction
- Think of it as taking dictation from your deeper mind
- Don't worry about coherence or quality
- Trust that patterns and meaning will emerge

Practical Tools

Pre-Writing Ritual

- Begin each writing session with the provided self-hypnosis process (***The Subconscious Story Writing Process)***
- Create a consistent environment that signals "writing time"
- Clear your space of distractions
- Take a few centering breaths
- Remind yourself: "I am open to the story that wants to be told"

Character Development

- Interview your characters in the workbook's Ideas section
- Let them surprise you with their answers
- Ask about their:

    - Fears and desires
    - Hidden secrets
    - Relationships
    - Past experiences
    - Future hopes
- Record their responses without censoring

Plot Development

- When stuck, list your hero's daily movements
- Focus on physical actions to unlock emotional insights
- Ask: What would this character naturally do next?
- Let the character's choices drive the plot
- Trust that meaningful patterns will emerge

Troubleshooting

When You're Stuck

- Return to telling yourself the story (this is why it's called ***STORYTELLING***)
- List physical actions and locations (follow your hero through all his daily actions and make a list of his every movement and afterwards you choose whatever actions are the true important ones to the story)
- Interview your characters (get to know them intimately) *See ***Character Interview Guide for Subconscious Story Development***
- Use the Sleep Story Seeding Method (this is one of the best tools you can use)
- Trust the process ("blocks" often precede breakthroughs, don't ever *think* you are stuck, because in reality you aren't stuck, you're just too "conscious". Release the fear of being stuck by trusting your subconscious mind to do the heavy lifting. Remember you already have

all the answers inside of you.

- Take a break (Going for a walk is highly recommended)
- Read a novel in the same genre you're writing or from one of your favorite authors (Inspiration is always a great way to refresh and snap out of a negative trance)
- Watch a good movie

When You're Overwhelmed

- Return to modest daily goals
- Focus on one scene at a time
- Remember you're discovering, not creating (especially in the outlining stage)
- Practice the self-hypnosis sessions provided for each day or do ***The Subconscious Writing Process*** (it will get you back in a creative state)
- Trust your subconscious mind's timing (seriously, your subconscious is the boss, all you need to do "consciously" is show up (like a good employee) and let the boss show you how to do the work (you're just taking down notes)

Remember

Your subconscious mind is an infinite source of creativity. Your job is to show up consistently, remain open to what emerges, and record what comes. Trust the process, practice regularly, and let your story reveal itself in its own perfect way.

CHAPTER 6

Getting Started with The Subconscious Story Writing System

Let's talk about how to unlock your story's potential using your most powerful creative tool: your subconscious mind. I've developed this system through years of working as a professional hypnotist, novelist, and writing coach. While it's proven incredibly effective, remember—it's a framework, not a cage. Feel free to adapt it to your creative style once you understand its core principles.

Starting Your Creative Journey

Before you dive into the structure of your story, I always recommend to let your creative mind play. There's a section I've included in ***The Subconscious Novelist Workbook*** titled the ***Free Association Play-Sheets***—they're your creative playground. They are blank sheets where you can write, draw, doodle, scribble, make notes, and free associate everything, allowing your subconscious mind to play and immerse you in the world of your story. It activates the kinesthetic part of your subconscious mind. If you don't have the workbook, you can always use loose printer paper or index cards, but make sure you keep these in a folder because everything you write down is more important than you may realize. They are part of Day 1 of the program, and as always I recommend, you should start your writing session by entering the world of your story:

- Think about characters, events, scenes, settings
- Note connections, mood, atmosphere, ambiance
- Write down everything that pops into your mind
- Don't filter or judge—just let it flow

Accessing Your Subconscious Mind

If you don't have any ideas for a story yet, I've created a special hypnotic relaxation process called "***The Subconscious Story Writing Process***." This technique helps you enter an alpha or even theta state where ideas flow naturally. You can also try these other creative tools:

Using Tarot for Story Development

The tarot serves as a powerful gateway to your subconscious storytelling mind. What I'm sharing here represents just the tip of the iceberg regarding tarot's applications for creative writing. The connection between tarot and storytelling runs remarkably deep, allowing writers to harness tarot's archetypal wisdom to develop compelling characters, intricate plot lines, and resonant themes. Through its rich symbolic language, tarot provides direct access to the universal patterns and psychological truths that form the foundation of powerful narratives.

I recommend using either the Tarot de Marseille or the Rider-Waite-Smith deck, as each offers unique benefits for writers:

Tarot de Marseille:

- Older, more archetypal imagery
- Less specific symbolism allows freer interpretation
- Excellent for plot structure and character dynamics
- Numbers and court cards especially useful for story beats
- Great for discovering underlying themes and motivations

Rider-Waite-Smith:

- Rich in symbolic detail and narrative elements
- Each card tells its own story
- Excellent for scene development and character backgrounds
- Minor Arcana more detailed for subplots
- Perfect for visual writers and scene construction

In the following pages I provide a basic yet through complete reference guide to the Tarot card meanings and several ways to use them to subconsciously discover story:

Guide to the 78 Cards of the Tarot for Subconscious Story Development

Major Arcana Cards

0. The Fool

Keywords & Storytelling Applications: New beginnings • naive protagonist • coming-of-age journey • leap of faith • the hero's call to adventure • untested potential • innocence before experience • tabula rasa character • spontaneous decision-maker • risk-taker • the wanderer • characters who ignore warnings • trickster archetype • court jester • wild card personality • unconventional problem solver • character lacking self-preservation • impulsive choices • optimist in pessimistic settings • fish out of water • stranger in a strange land • trust in the universe • characters who live in the moment • the spiritual innocent • characters who break social norms • the foolish wisdom-keeper • intuitive genius • characters who make lucky escapes • divine protection • one who begins the journey unprepared • the unexpected hero

Storytelling Scenarios: A young protagonist leaving home for the first time • A character making a decision others consider foolish • An impulsive leap that changes everything • A naive character entering a dangerous world • Someone who accidentally stumbles into greatness • A character who succeeds through innocence rather than skill • The unprepared adventurer • Someone stepping off a metaphorical cliff • A character whose seeming foolishness masks deeper wisdom • The one person willing to try what experts claim impossible • Stories that begin with a character taking a risk • Tales where innocence proves more valuable than experience • The unexpected savior whose unconventional approach solves the problem • A character whose openness to experience leads to discovery • Stories exploring the power of beginnings and fresh starts

1. The Magician

Keywords & Storytelling Applications: Manifestation • skilled protagonist • mastery of tools • the manipulator • confidence personified • trickster • con artist • stage magician • actual wizard/witch • technological genius • charismatic leader • smooth-talking character • catalyst character • mentor figure • knowledge broker • character with hidden skills • master of illusion • character at the height of their power • someone with mysterious abilities • the bridge between worlds • communicator between realms • translator of ancient knowledge • wielder of focused will • character who makes the impossible possible • master of elements • character who understands hidden connections • the one who sees the patterns • alchemist • transformer • character who channels higher power • one who bends reality

Storytelling Scenarios: A character discovering their hidden talents • The moment when skills are put to the ultimate test • A con artist's elaborate scheme • A mentor showing a protagonist their potential • A scientific genius creating something world-changing • A magician whose tricks are actually real • Someone manipulating others through charisma • A character bringing diverse elements together to create something new • A story about transformation through focused will • A protagonist learning to channel their abilities • A character who serves as a conduit for greater powers • Tales exploring the line between illusion and reality • Stories about manifesting desires into reality • The journey from amateur to master • Characters who bridge different worlds or realms • Narratives about the responsible use of power • Stories exploring the price of great skill or ability

2. The High Priestess

Keywords & Storytelling Applications: Mystery • intuition • the unconscious mind • hidden knowledge • secrets keeper • oracle • psychic character • enigmatic mentor • veiled antagonist • unreliable narrator • guardian of thresholds • dream interpreter • mystic • seer • librarian of forbidden texts • keeper of ancient wisdom • silent observer • character with second sight • the one who knows but doesn't tell • intuitive detective • prophetic character • character connected to the moon • guardian of women's mysteries • mysterious stranger • character who speaks in riddles • one who sees beneath surfaces • guide to the underworld • character who understands symbols • priestess • nun • witch • the woman no one truly knows • character who lives between worlds

Storytelling Scenarios: A character receiving cryptic visions • The discovery of hidden knowledge that changes everything • A mysterious mentor who speaks in riddles • A protagonist learning to trust their intuition over logic • A character who guards ancient secrets • Stories set in dreams or the unconscious • A mystery that can only be solved through intuition • Tales exploring women's hidden power • A character who sees what others cannot • Stories about knowledge that shouldn't be revealed • The silent character who knows more than they say • Narratives exploring the thin veil between worlds • A protagonist journeying into the unconscious mind • Characters who receive messages from another realm • Stories about the price of forbidden knowledge • Tales of prophetic dreams or visions • A character whose silence speaks volumes • Stories exploring the power of what remains hidden

3. The Empress

Keywords & Storytelling Applications: Abundance • fertility • motherhood • nature's power • creative expression • sensual character • earth mother • goddess figure • queen • nurturing mentor • matriarch • creative muse • pregnant character • female ruler • character in touch with nature • agricultural deity • provider character • mother-figure • seductress • character of luxury and comfort • one who creates life • character of beauty and grace • character representing spring or summer • the nurturer • one who empowers others to grow • female character at the height of her power • the embodiment of feminine energy • character who heals through love • one who brings prosperity • the creatrix • the green woman • character representing biological fertility or creative fertility

Storytelling Scenarios: A character discovering their own creative power • The birth of something significant • A tale centered around motherhood or pregnancy • A story set in lush, abundant nature • A character who nurtures others to greatness • A queen or empress wielding power through abundance rather than force • A narrative about creating something beautiful • Tales exploring the power of feminine energy • Stories about growth, blossoming, or ripening • A protagonist healing a damaged land • Characters finding abundance in unexpected places • Stories about the relationship between humans and the natural world • A tale exploring sensual pleasures • Narratives about the responsibility of creation • Stories where fertility (creative or literal) is central • Tales of strong maternal figures • A character who must learn to balance giving with self-care

4. The Emperor

Keywords & Storytelling Applications: Authority • structure • father figure • order from chaos • ruler • king • CEO • general • judge • lawmaker • empire builder • patriarch • disciplinarian • logical character • strategic thinker • protector • provider • establishment figure • character representing societal rules • authority figure • mentor who teaches discipline • character representing masculine energy • leader • command • control • stability • steadfast character • unyielding figure • character representing tradition • the voice of reason • character who values order above all • one who creates systems • the ultimate authority • character wearing a mask of strength • character representing winter or autumn

Storytelling Scenarios: A character establishing order in a chaotic situation • The coronation of a new ruler • A tale exploring the relationship between father and child • A protagonist learning to command respect • A leader facing a crisis that tests their authority • Stories about the creation or maintenance of empires • Tales exploring the price of order and stability • A character whose rigid thinking creates problems • Narratives about rebellion against authority • Stories exploring effective vs. tyrannical leadership • A character learning to balance flexibility with structure • Tales about the burden of leadership • A protagonist stepping into a position of authority • Stories exploring masculine energy or traditional male roles • Narratives about the creation of laws or systems • A character who must decide between compassion and order • Tales of wise rulers or foolish kings

5. The Hierophant

Keywords & Storytelling Applications: Tradition • conformity • religion • education • mentor • priest • rabbi • imam • spiritual leader • teacher • professor • keeper of tradition • cultural guardian • conventional thinker • by-the-book character • mediator between heaven and earth • religious institution • dogmatic character • orthodox believer • ritual master • ceremonial figure • wisdom within convention • the respectable facade • established beliefs • spiritual interpreter • translator of divine will • bridge between spiritual and material • keeper of sacred knowledge • conservator • preserver of culture • guardian of established ways • character representing societal expectations • one who bridges divine and mundane

Storytelling Scenarios: A character questioning their faith or beliefs • A tale set within a religious institution • A protagonist learning from a traditional mentor • Stories exploring the value or limitations of tradition • A character mediating between worldly and spiritual concerns • Tales about initiation into established systems • A narrative about rebellion against or return to tradition • Stories exploring the role of ceremony and ritual • A character finding freedom within structure • Tales about the tension between individual belief and organized religion • A protagonist seeking spiritual guidance • Narratives exploring the power of education and learning • A character preserving ancient ways in changing times • Stories about the passing down of wisdom • Tales exploring the comfort and constraints of conformity • A character finding personal meaning in collective traditions • Narratives about the transformation of established institutions

6. The Lovers

Keywords & Storytelling Applications: Choice • partnership • values alignment • romantic love • temptation • integration of opposites • soul connections • relationships • moral choices • crossroads • decision points • duality • passion • commitment • characters at a decision point • star-crossed lovers • perfect match • complementary characters • rival suitors • forbidden romance • sacred marriage • union of opposites • characters representing different sides of the protagonist • ethical dilemma • character torn between two paths • testing of values • heart versus head decisions • sexual awakening • character choosing their identity • merging of disparate elements • harmony between conflicting aspects • choice with significant consequences • alignment with one's higher self

Storytelling Scenarios: A character making a life-altering choice • A romance facing significant obstacles • A protagonist torn between two paths • Stories of forbidden love • Tales exploring the integration of different aspects of self • A character choosing between passion and responsibility • Narratives about finding one's perfect match or counterpart • Stories about the consequences of choice • A protagonist facing a moral dilemma • Tales of unions that transform the individuals involved • Stories exploring sexual awakening or discovery • Narratives about commitments and their implications • A character choosing which values to honor • Tales of partnerships that create something greater than the sum of their parts • Stories about the choice to be vulnerable with another • Narratives exploring the healing power of love • Tales about the alignment of oneself with higher principles

7. The Chariot

Keywords & Storytelling Applications: Willpower • determination • victory • control • forward movement • triumph over obstacles • ambition • drive • focus • competing forces harnessed • discipline • character on a mission • conqueror • warrior • competitor • athlete • race car driver • military leader • dominant personality • character maintaining control under pressure • character balancing opposing forces • single-minded pursuer • tunnel vision • journey • physical movement • migration • travel • character on a quest • unstoppable force • character who refuses to quit • victory through perseverance • focused movement toward a goal • character integrating conflicting aspects • triumph through determination

Storytelling Scenarios: A character overcoming seemingly impossible odds • A tale about a journey or quest • A protagonist learning to harness conflicting forces • Sports stories or tales of competition • Military campaigns or strategic conquests • A character whose determination becomes obsession • Stories about the price of victory • Tales of journeys both physical and metaphorical • A protagonist bringing disparate elements under control • Narratives about triumph through perseverance • Stories exploring the tension between control and surrender • A character mastering their impulses • Tales about maintaining balance amid forward motion • War stories or battle narratives • A protagonist whose single-minded focus creates blind spots • Stories about racing against time or opponents • Narratives exploring the costs and rewards of ambition

8. Strength

Keywords & Storytelling Applications: Courage • compassion • patience • gentle power • inner strength • taming the beast within • character with hidden power • the quiet force • unlikely hero • character with influence over wild things • beast tamer • animal whisperer • character who overcomes through compassion • survivor • character who transforms rage • the soft-spoken powerhouse • character with unexpected courage • character whose gentleness is their strength • one who faces fears • character with moral courage • the merciful victor • character who chooses compassion over vengeance • endless patience • character who understands their dark side • one whose vulnerability becomes strength • character who masters primal instincts • the brave heart • character with quiet confidence • one who stands firm • character who demonstrates true courage

Storytelling Scenarios: A character taming a wild beast or force • Tales exploring inner demons or shadow aspects • A protagonist finding courage in a moment of fear • Stories about power used with restraint • A character whose compassion changes an enemy • Narratives about patience overcoming aggression • Tales exploring different kinds of strength • A protagonist whose gentleness proves more powerful than force • Stories about mastering one's own instincts or passions • A character facing their greatest fear • Tales of unexpected courage in unlikely heroes • Narratives examining the relationship between humans and animals • A protagonist choosing mercy when vengeance seems justified • Stories exploring moral courage versus physical strength • Tales about standing firm against overwhelming opposition • A character drawing strength from vulnerability • Narratives about the quiet power of endurance

9. The Hermit

Keywords & Storytelling Applications: Solitude • introspection • inner guidance • withdrawal • seeking wisdom • soul-searching • mentor character • wise elder • lighthouse keeper • monk • nun • desert dweller • mountain sage • character on retreat • the wisdom of isolation • character seeking truth • inner light • spiritual guide • character who chooses solitude • the lone wolf • the recluse • introspective character • seeker • pilgrim • guardian of hidden knowledge • the one who walks alone • guide in darkness • character on a vision quest • one who withdraws from society • character seeking answers within • voluntary exile • the silent observer • teacher who appears when needed • bearer of hidden light • one who illuminates the path

Storytelling Scenarios: A character withdrawing from society to find answers • A tale about a journey of self-discovery • A protagonist seeking a reclusive mentor • Stories set in isolated locations • A character learning to trust their inner guidance • Tales of spiritual retreat or pilgrimage • A narrative about finding light in darkness • Stories exploring the wisdom gained through solitude • A character serving as a beacon for others • Tales about the tensions between society and solitude • A protagonist on a vision quest • Narratives about aging and the wisdom it brings • A character who must go within to find answers • Stories about mentorship and guidance • Tales exploring silence and its power • A character who illuminates the path for others • Narratives about voluntary exile or retreat

10. Wheel of Fortune

Keywords & Storytelling Applications: Cycles • turning points • destiny • luck • fortune • fate • change • karma • what goes around comes around • character experiencing dramatic reversal • rags to riches • riches to rags • gambling character • risk-taker • character subject to forces beyond control • lottery winner • character experiencing sudden change • the rise and fall • cyclical events • recurring patterns • character riding the wheel of fate • prophetic moment • destined encounter • character at mercy of larger forces • tipping points • inevitable change • character experiencing dramatic success or failure • the moment everything changes • patterns of history • character breaking a cycle • the unexpected twist • divine timing • character learning from the cycles of life

Storytelling Scenarios: A character experiencing a sudden change in fortune • Tales of fate or destiny • A protagonist gambling everything on one chance • Stories exploring karmic patterns or consequences • A character's rise to power followed by a fall • Tales about breaking free from recurring cycles • A narrative centered around a sudden windfall or loss • Stories examining luck versus skill • A character trying to control uncontrollable circumstances • Tales of prophetic moments or destined encounters • A protagonist recognizing patterns in their life

• Narratives about the cyclical nature of history or events • A character learning to ride the waves of change • Stories about accepting the ups and downs of life • Tales exploring divine timing or intervention • A narrative structured around cycles or seasons • Stories where past actions return with consequences

11. Justice

Keywords & Storytelling Applications: Fairness • truth • law • cause and effect • balance • consequences • accountability • karma • legal proceedings • judge character • lawyer • police officer • ethical decisions • moral dilemmas • character facing consequences • the scales being balanced • truth revealed • character seeking justice • fair judgment • impartial decisions • character representing equity • cosmic justice • karmic return • character weighing evidence • objective analysis • legal thriller elements • character committed to fairness • one who rights wrongs • truth-seeker • character representing conscience • impartial observer • one who holds others accountable • character who brings balance • the mediator • character facing their own actions' results • one who separates truth from falsehood

Storytelling Scenarios: A character seeking justice for a wrong • Legal thrillers or courtroom dramas • A protagonist facing the consequences of past actions • Stories exploring moral or ethical dilemmas • A character discovering harsh truths • Tales about the balance between mercy and justice • A narrative examining cause and effect • Stories about karma or cosmic balance • A character serving as judge or arbitrator • Tales exploring what is truly fair versus technically legal • A protagonist caught between competing claims of justice • Narratives about the search for truth • A character bringing balance to an unfair situation • Stories about accountability and responsibility • Tales examining impartiality versus compassion • A protagonist whose sense of justice is challenged • Narratives exploring systems of law or ethics

12. The Hanged Man

Keywords & Storytelling Applications: Suspension • surrender • letting go • sacrifice • new perspective • waiting • martyrdom • character in limbo • suspended animation • different point of view • character who gives up something important • voluntary sacrifice • one who sees differently • paradoxical character • unconventional viewpoint • character between worlds • one who surrenders to win • the willing victim • character in transition • spiritual surrender • character gaining wisdom through surrender • one who chooses sacrifice • suspended character • one who waits • character seeing the world upside down • paradoxical wisdom • between life and death • character in gestation • one who surrenders control • character facing a necessary loss • spiritual initiation • one who transcends normal perspective

Storytelling Scenarios: A character sacrificing something valuable for a greater good • Tales about seeing familiar situations from new angles • A protagonist in a state of limbo or waiting • Stories exploring willing surrender • A character suspended between different worlds or states • Tales of martyrdom or self-sacrifice • A narrative about gaining wisdom through letting go • Stories about characters whose worlds have been turned upside down • A protagonist who must surrender control to succeed • Tales exploring paradoxical situations • A character undergoing spiritual initiation • Narratives about the power of passivity or non-action • A protagonist trapped or suspended physically • Stories about waiting as a spiritual practice • Tales exploring sacrificial figures or archetypes • A character who gains by losing • Narratives examining the wisdom found in reversals or inversions

13. Death

Keywords & Storytelling Applications: Transformation • endings • rebirth • profound change • letting go • character experiencing major life shift • transitional figure • harbinger of change • the necessary end • funeral director • psychopomp • character facing mortality • one who facilitates transitions • the grim reaper • character experiencing ego death • the end of an era • character shedding old identity • one who survives great loss • character facilitating necessary endings • profound metamorphosis • the phoenix figure • character who dies symbolically • one who guides through transitions • radical transformation • character at the end of their rope • one who embodies impermanence • character facing the inevitable • dramatic plot twist • one who emerges transformed • pruning to promote growth • character representing decay and renewal • devastating loss leading to new beginning

Storytelling Scenarios: A character experiencing a profound personal transformation • Stories about the end of a way of life • A protagonist facing mortality • Tales of symbolic death and rebirth • A character guiding others through major transitions • Narratives about necessary endings • Stories exploring grief and its transformative potential • A character shedding an old identity • Tales about facing the inevitable • A protagonist experiencing the death of illusions • Stories structured around endings that lead to new beginnings • A character serving as a harbinger of necessary change • Tales exploring impermanence and its lessons • A protagonist dying to old ways of being • Narratives about cultural or societal transformation • A character who must let go to move forward • Stories about facing fear of change or ending

14. Temperance

Keywords & Storytelling Applications: Balance • moderation • harmony • blending • middle path • synthesis • healing • patience • character who brings opposites together • alchemist • healer • peacemaker • mediator • character representing the golden mean • one who tempers extremes • character with perfect timing • one who finds the middle way • character blending disparate elements • bridge between opposites • the careful mixer • character practicing moderation • one who harmonizes conflicts • character representing patience • the balanced soul • character avoiding extremes • one who creates something new through combination • the divine chemist • character who heals through balance • one who flows between worlds • character embodying grace • one who knows the right measure • angel figure • character with healing abilities

Storytelling Scenarios: A character bringing opposing factions together • Tales about healing after conflict or injury • A protagonist learning the value of moderation • Stories exploring the balancing of different elements • A character serving as mediator between opposing forces • Narratives about patience and perfect timing • Tales of alchemy or transformation • A protagonist creating harmony from discord • Stories about finding middle ground • A character whose strength comes from balance • Tales exploring recovery or rehabilitation • A protagonist bringing together different worlds or viewpoints • Narratives about the blending of opposing qualities • A character whose patience achieves what force cannot • Stories about spiritual or emotional healing • Tales exploring the power of moderation in an extreme world • A character who embodies grace under pressure

15. The Devil

Keywords & Storytelling Applications: Bondage • addiction • materialism • shadow aspects • illusion of being trapped • sexuality • temptation • character in self-imposed chains • addict • character bound by limiting beliefs • one enslaved to desire • manipulator • tempter/temptress • character representing unexpressed shadow • one dealing with dark urges • character facing their demons • one exposing hidden darkness • the ultimate antagonist • character representing material obsession • one who reveals uncomfortable truths • character offering forbidden knowledge • the scapegoat • character bound by illusions • one trapped in patterns • character representing unhealthy attachments • the fear-monger • character embodying chaos • one who tests morality • character representing untamed instincts • the forbidden • one who offers easy but costly solutions • character representing what we deny • the taboo breaker

Storytelling Scenarios: A character struggling with addiction or obsession • Tales exploring shadows, vices, or repressed aspects • A protagonist bound by self-limiting beliefs • Stories about temptation and its consequences • A character facing their darkest impulses • Narratives about breaking free from mental or emotional chains • Tales exploring the shadow side of human nature • A protagonist dealing with unhealthy attachments • Stories about the illusion of powerlessness • A character confronting what they've denied in themselves • Tales exploring materialism and its pitfalls • A protagonist tempted by what seems too good to be true • Narratives about escaping self-imposed limitations • A character grappling with forbidden desires • Stories exploring taboo subjects • Tales about the things that bind us to unhealthy patterns • A character who must name their demons to be free of them

16. The Tower

Keywords & Storytelling Applications: Sudden change • crisis • revelation • upheaval • breakdown leading to breakthrough • catastrophe • awakening • character experiencing sudden reversal • disaster • paradigm shift • character's world falling apart • revelation of truth • one whose foundations are shaken • character amid chaos • the moment of collapse • one experiencing divine intervention • character struck by sudden insight • the necessary destruction • one who survives catastrophe • character experiencing revelation through crisis • sudden plot twist • lightning strike moment • character amid revolutionary change • the breaking of illusions • one whose false security is shattered • character amid sudden transformation • destruction preceding creation • one who witnesses collapse • character at ground zero • the moment when everything changes • one surviving the storm

Storytelling Scenarios: A character experiencing a sudden, life-changing crisis • Tales of disasters, natural or man-made • A protagonist whose secure world suddenly collapses • Stories about revelations that change everything • A character experiencing an awakening through crisis • Narratives about the destruction of false structures • Tales exploring sudden, revolutionary change • A protagonist struck by a revelation or epiphany • Stories structured around major plot twists or reversals • A character whose illusions are suddenly shattered • Tales about surviving catastrophe • A protagonist experiencing divine intervention • Narratives exploring how breakdown leads to breakthrough • A character rebuilding after complete destruction • Stories about the liberation that comes through loss • Tales exploring moments when everything changes • A protagonist whose certainties are suddenly challenged

17. The Star

Keywords & Storytelling Applications: Hope • inspiration • serenity • renewal • healing • optimism • calm after storm • guiding light • beacon in darkness • character finding hope • healer • inspiring figure • one who offers peace • character representing renewal • guiding figure • one who brings calm after chaos • character representing higher aspirations • celestial connection • one who renews faith • character embodying hope • the peaceful presence • one who sees the way forward • character reconnecting to source • divine inspiration • one who trusts the universe • character representing pure potential • the gift-giver • one who replenishes • character who brings light • the quiet optimist • one who sees possibilities • character who inspires others • the faith keeper • one connected to cosmic forces

Storytelling Scenarios: A character finding hope in a desperate situation • Tales of healing after trauma • A protagonist guided by a distant light • Stories about renewal after destruction • A character serving as inspiration for others • Narratives exploring calm after chaos • Tales of quiet hope and optimism • A protagonist reconnecting with faith or purpose • Stories about the gifts that come after suffering • A character serving as a guiding star for others • Tales exploring serenity amid difficulty • A protagonist finding their way by looking up • Narratives about naked vulnerability and its power • A character who embodies quiet confidence • Stories exploring the renewal of faith or trust • Tales about finding direction when lost • A protagonist discovering the beauty of simplicity • Narratives examining the healing power of nature

18. The Moon

Keywords & Storytelling Applications: Illusion • intuition • dreams • subconscious • uncertainty • mystery • character facing fears • one navigating illusions • dream walker • intuitive character • one confronting the shadow • character in a world of illusion • psychic • one experiencing confusion • character representing hidden knowledge • nightmare figure • one lost in darkness • character uncovering buried truths • sleepwalker • one experiencing altered states • character representing the mysterious feminine • fear-faced • one whose path is unclear • character representing intuitive wisdom • madness • one who sees what others miss • character in twilight realms • the beast within • one walking between worlds • character discovering hidden meanings • shape-shifter • one who thrives in darkness • character representing primal fears • the night journey • one who trusts the unseen path

Storytelling Scenarios: A character journeying through a dreamlike or surreal landscape • Tales exploring the thin line between reality and illusion • A protagonist relying on intuition when logic fails • Stories set in twilight or darkness • A character facing their deepest fears • Narratives about the subconscious mind • Tales exploring madness or altered perception • A protagonist navigating uncertainty or confusion • Stories about hidden enemies or dangers • A character discovering buried memories or truths • Tales examining the power of intuition • A protagonist on a night journey • Narratives set in liminal spaces • A character whose perception cannot be trusted • Stories exploring primitive fears • Tales about trusting an unclear path • A protagonist whose dreams reveal important truths • Narratives examining the cyclical nature of emotions

19. The Sun

Keywords & Storytelling Applications: Joy • success • radiance • vitality • enlightenment • character achieving clarity • one who brings illumination • child figure • character representing innocence • one who achieves success • character radiating confidence • the victorious • one who sees clearly • character representing truth revealed • the optimist • one who brings joy • character embodying vitality • the enlightened • one whose true self shines • character at their peak • the innocent wise one • one who represents perfect harmony • character who illuminates others • the accomplished • one who embodies success • character representing revelation • the truth-bearer • one whose light dispels darkness • character representing ideal outcome • the revelator • one who represents divine child • character embodying pure joy • the radiant presence

Storytelling Scenarios: A character experiencing complete success or triumph • Tales exploring innocence and wisdom combined • A protagonist achieving clarity after confusion • Stories about truth being revealed • A character bringing joy to a dark situation • Narratives exploring enlightenment or awakening • Tales of perfect moments of happiness • A protagonist whose authentic self emerges • Stories about vitality and health • A character whose transparency changes everything • Tales exploring the wisdom of children • A protagonist whose optimism is vindicated • Narratives about achievement and recognition • A character who illuminates others • Stories exploring the height of success • Tales about truth dispelling illusion • A protagonist experiencing perfect harmony • Narratives examining the power of authenticity

20. Judgement

Keywords & Storytelling Applications: Awakening • rebirth • reckoning • evaluation • calling • character experiencing spiritual awakening • one who faces final judgment • character answering a calling • the reborn • one who evaluates fairly • character representing absolution • the forgiven • one who rises again • character at moment of truth • the fairly judged • one who hears the call • character representing karmic resolution • the resurrected • one who experiences revelation • character representing divine justice • the awakened • one who rises from ashes • character who judges fairly • the reconciler • one who brings closure • character representing rebirth • the evaluator • one who awakens others

• character responding to higher calling • the absolved • one who faces their life review • character experiencing profound realization

Storytelling Scenarios: A character experiencing a profound awakening or call • Tales exploring resurrection or rebirth • A protagonist facing judgment for past actions • Stories about answering a calling or purpose • A character awakening to their true nature • Narratives examining forgiveness and absolution • Tales of reconciliation • A protagonist experiencing a life review • Stories about rising to a higher level of consciousness • A character serving as judge or evaluator • Tales exploring karmic resolution or closure • A protagonist hearing a call they cannot ignore • Narratives about transcending past limitations • A character experiencing spiritual awakening • Stories examining final judgments or reckonings • Tales about making peace with one's past • A protagonist rising from metaphorical death or ashes

21. The World

Keywords & Storytelling Applications: Completion • integration • accomplishment • wholeness • fulfillment • character achieving integration • one who completes the journey • world traveler • character representing accomplishment • one who dances with life • character at journey's end • the complete one • one who integrates opposites • character representing wholeness • the accomplished • one who synthesizes experience • character who transcends limitations • the world dancer • one who achieves harmony • character representing fulfillment • the journey completer • one who embodies completion • character at the height of achievement • the unified • one who brings resolution • character representing cosmic harmony • the master • one who has arrived • character representing perfect balance • the whole • one who unites all elements • character at story's end • the integrated self

Storytelling Scenarios: A character completing a significant journey or quest • Tales exploring the integration of all parts of self • A protagonist achieving mastery or accomplishment • Stories about coming full circle • A character achieving wholeness or completion • Narratives examining the synthesis of experience • Tales of final fulfillment or achievement • A protagonist dancing with life rather than struggling • Stories about transcending limitations • A character who embodies harmony and balance • Tales exploring the end of a significant cycle • A protagonist whose story reaches satisfying completion • Narratives about the unity of all things • A character who has integrated opposing aspects • Stories examining what comes after achievement • Tales about characters who have "arrived" • A protagonist experiencing the joy of completion

Minor Arcana Cards:

Wands (Fire)

Ace of Wands

Keywords & Storytelling Applications: Creative spark • initial inspiration • new project • brilliant idea • character struck by inspiration • one who begins a creative journey • visionary starter • innovative thinker • character with entrepreneurial spirit • one experiencing a flash of insight • character at the beginning of passion • the initiator • one who ignites change • character with untapped potential • the spark of life • one with a new opportunity • character with creative passion • the genesis moment • one who plants the first seed • character with innovative vision • the flame bearer • one with pure creative potential • character receiving the divine spark • the inspired • one filled with enthusiasm • character with unlimited possibilities • one about to embark on adventure • character receiving a calling • the awakener • one who brings the first light

Storytelling Scenarios: A character suddenly struck by a brilliant idea or vision • The moment a protagonist decides to start a new venture • Tales about the birth of a creative project • A character receiving a spark of divine inspiration • Stories exploring the excitement of new beginnings • A protagonist discovering a passion or calling • Narratives about the conception of an invention or art piece • A character planting the first seed of something that will grow • Tales examining the initial excitement of creation • A protagonist experiencing a sudden urge to create or build • Stories about the first glimmer of a new path • A character igniting change in a stagnant situation • Narratives exploring those precious moments when inspiration strikes • Tales about characters who bring new energy to situations • A protagonist at the very beginning of their hero's journey • Stories examining how small sparks lead to great fires

Two of Wands

Keywords & Storytelling Applications: Planning • future vision • decision point • power in balance • character at a crossroads • one making strategic plans • visionary leader • global thinker • character overseeing their domain • one contemplating expansion • character with the world in their hands • the strategist • one who sees potential futures • character with established power seeking more • the planner • one between familiar and unknown • character making far-reaching decisions • the visionary • one contemplating their empire • character balancing risk and security • the decision-maker • one with the world at their feet • character choosing between options • the worldly character • one who looks to distant horizons • character planning their next move • the empire builder • one who holds power • character discovering their personal power • the future planner • one weighing alternatives

Storytelling Scenarios: A character who has achieved initial success now planning their next move • Tales about choosing between safety and adventure • A protagonist mapping out a strategy for expansion • Stories examining the weight of decision-making • A character standing at their castle wall looking toward distant horizons • Narratives about the early stages of building an empire • Tales of characters discovering their personal power • A protagonist facing a choice between two significant paths • Stories about visionaries planning ambitious projects • A character holding metaphorical or literal power • Tales examining the responsibility of leadership • A protagonist considering worldwide or far-reaching implications • Narratives about characters who must decide when to make their move • Stories exploring the tension between planning and action • A character who sees potential where others don't • Tales about the moment of commitment to a direction

Three of Wands

Keywords & Storytelling Applications: Expansion • foresight • enterprise • looking ahead • character awaiting results • one who ventures beyond boundaries • international trader • visionary entrepreneur • character watching for ships to come in • one who takes calculated risks • character seeing early signs of success • the venture launcher • one who expands horizons • character with entrepreneurial vision • the explorer • one who goes beyond limits • character watching plans unfold • the opportunity seeker • one who pioneers new territory • character with commercial instinct • the venture capitalist • one with business acumen • character looking toward future returns • the trader • one expanding their influence • character with leadership vision • the far-sighted • one waiting for efforts to bear fruit • character who ventures forth • the horizon watcher • one who anticipates growth

Storytelling Scenarios: A character watching for the results of their ventures from a high vantage point • Tales about expansion into new territories or markets • A protagonist with the vision to see beyond current horizons • Stories examining international trade or commerce • A character launching ventures that will take time to materialize • Narratives about pioneers or explorers • Tales of entrepreneurs who take calculated risks • A protagonist whose plans are beginning to show early promise • Stories about characters who push beyond established boundaries • A business-focused character evaluating opportunities • Tales examining what happens after the initial commitment • A protagonist whose vision extends beyond the immediate • Narratives about characters waiting for their "ships to come in" • Stories exploring the early stages of expansion • A character leveraging current success to build something greater • Tales about the anticipation of future growth or returns

Four of Wands

Keywords & Storytelling Applications: Celebration • homecoming • milestone • harmony • community joy • character experiencing triumph • one who creates community • wedding planner • party organizer • character building foundations • one who brings people together • character celebrating achievement • the community builder • one who creates safe spaces • character establishing traditions • the celebrant • one who marks milestones • character creating stability • the homemaker • one who builds foundations for future • character returning home victorious • the reunion organizer • one who creates harmony • character achieving security • the foundation layer • one who establishes community • character bringing family together • the welcoming host • one who celebrates accomplishments • character creating lasting structures • the milestone marker • one who provides sanctuary

Storytelling Scenarios: A character celebrating a significant achievement or milestone • Tales about homecomings or returns • A protagonist creating community or found family • Stories examining the joy of shared accomplishment • A character organizing a wedding, celebration, or festival • Narratives about building foundations for the future • Tales exploring the creation of safe spaces or sanctuaries • A protagonist establishing a home or headquarters • Stories about characters who bring people together • Wedding or commitment ceremonies that mark new beginnings • Tales examining the stabilization of a project or relationship • A protagonist finding security after uncertainty • Narratives about communities coming together • A character who creates harmony in chaotic situations • Stories exploring the creation of traditions or rituals • Tales about characters who build lasting structures • A protagonist experiencing the joy of belonging

Five of Wands

Keywords & Storytelling Applications: Competition • conflict • rivalry • debate • character amid chaos • one involved in heated competition • tournament fighter • debate participant • character in pointless struggle • one facing opposition • character amid friendly rivalry • the competitor • one who thrives on challenge • character in creative chaos • the challenger • one fighting for position • character testing their skills • the opposition • one who creates tension • character in productive conflict • the rival • one struggling to be heard • character amid group discord • the wrestler • one who pushes boundaries • character facing multiple opponents • the contender • one fighting for recognition • character amid creative differences • the fighter • one engaged in healthy competition

Storytelling Scenarios: A character engaged in a competition, tournament, or contest • Tales exploring rivalry between individuals or groups • A protagonist facing opposition to their ideas or plans • Stories examining the creative chaos of collaborative efforts • A character dealing with multiple people talking over each other • Narratives about testing skills against worthy opponents • Tales exploring the productive aspects of conflict • A protagonist fighting to be heard in a chaotic situation • Stories about friendly competition that pushes everyone to excel • A character striving to prove themselves among peers • Tales examining group discord or lack of coordination • A protagonist navigating a situation with unclear leadership • Narratives about debates or arguments • A character in sports or competitive environments • Stories exploring how friction can generate creative energy • Tales about jockeying for position or status • A protagonist facing challenges that test their resolve

Six of Wands

Keywords & Storytelling Applications: Victory • recognition • success • acclaim • character receiving acclaim • one who achieves public success • champion • award winner • character returning victorious • one recognized for achievements • character experiencing triumph • the victor • one who receives accolades • character gaining followers • the celebrated hero • one who earns respect • character winning against odds • the champion • one who returns triumphant • character receiving validation • the acclaimed • one who gains leadership through merit • character experiencing moment of glory • the success story • one who overcomes obstacles • character receiving public praise • the recognized leader • one who enjoys their moment • character validated by community • the praised one • one who earns their position

Storytelling Scenarios: A character receiving public recognition for their achievements • Tales about victory parades or celebrations • A protagonist winning against significant odds • Stories examining the aftermath of success • A character returning home after triumph abroad • Narratives about leaders who have earned their position • Tales exploring the feeling of validation after long struggle • A protagonist experiencing their moment of glory • Stories about awards ceremonies or public acclaim • A character whose success attracts followers or admirers • Tales examining how achievement changes one's standing • A protagonist who becomes a symbol of victory for others • Narratives about characters who have overcome significant challenges • Stories exploring the personal experience of triumph • A character navigating the responsibilities that come with recognition • Tales about the culmination of effort in public acclaim • A protagonist whose success inspires others

Seven of Wands

Keywords & Storytelling Applications: Defense • standing ground • perseverance • challenge • character defending position • one who holds their ground • underdog fighter • principled defender • character facing multiple challenges • one maintaining advantage • character standing up for beliefs • the defender • one who refuses to yield • character protecting what they've built • the challenged leader • one who perseveres against opposition • character holding the high ground • the principled fighter • one defending against competitors • character standing alone • the outnumbered • one fighting for their position •

character defending their territory • the last stand • one who won't back down • character facing opposition bravely • the determined fighter • one who maintains boundaries • character protecting their achievements • the steadfast • one who resists pressure

Storytelling Scenarios: A character defending their position or territory against challengers • Tales about standing firm when outnumbered • A protagonist refusing to back down from their principles • Stories examining the defense of hard-won achievements • A character maintaining boundaries against intrusion • Narratives about holding the high ground in conflict • Tales exploring the challenges of maintaining leadership • A protagonist facing multiple opponents or challenges simultaneously • Stories about characters who must prove themselves repeatedly • A character defending their beliefs against popular opinion • Tales examining courage in the face of overwhelming odds • A protagonist who stands alone in their convictions • Narratives about protecting what one has built • A character who refuses to surrender their advantage • Stories exploring the determination required to maintain position • Tales about characters who defend others from their position of strength

Eight of Wands

Keywords & Storytelling Applications: Swift action • rapid developments • momentum • communication • character amid fast changes • one delivering urgent messages • news bearer • rapid communicator • character in accelerating events • one experiencing sudden progress • character riding momentum • the messenger • one caught in swift developments • character seeing immediate results • the accelerator • one communicating across distances • character in fast-moving plot • the momentum rider • one delivering important news • character amid quick developments • the swift traveler • one whose actions bring rapid results • character experiencing breakthroughs • the communicator • one in synchronistic events • character amid aligned circumstances • the quick mover • one whose message arrives just in time • character in sudden motion • the synchronizer • one caught in fast-moving events

Storytelling Scenarios: A character experiencing a sudden acceleration of events • Tales about urgent messages or communications • A protagonist caught in rapidly developing situations • Stories examining moments when everything happens at once • A character delivering news that changes everything • Narratives about journeys or projects that suddenly gain momentum • Tales exploring synchronicity or perfect timing • A protagonist whose plans suddenly come together • Stories about characters who must act quickly when opportunity appears • A sudden flurry of activity after a period of waiting • Tales examining what happens when communication barriers fall • A protagonist navigating a situation where events move faster than expected • Narratives about technology that speeds up communication • A character riding the wave of sudden momentum • Stories exploring the exhilaration of swift progress • Tales about characters who must deliver important information quickly

Nine of Wands

Keywords & Storytelling Applications: Resilience • persistence • last stand • vigilance • character maintaining vigilance • one who's been wounded but stands • battle-weary fighter • persistent defender • character who won't give up • one who remains alert to danger • character drawing on inner reserves • the last defender • one who persists despite injury • character showing resilience • the vigilant guard • one who sees potential threats • character who's been through battles • the survivor • one prepared for final challenge • character maintaining defensive position • the persistent one • one who continues despite exhaustion • character who's almost at the finish line • the watchful guardian • one who anticipates attack • character who's learned from past struggles • the boundary keeper • one who draws on experience • character who won't be defeated

Storytelling Scenarios: A character who continues to stand despite being battle-weary • Tales about maintaining vigilance when exhausted • A protagonist making their last stand against opposition • Stories examining resilience after repeated challenges • A character who has learned caution from past wounds • Narratives about guarding what matters most • Tales exploring the determination to continue despite setbacks • A protagonist who is bruised but not beaten • Stories about characters who remain alert to danger • The moment before final victory when endurance is most tested • Tales examining what keeps someone fighting when they could surrender • A protagonist drawing on reserves of inner strength • Narratives about characters who maintain boundaries despite pressure • Stories exploring the wisdom gained through struggle • A character who anticipates challenges based on experience • Tales about the courage to stand one's ground when weary • A protagonist who refuses to back down at the crucial moment

Ten of Wands

Keywords & Storytelling Applications: Burden • responsibility • overcommitment • exhaustion • character carrying too much • one burdened by responsibilities • overworked executive • exhausted caregiver • character bearing others' burdens • one who can't delegate • character approaching burnout • the burden bearer • one overwhelmed by duties • character who takes on too much • the responsible one • one carrying the load alone • character near breaking point • the overcommitted • one who can't say no • character crushed by expectations • the duty-bound • one who sacrifices for others • character carrying legacy burdens • the workaholic • one weighed down by obligations • character completing difficult journey • the weight bearer • one who needs to share load • character fulfilling final obligations • the overtaxed • one who bears weight of leadership

Storytelling Scenarios: A character struggling under the weight of too many responsibilities • Tales about burnout or exhaustion • A protagonist who can't delegate or share burdens • Stories examining the cost of taking on too much • A character nearing the end of a difficult journey • Narratives about the isolation of leadership • Tales exploring the physical and emotional toll of overcommitment •

A protagonist who can't say no to additional responsibilities • Stories about characters who bear others' burdens • The final stretch before completion when everything feels heaviest • Tales examining workaholism or unhealthy sacrifice • A protagonist whose sense of duty becomes self-destructive • Narratives about characters who must learn to share responsibilities • Stories exploring the pressure of expectations • A character fulfilling obligations at great personal cost • Tales about the need for boundaries and self-care • A protagonist realizing they don't have to carry everything alone

Page of Wands

Keywords & Storytelling Applications: Exploration • discovery • enthusiasm • potential • character full of enthusiasm • one discovering their passion • young explorer • enthusiastic messenger • character with creative potential • one starting creative journey • character bringing exciting news • the adventurous youth • one filled with energy • character discovering new interests • the free spirit • one exploring creative talents • character with boundless enthusiasm • the messenger • one open to new experiences • character representing potential • the excitable novice • one with news of opportunity • character embarking on adventure • the passionate beginner • one exploring their world • character representing enthusiasm • the spark igniter • one who asks "what if?" • character representing creative potential • the inspired youth • one beginning journey of passion

Storytelling Scenarios: A young or youthful character discovering their passion • Tales about enthusiasm and unbridled energy • A protagonist receiving news of an opportunity or adventure • Stories examining the early stages of creative discovery • A character setting out on their first independent journey • Narratives about messengers bringing exciting news • Tales exploring untapped potential or talent • A protagonist who brings fresh perspective to old situations • Stories about characters who ask "what if?" • The spark of curiosity that leads to exploration • Tales examining the joy of discovering one's gifts • A protagonist whose enthusiasm inspires others • Narratives about characters at the beginning of their learning curve • Stories exploring the excitement of new possibilities • A character whose energy disrupts comfortable routines • Tales about the courage to try something new • A protagonist whose inexperience is balanced by enthusiasm

Knight of Wands

Keywords & Storytelling Applications: Action • adventure • impulsiveness • passion • character rushing into action • one driven by passion • adventurous traveler • impetuous warrior • character making bold moves • one who acts without planning • character bringing dynamic change • the courageous knight • one following creative impulses • character who can't sit still • the passionate pursuer • one who charges ahead • character living for excitement • the freedom seeker • one who brings energy • character representing action over thought • the thrill-seeker • one who acts first, thinks later • character who inspires through boldness • the adventurer • one who creates excitement • character who stirs up change • the charger • one who breaks stagnation • character representing passionate pursuit • the impulsive hero • one who lives in the moment

Storytelling Scenarios: A character who charges into situations without planning • Tales about the pursuit of passion or excitement • A protagonist whose energy transforms static situations • Stories examining the consequences of impulsive decisions • A character who brings chaos through well-intended actions • Narratives about adventurers who live for the thrill • Tales exploring the tension between passion and practicality • A protagonist whose courage outpaces their caution • Stories about characters who inspire others through bold action • The whirlwind romance or passionate affair • Tales examining the charisma of the adventure-seeker • A protagonist who acts as a catalyst for change • Narratives about characters who break through stagnation • Stories exploring the benefits and costs of living in the moment • A character whose enthusiasm sweeps others along • Tales about journeys undertaken on impulse • A protagonist who brings creative fire to situations

Queen of Wands

Keywords & Storytelling Applications: Confidence • determination • passion • charisma • character radiating confidence • one who leads with passion • charismatic leader • determined achiever • character with magnetic presence • one who inspires action • character with clear vision • the confident leader • one who balances passion with wisdom • character representing feminine fire • the charismatic host • one who nurtures creativity • character with social intelligence • the passionate creator • one who commands respect • character embodying warmth and power • the inspirational leader • one who encourages others • character with vibrant energy • the social connector • one who gets things done • character representing determined femininity • the warm authority • one who leads by example • character balancing strength with approachability • the magnetic personality • one who nurtures creative fire

Storytelling Scenarios: A character whose confidence and charisma draw others to them • Tales about leadership through inspiration rather than force • A protagonist who balances passion with wisdom • Stories examining strong feminine energy • A character who creates warmth and welcome for others • Narratives about visionaries who also implement • Tales exploring the power of social intelligence • A protagonist who nurtures creativity in themselves and others • Stories about characters who command respect through authenticity • A hostess or host who creates memorable experiences • Tales examining confident sexuality or sensuality • A protagonist whose determination overcomes obstacles • Narratives about characters who lead by example • Stories exploring the balance of warmth and authority • A character whose enthusiasm inspires action in others • Tales about the power of optimism coupled with practical action • A protagonist who creates community through their magnetic presence

King of Wands

Keywords & Storytelling Applications: Leadership • vision • inspiration • authority • character with bold leadership • one who inspires loyalty • visionary leader • charismatic authority • character representing mature masculine fire • one who commands through respect • character with creative authority • the visionary king • one who leads with passion • character balancing power with creativity • the inspirational mentor • one with entrepreneurial spirit • character representing moral authority • the creative director • one who sets vision for others • character representing mastered passion • the bold leader • one who inspires from the throne • character with natural authority • the charismatic executive • one who leads projects • character representing expansive vision • the passionate authority • one who transforms through leadership • character representing creative mastery • the fire king • one who combines vision with action

Storytelling Scenarios: A character whose vision inspires others to follow • Tales about leadership that transforms organizations or groups • A protagonist who masters their passionate nature • Stories examining the responsible use of power • A character who inspires loyalty through authentic leadership • Narratives about visionaries who create lasting change • Tales exploring the balance of authority and creativity • A protagonist who leads with both passion and wisdom • Stories about characters who command natural respect • The mentor who pushes others to achieve their potential • Tales examining charismatic leadership • A protagonist combining creative vision with practical implementation • Narratives about characters who build something significant • Stories exploring mature masculine energy • A character whose personal power serves a greater vision • Tales about entrepreneurs or founders • A protagonist who must learn to direct their fire constructively • Narratives about the journey from impulsiveness to mastered passion

Cups (Water)

Ace of Cups

Keywords & Storytelling Applications: New emotions • love • intuition • compassion • character experiencing emotional awakening • one whose heart opens • new lover • spiritual seeker • character experiencing divine love • one beginning emotional journey • character with pure feelings • the heart opener • one who offers emotional gift • character whose compassion flows • the intuitive • one beginning love story • character experiencing emotional rebirth • the emotional healer • one who nurtures others • character representing new relationship • the love receiver • one whose emotions overflow • character with spiritual connection • the empathic one • one experiencing baptism • character representing emotional potential • the cup bearer • one whose feelings are pure • character offering emotional abundance • the spiritually awakened • one experiencing emotional renewal

Storytelling Scenarios: A character experiencing the beginning of a significant love story • Tales about emotional awakening or renewal • A protagonist whose heart opens after being closed • Stories examining the first stirrings of compassion • A character experiencing spiritual connection or divine love • Narratives about intuitive awakening • Tales exploring emotional healing after wounding • A protagonist offering forgiveness or compassion • Stories about characters whose sensitivity becomes their strength • The beginning of a significant emotional journey • Tales examining the moment when one's cup begins to overflow • A protagonist experiencing baptism or spiritual cleansing • Narratives about characters who discover their capacity to love • Stories exploring unconditional love or compassion • A character whose intuition awakens • Tales about the birth of empathy • A protagonist whose emotions begin to flow after being blocked

Two of Cups

Keywords & Storytelling Applications: Partnership • connection • attraction • union • character finding their match • one experiencing mutual attraction • new lovers • business partners • character forming deep connection • one experiencing soul recognition • character in harmonious relationship • the partner finder • one who connects deeply • character experiencing romantic beginning • the soul mate • one who forms alliance • character in perfect balance with another • the harmonizer • one who experiences mutual respect • character forming meaningful bond • the relationship builder • one who balances opposites • character offering emotional exchange • the connector • one recognizing their counterpart • character experiencing lover's gaze • the union maker • one committed to equal partnership • character experiencing chemistry • the reconciler • one who heals through relationship

Storytelling Scenarios: A character experiencing the magic of mutual attraction • Tales about the formation of significant partnerships • A protagonist meeting their match or counterpart • Stories examining the early stages of romance • A character recognizing a soul connection with another • Narratives about healing through connection • Tales exploring balanced relationships or partnerships • A protagonist forming an alliance with an equal • Stories about characters who complement each other perfectly • The moment when two people recognize something special in each other • Tales examining chemistry between individuals • A protagonist experiencing reconciliation after conflict • Narratives about business or creative partnerships • Stories exploring the power of mutual respect • A character finding someone who truly sees them • Tales about the formation of deep friendship • A protagonist experiencing the power of emotional exchange

Three of Cups

Keywords & Storytelling Applications: Celebration • friendship • collaboration • joy • character amid celebration • one surrounded by friends • party attendee • team member • character experiencing shared joy • one who celebrates life • character in harmonious group • the celebrator • one who brings people together • character experiencing emotional abundance • the friend • one who collaborates creatively • character with supportive community • the joy sharer • one who thrives in groups • character experiencing momentary bliss • the community builder • one who celebrates accomplishment • character with female friendships • the team player • one who creates festive atmosphere • character in creative collaboration • the happiness multiplier • one who toasts success • character experiencing communal joy • the gathering creator • one who harmonizes with others

Storytelling Scenarios: A character celebrating a significant achievement with friends • Tales about the power of supportive community • A protagonist finding joy in collaboration • Stories examining female friendship or sisterhood • A character creating or attending a celebration • Narratives about creative teams or collaborations • Tales exploring moments of shared happiness • A protagonist surrounded by supportive companions • Stories about characters who bring people together • The healing power of celebration after hardship • Tales examining the emotional abundance of community • A protagonist who thrives through connection with others • Narratives about characters raising a toast to success • Stories exploring the creative energy of harmonious groups • A character whose joy is multiplied through sharing • Tales about milestone celebrations or gatherings • A protagonist who creates festive atmosphere for others

Four of Cups

Keywords & Storytelling Applications: Contemplation • apathy • reevaluation • discontent • character experiencing emotional stagnation • one who refuses offers • bored protagonist • contemplative thinker • character blind to opportunities • one who takes things for granted • character reassessing priorities • the discontented • one lost in thought • character experiencing emotional withdrawal • the opportunity misser • one who seeks deeper meaning • character amid emotional reassessment • the contemplator • one who feels unfulfilled • character oblivious to blessings • the introspective one • one experiencing ennui • character in emotional meditation • the seeker of meaning • one rejecting the obvious • character who wants more • the self-absorbed • one who questions emotional choices • character at emotional crossroads • the meditator • one experiencing divine discontent

Storytelling Scenarios: A character experiencing boredom or dissatisfaction with current circumstances • Tales about refusing what is freely offered • A protagonist failing to notice an opportunity right before them • Stories examining the search for deeper meaning • A character taking time for contemplation or meditation • Narratives about emotional withdrawal or self-absorption • Tales exploring the feeling that something is missing • A protagonist questioning their emotional choices • Stories about characters who have become complacent • The moment when dissatisfaction leads to reevaluation • Tales examining divine discontent that precedes growth • A protagonist who has everything but feels nothing • Narratives about characters who seek more than surface pleasures • Stories exploring the tension between contemplation and action • A character who must decide whether to accept what's offered • Tales about characters lost in their own thoughts • A protagonist experiencing emotional apathy or numbness

Five of Cups

Keywords & Storytelling Applications: Loss • disappointment • regret • grief • character experiencing heartbreak • one mourning what's lost • grieving lover • disappointed optimist • character focusing on loss • one unable to see what remains • character facing emotional setback • the grief-stricken • one processing disappointment • character experiencing emotional aftermath • the regretful one • one dwelling on past mistakes • character in emotional recovery • the mourner • one learning from loss • character refusing to see hope • the disappointed • one experiencing necessary grief • character with unprocessed emotions • the loss dweller • one who must turn around • character coping with bereavement • the emotionally wounded • one experiencing betrayal • character with shattered expectations • the inconsolable • one who eventually must move forward

Storytelling Scenarios: A character grieving a significant loss or disappointment • Tales about focusing on what's been lost rather than what remains • A protagonist experiencing the aftermath of betrayal • Stories examining the process of mourning or bereavement • A character whose expectations have been shattered • Narratives about regret over past choices • Tales exploring necessary grief or emotional processing • A protagonist learning to turn from loss toward what remains • Stories about characters who must face emotional pain • The process of recovering from heartbreak or disappointment • Tales examining how grief can blind us to remaining blessings • A protagonist dealing with the emotional aftermath of failure • Narratives about characters who must learn from painful experiences • Stories exploring the slow process of emotional healing • A character fixated on what might have been • Tales about the journey from despair toward hope • A protagonist who must decide whether to remain in grief or move forward

Six of Cups

Keywords & Storytelling Applications: Nostalgia • memories • innocence • childhood • character revisiting the past • one reconnecting with childhood • nostalgic reminiscer • innocent child • character giving from the heart • one experiencing simple joy • character receiving unexpected gift • the memory keeper • one who returns home • character experiencing childhood flashbacks • the innocent • one sharing simple pleasures • character representing past happiness • the gift giver • one who remembers simpler times • character experiencing reunion • the childhood friend • one revisiting old haunts • character representing uncomplicated love • the nostalgic one • one who holds onto the past • character experiencing déjà vu • the pure-hearted • one connected to their inner child • character sharing memories • the time traveler • one finding comfort in the familiar

Storytelling Scenarios: A character revisiting their childhood home or hometown • Tales about unexpected reunions with old friends • A protagonist experiencing powerful nostalgic memories • Stories examining the innocence of childhood • A character giving or receiving gifts from the heart • Narratives about simple, uncomplicated pleasures • Tales exploring the bittersweet nature of remembrance • A protagonist reconnecting with their inner child • Stories about characters who share meaningful memories • The healing power of remembering happier times • Tales examining past relationships that shaped us • A protagonist experiencing déjà vu or memory triggers • Narratives about characters who find comfort in familiar places or people • Stories exploring the contrast between childhood and adult perspectives • A character whose past holds keys to present happiness • Tales about generational connections or shared family memories • A protagonist who must revisit the past to move forward

Seven of Cups

Keywords & Storytelling Applications: Choices • fantasy • illusion • possibilities • character facing too many options • one lost in daydreams • fantasy creator • option overloader • character seeing illusions • one experiencing temptation • character immersed in imagination • the daydreamer • one confronting illusions • character paralyzed by choices • the fantasizer • one creating mind castles • character seeing what isn't there • the option juggler • one experiencing escapism • character facing tempting visions • the possibility explorer • one lacking discernment • character in dream world • the illusionist • one needing to choose • character seeing mirages • the vision seeker • one overwhelmed by possibilities • character creating fantasy life • the escapist • one refusing reality

Storytelling Scenarios: A character overwhelmed by too many choices or possibilities • Tales about being lost in daydreams or fantasies • A protagonist tempted by illusions or false promises • Stories examining escapism or avoidance of reality • A character whose imagination creates castles in the air •

Narratives about the need for discernment among options • Tales exploring the tension between fantasy and reality • A protagonist paralyzed by the inability to choose • Stories about characters who create elaborate mental worlds • The moment when tempting visions must be evaluated realistically • Tales examining how varied options can prevent committed action • A protagonist who must distinguish between authentic desires and fantasies • Narratives about characters confronting their illusions • Stories exploring the appeal and danger of escapism • A character facing temptations that distract from genuine needs • Tales about the scattered energy of pursuing too many possibilities • A protagonist whose dreams need grounding in reality

Eight of Cups

Keywords & Storytelling Applications: Abandonment • withdrawal • seeking more • emotional journey • character walking away • one seeking deeper meaning • emotional pilgrim • spiritual seeker • character leaving comfort behind • one who outgrows situation • character on emotional quest • the seeker • one who abandons the unfulfilling • character pursuing deeper truth • the emotional nomad • one who leaves in darkness • character feeling called elsewhere • the truth pursuer • one who needs more than material success • character at turning point • the night traveler • one who follows inner call • character abandoning what once mattered • the deeper seeker • one who rejects the incomplete • character on moonlit path • the emotional explorer • one who leaves success for meaning • character following intuitive path • the meaning seeker • one who walks away from the known

Storytelling Scenarios: A character walking away from a comfortable but unfulfilling situation • Tales about the search for deeper meaning or purpose • A protagonist embarking on a pilgrimage or spiritual quest • Stories examining the courage to abandon what no longer serves • A character following an inner calling or intuition • Narratives about leaving success to find fulfillment • Tales exploring the journey into the unknown • A protagonist who feels that something essential is missing • Stories about characters who outgrow relationships or circumstances • The emotional journey away from material success toward authenticity • Tales examining the quest for deeper emotional truth • A protagonist making a difficult but necessary departure • Narratives about characters following the moonlit path of intuition • Stories exploring the bittersweet nature of necessary endings • A character who recognizes the incompleteness of apparent success • Tales about the calling to move beyond comfortable limitations • A protagonist leaving in darkness to find a new dawn

Nine of Cups

Keywords & Storytelling Applications: Satisfaction • contentment • wish fulfillment • pleasure • character experiencing satisfaction • one who gets their wish • wish granter • pleasure seeker • character experiencing emotional fulfillment • one surrounded by abundance • character with material and emotional wealth • the wish manifester • one who enjoys sensual pleasures • character experiencing contentment • the happy one • one whose cup runneth over • character at emotional peak • the contented one • one granting wishes to others • character experiencing dream come true • the emotional provider • one experiencing complete satisfaction • character enjoying the moment • the pleasure enjoyer • one whose wishes manifest • character exuding self-satisfaction • the abundance keeper • one experiencing peak happiness • character with everything they desire • the fulfilled one • one basking in success

Storytelling Scenarios: A character experiencing the fulfillment of a long-held wish • Tales about moments of complete contentment or satisfaction • A protagonist enjoying the fruits of their labors • Stories examining what happens after getting what you want • A character surrounded by emotional and material abundance • Narratives about the pleasures of sensual enjoyment • Tales exploring the feeling of having "made it" • A protagonist who grants wishes or brings joy to others • Stories about characters who have achieved their heart's desire • The satisfaction of a dream finally realized • Tales examining the importance of gratitude for abundance • A protagonist experiencing a perfect moment of happiness • Narratives about characters who embody generous satisfaction • Stories exploring the zenith of emotional fulfillment • A character whose happiness seems complete • Tales about the moment when all wishes come true • A protagonist who must learn whether fulfillment comes from within or without

Ten of Cups

Keywords & Storytelling Applications: Harmony • family • emotional fulfillment • happiness • character experiencing perfect harmony • one amid family bliss • happy family member • community leader • character experiencing domestic bliss • one who creates emotional harmony • character representing ideal family • the harmonizer • one who builds loving home • character experiencing emotional completion • the happy family member • one who achieves emotional ideal • character representing domestic happiness • the community builder • one who creates safe haven • character experiencing rainbow after storm • the happy ending • one who brings family together • character representing emotional wealth • the peacemaker • one who nurtures family bonds • character experiencing shared joy • the home builder • one who creates lasting harmony • character representing family traditions • the family connector • one who brings emotional closure

Storytelling Scenarios: A character experiencing perfect harmony within a family or community • Tales about achieving emotional fulfillment through connection • A protagonist creating or finding their ideal home • Stories examining what happens after "happily ever after" • A character whose emotional journey finds completion • Narratives about the rainbow after the storm • Tales exploring the ideal of family or community unity • A protagonist creating a haven of emotional safety for others • Stories about characters who build meaningful traditions • The culmination of an emotional quest in shared happiness • Tales examining the power of belonging and acceptance • A protagonist experiencing the joy of being truly at home • Narratives about characters who create harmony in their environment • Stories exploring family bonds and their healing power • A character whose emotional wounds find healing through community • Tales about the creation of chosen family • A protagonist who completes an emotional cycle in fulfillment

Page of Cups

Keywords & Storytelling Applications: Intuition • emotional messages • sensitivity • creativity • character with emotional sensitivity • one receiving intuitive messages • creative dreamer • emotional student • character with artistic sensitivity • one open to feelings • character receiving unexpected news • the emotional messenger • one with creative imagination • character with childlike wonder • the intuitive youth • one exploring emotional depths • character representing emotional potential • the imaginative one • one whose feelings speak truth • character with empathic gifts • the sensitive soul • one beginning creative journey • character representing emotional learning • the dreamer • one who hears inner voice • character with psychic sensitivity • the emotional explorer • one surprised by feelings • character representing emotional curiosity • the feelings novice • one with pure emotional response

Storytelling Scenarios: A character who receives unexpected emotional messages or insights • Tales about the beginning of creative or artistic development • A protagonist whose sensitivity becomes their strength • Stories examining childlike emotional openness • A character receiving surprising news that touches the heart • Narratives about learning the language of emotions • Tales exploring the early stages of intuitive development • A protagonist whose imagination brings unexpected gifts • Stories about characters who represent emotional potential • The moment when intuition delivers an important message • Tales examining the surprise of new emotional discoveries • A protagonist navigating the waters of feeling • Narratives about characters whose hearts speak louder than their minds • Stories exploring the unexpected wisdom of emotional youth • A character whose dreams contain important messages • Tales about artistic or creative beginnings • A protagonist whose emotional innocence sees truth that others miss

Knight of Cups

Keywords & Storytelling Applications: Romance • imagination • charm • gallantry • character on romantic quest • one following heart's desire • romantic idealist • emotional messenger • character guided by feelings • one pursuing artistic vision • character representing emotional courage • the romantic knight • one delivering emotional messages • character following creative inspiration • the sensitive warrior • one on quest for love • character combining courage with sensitivity • the emotional pilgrim • one who woos with words • character representing emotional idealism • the charming one • one who follows emotional impulses • character bringing important news • the poetic warrior • one swept away by feelings • character embodying romantic love • the dreamy knight • one whose imagination guides • character representing emotional yearning • the seeker of beauty • one driven by artistic passion

Storytelling Scenarios: A character embarking on a quest for love or beauty • Tales about following one's heart despite practical concerns • A protagonist delivering messages of emotional importance • Stories examining romantic idealism and its consequences • A character swept away by emotional currents • Narratives about the courage required to follow feelings • Tales exploring the tension between dreams and reality • A protagonist whose imagination leads to unexpected places • Stories about characters who embody both sensitivity and courage • The journey of an artist following their creative vision • Tales examining the power and pitfalls of charm • A protagonist whose poetry or art expresses deep emotion • Narratives about characters whose feelings drive their actions • Stories exploring romantic pursuits or courtship • A character whose sensitivity may be both strength and weakness • Tales about messengers bearing emotional news • A protagonist whose idealism creates both beauty and challenge

Queen of Cups

Keywords & Storytelling Applications: Intuition • empathy • emotional wisdom • compassion • character with deep intuition • one who nurtures emotions • emotional healer • compassionate counselor • character with psychic ability • one who embodies emotional wisdom • character representing feminine intuition • the emotional nurturer • one who listens deeply • character whose heart understands • the empathic one • one who sees beneath surfaces • character embodying maternal love • the intuitive guide • one who feels others' pain • character with emotional intelligence • the compassionate one • one who holds emotional space • character representing emotional depth • the feeling wisdom keeper • one connected to unconscious • character who nurtures creativity • the dream interpreter • one with healing presence • character representing receptive love • the emotional mirror • one who reflects truth

Storytelling Scenarios: A character whose intuition reveals hidden truths • Tales about healing through emotional understanding • A protagonist who nurtures others' emotional growth • Stories examining the power of deep empathy • A character whose compassion transforms situations • Narratives about the wisdom that comes through feeling • Tales exploring maternal love and nurturing • A protagonist whose emotional intelligence guides others • Stories about characters who mirror emotional truth • The healing presence that creates safe space for vulnerability • Tales examining psychic or intuitive abilities • A protagonist who understands the language of dreams • Narratives about characters who embody receptive feminine energy • Stories exploring the depth of emotional waters • A character whose compassion extends to the unlovable • Tales about healers who work through heart connection • A protagonist whose emotional wisdom comes from their own wounds

King of Cups

Keywords & Storytelling Applications: Emotional mastery • compassion with boundaries • wisdom • diplomacy • character with emotional control • one who balances heart and mind • compassionate authority • diplomatic leader • character representing mature emotion • one who manages feelings wisely • character combining power with empathy • the emotional master • one who rules with compassion • character representing emotional maturity • the wise counselor • one who navigates emotional complexities • character with balanced feelings • the diplomatic one • one who harnesses emotions • character representing emotional stability • the compassionate judge • one who leads with heart • character with emotional authority • the balanced one • one whose feelings serve wisdom • character representing mature masculine feeling • the emotional king • one who contains powerful emotions • character embodying emotional intelligence • the feeling mediator • one who brings emotional clarity

Storytelling Scenarios: A character who maintains emotional balance in crisis • Tales about leadership that combines heart with boundaries • A protagonist navigating complex emotional situations with wisdom • Stories examining mature emotional expression • A character whose compassion is tempered with clarity • Narratives about emotional mastery after long struggle • Tales exploring wise counsel or guidance • A protagonist who mediates emotional conflicts • Stories about characters who embody mature masculine emotional energy • The power that comes from integrating heart and mind • Tales examining emotional intelligence in action • A protagonist whose authority comes from emotional wisdom • Narratives about characters who can feel deeply without being overwhelmed • Stories exploring diplomatic solutions to emotional problems • A character whose stability helps others through emotional storms • Tales about therapists, counselors, or wise emotional guides • A protagonist who teaches others to navigate emotional waters

Swords (Air)

Ace of Swords

Keywords & Storytelling Applications: Clarity • breakthrough • mental power • truth • character experiencing mental breakthrough • one who cuts through confusion • truth seeker • clarity finder • character with mental sharpness • one who achieves breakthrough • character representing pure intellect • the truth revealer • one who achieves clarity • character experiencing cognitive shift • the clear thinker • one who wields intellectual power • character representing breakthrough moment • the fog cutter • one who brings mental focus • character embodying logical force • the sharp mind • one who speaks truth • character experiencing intellectual victory • the breakthrough achiever • one who dispels illusions • character representing mental force • the clarity bringer • one whose mind awakens • character discovering fundamental truth • the sword wielder • one whose thoughts pierce veils

Storytelling Scenarios: A character experiencing a moment of perfect clarity or understanding • Tales about intellectual breakthroughs or discoveries • A protagonist cutting through confusion or deception • Stories examining the power of truth to transform situations • A character whose mind suddenly grasps a complex problem • Narratives about the moment when mental fog clears • Tales exploring the double-edged nature of intellectual power • A protagonist whose clarity of thought changes everything • Stories about characters who speak truth to power • The triumph of rationality over chaos or confusion • Tales examining the moment when understanding dawns • A protagonist whose mental acuity solves seemingly unsolvable problems • Narratives about characters who dispel illusions with clear thinking • Stories exploring the birth of new ideas or paradigms • A character whose analytical powers cut through complexity • Tales about the discovery of hidden truth • A protagonist experiencing intellectual awakening

Two of Swords

Keywords & Storytelling Applications: Decision • stalemate • neutrality • difficult choice • character at decision point • one maintaining precarious balance • undecided chooser • blindfolded decision-maker • character refusing to choose • one caught between options • character in emotional numbness • the fence-sitter • one blocking emotional input • character creating temporary peace • the balancer • one weighing equal options • character in denial of problem • the choice avoider • one maintaining equilibrium • character in mental stalemate • the blindfolded one • one creating artificial calm • character seeking neutrality • the decision postponer • one caught in dilemma • character achieving temporary truce • the equilibrium seeker • one blocking outside influence • character between difficult options • the emotional blocker • one creating mental barriers

Storytelling Scenarios: A character caught between equally difficult choices • Tales about the refusal to see or decide • A protagonist maintaining a precarious balance between opposing forces • Stories examining emotional numbness as protection • A character who creates temporary peace through denial • Narratives about the tension of unresolved choices • Tales exploring the blindfolded state of indecision • A protagonist whose neutrality cannot be maintained indefinitely • Stories about characters who block emotional input to make decisions • The temporary truce that postpones inevitable conflict • Tales examining the paralysis of equally weighted options • A protagonist caught in mental stalemate • Narratives about characters who create barriers against painful awareness • Stories exploring the tension of suspended decision • A character who must eventually remove the blindfold • Tales about situations where refusing to choose is itself a choice • A protagonist balancing between competing loyalties or values

Three of Swords

Keywords & Storytelling Applications: Heartbreak • sorrow • grief • painful truth • character experiencing heartbreak • one suffering painful truth • betrayed lover • grief-stricken individual • character amid emotional pain • one whose heart is pierced • character facing painful reality • the heartbroken • one processing deep hurt • character experiencing necessary pain • the grief bearer • one betrayed by trusted other • character confronting painful truth • the sorrow carrier • one whose illusions are shattered • character amid emotional storm • the pain experiencer • one whose trust is broken • character learning through suffering • the truth acceptor • one facing relationship end • character with pierced illusions • the betrayed • one whose heart must heal • character amid necessary suffering • the disillusioned • one who faces harsh reality

Storytelling Scenarios: A character experiencing the sharp pain of betrayal or heartbreak • Tales about the shattering of romantic illusions • A protagonist confronting painful truth about a relationship • Stories examining grief after significant loss • A character whose heart is literally or metaphorically pierced • Narratives about the storm of emotions that follows betrayal • Tales exploring the pain necessary for growth or clarity • A protagonist whose trust has been violated • Stories about characters facing the reality of a situation despite pain • The moment when a character realizes they've been deceived • Tales examining how heartbreak transforms perspective • A protagonist processing deep emotional wounds • Narratives about characters whose illusions are painfully shattered • Stories exploring the physical manifestations of emotional pain • A character learning important lessons through suffering • Tales about the end of significant relationships • A protagonist whose pain eventually leads to healing or growth

Four of Swords

Keywords & Storytelling Applications: Rest • recuperation • sanctuary • stillness • character needing recovery • one in retreat • exhausted warrior • meditation practitioner • character in forced rest • one seeking sanctuary • character in mental retreat • the recuperator • one in recovery mode • character taking timeout • the sanctuary seeker • one finding mental peace • character recharging energy • the meditator • one lying in repose • character requiring stillness • the mind quieter • one recovering from battle • character in protected space • the still point • one healing mental wounds • character in sabbatical • the hermit • one preparing for future challenges • character representing withdrawal • the interval • one between battles • character in convalescence

Storytelling Scenarios: A character forced to rest or recuperate after major exertion • Tales about strategic withdrawal from conflict • A protagonist finding sanctuary or safe harbor • Stories examining the healing power of stillness • A character in recovery mode after illness or trauma • Narratives about mental or spiritual retreat • Tales exploring the necessary pause between challenges • A protagonist seeking quiet to prepare for future trials • Stories about characters who must heal before moving forward • The power found in surrender to necessary rest • Tales examining forced stillness as blessing in disguise • A protagonist learning the value of timeout or sabbatical • Narratives about characters who find sanctuary in unexpected places • Stories exploring meditation or contemplative practices • A character whose strength returns through strategic rest • Tales about the quiet interval between significant life chapters • A protagonist recovering from mental or emotional battles

Five of Swords

Keywords & Storytelling Applications: Conflict • defeat • humiliation • win at all costs • character experiencing defeat • one who wins pyrrhic victory • sore loser • gloating winner • character amid conflict aftermath • one who goes too far • character experiencing humiliation • the hollow victor • one left defeated on battlefield • character facing loss of respect • the conflict creator • one willing to sacrifice honor • character experiencing painful lesson • the bitter winner • one who suffers defeat • character using questionable tactics • the ruthless one • one who must face consequences • character amid social conflict • the aftermath survivor • one experiencing cost of victory • character embodying win-at-all-costs • the defeated • one gathering scattered pieces • character learning from loss • the humiliated • one experiencing social rejection

Storytelling Scenarios: A character who wins but at too great a cost • Tales about pyrrhic victories or hollow triumphs • A protagonist dealing with humiliation after defeat • Stories examining the aftermath of conflict • A character who uses questionable tactics to succeed • Narratives about the cost of winning at all costs • Tales exploring the pain of defeat or humiliation • A protagonist picking up the pieces after a battle lost • Stories about characters who must face the consequences of their actions • The bitterness that remains after conflict • Tales examining the emotions of the vanquished • A protagonist who must learn from painful loss • Narratives about characters whose ambition overreaches their ethics • Stories exploring the tension between winning and maintaining integrity • A character who must recover their honor after defeat • Tales about conflicts where everyone loses something • A protagonist dealing with the shame of defeat or poor performance

Six of Swords

Keywords & Storytelling Applications: Transition • passage • leaving behind • moving on • character in transition • one being guided to safety • refugee • emigrant • character leaving troubled waters • one carrying mental baggage • character moving toward peace • the passage maker • one guided through transition • character carrying past with them • the mental traveler • one on healing journey • character in between states • the transition passenger • one moving from chaos to calm • character on necessary journey • the refugee • one escorted to safety • character in emotional transition • the migrant • one carried by others' help • character moving toward healing • the guided one • one leaving difficulty behind • character in liminal space • the between-worlds traveler • one on journey of emotional recovery

Storytelling Scenarios: A character departing from a troubled situation toward something better • Tales about necessary journeys or migrations • A protagonist being guided through a difficult transition • Stories examining the process of leaving the past behind • A character physically or emotionally relocating • Narratives about refugees or those seeking asylum • Tales exploring the liminal space between old and new • A protagonist carrying baggage from past experiences • Stories about characters who must accept help during transition • The journey from turbulent waters toward calmer seas • Tales examining what we take with us when we leave • A protagonist whose mind is transitioning to new understanding • Narratives about characters who must physically relocate to heal emotionally • Stories exploring the bittersweet nature of necessary departures • A character whose journey represents emotional or mental process • Tales about guided passages through difficult terrain • A protagonist experiencing the uncertainty of being between worlds

Seven of Swords

Keywords & Storytelling Applications: Deception • strategy • stealth • cunning • character using stealth • one who deceives • strategic thief • clever manipulator • character attempting escape • one who acts covertly • character employing strategy • the secret agent • one who works alone • character avoiding confrontation • the strategist • one implementing plans • character representing partial victory • the cunning one • one avoiding direct conflict • character stealing ideas • the spy • one who hides truth • character employing mental agility • the escape artist • one who operates in shadows • character with hidden agenda • the trickster • one who uses wit over force • character with secret plan • the lone operator • one who bends rules • character representing strategic retreat

Storytelling Scenarios: A character using stealth or cunning rather than direct confrontation • Tales about strategic theft or deception • A protagonist who must work alone on a risky venture • Stories examining the ethics of necessary deception • A character implementing a secret plan or strategy • Narratives about spies or intelligence operations • Tales exploring the advantages of wit over force • A protagonist stealing information or ideas • Stories about characters who operate in the shadows • The partial victory achieved through cunning • Tales examining strategic retreat or tactical withdrawal • A protagonist whose ethical boundaries are tested • Narratives about characters with hidden agendas • Stories exploring the consequences of deception • A character whose clever plan has unforeseen consequences • Tales about those who bend rules to achieve goals • A protagonist who must use mental agility to overcome powerful opposition

Eight of Swords

Keywords & Storytelling Applications: Restriction • limitation • imprisonment • victim mindset • character feeling trapped • one in self-imposed prison • bound captive • restricted thinker • character amid mental constraints • one surrounded by problems • character blinded to options • the prisoner • one trapped by mental constructs • character in situation of limited options • the self-restricted • one unable to see way out • character with victim mentality • the bound one • one trapped in mental paradigm • character amid external restrictions • the limitation experiencer • one surrounded by obstacles • character unable to move • the captive • one with freedom close but unseen • character accepting false limitations • the blindfolded one • one restricted by beliefs • character needing to remove own blindfold • the constrained • one whose thoughts create prison

Storytelling Scenarios: A character trapped in a situation with seemingly no escape • Tales about self-imposed limitations or restrictions • A protagonist unable to see available options • Stories examining the victim mindset • A character bound by societal or external constraints • Narratives about psychological imprisonment • Tales exploring the power of limiting beliefs • A protagonist who must remove their own blindfold • Stories about characters trapped by their own thought patterns • The moment when one realizes their prison is self-created • Tales examining situations of constraint where escape is actually possible • A protagonist surrounded by obstacles but unable to move • Narratives about characters whose freedom is within reach but unseen • Stories exploring the restricted options of the vulnerable • A character whose mindset creates their limitations • Tales about the realization that freedom requires courage • A protagonist who must challenge their perception of helplessness

Nine of Swords

Keywords & Storytelling Applications: Anxiety • nightmares • worry • despair • character experiencing insomnia • one plagued by nightmares • anxiety sufferer • guilt carrier • character in mental anguish • one tormented by thoughts • character experiencing dark night of soul • the worried one • one facing inner demons • character amid psychological suffering • the nightmare experiencer • one overwhelmed by fear • character in mental crisis • the despair sufferer • one haunted by past actions • character experiencing guilt • the midnight worrier • one facing worst fears • character in deep distress • the anxiety carrier • one whose thoughts torture • character representing mental suffering • the sleepless one • one whose mind creates worst scenarios • character haunted by regrets • the tormented • one in darkest hour before dawn

Storytelling Scenarios: A character experiencing crippling anxiety or worry • Tales about insomnia and nighttime torment • A protagonist facing their worst fears in the darkness • Stories examining the suffering caused by one's own thoughts • A character haunted by guilt or regret • Narratives about psychological anguish or mental crisis • Tales exploring the dark night of the soul • A protagonist tormented by recurring nightmares • Stories about characters battling inner demons • The amplification of fears in the darkness of night • Tales examining how the mind can become its own torturer • A protagonist overwhelmed by grief or despair • Narratives about characters who find no respite from mental suffering • Stories exploring anxiety disorders or psychological distress • A character who cannot escape their own thoughts • Tales about hitting emotional rock bottom • A protagonist experiencing the darkest hour before potential dawn

Ten of Swords

Keywords & Storytelling Applications: Ending • rock bottom • failure • crisis •

character at absolute bottom • one experiencing total defeat • fallen warrior • crisis experiencer • character facing painful ending • one betrayed completely • character amid dramatic conclusion • the rock-bottom hitter • one experiencing necessary ending • character facing painful truth • the defeated • one whose situation must change • character experiencing betrayal • the transformation experiencer • one facing painful but necessary end • character amid destruction before renewal • the ended • one experiencing complete collapse • character at point of no return • the crisis survivor • one experiencing worst-case scenario • character facing devastating loss • the phoenix potential • one experiencing necessary death • character at transformative moment • the cycle ender • one facing painful rebirth

Storytelling Scenarios: A character experiencing complete defeat or failure • Tales about hitting absolute rock bottom • A protagonist betrayed in the worst possible way • Stories examining the end of a significant life chapter • A character whose situation has completely collapsed • Narratives about the moment when things cannot get worse • Tales exploring necessary endings despite their pain • A protagonist facing the painful truth of complete failure • Stories about characters who must experience death before rebirth • The crisis that completely transforms one's reality • Tales examining the aftermath of devastating betrayal • A protagonist whose old life or identity is completely destroyed • Narratives about characters at the point of no return • Stories exploring the painful clarity that comes with complete collapse • A character experiencing the darkest moment before potential rebirth • Tales about the phoenix rising from complete destruction • A protagonist whose suffering marks the end of a difficult cycle

Page of Swords

Keywords & Storytelling Applications: Curiosity • vigilance • new ideas • preparation • character full of curiosity • one watching for danger • young thinker • idea explorer • character with mental alertness • one preparing for challenges • character representing intellectual beginnings • the truth seeker • one with curious mind • character representing vigilant awareness • the watchful one • one who questions everything • character with fresh perspective • the mental explorer • one ready for anything • character representing new understanding • the messanger • one quick of thought • character who sees clearly • the observer • one beginning intellectual journey • character representing mental acuity • the idea generator • one watching the horizon • character starting new learning • the vigilant youth • one whose mind is opening

Storytelling Scenarios: A character whose curiosity leads to important discoveries • Tales about vigilant observation or watchfulness • A protagonist at the beginning of intellectual exploration • Stories examining the fresh perspective of the uninitiated • A character who questions established ideas or customs • Narratives about preparation for intellectual challenges • Tales exploring the energy of new ideas or concepts • A protagonist whose alertness prevents disaster • Stories about characters who maintain careful watch • The enthusiasm of beginning a journey of learning • Tales examining the power of seeing with fresh eyes • A protagonist who brings new perspective to old problems • Narratives about characters who challenge accepted truths • Stories exploring the mindset of preparation and readiness • A character whose quick mind grasps important details • Tales about the messenger who brings important information • A protagonist whose mind is just awakening to its potential

Knight of Swords

Keywords & Storytelling Applications: Action • impulsiveness • directness • aggression • character charging forward • one pursuing truth relentlessly • forceful communicator • determined pursuer • character with aggressive approach • one focused on goal • character representing mental charge • the truth warrior • one who acts without caution • character representing direct action • the focused attacker • one who speaks without filter • character in mental pursuit • the charger • one with single-minded focus • character representing intellectual force • the direct one • one whose words cut • character with unwavering determination • the relentless pursuer • one who overcomes obstacles • character representing mental aggression • the verbal warrior • one who acts before thinking • character cutting through resistance • the blunt speaker • one who charges ahead

Storytelling Scenarios: A character who charges ahead without considering consequences • Tales about the relentless pursuit of truth or goals • A protagonist whose directness creates both progress and problems • Stories examining the consequences of acting without planning • A character whose words cut like swords • Narratives about the power and danger of intellectual aggression • Tales exploring single-minded focus or determination • A protagonist who overcomes obstacles through sheer force of will • Stories about characters who speak bluntly or without filter • The double-edged nature of forceful communication • Tales examining the tension between action and wisdom • A protagonist whose impulsiveness leads to unexpected situations • Narratives about characters who prioritize truth over tact • Stories exploring the mindset of the intellectual warrior • A character whose mental agility becomes aggressive force • Tales about breaking through resistance or barriers • A protagonist whose determination borders on obsession

Queen of Swords

Keywords & Storytelling Applications: Perception • independence • clear communication • complexity • character with perceptive insight • one who sees truth • independent thinker • clear communicator • character who cuts through deception • one who stands alone • character representing intellectual discernment • the truth speaker • one who values honesty • character representing emotional independence • the perceptive one • one with analytical mind • character who speaks directly • the independent one • one who has survived difficulty • character representing clarity through pain • the unsentimental • one whose words have precision • character with emotional boundaries • the sharp-eyed • one who offers honest feedback • character representing mature intellectual femininity • the clarity keeper • one who combines wisdom with truth • character who stands in personal power • the boundary setter • one whose mind is not clouded

Storytelling Scenarios: A character whose perceptive insights reveal hidden truth • Tales about maintaining independence in challenging circumstances • A protagonist who speaks truth without emotional cushioning • Stories examining wisdom gained through difficult experiences • A character who establishes clear boundaries • Narratives about the power of direct, honest communication • Tales exploring emotional independence after painful experiences • A protagonist whose analytical mind cuts through confusion • Stories about characters who maintain objectivity despite personal cost • The strength found in standing alone with one's truth • Tales examining unsentimental wisdom or perspective • A protagonist who values honesty above comfort • Narratives about characters who see clearly what others miss • Stories exploring the complexity of the intellectual feminine • A character who has learned to balance head and heart • Tales about finding one's voice after silencing • A protagonist whose boundaries protect their hard-won wisdom

King of Swords

Keywords & Storytelling Applications: Authority • truth • ethical leadership • mental mastery • character with intellectual authority • one who judges fairly • ethical leader • truth upholder • character with mental mastery • one who makes clear decisions • character representing intellectual maturity • the just ruler • one who upholds principles • character representing ethical authority • the fair judge • one who speaks with clarity • character with intellectual power • the truth commander • one who uses logic and ethics • character representing mature masculine intellect • the principled one • one whose word is law • character with mastered thought • the mental master • one who cuts through complexity • character representing clear judgment • the authority figure • one who upholds justice • character with power of discernment • the wise ruler • one whose mind creates order

Storytelling Scenarios: A character whose intellectual authority commands respect • Tales about leadership based on ethical principles • A protagonist who must judge a complex situation fairly • Stories examining the responsibility of intellectual power • A character who creates order through clear thinking • Narratives about difficult decisions made with ethical clarity • Tales exploring the mature masculine intellect • A protagonist whose words carry the weight of authority • Stories about characters who uphold truth despite consequences • The power of clear judgment in chaotic situations • Tales examining the tension between justice and mercy • A protagonist whose mind has mastered emotion without denying it • Narratives about characters who create structures based on principles • Stories exploring the archetype of the wise king or judge • A character whose clarity helps others find their way • Tales about leadership that balances intellect with ethics • A protagonist who must use their authority to protect truth or justice

Pentacles (Earth)

Ace of Pentacles

Keywords & Storytelling Applications: Opportunity • prosperity • beginning • manifestation • character receiving opportunity • one manifesting material success • new entrepreneur • financial opportunity recipient • character at prosperity threshold • one receiving physical gift • character embarking on material journey • the manifestor • one planting prosperity seed • character receiving tangible opportunity • the opportunity receiver • one beginning prosperous path • character with new job or business • the seed planter • one with material potential • character at gateway to abundance • the physical creator • one whose work bears fruit • character starting financial venture • the resource finder • one receiving earthly blessing • character with material potential • the wealth seeker • one at beginning of practical journey • character entering gate of opportunity • the physical beginner • one whose dreams manifest

Storytelling Scenarios: A character receiving an unexpected financial opportunity • Tales about the beginning of a business or entrepreneurial venture • A protagonist standing at the threshold of prosperity • Stories examining the seed stage of material manifestation • A character receiving a tangible gift or inheritance • Narratives about the start of a career or practical path • Tales exploring the moment when potential becomes opportunity • A protagonist receiving the fruits of previous efforts • Stories about characters who discover resources or riches • The initial investment that promises future returns • Tales examining the birth of material projects • A protagonist stepping through a gateway to abundance • Narratives about characters planting seeds for future harvest • Stories exploring the physical manifestation of ideas • A character whose dreams begin to take tangible form • Tales about the beginning of financial independence • A protagonist receiving their first substantial paycheck or commission

Two of Pentacles

Keywords & Storytelling Applications: Balance • adaptability • juggling priorities • change • character balancing responsibilities • one juggling multiple tasks • busy multitasker • adaptable worker • character amid financial ups and downs • one managing change • character handling multiple responsibilities • the juggler • one dancing through obstacles • character adapting to circumstances • the balancer • one navigating fluctuations • character managing competing demands • the flexible one • one prioritizing resources • character amid physical change • the resource manager • one responding to shifting tides • character maintaining equilibrium • the adaptable one • one choreographing life demands • character keeping many plates spinning • the choreographer • one embracing life's rhythm • character balancing work and play • the prioritizer • one making multiple commitments work

Storytelling Scenarios: A character juggling multiple responsibilities or commitments • Tales about maintaining balance during periods of change • A protagonist adapting to fluctuating circumstances • Stories examining how to prioritize competing demands • A character dancing between different aspects of life • Narratives about handling financial ups and downs • Tales exploring the skill of flexibility in changing times • A protagonist managing multiple projects simultaneously • Stories about characters who must maintain equilibrium amid chaos • The challenge of keeping multiple "plates spinning" • Tales examining work-life balance • A protagonist whose adaptability becomes their strength • Narratives about characters navigating through unpredictable circumstances • Stories exploring the rhythm of constant adjustment • A character who must allocate limited resources wisely • Tales about managing during times of financial uncertainty • A protagonist whose juggling act becomes increasingly complex

Three of Pentacles

Keywords & Storytelling Applications: Collaboration • skill • teamwork • craftsmanship • character displaying craftsmanship • one working with team • skilled artisan • collaborative worker • character receiving recognition for skills • one building something lasting • character amid project collaboration • the craftsperson • one whose work is appreciated • character developing expertise • the collaborator • one working with specialists • character creating quality work • the team member • one building something significant • character refining skills • the quality creator • one whose talents are recognized • character participating in group effort • the skilled worker • one combining talents with others • character laying foundations • the apprentice • one learning craft • character receiving guidance from masters • the foundation builder • one creating excellence through teamwork

Storytelling Scenarios: A character whose craftsmanship or skill receives recognition • Tales about successful collaboration on important projects • A protagonist working with others to build something significant • Stories examining the development of expertise or craftsmanship • A character learning from masters in their field • Narratives about laying foundations for future achievements • Tales exploring the synergy that comes from teamwork • A protagonist whose skills contribute to a larger purpose • Stories about characters who take pride in quality work • The satisfaction of creating something built to last • Tales examining the apprenticeship journey • A protagonist finding their place within a team • Narratives about characters whose different talents create something greater • Stories exploring the satisfaction of work well done • A character receiving appreciation for their contribution • Tales about the building of cathedrals, bridges, or other lasting structures • A protagonist whose individual efforts harmonize with others'

Four of Pentacles

Keywords & Storytelling Applications: Security • control • conservation • hoarding • character seeking security • one holding onto possessions • careful saver • resource controller • character fearing loss • one with scarcity mindset • character protecting assets • the hoarder • one refusing to share • character seeking financial control • the security seeker • one clinging to stability • character with fear-based relationship to money • the miser • one who grasps too tightly • character establishing foundations • the stable one • one whose possessions possess them • character representing material stability • the control seeker • one building financial security • character afraid of change • the foundation keeper • one whose world is too small • character protecting what they've earned • the conserver • one creating material boundaries

Storytelling Scenarios: A character who clings too tightly to possessions or money • Tales about the search for security and stability • A protagonist whose fear of loss prevents growth • Stories examining the line between prudence and hoarding • A character building foundations for their security • Narratives about control issues related to resources • Tales exploring the prison created by excessive caution • A protagonist whose possessions begin to possess them • Stories about characters who cannot share or give • The stability found in careful management of resources • Tales examining the scarcity mindset • A protagonist creating boundaries around their resources • Narratives about characters whose world becomes too small • Stories exploring the tension between security and generosity • A character whose stability becomes stagnation • Tales about the psychological aspects of wealth protection • A protagonist who must learn to loosen their grip on control

Five of Pentacles

Keywords & Storytelling Applications: Hardship • struggle • isolation • poverty • character experiencing material hardship • one excluded from prosperity • poverty experiencer • health struggler • character facing financial crisis • one excluded from group • character amid physical suffering • the outsider • one enduring hardship • character experiencing unemployment • the impoverished • one facing illness or disability • character left out in cold • the excluded • one experiencing isolation • character amid material challenge • the struggling one • one whose resources are depleted • character facing hard times • the resilient poor • one seeking assistance • character representing financial difficulty • the down-and-out • one whose situation worsens • character experiencing scarcity • the outcast • one surviving despite hardship

Storytelling Scenarios: A character experiencing financial hardship or poverty • Tales about enduring through times of scarcity • A protagonist facing unemployment or financial crisis • Stories examining social exclusion or marginalization • A character dealing with illness without adequate resources • Narratives about homelessness or economic struggle • Tales exploring the experience of being an outsider • A protagonist enduring harsh conditions with limited support • Stories about characters who face physical hardship • The loneliness of struggling while others prosper nearby • Tales examining how crisis reveals true friends • A protagonist seeking assistance during difficult times •

Narratives about characters whose resources have been depleted • Stories exploring resilience in the face of adversity • A character who must navigate systems while disadvantaged • Tales about the invisible suffering of those in need • A protagonist who finds unexpected resources in times of scarcity

Six of Pentacles

Keywords & Storytelling Applications: Generosity • giving • receiving • charity • character displaying generosity • one who gives to others • charitable donor • grant recipient • character in position to help • one receiving assistance • character distributing resources • the philanthropist • one experiencing generosity • character sharing wealth • the benefactor • one accepting help with grace • character creating financial balance • the donor • one weighing where help is needed • character experiencing prosperity • the almsgiver • one receiving timely assistance • character representing benevolence • the grace receiver • one who assesses worthiness • character distributing fairly • the balance keeper • one demonstrating abundance mentality • character receiving needed help • the generous one • one who understands giving and receiving

Storytelling Scenarios: A character in a position to help others financially • Tales about giving or receiving necessary assistance • A protagonist who must learn to accept help graciously • Stories examining the dynamics of charity or philanthropy • A character who distributes resources to those in need • Narratives about the circulation of prosperity • Tales exploring the power imbalance in giving relationships • A protagonist who must determine who deserves assistance • Stories about characters who share their abundance • The dignity or humiliation in receiving charity • Tales examining different forms of generosity • A protagonist whose timely gift changes someone's circumstances • Narratives about characters who give without expecting return • Stories exploring the psychological aspects of charity • A character who holds the scales of giving and receiving • Tales about the responsibility that comes with wealth • A protagonist experiencing unexpected generosity in time of need

Seven of Pentacles

Keywords & Storytelling Applications: Assessment • patience • investment • growth • character evaluating progress • one waiting for harvest • patient investor • project assessor • character amid slow growth • one evaluating long-term work • character pausing to reflect • the long-term planner • one viewing growth of efforts • character awaiting return on investment • the patient one • one planning next phase • character taking stock • the crop watcher • one in growth pause • character evaluating project • the assessor • one watching seeds grow • character amid necessary pause • the investor • one seeing first fruits • character questioning efforts • the evaluator • one experiencing delayed gratification • character amid long-term process • the planner • one reflecting on progress

Storytelling Scenarios: A character pausing to evaluate the progress of their work • Tales about patience during long-term projects • A protagonist awaiting returns on their investment • Stories examining the frustration and necessity of delayed gratification • A character taking stock of what they've accomplished • Narratives about the slow growth of worthwhile endeavors • Tales exploring the assessment phase of significant work • A protagonist questioning whether their efforts will bear fruit • Stories about characters who must decide whether to continue or change course • The moment of reflection between planting and harvesting • Tales examining how we measure progress or success • A protagonist who must develop patience with natural processes • Narratives about characters who have invested significant time • Stories exploring the tension between continuing or abandoning projects • A character seeing the first fruits of long labor • Tales about planning next steps after evaluation • A protagonist experiencing the satisfaction of witnessed growth

Eight of Pentacles

Keywords & Storytelling Applications: Dedication • skill development • craftsmanship • diligence • character developing skills • one dedicated to craft •

apprentice • detail-focused worker • character showing diligence • one mastering trade • character amid skill refinement • the craftsperson • one focused on excellence • character showing attention to detail • the dedicated worker • one improving through practice • character representing focused work • the apprentice • one mastering practical skills • character showing commitment to quality • the skill developer • one in focused learning • character demonstrating work ethic • the detail master • one repeating until perfect • character representing dedication • the quality pursuer • one showing methodical approach • character refining abilities • the persistent learner • one building reputation through work

Storytelling Scenarios: A character dedicating themselves to mastering a craft or skill • Tales about apprenticeship or skill development • A protagonist whose attention to detail creates excellence • Stories examining the satisfaction of work well done • A character building a reputation through consistent quality • Narratives about the discipline required for mastery • Tales exploring the focus required for craftsmanship • A protagonist improving their skills through diligent practice • Stories about characters who find meaning in work itself • The gradual process of developing expertise in a field • Tales examining the satisfaction of tangible accomplishment • A protagonist whose methodical approach yields results • Narratives about characters who pursue quality above all • Stories exploring the relationship between dedication and growth • A character whose work ethic transforms their circumstances • Tales about learning through doing • A protagonist whose commitment to excellence sets them apart

Nine of Pentacles

Keywords & Storytelling Applications: Independence • self-sufficiency • refinement • accomplishment • character enjoying earned luxury • one who is self-sufficient • refined individual • garden cultivator • character with financial independence • one enjoying fruits of labor • character representing material success • the self-made one • one who has created beauty • character with cultivated taste • the independent one • one enjoying solitary accomplishment • character amid luxurious surroundings • the garden tender • one whose discipline brought rewards • character representing cultured wealth • the accomplished one • one who enjoys refined pleasures • character with material security • the graceful achiever • one surrounded by beauty • character who built own success • the solo achiever • one with cultivated surroundings • character enjoying well-earned rest • the luxury enjoyer • one in harmonious environment

Storytelling Scenarios: A character enjoying the fruits of their labor and discipline • Tales about achieving financial or material independence • A protagonist who has created beauty in their surroundings • Stories examining the satisfaction of self-made success • A character who enjoys refined or cultivated pleasures • Narratives about the garden as metaphor for cultivated life • Tales exploring the joy of accomplishment enjoyed in solitude • A protagonist who has achieved security through their own efforts • Stories about characters who create personal sanctuaries • The quiet pride in having built something substantial • Tales examining what happens after achieving material goals • A protagonist whose discipline has created freedom • Narratives about characters who enjoy cultured or refined living • Stories exploring the balance between solitude and companionship • A character who has trained wild impulses into beautiful expression • Tales about the creation of personal paradise • A protagonist who has mastered their material world

Ten of Pentacles

Keywords & Storytelling Applications: Legacy • inheritance • family wealth • permanence • character amid family prosperity • one who establishes dynasty • wealth inheritor • legacy builder • character representing family security • one creating lasting structures • character amid generational wealth • the dynasty founder • one who leaves inheritance • character establishing lasting success • the tradition keeper • one enjoying family security • character representing material legacy • the wealth steward • one amid permanence • character creating generational security • the legacy leaver • one experiencing family wealth • character representing permanence • the estate manager • one building for future generations • character establishing traditions • the foundation builder • one passing down values with wealth • character representing ancestral connection • the succession planner • one creating secure future

Storytelling Scenarios: A character building something meant to last for generations • Tales about family businesses or dynasties • A protagonist managing or receiving significant inheritance • Stories examining the privileges and burdens of family wealth • A character creating institutions or foundations • Narratives about establishing lasting legacies • Tales exploring the transfer of values along with assets • A protagonist navigating family traditions and expectations • Stories about characters who build security for future generations • The satisfaction of establishing something permanent • Tales examining what we pass down to those who follow • A protagonist preserving family heritage or traditions • Narratives about characters who must decide what legacy to leave • Stories exploring the relationship between material and spiritual inheritance • A character whose success extends beyond their lifetime • Tales about the foundations that support extended families • A protagonist creating financial stability that outlasts them

Page of Pentacles

Keywords & Storytelling Applications: Study • application • new opportunity • curiosity • character beginning practical learning • one curious about material world • student of craft • opportunity explorer • character receiving practical opportunity • one beginning material path • character studying diligently • the practical student • one open to earthly learning • character with scholarship • the opportunity noticer • one taking first steps • character representing new study • the apprentice • one practicing new skills • character discovering talents • the careful student • one examining details • character representing new resources • the opportunity seeker • one with practical curiosity • character beginning training • the diligent learner • one attentive to physical world • character with new interest • the resource examiner • one starting practical journey

Storytelling Scenarios: A character at the beginning of practical study or training • Tales about discovering new talents or abilities • A protagonist noticing opportunities others miss • Stories examining the early stages of learning a craft • A character receiving news about material or financial matters • Narratives about scholarship or educational opportunities • Tales exploring curiosity about how things work • A protagonist taking first steps on a practical path • Stories about characters who pay attention to details • The excitement of discovering one's aptitudes • Tales examining the student mindset or approach • A protagonist finding unexpected resources or support • Narratives about characters who approach material matters with curiosity • Stories exploring the early stages of career development • A character with a fresh perspective on practical matters • Tales about beginning apprenticeship or internship • A protagonist whose careful attention reveals hidden value

Knight of Pentacles

Keywords & Storytelling Applications: Reliability • responsibility • patience • methodical approach • character showing reliability • one with methodical approach • dependable worker • patient planner • character representing steady progress • one who follows through • character with strong work ethic • the reliable one • one who takes responsibility • character making steady progress • the patient knight • one committed to duty • character representing methodical approach • the responsible one • one focused on practical matters • character making slow, sure progress • the steady worker • one who finishes what they start • character representing dependability • the methodical one • one with farmer's patience • character valuing routine • the duty-bound • one who shows up consistently • character representing reliability • the plodder • one who values practical results

Storytelling Scenarios: A character whose reliability makes them indispensable

• Tales about the steady pursuit of practical goals • A protagonist who approaches challenges methodically • Stories examining the value of consistency over flash • A character who patiently works toward tangible results • Narratives about taking responsibility for practical matters • Tales exploring the tension between methodical and dynamic approaches • A protagonist whose slow, steady effort ultimately succeeds • Stories about characters who fulfill their duties without complaint • The gradual progress that eventually reaches impressive goals • Tales examining the psychological benefits of routine and structure • A protagonist who finishes what others start • Narratives about characters whose patient approach proves wise • Stories exploring the farmer mentality versus the hunter mentality • A character whose mundane efforts create extraordinary results • Tales about the reliability that forms the foundation for others' success • A protagonist who remains steady while others chase shiny objects

Queen of Pentacles

Keywords & Storytelling Applications: Nurturing • abundance • practicality • generosity • character creating abundance • one nurturing through practical means • nurturing provider • prosperity creator • character with practical wisdom • one creating comfortable home • character representing material nurturing • the domestic manager • one creating security for others • character with green thumb • the nurturer • one with financial acumen • character combining warmth with practicality • the prosperity nurturer • one with domestic skills • character creating welcoming environment • the earth mother • one who nurtures growth • character representing practical abundance • the resource manager • one securing others' well-being • character making others comfortable • the hearth keeper • one with natural prosperity • character representing nurturing wealth • the provider • one who creates fertile conditions

Storytelling Scenarios: A character who creates a nurturing and abundant environment • Tales about the practical aspects of caregiving • A protagonist who combines warmth with financial acumen • Stories examining the creation of comfortable, welcoming spaces • A character who ensures others' practical needs are met • Narratives about the management of household or family resources • Tales exploring the nurturing of growth in practical realms • A protagonist whose practicality creates security for others • Stories about characters with a natural ability to generate prosperity • The creation of fertile conditions for others to flourish • Tales examining the domestic arts as expressions of love • A protagonist who tends the garden of practical affairs • Narratives about characters whose nurturing extends to material provision • Stories exploring the earth mother archetype • A character whose generosity flows from abundance • Tales about the management of resources for common good • A protagonist who creates wealth to share rather than hoard

King of Pentacles

Keywords & Storytelling Applications: Wealth • success • leadership • abundance • character with material success • one who leads enterprises • successful businessman • financial leader • character representing material mastery • one creating material success • character with business acumen • the wealth builder • one who secures kingdom • character with prosperity wisdom • the enterprise leader • one managing resources wisely • character representing material leadership • the abundance creator • one with practical authority • character with financial security • the business leader • one who creates stable empire • character representing material authority • the resource master • one who builds lasting wealth • character with enterprise success • the kingdom builder • one representing material achievement • character with financial wisdom • the prosperity ruler • one whose leadership creates wealth

Storytelling Scenarios: A character who has achieved significant material success • Tales about leadership in business or finance • A protagonist who builds enterprises or organizations • Stories examining the wise management of resources • A character who creates stability and security for many • Narratives about the responsibility that comes with wealth • Tales exploring the creation of lasting economic structures • A protagonist who combines practical wisdom with authority • Stories about characters who master the material realm • The establishment of prosperous kingdoms or enterprises • Tales examining the balance between prosperity and ethics • A protagonist whose leadership creates opportunities for others • Narratives about characters who build financial dynasties • Stories exploring the archetype of the benevolent ruler • A character whose practical wisdom benefits their community • Tales about leaders who understand physical realities • A protagonist who brings order and abundance to chaotic situations

Remember

These keywords are jumping-off points for your imagination. Let your subconscious mind play with them freely - sometimes the most unexpected combinations lead to the most interesting stories.

Tarot for Storytellers: Accessing the Subconscious Novelist Within

The Tarot as a Storytelling Tool

The tarot deck is a treasure trove of archetypal imagery, symbolic connections, and narrative possibilities. Each of the 78 cards represents not just a character or situation, but an entire universe of storytelling potential. As writers, we can use these symbols to bypass our conscious, analytical mind and tap directly into the wellspring of creativity that lies beneath.

Remember that the interpretations and keywords provided for each card are merely jumping-off points for your imagination. The true power of tarot for storytelling lies in allowing your subconscious mind to play with these symbols freely. Sometimes the most unexpected combinations lead to the most original and compelling stories.

Working with the Elements

Before diving into specific spreads, understanding the four elemental suits can help you recognize broader patterns and themes in your readings:

Water (Cups)

- **Storytelling Focus:** Emotional narratives, relationships, inner journeys, psychological transformation
- **Genre Affinity:** Romance, family drama, coming-of-age, psychological fiction
- **Character Development:** Emotional growth, healing journeys, relationship dynamics
- **Plot Elements:** Falling in love, reconciliation, emotional revelations, healing from past wounds
- **Atmosphere:** Introspective, emotionally rich, intimate, sometimes melancholic

Fire (Wands)

- **Storytelling Focus:** Action, passion, creativity, spiritual quests, ambition
- **Genre Affinity:** Adventure, spiritual journey, creative process narratives, entrepreneurial tales
- **Character Development:** Finding purpose, creative awakening, spiritual growth
- **Plot Elements:** Quests, competitions, artistic endeavors, passionate pursuits
- **Atmosphere:** Dynamic, energetic, inspirational, transformative

Earth (Pentacles)

- **Storytelling Focus:** Material concerns, practical challenges, resources, physical world
- **Genre Affinity:** Historical fiction, realistic fiction, financial thrillers,

agricultural tales

- **Character Development:** Building security, learning craftsmanship, creating legacy
- **Plot Elements:** Building businesses or homes, financial challenges, apprenticeship
- **Atmosphere:** Grounded, sensory-rich, practical, traditional

Air (Swords)

- **Storytelling Focus:** Mental challenges, communication, conflict, truth
- **Genre Affinity:** Mystery, psychological thriller, debate narratives, intellectual journeys
- **Character Development:** Intellectual growth, overcoming mental obstacles, finding truth
- **Plot Elements:** Arguments, revelations, mental breakthroughs, ethical dilemmas
- **Atmosphere:** Intellectually stimulating, sometimes tense or conflicted, clarity-seeking

When multiple cards from a single element appear in your spread, this suggests your story might particularly emphasize the themes associated with that element. A predominance of Cups cards might indicate a deeply emotional narrative centered on relationships and inner growth, while an abundance of Swords could suggest a story driven by conflict, communication, and the pursuit of truth.

Expanded Story Development Spreads

1. The Three-Act Structure

This classic spread maps perfectly to traditional story structure, providing insights into your narrative's beginning, middle, and end.

Card 1: Beginning (Act 1)

- Character's ordinary world
- Inciting incident
- Call to adventure
- Setup of central conflict

Card 2: Middle (Act 2)

- Challenges and complications
- Tests and tribulations
- Rising action and stakes
- Darkest moment/low point

Card 3: End (Act 3)

- Climax and resolution
- Character transformation
- Thematic statement
- Final image or message

Example Interpretation:

- The Fool (Beginning): A story starting with a naive protagonist stepping blindly into a new adventure, unaware of the dangers ahead. The character's innocence and optimism set them apart in their world.
- Five of Swords (Middle): The protagonist faces betrayal and conflict, perhaps learning that their trusted companions have their own agendas. They experience the humiliation of defeat or the hollow victory of winning at too great a cost.
- Six of Cups (End): The story resolves with reconciliation, forgiveness, or a return to innocence with newfound wisdom. Childhood connections or memories play a crucial role in the resolution, suggesting the healing power of nostalgia or the completion of an emotional cycle.

2. Character Development Spread

This expanded version of the Character Triangle provides deeper insight into your central characters and their relationships.

Card 1: Protagonist's Nature

- Core personality
- Strengths and talents
- Internal landscape
- Default approach to problems

Card 2: Protagonist's Challenge

- Internal obstacle
- What they must overcome
- Shadow aspects
- The lesson they need to learn

Card 3: Antagonist/Opposition

- Nature of opposing force
- Motivation of the antagonist
- Mirror to protagonist
- External challenge

Card 4: Key Relationship/Ally

- Important supporting character
- Nature of their support
- What they represent for protagonist
- How they influence the journey

Card 5: Protagonist's Transformation

- How they change
- What they become
- Realized potential
- New understanding

Example Interpretation:

- Four of Pentacles (Protagonist's Nature): A character who begins as overly cautious, protective of what they have built, possibly fearful of change or loss. They value security and stability above all.
- The Hermit (Protagonist's Challenge): They must learn to look inward for answers, to step away from their material concerns and find wisdom in solitude and reflection. Their journey requires spiritual growth beyond material security.
- Knight of Wands (Antagonist/Opposition): They face opposition from an impulsive, action-oriented force—perhaps someone who threatens their security through reckless behavior or represents the freedom and adventure they secretly crave.
- Queen of Cups (Key Relationship/Ally): A nurturing, emotionally intuitive ally who helps the protagonist connect with their feelings and develop emotional intelligence. This character provides compassionate guidance without judgment.
- Ten of Pentacles (Protagonist's Transformation): The protagonist ultimately creates a more meaningful form of security—one based on legacy, community, and shared abundance rather than personal hoarding. They learn that true security comes from connection rather than isolation.

3. Scene Development Spread

Use this expanded spread to develop a pivotal scene in your narrative with greater depth and nuance.

Card 1: Setting/Atmosphere

- Physical location
- Emotional atmosphere
- Time and context
- Symbolic environment

Card 2: Character Motivation

- What the viewpoint character wants
- Underlying emotional need
- Stakes involved
- Pressure points

Card 3: Conflict/Obstacle

- What stands in the way
- Nature of the opposition
- External or internal barriers
- Complications

Card 4: Turning Point

- Moment of change
- Revelation or decision
- Power shift
- Unexpected element

Card 5: Resolution/Consequence

- Immediate outcome
- Character reaction
- Seeds planted for future
- Thematic resonance

Example Interpretation:

- The Moon (Setting/Atmosphere): A scene set in a dreamlike, uncertain environment—perhaps at night, near water, or in a situation where nothing is quite as it seems. The atmosphere is one of mystery, hidden danger, and psychological unease.
- Two of Wands (Character Motivation): The character is at a decision point, contemplating a bold move or expansion. They desire to extend their influence or explore beyond current boundaries, feeling pulled toward the unknown despite their fears.

- Seven of Swords (Conflict/Obstacle): Deception complicates the scene—either the character contemplates using stealth or subterfuge, or they discover someone else's deception. Trust issues and ethical dilemmas arise.
- The Tower (Turning Point): A sudden, shocking revelation or event completely disrupts expectations. The character's plans or assumptions are shattered, forcing an immediate recalibration of their understanding.
- Ace of Cups (Resolution/Consequence): Despite the chaos and deception, the scene ends with an emotional opening or new beginning. The disruption creates space for emotional truth, perhaps the start of a genuine connection where false premises once stood.

4. Theme and Motif Exploration

This spread helps you develop the deeper thematic elements of your story.

Card 1: Central Theme

- Core message or question
- What the story is really about
- Universal truth explored

Card 2: Symbol or Motif

- Recurring image
- Meaningful object
- Visual metaphor
- Symbolic action

Card 3: Character Embodiment

- Character who represents the theme
- How theme manifests in personality
- Living example of the concept

Card 4: Thematic Opposition

- Counterargument or antithesis
- Challenging perspective
- What complicates the theme

Card 5: Resolution or Synthesis

- How theme resolves
- Evolved understanding
- Final statement on the question

Example Interpretation:

- Justice (Central Theme): A story exploring the nature of fairness, consequence, and moral balance. The narrative questions what true justice means beyond mere legality.
- Eight of Swords (Symbol or Motif): Recurring imagery of self-imposed limitations or blindness. Perhaps characters repeatedly find themselves in situations where they cannot see their own options, or bind themselves through belief systems.
- King of Swords (Character Embodiment): A character who represents intellectual authority and adherence to principles. This person embodies the rational, impartial approach to justice and serves as a standard against which others are measured.
- The Devil (Thematic Opposition): The theme is complicated by explorations of temptation, materialistic concerns, and situations where people become enslaved to their desires or fears. This represents how justice can be corrupted or compromised.
- Six of Pentacles (Resolution or Synthesis): The thematic resolution suggests that true justice involves generosity, proper distribution of resources, and acknowledging power imbalances. It proposes a more compassionate form of justice that considers circumstance and need.

Advanced Storytelling Techniques

1. The Open Reading Technique

One of the most powerful ways to use tarot for story development is through what is known as the "open reading" approach. This technique maximizes the involvement of your subconscious mind in the creative process.

Step-by-Step Process:

1. Clear your mind and focus on your desire to discover a story
2. Pull three to five cards without assigning preset positions
3. Arrange the cards in the order that feels right intuitively
4. Observe your immediate reactions and emotional responses
5. Notice which visual elements in each card draw your attention
6. Look for visual connections between cards (colors, directions, symbols)
7. Allow your mind to freely associate with the imagery
8. Watch for narrative patterns that emerge naturally
9. Record your initial impressions without censoring

Interpreting Open Readings: Consider how the cards might represent:

- Different characters or aspects of the same character
- Stages of a physical or emotional journey
- Contrasting worldviews or perspectives
- Setting elements and atmosphere
- Plot developments and complications
- Symbolic representations of internal states
- Theme and subtext

The beauty of open reading is that it allows your subconscious mind maximum freedom to make connections. When you look at the cards without predetermined positions or meanings, your mind naturally begins to weave narratives between them. You might notice how the figure in one card seems to be looking at another card, or how colors and symbols repeat across the spread.

These natural connections often reveal story elements you wouldn't have consciously created. For instance, you might pull the Tower, the Six of Cups, and the Moon. Without assigning specific positions, you might notice how the Tower's destruction connects to the nostalgic memories of the Six of Cups, suggesting a story about how a present crisis forces a character to confront their past. The Moon's presence might suggest that not all these memories are reliable, or that the truth about the past is obscured by time and emotion.

The real magic happens when you let these connections simmer in your mind without forcing interpretations. Sometimes the most powerful story insights come hours or even days after an open reading, when your subconscious mind has had time to process the symbols and patterns. You might suddenly realize that the posture of a figure in one card reflects your protagonist's emotional state, or that the geometric patterns across the spread suggest a subplot or character connection you wouldn't have considered otherwise.

2. Character Voice Development

This technique helps you access different narrative voices and character perspectives.

Process:

1. Select a court card (Page, Knight, Queen, King) that represents a character you're developing
2. Place this card in the center
3. Draw three cards and place them around the central card
4. Interpret these cards as:
    - Card 1: How this character sees themselves
    - Card 2: How others see this character
    - Card 3: What this character rarely reveals
5. Write a first-person monologue from the character's perspective, incorporating elements from all four cards
6. Pay attention to word choice, rhythm, and speech patterns that emerge

Example:

- Central Card (Character): Knight of Cups (romantic, idealistic, emotionally-driven character)
- How they see themselves (Nine of Wands): A battle-weary romantic who has suffered for love but still stands ready to defend their ideals
- How others see them (Three of Pentacles): A talented collaborator, someone whose artistic or emotional contributions are valued
- What they rarely reveal (Ten of Swords): A profound sense of betrayal and defeat, perhaps a past emotional devastation that shapes their romantic idealism

This spread reveals a character with a complex emotional landscape—someone who presents as a romantic idealist and is valued for their emotional intelligence and creativity, but harbors deep wounds from past betrayals. Their idealism might be a response to profound disappointment, a way of maintaining hope despite evidence to the contrary.

3. Plot Complication Generator

When your story feels too straightforward or predictable, use this technique to introduce organic complications.

Process:

1. Lay out three cards representing your current story situation:
    - Card 1: Protagonist's position
    - Card 2: Current goal or direction
    - Card 3: Main obstacle
2. Draw one card and place it perpendicular to these three, crossing over them
3. This crossing card represents an unexpected complication or twist
4. Draw a final card representing how this complication changes the trajectory

Example:

- Protagonist's position (Queen of Wands): A confident, charismatic character in a position of creative leadership
- Current goal (Three of Wands): Expansion, launching enterprises, seeing initial success in ventures
- Main obstacle (Five of Pentacles): Limited resources, possibly rejection from established institutions, hardship
- Complication (Seven of Swords): Deception within the ranks, theft of ideas, strategic undermining
- Changed trajectory (The Hermit): The protagonist withdraws to reassess, seeks wisdom in solitude, follows an inner light rather than external validation

This spread suggests a story about a charismatic leader whose expanding enterprise faces both resource challenges and internal betrayal, forcing them to abandon their original approach and seek a more solitary, wisdom-focused path forward. The complication transforms what might have been a straightforward tale of overcoming external obstacles into a story about discernment, inner guidance, and redefining success.

4. World-Building Spread

For speculative fiction writers, this spread helps develop rich, coherent fictional worlds.

Process:

1. Draw cards for the following aspects of your world:
    - Card 1: Physical environment/geography
    - Card 2: Social/political structure
    - Card 3: Value system/beliefs
    - Card 4: Unique challenge or conflict
    - Card 5: Hidden or magical element

    - Card 6: Historical influence
2. Look for connections between the cards that suggest how these elements interact
3. Pay special attention to repeated symbols, colors, or themes

Example:

- Physical environment (The Moon): A world of shifting landscapes, tidal influences, mysterious waters, and hidden dangers. Perhaps reality itself is somewhat fluid or dreamlike.
- Social structure (Four of Wands): Communities centered around celebrations, gathering places, or creative collectives. Social harmony is highly valued.
- Value system (Six of Swords): A culture that prizes transition, journey, and the guidance of others. Knowledge is passed through mentorship and movement.
- Unique challenge (Knight of Pentacles): The slow, plodding nature of material progress creates tension with the fluid environment. Persistence versus adaptation.
- Hidden element (The High Priestess): Secret knowledge accessible only to the initiated; intuitive understanding as a form of power; hidden connections between the conscious and unconscious realms.
- Historical influence (The Tower): A cataclysmic event in the past that destroyed previous structures and forced new beginnings. This shapes current attitudes toward change and stability.

This spread suggests a fascinating world where communities live in harmony despite shifting, dreamlike environments. The society values transition and journey, perhaps because their physical world is unstable, yet they also recognize the need for the steady building of resources and infrastructure (creating tension). Secret knowledge about navigating this reality is closely guarded by intuitive adepts, and all of this exists in the shadow of a historical catastrophe that continues to influence their approach to change.

5. Story Evolution Spread

This technique helps you explore how a story idea might develop over time, revealing its potential arc.

Process:

1. Begin with a single card representing your initial story idea or concept
2. Draw seven cards and arrange them in a row below this card
3. These seven cards represent the evolution of your story idea through:
    - Card 1: Initial situation
    - Card 2: Complicating factor
    - Card 3: Raising the stakes
    - Card 4: Central crisis/midpoint
    - Card 5: Response to crisis
    - Card 6: Climactic challenge
    - Card 7: Resolution/new understanding
4. Pay attention to patterns in suits (elements) and numbers, as well as the narrative flow

Example:

- Initial concept (Queen of Cups): A story centered on an intuitive, emotionally nurturing character with possible psychic abilities
- Initial situation (Six of Cups): The character uses their gifts to help others connect with past memories or heal childhood wounds
- Complicating factor (Three of Swords): A heartbreaking discovery or betrayal disrupts the character's work
- Raising the stakes (The Magician): The character discovers greater powers or abilities that come with increased responsibility
- Central crisis (Eight of Swords): A situation where the character feels trapped, possibly by their own perceptions or fears
- Response to crisis (Knight of Wands): Taking bold, passionate action despite uncertainties; a quest or mission

- Climactic challenge (Ten of Pentacles): Confronting issues related to legacy, family structures, or established institutions
- Resolution (The World): Integration of all experiences into a new level of understanding; completion of a significant cycle

This spread reveals a potentially rich story about an emotionally intuitive healer who faces betrayal, discovers greater powers, endures a period of feeling trapped by their gift, then embarks on a passionate quest that ultimately brings them into conflict with established family or institutional structures. The story resolves with a sense of completion and integration, suggesting the character achieves a holistic understanding of their gifts and place in the world.

Practical Tips for Subconscious Story Development

Capturing Insights

- Keep a dedicated journal for your tarot story readings
- Sketch the card layouts or take photos of significant spreads
- Record your immediate, unfiltered impressions before analyzing
- Note which card elements particularly draw your attention
- Return to readings days or weeks later to see new connections

Developing Trust in the Process

- Allow contradictions and paradoxes to exist without immediate resolution
- Give yourself permission to follow associations that seem illogical
- Remember that symbolic meanings are often multifaceted and complex
- Trust that your subconscious mind is making connections beyond your awareness
- Resist the urge to force cards to fit your preconceived story ideas

Deepening the Practice

- Study the visual details of cards beyond their traditional meanings
- Notice your emotional responses to certain cards and explore why they affect you
- Allow the cards to suggest sensory details—sounds, smells, textures
- Consider how card combinations might suggest dialogue between characters
- Use problematic or challenging card combinations as opportunities for complex storytelling

When You Feel Stuck

- Try reading the cards in reverse order for a new perspective
- Focus on a single detail from one card and free-associate
- Ask "what if" questions about unexpected card combinations
- Draw an additional card for clarification or a new direction
- Temporarily set aside traditional meanings and respond purely to the imagery

Integration with Other Creative Practices

- Use tarot-inspired characters or situations as writing prompts
- Create playlists that evoke the energy of significant cards in your story
- Collect images that capture the essence of recurring cards
- Use physical movement to embody the energy of important cards
- Sketch scenes or characters based on card imagery

Embracing Synchronicity and Intuition

The true power of tarot for storytelling lies in its ability to access parts of your creative mind that logical thought cannot reach. When apparent coincidences, surprising connections, or unexpected patterns emerge in your readings, pay special attention—these synchronicities often point to the most fertile ground for storytelling.

The cards you draw will sometimes seem eerily appropriate to your story questions, offering exactly the insight you need. Other times, they may seem completely unrelated, challenging you to make creative leaps that lead to original narrative directions. Both experiences are valuable. The seemingly perfect card validates your intuitive understanding of your story, while the apparently unrelated card pushes you beyond your conscious limitations.

Remember that the meaning of the cards is less important than your response to them. A card that "traditionally" represents joy might trigger thoughts of sadness in your mind—follow that response rather than the textbook meaning. Your subconscious is speaking through these associations, offering narrative possibilities unique to your creative vision.

By developing a regular practice of working with tarot for storytelling, you'll strengthen the connection between your conscious crafting abilities and your subconscious creative wellspring. Over time, you'll find yourself accessing deeper levels of creativity with increasing ease, developing stories that resonate with authentic emotion and archetypal power.

The cards are simply tools to help you access what you already know at some level—the stories that only you can tell. Trust the process, embrace the mystery, and watch as your writing transforms through this dialogue with your deeper creative self.

The Tarot Character Development System: From Archetypes to Living Characters

The Bridge Between Tarot and Character Creation

While our previous explorations focused on general storytelling applications of tarot, this system delves specifically into character development—arguably the most crucial element of compelling fiction. The Tarot Character Development

System creates a direct bridge between the archetypal wisdom embedded in the 78 cards and the complex, nuanced characters that drive memorable stories.

The system works because both tarot and character development draw from the same well of human experience and psychological truth. Each tarot card represents not just a concept but a fully realized archetype with motivations, conflicts, strengths, and weaknesses—all the elements needed for dimensional characters. By systematically applying tarot imagery to character creation, we access deeper, more authentic character insights than conscious planning alone can provide.

The Four Principles of Tarot Character Development

1. Attention: Deep Character Immersion

The foundation of this system is the quality of attention you bring to the process. Unlike analytical character development methods that begin with lists or questionnaires, this approach starts with immersion in imagery and symbolism.

Enhanced Practice:

- Begin each session with 2-3 minutes of mindful breathing to enter a receptive state
- Allow your eyes to move freely across card imagery without forcing focus
- Notice which elements naturally draw your attention—colors, symbols, figures, or emotions
- Pay attention to physical sensations or emotional responses that arise
- Record immediate impressions using voice notes to capture spontaneous insights
- Ask open-ended questions like "Who is this person?" or "What matters most to them?"
- Allow time for insights to emerge naturally without rushing

Integration with Card Meanings: The comprehensive card meanings we've explored provide rich material for character work, but approach them as possibilities rather than definitions. When a card appears in a character spread, first notice your intuitive response, then supplement with the card's traditional associations if helpful.

2. Bypassing the Critical Mind

The analytical, critical part of our mind is essential for story structure and editing but can inhibit the deeper character insights that arise from the subconscious. This principle focuses on temporarily setting aside critical analysis to access deeper character truths.

Enhanced Practice:

- Resist the urge to immediately name or categorize character traits
- Record impressions without judging them as "good" or "bad" for your story
- Allow contradictions and complexities to exist without resolution
- Use "yes, and" thinking instead of "either/or" analysis
- If your critical mind offers objections, acknowledge them and gently set them aside
- Practice stream-of-consciousness writing about the cards without stopping
- Embrace playfulness and experimentation without concern for "getting it right"
- Notice when you're analyzing rather than experiencing, and gently return to direct experience

Manifestations in Character Development:

- Characters with authentic contradictions and complexities
- Motivations that arise from deep psychological truths rather than plot necessity

- Personality traits that surprise even you as the author
- Characters who resist simple categorization or stereotyping
- Authentic character voices that seem to speak independently
- Character actions that feel inevitable rather than contrived

3. Connecting with the Creative Subconscious

This principle focuses on strengthening the bridge between your conscious writing mind and the vast creative resources of your subconscious.

Enhanced Practice:

- Notice patterns across cards without forcing connections
- Pay attention to recurring symbols, colors, or elements
- Allow metaphorical thinking to flourish without immediate translation
- Trust that meaningful connections are forming beneath conscious awareness
- Record dreams or insights that arise between sessions
- Use embodiment techniques—physically move like the character might
- Speak aloud in the character's voice without planning what you'll say
- Create space for insights to emerge through non-writing activities like walking or showering

Subconscious Integration Techniques:

- After a session, “assign” a question about your character to your subconscious
- Before sleep, briefly review the cards and ask for clarity
- Upon waking, immediately record any character insights
- Take breaks from active development to allow subconscious processing
- Notice “coincidences” related to your character in daily life
- Pay attention to songs, images, or phrases that suddenly seem relevant

4. Direct Experience

Rather than thinking about your character, this principle encourages experiencing the world from within your character's perspective.

Enhanced Practice:

- Allow yourself to temporarily inhabit the perspective revealed by the cards
- Experience sensory impressions as your character would perceive them
- Notice how your body posture or breathing shifts when connecting with the character
- Speak or write in first person from the character's viewpoint without planning
- Experience emotional responses to scenarios through your character's lens
- Consider how the character's past would shape their perception of present events
- Allow yourself to be surprised by the character's reactions or thoughts

Embodiment Exercises:

- Select a card that represents your character's core essence
- Physically adopt the posture or stance of the figure in the card
- Breathe as this character would breathe—shallow, deep, measured, or erratic
- Allow your facial expressions to align with the character's emotional state
- Speak aloud, letting the character's voice emerge through your own
- Move through space as this character would move
- Interact with objects from this character's perspective

Expanded Character Development Spreads

The Character Core Spread (5 Cards)

This fundamental spread reveals the essential nature of your character across multiple dimensions. The five-card layout creates a cross pattern that allows for powerful interactions between the central essence and the four influencing aspects.

Card Positions:

1. **Character's Essence** (Center Card) - The fundamental nature or core identity
2. **External Persona** (Above) - How the character presents themselves to the world
3. **Hidden Self** (Below) - What the character conceals or represses
4. **Past Influence** (Left) - Formative experiences or inherited traits
5. **Future Potential** (Right) - What the character might become

Enhanced Analysis Techniques:

For **Character's Essence** (Center Card):

- Note your immediate emotional response to this card
- Consider both the figure's posture and the card's background elements
- Ask yourself: "What is this character's fundamental relationship to the world?"
- Look for the character's primary element (fire/wands, water/cups, air/swords, earth/pentacles)
- Consider how Major Arcana cards suggest archetypal journeys while Minor Arcana cards indicate specific traits
- Notice what the character is doing in the card—action often reveals essence

Example with **The Empress**: A character whose essence is nurturing, creative, and connected to the natural world. Their core strength lies in fertility (of ideas, creations, or literal children) and abundance. Their fundamental approach to life is through sensory experience and creation.

For **External Persona** (Above):

- Look for how this card differs from or aligns with the essence card
- Consider what aspects of the essence this persona amplifies or diminishes
- Note symbols of masks, clothing, or presentation
- Ask: "What does this character want others to see about them?"
- Consider how the character's element manifests in social situations
- Look for evidence of conscious versus unconscious self-presentation

Example with **Knight of Swords**: The character presents themselves as direct, intellectual, and perhaps aggressive. They want to be seen as decisive and forceful, moving swiftly toward goals. This creates interesting tension with an Empress essence—perhaps they hide their nurturing nature behind intellectual prowess.

For **Hidden Self** (Below):

- Look for shadows, depths, or concealed elements in the card
- Consider what this character fears about themselves
- Note elements that contrast sharply with the external persona
- Ask: "What would devastate this character if others discovered it?"
- Look for repressed strengths as well as weaknesses
- Consider how this hidden aspect might emerge under stress

Example with **Four of Cups**: Beneath their nurturing, abundant exterior and sharp, intellectual presentation, this character harbors apathy, disillusionment, or emotional withdrawal. They may secretly feel that what they offer is unwanted or insufficient, or they might struggle with appreciating what they have.

For **Past Influence** (Left):

- Look for evidence of formative experiences or inherited patterns
- Consider both positive and negative influences

- Note how this card might explain tensions between essence and persona
- Ask: "How did the character become who they are today?"
- Look for elements that shaped the character's worldview
- Consider whether the character embraces or rejects this influence

Example with **Five of Pentacles**: This character's background includes material hardship, exclusion, or health struggles. Their abundant nature might have developed as a response to early deprivation. Their sharp intellect could be a tool developed to ensure they never experience such hardship again.

For **Future Potential** (Right):

- Look for evidence of growth direction or unfulfilled potential
- Consider how this card might resolve tensions in the other positions
- Note elements that surprise you or contradict current character traits
- Ask: "What might this character become under ideal circumstances?"
- Look for both positive potentials and possible pitfalls
- Consider how this potential connects to the story's thematic elements

Example with **The Star**: This character has the potential to develop profound hope, authenticity, and generosity. Their journey might involve moving from intellectual sharpness and nurturing others to finding deep healing and peace for themselves. Their hardship background could transform into wisdom that guides others.

Integration with Previous Card Meanings: When working with the Character Core Spread, reference our comprehensive card meanings for additional insights. For each position, consider:

- How the card's physical qualities might manifest in your character's appearance or mannerisms
- How the emotional qualities might influence their internal landscape
- How the energetic qualities might appear in their actions and relationships
- How the spiritual qualities might reflect their deeper purpose or conflicts

Character Type Integration: Different character types will emerge naturally from various card combinations. Notice how the spread might reveal:

- **Protagonist patterns**: Strong tension between essence and future potential
- **Antagonist patterns**: Significant dissonance between external persona and hidden self
- **Mentor patterns**: Past influence and essence in strong alignment
- **Sidekick patterns**: External persona that complements another character's weaknesses
- **Threshold guardian patterns**: External persona that directly challenges another character's journey

The 12-Beat Character Journey Spread

This comprehensive spread maps your character's development through the classic three-act structure, revealing not just who they are but how they change throughout your story. This spread is particularly powerful for ensuring character arcs that feel both surprising and inevitable.

ACT 1 (4 Cards)

1. Status Quo (Set Up) This card reveals the character's initial state before the story's events begin to unfold.

Enhanced Analysis:

- Note the character's environment and relationships suggested by the card
- Consider whether they appear comfortable or restless in their current state
- Look for symbols of limitation, protection, or stagnation
- Identify unfulfilled needs or dormant potential
- Consider how this starting point relates to your story's theme
- Look for what the character values or believes at the beginning

Example with **Four of Cups**: A character who begins in a state of emotional apathy or discontentment. They may have material comfort but feel something is missing. Their unfulfilled need might be genuine connection or purpose. They might value security but secretly crave meaning.

2. Inciting Incident This card reveals the external event that disrupts their life and begins their journey.

Enhanced Analysis:

- Look for elements of surprise, disruption, or revelation in the card
- Consider how this event challenges the status quo
- Note symbols that suggest no return to previous conditions is possible
- Identify stakes or consequences suggested by the card
- Look for how this incident might connect to the character's unfulfilled needs
- Consider both external and internal dimensions of the disruption

Example with **The Tower**: A sudden, catastrophic disruption—perhaps the collapse of a relationship, belief system, or physical structure they depended on. This event is likely traumatic but necessary, forcing them out of apathy. The stakes are existential—their entire understanding of reality might be challenged.

3. Internal Wrestling This card shows the character's internal response to the inciting incident, revealing their preliminary adjustment to change.

Enhanced Analysis:

- Note emotional qualities and internal conflict in the card
- Look for evidence of resistance or acceptance
- Consider how past experiences (from the Core Spread) influence this response
- Identify defense mechanisms or coping strategies
- Look for the tension between fear and desire
- Consider what preliminary lessons they might be learning

Example with **Two of Swords**: The character responds to their disruptive event by trying to maintain emotional equilibrium through detachment or indecision. They may be blindfolding themselves to the full implications of what's happened, creating a temporary truce within themselves but postponing necessary decisions.

4. Welcome to the Jungle (Plot Point 1) This card represents the character's definitive entry into the journey or special world of Act 2.

Enhanced Analysis:

- Look for symbols of threshold crossing or commitment
- Note how this differs from their status quo
- Consider what is left behind and what is embraced
- Identify new rules or conditions they must navigate
- Look for evidence of the character's approach to this new territory
- Consider how this moment crystallizes the nature of their journey

Example with **Eight of Cups**: The character definitively leaves behind their emotional stagnation, walking away from what was familiar toward something deeper or more meaningful. This journey looks solitary and might happen in darkness or uncertainty, suggesting an internal quest for meaning rather than external adventure.

ACT 2 (5 Cards)

5. Subplot & Support This card reveals key relationships or secondary plotlines that will influence the character's journey.

Enhanced Analysis:

- Identify potential mentor figures, allies, or love interests
- Consider how these relationships might support or complicate the main journey
- Note what lessons or gifts these connections might offer
- Look for how these elements connect to the character's unfulfilled needs

- Consider both positive and challenging relationship dynamics
- Look for how these connections might test or affirm the character's values

Example with **Six of Cups**: The character encounters relationships characterized by nostalgia, innocence, or past connections. Perhaps they reconnect with childhood friends or places that remind them of simpler times. These relationships offer emotional gifts but might initially keep them looking backward rather than forward.

6. Trials This card indicates the nature of the tests and challenges the character will face in pursuit of their goal.

Enhanced Analysis:

- Note the specific type of challenge suggested by the card (physical, emotional, intellectual, spiritual)
- Consider how these trials relate to the character's weaknesses or fears
- Look for skills or qualities being tested or developed
- Identify patterns of resistance the character might experience
- Consider how these challenges escalate in difficulty
- Look for how these trials connect to the character's core wound

Example with **Seven of Wands**: The character faces challenges that require them to defend their position or stand their ground against opposition. They may feel outnumbered but have the advantage of higher ground. These trials will test their conviction, courage, and ability to maintain boundaries when under pressure.

7. Midpoint Revelation This pivotal card shows the crucial discovery or change that occurs at the story's middle, shifting the character's understanding and approach.

Enhanced Analysis:

- Look for symbols of revelation, transformation, or perspective shift
- Note how this revelation might change the character's goals

- Consider how this connects to the story's thematic statement
- Identify what the character learns about themselves or their situation
- Look for how this revelation raises the stakes
- Consider how this might begin a shift from reactive to proactive behavior

Example with **The Hanged Man**: At the midpoint, the character experiences a profound perspective shift through surrender or sacrifice. They may voluntarily put themselves in a vulnerable position to gain new insight. This revelation likely involves seeing their situation from a completely different angle, perhaps recognizing that their pursuit of meaning requires sacrifice.

8. Complications This card reveals how challenges intensify following the midpoint revelation, creating mounting pressure on the character.

Enhanced Analysis:

- Note how difficulties escalate or compound
- Consider how external and internal pressures might combine
- Look for evidence of the character's response to increasing pressure
- Identify what begins to break down or fail
- Consider how these complications test the midpoint revelation
- Look for how these challenges push the character toward crisis

Example with **Five of Pentacles**: The character experiences increasing hardship, possibly including material loss, health issues, or social exclusion. Their new perspective gained at the midpoint is severely tested by these practical difficulties. They may feel abandoned by institutions or support systems they once relied upon.

9. Crisis (Dark Night) This card shows the character's lowest point, where their journey seems to fail and old paradigms completely collapse.

Enhanced Analysis:

- Look for symbols of loss, defeat, or despair
- Note what must be completely surrendered or released

- Consider how this crisis relates to the character's deepest fears
- Identify the wisdom that might be found only through this collapse
- Look for seeds of transformation within the darkness
- Consider what false beliefs or approaches are proven unsustainable

Example with **Ten of Swords**: The character experiences a complete collapse or defeat—the death of their old approach or identity. This may feel like betrayal or overkill, with no possibility of continuing as before. While painful, this collapse is necessary for rebirth and clearly marks the end of a cycle.

10. Critical Choice This card reveals the character's moment of truth where they must make a fundamental decision that defines their path forward.

Enhanced Analysis:

- Look for symbols of decision, judgment, or choosing
- Note how this choice relates to the character's core values
- Consider what competing values or desires must be reconciled
- Identify what the character must risk or sacrifice
- Look for how this choice connects to the initial disruption
- Consider how this decision crystallizes the character's growth

Example with **Justice**: The character faces a choice that requires them to weigh various factors with complete honesty. This decision demands fairness, balance, and clear-sighted assessment of cause and effect. Their choice will have significant consequences and likely involves accepting responsibility for past actions while establishing new karmic patterns.

ACT 3 (2 Cards)

11. Welcome to the End (Plot Point 2) This card shows the character's entry into the final act, where they must apply their transformation to resolve their journey.

Enhanced Analysis:

- Look for symbols of return or application of lessons learned
- Note connections to earlier cards, particularly the status quo and inciting incident
- Consider what new resources or perspectives the character now brings
- Identify the nature of the final challenge or test
- Look for evidence of how the character has fundamentally changed
- Consider how their approach differs from what it would have been earlier

Example with **Six of Wands**: The character enters the final phase with newfound recognition, confidence, and support from others. Having endured trials and made difficult choices, they now move forward with victory in sight. This suggests they'll face their final challenges with well-earned confidence rather than the apathy or indecision of earlier states.

12. Theme Triumphant This final card reveals the character's ultimate transformation and how they embody the story's thematic truth.

Enhanced Analysis:

- Look for symbols of completion, integration, or understanding
- Note the distance traveled from the status quo card
- Consider how the character has resolved their core conflicts
- Identify what the character has gained and lost through their journey
- Look for how this transformation reflects the story's central theme
- Consider what new potential now exists for the character

Example with **Nine of Cups**: The character's journey culminates in emotional fulfillment and satisfaction. From their initial apathy and subsequent trials, they've arrived at a place of genuine contentment and wish fulfillment. The theme might involve learning to recognize and appreciate abundance after experiencing both emotional emptiness and material hardship.

Journey Integration Techniques:

- After completing the spread, arrange the cards in sequence to visualize the character's journey

- Notice patterns in suits (elements) that might suggest the primary arena of growth
- Look for repeated numbers or court cards that might indicate recurring patterns
- Identify where the character moves between Major and Minor Arcana, suggesting shifts between archetypal experiences and everyday reality
- Consider how this character's journey relates to others in your story
- Look for natural plot points and pacing suggestions in the card sequence

The Character Relationships Spread (6 Cards)

This spread reveals how your character relates to themselves and others, exposing the complex web of connections that define their social and internal world.

Card Positions:

1. **Self-Image** - How the character perceives themselves
2. **Public Persona** - How they present themselves to the general world
3. **Private Self** - Who they are in intimate settings or when alone
4. **Relationship with Allies** - How they interact with supporters
5. **Relationship with Antagonists** - How they respond to opposition
6. **Hidden Relationship Potential** - Unexplored relationship dynamics

Enhanced Analysis Techniques:

For **Self-Image**:

- Note whether the self-image seems accurate or delusional based on other spread positions
- Consider how this perception helps or hinders the character
- Look for evidence of pride or shame in how they see themselves
- Identify the origins of this self-perception (possibly connecting to the Core Spread's Past Influence)
- Consider what would happen if this self-image were threatened

- Look for what the character values about themselves

Example with **Knight of Cups**: The character sees themselves as romantic, idealistic, and emotionally driven. They value their sensitivity and imaginative nature, identifying as someone who pursues beauty and meaning with dedication. They might over-emphasize their emotional qualities while underestimating other aspects of themselves.

For **Public Persona**:

- Compare this position with the Self-Image to identify potential dissonance
- Note masks, performances, or protective strategies
- Consider what the character hopes to gain through this presentation
- Identify social contexts where this persona is most active
- Look for what the character conceals from the public
- Consider how much energy this persona requires to maintain

Example with **King of Swords**: In public, this same character presents as authoritative, rational, and clear-thinking. They want others to see them as someone who makes reasonable decisions and wields intellectual authority. This creates tension with their self-image—they perceive themselves as emotional but present as logical.

For **Private Self**:

- Look for revelations about who the character is when masks come off
- Consider who (if anyone) gets to see this aspect of the character
- Note how this private self might contradict or complement other aspects
- Identify what conditions allow this self to emerge
- Look for what the character fears about this private self
- Consider whether this represents their truest self or another form of protection

Example with **Nine of Pentacles**: In private or intimate settings, this character enjoys solitude, self-sufficiency, and refined pleasures. Despite their romantic self-image and intellectual public persona, they are actually quite self-contained and appreciate luxury and accomplishment. They may fear appearing selfish by revealing how much they enjoy independence.

For **Relationship with Allies**:

- Note how the character behaves with supporters and friends
- Consider what they seek from supportive relationships
- Identify what they offer to their allies
- Look for patterns of healthy or unhealthy attachment
- Consider how these relationships might evolve through their journey
- Look for how these relationships reflect or challenge their self-perception

Example with **Three of Cups**: With allies, this character thrives in celebratory, emotionally supportive group dynamics. They seek joy, creative collaboration, and emotional connection from these relationships. They offer heartfelt celebration of others' successes and create spaces for shared happiness. These relationships allow their emotional self-image to find expression.

For **Relationship with Antagonists**:

- Note the character's typical response to opposition or conflict
- Consider what triggers defensive or aggressive reactions
- Identify patterns from past conflicts that might repeat
- Look for how antagonistic relationships might transform
- Consider what the character projects onto their opponents
- Look for how these relationships might reveal the character's fears

Example with **Five of Swords**: When facing opposition, this character tends toward hollow victories or painful defeats. They might employ questionable tactics to win arguments or conflicts, then find the victory unsatisfying. They may project their own intellectual insecurities onto opponents, turning disagreements into intellectual combat to validate their King of Swords persona.

For **Hidden Relationship Potential**:

- Look for unexplored ways the character might connect with others
- Consider relationships that might transform their journey
- Identify relationship patterns they need to break or develop
- Look for relationship needs they haven't acknowledged
- Consider how their journey might open new relationship possibilities
- Look for relationship dynamics that might resolve their core conflicts

Example with **Two of Cups**: This character has untapped potential for a deeply balanced, mutually supportive partnership. Despite their self-sufficient private nature, they have capacity for a profound connection that balances giving and receiving. This relationship would allow integration of their emotional self-image and intellectual persona through authentic exchange with an equal.

Relationship Dynamics Integration: After completing this spread, consider how these different relationship modes interact:

- Notice tensions between how the character relates to themselves versus others
- Consider which relationships allow for authentic expression
- Identify relationships that might catalyze growth or change
- Look for how relationship patterns connect to the character's journey
- Consider how relationships might evolve through the story
- Look for relationship transformations that mirror inner growth

Expanded Character Integration Techniques

Deep Character Development Process

This five-stage process guides you from initial character concept through complete integration, ensuring your character has both depth and coherence.

1. Initial Character Seed

Begin with a single card that represents the essential spark of your character.

Enhanced Process:

- Shuffle while focusing on discovering a new character
- Draw one card and place it before you
- Study the image without immediately interpreting it
- Notice which elements of the card naturally draw your attention
- Allow your first impressions to form without analysis
- Record immediate sensory impressions—colors, textures, emotions
- Ask open-ended questions: "Who is this person?" "What matters to them?"
- Allow the character to begin speaking or moving in your imagination
- Note any immediate story possibilities that arise

Example with **The Empress**: Initial impressions might include abundance, sensuality, connection to nature, creativity, and nurturing energy. Perhaps you notice the lush surroundings first, suggesting someone deeply connected to natural cycles. The character might begin to reveal themselves as someone who creates environments where things and people can flourish.

2. Character Deepening

Use the Character Core Spread to expand your understanding of this character's complexity.

Enhanced Process:

- Place your seed card in the center position
- Draw four additional cards for the remaining positions
- Allow each card to reveal different dimensions of your character
- Notice tensions or harmonies between different aspects
- Let unexpected combinations spark new character insights
- Consider how these different facets might emerge in different contexts
- Allow contradictions to exist without immediate resolution
- Notice which aspects feel most alive or interesting to you
- Begin to sense the character's internal landscape and external presentation

Example: Building on **The Empress** as the character's essence, you might discover:

- External Persona (**Knight of Wands**): They present as more adventurous and impulsive than their nurturing core
- Hidden Self (**Eight of Swords**): Beneath their abundant exterior lies a feeling of restriction or helplessness
- Past Influence (**Ten of Pentacles**): Their foundation includes family wealth, tradition, and established structures
- Future Potential (**The Fool**): They have the potential to embrace new beginnings with complete openness

These combinations reveal a character with fascinating tensions—someone whose nurturing essence is partially hidden behind adventurous energy, who feels secretly restricted despite coming from abundance, and whose journey might involve breaking free from tradition to embrace new possibilities.

3. Character Journey Mapping

Apply the Character Journey Spread to discover how your character changes through your story.

Enhanced Process:

- Complete the 12-card journey spread with your character in mind
- Notice the emotional and psychological journey revealed
- Allow plot elements to emerge organically from character development
- Consider how external events reflect internal transformations
- Look for natural turning points and revelations
- Allow supporting characters to emerge from relationship cards
- Notice how complications and challenges test the character's core nature
- Consider how the resolution authentically emerges from the character's journey

Example: For our Empress-centered character, the journey might reveal:

- Beginning in comfortable abundance but feeling unfulfilled (**Four of Pentacles**)
- Disrupted by sudden loss of security or position (**The Tower**)
- Responding with careful assessment of options (**Seven of Pentacles**)
- Entering the journey through deliberate sacrifice of privilege (**The Hanged Man**)
- Finding support through creative collaboration (**Three of Pentacles**)
- Facing trials that test their nurturing abilities in harsh conditions (**Five of Pentacles**)
- Experiencing a midpoint revelation about inner strength (**Strength**)
- Confronting complications when old patterns resurface (**The Devil**)
- Reaching crisis when forced to choose between security and freedom (**Four of Swords**)
- Making the critical choice to embrace their own path (**The Chariot**)
- Entering the final phase with newfound independence (**Nine of Pentacles**)
- Achieving transformation through integration of nurturing and freedom (**The World**)

This journey reveals a character arc about moving from comfortable but constrained abundance to chosen, authentic nurturing that integrates freedom and responsibility.

4. Relationship Web Development

Use the Character Relationships Spread to understand how your character connects with themselves and others.

Enhanced Process:

- Complete the 6-card relationship spread
- Notice patterns in how the character relates in different contexts
- Allow supporting characters to emerge from these relationship dynamics
- Consider how relationships evolve through the character's journey

- Look for relationship transformations that mirror internal growth
- Allow tensions between different relationship modes to create depth

Example: Our Empress-centered character might reveal:

- Self-Image (**Queen of Pentacles**): Sees themselves as practical, nurturing, and abundant
- Public Persona (**The Sun**): Presents as joyful, confident, and radiantly successful
- Private Self (**Eight of Cups**): In private, experiences restlessness and a sense that something is missing
- Relationship with Allies (**Two of Cups**): Forms deep, meaningful connections with chosen companions
- Relationship with Antagonists (**Seven of Swords**): Faces opponents who use deception or strategy against them
- Hidden Relationship Potential (**Ace of Wands**): Has unexplored capacity for passionate new connections that spark transformation

These patterns suggest a character who appears successful and nurturing but privately feels unfulfilled, who values deep connections with allies while struggling with deceptive opponents, and who has untapped potential for transformative new relationships.

5. Integration and Refinement

Review all spreads together to identify cohesive patterns and resolve contradictions.

Enhanced Process:

- Arrange all cards from your various spreads where you can see them simultaneously
- Notice recurring cards, suits, numbers, or themes
- Look for how different aspects of the character connect across spreads
- Identify the most compelling tensions or contradictions
- Consider how these tensions might drive the character's story

- Allow deeper patterns to emerge from the complete picture
- Trust your subconscious to reveal connections you didn't consciously plan
- Note which aspects feel most alive or interesting to explore
- Begin to sense the character as a complete, complex entity
- Allow final refinements or adjustments based on the integrated picture

Example: Looking at all spreads for our Empress-centered character, you might notice:

- A recurring pattern of abundance and restriction (Empress essence with Eight of Swords hidden self)
- Tension between stability and restlessness (Ten of Pentacles influence with Eight of Cups private self)
- A journey from external abundance to authentic creation (Four of Pentacles start to The World completion)
- Evolution from defined roles to self-determined identity (Queen of Pentacles self-image to Ace of Wands potential)

These patterns suggest a character whose journey involves moving from inherited or expected forms of nurturing and abundance toward authentic, chosen creation and connection—someone who must leave behind golden cages to find true fulfillment.

Advanced Integration Techniques

The Shadow Character Method

This technique helps you explore the tension between a character's conscious identity and their disowned or repressed aspects, creating rich psychological depth.

Enhanced Process:

1. Identify a card that represents the character's primary conscious identity

2. Draw a card specifically to represent their shadow aspect
3. Note the tension or complementary relationship between these cards
4. Consider how this tension might drive internal conflict
5. Explore how external characters might embody shadow aspects
6. Allow the shadow to reveal both weaknesses and untapped strengths
7. Consider what situations might cause the shadow to emerge
8. Explore how integration of shadow aspects might lead to character growth

Example: For a character represented by **The Hierophant** (tradition, conventional wisdom, established institutions), you might draw **The Fool** as their shadow aspect. This suggests someone who consciously identifies with structure and tradition while repressing their desire for spontaneity and new beginnings. Their journey might involve recognizing how their conventional approach limits their growth, perhaps through encountering a free-spirited character who embodies their disowned qualities. Integration would involve finding ways to honor tradition while embracing innovation and personal discovery.

The Character Evolution Path

This technique focuses specifically on how your character transforms through time, revealing their developmental arc.

Enhanced Process:

1. Draw three cards representing the character's past, present, and future
2. For more nuance, expand to five cards (distant past, recent past, present, near future, distant future)
3. Note the progression of elements, numbers, or archetypes across this timeline
4. Consider how earlier experiences shaped current patterns
5. Explore how present circumstances are preparing for future development
6. Look for both evolution and potentially recurring patterns

7. Consider what must be released for growth to occur
8. Identify catalysts or thresholds between different phases

Example: A character's evolution path might show:

- Distant Past (**Ten of Swords**): A devastating ending or betrayal
- Recent Past (**Four of Swords**): A period of withdrawal and healing
- Present (**Temperance**): A time of finding balance and moderation
- Near Future (**Eight of Wands**): Rapid progress and communication
- Distant Future (**The Sun**): Ultimate clarity, joy, and authentic expression

This progression reveals a healing journey from devastation through restoration to balanced growth, eventually leading to genuine joy and success. The cards suggest that the character's suffering created necessary space for healing, which enabled them to find balance, leading to accelerated growth and ultimately to authentic happiness.

The Relationship Matrix

This technique explores the complex web of connections between multiple characters, revealing relationship dynamics and potential developments.

Enhanced Process:

1. Select cards representing key characters in your story
2. Draw cards specifically for the relationships between these characters
3. Arrange these in a matrix format where each intersection shows the relationship dynamic
4. Look for patterns, complementary relationships, and potential conflicts
5. Consider how different character combinations might create unexpected alliances or tensions
6. Allow natural conflicts and alliances to emerge from card combinations
7. Notice power dynamics suggested by the cards
8. Explore how these relationships might evolve through your story
9. Look for triangular relationships that might create compelling subplots

Example Implementation: For a story with three main characters, you might create this matrix:

Character	Protagonist (The Empress)	Ally (Knight of Cups)	Antagonist (King of Swords)
Protagonist (The Empress)	*Self-relationship* - Night of Cups - Seeks something deeper	*Relationship with Ally* - Two of Cups - Mutual connection	*Relationship with Antagonist* - Five of Wands - Competitive conflict
Ally (Knight of Cups)	*Relationship with Protagonist* - Page of Pentacles - Eager to learn from	*Self-relationship* - Seven of Cups - Internal confusion	*Relationship with Antagonist* - The Moon - Fear and uncertainty
Antagonist (King of Swords)	*Relationship with Protagonist* - The Emperor -Wishes to control	*Relationship with Ally* - Eight of Swords - Dismisses as trapped	*Self-relationship* - Justice - Believes in own righteousness

This matrix reveals fascinating relationship dynamics:

- The protagonist seeks something deeper from life (Eight of Cups) while experiencing genuine connection with their ally (Two of Cups) and competitive conflict with the antagonist (Five of Wands)
- The ally experiences internal confusion about their direction (Seven of Cups), looks to the protagonist for practical guidance (Page of Pentacles), and fears the antagonist (The Moon)
- The antagonist believes in their own righteousness (Justice), wishes to control the protagonist (The Emperor), and dismisses the ally as trapped or irrelevant (Eight of Swords)

These dynamics suggest potential story developments:

- The protagonist's search for deeper meaning might eventually require leaving the ally behind
- The ally's confusion and fear might make them vulnerable to manipulation by the antagonist
- The antagonist's rigid righteousness might eventually be their downfall

- The protagonist and antagonist have parallels in their authority archetypes (Empress/Emperor) suggesting they might understand each other better than they admit

By exploring these relationships through tarot imagery, you discover connections and tensions that plot planning alone might miss, creating a rich web of interactions that drive your story forward.

Character Archetype Exploration

The tarot is fundamentally based on archetypes—universal character patterns that resonate across cultures and time periods. By intentionally working with these archetypes, you can create characters with psychological depth that connect with readers at a subconscious level.

Major Arcana Archetypes

The 22 Major Arcana cards represent powerful archetypal energies that can form the foundation of compelling characters. These archetypes transcend simple character traits, embodying complete psychological patterns and developmental stages.

Character Development Application:

1. Select a Major Arcana card that resonates with your character concept
2. Study the traditional meanings and symbolism of this archetype
3. Consider both positive and shadow expressions of this energy
4. Explore how this archetypal energy might manifest in modern contexts
5. Identify other characters in literature or film who embody this archetype
6. Use Minor Arcana cards to add nuance and individuality to the archetype

Examples of Major Arcana Character Archetypes:

The Magician archetype creates characters who:

- Channel power or knowledge from higher sources

- Transform situations through skill and focused will
- Bridge different worlds or realms of experience
- May struggle with using their gifts ethically
- Often serve as catalysts who set events in motion
- Modern examples might include: innovative tech genius, influential social media personality, skilled negotiator, charismatic political figure

The High Priestess archetype creates characters who:

- Guard hidden knowledge or secrets
- Access intuitive wisdom beyond rational understanding
- Maintain boundaries between known and unknown realms
- May struggle with expressing their wisdom in practical ways
- Often serve as guides who reveal only what others are ready to see
- Modern examples might include: research scientist, psychotherapist, mystery writer, ethical hacker, keeper of family secrets

The Hermit archetype creates characters who:

- Have withdrawn from conventional society to find wisdom
- Carry light or knowledge through dark places
- Have learned through solitude and contemplation
- May struggle with human connection and relationship
- Often serve as mentors who guide others on their own paths
- Modern examples might include: reclusive expert, wilderness guide, retired professional sought for advice, social critic, independent researcher

Court Card Character Types

The 16 Court Cards (Pages, Knights, Queens, and Kings of each suit) offer a system for creating characters with specific elemental combinations and developmental stages.

Character Development Application:

1. Explore the court card that best represents your character's approach to life
2. Consider both the rank (Page, Knight, Queen, King) and suit (Wands, Cups, Swords, Pentacles)
3. The rank suggests their developmental stage and expression style
4. The suit suggests their primary element and area of focus
5. Use this combination to develop consistent character traits and behaviors
6. Add depth by exploring how they might act when under pressure or in different contexts

Court Card Development Framework:

Pages represent:

- Beginners or students in their element
- Curiosity and openness to learning
- Messengers or harbingers of their element
- Youthful or fresh perspective
- Potential not yet fully realized
- Characters at the start of their journey

Knights represent:

- Active, mobile expression of their element
- Action-oriented approach, sometimes to extremes
- Questing or seeking energy
- Skill development through movement and testing
- Passionate but sometimes unbalanced application
- Characters in the midst of their quest or journey

Queens represent:

- Mastery of the internal aspects of their element
- Nurturing and developing their element's qualities
- Receptive but powerful expression
- Creating environments where their element thrives

- Wisdom through feeling and intuitive understanding
- Characters who influence through presence and nurturing

Kings represent:

- Mastery of the external application of their element
- Authority and responsibility within their domain
- Decisive and outwardly focused expression
- Creating structures that embody their element
- Wisdom through experience and manifestation
- Characters who influence through direct action and leadership

Elemental Qualities:

Wands (Fire) characters focus on:

- Passion, creativity, and inspiration
- Action, energy, and initiative
- Growth, expansion, and adventure
- Spirit, vision, and transformation
- When challenged: impulsiveness, burnout, aggression

Cups (Water) characters focus on:

- Emotions, relationships, and connections
- Intuition, dreams, and the unconscious
- Love, compassion, and empathy
- Imagination, reflection, and feeling
- When challenged: emotional overwhelm, escapism, manipulation

Swords (Air) characters focus on:

- Intellect, communication, and ideas
- Analysis, strategy, and decision-making
- Truth, justice, and ethical principles
- Clarity, perception, and discernment
- When challenged: overthinking, conflict, detachment

Pentacles (Earth) characters focus on:

- Practical matters, resources, and physical reality
- Stability, security, and methodical progress
- Craftsmanship, tangible results, and reliability
- Sensory experience, comfort, and embodiment
- When challenged: stubbornness, materialism, excessive caution

By combining ranks and suits, you create characters with specific approaches to life:

Example: Knight of Wands This creates a character who:

- Approaches life with passionate energy and enthusiasm
- Acts quickly, sometimes impulsively, on creative inspirations
- Seeks adventure and new experiences actively
- May struggle with completing projects before moving to the next
- Brings excitement and transformation wherever they go
- Under pressure, might become aggressive or burn out completely
- Modern examples might include: adventure travel blogger, serial entrepreneur, inspirational speaker, activist leading demonstrations

Example: Queen of Swords This creates a character who:

- Approaches life with intellectual clarity and perceptiveness
- Creates environments where truth and communication flourish
- Has learned wisdom through difficult experiences
- May struggle with appearing cold or intimidating to others
- Brings discernment and ethical consideration to situations
- Under pressure, might become cutting or isolate themselves
- Modern examples might include: investigative journalist, judge, literary critic, ethical AI researcher

Practical Exercises for Character Development

Basic Character Discovery

This foundational exercise helps you meet a new character through direct tarot imagery.

Enhanced Process:

1. Create quiet, receptive space without distractions
2. Take several deep breaths to center yourself
3. Shuffle your deck while focusing on discovering a new character
4. Ask aloud: "What character wants to emerge in my story?"
5. Draw one card and place it before you
6. Study the image without immediately analyzing or interpreting
7. Notice which elements naturally draw your attention
8. Allow first impressions to form—physical traits, emotional qualities, energy
9. Record these impressions without judgment
10. Begin free-writing from the character's perspective, letting their voice emerge
11. Ask the character questions and record their responses
12. Notice physical sensations or emotional responses in yourself
13. Allow the character to surprise you with unexpected traits or histories
14. Draw a second card if you need more information about the character

Reflection Questions:

- What was your immediate emotional response to this character?
- Which physical or visual elements of the card connected with the character?
- What voice or speech pattern emerged naturally for this character?
- What surprised you about this character?
- What questions do you still have about them?

- What kind of story does this character seem to belong in?

Character Deepening Through Elemental Balancing

This exercise helps you develop more balanced, three-dimensional characters by exploring their relationship with all four elements.

Enhanced Process:

1. Identify a card that represents your character's primary energy
2. Note which element this card represents (Wands/Fire, Cups/Water, Swords/Air, Pentacles/Earth)
3. Draw one card from each of the other three elements
4. These cards represent how your character relates to these complementary energies
5. Consider how your character integrates or struggles with these different aspects
6. Look for imbalances—elements they over-emphasize or neglect
7. Explore how these elemental relationships might create internal conflicts
8. Consider how elemental balance or imbalance affects their relationships
9. Identify potential growth through better elemental integration

Example: For a character represented by the Knight of Wands (Fire):

- Relationship with Water (Emotions): Eight of Cups—they tend to walk away from emotional situations when they become too deep, seeking new experiences instead of emotional processing
- Relationship with Air (Intellect): Two of Swords—they often reach intellectual stalemates or indecision, preferring action over careful analysis
- Relationship with Earth (Material): Four of Pentacles—they might be surprisingly conservative with resources, perhaps due to past insecurity

This elemental profile reveals a character who leads with passionate action but struggles with emotional depth, intellectual clarity, and may have unresolved issues with material security. Their growth might involve learning to stay present with emotions, developing decisiveness, and finding a more balanced relationship with resources.

Voice Development Through Tarot Dialogue

This exercise helps you discover and refine authentic character voices through directed tarot dialogue.

Enhanced Process:

1. Select a card representing your character
2. Place this card in front of you
3. Draw three additional cards and place them in a row below your character card
4. These cards represent topics or situations your character will address
5. For each card, write a brief monologue in your character's voice
6. Allow the character's specific speech patterns, vocabulary, and perspective to emerge
7. Notice how their voice shifts when addressing different topics
8. Pay attention to what they avoid saying as well as what they express
9. Draw an additional card if you want to see how they respond to a specific challenge
10. Review the monologues to identify consistent voice elements

Example: For a character represented by The Empress:

- Responding to Three of Swords (heartbreak): Their language might be nurturing and healing, focusing on growth that comes through pain, using natural metaphors and sensory details
- Responding to Seven of Wands (defensiveness): Their language might become more protective, revealing fierceness beneath nurturing, perhaps using maternal imagery
- Responding to The Fool (new beginnings): Their language might show

enthusiasm for potential, emphasizing how they'll support growth, using abundant and generous phrasing

Through these varied responses, you might discover this character uses sensory-rich language, speaks in nurturing but firm tones, employs natural metaphors, and maintains a consistent focus on growth and potential even when addressing difficult topics.

Character Conflict Exploration

This exercise helps you uncover authentic sources of conflict and tension for your character.

Enhanced Process:

1. Draw a card representing your character's core desire or motivation
2. Draw a second card representing their fear or what blocks them
3. Draw a third card representing their typical approach to conflict
4. Draw a fourth card representing what they need to learn about conflict
5. Study the relationships between these cards
6. Note whether their approach aligns with their true needs
7. Consider internal and external manifestations of this conflict pattern
8. Explore how this conflict pattern might evolve through your story
9. Identify characters or situations that might trigger this conflict

Example:

- Core Desire (**Nine of Pentacles**): Self-sufficiency, independence, cultivated abundance
- Fear/Block (**Six of Cups**): Childhood patterns, nostalgia, dependency on past relationships
- Typical Approach to Conflict (**Eight of Swords**): Self-restriction, victim mentality, seeing no options
- Needed Lesson (**The Chariot**): Assertiveness, controlled action, moving forward despite opposition

This conflict profile reveals a character who desires independence but is blocked by emotional attachments to the past. When facing conflict, they tend to feel trapped and victimized rather than taking action. Their growth requires learning to harness opposing forces and move forward decisively despite emotional pulls toward the past. This pattern might manifest in career situations where they need to assert independence from family expectations, or in relationships where they must break free from comfortable but limiting dynamics.

Final Integration: The Living Character

The ultimate goal of the Tarot Character Development System is to create characters who feel alive—who surprise, challenge, and engage both you and your readers with their authenticity and depth. A fully integrated character transcends the individual cards or techniques used to create them, emerging as a cohesive, complex entity with their own voice, motivations, and journey.

Signs that your character has achieved this integration include:

- You can easily imagine how they would respond in new situations
- They occasionally surprise you with their choices or reactions
- Their voice comes naturally when you write from their perspective
- Their motivations feel complex but coherent
- You can sense both their strengths and vulnerabilities
- Their journey feels both surprising and inevitable
- You feel emotional investment in their development
- Other characters develop naturally in relation to them
- They seem to generate their own storylines and conflicts

Remember that the tarot is simply a bridge to your own creative subconscious. These cards and techniques help you access what you already know intuitively about human nature, psychological truth, and compelling character development. As you become more familiar with this system, you'll likely find yourself needing fewer cards and more direct access to your character's authentic voice and journey.

The most powerful characters are those who seem to exist beyond the page—who continue to live in your imagination and your readers' minds long after the story ends. By accessing the archetypal wisdom of the tarot through this system, you open yourself to creating characters with this rare and precious quality of autonomous life.

CHAPTER 7

The Thirty-Six Dramatic Situations

Introduction to Polti's 36 Dramatic Situations

In 1895, French writer Georges Polti published "The Thirty-Six Dramatic Situations," arguing that all stories, regardless of their apparent diversity, can be boiled down to just three dozen basic dramatic situations. Building on work by Carlo Gozzi, a Venetian playwright who first claimed the existence of only 36 plots, Polti meticulously cataloged these fundamental situations with their variations.

Each dramatic situation represents a core human conflict or relationship dynamic that creates tension, emotional involvement, and narrative drive. These situations have proven remarkably durable across cultures, time periods, and storytelling mediums, from ancient Greek tragedies to modern films.

What makes Polti's work particularly valuable is his detailed classification system. For each situation, he identifies:

- The core dynamic or relationship
- The essential elements or roles required
- Numerous variations and subcategories
- Examples from literature, drama, and mythology

Understanding these dramatic situations provides writers with archetypal patterns that can be infinitely adapted and combined to create fresh narratives while still tapping into deeply resonant human experiences.

The Thirty-Six Dramatic Situations in Detail

1. Supplication

Core Dynamic: A Persecutor threatens a Suppliant who appeals to a Power in authority for protection or intervention.

Essential Elements:

- The Suppliant: One who pleads or begs for mercy or assistance
- The Persecutor: One who threatens or pursues the Suppliant
- The Power: A person or entity with authority to grant or deny the supplication

Variations:

- The Power is hesitant to help
- The Suppliant is guilty of past wrongdoing
- The Suppliant and Power are related, creating conflicting loyalties
- The Persecutor also appeals to the Power, creating competing claims
- The supplication fails, leading to tragedy
- The supplication succeeds despite obstacles

Classic Examples: The Suppliants (Aeschylus), King Lear begging his daughters, refugees seeking asylum

Psychological Core: This situation explores themes of mercy, justice, compassion, and the dynamics of power imbalance. It asks when we should shield others from consequences and when we should let justice take its course.

2. Deliverance

Core Dynamic: An Unfortunate is threatened by a Threatener and rescued by a Rescuer.

Essential Elements:

- The Unfortunate: A victim or person in peril
- The Threatener: The source of danger or persecution
- The Rescuer: The deliverer who intervenes

Variations:

- The rescue appears impossible but succeeds
- The rescuer has personal interest in the unfortunate

- The rescuer discovers the unfortunate by chance
- The rescue requires sacrifice by the rescuer
- The rescue reveals unknown connections between characters
- The unfortunate does not wish to be rescued

Classic Examples: Perseus rescuing Andromeda, Lancelot saving Guinevere, superheroes saving civilians

Psychological Core: This situation examines courage, intervention, and the moral obligation to help others. It resonates with our desire to believe in protection from harm and celebrates heroic action.

3. Crime Pursued by Vengeance

Core Dynamic: An Avenger pursues a Criminal who has harmed the Victim.

Essential Elements:

- The Avenger: One who seeks retribution
- The Criminal: One who committed the wrong
- The Victim: One who was harmed (may be the Avenger or someone connected to them)

Variations:

- Professional pursuit (detective stories)
- The criminal is unaware of pursuit
- The avenger is related to both victim and criminal
- Disguised pursuit
- The avenger becomes as criminal as the pursued
- The vengeance destroys the avenger

Classic Examples: Hamlet, The Count of Monte Cristo, revenge films

Psychological Core: This situation explores justice, retribution, obsession, and the psychological price of revenge. It questions whether personal vengeance can ever bring true resolution.

4. Vengeance Taken for Kindred upon Kindred

Core Dynamic: An Avenging Kinsman seeks revenge against a Guilty Kinsman for harm done to a Victim Kinsman.

Essential Elements:

- The Avenging Kinsman: Family member seeking revenge
- The Guilty Kinsman: Relative who committed the crime
- The Victim Kinsman: Relative who was harmed

Variations:

- Revenge for a murder
- Revenge for dishonor or betrayal within a family
- Revenge unknowingly taken against a relative
- Revenge revealing unknown family connections
- Conflict between family loyalty and justice

Classic Examples: Electra, blood feuds in various cultures, family revenge dramas

Psychological Core: This situation intensifies the vengeance theme by adding family ties, forcing characters to choose between blood loyalty and justice. It examines how betrayal within family creates uniquely profound wounds.

5. Pursuit

Core Dynamic: A Fugitive is pursued by a Pursuer.

Essential Elements:

- The Fugitive: One who flees
- The Pursuer: One who chases
- Often includes the Object of pursuit (what the pursuer wants from the fugitive)

Variations:

- Pursuit for punishment of crime
- Pursuit for recapture of escaped prisoner
- Pursuit of one in hiding
- Pursuit of someone falsely accused
- Pursuit involving disguise or mistaken identity
- Psychological pursuit where the chase is internal

Classic Examples: Les Misérables (Javert pursuing Valjean), fugitive films, chase thrillers

Psychological Core: This situation creates tension through the constant threat of capture. It examines persistence, desperation, and the psychological effects of being hunted or being a hunter.

6. Disaster

Core Dynamic: A Vanquished Power falls from position or happiness through calamity or defeat.

Essential Elements:

- The Vanquished Power: One who falls from grace
- The Victorious Enemy or Force: That which causes the fall
- Often includes Witnesses to the disaster

Variations:

- Overthrow of ruler or empire
- Fall from prosperity to poverty
- Natural disaster overwhelming characters
- Defeat in battle or competition
- Loss of loved ones
- Reversal of fortune

Classic Examples: The fall of Troy, Job's trials, disaster films

Psychological Core: This situation explores how characters respond to catastrophic loss and tests their resilience. It examines human vulnerability to forces beyond our control and our capacity to endure.

7. Falling Prey to Cruelty or Misfortune

Core Dynamic: An Unfortunate suffers from the Misfortune and/or from a Master/Tormentor.

Essential Elements:

- The Unfortunate: Victim of cruelty or circumstance
- The Master or Tormentor: One inflicting suffering (if present)
- The Misfortune: Adverse circumstances causing suffering

Variations:

- The unfortunate suffering from persecution
- The unfortunate abandoned or cast out
- The unfortunate exposed to public contempt
- The unfortunate suffering physical torture
- The unfortunate suffering psychological torment
- The unfortunate experiencing extreme misfortune or tragedy

Classic Examples: Prometheus Bound, enslaved characters, victims of torture

Psychological Core: This situation examines human suffering, resilience, and dignity under extreme duress. It confronts us with the reality of cruelty and invites empathy with those who suffer.

8. Revolt

Core Dynamic: A Conspirator leads a revolt against a Tyrant/Authority.

Essential Elements:

- The Tyrant/Authority: The figure or system being opposed
- The Conspirator: The leader of the rebellion

- The Cause: The reason for the uprising

Variations:

- Rebellion against political oppression
- Rebellion against social norms or conventions
- Familial rebellion (against parental authority)
- Institutional rebellion (against organizational rules)
- Individual rebellion against societal expectations
- Rebellion that becomes tyranny itself

Classic Examples: Robin Hood, revolutionary stories, dystopian rebellions

Psychological Core: This situation explores the tension between authority and freedom, examining when rebellion is justified and the corrupting potential of power even for those who initially fight against it.

9. Daring Enterprise

Core Dynamic: A Bold Leader and Associates undertake a daring mission for a certain Object.

Essential Elements:

- The Bold Leader: One who initiates the enterprise
- The Object of the Enterprise: The goal or prize
- The Adversary/Obstacle: What stands in the way

Variations:

- Dangerous quest or mission
- Adventurous expedition
- Obtaining an object of desire
- Daring rescue mission
- Ambitious scheme or heist
- Scientific or exploratory venture

Classic Examples: Jason and the Golden Fleece, heist films, exploration narratives

Psychological Core: This situation celebrates courage, ingenuity, and ambition. It examines leadership under pressure and the human drive to accomplish difficult goals despite significant risks.

10. Abduction

Core Dynamic: An Abductor takes a Victim by force, often pursued by a Guardian.

Essential Elements:

- The Abductor: One who takes another by force
- The Abducted: The person taken
- Often includes a Guardian who pursues

Variations:

- Abduction of a lover
- Abduction for ransom
- Kidnapping for political leverage
- Abduction revealing unknown connections
- Abduction that leads to unexpected consequences
- Stockholm syndrome where abducted bonds with abductor

Classic Examples: The Rape of the Sabine Women, kidnapping stories, hostage films

Psychological Core: This situation explores control, freedom, and power dynamics. It examines the psychological effects of captivity on both captive and captor, and the lengths to which loved ones will go to rescue the abducted.

11. The Enigma

Core Dynamic: A Problem Solver works to answer a question or solve a puzzle presented by an Interrogator or Situation.

Essential Elements:

- The Interrogator: One who poses the enigma
- The Seeker: One who attempts to solve it
- The Problem: The enigma itself

Variations:

- Riddles with life-or-death consequences
- Mystery requiring investigation
- Test of character through puzzles
- Prophetic enigma requiring interpretation
- Scientific or philosophical problem seeking solution
- Psychological enigma or identity question

Classic Examples: Oedipus and the Sphinx, detective stories, puzzle films

Psychological Core: This situation examines human curiosity, intelligence, and our need to make sense of confusing circumstances. It explores how we approach problems and what solving or failing to solve them reveals about us.

12. Obtaining

Core Dynamic: A Solicitor and Adversary compete for a Coveted Thing, requiring an Arbitrator to decide.

Essential Elements:

- The Solicitor: One who desires to obtain something
- The Adversary: One who opposes the solicitor
- The Coveted Thing: What is being sought
- Often includes an Arbitrator who decides

Variations:

- Competition for love or affection

- Contest for a prize or position
- Legal battle over property or rights
- Negotiation for valuable object or opportunity
- Rivalry for status or recognition
- Struggle for limited resource

Classic Examples: The Judgment of Paris, custody battles, competition stories

Psychological Core: This situation explores desire, ambition, and fair distribution of limited resources. It examines how we pursue what we want when others want the same thing, and the moral questions of who deserves to obtain their desire.

13. Enmity of Kinsmen

Core Dynamic: A Malevolent Kinsman hates and acts against a Hated Kinsman.

Essential Elements:

- The Malevolent Kinsman: Family member who hates
- The Hated Kinsman: Family member who is hated
- Often includes a Reason for the hatred

Variations:

- Hatred between brothers
- Hatred between relatives by marriage
- Hatred between parent and child
- Family feuds spanning generations
- Hatred based on envy or jealousy within family
- Hatred based on competing claims to inheritance or position

Classic Examples: Biblical Cain and Abel, Richard III, dysfunctional family dramas

Psychological Core: This situation explores how the closest bonds can transform into the deepest animosity. It examines how shared blood intensifies conflicts and how family dynamics can create lasting psychological wounds.

14. Rivalry of Kinsmen

Core Dynamic: A Preferred Kinsman competes with a Rejected Kinsman for a shared goal or person's favor.

Essential Elements:

- The Preferred Kinsman: The one who is favored
- The Rejected Kinsman: The one who is less favored
- The Object of Rivalry: What they compete for
- Often includes the Preference Giver who favors one over the other

Variations:

- Rivalry between siblings for parental affection
- Rivalry between relatives for inheritance
- Rivalry between family members for the same love interest
- Rivalry between kinsmen for political position
- Rivalry revealing true character of each kinsman
- Rivalry that destroys the family bond

Classic Examples: Jacob and Esau, sibling rivalry stories, family succession dramas

Psychological Core: This situation examines the pain of unequal treatment within what should be equal relationships. It explores how comparison and competition within families shapes identity and drives behavior.

15. Murderous Adultery

Core Dynamic: Two Adulterers conspire to kill a betrayed spouse.

Essential Elements:

- The Two Adulterers: The unfaithful spouse and lover
- The Betrayed Spouse: The murder victim
- Often includes an Avenger who discovers the crime

Variations:

- Murder planned but not executed
- Murder committed then discovered
- Murder with mistaken identity or unintended victim
- Murder followed by remorse or haunting
- Murder revealing unexpected connections
- Murder leading to further betrayals

Classic Examples: Clytemnestra and Aegisthus killing Agamemnon, noir films about murderous spouses

Psychological Core: This situation explores the darkest consequences of betrayal, examining how broken trust can escalate to violence. It confronts the tension between desire and loyalty, and how passion can override moral boundaries.

16. Madness

Core Dynamic: A Madman harms a Victim through their derangement.

Essential Elements:

- The Madman: One whose mental state causes harm
- The Victim: One who suffers from the madness
- Often includes a Witness to the madness

Variations:

- Temporary insanity leading to regrettable actions
- Deliberate feigning of madness for strategic purposes
- Madness induced by trauma or manipulation
- Madness revealing hidden truths

- Hallucination or delusion causing harmful behavior
- Obsession driving character to extremes

Classic Examples: Hamlet's feigned madness, King Lear, psychological thrillers

Psychological Core: This situation examines the fragility of the human mind and the thin line between sanity and madness. It explores how mental disturbance affects both the sufferer and those around them, and questions the nature of reality and perception.

17. Fatal Imprudence

Core Dynamic: The Imprudent One makes a fatal mistake that harms self or others.

Essential Elements:

- The Imprudent One: Person who makes the mistake
- The Victim: Person harmed by the mistake
- The Error: The fatal mistake itself

Variations:

- Error through ignorance or naivety
- Error through carelessness
- Error through curiosity
- Error through misunderstanding
- Error through neglect of warning
- Error through excessive trust

Classic Examples: Pandora opening the box, tragic accidents, cautionary tales

Psychological Core: This situation explores the consequences of carelessness, curiosity, or ignorance. It examines human fallibility and how momentary lapses in judgment can have permanent consequences.

18. Involuntary Crimes of Love

Core Dynamic: A Lover discovers they have unknowingly committed a taboo relationship.

Essential Elements:

- The Lover: One who discovers the taboo
- The Beloved: The forbidden person
- The Revealer: Person or event that reveals the truth

Variations:

- Discovery of incest after the fact
- Love for one forbidden by family enmity
- Love discovered to be adulterous unknowingly
- Love for one bound by religious vows
- Love forbidden by class or social boundaries
- Love that violates professional ethics

Classic Examples: Oedipus and Jocasta, stories of unknowing incest, forbidden love

Psychological Core: This situation explores how we respond when natural feelings collide with social taboos or moral prohibitions. It examines the psychological aftermath of discovering that what felt right is considered deeply wrong.

19. Slaying of a Kinsman Unrecognized

Core Dynamic: A Slayer kills a Victim, then discovers the Victim was related to them.

Essential Elements:

- The Slayer: One who kills
- The Unrecognized Victim: The relative who is killed
- The Recognition: The moment of discovery

- Often includes a Revealer who exposes the truth

Variations:

- Parent unknowingly killing child
- Child unknowingly killing parent
- Siblings killing each other unaware
- Killing someone then discovering family connection
- Near-miss where recognition happens just in time
- Recognition coming too late to prevent tragedy

Classic Examples: Greek tragedies involving unrecognized relatives, mistaken identity killings

Psychological Core: This situation creates horror through dramatic irony, as the audience often knows what the character doesn't. It examines how incomplete knowledge can lead to irreversible tragedy and explores guilt that comes from unintentional wrongdoing.

20. Self-Sacrificing for an Ideal

Core Dynamic: A Hero sacrifices themself for a Cause, Ideal, or Beneficiary.

Essential Elements:

- The Hero: One who makes the sacrifice
- The Ideal or Cause: What is being sacrificed for
- Often includes the Beneficiary who benefits from the sacrifice

Variations:

- Sacrifice of life for principle
- Sacrifice of personal happiness for duty
- Sacrifice of worldly success for spiritual value
- Sacrifice to protect loved ones
- Sacrifice to uphold justice or truth
- Sacrifice that inspires others to similar nobility

Classic Examples: Religious martyrs, self-sacrificing heroes, characters who give up personal happiness for greater good

Psychological Core: This situation examines what we value more than our own welfare or happiness. It explores transcendent values and the human capacity to subordinate self-interest to higher principles.

21. Self-Sacrifice for Kindred

Core Dynamic: A Hero sacrifices themself for a family member or loved one.

Essential Elements:

- The Hero: One who makes the sacrifice
- The Kinsman: The relative benefiting from sacrifice
- The Creditor/Person or Thing threatening Kinsman

Variations:

- Sacrifice of life to save family member
- Sacrifice of freedom for relative's benefit
- Sacrifice of reputation to protect family member
- Sacrifice of love or happiness for family duty
- Sacrifice revealing true character or devotion
- Sacrifice that resonates beyond the immediate family

Classic Examples: Tales of parental sacrifice, siblings taking blame for each other, family loyalty stories

Psychological Core: This situation focuses the self-sacrifice theme specifically on family bonds. It examines the depth of familial love and duty, exploring what we're willing to give up for those connected to us by blood or deep affection.

22. All Sacrificed for a Passion

Core Dynamic: A Lover sacrifices everything for an overwhelming passion or desire.

Essential Elements:

- The Lover: One consumed by passion
- The Object of Passion: Person or thing desired
- The Sacrificed: What is given up (career, reputation, relationships, etc.)

Variations:

- Sacrifice of honor or integrity for desire
- Sacrifice of family ties for passionate love
- Sacrifice of wealth or position for obsession
- Sacrifice leading to destruction
- Sacrifice revealing the true nature of desire
- Sacrifice that ultimately proves empty

Classic Examples: Characters who abandon everything for love, obsession stories, cautionary tales about desire

Psychological Core: This situation explores the overwhelming power of passion and its ability to override other values and commitments. It examines the fine line between dedication and obsession, and questions whether anything is worth sacrificing everything else.

23. Necessity of Sacrificing Loved Ones

Core Dynamic: A Hero must sacrifice a Beloved Victim due to Necessity.

Essential Elements:

- The Hero: One who must make the sacrifice
- The Beloved Victim: The loved one who must be sacrificed
- The Necessity: The force requiring the sacrifice

Variations:

- Sacrifice demanded by duty to state
- Sacrifice required by religious obligation
- Sacrifice necessary to save many others

- Sacrifice to fulfill prophecy or destiny
- Sacrifice averted at last moment
- Sacrifice revealing moral complexity

Classic Examples: Abraham and Isaac, Agamemnon sacrificing Iphigenia, moral dilemma stories

Psychological Core: This situation examines the ultimate moral dilemma—choosing between love for an individual and broader obligations. It explores how we navigate conflicting values when both choices involve profound loss.

24. Rivalry of Superior and Inferior

Core Dynamic: A Superior Rival and Inferior Rival compete, with the outcome challenging expectations.

Essential Elements:

- The Superior Rival: One with advantages
- The Inferior Rival: One with disadvantages
- The Object of Rivalry: What they compete for
- Often includes a Judge who decides between them

Variations:

- David and Goliath situations (underdog victories)
- Competition across class or social barriers
- Rivalry between mentor and student
- Rivalry revealing that apparent disadvantage is actually strength
- Rivalry where superior becomes inferior through pride
- Rivalry exposing the true meaning of superiority

Classic Examples: Underdog stories, competitions across social classes, mentor-student conflicts

Psychological Core: This situation explores power imbalance, expectations, and the nature of true advantage. It examines how apparent weakness can become strength and how different forms of power operate in competition.

25. Adultery

Core Dynamic: A Deceived Spouse is betrayed by an Adulterous Spouse and Paramour.

Essential Elements:

- The Deceived Spouse: The betrayed partner
- The Adulterous Spouse: The unfaithful partner
- The Paramour: The lover outside the marriage

Variations:

- Discovery of the affair leading to confrontation
- Long-term deception with mounting complications
- Adultery motivated by genuine love versus desire
- Adultery as revenge or rebellion
- Adultery leading to deeper understanding of marriage
- Adultery forgiven and marriage rebuilt

Classic Examples: Anna Karenina, Madame Bovary, marital infidelity stories

Psychological Core: This situation examines trust, loyalty, and desire within committed relationships. It explores the consequences of betrayal not just for the betrayed but for all parties involved.

26. Crimes of Love

Core Dynamic: A Lover and Beloved enter a relationship that society forbids.

Essential Elements:

- The Lover: One participant in the forbidden love
- The Beloved: The other participant
- The Forbidder: Person or societal force opposing the relationship

Variations:

- Love forbidden by family opposition
- Love forbidden by societal prejudice
- Love forbidden by religious restrictions
- Love forbidden by professional boundaries
- Love that violates cultural taboos
- Love considered inappropriate due to age difference

Classic Examples: Romeo and Juliet, forbidden love stories across cultures

Psychological Core: This situation explores the tension between individual desire and social norms. It examines how love can become intensified when forbidden and the price people are willing to pay to follow their hearts against external opposition.

27. Discovery of the Dishonor of a Loved One

Core Dynamic: A Discoverer finds that a Loved One has committed an act bringing dishonor.

Essential Elements:

- The Discoverer: One who learns the truth
- The Guilty Loved One: Person who has committed the dishonorable act
- The Dishonor: The shameful action or secret

Variations:

- Discovery of loved one's criminal past
- Discovery of deception or betrayal
- Discovery of moral failing or cowardice
- Discovery forcing choice between love and honor
- Discovery leading to attempt to hide or resolve dishonor
- Discovery that changes perception of loved one forever

Classic Examples: Stories where characters discover dark secrets about family members, revelations about respected figures

Psychological Core: This situation examines how we respond when our image of someone we love is shattered. It explores the conflict between love and moral judgment, and how we reconcile care for someone with disapproval of their actions.

28. Obstacles to Love

Core Dynamic: Two Lovers face Obstacles to their union.

Essential Elements:

- The Two Lovers: Those who wish to be together
- The Obstacle(s): What prevents their union
- Often includes a Mediator who helps or hinders

Variations:

- External obstacles (family opposition, distance, war)
- Internal obstacles (fear, pride, misunderstanding)
- Social obstacles (class difference, cultural barriers)
- Psychological obstacles (past trauma, trust issues)
- Physical obstacles (illness, imprisonment)
- Obstacles overcome through persistence or sacrifice

Classic Examples: Pride and Prejudice, romantic comedies, love stories with complications

Psychological Core: This situation explores commitment, perseverance, and the value we place on connection. It examines whether love is strengthened or weakened by difficulties, and what lovers are willing to overcome to be together.

29. An Enemy Loved

Core Dynamic: A Lover discovers their Beloved is actually their Enemy.

Essential Elements:

- The Lover: One who loves
- The Beloved Enemy: One who is both loved and enemy
- The Revelation: The discovery of the conflict

Variations:

- Love for someone from an enemy family or group
- Love discovered after enmity is established
- Love for someone who has caused personal harm
- Professional enemies who develop personal feelings
- Enemies who must work together despite feelings
- Enemy pretending love as strategic deception

Classic Examples: Spy stories with romantic complications, tales of love across battle lines, romantic conflicts of loyalty

Psychological Core: This situation explores the tension between personal feeling and external loyalty. It examines how love can transcend group identity and how individuals navigate conflicting commitments to heart and cause.

30. Ambition

Core Dynamic: An Ambitious Person seeks a Coveted Thing but faces Opposition.

Essential Elements:

- The Ambitious Person: One who desires greatness
- The Coveted Thing: Object of ambition (power, wealth, fame, etc.)
- The Adversary or Obstacle: What stands in the way

Variations:

- Ambition pursued regardless of cost
- Ambition revealing true character
- Ambition achieved but proving hollow
- Ambition destroying what was truly valuable

- Ambition redirected to worthy purpose
- Ambition leading to downfall

Classic Examples: Macbeth, Citizen Kane, rise-and-fall stories

Psychological Core: This situation explores the human drive for achievement and recognition. It examines the fine line between healthy aspiration and destructive obsession, and questions what success truly means.

31. Conflict with a God

Core Dynamic: A Mortal comes into conflict with a Deity or powerful supernatural force.

Essential Elements:

- The Mortal: The human challenger
- The Deity: The supernatural power
- The Cause: Reason for the conflict

Variations:

- Defiance of divine command or law
- Rebellion against fate or prophecy
- Challenge to divine authority or judgment
- Attempt to transcend mortal limitations
- Competition with divine power
- Struggle to understand divine purpose

Classic Examples: Prometheus, Job, mortal-divine conflict myths

Psychological Core: This situation explores human relationship with higher powers, fate, and ultimate authority. It examines the tension between acceptance and rebellion against what seems predetermined or beyond human control.

32. Mistaken Jealousy

Core Dynamic: A Jealous One mistakenly suspects a Partner of infidelity with a

Perceived Rival.

Essential Elements:

- The Jealous One: Person experiencing unfounded jealousy
- The Partner: Person wrongly suspected
- The Perceived Rival: Person wrongly believed to be involved
- The Mistake: What causes the false suspicion

Variations:

- Jealousy based on misinterpreted evidence
- Jealousy manipulated by outside party
- Jealousy rooted in projecting one's own desires
- Jealousy driven by past betrayal
- Jealousy revealing deeper relationship issues
- Jealousy creating the very problem feared

Classic Examples: Othello, comedies of misunderstanding, paranoid partner narratives

Psychological Core: This situation explores insecurity, trust, and the power of imagination to create its own reality. It examines how fear of loss can itself become the agent of destruction.

33. Erroneous Judgment

Core Dynamic: A Mistaken One forms a false judgment about a Victim, leading to error.

Essential Elements:

- The Mistaken One: Person who judges erroneously
- The Victim: Person misjudged
- The Cause of Mistake: What leads to the error
- Often includes the Author of Mistake who creates confusion

Variations:

- False suspicion of crime
- Misinterpreted actions or intentions
- Prejudice leading to misjudgment
- Circumstantial evidence creating false picture
- Deliberate deception causing erroneous judgment
- Error maintained through confirmation bias

Classic Examples: To Kill a Mockingbird, mistaken identity plots, false accusation stories

Psychological Core: This situation explores the fallibility of human judgment and perception. It examines how preconceptions, limited information, and psychological biases affect our assessment of others and situations.

34. Remorse

Core Dynamic: A Guilty One is consumed by guilt over a Misdeed and seeks resolution.

Essential Elements:

- The Guilty One: Person experiencing remorse
- The Misdeed: Action causing guilt
- Often includes the Victim of misdeed
- May include a Interrogator or Confessor who hears admission

Variations:

- Remorse leading to confession
- Remorse driving attempts at atonement
- Remorse without possibility of restitution
- Remorse revealing changed character
- Remorse as catalyst for broader change
- Remorse rejected as insufficient by victims

Classic Examples: Crime and Punishment, redemption arcs, guilt-driven character studies

Psychological Core: This situation explores conscience, moral responsibility, and the possibility of redemption. It examines how we live with the consequences of our actions and whether genuine remorse can lead to forgiveness or healing.

35. Recovery of a Lost One

Core Dynamic: A Seeker finds a Lost One who had disappeared or been taken.

Essential Elements:

- The Seeker: Person searching
- The Lost One: Person who was missing
- The Recognition: Moment of rediscovery
- Often includes the Circumstance of loss

Variations:

- Recovery of family member thought dead
- Recovery of person with altered identity
- Recovery revealing secrets or deceptions
- Recovery after deliberate disappearance
- Recovery changing both seeker and found
- Recovery bringing complications rather than resolution

Classic Examples: The Odyssey (Odysseus returning home), missing person stories, reunion narratives

Psychological Core: This situation explores loss, persistence, and the complexity of reunion. It examines how separation changes both the lost and those left behind, and whether reconnection can truly restore what was broken.

36. Loss of Loved Ones

Core Dynamic: A Kinsman Slain, Witness, and Executioner engage in a tragedy of loss.

Essential Elements:

- The Kinsman Slain: Loved one who dies
- The Witness: One who experiences the loss
- The Executioner: Agent of death (person, force, fate)

Variations:

- Death of loved one by violence
- Death by accident or natural disaster
- Death by illness or natural causes
- Death revealing unknown connections
- Death transforming the survivor
- Anticipated death with time for reconciliation

Classic Examples: Tragedies focusing on bereavement, narratives of devastating loss, survivor stories

Psychological Core: This situation explores grief, mortality, and the reconstruction of life after profound loss. It examines how the death of those closest to us challenges our identity and forces confrontation with our own mortality.

Practical Applications of the 36 Dramatic Situations

Polti's framework offers writers several practical advantages:

1. **Breaking Creative Blocks**: When stuck, randomly selecting one of the 36 situations can spark new narrative directions.
2. **Deepening Conflict**: Identifying the core situation at the heart of your story allows you to explore its variations and intensify its dramatic potential.
3. **Character Development**: Characters can be more fully realized by understanding their function within classic dramatic situations.

4. **Plot Refinement**: Recognizing which situation drives your narrative helps eliminate extraneous elements and strengthen core dramatic tensions.
5. **Combining Situations**: Most complex narratives interweave multiple situations, creating rich tapestries of conflict and resolution.
6. **Testing Story Strength**: If your narrative doesn't align with any of these fundamental situations, it may lack the essential tension that drives compelling stories.
7. **Universal Appeal**: By connecting your unique story to archetypal situations, you tap into patterns that resonate across cultural and historical

The Tarot-36: Integrating Dramatic Situations with Tarot for Subconscious Story Development

The Marriage of Two Ancient Systems

The tarot and Polti's 36 dramatic situations represent two profound systems for understanding human experience. Both evolved from centuries of accumulated wisdom about the patterns that shape our lives and stories. While they emerged from different traditions—tarot from esoteric symbolism and the dramatic situations from literary analysis—they share a remarkable resonance in their ability to illuminate the fundamental dynamics that drive human narrative.

The integration of these systems creates a powerful tool for subconscious story development. The Tarot-36 system doesn't simply lay these approaches side by side but weaves them together into a unified framework that amplifies the strengths of each. The archetypal imagery of tarot provides intuitive access to the subconscious, while the dramatic situations offer structural clarity about core conflicts and relationships.

This integration works so effectively because both systems function as mirrors reflecting the full spectrum of human experience. By mapping the dramatic situations onto the tarot's rich symbolic landscape, we create a dimensional storytelling matrix where character, conflict, and theme emerge organically from the dance between conscious craft and subconscious creativity.

Core Principles of the Tarot-36 Integration

1. Archetypal Resonance

Each of the 78 tarot cards contains multiple potential dramatic situations within its imagery and symbolism. Conversely, each dramatic situation finds expression across various tarot cards, appearing in different aspects and variations. This natural resonance creates a rich field of associations that the subconscious mind can navigate intuitively, discovering connections that might elude conscious analysis.

2. Dimensional Story Development

While traditional approaches might assign a single meaning or function to a card, the Tarot-36 system reveals how each card operates across multiple dimensions simultaneously:

- As character archetype
- As relationship dynamic
- As situational conflict
- As thematic element
- As plot catalyst

This multidimensional quality allows stories to develop organically, with each card revealing different aspects depending on the dramatic situation it connects with.

3. Subconscious-Conscious Dialogue

The integration creates a direct channel between subconscious narrative impulses and conscious storytelling craft. The tarot's symbolic language speaks directly to the subconscious mind, while the dramatic situations provide conscious structural understanding. Together, they create a dialogue between these two aspects of creativity, with each informing and enriching the other.

4. Infinite Variation Through Combination

With 78 tarot cards and 36 dramatic situations, the possible combinations create an essentially infinite landscape of narrative possibilities. This system doesn't constrain creativity but rather provides navigation tools for exploring the vast territory of potential stories that exist within the creative subconscious.

The Tarot-36 Mapping: Major Arcana

The Major Arcana cards, with their powerful archetypal imagery, serve as particularly resonant vessels for the dramatic situations. While each card can potentially connect with many situations, certain affinities are especially strong. Here we explore these primary resonances while acknowledging the multidimensional nature of each card.

0. The Fool

Primary Dramatic Situations:

- **Daring Enterprise (#9)** - The Fool embarks on a journey without knowing the dangers ahead, representing the ultimate daring enterprise undertaken with optimism and faith.
- **Fatal Imprudence (#17)** - The Fool's step off the cliff edge embodies the potential for mistakes made through innocence, naivety, or carelessness.
- **Pursuit (#5)** - Often the Fool becomes a figure pursued by consequences, reality, or those who wish to prevent the journey.

Storytelling Integration: When The Fool appears in your tarot spread, consider how these dramatic situations might manifest in your narrative. Is your character embarking on a journey with innocent optimism? Might their naivety lead to significant error? Are they being pursued or about to be pursued by forces they've unwittingly set in motion?

The Fool invites stories about beginnings, leaps of faith, and the price of innocence. Combined with cards from the Swords suit, the Fatal Imprudence aspect may dominate. Paired with Wands, the Daring Enterprise becomes more prominent. Cup cards might emphasize the emotional journey aspects.

1. The Magician

Primary Dramatic Situations:

- **Obtaining (#12)** - The Magician uses skill and focus to obtain or manifest desires, competing with opposing forces.
- **Ambition (#30)** - The Magician represents focused will directed toward achievement and the mastery of elements to reach goals.
- **The Enigma (#11)** - The Magician possesses secret knowledge and the ability to solve problems through hidden wisdom.

Storytelling Integration: When The Magician appears, explore characters who actively manifest their desires through skill, concentration, and knowledge. Consider stories about the pursuit of mastery, the responsible use of power, or the solving of complex problems through unexpected connections.

The Magician suggests narratives where characters must integrate different elements (shown by the four suits on the Magician's table) to achieve their aims. The card invites consideration of what your character wishes to manifest and what skills or resources they must harness to do so.

2. The High Priestess

Primary Dramatic Situations:

- **The Enigma (#11)** - The High Priestess guards mysteries and represents knowledge that must be intuited rather than directly obtained.
- **Discovery of the Dishonor of a Loved One (#27)** - She often reflects

hidden knowledge about others that will eventually come to light.

- **Conflict with a God (#31)** - She mediates between worlds and represents the human relationship with divine or unconscious forces.

Storytelling Integration: The High Priestess invites stories involving secrets, intuition, and the unveiling of hidden knowledge. When she appears, consider what mysteries lie at the heart of your narrative and how characters might access truth through non-rational means.

This card suggests plots where important information remains veiled until the protagonist develops the wisdom to perceive it. It indicates narratives where what is not said may be more important than what is, and where meaning must be intuited from symbols and indirect communication.

3. The Empress

Primary Dramatic Situations:

- **Recovery of a Lost One (#35)** - The Empress represents nurturing reunion, the return to source, and the healing embrace of the maternal.
- **All Sacrificed for a Passion (#22)** - She embodies abundance, fertility, and passionate creative energy that can consume everything else.
- **Necessity of Sacrificing Loved Ones (#23)** - She may represent the painful aspects of nurturing, including letting go for growth.

Storytelling Integration: When The Empress appears, consider stories involving creation, nurturing, abundance, and the complex dynamics of maternal relationships. This card suggests narratives about reconnection with essential aspects of self or others, the power of creative passion, and the tension between holding close and releasing for growth.

The Empress indicates characters with nurturing power, creative fertility, or deep connection to natural cycles. Her presence might indicate stories about creation (of art, children, or projects), the return to wholeness after loss, or the challenging aspects of love that both embraces and must eventually release.

4. The Emperor

Primary Dramatic Situations:

- **Revolt (#8)** - The Emperor represents authority that may be either justly exercised or rebelled against.
- **Vengeance Taken for Kindred upon Kindred (#4)** - He embodies patriarchal authority and family leadership that enforces consequences.
- **Rivalry of Superior and Inferior (#24)** - He represents established power that may be challenged by emerging strength.

Storytelling Integration: The Emperor suggests stories involving authority, structure, order, and the exercise of power. When this card appears, consider narratives about the establishment or challenging of rules, the protection of what has been built, or the conflict between stability and change.

This card indicates characters who create order from chaos, establish foundations, or must decide how to use their authority. It may suggest stories exploring the legitimate use of power versus tyranny, the need for structure versus the desire for freedom, or the father-figure as both protector and potential oppressor.

5. The Hierophant

Primary Dramatic Situations:

- **Supplication (#1)** - The Hierophant represents spiritual authority that can grant or deny petitions and intercede with higher powers.
- **Crime of Love (#26)** - He often represents social or religious conventions that may forbid certain relationships.
- **Erroneous Judgment (#33)** - He can represent judgment based on doctrine or convention rather than true understanding.

Storytelling Integration: When The Hierophant appears, consider stories involving tradition, institutions, conventional wisdom, and the tension between established teaching and personal truth. This card suggests narratives exploring membership in groups, initiation into established systems, or the challenge of finding individual meaning within collective structures.

The Hierophant indicates characters who uphold tradition, seek conventional approval, or mediate between individuals and institutions. His presence might suggest stories about conformity versus individual conscience, the value and limitations of established wisdom, or the search for enlightenment through traditional pathways.

6. The Lovers

Primary Dramatic Situations:

- **Obstacles to Love (#28)** - The Lovers represents connection that must overcome various barriers to unite.
- **Crimes of Love (#26)** - This card can indicate love that society forbids or relationship choices that violate conventional boundaries.
- **Adultery (#25)** - The Lovers may represent the choice between committed partnership and new attraction.

Storytelling Integration: The Lovers suggests stories involving significant choices, value alignment, and the integration of seemingly opposite elements. When this card appears, consider narratives about choosing between competing desires, finding union after separation, or aligning external choices with internal values.

This card indicates characters facing heart-versus-head decisions, seeking their other half, or attempting to integrate different aspects of themselves. The presence of The Lovers might suggest stories about true partnership, the challenges of making authentic choices, or the healing power of love to unite what has been divided.

7. The Chariot

Primary Dramatic Situations:

- **Pursuit (#5)** - The Chariot represents active chase, whether pursuing goals or fleeing consequences.
- **Daring Enterprise (#9)** - This card embodies the disciplined courage needed to undertake challenging quests or missions.
- **Ambition (#30)** - The Chariot shows ambition channeled through disciplined will and the mastery of opposing forces.

Storytelling Integration: When The Chariot appears, consider stories involving determined movement, the control of opposing forces, and victories achieved through focus and will. This card suggests narratives about quests, competitions, campaigns, or journeys that require both discipline and momentum.

The Chariot indicates characters who harness contrary impulses to move forward, maintain control under pressure, or pursue goals with single-minded determination. Its presence might suggest stories about competitive endeavors, military campaigns, difficult journeys, or the triumph of will over instinct.

8. Strength

Primary Dramatic Situations:

- **Self-Sacrifice for an Ideal (#20)** - Strength represents the courage to endure hardship for higher principles.
- **Rivalry of Superior and Inferior (#24)** - This card shows the gentle overcoming the fierce, inner strength defeating brute force.
- **Conflict with a God (#31)** - Strength can represent the human spirit's courage in facing overwhelming forces.

Storytelling Integration: Strength suggests stories involving courage, gentle power, the taming of primal forces, and endurance through difficulty. When this card appears, consider narratives about inner strength prevailing over external force, compassion transforming aggression, or sustained courage rather than momentary bravery.

This card indicates characters who master their own impulses, transform potentially destructive energy into creative power, or demonstrate resilience in the face of overwhelming challenges. Its presence might suggest stories about the patient taming of wild forces (within or without), the power of compassion over coercion, or triumph through endurance rather than force.

9. The Hermit

Primary Dramatic Situations:

- **Enigma (#11)** - The Hermit holds wisdom that must be sought and represents the journey toward understanding.
- **Recovery of a Lost One (#35)** - Though seemingly about isolation, The Hermit often represents finding what was lost within oneself.
- **Obtaining (#12)** - The Hermit seeks to obtain wisdom and self-knowledge through withdrawal and reflection.

Storytelling Integration: When The Hermit appears, consider stories involving inner searching, voluntary withdrawal, guidance through darkness, or the seeking of wisdom in solitude. This card suggests narratives about journeys of self-discovery, the finding of inner light during dark times, or the guidance that comes through isolation.

The Hermit indicates characters who step back from conventional life to find deeper truth, serve as guides for others' journeys, or carry light through dark places. His presence might suggest stories about retreat as a path to wisdom, the mentor figure who appears when needed, or the courage to walk alone when necessary.

10. Wheel of Fortune

Primary Dramatic Situations:

- **Disaster (#6)** - The Wheel represents the impersonal forces that can suddenly change fortune for better or worse.
- **Ambition (#30)** - This card shows the cyclical nature of success and

failure in the pursuit of goals.

- **Erroneous Judgment (#33)** - The Wheel reminds us how misperception of our position in the cycle leads to error.

Storytelling Integration: The Wheel of Fortune suggests stories involving fate, cycles, sudden changes in fortune, and the impersonal forces that shape human destiny. When this card appears, consider narratives about unexpected reversals, the cyclical nature of success and failure, or the challenge of maintaining equilibrium amid life's ups and downs.

This card indicates characters experiencing dramatic shifts in circumstances, learning to adapt to changing fortunes, or coming to terms with forces beyond their control. Its presence might suggest stories about the irony of success leading to failure (or vice versa), the wisdom of accepting life's cycles, or the role of chance and synchronicity in human affairs.

11. Justice

Primary Dramatic Situations:

- **Crime Pursued by Vengeance (#3)** - Justice represents the consequences that follow actions and the balancing of scales.
- **Adultery (#25)** - This card can represent the judgments and consequences that follow betrayal of trust.
- **Erroneous Judgment (#33)** - Justice reminds us of the challenge of judging fairly and seeing clearly.

Storytelling Integration: When Justice appears, consider stories involving cause and effect, the consequences of past actions, ethical decisions, or the search for truth and fairness. This card suggests narratives about moral choices, legal proceedings, the restoration of balance, or the challenge of reconciling mercy with judgment.

Justice indicates characters facing the consequences of earlier choices, seeking to establish fairness in unfair situations, or struggling to discern truth amid deception. Its presence might suggest stories about characters receiving their due (good or bad), the complexity of determining what is truly fair, or the tension between letter and spirit of law.

12. The Hanged Man

Primary Dramatic Situations:

- **Self-Sacrifice for an Ideal (#20)** - The Hanged Man represents willing sacrifice for higher understanding or principle.
- **Remorse (#34)** - This card can indicate the suspended state that follows recognition of error, leading to new perspective.
- **The Enigma (#11)** - The Hanged Man embodies the paradoxical nature of certain wisdom that can only be gained through surrender.

Storytelling Integration: The Hanged Man suggests stories involving voluntary sacrifice, suspended action, surrender, or gaining wisdom through reversed perspective. When this card appears, consider narratives about letting go of control to gain insight, the productive pause between phases, or finding strength through surrender.

This card indicates characters who must surrender to win, gain by losing, or find new perspectives by inverting their viewpoint. Its presence might suggest stories about willing sacrifice for spiritual growth, the liminal space between life phases, or the wisdom gained by stepping outside conventional perspectives.

13. Death

Primary Dramatic Situations:

- **Loss of Loved Ones (#36)** - Death represents the universal experience of losing what we cherish.
- **Falling Prey to Cruelty or Misfortune (#7)** - This card can represent the impersonal but profound suffering that transformation often requires.
- **Recovery of a Lost One (#35)** - Paradoxically, Death often leads to

rebirth and the recovery of essential aspects of self.

Storytelling Integration: When Death appears, consider stories involving necessary endings, profound transformation, release of the outdated, or the painful transitions that lead to renewal. This card suggests narratives about letting go of identities that no longer serve, experiences that permanently alter perception, or the fertile void that precedes new growth.

Death indicates characters experiencing inevitable transitions, releasing what must be released, or undergoing identity death and rebirth. Its presence might suggest stories about characters forced to let go of who they thought they were, the end of one life chapter that enables the beginning of another, or the transformation of form while essence remains.

14. Temperance

Primary Dramatic Situations:

- **Remorse (#34)** - Temperance represents the healing integration that follows recognition of past imbalance.
- **Conflict with a God (#31)** - This card shows the harmonious flow between human and divine, material and spiritual.
- **Rivalry of Superior and Inferior (#24)** - Temperance blends seemingly opposed elements, finding complementarity rather than conflict.

Storytelling Integration: Temperance suggests stories involving integration of opposites, balanced exchange, moderation, or healing through proper combination. When this card appears, consider narratives about finding the middle path, harmonizing conflicting elements, or creating something new through the balanced blending of diverse ingredients.

This card indicates characters who mediate between opposing forces, heal through balanced exchange, or find the perfect measure in all things. Its presence might suggest stories about alchemical transformation, the healing of divisions within self or community, or the creation of harmony from apparent discord.

15. The Devil

Primary Dramatic Situations:

- **All Sacrificed for a Passion (#22)** - The Devil represents obsession and the sacrifice of freedom for desire.
- **Adultery (#25)** - This card often represents illicit attraction and the bondage created by betrayal.
- **Falling Prey to Cruelty or Misfortune (#7)** - The Devil shows entrapment, whether by external forces or internal compulsion.

Storytelling Integration: When The Devil appears, consider stories involving bondage (literal or figurative), unhealthy attachments, the shadow self, or the illumination that can come through confronting our darkest aspects. This card suggests narratives about breaking free from self-imposed limitations, confronting repressed desires, or recognizing how we participate in our own entrapment.

The Devil indicates characters bound by their own desires, confronting their shadow aspects, or discovering unexpected freedom through facing what they fear or deny. Its presence might suggest stories about addiction and recovery, the projection of inner demons onto others, or the transformative potential of accepting our complete nature, including parts we deem unacceptable.

16. The Tower

Primary Dramatic Situations:

- **Disaster (#6)** - The Tower represents sudden catastrophe that destroys existing structures.
- **Revolt (#8)** - This card shows the violent overthrow of established order, whether external or internal.
- **Discovery of the Dishonor of a Loved One (#27)** - The Tower often reveals what has been hidden, bringing painful truths to light.

Storytelling Integration: The Tower suggests stories involving sudden revelation, the necessary destruction of false structures, divine intervention, or moments when reality breaks through illusion. When this card appears, consider narratives about catastrophic events that ultimately lead to liberation, shocking truths that shatter worldviews, or the collapse that must precede authentic rebuilding.

This card indicates characters experiencing profound disillusionment, unexpected liberation through loss, or the shock of seeing reality clearly for the first time. Its presence might suggest stories about characters whose comfortable illusions are shattered, crises that reveal what truly matters, or the painful but necessary destruction of what is built on false premises.

17. The Star

Primary Dramatic Situations:

- **Recovery of a Lost One (#35)** - The Star represents finding hope and healing after loss.
- **Supplication (#1)** - This card shows the vulnerable asking for and receiving divine assistance.
- **Daring Enterprise (#9)** - The Star embodies the hope and guidance needed for ambitious undertakings.

Storytelling Integration: When The Star appears, consider stories involving healing after trauma, naked vulnerability that becomes strength, or the guiding vision that provides direction through darkness. This card suggests narratives about renewal after devastation, the restoration of faith, or the quiet hope that persists even in difficult circumstances.

The Star indicates characters finding hope when all seemed lost, receiving guidance through difficult passages, or discovering authentic expression after removing false coverings. Its presence might suggest stories about healing after The Tower's destruction, the replenishment of depleted emotional wells, or the quiet certainty that guides meaningful action.

18. The Moon

Primary Dramatic Situations:

- **The Enigma (#11)** - The Moon represents mysteries that must be navigated through intuition rather than logic.
- **Madness (#16)** - This card shows the thin line between intuition and delusion, vision and hallucination.
- **Erroneous Judgment (#33)** - The Moon reminds us how easily we misperceive reality when moving through unfamiliar territory.

Storytelling Integration: The Moon suggests stories involving uncertainty, intuitive navigation through confusion, confrontation with fears, or the thin boundary between reality and illusion. When this card appears, consider narratives about journeys through psychological darkness, the confrontation with what lurks below conscious awareness, or the challenges of finding path when landmarks are unclear.

This card indicates characters moving through unfamiliar psychological territory, confronting primal fears, or developing intuition to navigate where logic fails. Its presence might suggest stories about dreams and their messages, the confrontation with repressed material, or the disorientation that precedes psychological integration.

19. The Sun

Primary Dramatic Situations:

- **Recovery of a Lost One (#35)** - The Sun represents the joyful reunion with essential aspects of self or others.
- **Discovery of the Dishonor of a Loved One (#27)** - Paradoxically, The Sun's clarity can reveal what has been hidden, though with healing light rather than harsh exposure.
- **Deliverance (#2)** - This card shows liberation from darkness, limitation, or confusion.

Storytelling Integration: When The Sun appears, consider stories involving illumination, joyful success, innocent wisdom, or the vitality that comes with authentic self-expression. This card suggests narratives about emerging from darkness into light, achieving clarity after confusion, or experiencing the pure joy of being fully alive.

The Sun indicates characters discovering or rediscovering their essential nature, experiencing the clarity that comes with complete honesty, or finding joy beyond happiness. Its presence might suggest stories about the triumph of truth over deception, the integration of masculine and feminine principles (sun and child), or the achievement of success that brings benefit to all.

20. Judgment

Primary Dramatic Situations:

- **Slaying of a Kinsman Unrecognized (#19)** - Judgment represents the moment of recognition that transforms understanding of past actions.
- **Remorse (#34)** - This card shows the awakening that follows acknowledgment of past error.
- **Necessity of Sacrificing Loved Ones (#23)** - Judgment can represent the difficult choices required by higher calling.

Storytelling Integration: Judgment suggests stories involving awakening to calling, rebirth after symbolic death, reconciliation with the past, or moments of profound realization that change everything. When this card appears, consider narratives about characters hearing and responding to their true calling, reconciling with past actions through forgiveness, or experiencing spiritual awakening that transforms their identity.

This card indicates characters experiencing resurrection after metaphorical death, hearing the call that gives life meaning, or reconciling divided aspects of self or community. Its presence might suggest stories about answering the call to authentic purpose, the moment when past actions are seen in new light, or the integration of past experience into renewed identity.

21. The World

Primary Dramatic Situations:

- **Recovery of a Lost One (#35)** - The World represents the ultimate recovery—finding wholeness and integration after the journey.
- **Self-Sacrifice for an Ideal (#20)** - This card shows the completion that follows dedication to the full journey of development.
- **Obtaining (#12)** - The World represents the attainment of wholeness, the successful culmination of the quest.

Storytelling Integration: When The World appears, consider stories involving completion of cycles, integration of all elements, achievement of wholeness, or successful culmination of lengthy endeavors. This card suggests narratives about bringing disparate elements into harmony, achieving mastery through full development, or experiencing the joy of completion while preparing for new beginnings.

The World indicates characters achieving integration of all aspects of self, completing significant life cycles, or experiencing the dance of life in its fullness. Its presence might suggest stories about characters who have completed their hero's journey and integrated its lessons, the harmony that comes when nothing essential is excluded, or the mastery that allows simultaneous engagement with all dimensions of existence.

The Tarot-36 Mapping: Minor Arcana - Wands (Fire)

The Minor Arcana suits each connect to dramatic situations through their elemental associations. The Wands, associated with fire, naturally resonate with situations involving action, passion, creativity, ambition, and conflict.

Ace of Wands

Primary Dramatic Situations:

- **Daring Enterprise (#9)** - The Ace of Wands represents the initial spark of inspiration that ignites ambitious projects.
- **Ambition (#30)** - This card shows the seed of creative ambition and passionate purpose.
- **All Sacrificed for a Passion (#22)** - The Ace of Wands can represent the beginning of overwhelming passion.

Storytelling Integration: Consider how this card might indicate a character receiving divine inspiration, discovering their creative purpose, or feeling the first spark of passion that will drive their journey. The Ace of Wands suggests stories that begin with a flash of insight, a creative awakening, or the first kindling of a fire that will eventually transform a situation or relationship.

Two of Wands

Primary Dramatic Situations:

- **Obtaining (#12)** - The Two of Wands represents the planning stage of acquiring what one desires.
- **Ambition (#30)** - This card shows contemplation of expanded horizons and future conquests.
- **Daring Enterprise (#9)** - The Two of Wands involves planning bold ventures while standing at the threshold.

Storytelling Integration: This card suggests a character at the planning stage of an enterprise, contemplating expansion, or considering their next move from a position of initial accomplishment. Consider stories about characters making decisions that will shape their future direction, planning ambitious ventures, or standing at the threshold between familiar territory and new horizons.

Three of Wands

Primary Dramatic Situations:

- **Daring Enterprise (#9)** - The Three of Wands represents the launch of ventures and awaiting their results.
- **Ambition (#30)** - This card shows leadership and the expansion of vision into new territories.
- **Pursuit (#5)** - The Three of Wands can represent pursuing opportunities beyond current horizons.

Storytelling Integration: Consider characters who have launched their ships and now watch for results, leaders overseeing expanding enterprises, or visionaries whose perspective encompasses distant possibilities. The Three of Wands suggests stories about the early stages of expansion, leadership that looks toward broader horizons, or the forward-thinking vision required for business or creative ventures.

Four of Wands

Primary Dramatic Situations:

- **Recovery of a Lost One (#35)** - The Four of Wands represents homecoming, reunion, and celebration of connection.
- **Obstacles to Love (#28)** - This card shows the successful overcoming of barriers to harmonious relationship.
- **Revolt (#8)** - The Four of Wands can represent the celebration that follows successful revolution.

Storytelling Integration: This card suggests characters celebrating milestones, creating community, or establishing foundations for future growth. Consider stories about homecomings, community celebrations, successful completion of preliminary phases, or the creation of secure foundations that support further development.

Five of Wands

Primary Dramatic Situations:

- **Rivalry of Superior and Inferior (#24)** - The Five of Wands represents competition between various rivals of different abilities.
- **Revolt (#8)** - This card shows conflict against established structure, often in chaotic form.
- **Enmity of Kinsmen (#13)** - The Five of Wands can represent conflict within groups that should be cooperative.

Storytelling Integration: Consider characters engaged in competition, struggling amid chaos, or participating in conflict that tests their abilities. The Five of Wands suggests stories about competitive environments, the proving ground of ability, or conflicts that ultimately develop skills rather than causing serious harm.

Six of Wands

Primary Dramatic Situations:

- **Obtaining (#12)** - The Six of Wands represents successful achievement of recognition or victory.
- **Ambition (#30)** - This card shows ambition realized and publicly acknowledged.
- **Rivalry of Superior and Inferior (#24)** - The Six of Wands represents victory in competition.

Storytelling Integration: This card suggests characters experiencing public recognition, achieving victory after struggle, or receiving acknowledgment for their accomplishments. Consider stories about triumphant returns, public acclaim after achievement, or the social validation that comes with successful ventures.

Seven of Wands

Primary Dramatic Situations:

- **Pursuit (#5)** - The Seven of Wands represents standing one's ground against pursuers or challengers.
- **Revolt (#8)** - This card shows defense against overwhelming opposition or system.
- **Rivalry of Superior and Inferior (#24)** - The Seven of Wands represents the underdog defending their position.

Storytelling Integration: Consider characters defending their position, standing firm despite opposition, or maintaining their ground when challenged. The Seven of Wands suggests stories about holding boundaries against opposition, defending hard-won territory, or the courage to stand alone against multiple challengers.

Eight of Wands

Primary Dramatic Situations:

- **Pursuit (#5)** - The Eight of Wands represents swift movement toward a target.
- **Daring Enterprise (#9)** - This card shows rapid action to accomplish goals.
- **Abduction (#10)** - The Eight of Wands can represent swift action to capture or retrieve.

Storytelling Integration: This card suggests characters experiencing rapid developments, taking swift action, or receiving important communications that accelerate events. Consider stories about sudden momentum after delay, the swift convergence of events, or communication that bridges distances and creates immediate connection.

Nine of Wands

Primary Dramatic Situations:

- **Pursuit (#5)** - The Nine of Wands represents the final stand against pursuers.

- **Falling Prey to Cruelty or Misfortune (#7)** - This card shows endurance despite wounds and hardship.
- **Self-Sacrifice for an Ideal (#20)** - The Nine of Wands represents persistence for a cause despite personal cost.

Storytelling Integration: Consider characters at their last line of defense, persisting despite exhaustion, or maintaining vigilance after being wounded. The Nine of Wands suggests stories about resilience in the face of repeated challenges, the determined stand that comes from experience, or the wary vigilance of those who have been hurt but remain standing.

Ten of Wands

Primary Dramatic Situations:

- **Necessity of Sacrificing Loved Ones (#23)** - The Ten of Wands represents burden that requires sacrifice of other aspects of life.
- **All Sacrificed for a Passion (#22)** - This card shows overwhelming commitment that burdens the bearer.
- **Ambition (#30)** - The Ten of Wands represents the heavy price of ambitious endeavor.

Storytelling Integration: This card suggests characters bearing heavy burdens, suffering from overcommitment, or nearing completion of difficult tasks. Consider stories about the final stretch of demanding projects, the burden of responsibility, or the exhaustion that comes from carrying too much for too long.

Page of Wands

Primary Dramatic Situations:

- **Daring Enterprise (#9)** - The Page of Wands represents the enthusiastic messenger or initiator of ventures.
- **The Enigma (#11)** - This card shows the bearer of creative puzzles or

inspirational questions.

- **Pursuit (#5)** - The Page of Wands can represent the explorer pursuing new discoveries.

Storytelling Integration: Consider characters discovering new passions, delivering exciting news, or exploring creative possibilities with youthful enthusiasm. The Page of Wands suggests stories about the first awakening of creative talent, the excitement of new discoveries, or the messages that ignite passion and inspiration.

Knight of Wands

Primary Dramatic Situations:

- **Pursuit (#5)** - The Knight of Wands represents the active chase of desires or goals.
- **Daring Enterprise (#9)** - This card shows the enthusiastic pursuit of adventure and challenge.
- **All Sacrificed for a Passion (#22)** - The Knight of Wands represents impulsive pursuit of passion.

Storytelling Integration: This card suggests characters acting on impulse, pursuing passions with enthusiasm, or bringing energy and excitement to situations. Consider stories about adventurous quests, passionate pursuits, or the dynamic but sometimes unstable energy that catalyzes transformation.

Queen of Wands

Primary Dramatic Situations:

- **Daring Enterprise (#9)** - The Queen of Wands represents confident leadership of creative ventures.
- **Rivalry of Superior and Inferior (#24)** - This card shows natural authority and charismatic power.
- **Obtaining (#12)** - The Queen of Wands represents successful

manifestation through confident action.

Storytelling Integration: Consider characters who lead with natural authority, inspire others through their confident presence, or create welcoming environments where creativity flourishes. The Queen of Wands suggests stories about charismatic leadership, the power of confident self-expression, or the ability to manifest desires through clear intention and social intelligence.

King of Wands

Primary Dramatic Situations:

- **Ambition (#30)** - The King of Wands represents mastered ambition and visionary leadership.
- **Revolt (#8)** - This card shows the charismatic leader who can inspire revolution or transformation.
- **Conflict with a God (#31)** - The King of Wands represents the human who harnesses divine creative fire.

Storytelling Integration: This card suggests characters with mature mastery of creative power, visionary leadership, or the ability to inspire others toward transformation. Consider stories about charismatic leaders, creative visionaries whose passion has matured into wisdom, or those who channel creative fire in service of larger vision rather than personal glory.

The Tarot-36 Mapping: Minor Arcana - Cups (Water)

The Cups suit, associated with water, naturally resonates with dramatic situations involving emotions, relationships, love, intuition, and psychological transformation.

Ace of Cups

Primary Dramatic Situations:

- **Crime of Love (#26)** - The Ace of Cups represents the beginning of emotional or spiritual connection that transcends ordinary boundaries.

- **Recovery of a Lost One (#35)** - This card shows the rebirth of emotional capacity or reconnection with heart.
- **Remorse (#34)** - The Ace of Cups can represent emotional renewal after regret.

Storytelling Integration: Consider characters experiencing emotional awakening, opening to new love, or connecting with deeper spiritual waters. The Ace of Cups suggests stories about the first stirrings of significant emotional connection, spiritual awakening that opens the heart, or the renewal of emotional capacity after a period of drought.

Two of Cups

Primary Dramatic Situations:

- **Crimes of Love (#26)** - The Two of Cups represents connection that may transcend social boundaries.
- **An Enemy Loved (#29)** - This card shows connection that might bridge opposing sides.
- **All Sacrificed for a Passion (#22)** - The Two of Cups represents the beginning of potentially all-consuming love.

Storytelling Integration: This card suggests characters forming significant emotional bonds, establishing balanced partnerships, or experiencing the mutual recognition that initiates romance. Consider stories about the formation of relationships that have transformative potential, the healing that comes through genuine connection, or the balancing of opposing energies through partnership.

Three of Cups

Primary Dramatic Situations:

- **Recovery of a Lost One (#35)** - The Three of Cups represents reunion with loved ones and celebration of connection.

- **Deliverance (#2)** - This card shows the joy of emotional rescue or release from isolation.
- **Obstacles to Love (#28)** - The Three of Cups represents the overcoming of barriers to emotional connection.

Storytelling Integration: Consider characters celebrating emotional connection, experiencing the joy of community, or finding support through friendship. The Three of Cups suggests stories about the healing power of friendship, the celebration that follows emotional reunion, or the abundance that comes through shared feeling.

Four of Cups

Primary Dramatic Situations:

- **Erroneous Judgment (#33)** - The Four of Cups represents misjudgment of what is offered due to emotional stagnation.
- **Remorse (#34)** - This card shows contemplation of emotional dissatisfaction that may lead to regret.
- **Enigma (#11)** - The Four of Cups represents the puzzle of why abundance fails to satisfy.

Storytelling Integration: This card suggests characters experiencing emotional disconnection, failing to recognize opportunities due to apathy, or contemplating the cause of inner dissatisfaction. Consider stories about characters who have everything yet feel nothing, the opportunity that arrives when least expected (or wanted), or the dissatisfaction that precedes meaningful change.

Five of Cups

Primary Dramatic Situations:

- **Loss of Loved Ones (#36)** - The Five of Cups represents grief, mourning, and the processing of emotional loss.
- **Falling Prey to Cruelty or Misfortune (#7)** - This card shows emotional

suffering and the focus on what has been lost.

- **Remorse (#34)** - The Five of Cups represents regret over spilled cups and the challenge of seeing what remains.

Storytelling Integration: Consider characters processing grief, focusing on loss while missing what remains, or beginning the journey from despair toward acceptance. The Five of Cups suggests stories about the aftermath of emotional disappointment, the challenge of acknowledging loss without being defined by it, or the subtle presence of hope (the remaining cups) amid overwhelming grief.

Six of Cups

Primary Dramatic Situations:

- **Recovery of a Lost One (#35)** - The Six of Cups represents reconnection with childhood innocence or past relationships.
- **Involuntary Crimes of Love (#18)** - This card shows connections from the past that may have unrecognized complications.
- **Remorse (#34)** - The Six of Cups can represent nostalgic regret for simpler, more innocent times.

Storytelling Integration: This card suggests characters experiencing nostalgia, revisiting childhood memories, or receiving emotional gifts that connect past and present. Consider stories about returning to childhood places or relationships, the healing that comes through remembering innocence, or the bittersweet quality of memories that cannot be recaptured but continue to nourish.

Seven of Cups

Primary Dramatic Situations:

- **Fatal Imprudence (#17)** - The Seven of Cups represents the danger of choosing illusions or being lost in fantasy.
- **Madness (#16)** - This card shows the thin line between imagination and delusion.

- **The Enigma (#11)** - The Seven of Cups represents the puzzle of discerning authentic desires amid illusions.

Storytelling Integration: Consider characters faced with too many choices, lost in fantasy or illusion, or struggling to discern what they truly desire amid confusing options. The Seven of Cups suggests stories about the paralysis that comes with too many possibilities, the challenge of distinguishing genuine desires from escapist fantasies, or the seductive power of illusion.

Eight of Cups

Primary Dramatic Situations:

- **Daring Enterprise (#9)** - The Eight of Cups represents the courage to leave comfort in search of deeper meaning.
- **The Enigma (#11)** - This card shows the quest to resolve the mystery of emotional dissatisfaction.
- **All Sacrificed for a Passion (#22)** - The Eight of Cups represents abandoning established emotional security for deeper calling.

Storytelling Integration: This card suggests characters walking away from emotional investments that no longer serve, seeking deeper fulfillment beyond material or emotional comfort, or following intuitive calling despite the cost. Consider stories about spiritual pilgrimage, the courage to acknowledge when enough is not enough, or the sometimes solitary journey toward authentic emotional fulfillment.

Nine of Cups

Primary Dramatic Situations:

- **Obtaining (#12)** - The Nine of Cups represents successful attainment of emotional desires.
- **Recovery of a Lost One (#35)** - This card shows the return of emotional wholeness and satisfaction.

- **Ambition (#30)** - The Nine of Cups represents the achievement of emotional and material well-being.

Storytelling Integration: Consider characters experiencing wish fulfillment, emotional contentment, or the satisfaction of desires. The Nine of Cups suggests stories about the achievement of emotional abundance, the fulfillment that comes when desires are realized, or the pleasure of having enough to share with others.

Ten of Cups

Primary Dramatic Situations:

- **Recovery of a Lost One (#35)** - The Ten of Cups represents the ultimate emotional homecoming and fulfillment.
- **Deliverance (#2)** - This card shows emotional rescue and the happiness of complete belonging.
- **Obstacles to Love (#28)** - The Ten of Cups represents the transcendence of all barriers to emotional harmony.

Storytelling Integration: This card suggests characters experiencing perfect emotional harmony, creating or finding their ideal community, or achieving the rainbow after the storm. Consider stories about emotional completion, the creation of family or community that represents emotional home, or the harmony that comes when all aspects of emotional life are integrated.

Page of Cups

Primary Dramatic Situations:

- **The Enigma (#11)** - The Page of Cups represents the messenger of intuitive insights and emotional discoveries.
- **Recovery of a Lost One (#35)** - This card shows the reconnection with emotional innocence and openness.
- **Madness (#16)** - The Page of Cups can represent the thin line between intuitive wisdom and illogical fancy.

Storytelling Integration: Consider characters discovering their emotional or intuitive gifts, receiving surprising emotional messages, or approaching life with open-hearted innocence. The Page of Cups suggests stories about emotional awakening, the surprising wisdom that comes through intuitive channels, or the courage to remain emotionally authentic in a cynical world.

Knight of Cups

Primary Dramatic Situations:

- **Crimes of Love (#26)** - The Knight of Cups represents romantic pursuit that may transcend conventional boundaries.
- **All Sacrificed for a Passion (#22)** - This card shows the pursuit of love or beauty at the expense of practicality.
- **Daring Enterprise (#9)** - The Knight of Cups represents the quest for emotional or artistic fulfillment.

Storytelling Integration: This card suggests characters on romantic quests, following creative inspiration, or bringing beauty and emotion into practical situations. Consider stories about romantic pursuit, artistic journeys, or the introduction of emotional values into environments governed by more pragmatic concerns.

Queen of Cups

Primary Dramatic Situations:

- **The Enigma (#11)** - The Queen of Cups represents intuitive wisdom that solves emotional puzzles.
- **Supplication (#1)** - This card shows compassionate response to emotional needs and requests.
- **Recovery of a Lost One (#35)** - The Queen of Cups represents emotional healing and the restoration of heart connection.

Storytelling Integration: Consider characters with deep emotional wisdom, intuitive gifts, or the ability to create emotionally nurturing environments. The Queen of Cups suggests stories about intuitive healing, compassionate support that transforms suffering, or the wisdom that comes through deep emotional sensitivity.

King of Cups

Primary Dramatic Situations:

- **Self-Sacrifice for an Ideal (#20)** - The King of Cups represents emotional wisdom that serves higher principles.
- **Conflict with a God (#31)** - This card shows mastery of emotional depths that connects human and divine realms.
- **Madness (#16)** - The King of Cups represents the balance between emotional depth and rational control that prevents being overwhelmed.

Storytelling Integration: This card suggests characters with emotional mastery, the ability to remain calm in emotional storms, or the wisdom to balance heart and head. Consider stories about emotional leadership during crisis, the mature integration of feeling and thought, or the diplomatic skill that comes from genuine emotional understanding combined with clear boundaries.

The Tarot-36 Mapping: Minor Arcana - Swords (Air)

The Swords suit, associated with air, naturally resonates with dramatic situations involving conflict, intellect, communication, truth, and mental challenges.

Ace of Swords

Primary Dramatic Situations:

- **Crime Pursued by Vengeance (#3)** - The Ace of Swords represents the sharp truth that cuts through deception and demands justice.
- **Enigma (#11)** - This card shows the clarity that solves intellectual puzzles and reveals truth.

- **Revolt (#8)** - The Ace of Swords represents the clarity that cuts through oppressive confusion.

Storytelling Integration: Consider characters experiencing breakthrough clarity, discovering essential truth, or wielding intellectual power that cuts through confusion. The Ace of Swords suggests stories about moments of revelation, the double-edged nature of truth, or the mental clarity that both liberates and challenges.

Two of Swords

Primary Dramatic Situations:

- **Erroneous Judgment (#33)** - The Two of Swords represents the precarious balance of decision making without sufficient information.
- **An Enemy Loved (#29)** - This card shows the tension of conflicting loyalties and difficult choices.
- **Mistaken Jealousy (#32)** - The Two of Swords represents emotional blindness that prevents clear perception.

Storytelling Integration: This card suggests characters at decision points, maintaining difficult emotional or mental balance, or temporarily blocking information to maintain peace. Consider stories about the tension of unresolved choice, the temporary peace that comes through refusing to see, or the difficult balance required when faced with equally challenging options.

Three of Swords

Primary Dramatic Situations:

- **Loss of Loved Ones (#36)** - The Three of Swords represents heartbreak, grief, and emotional wounding.
- **Discovery of the Dishonor of a Loved One (#27)** - This card shows the pain of discovering betrayal or deception.
- **Adultery (#25)** - The Three of Swords represents the painful triangle of

infidelity.

Storytelling Integration: Consider characters experiencing heartbreak, processing painful truth, or suffering the necessary pain of growth. The Three of Swords suggests stories about emotional wounds that cannot be avoided, the clarity that comes through painful experience, or the breaking open of the heart that ultimately allows greater depth of feeling.

Four of Swords

Primary Dramatic Situations:

- **Remorse (#34)** - The Four of Swords represents the contemplative stillness that follows recognition of error.
- **Falling Prey to Cruelty or Misfortune (#7)** - This card shows recovery from wounds inflicted by others or circumstance.
- **Madness (#16)** - The Four of Swords represents the rest needed to restore mental balance and prevent breakdown.

Storytelling Integration: This card suggests characters in recovery, finding sanctuary from mental battles, or gaining perspective through strategic withdrawal. Consider stories about healing after conflict, the wisdom gained through forced rest, or the sanctuary that provides respite and restoration before returning to life's battles.

Five of Swords

Primary Dramatic Situations:

- **Crime Pursued by Vengeance (#3)** - The Five of Swords represents the hollow victory that may invite future retribution.
- **Rivalry of Superior and Inferior (#24)** - This card shows conflict where one side wins at the expense of relationship.
- **Enmity of Kinsmen (#13)** - The Five of Swords represents conflict within groups that should be united.

Storytelling Integration: Consider characters experiencing pyrrhic victory, the aftermath of conflict where winning feels like losing, or the consequences of prioritizing being right over being in relationship. The Five of Swords suggests stories about the cost of victory at all costs, the aftermath of betrayal, or the emptiness of triumph achieved through questionable means.

Six of Swords

Primary Dramatic Situations:

- **Deliverance (#2)** - The Six of Swords represents passage from troubled waters toward calmer shores.
- **Supplication (#1)** - This card shows being guided or assisted through difficult transition.
- **Pursuit (#5)** - The Six of Swords can represent moving away from threats toward safety.

Storytelling Integration: This card suggests characters in transition, moving away from difficulty toward peace, or being guided through challenging passage. Consider stories about necessary departures, the quiet passage between life phases, or the assistance that helps navigation through troubled waters toward calmer seas.

Seven of Swords

Primary Dramatic Situations:

- **Crime Pursued by Vengeance (#3)** - The Seven of Swords represents actions that may seem clever but invite future consequences.
- **Abduction (#10)** - This card shows taking what belongs to others through stealth or cunning.
- **Daring Enterprise (#9)** - The Seven of Swords represents cunning strategies and covert operations.

Storytelling Integration: Consider characters using strategy or deception, attempting to escape consequences, or using intelligence rather than force to achieve aims. The Seven of Swords suggests stories about strategic withdrawal, ethical compromises made for perceived necessity, or the complex moral territory of using deception to achieve possibly justified ends.

Eight of Swords

Primary Dramatic Situations:

- **Falling Prey to Cruelty or Misfortune (#7)** - The Eight of Swords represents the experience of restriction and helplessness.
- **Erroneous Judgment (#33)** - This card shows how misperception creates the illusion of being trapped.
- **Madness (#16)** - The Eight of Swords represents mental constructs that create psychological imprisonment.

Storytelling Integration: This card suggests characters feeling trapped by circumstances, restricted by their own thinking, or unable to see available options due to fear or limited perspective. Consider stories about self-imposed limitations, the prison created by false beliefs, or the process of recognizing that what seems like external restriction is actually internal constraint.

Nine of Swords

Primary Dramatic Situations:

- **Remorse (#34)** - The Nine of Swords represents anguish over past actions or choices.
- **Madness (#16)** - This card shows anxiety, worry, and mental torment that approach breakdown.
- **Discovery of the Dishonor of a Loved One (#27)** - The Nine of Swords can represent the midnight anguish of discovering painful truth.

Storytelling Integration: Consider characters experiencing anxiety, night terrors, or the mental anguish that comes from guilt, worry, or fear. The Nine of

Swords suggests stories about the dark night of the soul, the weight of conscience, or the psychological suffering that precedes either breakdown or breakthrough.

Ten of Swords

Primary Dramatic Situations:

- **Disaster (#6)** - The Ten of Swords represents complete defeat or collapse.
- **Loss of Loved Ones (#36)** - This card shows the experience of absolute ending and the grief that follows.
- **Necessity of Sacrificing Loved Ones (#23)** - The Ten of Swords represents painful but necessary ending.

Storytelling Integration: This card suggests characters experiencing complete ending, the darkest moment before dawn, or the release that comes only through total surrender. Consider stories about hitting rock bottom, the necessary death of old paradigms, or the painful clarity that comes when illusions are completely shattered and only truth remains.

Page of Swords

Primary Dramatic Situations:

- **Pursuit (#5)** - The Page of Swords represents vigilant observation and the gathering of information.
- **The Enigma (#11)** - This card shows intellectual curiosity and the investigation of puzzles.
- **Obtaining (#12)** - The Page of Swords represents strategic planning to acquire knowledge or advantage.

Storytelling Integration: Consider characters with keen mental acuity, intellectual curiosity, or vigilant attention to potential threats. The Page of Swords suggests stories about the first application of mental ability, the gathering of intelligence, or the watchful vigilance that prepares for potential challenge.

Knight of Swords

Primary Dramatic Situations:

- **Pursuit (#5)** - The Knight of Swords represents aggressive chase or determined pursuit.
- **Revolt (#8)** - This card shows charging against opposition or established order.
- **Crime Pursued by Vengeance (#3)** - The Knight of Swords represents forceful pursuit of what is perceived as justice.

Storytelling Integration: This card suggests characters taking direct action, charging toward goals with single-minded focus, or cutting through obstacles with mental force. Consider stories about determined pursuit of goals regardless of obstacles, the power and limitation of intellectual force, or the courage to charge directly at challenges rather than maneuvering around them.

Queen of Swords

Primary Dramatic Situations:

- **Crime Pursued by Vengeance (#3)** - The Queen of Swords represents clear perception of truth and the demand for justice.
- **Discovery of the Dishonor of a Loved One (#27)** - This card shows the clear sight that perceives deception or dishonor.
- **Erroneous Judgment (#33)** - The Queen of Swords represents the challenge of balancing perceptiveness with compassion in judgment.

Storytelling Integration: Consider characters with penetrating perception, the ability to see truth without emotional distortion, or wisdom gained through difficult experience. The Queen of Swords suggests stories about clarity born from suffering, the strength that comes through independence, or the compassion that can exist alongside unflinching honesty.

King of Swords

Primary Dramatic Situations:

- **Erroneous Judgment (#33)** - The King of Swords represents the power and responsibility of intellectual authority and judgment.
- **Rivalry of Superior and Inferior (#24)** - This card shows intellectual authority that may be challenged by emerging thought.
- **Conflict with a God (#31)** - The King of Swords represents human intellect attempting to comprehend divine or universal law.

Storytelling Integration: This card suggests characters with intellectual authority, the power to render judgment, or the ability to create order through clear thinking. Consider stories about ethical leadership, the use of intellectual power to create justice, or the challenge of balancing truth with compassion when in position of authority.

The Tarot-36 Mapping: Minor Arcana - Pentacles (Earth)

The Pentacles suit, associated with earth, naturally resonates with dramatic situations involving material concerns, resources, physical well-being, security, and practical matters.

Ace of Pentacles

Primary Dramatic Situations:

- **Obtaining (#12)** - The Ace of Pentacles represents the seed of material prosperity and opportunity.
- **Daring Enterprise (#9)** - This card shows the beginning of practical ventures with tangible rewards.
- **Recovery of a Lost One (#35)** - The Ace of Pentacles can represent reconnection with physical well-being or material security.

Storytelling Integration: Consider characters receiving material opportunity, planting the seeds of future prosperity, or connecting with the physical world in new ways. The Ace of Pentacles suggests stories about new financial beginnings, gifts that have practical value, or the first step on a path toward material security and abundance.

Two of Pentacles

Primary Dramatic Situations:

- **Pursuit (#5)** - The Two of Pentacles represents maintaining balance while in motion or under pressure.
- **Falling Prey to Cruelty or Misfortune (#7)** - This card shows the adaptive response to fluctuating circumstances.
- **Enigma (#11)** - The Two of Pentacles represents the puzzle of maintaining equilibrium amid change.

Storytelling Integration: This card suggests characters balancing multiple responsibilities, adapting to changing circumstances, or finding harmony amid flux. Consider stories about maintaining grace under pressure, the dance of multiple priorities, or finding balance when nothing stays still.

Three of Pentacles

Primary Dramatic Situations:

- **Daring Enterprise (#9)** - The Three of Pentacles represents collaborative effort toward ambitious physical creation.
- **Obtaining (#12)** - This card shows the focused work required to manifest material goals.
- **Revolt (#8)** - The Three of Pentacles can represent the building of new structures to replace outdated ones.

Storytelling Integration: Consider characters collaborating on meaningful work, receiving recognition for skill, or laying foundations for significant projects. The Three of Pentacles suggests stories about the satisfaction of craftsmanship, the power of collaboration between different skills, or the process of building something that will endure.

Four of Pentacles

Primary Dramatic Situations:

- **Obtaining (#12)** - The Four of Pentacles represents holding onto resources and establishing security.
- **Disaster (#6)** - This card shows the attempt to prevent loss or protect against catastrophe.
- **Ambition (#30)** - The Four of Pentacles represents the challenge of security becoming limitation to growth.

Storytelling Integration: This card suggests characters establishing material security, holding tightly to resources, or becoming defined by what they possess. Consider stories about the tension between security and growth, the prison created by excessive attachment, or the challenge of determining when enough is enough.

Five of Pentacles

Primary Dramatic Situations:

- **Falling Prey to Cruelty or Misfortune (#7)** - The Five of Pentacles represents material hardship, exclusion, and physical suffering.
- **Supplication (#1)** - This card shows the need for assistance during times of material difficulty.
- **Obtaining (#12)** - The Five of Pentacles represents the struggle to obtain basic resources for survival.

Storytelling Integration: Consider characters experiencing material hardship, feeling excluded from prosperity, or struggling with health challenges. The Five of Pentacles suggests stories about economic struggle, the experience of being outsiders looking in, or the challenge of maintaining faith when physical circumstances are dire.

Six of Pentacles

Primary Dramatic Situations:

- **Supplication (#1)** - The Six of Pentacles represents the dynamic between those who give and those who receive assistance.
- **Obtaining (#12)** - This card shows the distribution of resources and the power dynamics involved.
- **Rivalry of Superior and Inferior (#24)** - The Six of Pentacles represents the complex relationship between those who have and those who need.

Storytelling Integration: This card suggests characters in position to give or receive, the circulation of resources within community, or the power dynamics inherent in generosity. Consider stories about the complexity of charity, the balance of giving and receiving, or the challenge of maintaining dignity when in need or respect when in abundance.

Seven of Pentacles

Primary Dramatic Situations:

- **Daring Enterprise (#9)** - The Seven of Pentacles represents the patience required for long-term ventures.
- **Ambition (#30)** - This card shows the assessment of progress toward material goals.
- **Enigma (#11)** - The Seven of Pentacles represents the puzzle of when to harvest and when to continue investing.

Storytelling Integration: Consider characters evaluating the results of their efforts, exercising patience during growth phases, or making decisions about future investment of resources. The Seven of Pentacles suggests stories about the challenging middle phase of projects, the patience required for natural growth, or the assessment that precedes decisions about future direction.

Eight of Pentacles

Primary Dramatic Situations:

- **Ambition (#30)** - The Eight of Pentacles represents disciplined effort toward mastery and achievement.
- **Daring Enterprise (#9)** - This card shows the detailed work that supports ambitious projects.
- **Obtaining (#12)** - The Eight of Pentacles represents skill development that creates material success.

Storytelling Integration: This card suggests characters developing expertise through practice, focusing on detailed craftsmanship, or building reputation through consistent quality. Consider stories about apprenticeship, the satisfaction of work well done, or the power of focused attention to detail in creating excellence.

Nine of Pentacles

Primary Dramatic Situations:

- **Obtaining (#12)** - The Nine of Pentacles represents successful attainment of material abundance and security.
- **Ambition (#30)** - This card shows ambition realized through disciplined effort.
- **Crime of Love (#26)** - The Nine of Pentacles can represent the choice of self-sufficient independence over relationship.

Storytelling Integration: Consider characters enjoying well-earned prosperity, savoring the fruits of disciplined effort, or creating personal sanctuary. The Nine of Pentacles suggests stories about independence and self-sufficiency, the refinement that comes through material success, or the garden one creates through patient cultivation.

Ten of Pentacles

Primary Dramatic Situations:

- **Recovery of a Lost One (#35)** - The Ten of Pentacles represents connection with ancestral roots and the full circle of physical security.
- **Obtaining (#12)** - This card shows the ultimate attainment of material prosperity and security.
- **Ambition (#30)** - The Ten of Pentacles represents ambition fulfilled not just for self but for generations.

Storytelling Integration: This card suggests characters establishing lasting legacy, creating security that extends beyond individual life, or connecting with ancestral tradition. Consider stories about family wealth and its complexities, the establishment of institutions that will outlast their founders, or the deep security that comes when material and spiritual abundance align.

Page of Pentacles

Primary Dramatic Situations:

- **Obtaining (#12)** - The Page of Pentacles represents the first steps toward material or educational goals.
- **Daring Enterprise (#9)** - This card shows the initial phase of practical ventures or learning.
- **The Enigma (#11)** - The Page of Pentacles represents the study required to solve material puzzles.

Storytelling Integration: Consider characters beginning practical studies, receiving news about material matters, or approaching physical reality with fresh perspective. The Page of Pentacles suggests stories about scholarship, apprenticeship, or the fresh eyes that see value where others might miss it.

Knight of Pentacles

Primary Dramatic Situations:

- **Obtaining (#12)** - The Knight of Pentacles represents methodical pursuit of material goals.
- **Daring Enterprise (#9)** - This card shows the reliable execution that supports ambitious ventures.
- **Pursuit (#5)** - The Knight of Pentacles represents steady pursuit that eventually reaches its target.

Storytelling Integration: This card suggests characters with methodical persistence, reliable follow-through, or the patience to build step by step. Consider stories about the power of consistency, the slow but steady approach that ultimately succeeds, or the grounding influence amid more volatile energies.

Queen of Pentacles

Primary Dramatic Situations:

- **Recovery of a Lost One (#35)** - The Queen of Pentacles represents nurturing connection with physical well-being and material needs.
- **Obtaining (#12)** - This card shows practical wisdom that creates material abundance.
- **Self-Sacrifice for Kindred (#21)** - The Queen of Pentacles represents nurturing that provides practical support for others.

Storytelling Integration: Consider characters with practical nurturing ability, the wisdom to create abundance, or the capacity to make others feel physically cared for. The Queen of Pentacles suggests stories about the creation of nurturing environments, the practical wisdom that comes from earth connection, or the warm security created by those who understand physical needs.

King of Pentacles

Primary Dramatic Situations:

- **Obtaining (#12)** - The King of Pentacles represents mastery in the material realm and the ability to generate prosperity.
- **Ambition (#30)** - This card shows materialized ambition and the authority that comes with proven success.
- **Rivalry of Superior and Inferior (#24)** - The King of Pentacles represents established material authority that may face challenge.

Storytelling Integration: This card suggests characters with material authority, proven success in business or practical matters, or the ability to create prosperity for many. Consider stories about financial leadership, the responsibilities that come with material success, or the challenge of maintaining connection with earth values amid position and power.

Practical Applications of the Tarot-36 System

Now that we've explored the resonance between tarot cards and dramatic situations, let's examine how to practically apply this integrated system for subconscious story development.

The Situation-Character Spread

This spread is designed to reveal both the core dramatic situation driving your story and the key characters who embody its essential elements.

Layout:

1. Center Card: The Core Dramatic Situation
2. Upper Left: The Primary Character/Element
3. Upper Right: The Secondary Character/Element
4. Lower Left: The Complicating Factor
5. Lower Right: The Resolution Potential

Process:

1. Shuffle the deck while focusing on your story's essential conflict
2. Draw five cards and place them in the positions described above

3. First, identify which of the 36 dramatic situations most resonates with the center card
4. Then explore how the surrounding cards embody the key roles or elements of that situation
5. Notice how the combination of cards creates a unique expression of the dramatic situation
6. Allow your subconscious to recognize patterns and connections beyond logical analysis

Example: Center Card: Five of Swords (Core Situation)

- This card strongly suggests Dramatic Situation #3: Crime Pursued by Vengeance
- The hollow victory and aftermath of conflict points to actions that invite retribution

Upper Left: Knight of Cups (Primary Character)

- This represents the Avenger, but in an unexpected form—romantic, idealistic, emotional
- Suggests vengeance driven by heartbreak rather than cold calculation

Upper Right: Queen of Pentacles (Secondary Character)

- This represents the Criminal, again in surprising form—nurturing, practical, abundant
- Suggests wrongdoing stemming from misguided protection rather than malice

Lower Left: The Tower (Complicating Factor)

- Sudden revelation that changes understanding of the original crime
- Suggests the vengeance quest will be disrupted by unexpected truth

Lower Right: Temperance (Resolution Potential)

- Integration, healing, and balance as alternative to continued cycle of revenge

- Suggests reconciliation rather than retribution as potential resolution

This spread reveals a story about romantic betrayal where what seems like nurturing protection is experienced as criminal harm. The vengeance quest is disrupted by revelations that change understanding of the original offense, potentially leading to healing integration rather than continued conflict.

The Situation Evolution Spread

This spread explores how a single dramatic situation might evolve through different expressions or dimensions throughout a story.

Layout:

1. Center Card: The Core Dramatic Situation
2. Position 1: Initial Expression
3. Position 2: Complication/Development
4. Position 3: Crisis/Climax
5. Position 4: Resolution/Transformation

Process:

1. Shuffle while contemplating a core conflict or situation for your story
2. Draw one card and place it in the center
3. Identify which dramatic situation most resonates with this card
4. Draw four additional cards for the evolution positions
5. Explore how each card represents a different expression or phase of the core situation
6. Notice how the situation transforms while maintaining its essential nature

Example: Center Card: The Lovers (Core Situation)

- This suggests Dramatic Situation #28: Obstacles to Love
- The fundamental conflict involves barriers to union between lovers

Position 1: Two of Cups (Initial Expression)

- Initial mutual attraction and connection established

- Obstacles not yet apparent but suggested by surrounding cards

Position 2: Knight of Wands (Complication/Development)

- Passionate pursuit despite emerging barriers
- Energy and impulsiveness that may create

Position 3: Five of Swords (Crisis/Climax)

- Conflict reaches breaking point, with apparent defeat or betrayal
- The obstacles appear to have triumphed, with relationship in ruins

Position 4: Six of Cups (Resolution/Transformation)

- Resolution through reconnection with innocent love and forgiveness
- The obstacle is transcended through remembrance of original emotional bond

This spread reveals a love story where initial connection (Two of Cups) faces obstacles that are approached with passion and perhaps impulsiveness (Knight of Wands), leading to apparent defeat or betrayal (Five of Swords), but ultimately resolving through reconnection with the innocent core of the relationship (Six of Cups). The dramatic situation of "Obstacles to Love" remains consistent throughout but transforms in expression from initial connection to conflict to reconciliation.

The Multiple Situation Integration Spread

This advanced spread reveals how different dramatic situations interact within a complex narrative, creating the rich tapestry of subplots and thematic dimensions that characterize sophisticated storytelling.

Layout:

1. Center Card: Core Theme or Unifying Element
2. Upper Position: Primary Dramatic Situation
3. Right Position: Secondary Dramatic Situation
4. Lower Position: Hidden or Emerging Dramatic Situation

5. Left Position: Opposing or Contrasting Dramatic Situation

Process:

1. Shuffle while focusing on the overall theme or feeling of your story
2. Draw five cards and place them in the positions described above
3. For each position, identify which dramatic situation most resonates with the card
4. Explore how these different situations interact and influence each other
5. Consider how characters might move between situations or embody multiple dynamics
6. Notice thematic connections or contrasts between the different situations

Example: Center Card: The World (Core Theme)

- Suggests completion, integration, and wholeness as the unifying theme
- Characters seeking completion in different ways and spheres

Upper Position: Ten of Cups (Primary Dramatic Situation)

- Suggests Dramatic Situation #35: Recovery of a Lost One
- The central narrative involves emotional reunion and healing of family bonds

Right Position: King of Swords (Secondary Dramatic Situation)

- Suggests Dramatic Situation #33: Erroneous Judgment
- A subplot involves intellectual authority and the consequences of judgment

Lower Position: Seven of Pentacles (Hidden Situation)

- Suggests Dramatic Situation #9: Daring Enterprise
- An emerging storyline involves patient investment toward ambitious goals

Left Position: Five of Wands (Opposing Situation)

- Suggests Dramatic Situation #8: Revolt

- A contrasting dynamic involves conflict against established structures

This spread reveals a multidimensional story centered on completion and integration. The primary narrative involves emotional reunion and healing (Recovery of a Lost One), complicated by themes of judgment and its consequences (Erroneous Judgment). Beneath the surface lies patient work toward ambitious goals (Daring Enterprise), while conflict against established structures (Revolt) provides contrast and tension. Characters might move between these situations—perhaps a judge who makes an erroneous judgment must revolt against the very system they upheld to ultimately find emotional healing and completion.

Dramatic Situation Transformation Technique

This technique allows you to intentionally transform one dramatic situation into another, creating dynamic character and plot development.

Process:

1. Identify the dominant dramatic situation in your current story phase
2. Determine which situation would create meaningful evolution or contrast
3. Draw three cards that bridge between these situations
4. Use these cards to develop the transitional phases of your narrative
5. Notice how character motivations and relationships must shift to accommodate this transformation

Example: Current Situation: #3 Crime Pursued by Vengeance

- Protagonist is pursuing someone who harmed a loved one
- Story feels stuck in cycles of revenge and counter-revenge

Target Situation: #34 Remorse

- Want to transform to a story about guilt, accountability, and potential redemption
- Need to develop credible path from vengeance to remorse

Bridging Cards:

1. Three of Swords: The painful truth that disrupts pursuit
2. The Hanged Man: The suspended perspective that allows new seeing
3. Nine of Cups: The emotional satisfaction that comes through different resolution

This transformation suggests a narrative where the vengeful protagonist discovers painful truth (Three of Swords) that challenges their understanding of the original crime. This forces a period of suspended action and shifted perspective (The Hanged Man), ultimately leading to an unexpected form of emotional satisfaction (Nine of Cups) through forgiveness or understanding rather than revenge. The character's motivation transforms from pursuing external justice to processing internal truth.

The Character-Situation Alignment Technique

This technique helps determine which dramatic situations most authentically align with specific character archetypes, creating narrative dynamics that feel both surprising and inevitable.

Process:

1. Draw a card representing your character's core archetype
2. Identify 3-5 dramatic situations that could naturally involve this character type
3. Draw additional cards to reveal which situation currently has strongest energy
4. Explore how this character might function differently in each potential situation
5. Consider how the character might transform as they move between situations

Example: Character Card: Queen of Wands

- Represents confident, charismatic leadership with creative and passionate

energy
- Natural authority with warmth and inspiration

Potential Dramatic Situations:

- #9 Daring Enterprise (natural leader of bold ventures)
- #24 Rivalry of Superior and Inferior (charismatic authority challenged)
- #8 Revolt (inspiring leader of transformation)
- #30 Ambition (passionately pursuing goals with confidence)

Alignment Card: The Tower

- Suggests strongest resonance with Situation #8: Revolt
- Indicates sudden, disruptive transformation of established structures

This alignment reveals that while this Queen of Wands character could authentically function in multiple dramatic situations, the current narrative energy strongly supports her role in revolutionary transformation. The Tower's appearance suggests her confident leadership will involve disrupting established structures rather than working within them. This creates interesting tension, as the Queen of Wands typically represents established feminine power rather than revolutionary force.

The Tarot-36 as Subconscious Navigation System

The true power of the Tarot-36 system emerges when we understand it not simply as a storytelling technique but as a navigation system for thc vast territory of the creative subconscious. By integrating the rich symbolic language of tarot with the structural clarity of the dramatic situations, we create a bridge between the mysterious depths of imagination and the practical craft of storytelling.

Why This System Works on a Psychological Level

The Tarot-36 system functions effectively because it operates at multiple levels of consciousness simultaneously:

1. **Conscious Analytical Level** The 36 dramatic situations provide clear structural understanding of narrative dynamics, giving the conscious mind reliable frameworks for story development.
2. **Pre-conscious Associative Level** The visual symbols and archetypal elements of tarot cards trigger chains of association, connecting current creative questions with the vast network of stories, symbols, and patterns stored in memory.
3. **Subconscious Symbolic Level** The archetypal images speak directly to deeper layers of imagination, activating narrative possibilities that might remain inaccessible through logical processes alone.
4. **Collective Mythic Level** Both tarot and the dramatic situations connect to universal human experiences and myths, allowing stories to resonate with the shared psychological inheritance of humanity.

By engaging all these levels simultaneously, the system creates a dialogue between different aspects of creative intelligence, resulting in stories that feel both freshly original and deeply familiar.

Beyond Planning: The Emergent Narrative

Unlike conventional story planning tools that attempt to predetermine narrative elements, the Tarot-36 system creates conditions for emergent storytelling—where complex, coherent narratives arise organically from the interaction of simpler elements.

This approach honors the mysterious nature of creativity while providing enough structure to shape raw inspiration into effective storytelling. Rather than forcing the subconscious to conform to conscious plans, it invites conscious craft to partner with subconscious wisdom, creating stories that surprise their own authors while maintaining internal coherence and purpose.

Integrating with the Full Subconscious Novelist System

The Tarot-36 system functions as a powerful complement to the other elements of the Subconscious Novelist approach:

- **Character Development System**: The dramatic situations provide natural arenas for characters to reveal their essential nature through challenging circumstances.
- **Elemental Storytelling**: The four suits' elemental associations align naturally with different types of dramatic situations, creating resonant combinations.
- **Open Reading Technique**: The dramatic situations provide additional interpretive frameworks for understanding open readings.
- **Story Evolution Patterns**: The dramatic situations reveal underlying structure within seemingly random card sequences.

By adding the 36 dramatic situations to your Subconscious Novelist toolkit, you enhance your ability to recognize and develop the narrative potential within any tarot reading or creative impulse.

Final Insights: The Dance of Structure and Freedom

The ultimate aim of the Tarot-36 system is not to constrain creativity within formulaic patterns but to provide just enough structure to amplify the voice of your creative subconscious. Like the banks of a river that don't create the water but channel its flow, the dramatic situations don't create your unique stories but help shape their expression.

The most powerful storytelling emerges from the dance between structure and freedom—between the familiar patterns that allow readers to orient themselves and the surprising innovations that keep narratives alive. By integrating two profound systems for understanding human experience, the Tarot-36 approach creates the optimal conditions for this dance to unfold naturally in your creative process.

Remember that the associations provided are starting points rather than limitations. As you work with this system, you'll discover unique resonances between cards and situations that reflect your personal creative voice. Trust these discoveries, even when they differ from established associations, for they represent the emergence of your authentic storytelling wisdom.

In the end, the Tarot-36 system is not about following external formulas but about creating a dialogue with your own deepest creative resources. The cards and situations are simply the language of this dialogue—a bridge between the known and unknown territories of imagination.

CHAPTER 8

Keyword Story Development System: Story Elements by Category

CHARACTERS

PROTAGONISTS/ALLIES

1. Detective
2. Whistleblower
3. Street Urchin
4. Teacher
5. Artist
6. Scholar
7. Healer
8. Protector
9. Champion
10. Mystic
11. Wanderer
12. Mentor
13. Apprentice
14. Underdog
15. Activist

ANTAGONISTS/OPPOSITION

1. Hitman
2. Corrupt Judge
3. Crime Boss
4. Serial Killer
5. Con Artist
6. Puppet Master

7. Kingmaker
8. Blackmailer
9. Stalker
10. Saboteur
11. Double Agent
12. Assassin
13. Embezzler
14. Cultist
15. False Prophet

SUPPORTING CHARACTERS

1. Informant
2. Fence
3. Bartender
4. Trophy Wife
5. Last Witness
6. Silent Partner
7. Grieving Widow
8. Office Worker
9. Mortician
10. Private Investigator
11. Funeral Director
12. Embalmer
13. Agent
14. Courier
15. Accomplice

AUTHORITY FIGURES

1. Police Chief
2. Mayor

3. Cardinal
4. CEO
5. General
6. Principal
7. Prison Warden
8. District Attorney
9. Senator
10. Intelligence Director
11. Ship Captain
12. Hospital Administrator
13. Union Leader
14. Bank President
15. Military Commander

SPECIALISTS/EXPERTS

1. Forensic Expert
2. Code Breaker
3. Art Authenticator
4. Profiler
5. Archaeologist
6. Hacker
7. Explosives Expert
8. Toxicologist
9. Safe Cracker
10. Surveillance Expert
11. Interrogator
12. Forger
13. Antiquities Expert
14. Negotiator
15. Behavioral Analyst

OUTLIERS/OUTSIDERS

1. Conspiracy Theorist
2. Reformed Criminal
3. Disgraced Officer
4. Exiled Royal
5. Defector
6. Rogue Agent
7. Whistleblower
8. Survivor
9. Vigilante
10. Underground Leader
11. Black Sheep
12. Refugee
13. Deserter
14. Outcast Genius
15. Lone Wolf

LOCATIONS/SETTINGS

URBAN

1. Opium Den
2. Steam Tunnels
3. Private Club
4. Underground Fight Club
5. Embassy
6. Industrial Wasteland
7. Abandoned Hospital
8. Police Precinct
9. Law Office
10. Art Gallery

11. Casino
12. Nightclub
13. Theater
14. Museum
15. Stock Exchange

INSTITUTIONAL

1. Boarding School
2. Asylum
3. Prison
4. Laboratory
5. Monastery
6. Military Base
7. Corporate Headquarters
8. Court House
9. University
10. Orphanage
11. Hospital
12. Research Facility
13. Government Building
14. Archive
15. Secret Facility

OTHER LOCATIONS

1. Luxury Yacht
2. Castle
3. Temple Ruins
4. Wilderness Retreat
5. Remote Island
6. Mountain Lodge

7. Underground Bunker
8. Desert Compound
9. Haunted Manor
10. Ancient Tomb
11. Submarine
12. Arctic Station
13. Ghost Town
14. Hidden Valley
15. Excavation Site

INTERNATIONAL/EXOTIC

1. Bazaar
2. Opium Fields
3. Diamond Mine
4. Ancient Monastery
5. Sacred Temple
6. Smuggler's Cove
7. Refugee Camp
8. War Zone
9. Black Market
10. Exotic Resort
11. Foreign Embassy
12. Border Crossing
13. Spice Market
14. Hidden Village
15. Ancient Ruins

CONTEMPORARY/MODERN

1. Tech Startup
2. Social Media HQ

3. Data Center
4. Virtual Reality Lab
5. Drone Base
6. Smart Building
7. Biotech Facility
8. Crypto Mining Farm
9. AI Research Lab
10. Space Launch Site
11. Green Energy Plant
12. Surveillance Hub
13. Digital Archive
14. Robot Factory
15. Quantum Lab

MOTIVES

PERSONAL

1. Lost Inheritance
2. Family Honor
3. Hidden Addiction
4. Stolen Identity
5. Revenge
6. Jealousy
7. Obsession
8. Redemption
9. Survival
10. Protection
11. Recognition
12. Freedom
13. Justice
14. Love

15.Greed

PROFESSIONAL/POLITICAL

1. Corporate Sabotage
2. Political Blackmail
3. Class Revenge
4. Professional Rivalry
5. Power Grab
6. Cover-up
7. Whistle-blowing
8. Market Manipulation
9. Election Rigging
10. Arms Dealing
11. Information Theft
12. Territory Control
13. Military Coup
14. Hostile Takeover
15. Scientific Discovery

PSYCHOLOGICAL/EMOTIONAL

1. Fear of Exposure
2. Need for Control
3. Desire for Fame
4. Search for Truth
5. Quest for Power
6. Fear of Death
7. Need for Acceptance
8. Desire for Revenge
9. Search for Identity
10. Quest for Redemption

11. Fear of Failure
12. Need for Love
13. Desire for Freedom
14. Search for Meaning
15. Quest for Justice

CRIMINAL/DARK

1. Blackmail Opportunity
2. Drug Territory
3. Gang Initiation
4. Human Trafficking
5. Art Theft
6. Money Laundering
7. Identity Theft
8. Organ Trafficking
9. Weapons Dealing
10. Corporate Espionage
11. Data Theft
12. Contract Killing
13. Evidence Planting
14. Witness Elimination
15. Framework Operation

COMPLICATIONS

INITIAL COMPLICATIONS

1. Frame-up
2. Double-cross
3. False Identity
4. Missing Evidence

5. Deadly Secret
6. Missing Will
7. Staged Accident
8. Mistaken Identity
9. Hidden Connection
10. Anonymous Threat
11. Ticking Clock
12. Rising Tension
13. Betrayal
14. Sacrifice

ESCALATING COMPLICATIONS

1. Second Murder
2. New Evidence
3. Unexpected Witness
4. Hidden Agenda
5. Past Crime
6. Secret Identity
7. Double Agent
8. Missing Person
9. Conspiracy
10. Cover Up
11. False Lead
12. Dead End
13. Red Herring
14. Time Pressure

FINAL COMPLICATIONS

1. Ultimate Betrayal
2. Final Countdown

3. Point of No Return
4. Last Stand
5. Moral Choice
6. Sacrifice Required
7. True Identity
8. Hidden Truth
9. Final Test
10. Ultimate Price
11. Greater Evil
12. Higher Stakes
13. Impossible Choice
14. Final Battle
15. Ultimate Sacrifice

TONE/ATMOSPHERE

PSYCHOLOGICAL

1. Paranoia
2. Claustrophobia
3. Isolation
4. Persecution
5. Obsession
6. Madness
7. Delusion
8. Anxiety
9. Desperation
10. Guilt
11. Regret
12. Fear
13. Suspicion
14. Denial

15. Mania

ENVIRONMENTAL

1. Fog-shrouded
2. Storm-wracked
3. Snow-bound
4. Heat Wave
5. Darkness
6. Underground
7. Confined
8. Isolated
9. Decaying
10. Oppressive
11. Chaotic
12. Pristine
13. Sterile
14. Corrupt
15. Toxic

SOCIAL/CULTURAL

1. Class Divide
2. Cultural Clash
3. Religious Tension
4. Political Unrest
5. Social Upheaval
6. Racial Conflict
7. Gender Bias
8. Generation Gap
9. Wealth Disparity
10. Cultural Revolution

11. Social Change
12. Power Struggle
13. Ideological War
14. Cultural Shift
15. Social Movement

TEMPORAL/TIME BASED

1. Time Pressure
2. Historical Weight
3. Future Threat
4. Past Shadow
5. Present Crisis
6. Countdown
7. Deadline Looming
8. Race Against Time
9. Historical Echo
10. Future Impact
11. Past Consequences
12. Present Danger
13. Time Running Out
14. Historical Burden
15. Future Promise

Keyword Exploration Exercise

1. Choose 2 to 8 random keywords from the ***keyword story development system: story elements by categories*** section
2. Use corresponding words from the ***Keywords to Spark Story*** section to explore deeper alternatives
3. Combine with random dictionary/thesaurus words (optional)
4. Play the "what if?" game with your combinations

Example combinations:

- Detective + Serial Killer → "What if the detective is the killer?"
- Ghost + Unexpected Revelation → "What if the hero discovers they're a ghost?"

Keywords to Spark Story

1. Action
2. Drama
3. Romantic
4. Horror
5. War
6. Thriller
7. Hidden Truth
8. Stalker
9. Serial Killer
10. Heist
11. Road Trip
12. Fear
13. Bear
14. Jailed
15. Alligator
16. Cook
17. Swamp
18. Travel
19. Coma
20. Air
21. Blood Oath
22. Lost Soul
23. Time Loop

24.Mind Control
25.Secret Society
26.Murder
27.Gangster
28.Hitman
29.Mother
30.Mortician
31.Oracle
32.Bike
33.Doctor
34.Romantic Comedy
35.Ancient Power
36.Subconscious Mind
37.Conman
38.Handicapped
39.Astrology
40.Drugs
41.Detective
42.College
43.Rogue
44.Vatican
45.Activist
46.Fallen Hero
47.Vampire
48.Athlete
49.Killer
50.Space
51.Supernatural
52.Destiny
53.Family
54.Shop

55.Forbidden Love
56.Weirdo
57.Automaton
58.Haunting
59.Office Worker
60.CIA
61.Freedom
62.Contagious
63.Funeral Director
64.Magic
65.Trooper
66.Gambler
67.Shapeshifter
68.Castle
69.Mystery
70.Werewolf
71.Delivery
72.Morphing
73.Trauma
74.Father
75.Dark Secret
76.Embalmer
77.Octopus
78.Political
79.Race
80.Infinity
81.Scarecrow
82.FBI
83.Spiritual
84.Dogs
85.Disease

86.Fire
87.Playful
88.Ceremony
89.Evil
90.Adultery
91.Sci-Fi
92.Robot
93.Wedding
94.Comedy
95.Cousin
96.Masonic
97.Boat
98.Kabbalah
99.Ghost
100.Airplane
101.Rags to Riches
102.Bat
103.Underdog
104.Eternal Love
105.Informant
106.Water
107.Snakes
108.Death
109.Storm
110.Greed
111.Crime
112.Writer
113.Transformation
114.Historical
115.Assassin
116.Sect

117.Artist
118.Outside USA
119.Hacker
120.Body Switch
121.Monster
122.Selflessness
123.Lunatic
124.Conspiracy
125.Lawyer
126.Homeless
127.Hunting
128.Snow
129.USA
130.Primordial
131.Agent
132.Bartender
133.History
134.Art
135.Lust
136.Teen
137.Last Stand
138.Martial Arts
139.Faith
140.Unexpected Reveal
141.Police
142.Passion
143.Religious
144.Screenwriter
145.Ridicule
146.Legal
147.Teacher

148.Clown
149.Ranger
150.Moral Choice
151.Covenant
152.Lazy
153.Over Confident
154.Bad Decisions
155.Divine Task
156.Samurai
157.Cursed Gift
158.Inner Demon
159.Secret Regrets
160.Creature
161.Jealous
162.Inauthentic
163.Violent
164.Redemption
165.Nuclear
166.Frustrated
167.Intolerant
168.Empathetic
169.Grudge
170.Devastated
171.Grief
172.Break Up
173.Protective
174.Self Absorbed
175.Epic Journey
176.Reincarnation
177.Fatal Flaw
178.Forgiveness

179.Self Love
180.Acceptance
181.Responsibility
182.Survival
183.Trust
184.Dream Walker
185.Portal
186.Memory Thief
187.Soul Bond
188.Chosen One
189.Lost World
190.Oracle
191.Prophecy
192.Dragon
193.Spirit Guide
194.Astrologer
195.Warlord
196.Druid
197.Bard
198.Sentinel
199.Mentor
200.Apprentice
201.Time Jump
202.Soul Split
203.Dream Weave
204.Starborn
205.Moonweaver
206.Sun Crown
207.Geomancer
208.Stormcaller
209.Pyromancer

210.Tidecaller
211.Memory Lane
212.Future Sight
213.Present Mind
214.Past Ghost
215.Eternal Loop
216.Death Touch
217.Life Breath
218.Truth Light
219.Lie Shadow
220.Court House
221.Dark Power
222.Soulmate
223.Multiple Murders
224.Labyrinth
225.Citadel
226.Order
227.Cult
228.Path
229.Temple
230.Ruins
231.Scroll
232.Ritual
233.Light
234.Shadow
235.Truth
236.Deception
237.Hope
238.Fear
239.Love
240.Hatred

241.Joy
242.Pain
243.Peace
244.War
245.Dance
246.Stillness
247.Movement
248.Flight
249.Stealth
250.Agility
251.Curse
252.Blessing
253.Premonition
254.Harbinger
255.Dreams
256.Nightmares
257.Illusion
258.Reality
259.Dawn
260.Twilight
261.Storm
262.Tempest
263.Wilderness
264.Sanctuary
265.Flame
266.Ocean
267.Spirit
268.Telepathy
269.Empathy
270.Wisdom
271.Time

272. Space
273. Dimension
274. World
275. Universe
276. Betrayal
277. Sacrifice
278. Loyalty
279. Vengeance
280. Brotherhood
281. Sisterhood
282. Healer
283. Warrior
284. Scholar
285. Mystic
286. Prophecy
287. Seer
288. Outcast
289. Wanderer
290. Seeker
291. Protector
292. Avenger
293. Champion
294. Prophet
295. Sage
296. Hunter
297. Witch
298. Shaman
299. Paladin
300. Guardian

The Subconscious Story Elements Method

Your subconscious mind is a master at making connections and finding patterns. Here's how to use these story element lists in a way that taps into your subconscious storytelling power:

The Dream-Like Approach

Instead of consciously selecting elements from each category, try this more intuitive method:

1. **The First Glance**
    - Close your eyes and take three deep breaths
    - Flip through the book's story elements list or keyword section, open your eyes and quickly scan any category that draws you
    - Notice which words "light up" or catch your attention
    - Don't question why—just note them down
    - Let your eyes wander naturally between categories
2. **The Ripple Effect**
    - Start with the word that grabbed you most strongly
    - Let your mind drift to associated images or feelings
    - As scenes or ideas form, scan the lists again
    - Notice which new words connect to your mental images
    - Write down everything, even if the connections aren't clear yet
3. **The Subconscious Web**
    - Spread out your noted words
    - Draw lines between ones that feel connected
    - Don't worry about logic—trust your instincts
    - Look for patterns that emerge naturally
    - Let your mind weave a story web

Practical Example:

Let's say your eyes are drawn to:

- "Whistleblower" (Character)
- "Isolation" (Tone)
- "Underground Bunker" (Location)

Don't immediately try to plot a story. Instead:

1. Close your eyes and let these elements float in your mind
2. What emotions or images arise?
3. Open your eyes and scan the lists again
4. What new elements resonate with those feelings?
5. Let connections form organically

The Spiral Method

Think of story development as a spiral rather than a straight line:

1. **Center Point**
    - Choose any element that strongly attracts you
    - This is your spiral's center
    - Don't worry about whether it's the "right" starting point
2. **First Spiral**
    - Let your mind spiral outward from this point
    - What naturally connects to this element?
    - What feelings or images does it evoke?
    - What conflicts or tensions arise?
3. **Expanding Spirals**
    - Each new element creates its own spiral
    - Let them overlap and intersect
    - Notice where spirals create interesting patterns
    - These intersections often reveal story potential

Trusting the Process

Remember:

- Your subconscious mind is already making connections
- Don't force logical relationships
- Let meanings and patterns emerge naturally
- Write down everything, even if it seems unrelated
- Trust that your mind is building something meaningful

When You Feel Stuck

If you feel blocked:

1. Close your eyes and visualize your central element
2. What colors, sounds, or feelings come to mind?
3. Open your eyes and scan the lists
4. Which words match those sensations?
5. Let these new elements guide you

From Elements to Story

As your collection of elements grows:

1. Let them simmer in your mind
2. Notice which elements keep drawing your attention
3. What scenes naturally start forming?
4. Which characters want to speak?
5. What conflicts feel inevitable?

The story will begin to tell itself through these connections. Your job is to remain open to the process and record what emerges.

Final Note

This method combines the structure of story elements with the fluidity of subconscious creation. It gives your mind enough concrete material to work with while allowing your creative instincts to guide the process. The result is often richer and more surprising than conscious plotting alone could produce.

CHAPTER 9

Subconscious Story Development Questions

Deep Story Development Questions

Core Character Questions

- Who's involved in the story? Who is your protagonist (hero)? Who is the antagonist (villain)?
- What excites you about these characters?
- Do these characters have anything in common with other characters in history?
- How can you add undeserved or unjust actions that happen to your hero?
- How can you make the hero likable? Consider:
    - Showing them doing something universally positive
    - Showing them helping others
    - Displaying strong human sensibility
    - Demonstrating competence in their field
    - Revealing their sense of humor
- What are the worst-case scenarios for your hero?
- What is their worst nightmare?
- What do they fear most?
- What external events can push the hero to take action?
- What would be the absolute worst thing that could happen to them?
- What's important to these characters?
- How do they interact with each other?
- What are their relationships and connections?
- What are their histories and how do they intersect?
- What actions will these characters take and why?
- How will their actions cause events to occur?
- What's the general feeling for this story?
- What's the hero's clear goal?

- Is the goal difficult enough to carry them through the story?
- Do you know the end? Is it clear?

Theme Exploration

1. What universal truth does your story explore?
2. How does each character reflect or challenge the theme?
3. What scenes best demonstrate your theme?
4. How does your setting reinforce your theme?
5. What counter-arguments to your theme exist in the story?
6. How does the antagonist's arc relate to the theme?
7. What symbolic objects or events represent your theme?
8. How does the theme manifest in secondary characters?
9. What sacrifices does embracing the theme require?
10. How does the theme evolve through different acts?
11. What personal experiences informed your theme choice?

Plot Development

1. What's the worst thing that could happen to your protagonist?
2. What's the best thing that could happen but doesn't?
3. What seemingly small event triggers major consequences?
4. What subplot most challenges your protagonist's beliefs?
5. What coincidences could feel too convenient?
6. What information must be withheld until later?
7. Which character decisions drive major plot shifts?
8. What seemingly resolved conflicts resurface?
9. How do character weaknesses create plot opportunities?
10. What external events force character growth?
11. Which scenes serve multiple plot functions?

World Building

1. What rules govern your story world?

2. How does the setting influence character choices?
3. What aspects of your world create natural conflict?
4. What historical events shaped your story's present?
5. What social tensions exist in your world?
6. How does technology or magic affect daily life?
7. What economic factors influence character choices?
8. What cultural beliefs create conflict?
9. How do different social classes interact?
10. What physical environments affect the plot?
11. What traditions or customs impact character behavior?

Conflict Generation

1. What internal conflicts mirror external ones?
2. How do character flaws create plot complications?
3. What relationships generate natural tension?
4. What moral dilemmas have no clear solution?
5. How do characters' goals naturally oppose each other?
6. What societal pressures create personal conflicts?
7. What misunderstandings drive the plot?
8. How do past relationships complicate present actions?
9. What loyalty conflicts test characters?
10. What sacrifices create internal struggle?
11. How do character virtues create problems?

Enhanced Character Development

External Development

1. What physical traits define this character?
2. How do they present themselves to others?
3. What are their habitual gestures or expressions?
4. How do other characters react to them?
5. What's their social status and how does it affect them?

6. How does their voice reflect their personality?
7. What's their most distinctive physical habit under stress?
8. How has their appearance changed over time and why?
9. What do their living/working spaces reveal about them?
10. How do they dress differently in private vs. public?
11. What physical limitations or advantages shape their behavior?
12. How do they carry themselves in different social situations?
13. What unconscious physical tells reveal their emotions?

Internal Development

1. What childhood event shaped them most?
2. What's their greatest regret?
3. What do they want but won't admit?
4. What belief system guides their decisions?
5. What's their relationship with power?
6. What secret do they keep even from themselves?
7. How do they handle unexpected change?
8. What childhood dream did they abandon and why?
9. What moral compromises have they made?
10. What triggers their strongest emotional reactions?
11. What do they consider unforgivable?
12. How do their fears manifest in daily decisions?
13. What memory do they revisit most often?

Relationship Development

1. Who do they trust and why?
2. What's their attachment style?
3. How do they handle conflict?
4. What's their role in their family?
5. How do they show love?
6. Who disappointed them most deeply?

7. How do they behave in groups vs. one-on-one?
8. What kind of people do they instantly distrust?
9. How do they handle betrayal?
10. What relationship mistakes do they repeat?
11. Who do they envy and why?
12. How do they maintain boundaries?
13. What relationship dynamics trigger old wounds?

Goal Development

1. What's their conscious goal?
2. What's their unconscious goal?
3. What prevents them from achieving their goals?
4. What would they sacrifice for their goal?
5. How has their goal changed over time?
6. What do they believe success looks like?
7. What past failure still influences their choices?
8. What would make them abandon their goal?
9. How do their goals conflict with others' needs?
10. What do they tell themselves about why they want this goal?
11. What smaller goals support their main objective?
12. What would they do after achieving their goal?
13. How have their methods of pursuing goals evolved?

Using These Questions

Remember, these questions are tools to spark your creativity—not a checklist to complete. Use them when:

- You're stuck and need inspiration
- You want to deepen your understanding of a character
- You're looking for new plot complications
- You want to ensure your story's internal consistency

Let your subconscious mind guide you to the questions that resonate most with your story. Sometimes, a single question can unlock an entire plot-line or character arc.

The Creative Process

1. Start with free association (30-60 minutes minimum)
2. Review and highlight connecting themes
3. Use the question sets to deepen your exploration
4. Look for patterns and connections
5. Let your subconscious guide the process

Remember

Your subconscious mind is already telling the story. These tools just help you listen more closely and organize what you hear.

CHAPTER 10

Character Interview Guide for Subconscious Story Development

Understanding the Character Interview Process

The character interview is a creative exercise that allows writers to delve deeply into their characters' psyches by engaging in an imaginary conversation with them. This technique taps into the writer's subconscious understanding of the character, often revealing surprising insights that might not emerge through more analytical approaches.

How the Process Works:

1. **Create your storytelling sanctuary**
   Find a quiet, comfortable space where you won't be interrupted—your dedicated storytelling sanctuary. Sit in a comfortable chair with good back support, keeping your spine straight but relaxed. If you live with others, let them know you need 20 minutes of uninterrupted creative time for this character exploration.
2. **Enter the creative subconscious state**
   Adopt the "story-receptive attitude" where you're open to receive whatever character elements want to emerge. Begin with slow, deep breaths for about 30 seconds, each exhale releasing you deeper into your creative mind. Find a spot to rest your gaze, then soften it, letting the edges blur slightly. You might notice your breathing naturally slowing—these are signs you're entering the creative trance state ideal for character connection. Slowly begin opening and closing your eyes until they want to remain closed. Then bring awareness to the space between your eyebrows (the "third eye" point associated with imagination) and scan your body for tensions that might block creative flow, releasing them completely.
3. **Begin the dialogue**

Start by introducing yourself and explaining why you're interviewing them. From this receptive theta state, ask your first question and wait for the answer to form in your mind. You're now working from the alpha and theta brainwave states where breakthrough character insights naturally emerge.

4. **Record the conversation**

   Write down both your questions and the character's responses as they emerge. Don't censor or overthink their answers—let them flow naturally from your subconscious. The goal is to document the dialogue while maintaining the trance state, allowing the character's voice to come through authentically.

5. **Follow interesting threads**

   While having prepared questions is helpful, be willing to go off-script if the character says something intriguing or unexpected. These unexpected turns often represent your subconscious mind making connections and revealing insights about character development that your conscious mind hasn't yet recognized. Don't judge or edit during this process—that comes later in the beta state. Trust whatever emerges—even fragments are valuable connections to your creative subconscious.

6. **Thank the character**

   When you've finished, thank the character for their time and insights. This helps create a respectful relationship that makes future interactions easier. Take a moment to feel gratitude for whatever emerged. Let a small smile form—this signals to your brain that creative work is joyful work.

7. **Return to regular awareness**

   To return to regular awareness, either let yourself emerge naturally at your own pace or use a 1-to-5 count: "At the count of 5, I'll be fully alert, bringing with me all creative insights and character elements that emerged."

Pro Tips for Character Interviews:

- **Practice daily if possible** - Same time and place builds a creative ritual that strengthens the process through repetition.
- **Speak aloud** if it helps you distinguish between your voice and the character's voice—this can help maintain different states of consciousness.
- **Change perspective** by writing in first person as the character to access deeper theta state insights.
- **Keep a notebook handy** to record insights—write everything down, even fragments, as your subconscious mind will guide you to success through these seemingly minor details.
- **Be patient with silence**—sometimes the most revealing answers come after a pause as your subconscious works in the deeper theta state.
- **Accept surprises** about your character; these often lead to more authentic and complex portrayals.
- **Revisit the interview** at different stages of the writing process. Your character may reveal different aspects of themselves as your story develops.
- **The more you practice, the deeper you'll go**—this is more than just a hypnotic suggestion; it's a physiological and psychological phenomenon that strengthens your connection to your creative subconscious.

40 Character Development Questions

Background & Identity

1. What is your full name, and do you have any nicknames? How do you feel about them?
2. When and where were you born? Describe the place you grew up.
3. What is your earliest memory, and why do you think it stayed with you?
4. Who raised you, and what was your relationship with them like?

5. What was the most significant event of your childhood that shaped who you are today?
6. Do you have siblings or other close family members? How have these relationships evolved?
7. What is your educational background? Was school a positive or negative experience?
8. What cultural, religious, or philosophical beliefs were you raised with? Which have you kept or rejected?

Personality & Psychology

9. What three words would others use to describe you? Would you agree with their assessment?
10. What are you most proud of about yourself? Most ashamed of?
11. When do you feel most comfortable and authentic? When do you feel you're wearing a mask?
12. What makes you laugh? What makes you cry?
13. What are your greatest fears? Have you overcome any significant fears?
14. What personal rules do you live by that others might find strange or unnecessary?
15. How do you handle anger? Sadness? Joy? Fear?
16. What do you do when no one is watching?

Relationships & Social Life

17. Who is the most important person in your life right now? Why?
18. Have you ever been in love? What happened?
19. Who do you trust completely? How did they earn that trust?
20. Is there anyone you've cut out of your life? What happened?
21. How do you behave differently in different social contexts (work, family, friends)?
22. What type of people do you gravitate toward? What type do you avoid?

23. How do you handle conflict with others?
24. What's a secret you've never told anyone? Why do you keep it?

Motivations & Goals

25. What drives you to get up in the morning?
26. What long-term goals are you working toward? What short-term goals?
27. What would you sacrifice everything for?
28. If you knew you would die tomorrow, what would you do today?
29. What dream have you abandoned, and why?
30. What's the hardest choice you've ever had to make?
31. What are you willing to fight for? Die for?
32. What temptations do you struggle to resist?

Worldview & Story-Specific Questions

33. What do you believe happens after death?
34. What do you think is wrong with the world, and how would you fix it?
35. What experience changed your perspective on life the most?
36. What is your definition of success? Of happiness?
37. How do you feel about the primary conflict in your story?
38. What's your relationship with the antagonist or opposing forces?
39. What skills or knowledge do you possess that will help you overcome the challenges ahead?
40. What personal weakness might prevent you from achieving your goals in this story?

Bonus Questions for Deeper Exploration

41. What contradictions exist within your personality?
42. What metaphor or symbol best represents who you are?
43. If you could change one decision from your past, what would it be?
44. What do you want people to remember about you after you're gone?

45. What question have I not asked that you wish I would?

After the Interview

Once you've completed the interview, review the responses and look for:

- **Patterns** in how the character thinks and responds
- **Inconsistencies** that might reveal inner conflict
- **Surprising revelations** that could add depth to your story
- **Story possibilities** suggested by the character's history or desires
- **Character arc potential** based on their fears, desires, and weaknesses

Remember: The goal isn't to include all this information in your story but to develop a rich understanding that will inform how your character behaves, speaks, and reacts throughout your narrative. The most compelling characters often reveal themselves gradually through the story, allowing readers to discover them much as you have through this interview process.

CHAPTER 11

The 30-Chapter Novel Model Template

Format: 1-3 Scenes per Chapter (30-60 scenes total)

Prologue (Optional)

- Separate story element
- Theme setup potential
- Hook establishment
- World introduction
- Tension creation

Act One (Chapters 1-6)

Setup (Chapters 1-2)

Chapter 1

- World introduction
- Protagonist introduction
- Status quo establishment
- Initial tension

Chapter 2

- Theme expression
- Character deepening
- World expansion
- Conflict seeds

Inciting Incident (Chapter 3)

- Catalyst event

- Initial stakes
- Hero reaction
- World disruption

Internal Wrestling (Chapters 4-6)

Chapter 4

- Initial resistance
- Problem exploration
- Failed attempt #1
- Stakes escalation

Chapter 5

- Second attempt
- Complication introduction
- Support system reveal
- Internal conflict deepening

Chapter 6

- Final preparation
- Decision point
- Last resistance
- Point of no return setup

Act Two (Chapters 7-25)

Welcome to the Jungle (Chapter 7)

- New world entry
- Rule establishment
- First challenge

- No return point

Subplot Introduction (Chapter 8)

- B story launch
- New characters
- Theme support
- Main plot connection

Trials and Tribulations (Chapters 9-14)

Chapter 9-14

- Progressive challenges
- Skill development
- Relationship building
- Rising tension
- Support system testing
- Victory/failure cycles

Midpoint (Chapter 15)

- Major revelation
- Game changer
- Direction shift
- Stakes elevation

Complications (Chapters 16-20)

- Mounting pressure
- Support system stress
- Resource depletion
- Hope reduction
- Tension escalation

Crisis (Chapter 21)

- Ultimate test
- Major setback
- All is lost moment
- Maximum pressure

Critical Choice (Chapters 22-25)

- Internal struggle
- Theme crystallization
- Team rebuilding
- Final preparation
- Resolve strengthening

Act Three (Chapters 26-30)

Welcome to the End (Chapter 26)

- Final preparation
- Team assembly
- Plan completion
- Movement to climax

Theme Triumphant (Chapters 27-30)

Chapter 27

- Climax beginning
- Initial conflict
- Plan execution
- Stakes reminder

Chapter 28

- Major battle
- Plan adaptation
- Character testing
- Victory cost

Chapter 29

- Resolution beginning
- Relationship resolution
- World change
- Theme confirmation

Chapter 30

- Final resolution
- Character transformation
- World establishment
- Theme fulfillment

Epilogue (Optional)

- Future glimpse
- Theme echo
- Character evolution
- World aftermath
- Series setup potential

Complete Novel Chapter by Chapter Guide

Prologue (Optional)

A prologue should only be used if it provides crucial information that can't be naturally woven into the main narrative. This might be a historical event that shapes the main conflict, a threat from an antagonist's perspective, or a future scene that creates immediate intrigue. The key is to make it short but impactful, offering information that will make the main story more meaningful. End with a hook that connects directly to your main narrative, creating questions the reader needs answered.

Act 1

Chapter 1: Opening Hook

Open with your protagonist actively engaged in their normal world, handling a situation that showcases both their capabilities and flaws. This isn't a mundane day—it's a day that highlights what makes them interesting. Show their typical coping mechanisms, key relationships, and hints of underlying dissatisfaction. The chapter should end with a small disruption that foreshadows the bigger changes to come, creating immediate reader investment in your character's journey.

Chapter 2: World Building

Deepen the reader's understanding of your protagonist's world through meaningful interactions with supporting characters. Focus on conflicts and relationships that will matter later in the story. Show what your protagonist values most and what they're afraid to lose. This chapter should establish the status quo that will be disrupted, but make it dynamic—filled with existing tensions and small problems that hint at bigger issues to come.

Chapter 3: Inciting Incident

The big event crashes into your protagonist's life, disrupting everything they've taken for granted. This isn't just an inconvenience—it's something that forces them to act, challenging their normal coping mechanisms. Show their immediate reaction, which should demonstrate both their strengths and weaknesses. End the chapter with the stakes becoming crystal clear: they can't ignore this problem without serious consequences.

Chapter 4: First Attempt

Your protagonist tries to solve the new problem using their old methods and familiar approaches. These attempts should fail in ways that expose their character flaws and deepen the story's conflicts. Supporting characters express concern or offer alternative suggestions that the protagonist isn't ready to hear. The chapter should end with the realization that their usual solutions won't work this time—the problem is bigger than they thought. You could also show the protagonist in a preparation stage.

Chapter 5: Mounting Pressure

External forces begin pushing your protagonist toward change while they desperately try to maintain control. Their resistance to change creates new problems and strains key relationships. Show multiple areas of their life being affected by their refusal to adapt. The pressure builds through escalating consequences, leading to a situation where maintaining the status quo becomes increasingly costly. You could also show the protagonist in a preparation stage.

Chapter 6: Decision Point

The protagonist faces their final chance to cling to their old life. Their usual methods completely fail in a way that forces them to confront their deepest fears or flaws. Present them with a clear choice between painful growth or comfortable stagnation, but make the cost of not changing severe enough that they must act. End with their decision to step into unknown territory, even if they're doing it reluctantly. You could also show the protagonist in a preparation stage.

Act 2

Chapter 7: Welcome to the Jungle

Drop your protagonist into unfamiliar territory, whether physical or metaphorical. Show their discomfort through specific challenges that highlight how out of their depth they are. Establish new rules they must learn, introduce unfamiliar faces, and create situations where their old skills prove inadequate. End the chapter with a clear demonstration that there's no going back to their old life— they must adapt or fail.

Chapter 8: Subplot Introduction

Introduce a secondary storyline that seems separate from the main conflict but will ultimately connect thematically. This might be new relationships, a parallel problem, or a competing goal. Use this chapter to broaden the story's scope and add complexity to your protagonist's journey. The subplot should create new complications while offering opportunities for character growth.

Chapter 9: First Challenge (Begin Fun and Games Beat)

Present your protagonist with their first significant test in the new world. They should achieve a small victory, but it comes with complications that reveal how much they still need to learn. Show them beginning to develop new skills or approaches, while also exposing vulnerabilities. End with a mix of hope and concern about bigger challenges ahead.

Chapter 10: Team Building

Focus on developing relationships with allies and potential allies. Show your protagonist learning to work with others in new ways. Introduce conflicts within the support group that will create future complications. Make it clear that these relationships will be crucial for facing bigger challenges ahead, while also showing how they might become vulnerabilities.

Chapter 11: Rising Action

Present a bigger challenge that tests newly developed skills and team dynamics. Your protagonist should face stronger opposition that reveals the true scope of what they're up against. Show both growth and remaining weaknesses. End with a partial victory that suggests even greater challenges ahead.

Chapter 12: Complications

Multiple problems begin to converge. Team dynamics strain under pressure. The opposition reveals unexpected strengths or resources. Show how your protagonist's growth is still insufficient for the mounting challenges. End with a sense that things are starting to spiral out of control.

Chapter 13: Small Victory

The team achieves an important goal but at a significant cost. New information comes to light that raises the stakes substantially. The opposition's full strength begins to become apparent. This victory should feel temporary and incomplete, with clear signs that bigger problems are looming.

Chapter 14: Mounting Tension

Problems compound as earlier decisions create new complications. The team achieves its immediate goal but at the cost of creating bigger future problems. Show the opposition maneuvering for a major confrontation. Build tension toward the midpoint revelation that will change everything.

Chapter 15: Midpoint (Revelation or Plot Twist)

Deliver a major revelation that forces your protagonist to reevaluate everything they thought they knew. This might be about the nature of the conflict, their own capabilities, or the true motivations of others. Previous assumptions and plans become inadequate. End with the clear need for a completely new approach.

Chapter 16: Fallout (Begin Complications Beat)

Deal with the immediate aftermath of the midpoint revelation. Show how it affects team dynamics and individual motivations. Your protagonist must begin formulating a new strategy while dealing with the psychological impact of what they've learned. End with the first steps toward a new approach.

Chapter 17: Pressure Points

Multiple threats begin to converge. Support systems show serious strain. Resources start to deplete, and hard choices must be made about their allocation. Show the opposition taking advantage of the protagonist's moments of vulnerability and uncertainty.

Chapter 18: Losing Ground

The opposition gains significant advantages. Fractures in the team become serious problems. Earlier victories begin to unravel. Hope starts to fade as the full scope of the challenge becomes clear. End with the sense that defeat is becoming a real possibility.

Chapter 19: Desperate Measures

Your protagonist attempts increasingly risky solutions as safer options disappear. These attempts lead to more failures and complications. The opposition closes in, forcing desperate decisions. Show how each attempt to solve problems creates new ones.

Chapter 20: Last Stand

Final attempts to solve problems through conventional means fail completely. All resources are depleted. The opposition appears unbeatable. Show your protagonist trying everything they know while watching it all fall apart.

Chapter 21: Crisis

Everything falls apart in a spectacular way. The protagonist's worst fears are realized. Their team scatters, their resources are gone, and their plans are in ruins. This is the darkest moment where all hope seems lost and defeat appears certain.

Chapter 22: Rock Bottom

The protagonist faces their inner demons and confronts hard truths about themselves. Core beliefs are challenged. Show them at their most vulnerable, forcing them to question everything they thought they knew about themselves and their capabilities.

Chapter 23: New Understanding

A key realization emerges from the ashes of defeat. Your protagonist begins to see themselves and their situation in a new light. Show the first glimmers of a new approach based on what they've learned through failure. Begin rebuilding with a new perspective.

Chapter 24: Team Reunification

Start gathering remaining allies, now with new understanding and purpose. Show how previous conflicts and failures have transformed relationships. A new plan begins to form, built on hard-won wisdom and stronger bonds.

Chapter 25: Preparation

Complete final preparations for the climactic confrontation. The team unites with clear purpose, understanding both the cost and necessity of what's ahead. Show how each character has grown and changed while building tension for the final confrontation.

Act 3

Chapter 26: Welcome to the End

The final phase begins as your protagonist implements their new plan. Show

how they've grown through their journey as they make their first moves toward the climactic confrontation. Each team member understands their role and the stakes involved. End with the point of no return—the final commitment to seeing this through to the end.

Chapter 27: Initial Conflict

Launch into the first phase of the final battle. Plans are tested immediately and must be adapted. Show early victories and setbacks that demonstrate both how far your protagonist has come and how challenging the road ahead still is. End with momentum building toward the major confrontation.

Chapter 28: Major Battle

Core conflicts come to a head in intense confrontations. Your protagonist's character transformation is tested under maximum pressure. Show them implementing everything they've learned while facing their greatest challenges. Stakes escalate to their highest point.

Chapter 29: Climax Resolution

Bring the final confrontation to its conclusion. Show your protagonist's complete character arc through their actions and choices in this crucial moment. Demonstrate how they've changed through how they achieve their victory. Begin addressing the cost of victory and its implications.

Chapter 30: New World

Show the immediate impact of victory and how it has changed both the protagonist and their world. Demonstrate character growth through how they handle success and deal with the aftermath. Establish the new status quo while showing how the theme has played out through the protagonist's journey.

Optional Epilogue

An epilogue serves to provide a glimpse of the future after the dust has settled from your climax. Use this space to show the lasting impact of your protagonist's journey, both on them and their world. It might hint at future challenges, showcase character growth, or provide closure to subplots that couldn't be fully addressed in the final chapter. Keep it focused on demonstrating how the theme has manifested in the new status quo, and if writing a series, plant seeds for future stories without undermining the satisfaction of this book's ending.

CHAPTER 12

Understanding the Eight-Sequence Approach (optional approach)

The eight-sequence method is a powerful story structuring tool that originated in screenwriting but translates beautifully to novel writing. Each sequence functions as a "mini-movie" within your larger story, with its own beginning, middle, and end. This structure helps maintain momentum and reader engagement while ensuring proper pacing and development of both plot and character.

Why Use Sequences?

Think of sequences as the "chapters" of your acts. While traditional three-act structure gives you the macro view of your story, sequences provide the crucial middle layer between acts and scenes. They help you:

- Maintain consistent pacing
- Create natural ebbs and flows in tension
- Manage subplot integration
- Track character development
- Control information release
- Build and release tension systematically

Detailed Sequence Breakdown

Sequence One: Status Quo & Disruption

Purpose: Establish the hero's normal world and introduce the story problem

- Opens with a compelling hook
- Introduces protagonist in their natural environment
- Shows what's missing or wrong in hero's life

- Presents the inciting incident
- Creates immediate questions in reader's mind

Example: In "Silence of the Lambs," we're introduced to Clarice Starling at the FBI Academy, showing her training, ambitions, and position as a trainee—establishing both her current status and her aspirations.

Sequence Two: Predicament & Lock In

Purpose: Force the hero to engage with the story problem

- Hero's initial reaction to inciting incident
- Failed attempts to solve problem easily
- Introduction of stakes
- Point of no return decision
- Lock-in to the main conflict

Example: Clarice receives the assignment to interview Hannibal Lecter. Once she accepts and meets him, she's locked into a dangerous psychological game that will test everything she believes about herself.

Sequence Three: First Obstacles

Purpose: Introduce the new world and its challenges

- Hero enters unfamiliar territory
- Learning new rules
- Meeting allies and enemies
- First real conflicts
- Subplot introductions

Example: Clarice navigates the complex world of criminal profiling, dealing with Dr. Chilton's interference, learning to handle Lecter's psychological games, and beginning to understand the intricacies of Buffalo Bill's case.

Sequence Four: First Culmination/Midpoint

Purpose: Raise stakes and force character growth

- Major complications arise
- Initial strategy fails
- New information changes perspective
- Relationships deepen
- Clear shift in character's approach

Example: Clarice makes a breakthrough in the case by discovering the first victim's head in storage, but this raises the stakes as she realizes she's racing against time to save Catherine Martin. Her relationship with Lecter becomes more complex as she needs more from him.

Sequence Five: Subplot & Rising Action

Purpose: Deepen the story through relationships and complications

- B-story development
- New obstacles emerge
- Character relationships evolve
- Internal conflicts intensify
- Raising of stakes

Example: Clarice must navigate her deepening psychological engagement with Lecter while pursuing Buffalo Bill. The personal cost becomes evident as she's forced to reveal her childhood traumas to Lecter in exchange for help.

Sequence Six: Main Culmination

Purpose: Push protagonist to their lowest point

- Major setback occurs
- Allies lost or separated
- Plans fall apart

- All seems lost
- Internal crisis peaks

Example: Lecter escapes, leaving Clarice without her guide. The case seems to hit a dead end, and Catherine Martin's time is running out. Clarice faces professional skepticism and personal doubt.

Sequence Seven: New Tension & Twist

Purpose: Hero regroups and prepares for final battle

- New approach developed
- Team reassembly
- Final preparations
- Twist revelation
- Movement to climactic location

Example: Clarice decodes Lecter's clues about Buffalo Bill's identity and location, preparing herself for a confrontation she knows she'll likely face alone.

Sequence Eight: Resolution

Purpose: Resolve all conflicts and demonstrate change

- Climactic sequence
- Final battle
- Character transformation revealed
- Loose ends tied up
- New status quo established

Example: Clarice confronts Buffalo Bill in his lair, facing both physical danger and her deepest fears in the darkness. She emerges transformed, having proven herself while coming to terms with her past traumas.

Benefits of Sequence Integration

1. Pacing Control

Each sequence has natural rising and falling action, creating a rhythm that keeps readers engaged. This prevents the "saggy middle" common in novels by ensuring constant forward momentum.

2. Complexity Management

Sequences help you manage multiple plot threads by providing natural points for subplot integration and development. Each sequence can emphasize different aspects of your story while maintaining overall coherence.

3. Character Development

The sequence approach ensures character growth is steady and earned. Each sequence challenges your protagonist in new ways, forcing them to evolve gradually rather than change suddenly.

4. Theme Development

Sequences allow you to explore different facets of your theme, building complexity and depth throughout the story. Each sequence can illuminate a different aspect of your central theme.

Implementation Tips

1. **Sequence Transitions**
    - End each sequence with a significant event or revelation
    - Begin next sequence with reaction and adjustment
    - Use transitions to build momentum
2. **Length Management**
    - Each sequence roughly equals 12.5% of your novel

- Flexible based on story needs
- Can expand or contract slightly while maintaining purpose

3. **Tension Control**
   - Each sequence should have its own tension arc
   - Build to sequence-level climaxes
   - Vary intensity between sequences
4. **Character Focus**
   - Each sequence should challenge protagonist in new way
   - Balance external and internal conflicts
   - Use sequences to deepen relationships

Common Pitfalls to Avoid

1. **Rigid Adherence**
   - Don't force your story to fit exactly
   - Allow for natural variation
   - Maintain sequence purpose over exact length
2. **Lost Momentum**
   - Each sequence needs forward movement
   - Avoid static scenes
   - Keep raising stakes
3. **Disconnected Sequences**
   - Ensure each sequence builds on previous
   - Maintain cause-and-effect chain
   - Keep overall story arc in mind

By integrating the eight-sequence approach into your novel's structure, you create a robust framework that supports both plotting and character development while maintaining steady pacing and reader engagement. This method, while optional to this process, provides clear milestones for your writing process while ensuring your story maintains its organic flow and emotional impact.

Benefits of Eight Sequence Integration

1. Enhanced Pacing Control
   - Each sequence has a clear dramatic purpose
   - Natural rising and falling action within sequences
   - Built-in mini-arcs for better tension management

2. Clearer Story Milestones
   - Eight distinct units for easier progress tracking
   - Natural breakpoints for subplot integration
   - Clearer relationship between scenes and larger structure

3. Better Subplot Management
   - Each sequence can focus on different story threads
   - Easier to track multiple character arcs
   - Natural places for subplot (b-story) development

4. Stronger Scene Purpose
   - Every scene has clear sequence-level purpose
   - Easier to identify and cut unnecessary scenes
   - Better flow between major story beats

Implementation Guidelines

1. Sequence Transitions
   - End each sequence with a significant reversal or revelation
   - Begin each sequence with reaction to previous sequence
   - Use sequence breaks for major POV shifts if applicable

2. Character Development
   - Each sequence should advance character arc
   - Use sequence structure to pace internal growth
   - Balance external and internal conflicts within sequences

3. Theme Development
   - Each sequence explores different aspect of theme
   - Build thematic complexity through sequence progression
   - Use sequence endings to reinforce thematic elements

4. Tension Management
   - Each sequence has its own tension arc
   - Build to sequence-level climaxes
   - Use sequence structure to control pacing

Eight-Sequence Sequence Breakdown

Act One (Sequences 1-2)

- Sequence 1: Status Quo & Inciting Incident
  - Introduces the hero and their world
  - Presents the inciting incident
  - Roughly 12.5% of story

- Sequence 2: Predicament & Lock In
  - Hero reacts to the inciting incident
  - Commits to a course of action
  - Roughly 12.5% of story

Act Two-A (Sequences 3-4)

- Sequence 3: First Obstacles
  - Hero enters new world/situation
  - Faces initial challenges
  - Roughly 12.5% of story

- Sequence 4: First Culmination/Midpoint
  - Complications intensify

  - Leads to major turning point
  - Roughly 12.5% of story

Act Two-B (Sequences 5-6)
- Sequence 5: Subplot & Rising Action
  - Relationships deepen
  - New complications arise
  - Roughly 12.5% of story

- Sequence 6: Main Culmination
  - Major setback occurs
  - All seems lost
  - Roughly 12.5% of story

Act Three (Sequences 7-8)
- Sequence 7: New Tension & Twist
  - Hero regroups
  - Final preparations
  - Roughly 12.5% of story

- Sequence 8: Resolution
  - Climactic sequence
  - Final resolution
  - Roughly 12.5% of story

The following chart shows how the eight-sequence approach functions in the 3 Act Structure:

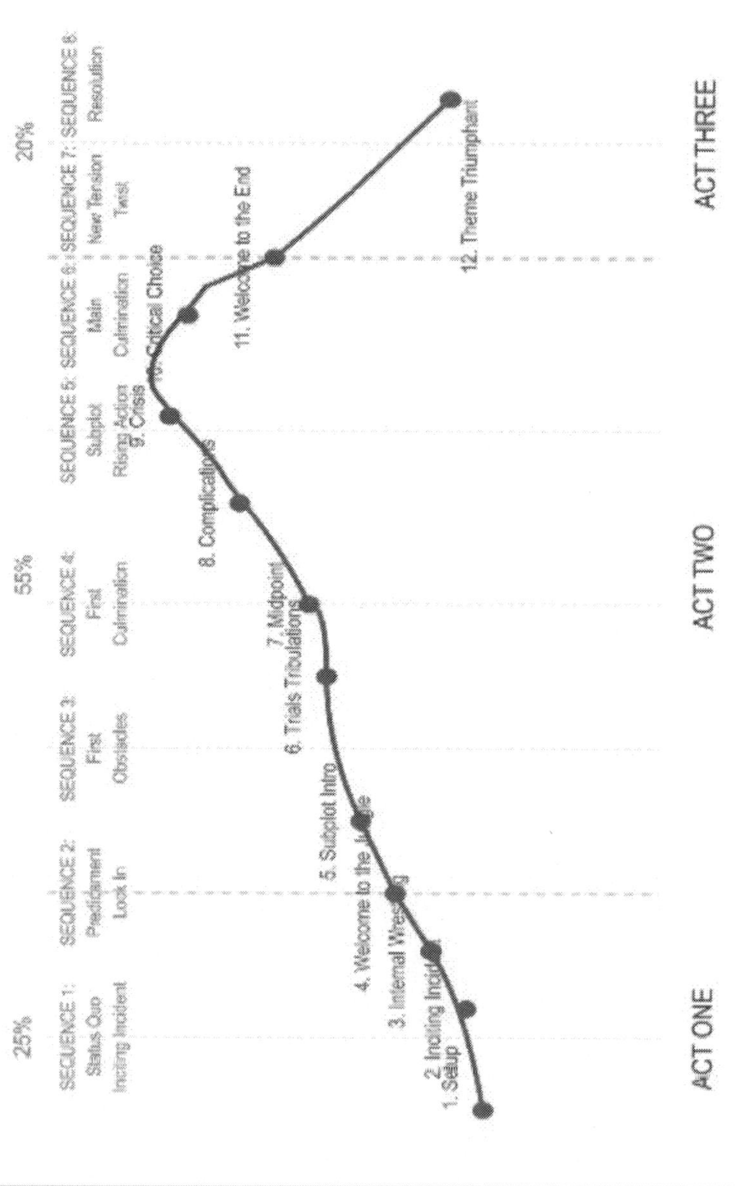

Below, I provide my 3 Act, 12 beat, 30 chapter template for you to follow. Keep in mind that this is a structure that works for all kinds of stories (but feel free to adjust it if you need to).

Eight-Sequence Approach Integrated with 30-Chapter Template

ACT ONE (25%)

SEQUENCE 1: Status Quo & Inciting Incident (Chapters 1-3)

Prologue (optional)

- A separate story element that sets up the world, theme, or conflict
- Often provides historical context or a glimpse of events to come
- Creates initial intrigue and tension without revealing too much
- May introduce a mystery that will be resolved by the story's end

Chapter 1: World and protagonist introduction, status quo establishment

- Introduces the protagonist in their ordinary world before transformation
- Establishes their current life, routines, relationships, and limitations
- Reveals character flaws, unfulfilled desires, or inner conflicts
- Creates reader empathy by showing both strengths and weaknesses

Chapter 2: Theme expression, character deepening, world expansion

- Further develops the protagonist's character and relationships
- Subtly introduces thematic elements that will be explored throughout
- Expands the story world, revealing more about its rules and society
- Plants seeds of the coming conflict or change

Chapter 3: Inciting Incident, catalyst event, initial stakes

- Presents the event that disrupts the protagonist's ordinary world
- Introduces the central conflict or problem that must be addressed
- Establishes initial stakes and shows why this matters to the protagonist
- Shows the protagonist's initial reaction (often reluctance or denial)

SEQUENCE 2: Predicament & Lock In (Chapters 4-6)

Chapter 4: Initial resistance, problem exploration, failed attempt

- Protagonist tries to avoid the call to action or solve the problem the wrong way
- Shows why the protagonist is not yet ready for the journey ahead
- Introduces complications that make the central problem more difficult
- Ends with a failure that raises the stakes

Chapter 5: Second attempt, complication introduction, support system

- Protagonist makes a more serious attempt to address the problem
- Introduces allies, mentors, or support systems that will aid the journey
- Adds new complications or reveals deeper aspects of the central conflict
- Deepens internal conflicts as the protagonist struggles with change

Chapter 6: Final preparation, decision point, point of no return setup

- Protagonist makes final preparations before fully committing to the journey
- Presents a major decision point where turning back becomes impossible
- Shows the protagonist's last resistance before accepting the challenge
- Sets up the threshold crossing into the "special world" of Act Two

ACT TWO (55%)

SEQUENCE 3: First Obstacles (Chapters 7-10)

Chapter 7: Welcome to the Jungle, new world entry, first challenge

- Protagonist enters the "special world" where different rules apply
- Establishes the new environment, its dangers, and opportunities
- Presents the first real challenge in this unfamiliar territory
- Marks the point of no return - the protagonist cannot go back to their old life

Chapter 8: Subplot introduction, B story launch, new characters

- Introduces a secondary storyline that complements the main plot
- Brings in new characters who will play important roles going forward
- Often introduces a relationship (romantic, mentorship, friendship) that supports theme
- Shows how the subplot connects to and enhances the main conflict

Chapter 9: First major challenge, skill development

- Protagonist faces their first significant test in the new world
- Begins developing new skills, perspectives, or approaches
- Shows both progress and continued weakness
- Raises the stakes as the protagonist better understands what they're up against

Chapter 10: Second challenge, relationship building

- Presents a more difficult challenge that builds on the first
- Develops relationships with allies, mentors, or antagonists
- Tests the protagonist's developing skills and resolve
- Deepens commitment to the goal despite growing difficulties

SEQUENCE 4: First Culmination (Chapters 11-15)

Chapter 11: Third challenge, rising tension

- Introduces an even more difficult obstacle or conflict
- Increases tension as problems compound and solutions become more complex
- Tests relationships established earlier in the story
- Shows protagonist's growing competence but also growing pressure

Chapter 12: Fourth challenge, support system testing

- Presents a challenge that tests the protagonist's support system
- May introduce conflict among allies or doubt in mentors

- Shows how external challenges affect internal growth
- Continues building toward the midpoint revelation

Chapter 13: Fifth challenge, victory/failure cycles

- Alternates between victories and setbacks to create rhythm
- Demonstrates the protagonist's improving abilities and persistent flaws
- Increases complexity of challenges as the story progresses
- Sets up expectations for a major turning point

Chapter 14: Final challenge before midpoint, mounting pressure

- Presents the last major obstacle before the midpoint revelation
- Creates maximum pressure on the protagonist and their allies
- Foreshadows the midpoint revelation or transformation
- Builds anticipation for a significant change in direction

Chapter 15: MIDPOINT, major revelation, game changer, direction shift

- Delivers a major revelation that changes the protagonist's understanding
- Transforms the nature of the quest or goal (often from reactive to proactive)
- Raises stakes dramatically through new information or a surprising event
- Represents a point of no return that fundamentally changes the story direction

SEQUENCE 5: Subplot & Rising Action (Chapters 16-20)

Chapter 16: Initial fallout from midpoint, mounting pressure

- Shows immediate consequences of the midpoint revelation
- Presents new challenges based on the changed understanding
- Increases pressure on the protagonist who must adapt to new information
- Often involves regrouping or forming a new plan

Chapter 17: Further complications, support system stress

- Introduces additional complications that test the protagonist's resolve

- Places stress on relationships and support systems
- Shows antagonist forces gaining strength or advantage
- Reveals deeper layers of conflict and thematic elements

Chapter 18: Resource depletion, hope reduction

- Protagonist begins losing resources (physical, emotional, allies)
- Hope diminishes as obstacles seem increasingly insurmountable
- Internal conflicts intensify, possibly causing mistakes or self-doubt
- The path to success becomes increasingly narrow and difficult

Chapter 19: Tension escalation, preparation for crisis

- Rapidly escalates tension as multiple story threads converge
- Shows protagonist preparing for an inevitable confrontation
- Foreshadows the coming "crisis" or "all is lost" moment
- Creates a sense of narrative momentum toward a breaking point

Chapter 20: Final complication leading to crisis

- Introduces the final complication that will trigger the crisis
- Positions all players for the major setback to come
- Heightens tension to maximum levels
- Creates a false sense of progress before the fall

SEQUENCE 6: Main Culmination (Chapters 21-25)

Chapter 21: CRISIS, ultimate test, major setback, all is lost moment

- Delivers the ultimate test or challenge that the protagonist fails
- Creates the "all is lost" moment where success seems impossible
- Often involves a personal loss, betrayal, or devastating revelation
- Represents the darkest moment when all hope seems gone

Chapter 22: Internal struggle, theme crystallization

- Shows the protagonist at their lowest point, struggling internally
- Crystallizes the story's theme through this moment of deep reflection

- Often involves confronting personal demons or fundamental flaws
- Plants the seed of the eventual solution or renewed determination

Chapter 23: Team rebuilding, resource gathering

- Protagonist begins to recover from the crisis and rebuild
- Reconnects with allies or finds new ones for the final challenge
- Gathers necessary resources (physical, emotional, informational)
- Shows the first steps toward the final resolution

Chapter 24: Final preparation, resolve strengthening

- Shows detailed preparation for the final confrontation
- Protagonist's determination grows stronger through overcoming doubt
- Characters have meaningful exchanges that resolve secondary conflicts
- Emotional preparedness develops alongside tactical planning

Chapter 25: Resolve fortified, final plan completion

- Protagonist's determination is now unwavering and complete
- Final plan is solidified with contingencies in place
- Emotional arcs reach pre-climax resolution points
- Sets the stage for entering the climactic sequence with full preparation

ACT THREE (20%)

SEQUENCE 7: New Tension & Twist (Chapter 26-27)

Chapter 26: Welcome to the End, team assembly, movement to climax

- Protagonist and allies move into position for the final confrontation
- Team is fully assembled with roles clearly defined
- Journey to the location of the climax often reveals final character moments
- Creates new tension through anticipation of the coming battle

Chapter 27: Climax beginning, initial conflict, plan execution

- Initial phase of the climactic sequence begins
- Protagonist puts their plan into action against the antagonist forces
- Early successes and failures test the plan's viability
- Often includes a surprise or complication that forces adaptation

SEQUENCE 8: Resolution (Chapters 28-30)

Chapter 28: Major battle, plan adaptation, character testing

- Central climactic confrontation reaches its peak intensity
- Plan must be adapted as unexpected challenges arise
- Characters are tested to their absolute limits
- Often includes a moment when all seems lost before a breakthrough

Chapter 29: Resolution beginning, relationship resolution, world change

- Shows the immediate aftermath of the climactic battle
- Begins resolving relationships and emotional arcs
- Demonstrates how the world has changed as a result
- Confirms the theme through the outcome of the central conflict

Chapter 30: Final resolution, character transformation, theme fulfillment

- Completes all remaining character arcs and relationship resolutions
- Shows the protagonist's final transformation compared to Chapter 1
- Fulfills thematic promises made throughout the story
- Establishes the new normal that will persist after the story ends

Epilogue (optional): Future glimpse, theme echo, world aftermath

- Provides a glimpse into the future beyond the main story
- Echoes the theme one final time through new context
- Shows the lasting impact of events on the world and characters
- May set up sequel potential if appropriate

CHAPTER 13

The Art of the Logline: Finding Your Story's Essence

What Is a Logline?

A logline is a concise, compelling 1-3 sentence summary that captures the essence of your story. It distills your entire narrative down to its most fundamental elements: protagonist, goal, motivation, and conflict. Think of it as the DNA of your story—a blueprint containing all the essential information needed to understand what your tale is fundamentally about.

Why Craft Your Logline After Your Three-Act Synopsis

Many writing guides suggest creating a logline before developing a full story. However, there's profound wisdom in reversing this approach. Here's why:

1. **Discovery Through Development**: When you complete your three-act synopsis first, you've already explored your story's depths. You understand your character arcs, plot twists, and thematic resonance in ways impossible to grasp initially.
2. **Distillation vs. Limitation**: Starting with a logline can inadvertently restrict your creative exploration. Writing the synopsis first allows your story to breathe and evolve organically before you crystallize its essence.
3. **Precision Through Knowledge**: With a completed synopsis, your logline becomes razor-sharp and authentic—rooted in the story you've actually crafted rather than the one you initially imagined.
4. **Course Correction**: The process of creating a post-synopsis logline often reveals if your story has strayed from its intended path or lacks cohesion.

The Logline as Your North Star

Once crafted, your logline serves as the guiding light throughout your writing journey:

- It keeps you focused on your core narrative when faced with creative decisions
- It helps identify scenes or characters that don't serve your central story
- It becomes an essential tool for pitching your work to agents, producers, or publishers
- It gives you clarity when revisions seem overwhelming

Crafting Your Perfect Logline

While there's no one-size-fits-all approach, here are several proven formulas for crafting compelling loglines:

The Classic Formula

This approach focuses on the four fundamental pillars of storytelling: character, desire, motivation, and opposition. It follows this structure:

The [hero] wants [goal] because [motivation] but [conflict(s)] are preventing them from achieving it.

Breaking it down:

1. **Hero**: Your protagonist with a brief, defining characteristic
2. **Goal**: The concrete, external objective they're pursuing
3. **Motivation**: The internal or emotional reason driving their pursuit
4. **Conflict**: The obstacles, antagonists, or forces standing in their way

Example for Rounders: "A gifted poker player turned law student wants to stay away from the underground gambling world because he nearly lost everything once before, but when his best friend accumulates a life-threatening debt to a vengeful Russian card shark, he must risk his legitimate future by returning to high-stakes poker games he swore to leave behind."

Example for The Bourne Identity: "An amnesiac found floating in the Mediterranean discovers he possesses extraordinary combat skills and must piece together his mysterious past while evading unknown assassins determined to eliminate him for reasons he can't remember."

This formula excels at:

- Stories with clear protagonist/antagonist dynamics
- Narratives driven by a specific, tangible goal
- Tales where inner motivation and external obstacles create dynamic tension
- Classical three-act structures with traditional story beats

The strength of this approach lies in its clarity and completeness—it ensures your logline captures the full dramatic essence of your story in a single compelling statement.

The "When" Structure

This approach centers around the inciting incident that propels your protagonist into the story's central conflict. It follows this pattern:

When [inciting incident happens], a [protagonist] must [take action] or risk [stakes].

Breaking it down:

1. **Inciting Incident**: The catalytic event that disrupts your protagonist's normal world
2. **Protagonist**: Your main character with a brief, defining trait
3. **Action**: The primary journey or task they must undertake
4. **Stakes**: What will be lost if they fail (personal, interpersonal, or global)

Example for The Matrix: "When a dissatisfied computer genius senses something wrong with reality itself, he follows a cryptic digital trail to a rebel leader hunted by mysterious agents, forcing him to confront an impossible choice: embrace a brutal truth that will forever alter his existence or retreat to the comfort of the only world he's ever known."

Example for Eastern Promises: "When a midwife discovers the diary of a dead

Russian teenager who died in childbirth, she must navigate the dangerous world of the London-based Russian mafia to find the baby's family, risking her own life as powerful men will kill to keep their secrets buried."

This formula works particularly well for:

- Stories with a clear moment that sets everything in motion
- Narratives where understanding the initial setup is crucial
- Tales that follow the "hero's journey" or "ordinary world disrupted" structure
- Stories where the stakes and consequences of failure are significant

The power of this approach comes from immediately establishing the dramatic situation and the urgent choice facing your protagonist, creating instant tension and a clear dramatic question for the audience to follow.

The Character-Driven Approach

This method places your protagonist's defining traits and internal journey at the center of your logline. It follows this structure:

A [character with defining trait(s)] must [overcome specific obstacle] to [achieve specific goal].

Breaking it down:

1. **Character with Defining Trait(s)**: Your protagonist described through their most significant qualities, flaws, or circumstances
2. **Obstacle**: The primary challenge they face (which may be internal, external, or both)
3. **Goal**: What they hope to achieve or become by the story's end

Example for Good Will Hunting: "A rebellious janitor with hidden mathematical genius must choose between loyalty to his working-class neighborhood friends and pursuing his extraordinary potential when a renowned professor and an unconventional therapist challenge his self-imposed limitations."

Example for The Machinist: "A dangerously emaciated industrial worker suffering from severe insomnia must discover why he's being stalked by a mysterious man no one else can see before his deteriorating mental state and physical condition destroy what remains of his life."

This approach is particularly effective for:

- Character studies where internal conflict drives the narrative
- Stories about personal transformation or self-discovery
- Narratives where the protagonist's unique traits or worldview are central
- Tales where the character's internal journey is as important as (or more important than) external plot events

The strength of this method lies in its ability to immediately establish what makes your protagonist compelling and different from other characters. By highlighting their unique qualities and internal struggles, you create immediate emotional investment in their journey. This approach also works well for stories where the protagonist's specific traits directly inform how they approach the central conflict.

The Situation-Character-Objective-Opponent (SCOO) Method

This approach breaks down your story into four distinct components and then combines them into a cohesive statement:

1. **Situation**: The unique world, setting, or circumstance where your story takes place
2. **Character**: Your protagonist with their defining attributes or qualities
3. **Objective**: What your character is trying to accomplish or achieve
4. **Opponent**: The antagonistic force (person, nature, society, self) preventing success

To craft this logline: *In [situation], [character] must [objective] despite/against [opponent].*

Example for No Country for Old Men: "In the desolate Texas borderlands of

1980, a Vietnam veteran who stumbles upon drug money must evade a merciless hitman with an unusual murder weapon and philosophical approach to fate."

This method excels at showcasing stories with unique worlds or circumstances while still maintaining focus on character and conflict. It's particularly useful for sci-fi, fantasy, period pieces, or stories where the setting significantly influences the narrative.

The Ironic Pairing Technique

This method identifies and highlights the central irony or contradiction that gives your story its unique tension. It typically follows this pattern:

A [protagonist] must [do something that contradicts their nature/belief/position] in order to [achieve goal].

The power comes from the inherent friction between who the character is and what they must do.

Example for Silence of the Lambs: "To catch a killer who skins women, an FBI trainee must seek the help of a brilliant psychiatrist who ate his patients."

Example for Fight Club: "A corporate drone obsessed with material possessions creates an anti-consumerist underground movement that threatens to destroy the capitalist system he depends on."

This approach is particularly effective for:

- Stories with protagonists forced to act against type
- Narratives with inherent philosophical contradictions
- High-concept premises with built-in irony
- Character journeys that subvert audience expectations

The ironic pairing creates immediate intrigue because readers instantly recognize the dramatic tension at the heart of the story.

Choose the formula that best highlights what makes your story unique:

- Is it character-driven? Focus more on the protagonist's traits and transformation
- Is it premise-driven? Emphasize the unique situation or concept
- Is it plot-driven? Highlight the central conflict and stakes

Masterful Examples from Cinema

Let's examine how this formula applies to some of Hollywood's most memorable films:

The Silence of the Lambs: An ambitious FBI trainee must gain the trust of an imprisoned, manipulative serial killer with a taste for human flesh to help catch another murderer who skins his female victims before time runs out for his latest captive.

Fight Club: A depressed insomniac trapped in a soul-crushing corporate job forms an underground fighting club with a charismatic soap salesman, but discovers their revolutionary partnership threatens to spiral beyond his control into something far more dangerous.

Good Will Hunting: A troubled janitor at MIT, who secretly possesses mathematical genius, must choose between pursuing his gift and remaining loyal to his working-class roots when a renowned professor and a therapist attempt to redirect his life.

The Matrix: A computer hacker discovers that his reality is an elaborate simulation controlled by sentient machines who have enslaved humanity, forcing him to choose between continuing his illusory existence or embracing his role as humanity's potential savior.

No Country for Old Men: When a Vietnam veteran stumbles upon the aftermath of a drug deal gone wrong and takes $2 million in cash, he triggers a relentless pursuit by a psychopathic hitman while a world-weary sheriff tries to understand the escalating violence that has invaded his once-peaceful region.

The Bourne Identity: An amnesiac rescued from the Mediterranean Sea discovers he's a highly trained assassin being hunted by his former employers, forcing him to recover his true identity while evading those determined to eliminate him.

The Departed: A police officer working undercover in an Irish mob and a mob member infiltrating the police force race to uncover one another's identity before their own covers are blown.

Rounders: A reformed poker prodigy must return to high-stakes underground gambling to help his recently paroled best friend pay off a dangerous debt, risking his law school career, relationship, and life savings against ruthless Russian mobsters.

The Machinist: An industrial worker who hasn't slept in a year begins to doubt his own sanity as he tries to understand why he's being stalked by a mysterious man that no one else can see and why his body is withering away.

Eastern Promises: A midwife investigating the identity of a Russian teenager who died in childbirth stumbles into the violent world of the Russian mafia in London, where she forms a dangerous bond with a mysterious driver who may be her only protection.

Red Dragon: A retired FBI profiler with a traumatic past must re-enter the mind of the serial killer who nearly destroyed him in order to catch a new murderer who targets entire families during the full moon.

The Logline's Power for Writers

Understanding and mastering your logline transforms your writing process in several ways:

1. **Clarifies Complex Ideas**: It forces you to identify and articulate your story's most essential components.
2. **Enhances Focus**: Keeps you on track during the long, often meandering process of completing your manuscript.
3. **Strengthens Narrative Unity**: Ensures that every scene, character, and

plot point serves your central story.

4. **Facilitates Effective Communication**: Gives you a powerful tool to share your vision with others.
5. **Reveals Structural Weaknesses**: A difficult-to-craft logline often signals fundamental story problems that need addressing.

When Your Logline Resists You

If you're struggling to create a compelling logline from your completed synopsis, this is valuable feedback. It may indicate:

- Your protagonist's goal isn't clear enough
- The central conflict lacks sufficient stakes
- Your character's motivation feels unconvincing or generic
- The story contains competing narrative threads that dilute its focus

Rather than viewing this as a failure, embrace it as an opportunity to strengthen your story before investing months in a draft that may require substantial revision.

Remember: The logline isn't just a marketing tool or a simple summary—it's the crystallization of your story's soul. By crafting it after developing your three-act synopsis, you honor the organic development of your narrative while gaining a powerful tool to guide your writing journey. Keep it visible as you write, let it be your compass when you feel lost, and use it to test every major story decision. Your logline is the promise you make to your reader. Make it impossible to resist.

CHAPTER 14

A Deeper Look into POV

Understanding POV Options

Point of view represents one of the most consequential decisions a novelist makes—perhaps the most intimate artistic choice in the writing process. This selection determines not only who tells your story but how readers will experience your fictional world. It establishes the psychological distance between reader and character, shapes how information is revealed, and influences every aspect of narrative from pacing to theme development. Far from a mere technical consideration, POV creates the foundational relationship between story and reader, affecting every word that follows.

The novelist's POV options can be understood as a spectrum of narrative distance, from the profound intimacy of first-person present tense to the Olympian perspective of third-person omniscient. Each position on this spectrum offers distinct advantages and limitations; none is inherently superior to others. The art lies in selecting the viewpoint that best serves your particular story's needs, then mastering the specific techniques that maximize its effectiveness.

First Person POV

First person viewpoint invites readers into direct communion with a character's consciousness, creating the literary equivalent of sustained eye contact. This perspective transforms readers from observers into participants, experiencing events through a character's unique sensory filters, thought patterns, and emotional responses. The intimate access creates immediate investment while simultaneously constraining the narrative within the boundaries of what this character could plausibly know, think, feel, and perceive.

First Person Present

The most immediate form of storytelling available to novelists, first-person present tense creates a sense of events unfolding in real time, collapsing the distance between experience and narration. When a protagonist declares, "I step into the darkened room, my heart pounding against my ribs," readers experience this action as simultaneous with its telling, creating a breathless immediacy that can prove particularly powerful for high-tension narratives.

This approach has found particular resonance in psychological thrillers and intense character studies. The rawness of emotion and thought finds natural expression in the unfiltered immediacy of present-tense narration. In "American Psycho" by Bret Easton Ellis, the disturbing present-tense narration places readers directly inside Patrick Bateman's fractured psyche, making his perceptions and delusions uncomfortably immediate. Similarly, "Fight Club" by Chuck Palahniuk uses first-person present tense to create a visceral, unprocessed experience of the narrator's fragmenting reality, allowing readers to inhabit the urgent experience of characters navigating profound psychological challenges without the mediating distance of retrospection.

Psychological thrillers similarly benefit from this perspective, as the claustrophobic confinement within a character's real-time perceptions heightens suspense and uncertainty. When a narrator observes, "She's smiling at me, but something flickers behind her eyes—something that makes my skin crawl," readers experience this dissonance directly, trapped within the narrator's limited understanding while sensing the significance of details the character might miss or misinterpret. This perspectival restriction becomes a powerful tool for creating tension, particularly when dealing with potentially unreliable narrators.

Stories requiring deep emotional connection find a natural home in this perspective. When readers experience a character's grief, love, fear, or triumph as it occurs, without the emotional processing that comes with retrospection, these feelings land with particular potency. The unmediated quality of emotion in first-person present creates a visceral reading experience well-suited to stories where emotional resonance drives engagement.

The advantages of this approach are substantial. The heightened tension and urgency created by present-tense narration makes it particularly effective for action sequences and high-stakes scenarios. Rather than being told what happened, readers experience what is happening, creating a cinematic immediacy that can prove irresistible in the right narrative context.

Internal monologue flows naturally in this perspective, without requiring the subtle shifts between past-tense narration and present-tense thought that characterize many first-person past narratives. When a character observes, "I wonder if she knows what I'm thinking. Can she see it on my face?" the wondering feels organic, captured in the moment of its occurrence rather than recalled after the fact.

This approach also facilitates the development of strong character voice, as every observation, action, and reflection comes filtered through the protagonist's unique perspective without the mediating distance of retrospection. Idiosyncratic speech patterns, thought processes, and perceptual quirks emerge naturally through this unprocessed narrative flow, creating distinctive voices that can become the heartbeat of compelling fiction.

However, first-person present comes with significant limitations. The restriction to the protagonist's knowledge creates both narrative intimacy and potential frustration. Readers cannot know more than the protagonist, which can complicate plots requiring multiple perspectives or information the protagonist couldn't plausibly access. This constraint requires careful handling, particularly in mysteries or complex narratives where the withholding and revelation of information drive engagement.

The perspective can feel artificial in certain genres, particularly those with established conventions of retrospective storytelling. Historical fiction, for instance, often benefits from the contextualizing distance of past tense, allowing narrators to place their experiences within larger historical movements they might not fully comprehend in the moment of occurrence.

Complex plots present particular challenges in this perspective, as the inability to shift viewpoints within scenes or chapters can create difficulties in managing multiple storylines or extensive casts of characters. Without the flexibility to follow different characters or jump forward and backward in time, novelists must find creative solutions for revealing essential information while maintaining the integrity of the protagonist's perspective.

First Person Past

The most traditional approach to first-person narration positions the narrator as the teller of their own story after the fact. This creates a dual consciousness within the narrative—the experiencing self who lives through events and the narrating self who relates them later, potentially with greater understanding, emotional processing, or ironic distance.

This approach finds natural expression in memoir-style narratives, where the tension between experience and retrospection creates rich opportunities for reflection. In “Interview with the Vampire” by Anne Rice, Louis recounts his centuries of vampire existence to a reporter, allowing him to contextualize his experiences with the benefit of immortal perspective. Similarly, in “The Legend of Bagger Vance” by Steven Pressfield, the narrator Junie relates events from decades earlier, providing both the immediacy of direct experience and the wisdom of retrospection. This dual perspective creates depth without sacrificing the intimacy of first-person narration.

Mystery novels and psychological thrillers frequently employ this approach, using the gap between experience and narration to control the revelation of information. In “The Beach” by Alex Garland, Richard's past-tense narration allows him to reflect on his experiences in Thailand with the benefit of hindsight, creating a layer of meaning unavailable in present-tense narration. Similarly, when detective protagonists like those in Thomas Harris's Hannibal Lecter series recount their investigations, the narrating consciousness can strategically withhold realizations or connections until the optimal moment for revelation, creating the satisfying cognitive click of pieces falling into place for both protagonist and reader simultaneously.

Character-driven stories benefit from the reflective quality this perspective enables, allowing protagonists to analyze their own motivations, mistakes, and growth with the benefit of hindsight. This creates opportunities for explicit character development that would feel unnaturally self-aware in present-tense narration, as characters can acknowledge how experiences changed them in ways they couldn't have articulated in the moment.

The advantages of first-person past include its natural storytelling feel, which aligns with how humans typically relate personal experiences. The “let me tell you what happened” framework feels organically human, creating an intuitive connection between narrator and reader that requires little adjustment from everyday modes of communication.

The allowance for reflection and hindsight creates opportunities for commentary, contextualization, and meaning-making that present-tense narration often precludes. When a narrator observes, “I didn't understand then what those words would come to mean to me,” they create anticipatory tension while signaling the significance of apparently mundane moments, guiding readers' attention and emotional investment.

Time jumps prove easier to handle in this perspective, as the narrating consciousness can move fluidly between timeframes, compressing uneventful periods and expanding significant moments with the natural selectivity of memory. This flexibility allows for sophisticated chronological manipulation without sacrificing narrative coherence or requiring elaborate structural devices.

However, this approach does introduce more distance between readers and action than present-tense narration. The implicit knowledge that the protagonist survived to tell the tale can reduce tension in life-threatening scenarios, requiring careful crafting to maintain suspense despite this inherent safety net. The retrospective quality can also dilute immediate emotional impact, trading raw feeling for processed understanding in ways that may not serve all narrative purposes equally well.

Third Person POV

Third-person narration introduces a mediating consciousness between reader and character, creating both greater flexibility and potential distance in the telling. This approach allows novelists to control precisely how much access readers have to characters' inner lives, from deeply intimate knowledge of thoughts and feelings to purely external observation of speech and action. The spectrum of possibilities within this perspective makes it perhaps the most versatile approach to narrative viewpoint.

Third Person Limited (Past or Present)

This approach combines the intimacy of first-person perspective with the flexibility of third-person narration by focusing closely on one character's viewpoint while maintaining the slight distance created by third-person pronouns. Readers experience events through a specific character's perceptual and psychological filters, but with the subtle mediating presence of a narrative consciousness distinct from the character.

This perspective proves particularly effective for character-driven narratives, where deep exploration of one person's development drives reader engagement. The close alignment with a specific consciousness creates investment in that character's journey, while the slight distance allows for nuances of characterization that might feel unnaturally self-aware in first-person narration. When the narrator observes that “Emma felt a surprising twinge of jealousy, though she would have denied it fiercely if asked,” this reveals aspects of character the protagonist herself might not fully acknowledge.

Genre fiction frequently employs this approach across categories from romance to thriller to fantasy, taking advantage of its balance between immersive character experience and narrative flexibility. The ability to follow one character deeply while occasionally shifting to others between chapters or sections allows for multi-faceted storytelling without sacrificing the emotional connection that drives reader engagement.

Complex plots requiring focus benefit from this perspective's ability to manage information revelation precisely. By limiting knowledge to what the viewpoint character could plausibly know while occasionally shifting perspectives, novelists can control exactly what readers learn and when, creating optimal conditions for mystery, suspense, or dramatic irony as the narrative requires.

The advantages of this approach are substantial. It combines the emotional intimacy of close character alignment with greater flexibility than first-person narration allows. Readers experience a character's thoughts, feelings, and perceptions almost as directly as in first person, but without the absolute restriction to that character's knowledge and awareness.

Deep character development flows naturally from this perspective, as the slight narrative distance allows for observations about the viewpoint character that they might not make about themselves. This creates opportunities for subtle characterization through the disconnect between self-perception and reality, revealing blind spots and defense mechanisms that characters themselves might not recognize.

Perhaps most significantly, this approach allows for viewpoint shifts between chapters or sections, creating the possibility of multi-perspective narratives without the disorientation that can accompany rapid viewpoint changes. By establishing clear boundaries for perspective shifts, novelists can explore multiple characters' experiences while maintaining the depth of engagement that comes from sustained immersion in a single consciousness.

However, limitations remain. The restriction to the chosen character's knowledge within scenes or chapters requires careful planning to ensure readers access essential information at appropriate moments. Novelists must consider what each viewpoint character could plausibly observe or deduce, structuring scenes to allow natural discovery of necessary plot elements.

Perspective shifts require particularly careful handling to prevent confusion or disengagement. Clear signaling of viewpoint changes, typically through chapter or section breaks, helps readers adjust to new perceptual filters without experiencing narrative whiplash. Maintaining distinct character voices and thought patterns for each perspective further supports smooth transitions between viewpoints.

Third Person Omniscient

The most expansive narrative perspective available to novelists, third-person omniscient introduces an all-knowing narrator who can access any character's thoughts, move freely between perspectives, reveal information unknown to any character, and even address readers directly. This godlike perspective creates maximum flexibility while potentially sacrificing the immediate emotional connection that comes from sustained immersion in a single consciousness.

Epic narratives with sweeping scope often employ this approach, using its flexibility to encompass vast timeframes, geographic expanses, or complex social systems. The Thomas Harris novels in the Hannibal Lecter series, particularly "Red Dragon," "The Silence of the Lambs," and "Hannibal," use omniscient narration to examine both intimate psychological experiences and broader criminal investigations, moving fluidly between the perspectives of investigators, victims, and the sophisticated serial killer himself. Mario Puzo's "The Godfather" similarly employs omniscient narration to capture the complex web of family dynamics, criminal enterprises, and societal contexts that shape the Corleone saga.

Stories involving multiple storylines find natural expression through this perspective, as the narrator can follow different characters pursuing separate objectives, revealing connections and contrasts invisible to the characters themselves. This bird's-eye view allows readers to perceive pattern and meaning across seemingly disparate narrative threads, creating satisfying moments of convergence when these strands ultimately intertwine.

Complex world-building benefits particularly from omniscient narration, as it allows direct communication of contextual information about history, culture, or physical environment without filtering it through character knowledge. This efficiency proves valuable in speculative fiction, where readers must quickly assimilate unfamiliar rules, systems, or settings to engage fully with the narrative.

The advantages of this approach center on its unparalleled flexibility. The omniscient narrator can reveal any information, explore any perspective, and make connections across vast narrative distances without the constraints that characterize more limited viewpoints. This freedom creates opportunities for sophisticated literary techniques from dramatic irony to thematic commentary to structural experimentation.

The ability to reveal multiple characters' thoughts—even within a single scene—allows for complex interpersonal dynamics unavailable to more restricted perspectives. When a narrator reveals that "James believed Sarah was angry about the promotion, while Sarah was actually concerned about his recent weight loss," this simple access to both characters' perceptions creates rich dramatic tension from misunderstanding.

For intricate plots with multiple moving pieces, omniscient narration proves particularly valuable, allowing readers to track developments across different locations or storylines simultaneously. This comprehensive awareness prevents confusion while creating opportunities for satisfying convergence when separate narrative threads ultimately intersect.

However, significant limitations counterbalance these advantages. The potential for emotional distance represents perhaps the greatest challenge of omniscient narration. Without sustained immersion in a single consciousness, readers may struggle to form the deep character attachments that drive emotional investment in many narratives. This distance requires deliberate countermeasures, such as moments of intensified character focus or particularly affecting character situations.

Maintaining reader engagement across perspective shifts demands considerable skill, particularly when moving between characters of varying interest or appeal. Without careful handling, readers may become invested in one narrative thread while viewing others as unwelcome interruptions, creating uneven engagement across the broader story.

Perhaps most significantly, the flexibility of omniscient narration creates constant risk of "head-hopping"—jarring, unpredictable shifts between character perspectives that disrupt reader immersion and create confusion about whose perceptions are being presented. Skilled omniscient narration typically signals perspective shifts clearly, maintaining consistent narrative distance within scenes and using paragraph breaks or other structural elements to indicate changes in perceptual focus.

POV Selection Guidelines

Selecting the optimal perspective for your novel requires thoughtful consideration of genre conventions, structural requirements, and character development needs. While no absolute rules govern these choices, understanding the typical patterns in your narrative category and the specific demands of your story will guide you toward the most effective approach.

Genre Considerations

Genre conventions, while not binding, provide useful guidance for POV selection based on reader expectations and narrative traditions. Thrillers and horror frequently employ first-person present or third-person limited perspectives to create maximal tension and uncertainty. The claustrophobic restriction to a protagonist's real-time perceptions heightens suspense, particularly when that character's understanding or reliability might be compromised. Gillian Flynn's "Gone Girl" alternates between two first-person narrators, creating shocking reversals when their deceptions are revealed. Similarly, Stephen King's "Pet Sematary" uses third-person limited perspective to gradually unveil supernatural horror through the increasingly desperate perceptions of its protagonist, allowing readers to experience the unfolding dread alongside the character.

Fantasy and science fiction narratives frequently utilize third-person limited or omniscient approaches to accommodate complex world-building and multiple storylines. The flexibility to provide direct contextual information about unfamiliar settings, systems, or histories proves particularly valuable in speculative genres, where readers must quickly assimilate new rules and realities. The ability to follow multiple characters through different aspects of an invented world allows for comprehensive exploration of complex fictional realities.

Literary fiction embraces the full spectrum of POV options, selecting viewpoint based on specific story needs rather than conventional patterns. From the multiple first-person perspectives in "House of Sand and Fog" by Andre Dubus III to the complex POV structure of "No Country for Old Men" by Cormac McCarthy, which combines third-person perspectives with first-person monologues, literary works choose POV based on thematic concerns, character psychology, or experimental purposes rather than genre expectations. This flexibility allows literary authors to select precisely the narrative distance that best serves their artistic intentions.

Romance typically employs either third-person limited (often alternating between both partners' perspectives) or first-person narration to create deep emotional investment in the central relationship. The ability to reveal both characters' feelings, misunderstandings, and attraction creates the tension of dramatic irony—readers recognize the potential for connection before the characters themselves, creating satisfying anticipation for eventual romantic resolution.

Story Structure Impact

The structural implications of POV selection must be considered during the outlining process, as viewpoint choices fundamentally shape how information can be revealed and how tension can be created. Multiple POVs require particularly careful planning, as novelists must determine not only what happens but who experiences (and thus narrates) each significant event. This decision affects everything from emotional impact to information control to pacing.

POV switches typically occur at chapter breaks or clearly marked section divisions, creating clean transitions between perspectives rather than the disorienting shifts that can accompany mid-scene viewpoint changes. This structural approach requires deliberate planning of chapter boundaries based not just on content but on optimal perspective for each narrative segment. When outlining, consider not only the events of each chapter but the most effective perceptual filter through which readers should experience those events.

The revelation of information must be planned based on POV limitations, particularly in mysteries or narratives where controlled disclosure drives engagement. Consider not only what readers need to know but how they will learn it given your chosen perspective. If essential information lies outside your protagonist's plausible knowledge, you'll need to create organic opportunities for discovery—a conversation overheard, a document discovered, a confession received—or consider whether a different viewpoint might better serve that narrative moment.

Subplot reveals must similarly be structured around POV access, particularly when dealing with narrative threads that do not directly involve your viewpoint character. If your protagonist cannot plausibly witness or learn about these developments, you may need additional viewpoint characters, narrative devices like letters or news reports, or restructuring to bring these elements within your protagonist's perceptual reach. Alternatively, you might embrace dramatic irony by allowing readers knowledge your protagonist lacks, creating tension through this asymmetrical awareness.

Character Development Considerations

The degree of internal access your story requires should significantly influence POV selection. Narratives centered on psychological transformation, emotional processing, or internal conflict naturally gravitate toward more intimate perspectives that allow direct access to character thoughts and feelings. Conversely, stories focusing primarily on action, plot twists, or external challenges might benefit from the greater flexibility and potential suspense created by more distanced viewpoints.

Consider which perspective best serves your protagonist's particular character arc. A journey of self-discovery might benefit from first-person narration, where readers experience revelations simultaneous with the character, as in "American Psycho" or "Fight Club." A story about a character with significant blind spots might be better served by third-person limited, allowing subtle indications of the gap between self-perception and reality, as in "The Talented Mr. Ripley" by Patricia Highsmith. A narrative about societal transformation might require the broader scope of omniscient narration to connect individual experiences to larger patterns of change, as Mario Puzo demonstrates in "The Godfather."

Stories requiring multiple character perspectives demand particular attention to POV selection. If understanding various characters' motivations, perceptions, and experiences proves essential to your narrative, you'll need either omniscient narration or a carefully structured approach to multiple limited viewpoints. Consider not only which characters deserve viewpoint status but how these different perspectives will complement each other, revealing different aspects of your story's central concerns.

The delivery of thematic content should similarly influence POV selection. If your novel explores the gap between appearance and reality, an unreliable first-person narrator might perfectly embody this theme through the disconnect between their narration and the truth readers gradually discern. If examining the interconnectedness of seemingly disparate lives, omniscient narration might allow the essential bird's-eye view of these connections. Consider how your chosen perspective might itself become a thematic element, reinforcing your novel's central concerns through its very structure.

Epistolary Novels

An additional POV option worth exploring is the epistolary form—novels composed entirely of documents such as letters, diary entries, newspaper clippings, transcripts, emails, or other documentary materials. This approach, with roots stretching back centuries, creates a unique relationship between reader and narrative by presenting the story as a collection of found texts rather than a traditional narrative.

The epistolary format creates an immediate sense of authenticity by mimicking real-world documents. When Mary Shelley's "Frankenstein" unfolds through Captain Walton's letters to his sister, which then contain Victor Frankenstein's narrative (itself containing the monster's account), readers experience the story as discovered rather than told. This layering of accounts creates a sense of historical veracity while allowing multiple perspectives on central events.

Bram Stoker's "Dracula" represents perhaps the most famous example of this approach, combining journal entries, letters, newspaper clippings, and phonograph recordings to create its vampire narrative. This documentary approach allows Stoker to present multiple perspectives on Count Dracula while maintaining the plausibility of each character's limited knowledge. The format naturally creates dramatic irony as readers piece together connections between separate accounts that the characters themselves cannot yet perceive.

The epistolary format offers distinct advantages, particularly for certain narrative types. The documentary presentation creates an inherent distance between events and their telling, allowing for the gradual revelation of information through incomplete or sequential documents. This structure naturally builds suspense as readers must actively assemble meaning from discrete texts, participating more actively in the construction of the narrative than in more conventional forms.

The format also allows for natural polyvocality—multiple distinct voices within a single narrative. Each letter writer or diarist can maintain their unique perspective, vocabulary, and sensibility, creating a chorus of viewpoints without the potential confusion of rapidly shifting third-person perspectives. This multiplicity proves particularly valuable for stories exploring how different characters perceive the same events or entities, as in “Dracula,” where each character perceives the vampire through their own psychological and cultural filters.

For contemporary novelists, the epistolary format has expanded to include modern communications—emails, text messages, social media posts, blog entries, audio or video transcripts, and digital records. This evolution maintains the documentary verisimilitude while reflecting current communication modes. Gillian Flynn's “Sharp Objects” incorporates elements of this approach through the protagonist's journal entries and notes, creating additional layers of revelation and concealment.

When considering this approach, remain aware of its particular challenges. The format inherently creates some distance from immediate action, as events must occur before they can be documented. This can reduce tension in life-threatening scenarios unless carefully managed through techniques like interrupted documents or real-time recordings. The plausibility of document creation and preservation also requires attention—why would characters write these texts, and how have they been preserved and assembled?

Despite these challenges, the epistolary format offers unique opportunities for novels concerned with the nature of truth, the reliability of perception, or the process of investigation and discovery. By structuring your narrative as documentary evidence rather than conventional storytelling, you invite readers into a more active interpretive relationship with your text, assembling meaning from fragments just as they might with real-world historical documents.

Conclusion

The selection of point of view represents far more than a technical decision about pronouns or tense. It establishes the fundamental relationship between reader and story, determining how directly readers experience events, how much they know and when they know it, and how closely they align with character consciousness. This choice influences every aspect of your novel from word choice to structure to thematic development.

While no perspective offers a perfect solution for all narrative needs, understanding the specific advantages and limitations of each approach allows you to select the viewpoint that best serves your particular story. Consider not only genre conventions and reader expectations but the specific emotional experience you wish to create, the information control your narrative requires, and the depth of character access that best supports your story's central concerns.

Remember that the most effective POV often feels inevitable in retrospect—so perfectly suited to the story that readers cannot imagine it told any other way. By thoughtfully aligning viewpoint with narrative purpose, you create this sense of perfect fit, this invisible rightness that allows readers to fall completely into your fictional world without the distraction of inappropriate narrative distance.

Ultimately, POV selection exemplifies the balance between conscious craft and intuitive artistry that characterizes all aspects of the novelist's work. Understand the options technically, consider the implications thoughtfully, then listen to your story's own inclinations—that quiet inner knowledge of how this particular tale wishes to be told. In the alignment between technical understanding and creative intuition, you'll discover the perfect lens through which your unique story can best be perceived.

CHAPTER 15

THE MOST IMPORTANT CRAFT ELEMENTS

Show, Don't Tell

When we speak of showing rather than telling in fiction, we're addressing one of the most fundamental transformations in a writer's journey. The difference between these approaches is the difference between summary and experience, between being informed and being immersed. To show is to create a direct sensory experience for your reader, allowing them to inhabit the world you've created rather than merely being told about it.

Engaging the senses forms the foundation of this craft element. Consider how reality flows into our consciousness—not as abstract concepts, but as a symphony of sensations. The bitter tang of coffee on the tongue, the whisper of leaves in a summer breeze, the cool smoothness of polished marble beneath fingertips. When you invite your readers to experience these sensations alongside your characters, you bridge the gap between their world and yours.

Specific details serve as the building blocks of showing. Rather than declaring a room "messy," reveal the empty coffee mugs collecting rings on the wooden table, the books splayed open and spine-up on the floor, the tangle of charging cables snaking across the carpet. Specificity creates authenticity, and authenticity breeds trust between writer and reader.

Actions reveal character more powerfully than any declaration ever could. Instead of telling readers that Thomas is dishonest, show him pocketing the extra change when the cashier makes a mistake, or maintaining two different stories about where he was last night. Through such actions, readers become active participants in the storytelling process, piecing together who your characters truly are based on what they do, not what you say about them.

This active partnership with your reader represents the ultimate triumph of showing—it allows readers to draw their own conclusions. When readers assemble meaning themselves, they become invested in your story in ways that straightforward telling could never achieve. The interpretive act becomes personal, and the story becomes theirs as much as yours.

Consider these transformations:

When you tell: “She was angry,” you place a simple label on a complex emotional state, keeping readers at a distance.

When you show: “Her fingers whitened around the coffee cup, her voice dropping to a whisper that somehow filled the entire room,” you invite readers to recognize the anger themselves, to feel its tension in their own bodies, to become participants rather than merely observers.

Mastering the art of showing requires patience and practice. It often demands more words than telling, asks more of both writer and reader, and sometimes feels counterintuitive to writers accustomed to efficiency. Yet this investment yields immeasurable returns in the depth and resonance of your fiction. The extra sentence or paragraph devoted to showing creates an experience that lingers in the reader's mind long after the more efficient telling would have faded.

Metaphor and Simile

At their essence, metaphors and similes represent language's most profound magic—the ability to transform one thing into another through the alchemy of comparison. These devices stretch beyond mere decoration to become instruments of perception, allowing readers to understand the unfamiliar through the lens of the familiar, to grasp the abstract through the concrete.

Understanding Metaphors and Similes

A simile creates a bridge between two unlike entities using the connecting words “like” or “as.” This explicit comparison maintains the separate identity of both elements while illuminating aspects of one through the qualities of the other. When Emily Dickinson writes that “Hope is the thing with feathers that perches in the soul,” she doesn't literally transform hope into a bird, but invites us to consider how hope might share qualities with our feathered companions—its lightness, its ability to rise above circumstances, its fragile yet persistent nature.

Metaphors perform a more radical transformation. They declare that one thing IS another, creating an equation that temporarily fuses two separate realities. When Shakespeare's Romeo declares "Juliet is the sun," he isn't merely suggesting a similarity—he's momentarily transforming his beloved into the celestial body around which his world revolves. This direct equation creates an immediate, visceral understanding that bypasses logical analysis and speaks directly to our intuitive comprehension.

Examples in Action

Consider how the abstract concept of tiredness transforms through the lens of these figurative devices:

The plain statement "She was tired" conveys information but fails to transmit experience.

Through simile, this state expands: "She was like a phone running on 1% battery," immediately conveying not just fatigue but the anxiety of imminent shutdown. "Her energy drained away as slowly as honey from a jar," suggests both the viscosity of her movements and the sweetness of potential rest. "She moved through the day like a sleepwalker," hints at a disconnection between consciousness and action. "Her mind felt as foggy as a coastal morning," transforms her mental state into a landscape the reader can visualize and perhaps recognize from their own experience.

Metaphor performs even more dramatic transformations: "She was a dead battery" creates an immediate equation between person and object, suggesting complete depletion. "Her energy was quicksand, pulling her down" introduces not just fatigue but the struggle against it. "She was a candle burning at both ends" invokes Edna St. Vincent Millay's famous line, suggesting not just tiredness but the self-destructive brilliance that often accompanies it. "Her mind was a computer in sleep mode" suggests both the conservation of resources and the potential for reawakening.

Similarly, the simple emotion of anger becomes multidimensional through these devices:

In simile form: "His rage built like a pressure cooker," suggests both containment and the danger of eventual explosion. "He exploded like a firecracker," captures the suddenness and spectacle of an angry outburst. "His words stung like wasps," transforms language into physical attack. "His face reddened as bright as a stop light," creates both visual imagery and suggests the implicit warning in his expression.

As metaphors: "He was a volcano ready to erupt" equates the man with a force of nature, suggesting both power and inevitability. "His words were daggers" transforms language into weapons that can pierce and wound. "He was a storm brewing" suggests both gathering intensity and the atmospheric change that accompanies profound anger. "His temper was a ticking bomb" introduces the element of time and inevitable destruction.

Advanced Usage

The true power of these devices emerges when developed beyond single comparisons into extended figurative landscapes that readers can inhabit.

An extended metaphor creates a sustained transformation that develops over several lines or even throughout an entire work: "His mind was a garden left untended. Weeds of worry had overtaken the flower beds of rational thought. The fence of logic had fallen into disrepair, letting wild anxieties roam freely. Only in sleep did the gentle rain of peace bring any relief to this overgrown landscape." Here, the initial metaphor of the garden becomes a complete world with its own internal logic, allowing complex emotional and psychological states to be explored through tangible imagery.

Extended similes perform similar work while maintaining the explicit comparison: "His thoughts raced like a hamster in its wheel, spinning endlessly through the night, generating lots of motion but getting nowhere, the constant movement becoming its own kind of stillness as dawn approached." The initial comparison expands into a complete scenario that illuminates not just the quality of the thoughts but their futility and the exhaustion they produce.

Tips for Effective Use

For metaphors and similes to resonate authentically, they should emerge organically from your character's consciousness and experience. A sailor will naturally think in terms of tides and currents, storms and calms; her metaphors should reflect this maritime perspective. A baker's comparisons might reference the transformation of ingredients under heat, the patience of waiting for dough to rise, the precision of measurements. A child's figurative language should reflect their more limited but often more magical worldview, perhaps comparing adults to giants or emotions to simple physical sensations.

Freshness proves essential in figurative language. The most effective comparisons create a spark of recognition and surprise in readers—the simultaneous reactions of "I've never thought of it that way" and "But of course, that's exactly how it is." When Cormac McCarthy describes the sky in "The Road" as "like the onset of some cold glaucoma dimming away the world," he creates an image both surprising and immediately recognizable, transforming an atmospheric condition into a visceral sensation of loss and gradual blindness that perfectly captures the novel's post-apocalyptic landscape.

Consistency within extended figurative passages creates coherence. If you begin with a gardening metaphor for emotional states, continue developing it with related imagery—pruning for self-discipline, blossoming for joy, withering for disappointment. This creates a complete figurative ecosystem that readers can navigate intuitively.

Perhaps most importantly, allow your metaphors and similes to arise naturally from your unconscious mind rather than being consciously manufactured. Our deepest minds constantly create connections between disparate elements; the most powerful figurative language often emerges when we trust these connections rather than forcing them. When drafting, let unexpected comparisons surface; during revision, refine them to their most essential and resonant form.

Description and Setting

The worlds we create in fiction exist first as sensory experiences, and it is through the careful orchestration of these sensations that our settings become places readers can truly inhabit. Effective description operates not as decoration but as revelation—each detail carefully selected to illuminate character, advance plot, establish mood, or develop theme.

Sensory Details

The rich tapestry of setting emerges through the full spectrum of sensory experience. Vision typically dominates our descriptions—the slant of light through venetian blinds, the faded blue of a childhood bedroom, the crimson splash of sunrise against mountain snow. Yet limiting ourselves to the visual diminishes the immersive potential of our settings.

Sound creates both atmosphere and intimacy—the distant wail of sirens suggesting urban danger, the rhythmic breathing of a sleeping lover conveying vulnerability and trust, the persistent drip of a faucet building tension through repetition. Smell offers perhaps the most direct connection to emotion and memory—the antiseptic sharpness of hospitals immediately conveying institutional sterility, the lingering scent of a departed parent's perfume evoking both presence and absence simultaneously.

Touch grounds readers in the physical reality of your world—the rough grain of weathered wood, the unexpected coolness of metal against skin, the clinging dampness of clothes in humid summer heat. Even taste, though used more sparingly, can create powerful connections—the metallic tang of fear, the bitterness of disappointment, the unexpected sweetness of a moment of grace.

Environmental Elements

Beyond immediate sensory input, settings exist within larger contexts that shape their meaning and impact. The physical space itself—whether expansive or confining, ordered or chaotic, natural or constructed—influences how characters move, interact, and feel within it. A character will behave differently in a cathedral's soaring space than in a cramped elevator, not just because of social conventions but because of how these spaces make them feel physically and emotionally.

Time creates another crucial dimension—not just the historical period with its technologies, social norms, and aesthetic qualities, but the time of day, the season, the era in a character's life or a society's development. A street corner appears profoundly different at noon than at midnight, in summer than in winter, in childhood than in adulthood, in times of peace than in times of conflict.

Weather serves as both literal atmosphere and emotional barometer. The relentless beat of summer sun can represent oppression or vitality; gathering storm clouds might signal impending conflict or necessary cleansing; gentle snow might suggest either peaceful silence or dangerous isolation. These meteorological conditions interact with character psychology in complex ways—sometimes reflecting internal states, sometimes contrasting with them for ironic effect.

The cultural context provides essential grounding for how characters interact with their environment. Religious beliefs, social hierarchies, economic systems, technological developments—all these elements determine what characters notice, how they interpret what they experience, what feels comfortable or foreign, safe or threatening. A character from a hunter-gatherer society will perceive a forest fundamentally differently than a character from modern urban America, noticing different details and assigning different meanings to what they observe.

All these elements combine to create not just a physical location but an emotional atmosphere—the ineffable mood that colors how readers experience your fictional world. This atmosphere might be one of nostalgic longing, simmering tension, dreamlike unreality, or countless other emotional textures that influence how readers interpret events and characters.

Pacing

The rhythm of storytelling—when to sprint, when to stroll, when to pause for contemplation—represents one of the novelist's most subtle and powerful tools. Pacing creates the temporal experience of your narrative, controlling not just how quickly events unfold but how readers emotionally process these events.

Control Through Structure

At the most granular level, sentence structure directly affects perceived time. Short, simple sentences accelerate experience: "Glass shattered. Footsteps pounded. Sarah ran." This telegraphic style creates immediacy and urgency, mimicking the fragmented awareness of high-stress situations. Conversely, complex sentences with multiple clauses, rich with qualifying phrases and sensory details, decelerate experience: "The afternoon light filtered through the dusty windowpane, casting long shadows across the faded carpet where Sarah's grandmother had once taught her to knit, creating a momentary illusion that the old woman's gentle hands might still be guiding the needles through yarn the color of forgotten summers."

Paragraph structure similarly modulates rhythm. Short paragraphs increase tempo, creating white space on the page that pulls readers forward. The single-sentence paragraph, used judiciously, can create a moment of startling impact. Longer paragraphs slow the reader's progress, encouraging deeper immersion in a moment, a memory, or a complex emotional state.

Scene length provides another layer of temporal control. Brief scenes—especially when juxtaposed in montage-like sequence—suggest acceleration and fragmentation, the breathless rush of events outpacing characters' ability to process them. Extended scenes allow for deeper exploration of character dynamics, complex emotions, or pivotal moments where every nuance matters.

Chapter breaks represent perhaps the most powerful pacing tool, creating natural pauses in the reading experience. Ending chapters at moments of revelation or danger encourages readers to continue immediately, while concluding at moments of resolution provides natural stopping points. The rhythm created by alternating between these approaches guides the overall arc of reader engagement.

Narrative distance—how closely we inhabit a character's consciousness—also affects perceived time. Deep immersion in a character's sensory and emotional experience typically slows pace, as readers process not just events but their psychological impact. Greater narrative distance, where events are summarized rather than experienced directly, accelerates time, allowing months or years to pass in a few paragraphs.

The masterful novelist orchestrates these elements like a composer, creating symphonic movements of acceleration and deceleration that guide readers through the emotional landscape of the story. Moments of crisis demand acceleration; moments of significance require deceleration. The contrast between these rhythms creates the dynamic tension that keeps readers engaged through hundreds of pages.

Tension and Conflict

At the heart of every compelling narrative lies conflict—the gap between desire and fulfillment, intention and outcome, expectation and reality. Without this essential friction, stories lack the energy that propels both characters and readers forward. Understanding the various forms conflict can take allows writers to create multidimensional tension that operates on multiple levels simultaneously.

External Conflict

The most visible conflicts occur between characters and forces outside themselves. Character versus character conflicts create the interpersonal dynamics that drive much of fiction—the clash of incompatible desires, competing values, or mutual misunderstanding. These conflicts reveal character through action and reaction, showing who people truly are when their needs collide with others'.

Character versus nature conflicts place humans against indifferent natural forces—storms, wilderness, disease, predators. These struggles often strip characters to their essential qualities, revealing what remains when social masks fall away. Such conflicts can function both literally and metaphorically, with natural obstacles representing internal or societal challenges.

Character versus society conflicts position individuals against cultural norms, institutional powers, or collective prejudices. These conflicts illuminate both individual courage and the powerful influence of social systems, exploring how people navigate, challenge, or succumb to the prevailing winds of their time and place. From Hester Prynne to Winston Smith, characters defined by their resistance to societal pressure reveal both the cost of nonconformity and its potential necessity.

In our contemporary world, character versus technology conflicts have emerged as particularly relevant. These struggles explore humanity's relationship with our own creations—how tools designed to serve human needs may transform, constrain, or even threaten those who created them. Such conflicts probe essential questions about what remains distinctly human in a world increasingly mediated by algorithms and interfaces.

Internal Conflict

Beneath these visible struggles lie the internal conflicts that often prove even more compelling. Moral dilemmas force characters to choose between competing values, revealing their true priorities when no perfect solution exists. The commander who must sacrifice some to save many, the friend who must decide between honesty and kindness, the citizen who weighs personal safety against collective justice—all these characters reveal themselves through impossible choices.

Personal fears create another dimension of internal conflict, as characters struggle against their own psychological limitations. The socially anxious character forced into public speaking, the acrophobic forced to scale heights to save another, the intimacy-avoidant gradually falling in love—these internal battles create compelling arcs of growth or tragic resistance to necessary change.

Competing desires create perhaps the most relatable internal conflicts. Characters rarely want just one thing; they want many things that may prove incompatible. Career advancement may conflict with family time; romantic passion may undermine long-term stability; artistic integrity may threaten financial security. These crossed purposes within a single character create realistic complexity and force meaningful choices that reveal true priorities.

Past trauma often generates ongoing internal conflict, as characters struggle between the protective adaptations developed in response to harm and the new possibilities that might require vulnerability. The hypervigilant survivor who cannot relax into intimacy, the abandoned child now resistant to forming attachments, the once-betrayed partner unable to trust again—these characters navigate the territory between self-protection and self-limitation.

The most compelling narratives often layer these conflicts, creating multidimensional tension that operates simultaneously across external and internal planes. A character facing external opposition must also overcome internal resistance; social barriers are mirrored by psychological ones; the natural world presents obstacles that reflect internal challenges. This layering creates the rich, complex experience that distinguishes truly memorable fiction.

Theme Development

The thematic dimension of fiction represents its philosophical heart—the underlying inquiries into meaning, value, and truth that transform entertainment into art. Yet the most powerful themes emerge organically through narrative elements rather than being imposed as didactic messages. Theme development requires a delicate balance between intentionality and discovery, between guiding readers toward significant questions and allowing them space for personal interpretation.

Through Narrative Elements

Character choices serve as the most natural vehicle for thematic exploration. When characters face meaningful decisions that reveal their values, readers naturally consider what they themselves might choose in similar circumstances. A character who sacrifices security for integrity implicitly raises questions about the relative worth of these values; a character who chooses vengeance over forgiveness invites readers to consider the true cost of both paths. Through these choices, themes emerge as lived questions rather than abstract propositions.

Plot events create consequences that illuminate thematic concerns. A seeming triumph that leads to unexpected loss, a terrible mistake that yields surprising grace, an act of kindness that ripples outward in unforeseen ways—these narrative developments naturally prompt reflection on causality, justice, redemption, and the pattern of human experience. The structure of events itself suggests meaning without stating it directly.

Symbolism offers perhaps the most subtle vehicle for thematic development. Objects, settings, weather, colors, recurring motifs—all can accumulate significance beyond their literal presence in the narrative. The persistent image of divided spaces in a story about cultural identity, the repeated motif of birds in a narrative about freedom, the gradual transformation of a landscape paralleling a character's internal journey—these symbolic elements speak to the unconscious mind, creating resonance beyond rational understanding.

Dialogue allows different perspectives on thematic questions to engage with one another directly. Characters may articulate opposing viewpoints, challenge each other's assumptions, or voice the very questions readers are considering. This dialectical approach prevents thematic exploration from becoming monological, acknowledging the complexity of significant human questions by presenting multiple valid perspectives.

Setting itself can embody thematic concerns. A border town becomes more than a location in a story exploring boundaries and crossing points; a decaying mansion speaks to faded glory and the weight of history; a spacecraft represents humanity's technological ambition and existential isolation. Physical spaces become externalizations of conceptual territories, allowing abstract ideas to take tangible form.

Integration

For themes to resonate authentically, they must emerge naturally from the story itself rather than being imposed upon it. Characters should act according to their own internal logic rather than serving as mouthpieces for authorial positions. Events should unfold according to the established rules of the fictional world rather than being manipulated to prove a point. When narrative integrity is sacrificed for thematic clarity, both typically suffer.

The most effective thematic development avoids preaching or explicit moralization. Readers resist being told what to think but engage deeply with stories that invite them to think for themselves. The question raised but not answered, the moral complexity presented without resolution, the legitimate perspective that challenges our assumptions—these create the conditions for genuine reflection rather than passive reception of conclusions.

Presenting multiple perspectives on significant questions acknowledges the complexity of human experience. Few important thematic concerns—justice, love, identity, freedom, connection, meaning—admit simple answers. By embodying different approaches to these questions in different characters, the novelist creates a conversation rather than a lecture, honoring readers' intelligence and life experience.

Ultimately, effective thematic development trusts readers to draw their own conclusions from the experiences presented. By creating rich, multidimensional scenarios that illuminate important questions from multiple angles, novelists invite readers into active participation in meaning-making rather than passive consumption of messages. This partnership between writer and reader creates the lasting resonance that distinguishes fiction that matters.

Voice and Style

The quality most resistant to formula yet most essential to distinctive fiction is the ineffable element we call voice—that unique literary fingerprint that makes a writer's work immediately recognizable. Voice emerges from the intersection of countless choices, creating a singular perspective through which readers experience the fictional world.

Elements of Voice

Word choice—from vocabulary level to connotative resonance, from specialized terminology to dialectal variations—creates the basic palette from which voice is painted. A writer who favors Anglo-Saxon monosyllables creates a different textural experience than one who employs polysyllabic Latinate terms; a voice rich in technical jargon suggests a different consciousness than one steeped in sensory language. These lexical preferences create both intellectual and emotional textures in prose.

Sentence structure shapes the rhythm of thought itself. Writers who favor short, declarative sentences create a different cognitive experience than those who construct elaborate syntactical architectures with multiple subordinate clauses. Some voices proceed with logical linearity; others circle associatively around their subjects. Some maintain consistent structures; others deliberately vary patterns for emphasis or surprise. These syntactical choices create the underlying architecture of voice.

Rhythm and flow emerge from the interplay of these elements—the alternation between long and short, the strategic placement of emphasis, the musicality of language as it moves through time. Some voices proceed with metronomic regularity; others syncopate unexpectedly. Some create gentle undulations; others jagged peaks and valleys. This rhythmic signature becomes as distinctive as a human fingerprint.

Tone represents the emotional coloration of voice—the attitude toward subject matter revealed through linguistic choices. A voice might be predominantly ironic, earnest, melancholic, exuberant, contemplative, sardonic, or any combination of these qualities. This tonal quality creates the feeling of a specific consciousness mediating between reader and fictional world.

Perspective encompasses not just the technical viewpoint (first person, close third, omniscient) but the specific angle of vision on events. The same scene viewed through the consciousness of a child, a cynic, a romantic, or a pragmatist becomes essentially different based on what details are noticed, what significance is assigned, what connections are made. This perspectival quality creates the sense of a particular mind making meaning of experience.

Development of Voice

The development of distinctive voice requires both conscious craft and unconscious emergence. Reading extensively across genres, styles, and eras exposes writers to the full range of possibilities in literary voice, creating an internal library of approaches that can be drawn upon, combined, and transformed. This literary metabolism builds the raw materials from which unique voice emerges.

Writing regularly allows voice to develop through practice, as self-consciousness gradually gives way to authentic expression. Early work often shows the visible influence of admired writers; with persistence, these influences become integrated rather than imitative, contributing to a new synthesis rather than remaining borrowed elements.

Experimentation proves essential to discovering one's natural voice. Trying different approaches—formal and informal, ornate and spare, distanced and intimate—helps writers identify what feels most authentic and effective for their particular sensibility and subject matter. This process of elimination gradually reveals the voice that feels simultaneously most natural and most powerful.

Trusting one's instincts becomes increasingly important as voice develops. The subconscious mind often recognizes the right word, rhythm, or structure before the conscious mind can articulate why it works. This intuitive element explains why voice remains somewhat mysterious even to those who have developed distinctive literary identities.

Perhaps most importantly, allowing the subconscious mind to guide stylistic choices leads to the deepest authenticity in voice. Our unconscious processes contain our true patterns of perception, association, and valuation—the unique ways we make meaning of experience. When we grant this deeper mind authority in our writing, voice emerges not as something constructed but as something revealed—the literary embodiment of our essential way of being in the world.

Integration

The craft elements explored in this chapter do not exist in isolation but work together in complex synergy. Showing illuminates character through sensory detail; metaphor creates fresh ways of showing; pacing controls emotional impact; setting embodies theme; conflict reveals character; voice unifies all elements through a consistent perspective.

In practice, writers typically focus on different elements at different stages of the writing process. First drafts might emphasize plot and character development, with later revisions addressing pacing, thematic coherence, and stylistic refinement. This sequential attention allows for depth in each dimension without overwhelming the writer's conscious capacity.

Ultimately, the subconscious mind becomes the true integrator of these elements. With sufficient practice and immersion in the craft, writers develop an intuitive sense of how these different aspects of fiction work together. The conscious mind may focus on plot structure while the subconscious mind simultaneously adjusts voice, develops symbols, and deepens characterization.

The most effective approach combines deliberate craft with intuitive development. Practice each element intentionally until it becomes second nature; read widely to internalize how other writers integrate these elements; trust your deeper mind to synthesize these learnings into organic whole cloth. With time and persistence, these craft elements transform from external techniques into internal capacities—not tools you use but lenses through which you naturally perceive and create fictional worlds.

Remember always that craft serves story, not the reverse. These elements exist not as checkboxes to mark or rules to follow but as capacities to develop in service of the tales that only you can tell. The subconscious novelist ultimately integrates craft not through intellectual mastery but through embodied practice—through telling stories so consistently and attentively that the artificial boundary between technique and intuition gradually dissolves.

Recommended Novels

VULTURE: A NOVEL (2024)

Author: A. M. Blanco

Book Details:

- POV: First Person (from Detective Tom Vogel's perspective)
- Tense: Present tense
- Publisher: 9th House Books
- **Year of Publication: December 2024**

SUCH SMALL HANDS (2017)

Author: Andrés Barba

Book Details:

- POV: Alternating between first-person and third-person
- Tense: Present tense
- Publisher: Transit Books
- Year of Publication: April 2017

SANATORIUM (2021)

Author: Sarah Pearse

Series: Detective Elin Warner Series (Book 1)

Book Details:

- POV: Third-person limited (primarily following Detective Elin Warner)
- Tense: Present tense
- Publisher: Pamela Dorman Books/Viking (US), Transworld/Bantam Press (UK)
- Year of Publication: February 2021

MEMORY MAN (2015)

Author: David Baldacci

Series: Amos Decker Series (Book 1)

Book Details:

- POV: Third-person limited
- Tense: Past tense
- Publisher: Grand Central Publishing
- Year of Publication: April 2015

THE OUTSIDER (2018)

Author: Stephen King

Book Details:

- POV: Third-person limited
- Tense: Past tense
- Publisher: Scribner
- Year of Publication: May 2018

THE INSTITUTE (2019)

Author: Stephen King

Book Details:

- POV: Third-person limited
- Tense: Past tense
- Publisher: Scribner
- Year of Publication: September 2019

FINAL GIRLS (2017)

Author: Riley Sager

Book Details:

- POV: First-person (Quincy Carpenter)
- Tense: Past tense with present tense sections
- Publisher: Dutton

- Year of Publication: July 2017

SHARP OBJECTS (2006)

Author: Gillian Flynn

Book Details:

- POV: First-person (Camille Preaker)
- Tense: Present tense
- Publisher: Shaye Areheart Books
- Year of Publication: September 2006

THOSE ACROSS THE RIVER (2011)

Author: Christopher Buehlman

Book Details:

- POV: First-person (Frank Nichols)
- Tense: Past tense
- Publisher: Ace Books
- Year of Publication: September 2011

THE LOST VILLAGE (2021)

Author: Camilla Sten

Book Details:

- POV: First-person (Alice Lindstedt) with alternating timelines
- Tense: Present tense (main narrative) and past tense (historical sections)
- Publisher: Minotaur Books
- Year of Publication: March 2021

TENDER IS THE FLESH (2020)

Author: Agustina Bazterrica (translated by Sarah Moses)

Book Details:

- POV: Third-person limited (following Marcos)
- Tense: Present tense
- Publisher: Scribner
- Year of Publication: August 2020

Recommended Novels with Film Adaptations to Study

DELIVERANCE (1970)

- **Novel**:
  - Author: James Dickey
  - POV: First-person
  - Tense: Past tense
  - Publisher: Houghton Mifflin
  - Year of Publication: 1970
- **Film Adaptation** (1972):
  - Director: John Boorman
  - Screenwriter: James Dickey

ABSOLUTE POWER (1996)

- **Novel**:
  - Author: David Baldacci
  - POV: Third-person
  - Tense: Past tense
  - Publisher: Warner Books
  - Year of Publication: 1996
- **Film Adaptation** (1997):
  - Director: Clint Eastwood
  - Screenwriter: William Goldman

FIGHT CLUB (1996)

- **Novel**:
    - Author: Chuck Palahniuk
    - POV: First-person
    - Tense: Present tense
    - Publisher: W.W. Norton
    - Year of Publication: 1996
- **Film Adaptation** (1999):
    - Director: David Fincher
    - Screenwriter: Jim Uhls

THE EXORCIST (1971)

- **Novel**:
    - Author: William Peter Blatty
    - POV: Third-person
    - Tense: Past tense
    - Publisher: Harper & Row
    - Year of Publication: 1971
- **Film Adaptation** (1973):
    - Director: William Friedkin
    - Screenwriter: William Peter Blatty

THE GODFATHER (1969)

- **Novel**:
    - Author: Mario Puzo
    - POV: Third-person
    - Tense: Past tense
    - Publisher: G.P. Putnam's Sons
    - Year of Publication: 1969
- **Film Adaptation** (1972):
    - Director: Francis Ford Coppola
    - Screenwriters: Mario Puzo, Francis Ford Coppola

AMERICAN PSYCHO (1991)

- **Novel**:
    - Author: Bret Easton Ellis
    - POV: First-person
    - Tense: Present tense
    - Publisher: Vintage Books
    - Year of Publication: 1991
- **Film Adaptation** (2000):
    - Director: Mary Harron
    - Screenwriters: Mary Harron, Guinevere Turner

THE BOURNE IDENTITY (1980)

- **Novel**:
    - Author: Robert Ludlum
    - POV: Third-person limited (primarily following Jason Bourne)
    - Tense: Past tense
    - Publisher: Richard Marek Books
    - Year of Publication: 1980
- **Film Adaptation** (2002):
    - Director: Doug Liman
    - Screenwriters: Tony Gilroy, William Blake Herron

RED DRAGON (1981)

- **Novel**:
    - Author: Thomas Harris
    - POV: Third-person omniscient
    - Tense: Past tense
    - Publisher: G.P. Putnam's Sons
    - Year of Publication: 1981
- **Film Adaptation** (2002):
    - Director: Brett Ratner
    - Screenwriter: Ted Tally
    - Note: Previously adapted as "Manhunter" (1986), directed by

Michael Mann

HANNIBAL (1999)

- **Novel**:
    - Author: Thomas Harris
    - POV: Third-person omniscient
    - Tense: Past tense
    - Publisher: Delacorte Press
    - Year of Publication: 1999
- **Film Adaptation** (2001):
    - Director: Ridley Scott
    - Screenwriters: David Mamet, Steven Zaillian

THE SILENCE OF THE LAMBS (1988)

- **Novel**:
    - Author: Thomas Harris
    - POV: Third-person omniscient
    - Tense: Past tense
    - Publisher: St. Martin's Press
    - Year of Publication: 1988
- **Film Adaptation** (1991):
    - Director: Jonathan Demme
    - Screenwriter: Ted Tally

PET SEMATARY (1983)

- **Novel**:
    - Author: Stephen King
    - POV: Third-person limited
    - Tense: Past tense
    - Publisher: Doubleday
    - Year of Publication: 1983
- **Film Adaptation** (2019):
    - Directors: Kevin Kölsch, Dennis Widmyer

  - Screenwriter: Matt Greenberg
  - Note: Previously adapted in 1989, directed by Mary Lambert with screenplay by Stephen King

INTERVIEW WITH THE VAMPIRE (1976)

- **Novel**:
  - Author: Anne Rice
  - POV: First-person (Louis)
  - Tense: Past tense
  - Publisher: Alfred A. Knopf
  - Year of Publication: 1976
- **Film Adaptation** (1994):
  - Director: Neil Jordan
  - Screenwriter: Anne Rice

GONE GIRL (2012)

- **Novel**:
  - Author: Gillian Flynn
  - POV: First-person (alternating narrators)
  - Tense: Present tense
  - Publisher: Crown Publishing Group
  - Year of Publication: 2012
- **Film Adaptation** (2014):
  - Director: David Fincher
  - Screenwriter: Gillian Flynn

LEGION/THE EXORCIST III (1983)

- **Novel** ("Legion"):
  - Author: William Peter Blatty
  - POV: Third-person
  - Tense: Past tense
  - Publisher: Simon & Schuster
  - Year of Publication: 1983

- **Film Adaptation** ("The Exorcist III," 1990):
    - Director: William Peter Blatty
    - Screenwriter: William Peter Blatty

THE ROAD (2006)

- **Novel**:
    - Author: Cormac McCarthy
    - POV: Third-person limited
    - Tense: Present tense
    - Publisher: Alfred A. Knopf
    - Year of Publication: 2006
- **Film Adaptation** (2009):
    - Director: John Hillcoat
    - Screenwriter: Joe Penhall

NO COUNTRY FOR OLD MEN (2005)

- **Novel**:
    - Author: Cormac McCarthy
    - POV: Multiple third-person perspectives with first-person monologues
    - Tense: Past tense
    - Publisher: Alfred A. Knopf
    - Year of Publication: 2005
- **Film Adaptation** (2007):
    - Directors: Joel and Ethan Coen
    - Screenwriters: Joel and Ethan Coen

HOUSE OF SAND AND FOG (1999)

- **Novel**:
    - Author: Andre Dubus III
    - POV: Multiple first-person perspectives
    - Tense: Present tense
    - Publisher: W.W. Norton & Company

    - Year of Publication: 1999
- **Film Adaptation** (2003):
    - Director: Vadim Perelman
    - Screenwriters: Vadim Perelman, Shawn Lawrence Otto

THE TALENTED MR. RIPLEY (1955)

- **Novel**:
    - Author: Patricia Highsmith
    - POV: Third-person limited (following Tom Ripley)
    - Tense: Past tense
    - Publisher: Coward-McCann
    - Year of Publication: 1955
- **Film Adaptation** (1999):
    - Director: Anthony Minghella
    - Screenwriter: Anthony Minghella

JAWS (1974)

- **Novel**:
    - Author: Peter Benchley
    - POV: Third-person
    - Tense: Past tense
    - Publisher: Doubleday
    - Year of Publication: 1974
- **Film Adaptation** (1975):
    - Director: Steven Spielberg
    - Screenwriters: Peter Benchley, Carl Gottlieb

VAMPIRES (1990, originally titled "Vampire$")

- **Novel**:
    - Author: John Steakley
    - POV: First-person and third-person
    - Tense: Past tense
    - Publisher: Roc Books

- Year of Publication: 1990
- **Film Adaptation** (1998):
    - Director: John Carpenter
    - Screenwriter: Don Jakoby

SPHERE (1987)

- **Novel**:
    - Author: Michael Crichton
    - POV: Third-person limited
    - Tense: Past tense
    - Publisher: Alfred A. Knopf
    - Year of Publication: 1987
- **Film Adaptation** (1998):
    - Director: Barry Levinson
    - Screenwriter: Kurt Wimmer

JURASSIC PARK (1990)

- **Novel**:
    - Author: Michael Crichton
    - POV: Third-person
    - Tense: Past tense
    - Publisher: Alfred A. Knopf
    - Year of Publication: 1990
- **Film Adaptation** (1993):
    - Director: Steven Spielberg
    - Screenwriters: Michael Crichton, David Koepp

THE BEACH (1996)

- **Novel**:
    - Author: Alex Garland
    - POV: First-person (Richard)
    - Tense: Past tense
    - Publisher: Viking Press

    - Year of Publication: 1996
- **Film Adaptation** (2000):
    - Director: Danny Boyle
    - Screenwriter: John Hodge

THE LEGEND OF BAGGER VANCE (1995)

- **Novel**:
    - Author: Steven Pressfield
    - POV: First-person (narrator Junie)
    - Tense: Past tense
    - Publisher: William Morrow
    - Year of Publication: 1995
- **Film Adaptation** (2000):
    - Director: Robert Redford
    - Screenwriter: Jeremy Leven

THE BLACK-EYED BLONDE (2014)

- **Novel**:
    - Author: Benjamin Black (pen name of John Banville)
    - POV: First-person (Philip Marlowe's perspective)
    - Tense: Past tense
    - Publisher: Henry Holt and Company
    - Year of Publication: 2014
- **Film Adaptation** ("Marlowe," 2022):
    - Director: Neil Jordan
    - Screenwriter: William Monahan
    - Note: The novel is an authorized continuation of Raymond Chandler's Philip Marlowe character

THE HAUNTING OF HILL HOUSE (1959)

- **Novel**:
    - Author: Shirley Jackson
    - POV: Third-person limited (following Eleanor Vance)
    - Tense: Past tense

    - Publisher: Viking Press
    - Year of Publication: October 1959
- **Film Adaptation: THE HAUNTING** (1963):
    - Director: Robert Wise
    - Screenwriter: Nelson Gidding
- **Film Adaptation: THE HAUNTING** (1999):
    - Director: Jan de Bont
    - Screenwriter: David Self
- **Television Series: THE HAUNTING OF HILL HOUSE** (2018):
    - Creator/Director: Mike Flanagan
    - Screenwriter: Mike Flanagan

Great Films With Great Novelizations

ROUNDERS (1998)

- **Director**: John Dahl
- **Screenwriters**: David Levien, Brian Koppelman
- **Novelization**:
    - Author: A.L. Singer
    - POV: First-person (from Mike McDermott's perspective)
    - Tense: Past tense
    - Publisher: Miramax Books
    - Year of Publication: 1998

CONSTANTINE (2005)

- **Director**: Francis Lawrence
- **Screenwriters**: Kevin Brodbin, Frank Cappello
- **Novelization**:
    - Author: John Shirley
    - POV: Third-person
    - Tense: Past tense
    - Publisher: Pocket Star Books
    - Year of Publication: 2005

THE GAME (1997)

Director: David Fincher

Screenwriters: John Brancato and Michael Ferris

Novelization:

- Author: A.L. Singer
- POV: Third-person limited (following Nicholas Van Orton's perspective)
- Tense: Past tense
- Publisher: Signet Books
- Year of Publication: 1997

FALLEN (1998)

Director: Gregory Hoblit

Screenwriter: Nicholas Kazan

Novelization:

- Author: Tom Sniegoski
- POV: First-person (primarily from Detective John Hobbes' perspective)
- Tense: Past tense
- Publisher: Signet Books
- Year of Publication: 1998

SEVEN (1995)

- **Director**: David Fincher
- **Screenwriter**: Andrew Kevin Walker
- **Novelization**:
    - Author: Anthony Bruno
    - POV: Third-person limited
    - Tense: Past tense
    - Publisher: St. Martin's Paperbacks
    - Year of Publication: 1995

CRIMSON PEAK (2015)

- **Director**: Guillermo del Toro
- **Screenwriters**: Guillermo del Toro, Matthew Robbins
- **Novelization**:
    - Author: Nancy Holder
    - POV: Third-person limited
    - Tense: Past tense
    - Publisher: Titan Books
    - Year of Publication: 2015

END OF DAYS (1999)

- **Director**: Peter Hyams
- **Screenwriter**: Andrew W. Marlowe
- **Novelization**:
    - Author: Frank Lauria
    - POV: Third-person omniscient
    - Tense: Past tense
    - Publisher: Doherty Associates, LLC, Tom
    - Year of Publication: 1999

BLADE (1998)

- **Director**: Stephen Norrington
- **Screenwriter**: David S. Goyer
- **Novelization**:
    - Author: Mel Odom
    - POV: Third-person
    - Tense: Past tense
    - Publisher: Pocket Books
    - Year of Publication: 1998

BLADE TRINITY (2004)

- **Director**: David S. Goyer
- **Screenwriter**: David S. Goyer

- **Novelization**:
  - Author: Natasha Rhodes
  - POV: Third-person
  - Tense: Past tense
  - Publisher: Black Flame
  - Year of Publication: 2004

THE TEXAS CHAINSAW MASSACRE (2003)

- **Director**: Marcus Nispel
- **Screenwriters**: Scott Kosar
- **Novelization**:
  - Author: Stephen Hand
  - POV: Third-person
  - Tense: Past tense
  - Publisher: Black Flame
  - Year of Publication: 2003

INDIANA JONES AND THE KINGDOM OF THE CRYSTAL SKULL (2008)

- **Director**: Steven Spielberg
- **Screenwriter**: David Koepp
- **Novelization**:
  - Author: James Rollins
  - POV: Third-person
  - Tense: Past tense
  - Publisher: Del Rey Books
  - Year of Publication: May 2008

TERMINATOR SALVATION (2009)

- **Director**: McG
- **Screenwriters**: John Brancato, Michael Ferris
- **Novelization**:
  - Author: Alan Dean Foster

- POV: Third-person
- Tense: Past tense
- Publisher: Titan Books
- Year of Publication: April 2009

DARKNESS FALLS (2003)

- **Director**: Jonathan Liebesman
- **Screenwriters**: Joe Harris, John Fasano, James Vanderbilt
- **Novelization**:
    - Author: Joe Harris
    - POV: Third-person
    - Tense: Past tense
    - Publisher: Pocket Star
    - Year of Publication: January 2003

COWBOYS AND ALIENS (2011)

- **Director**: Jon Favreau
- **Screenwriters**: Roberto Orci, Alex Kurtzman, Damon Lindelof, Mark Fergus, Hawk Ostby
- **Novelization**:
    - Author: Joan D. Vinge
    - POV: Third-person
    - Tense: Past tense
    - Publisher: Tor Books
    - Year of Publication: 2011

X (2022)

- **Director**: Ti West
- **Screenwriter**: Ti West
- **Novelization**:
    - Author: Tim Waggoner
    - POV: Third-person
    - Tense: Past tense

- Publisher: Titan Books
- Year of Publication: 2022

HALLOWEEN (2018)

- **Director**: David Gordon Green
- **Screenwriters**: David Gordon Green, Danny McBride, Jeff Fradley
- **Novelization**:
    - Author: John Passarella
    - POV: Third-person
    - Tense: Past tense
    - Publisher: Titan Books
    - Year of Publication: 2018

HALLOWEEN KILLS (2021)

- **Director**: David Gordon Green
- **Screenwriters**: David Gordon Green, Danny McBride, Scott Teems
- **Novelization**:
    - Author: Tim Waggoner
    - POV: Third-person
    - Tense: Past tense
    - Publisher: Titan Books
    - Year of Publication: 2021

IN THE LINE OF FIRE (1993)

- **Director**: Wolfgang Petersen
- **Screenwriter**: Jeff Maguire
- **Novelization**:
    - Author: Max Allan Collins
    - POV: Third-person
    - Tense: Past tense
    - Publisher: Jove Books
    - Year of Publication: 1993

DAWN OF THE DEAD (1978)

- **Novel**:
    - Author: George A. Romero and Susanna Sparrow
    - POV: Third-person
    - Tense: Past tense
    - Publisher: St. Martin's Press
    - Year of Publication: 1978
- **Original Film** (1978):
    - Director: George A. Romero
    - Screenwriter: George A. Romero

DARKMAN (1990)

- **Novel**:
    - Author: Randall Boyll (Novelization of film)
    - POV: Third-person
    - Tense: Past tense
    - Publisher: Jove Books
    - Year of Publication: 1990
- **Original Film** (1990):
    - Director: Sam Raimi
    - Screenwriters: Sam Raimi, Ivan Raimi, Chuck Pfarrer

A. M. BLANCO is a novelist and screenwriter residing in South Florida. A dramatist and prose stylist with a poetically hypnotic and cinematic voice, he combines dramatic storytelling with noir, crime, suspense, and horror to create visceral narratives. He is author of *Vulture*, and *The Mortician*. He coaches fiction writers on a one-on-one basis using his Subconscious Novelist Program. You can reach him directly at the 9th House Books website.

CONTACT

<u>9th House Books</u>

9thhousebooks@gmail.com

www.9thhousebooks.com

www.instagram.com/9th_House_Books

www.youtube.com/9th_House_Books

www.x.com/9th_House_Books

<u>A. M. Blanco</u>

Amblancowriter@gmail.com

www.instagram.com/a.m.blanco

www.tiktok.com/a_m_blanco

Made in United States
Orlando, FL
19 March 2025